MICHAEL RILEY

A CONCORDE IN MY TOY BOX

A PILOT'S CAREER, FROM THE SCHOOL GLIDER TO THE SOUND BARRIER

Mereo Books

2nd Floor, 6-8 Dyer Street, Cirencester, Gloucestershire, GL7 2PF
An imprint of Memoirs Book Ltd. www.mereobooks.com

A Concorde in my toy box: 978-1-86151-951-1

First published in Great Britain in 2019
by Mereo Books, an imprint of Memoirs Books Ltd.

A CIP catalogue record for this book is available from the British Library.

The address for Memoirs Books Ltd. can be found at www.memoirspublishing.com

Memoirs Books Ltd. Reg. No. 7834348

Typeset in 11/15pt Century Schoolbook
by Wiltshire Associates Ltd.
Printed and bound in Great Britain

CONTENTS

PREFACE

It was ten years after my last powered flight that my father's two 1939-1945 logbooks came to me. Having languished in two other family households this was fortunate: they might well have been thrown out eventually had my brother-in-law not decided that, as the only professional flyer in the family, I might like them. Thanks Alan.

Either side of the two year Operational Training Unit stint as an instructor were two bomber tours –1930s style map, compass and luck exploits, newly at night, then a concentrated Oboe Mosquito session – 106 bombing trips in all. He was lucky to have avoided the industrial level of the four engine offensive of the mid war years, it seems, but if we discard the flak and the night-fighters, it's best, where possible, not to trust to luck where flying is concerned.

I took the logbooks to the Public Records Office, Kew, and started my research. What happened on all these offensive flights into enemy territory, what was it like? Records of everyday flying things are scanty at Kew, if interesting, but the Operations Record Books, brief as each entry is, are comprehensive. Every one of the 83 and 109 Squadron flights was there, as were the four OTU thousand bomber participations (two Hampdens and two Wellingtons) with students, just as the intelligence officer had noted the details. - date, times, type, identification, target, bomb load, remarks.

This last item, when the whole squadron's experiences are considered, provides interesting reading, especially from the Hampden days. 'Navigator baled out over target. Target bombed successfully, returned to base, no damage.' The Hampden 'navigator' was usually a new pilot who did a few look-see trips as observer in the nose, with the map. Someone else: 'Icing in cloud during return. Got into a spin at 12,000 ft, recovered at 200 ft *(over the sea, in the dark: my note)*.

Sitting in the darkened box, peering at the microfiche reader screen, I was there. I could hear the remorseless drone of the engines, feel the tension, sense the concentration, feel the relief at seeing base reappear after nine hours, or surviving a wheels up landing in a farmer's field, somewhere, in early morning fog.

The many Mosquito missions are more orderly. High tech and high performance for the day. Very accurate instrument flying, reports such as 'saw T.I.s (target indicators) burning on runway intersection' are an example. This is astonishing accuracy for individual guidance from Britain, flying at 36,000ft in the dark. Instrument rating good pass. 2½ hours from Bedford to Germany and back was also a great improvement if you were fortunate to fly this remarkable twin. One of the few things my father told me about his wartime experience was an 'exceptional' assessment for his Oboe flying.

I gave the logbooks to the RAF Museum. They are primary history and much appreciated. The archive staff asked me about my 40 years of assorted flying. They requested a copy of the Concorde Stick and Rudder book, photocopied my logbooks, asked me to give a video interview (suitably controversial and opinionated - well, why not?) and then said 'What we would really like you to do is write a book about your flying history; we think we are the best place for collecting and storing it.

Hence this book.

CHAPTER 1

THE SCHOOL GLIDER

My first flight in an aeroplane took place in the late 1950s. It was also my first flight as a pilot – the only pilot. The Royal Air Force section of our school Combined Cadet Force had one of those two-dimensional Primary gliders (Grasshoppers). When I say one, I mean we only had one at a time – whenever it crashed a blue Queen Mary transporter brought another a few days later and took away the firewood. These simple flying machines can be very effective trainers; they can even soar and thermal in the right conditions, and the German original of this DIY design got many a would-be Luftwaffe pilot off to a basic, self-sufficient start in the 1930s. At school we had the same self-sufficient principle – there was no training programme or pre-flight briefing whatsoever for these catapult-launched forays into the Devonian sky.

Our commanding officer, a benign housemaster/chemistry teacher, dressed himself up as a sort of Flight Lieutenant on Thursday afternoons and oversaw our military activities. Good old Willy – he wasn't my housemaster or chemistry teacher so I don't know what he did behind the scenes (except play the same Bach (or probably pupil Krebs') organ beginner's prelude when called to stand in for Director of Music 'Jazz' Hall at morning chapel) – but in uniform not a lot: he just let us get on with it. This is very much the tradition at this kind of school – the boys run themselves, but usually within a pre-ordained structure.

It took two or three years in khaki to get there, but this was the cushy section, no doubt about it. On Thursday afternoons we usually paraded in semi-mufti (our normal school clothes plus blue shirt and webbing belt, RAF beret and black tie). After a perfunctory form-up in threes with fallout we would usually have a lecture from one of our number about lift and drag or carburettors. Sometimes we would see a training film – stiff, drab and dull for the Air Training Corps, or glamorous cautionary tales for USAAF throttle-benders. Both were in black and white, but the American leather-jacketed fly-boys who merrily bought the farm while hot-dogging over their girl's house, or forgot to read the NOTAMs, their carb heat, checks, airspeed, or landing gears portrayed a world of sunshine, Hollywood and dangerous fun – where image challenged responsibility. Where are those priceless 1943 reels today? I remember their messages still. But occasionally we got the glider out, about three times a term. Maybe Willy's nerves could only take this much exposure to his dodgy grass roots amateur flying school. (USAAC safety films can be found on YouTube.)

Later I came across the official training programme for this machine – ground slides at first to get the hang of effects-of-controls, with spoilers on the wings, restricted elevator movement, limited bungee power and so on. We had none of this. Maybe it was thought that the classroom lift and drag lessons were adequate, but not even a sit-in demo of up, down, left and right did we get.

The lucky tyro got two or three cat-shots. To my recollection the only briefing (from the overenthusiastic and totally unqualified members of the bungee team) occurred during the pushback between launches one and two, or also between two and three if progress was poor – two good sorties meant that it was someone else's turn. There was a considerable feeling of anticipation as the bungee catapult was extended. The beast was held back by a cable anchored to a corkscrew stake screwed into the turf astern. Someone held up a wingtip. Ahead, two teams of boys trudged into the distance bearing their ends of the rubber rope like acute-angled tug-of-war teams. A ball and string on the bungee indicated maximum acceptable tension for a full power blast-off, and the boys dutifully stopped heaving when ordered, but there was always an unofficial bonus: they ran frantically when the pilot cut himself loose – military power. A tug on the cable under the seat started this game with a solid jolt accompanied by a resonating 'thunk' – maximum acceleration at the start.

Exploratory waggles of the controls confirmed what I suspected – it was the same as a model aeroplane. After a few seconds of cruise at twenty feet it was time to brush the skid on to the grass with speed to spare before entering the cricket nets. The field was too small to contain many of our potentially successful flights: some did escape, but these, and several crashes, are other stories.

'Good show!' called a bemedalled real pilot with a wave of a gloved hand, down from Chivenor this afternoon for a liaison visit, standing on the touchline with Willy. The second flight confirmed something else. I'd found what I wanted to do, grasped the drowning man's straw. To play with such machines for ever represented a first attainable prospect of personal fulfilment and satisfaction, ending hope of further emotional growth. These full-size toys looked less frightening than people.

When I received my Swiss paraglider pilot's licence in 2000 it came with a booklet by Dr Bruno Banzer entitled *Human Error in Hang-glider Accidents*. Dr Banzer, himself a pilot, is a clinical psychologist at Zürich University, and this book, written on behalf of the National Accident (all kinds) Prevention Bureau, investigates possible reasons why otherwise rational pilots make the poor decisions (usually to take off against the evidence) that lead to a majority of accidents. The book, analytical, objective, and quite unlike the amateur DIY self-help touchy-feely rubbish that clutters the shelves of the English-speaking world's bookshops, made a lot of sense to me; but one hypothesis, initially discarded for reasons of vanity, I soon accepted – it's me, to a tee.

Why do pilots like to fly? Anyone with experience of contemporary 'train the trainers' education knows about the ideal 'doing things and feeling OK' emotional arousal level ('Angst' in German) to be found at the middle of the bell curve. Apart from those who normally spend their waking hours in the centre, there are pilots who inhabit the lower end. They like to fly because the demands of flight hoist them from their normal state of torpor and boredom to the ideal operating level. Then there are those from the 'too-high' end – really? It seems they like the excitement and challenge of successful flight because the sense of release and fulfilment they experience afterwards (coming down) provides relief from the chronic state of raised angst they live with as a result of unresolved childhood issues. They are contra-phobics. What wimps! Not me surely? Is this more self-help junk?

It took ten minutes' reflection... the man's right. Sometimes you have to accept the obvious when it stares you in the face.

CHAPTER 2

A FIRST LOOK AT THE SKY

I was born in Oxford, on January 22nd, 1942. My parents lived with my maternal grandparents at 1 Apsley Road, and my father had recently been posted to 16 OTU (Operational Training Unit) at Upper Heyford as an instructor. He'd completed a Hampden tour the previous November (83 Sqdn, Scampton). That had been 1941. Military aviation was to come a long way in the next few years.

Wars provide both opportunity and disaster for those involved: luck might have something to do with it, but choosing or falling into a job you happen to be good at helps a lot. Self-effacing and modest, but conscientious, reliable and good with figures, my father found his metier in the wartime Royal Air Force. After brief careers in the Vickers shipbuilding drawing office in Barrow-in-Furness and the Inland Revenue at Oxford he joined the RAFVR in 1939 as war threatened, and started to come to grips with the Tiger Moth at Kidlington, then at Marshalls of Cambridge.

Children are supposed to have little or no memory of events before the age of two. I have one or two short but clear recollections prior to this age – concern at the prospect of being pricked with my nappy pin, and a sense of dread upon hearing the switchbacking thirds of the air raid siren. We didn't have enemy action in Oxford, but the enthusiastic Observer Corps might consider a passing yellow trainer to be a daytime threat and hit the button. I didn't know what the siren meant, and certainly had no knowledge of the phrase 'air raid warning', but I clearly associated the sound with instant apprehension, even if no one else was in the room: it had to be telepathy.

The third clear memory was of a few days' residence in a dark and dingy flat in Deddington, across the valley from Upper Heyford. This must have been late 1943/early 44. It was an attempt to live as a family within commuting distance of 16 OTU, but my mother and I were soon back at Apsley Road (leaving my father to get on with the war, and try to teach his sprog crews the principles of getting a bomber to Germany and back in the dark, with map and compass only. There were plenty of training prangs – but these were urgent days).

From my third year, however, there are plenty of clear memories. Over the summer of 1944 my father was a member of 109 Squadron, Little Staughton – Mosquito target marking and precision bombing using Oboe VHF distance measurement guidance from two ground stations – very accurate if the navigation and instrument flying was good enough. Our garden faced south, and I clearly remember watching the little yellow aeroplane pass overhead from the south-east on a bright morning. This was the Little Staughton Proctor, and we drove to Kidlington to pick my father up. The next day I remember the departure procedures: 'Elevator up, elevator down,' said my grandfather, who knew nothing about aeroplanes, but did not lack a sense of occasion. This maternal side of the family came from a Gloucestershire agriculture-into-weaving background, and he had spent the last decades up to WW1 in Chipping Norton. He was an early member of Hartwells Motors when they progressed from agricultural machinery to cars, and had moved to Oxford as sales manager. Of course there was rationing during World War 2, but we didn't go without. Fiercely competitive Chipping Norton family gardeners and a close relationship with Oxford commercial circles helped us out – maybe Upper Heyford's enterprising pig and poultry section contributed as well.

The early summer of 1944 was sunny (as I remember) and some of the nights thundery – I remember the terror well, despite my father's reassurance (on his occasional home nightstops) that it was just 'Jack Frost rolling logs'. I was not convinced, and, many years later understood my young daughter's inconsolable fear at the same inexplicable thing: silly explanations don't work with perceptive kids. Aeroplanes were everywhere in 1944. I well recall a very noisy surprise treetop Mosquito run one morning along our gardens – west to east – probably a return to Little Staughton following a routine pre-op oboe calibration sortie over Wales; and a Sunday visit in best blue with my father's squadron other half, his Canadian ex-Lancaster navigator Dick McClelland from Alberta.

The sky was again blue the day I watched countless aeroplanes towing gliders west to east over our garden. An Abingdon neighbour in the 1990s, Peter Clarke, was piloting one of the gliders from Broadwell to Arnhem, a one-way trip. After landing he grabbed his gun and joined the battle, to be captured with many others at the Bridge Too Far (while I was being persuaded (no options anyway) to eat my tea in Apsley Road. I liked a boiled egg without salt, but was compelled to have salt with it: quite why I've never understood, but my mother's word was law; reasoning was defiance and not acceptable in our family, at all).

Dick McClelland and my father flew their 60+ Mosquito operations together, exclusively, with great precision, then went their separate ways – after the war Dick to his state-sponsored Canadian dentist's course, my father to assist my grandfather selling cars in Oxford. Christmas cards were exchanged for many years.

With 3500 flying hours, two bomber tours (106 trips) a couple of years' OTU instructing and, significantly, as one of Air Vice Marshal Don Bennett's experienced, reliable, careful and accurate pilots my father was exactly what the founder of British South American Airways was looking for, but this was not to be. My mother, convinced that flying was intrinsically dangerous, unreliable as employment and had no future anyway, threatened divorce if he did not give up what he was good at and enjoyed and get a safe and reliable little job that would keep him at home every day. We will never know whether her fears of a sudden loss of husband would have been justified. He died in 1981 aged 63, of quiet, cheerful but chronic domestic compliance.

CHAPTER 3

SCHOOL, 1947–1960

I first went to school in 1947 (aged 5); a Miss Gisborne's establishment at Forest Hill – mornings only. I was totally bemused; nonplussed. What was this all about? What was I here for? I'd never had anything to do with other children. They were different, bigger, strange and frightening, and the staff old and alien. Life had heretofore been a matter of accommodating numerous relatives; compliant, obedient, quiet and passive behaviour was expected and demanded. I was good at it. If I didn't exist life went along smoothly.

During my 35 years of trying to teach others about flying my ideas about how to do it changed enormously. They eventually acquired an academic perspective. This usually works best, and the first essential is a good briefing; in other words, tell the learners what they're there for. Until I was about 16 I never knew why I was at school. A decade of wasted opportunity. As a natural analyst my policy was always one of efficiency – minimum expenditure of effort to get by. 'Could do better' was the normal end-of-term report, always received with parental disappointment and disapproval; but what was the point of doing more than necessary – except to achieve an acceptable level of disapproval? To me, school was where you had to go, and survive by yourself. I did not think it was unrelieved fun, either.

In 1950, aged eight, I went to Christ Church Cathedral School, Oxford, as a day boy, but with a view to getting into the choir, so I became a 'learner'. These ancient cathedral choir schools originally catered only for the choirboys (16 in our case) who provided the treble line in the music for the daily cathedral services, but they have all become preparatory schools, thereby enlarging their business bases, with the members of the choir earning a proportion of their school fees as payment for their singing job. They are pro musicians. As a musical, teamwork, reliability and brain-training system I would recommend it. I don't think any of my forebears had ever been to a fee-paying school, let alone come into contact with such an historic establishment as Cardinal Wolsey's Oxford showpiece, but on both sides of the family the last couple of generations had benefitted from the basic 3Rs education encouraged by enlightened Victorian reformers and essential to parents who wanted better for their children. Many of the mid-19th century family members could not write their names, yet one great-great-great-grandfather, Jephtha Young, of the Gloucester weaving ancestors, was something of an amateur poet on the side, and a couple of collections of his homespun poems were published in the mid-19th century. Perfectly spelled, punctuated and rhymed, they have the style of a serious Pam Ayers, but are rather quaint and interesting commentaries on local characters, events, national politics and religious notions nonetheless – but I had no concept of what else school could be for: one went because one had to.

A term later I was accepted for the cathedral choir proper and became a boarder – at almost nine. By modern standards the early '50s were still austere times. The school food kept us alive; good enough, but not good. Our two cooks, Bent and Broad – one had a bow leg (just the one) and the other was broad in the beam – prepared 'socks on bricks' (cheese on toast) and 'dead man's leg' (meat loaf) among the range of dishes available with our collective ration books. Cabbage with slugs was what it says; no ration book coupons required for the slugs. Once a week a staff representative would go to the tiny sweet shop on Folly Bridge and blow our individual sweet rations on our choices of confectionary treats. Aniseed balls and gobstoppers were popular – a real aniseed at the centre, and many changes of colour inside the gob-stopper. Our teaching staff were a motley crew of regulars and cash-strapped temporaries. Regulars included a short-sighted lady who taught 10 minutes of arithmetic, then read us Enid Blyton while all but one of the class (standby reader) crept silently out of the window, and a pretentious spinster with claims of the Sorbonne. Then there was the pseudo Italian count con-man who purported to teach us geography, but only dictated the same paragraph about Argentina and the location of the Pampas. Not a trace of Italian or Spanish accent, but did he actually have Argentinian connections? We will never know. He also claimed to have been an RAF navigator, and I was rather miffed one day when I'd pointed out an Avro York on finals for Abingdon. 'No, definitely a Lancaster, with those rounded fins', he claimed, and the boys felt this had proved me wrong (navigator? I think not). Then there was a succession of university students who needed the money. Totally unsuited to teaching, they were either driven to distraction by our merciless ragging or attempted to keep order with displays of exasperated anger or missile throwing. One fiery and rather mean Vespa-riding Scotsman made the *Oxford Mail* for a display of drunken behaviour in the high street after either passing his finals or getting thrown out (rusticated). Aggressively noisy behaviour and knocking the top off a Belisha beacon were among the charges. We were delighted.

In 1955 I moved on to Blundell's in Devon. The school was older than many famous public schools, and did not suffer from the fabled excesses of many of them, but it was far from home and I survived without distinction, inhibited by a sense of desolation.

Time doesn't necessarily heal, but it does allow a slow adaptation to circumstances, and from around the time of the first Gornhay games field catapult glider sortie, things started to look up. With my bus warrant in hand I went to Exeter on three sunny Sundays in May 1958 and completed the Air Training Corps cadets' glider training syllabus – 25 winch launches including three solo circuits if you were good enough. Launch 21 was my pre-solo check and I sat in front of Sqn Ldr Mares (sounds like Maresh), a gruff central-European war hero. After release I set off around my 360, wobbling the stick in imitation of my usual instructor. Five seconds later the controls froze and 'Cut ziss out!' was growled from the back. An excellent lesson so early in my career, and he said nothing else – a real pilot, I think. After the three solo flights launch 25 was another dual with Mares, who intended to show me a spin, but he couldn't find the necessary climb to ensure our safety; however I came away with the impression that he could be a silent, dangerous and determined opponent in his Spitfire – good to have on your side. It's surprising how much a keen teenager can learn in a total flying experience of 2hrs 25mins and 30 seconds (counting the two Grasshopper bungee cat-shots, to be repeated many years later from the deck of the USN Eisenhower aircraft carrier – highly recommended). Add an engine or two and wheels for taxiing and there you have it.

During the same year I had gone to RAF Hornchurch in search of a flying scholarship. If you were successful in the aircrew selection procedure the RAF would pay for a private pilot's licence at an approved flying school. At the wash-up interview the officer told me the good news, but also that I would have to grow two inches if I wanted to join the Air Force. At the medical in London my eyesight turned out to be fantastic and my hearing so good (I could hear bats) that I was asked to come back at my leisure to help them calibrate a new testing gadget, but I had levelled off at sixteen so the height might be a problem. Sergeant Major Instructor (ret) Mundy was our PT teacher at Blundell's. Short, dapper, brisk and bouncy he was also sympathetic as befits a real pro, and advised stretching up exercises with my back against the wall. I sort of believed him for a few days even though two inches was a tall order, but I'm glad he didn't say 'no chance, sunshine'.

At around the same time we went to RAF Kinloss for our cadet camp. This was a grey, cold and wet affair and we didn't do much. An outdoor .303 rifle and Bren gun session was fun; no shortage of bullets here. We had an indoor .22 range at school. I was quite good but, as a musician, didn't have the time for real shooting. A section of pencil up the spout of a WW1-era Lee Enfield propelled by a blank was the nearest we got to real damage, once a year, on field day. Somebody dispatched a cow with this ordnance, not for one second imagining that such a schoolboy prank could have such tragic results. Boys sometimes do such things – but I do not know who it was, and would not say if I did. (This is what parents paid for, of course). At Kinloss we didn't get near a Shackleton, but I did make my first two flights with engines. The first was in an Anson, driven by two grinning Coastal Command losers who amused themselves by performing corkscrew evasion manoeuvres to make us sick (sorry chaps, it didn't work), then a nice Chipmunk ride with a Neptune pilot.

My Flying Scholarship was arranged for the summer of 1959. Before the end of the summer term a silent driver from Chivenor took me to their stores full of Hunter accessories, where I was issued with a grey flying suit (with built-in matching scarf), the white gloves and a leather helmet with Gosport tubes – 1 off, Tiger Moth pilots for the use of. Two out-and-backs across Devon for one little toff – but that was national service for my driver (to end in 1960).

On July 28th 1959 I took myself with my military kit to the Christchurch Aero Club to report for my Flying Scholarship course. This was the summer holidays and the family lived in Bournemouth, so this involved a bus ride there and back each day. A walk from Christchurch town centre zigzagged through a bungalow estate until one side of the road thinned out into scrappy buildings bordering on something of a grass field. This was the place – Somerton Airfield – and the brick hut with the Aero Club name on it would prove to be (though I didn't realise it at the time) the most unlikely-looking flying Eldorado.

Inside the hut there was a blackboard with the TTMF etc (trim, throttle friction, mixture...) checks written up, and that was about it. The CFI had an office in a corner, and there was tea-making equipment. This turned out to be the most delicious and welcome tea I have ever tasted. We had tea at home, at school, but the tea you brewed yourself after flying was something else. There are particular drinks that go with particular activities. The best alternative example I can think of is the rum and coke that balances perfectly the 28-degree sea water that accompanies a vigorous and salty tropical windsurfer wave sailing session.

My logbook shows me that I made a 45-minute Tiger Moth first flight on July 28th 1959 with John Stone, Assistant Chief Flying Instructor (later a well-known member of the staff at Air Service Training, Perth). Assistant CFI sounds quite impressive, but this was a small operation. There was the CFI, John Pothecary, and Stone – just the two. On this first flight we covered everything from exercise 1 to 9a, excluding 5. (What was 5? Not the foggiest.) This Tiger Moth tradition extended way back, and followed the training principles developed during and after WW1. I would not argue with them in 2014 (if you want real pilots). No radio, no checklist, a grass field (by the sea so you couldn't get lost), a windsock and a signals square – perfect. East of our grass was the old Airspeed factory where they now made Sea Vixens, and every week or so a brand new one would take off from the real runway the other side of a row of Scots pines. We didn't interfere with them and they didn't interfere with us. They never came back. We boys pushed the Tiger Moths around, did the fuel and oil, prop swinging and chocks away. John Pothecary had a little restoring business on the go – an ex-military Tiger cost about £300 then, so there was always one in bits requiring sandpapering. We always had something to do.

The next four weeks covered the whole PPL syllabus. The weather was wonderful. I went solo after something less than six hours, and ended up with 12 hours dual and 18 hours solo, making up the 30 hours required for the licence. The solo included a couple of hours' aerobatics. I was 17, and must have had a rudimentary idea of what flying was about. Spinning was interesting (in retrospect). Stick fully back, even up to the '*When the spinning stops, centralise the controls and pull out of the ensuing dive*' point. It works with a Tiger Moth with anti-spin strakes (maybe even without them). The rudder authority is enough (especially with up elevator) to stop the spin, and this feature is the basis of the Tiger Moth falling leaf manoeuvre.

Here might be a suitable place to say something about spinning (perhaps almost for the last time, because any mention of this subject raises hackles, especially from those who insist on clinging to the security of what they learned first). Spinning can be very different with different machines. You cannot understand or know too much, but the most important advice is to read the manual or listen carefully to someone who knows. It's a good start. Above all do not assume that your first Sky-God had the whole truth. He probably only told you enough to get you by as a crass beginner. My next aeroplane, the original Chipmunk (small rudder and no strakes), makes a perfect example. It could not have been more different – but no problem if you kept your head and followed the instructions: a good trainer (by traditional standards), but an expensive and distressing way of eliminating those prone to confusion.

The self-sufficiency policy also applied to cross country, and a trip to Thruxton and back with John Stone was the only dual away-landing flight. For my solo triangular cross country I again went to Thruxton, then continued over unexplored territory; first to Shoreham, where I stopped for more tea and watched Wing Commander Wallis flying his first autogyro (prototype of Little Nellie), before returning to Hampshire: and on the 16th of August, a Sunday, John Pothecary sent me to Weymouth to look at the USS *Skipjack* in Portland Harbour. I think this was the first US nuclear submarine. I had no trouble spotting it – it looked like its picture in the local paper; big, black, with the funny conning tower with wings, too near the front.

I see that my final flight was on August 20th 1959. I was 17, definitely wanted to be a pilot, and one year of school remained. My mother was not keen, my father conspiratorially non-committal.

CHAPTER 4

AIRLINE PILOT SELECTION

Round about 1959/60 the two state airlines, British Overseas Airways Corporation and British European Airways, acquired Air Service Training, Hamble for their own use, to be called the College of Air Training. This famous grass airfield near Southampton had, for many years, housed a commercial school for those who could pay. Students from all over the world had either financed themselves or been sponsored by airlines. The same facilities and many of the staff were retained, with plans for suitable improvements as appropriate.

Selection for the first year's intake took place in early 1960, by BOAC, the company with initial interest, and, as well as interviews etc., this followed the similar aptitude testing system used by the RAF: a logical reasoning paper (this wheel goes round this way so the other wheel etc), and the same machine-driving tests. These last are a fun challenge, and in the garage at Dormy House, BOAC's Heathrow aircrew resthouse in leafy A30 Sunningdale, I thought I must have done especially well on the wobbly steering wheel game and the left/right/up/down stick and rudder machine, together with its military throttle-slamming requirements. I had played with these before at RAF Hornchurch, but this second go was on shiny new ones – a delight to drive. Of course, all candidates had the same showroom condition advantage.

There was one test at Dormy House that I had not come across before. It is/was, in my opinion, a very effective simulation of mental overload and subsequent decision-making under pressure (simple and cheap as well) – the tapping test. In another Dormy House garage I sat at a table on which was a wide sheet of paper with two diagrams, one for each hand, each made up of a number of circles connected, one to the next, by arrowed tracks. They were not the same as each other. There was a pencil for each hand. Close by, sitting on top of another school desk, perched Denis Oram, urbane and balding, a pensioned-off captain battling Parkinson's disease, (my guess is one of nature's gentlemen, but I don't know) explained the rules: 'Take a pencil in each hand, and start on the left and right start circles. The tape recorder will play a sequence of taps. On each tap move the relevant pencil along its arrow to the next circle – right pencil, left pencil, right etc. You must follow the lines, and if you can't keep up stop, and continue when you can pick up the speed again.' Very simple instructions – clear priorities. 'You can have a 30 second practice run first, pencils reversed so you won't be drawing anything.' Great!

The practice run went well. Tap, move, look right, tap, move, look left, tap, move – and so on (I was good – this should be easy). So now the real thing: 'Turn the pencils round and draw along the lines, and we'll have a one minute thirty second run.' (Should be no problem – based on the practice). Off we go, initially just the same, well under control, then the taps got faster, and there were extra background noises. Hang in there – left, draw, right, draw, left, faster and faster. It's obvious that this will continue so follow the rules: stop and wait, take a breather, and pick it up again when you can cope (the tapping did slow down). There are many ways to get this test wrong. Ignore the taps and plod on at your own speed – wrong. Burst into tears and throw the pencils in the air – wrong. Scribble all over the paper in desperation – also wrong. These, I believe, were some candidates' reactions. There are many other possibilities. What a great simulation of overload – and inappropriate responses.

A few weeks later, as a result of significant weeding, I believe, I went to Heathrow (a rare awayday from school) for the next selection procedure – not in the huge concrete BOAC Kremlin building (with its splendid built-in hangars, worthy of Berlin), but a shed on the north side, a throwback to the early days (huddling in a Lancastrian for a number of teeth-juddering noisy and cold hours). I had a chat with Captain Abel, the other half of the selection team. He asked me to write an essay on why I wanted to be a pilot. No problem there, but then the Shorthouse problem came up. Unlike the military I have no recollection of a personal height limit featuring in the airline requirements, but he raised the 5 ft 4 fact, even though I was, even then, a qualified Tiger Moth pilot, and he ushered me to someone else and the huge hangars, to see if I could sit in a Comet 4. Whichever of these newish machines I then sat in (Captain's seat, no less) I will have later navigated it across the Bay of Bengal, the Borneo Straits and the trackless wastes of Australia, but what a shiny and fancy machine it then seemed to be. The stick was very similar to that of the Dragon Rapide and the Mosquito, very traditional De Havilland, but the Comet seat could be adjusted as well as the rudder pedals. The trial went well – it was not possible to see much out of the Comet windows anyway – and I made my way to Paddington and back to school, still in business.

In the July I was called to Hamble itself for flying grading. This consisted of a few basic dual flying exercises in the Chipmunk, much along the lines of my Tiger Moth experience of a year before. I flew with Cecil Pearce and Tubby Fieldhouse, both middle-aged (to me); quiet, businesslike and obviously very experienced instructors (as befitted their job).

Following my reported A level results and a couple of months' work experience at stationery manufacturer Hunt & Broadhurst of Oxford's delivery department (during which I earned enough money to buy the centre second sweep hand watch required by the college – but counting seconds never featured in the syllabus. It was a nice watch, stolen off my wrist in the street by an old crone one night in Singapore as I and Ron Boland made our way home to the Raffles hotel in about 1966. Stupid boy, I've never wasted good money on a prestige watch since.) I answered the call and reported to Hamble as requested, in the autumn of 1960.

CHAPTER 5

COLLEGE OF AIR TRAINING, HAMBLE 1960–1962

The initial 1960 intake of this airline pilot project was small, and divided into two waves of manageable classes, enabling the virtually emptied Air Service Training facilities to reinvent themselves as a shiny 'University of the Air'. There were two kinds of student – those who had not lived away from home before, and those who had. I had the impression that the former made up the first wave, 601 and 602, and the latter 603 and 604. Could it also be that these courses were made up in order of selection scores? I've no idea, but, in retrospect, the system worked well, having apparently first chosen candidates who would work hard, do what they were told and not seek individual expression – perfect airline pilots.

There were initial warnings of severe discipline and unbearably testing workloads, but the routine turned out differently. There were, of course, those who stayed in their rooms at night, studiously revising for fear of failure, and complained about poor catering and too many restrictions, but there were others who saw the rules for what they were, relished the facilities, freedoms and simplistic academic demands – and good food – and worked only as hard as was necessary. This was a holiday camp by the sea, with flying two days a week, and lessons the other three.

A few weeks into the first term the *Sunday Graphic* sent a team along to get what story they could out of this new venture. It was to be this paper's last issue, although I cannot be certain whether I was an unwitting part of this. We warranted a double page spread, and I had a starring role:

> **Jet-age swots – boys who must always be RIGHT**
>
> Little Michael Riley stands only 5ft 3½in his stockinged feet. He has blue eyes, fair, curly hair and a peaches and cream complexion. The sort of pink, angelic face that must have looked exactly right when he sang in Christ Church Cathedral Choir, Oxford.
>
> Four months ago he was playing the piano, organ and violin as a cloistered public schoolboy at Blundells School, Tiverton, Devon. Today he's engaged on one of the most gruelling physical and mental training courses in the world – **training to be a jet-age airline pilot.**
>
> *Soon he'll be throwing 140 tons of steel, worth £2,000,000, around the sky!*
>
> And in a few years a frighteningly heavy burden will be thrust upon his slight shoulders – the responsibility for 150 passengers speeding twice a day on 2,000 mph London-New York trips.
>
> **FOR THIS HE WILL BE PAID ABOUT £90 A WEEK.**
>
> The paper enlarged upon the future pay prospects:
>
> The boys do two years training at the college before taking £20-a-week 'learner jobs' with BOAC or BEA. But not for 10-15 years will they become captains earning £90 a week.

(I'm not sure about the 'learner jobs' to start with. I got £1230 a year as a BEA Vanguard co-pilot).

'Peaches and cream, peaches and cream!' parroted my more rugged and avuncular colleagues on the fateful publication day, but they soon tired of it. My family, on the other hand, were quite unfazed by the journalistic style. 'Ooh look – we must save a copy!' I imagine that after scouring the wartime papers for more serious aviation news this seemed harmless nonsense. Quite so. Would I get some fan mail from the public? Yes, just the one postcard, from as far away as the village. It mentioned my musical accomplishments and suggested I might like to join their chamber music activities – next Sunday lunch perhaps? Why not?

I knocked on the door of the Victorian terraced house and it was opened by a gorgeous eighteen-year-old blonde; lipstick, serious nails, Brigitte Bardot skirt, the lot. This was not one of the musicians but the daughter-in-law of the house who, notwithstanding the ongoing charm offensives of many of my colleagues over the next two years, turned out to be a good friend to this shy and unprepossessing teenager.

A blow by blow account of a two-year commercial pilot training course does not make exciting reading, but changing attitudes to pilot training over the last 60 years, mainly as a result of the technological advances which reduce the sophistication and cost of pilot training, and justify relatively lower pay scales, have made the ethos of the 1960s virtually unrecognisable in the modern industry, so the college is worth a few more words. The *Sunday Graphic* article, funny as it was, reflected much of how things were at the time. No mention was made of the new principal, a retired Australian Air Vice Marshall, who was settling in. He had told us that flying was fun but not funny – very wise – and wrote us an advice book which included 'Find a good tailor, and stick to him'. How true – even today. In fact cadet Tom Weller followed this advice when he left the college. His first BOAC uniform fitted him so well that he had a suit made by the makers, Frames of Reading. One good suit should suffice, and this one's still in good order after 50 years – but has become too narrow, he told me last week.

But the real power behind the scenes did get a picture and a few quotes in the Graphic. Sqn Ldr Nick Hoy, Chief Ground Instructor said 'In most jobs you learn by mistakes. Here you can't afford to. You might do 99 things right – and forget the 100th. And the 100th might be to lower the undercarriage.' (And there are more dangerous things to forget or buttons to press than that!) Nick rounded off with a run-down of the typical boy's start to the day: 'Just now the trainees are finding life no picnic':

AT 6.30 am they get up.

AT 6.45 am they're out in the open for PT.

AT 8.30 am they start lectures or flying.

And in the evenings – more lectures, and homework, too.

We did indeed start to do this 6:45 boot camp road work with a half-hearted shamble down the village and back, but this was unsupervised, and the request was initially complied with out of sympathy for the member of staff who had been given responsibility for seeing that this disciplinary demand was carried out. It was all rather silly. We were not meathead cannon fodder, nor had the staff much experience of this drill sergeant system themselves, so the tradition quickly died out. The lecturer who had been given this inappropriate task taught us the classroom intricacies of the Chipmunk, and introduced himself as the Deputy Chief Ground Instructor. The same day we were addressed by Sqn Ldr Nick. 'I am the Chief Ground Instructor; I have no deputy.' That seemed to indicate a little uncertainty regarding the holiday camp command structure (while the Antipodean AVM found his feet), and we remained free to enjoy what the college had to offer. After my school experience it was indeed a picnic – with nice food, no gates, boats to sail, village pubs within easy walking distance, plenty of free time and assorted sports facilities for those who were so inclined, including a manicured bowling green. In his introductory address to us CGI Nick had darkly threatened 'from time to time there will be workloads, of an intensity that will be impossible to bear' to academically toughen us up, one must suppose. Where did he get such bizarre and grandiose ideas for an aeroplane driving school? A world of fantasy in there somewhere.

(As I write these words in 2013 it occurs to me that Nick had been sent to America during WW2 for basic pilot training. This Officer and Gentleman experience and a life-changing incident there may explain his special ideas for our future, planned in his head while he had temporary control of the syllabus.)

The *Graphic* summarised the entry requirements:

> Only 41 out of the 1,000 who applied were up to the required fantastically high standard of education, physical fitness, personality and leadership. What sort of boys are the 41 who got through? Mainly middle-class, some working class. They come almost equally from public schools and grammar schools. Four are university graduates.

(And two of those got a little evening job teaching maths at Southampton Tech. One of their students taught us electronics.)

The journalist clearly had no problem with this off-the-cuff class assessment in 1960; perhaps the red-top readers expected it anyway, but the interesting factor about his conclusion was that there was in reality no correlation between the imagined class background, type of education or qualifications of the boys he would have encountered.

Sqn Ldr Nick had been a navigator, and teacher of all things navigatory, and his passion was astro-navigation. Not the sums, but the magic and mystical world of the heavens – Patrick Moore (another 1940s navigator) by way of Vincent Price and George Sanders, but much more stagey. His lectures about star recognition, based on a comprehensive knowledge of the constellations, finding one's way around the heavens from this one to that, were in the direct tradition of Arab traders sailing their dhows across the Arabian sea, long before the Three Wise Men made their astro-trip across the desert. Wonderful stuff – unchanged for the aeroplane navigator in a Lancaster winding up his clockwork sextant with a couple of minutes to go as he surveys the whole sky through his astrodome. This was nice to know, but mostly irrelevant for the periscopic sextant navigator of the pressurised jet age, with only a tiny circle of sky visible. But I remembered all he taught us, as a result of the theatrical delivery. 'The cold green light of Sirius… the angry red of…' was it Betelgeuse? I've forgotten most of it now – I never had to rely on the whole sky system in real life – but this was technical training as a performance, and a direct share in ancient history.

On a hot Saturday afternoon one summer, four of us – a public school flying scholarship boy and three of the university graduates (themselves all university air squadron members) – were tinkering with our model aeroplanes in our hobby room when, most unexpectedly, we were visited by a somewhat tired-looking Sqn Ldr Hoy, out of place and out of character. How strange: this is a Saturday, the place deserted, all staff at home, most boys elsewhere, not a hint of weekday office life anywhere. What was he doing here?

Without further ado Nick told us about his abbreviated and tragic piloting career. While part of a Boeing Stearman formation takeoff he had collided with another and crashed. He was badly injured, his piloting career was over, and after months of painful recovery he became a navigator, with a bad back. The Stearman is a friendly device, and formation great fun when you can do it in a relaxed frame of mind, but we do not know what went wrong. If the man next to you shies like a startled thoroughbred while still on the runway there's not much you can do. It may not have been Nick's fault at all. A promising career blighted by fate. This was a true tragedy, and I could understand why he felt the need to tell some of these privileged and untroubled cadets – some of whom might have enough experience to understand. Continuous and worsening pain distorts the personality, and may, in addition, need an element of self-medication to make each day almost as bearable as the one before.

Nick Hoy was easily the most interesting personality among the teaching staff, both airborne and classroom. This in no way denigrates the qualities of all the others; actually they were all, to a man, of great and varied experience, excellent teachers, and for these reasons quite at home doing a job they were used to and could do well. They were, in fact, as all good teachers should be, at one with themselves, and greatly responsible for the widely-held opinion that the College of Air Training, as it started out, was the best airline pilot training school of all time. This sounds a very bold claim – especially when quoted by a participant – but I don't think it is wrong. And, while not intending to identify those many who all did a great job, a lasting memory of excellent teaching has to mention Tony Palmer's pilot navigation lessons for Chipmunk pilots (to name just ourselves).

Chief Flying Instructor George Webb was quiet, sort of kindly, but fair – very fair. 'Tune the Hurn ILS, would you' in George's strangled tones was a well-known and ominous request, indicating a clear element of doubt as to a career future. I did not experience it myself, but during our first term I did get a ride in the back of an Airspeed Oxford for a tootle to the Hurn instrument approach. There was still a handful of Kuwaiti or Bahraini students resident, finishing their Air Service Training courses. How our pilot, Mohammed bin something important, got on I can't tell, but it all seemed under control, and George was quiet and reassuring (maybe). George had considerable wartime instructing experience on the Oxbox, when it was used as the principal basic twin-engined trainer, with much time spent learning the instrument/night flying techniques required for getting a night bomber back on the ground. He knew the required standard – exactly. This old wooden aeroplane looked chunky and agreeable, but had something of an asymmetric and spinning reputation. Instructor and ex-pathfinder pilot Tony Farrell, who had also spent much time with the Oxford, wrote that he found the (much higher performance) Mosquito much easier to fly. When you know what you are doing this is often the case, and, in the fullness of time, we were given a very clear impression that the control of a two-engine machine with only one engine available was a very important survival skill. The various instructors who lectured us about this on wet days were unanimous – and it was obvious that this priority for our future safety can only have come from real life experience. Paddy Kinnin started out by explaining that as beginners, we could be forgiven for thinking that to fly a Mosquito might be as easy as flying two Spitfires, but there would be more to it.

During our second term I had another of those lucky breaks – like the good fortune of arriving at the Christchurch Aero Club and my four weeks of ideal schoolboy Tiger Moth flying. Arrangements had been made for the Duke of Edinburgh to officially open the college. The Principal had some suitable ideas up his sleeve: 'What do you think, Riley, of you and Johnson playing the national anthem when the Duke arrives at the club for the official ceremony, speech and tea?' I was not happy. Somebody's band, maybe, but a crescendoing left hand drum roll on the club 88 for starters, joined by Tony and his clarinet to highlight this simple tune, would not have the gravitas required for the royal occasion, I thought – just too naff. Better forget it. Fortunately he did not press me, but he did come up with the arrival flypast. That was more like it.

The Duke was to arrive by Royal Flight helicopter on the dot, and as he stepped out to be greeted by the college principal five of our Chipmunk fleet would cruise regally over in perfect formation, all twenty pots firing strongly. Of course, instructors would be driving, but, if there were enough cadets to spare, these could ride along. Paddy Kinnin would lead, and the other spots would be taken, in landlubber positions, by Tony Farrell (2), Alan Smith (the flying) (3), Bill Anderson (4) and Tapps Tappin (5). During the Duke's tour around the college facilities the remainder of the 41 (no one chopped yet) cadets would be doing likely things – being taught in the classroom; in their flying suits getting their maps ready at Flights; driving the Link trainer; playing squash, maybe; thumbing through a book in the library. You get the idea: and clearly this had to be carefully planned so that these few could give the impression of a busy and confidence-inspiring outfit. Was the Duke intended to meet the best ones? Perhaps – anyway I got to fly with Tony Farrell. The Duke would not see me (or hear me on the ivories).

During the weeks beforehand we had a couple of practices. The basic formation flying of this newly assembled team had to gel, and Paddy's holding pattern over Bishop's Waltham rehearsed. Then there was the run in, timed to perfection; so there was quite a lot to do in the first flight, but it all seemed to go well, and Paddy's quiet and smooth leading, plus the accurate final timing at all of 90+kts (a bit downhill) without changes of power or aggressive manoeuvring all made it look very easy. Knowing what I know now, the comprehensive and catholic experience of our instructors and their leader could not have been better demonstrated.

On the next practice flight Tony Farrell told me that Paddy had decided that this was a good opportunity to teach the boys the rudiments of formation flying. This had not been discussed with us in public (I imagine because it was not part of the college syllabus and might have caused problems) so the elements of briefing had to be on the hoof. But it worked well: 'First thing – engine for forward and back. Not much throttle friction. You do the engine and I will fly.' After a couple of minutes 'Got the idea; now you fly and I will do the engine.' And so on. We had plenty of time cruising around before leaving our holding pattern and after a while Paddy's silky tones came over the radio: 'Hands up everyone who's not flying.' His face broke into a broad grin as he looked around.

On this dress rehearsal BEA Flight Ops Director Jimmy James played the Duke, and arrived in the bright red BEA Bristol Sycamore (blades made of sycamore?) The timing was perfect, but it took too long for the low-slung rotor to stop whirling, so he was late getting out. The AVM could only point into the distance – something to discuss with the Royal Flight Whirlwind crew. On the real day the whole thing went well and I saw the event (in black and white) on the television that evening. The Duke got out and shook hands with the AVM, who then pointed into the sky. The Duke looked up and there we were – perfect 5 vic. Paddy and the AVM had done a good job.

We flew the Chipmunk for the first year to fulfil the commercial licence requirements. These covered the routine single engine general handling exercises and included a lot of cross country and instrument flying – especially. A pair of us shared an instructor on flying days, and I was teamed up with John (Jeep) Jackson, from Norfolk. He had learned to fly the Tiger Moth at Little Snoring, and was also familiar with aerobatics. Sadly our instructor, Tubby Fieldhouse, was nursing an ailing wife and looking after a twelve-year-old daughter during our Chipmunk year. Though (also because) he was an excellent instructor, and we had some flying experience already, this meant that Jeep and I lucked out again – we did much more solo and mutual flying than most of the others. Once settled in Tubby would frequently meet us at the authorisation book first thing, ask us what we wanted to do (or suggest something perhaps), sign the book – and we shared, or had our own Chipmunks for the day, with the sunny south of England, including our local stamping ground, the Isle of Wight, at our disposal.

Mutual flying means sharing an aeroplane, the man in the back acting as safety pilot, keeping a look out while the other practised instrument flying – unable to see out. The safety pilot also gave the colleague things to do and kept an eye on where his navigational instructions were taking the pair. An hour of instrument flying was a little tedious, so we usually gave up after 30 or 40 minutes and spent the remainder amusing ourselves. Aerobatics was not part of the college syllabus, but I had done some with Tubby – he liked my slow rolls, which are the hardest of the three basic manoeuvres at this level. Jeep and I filled in our playtime with manoeuvring, or inventing combat moves, trying them out on unsuspecting cadets, imagining the farm workers below waving their pitchforks in support, or otherwise. It was difficult to identify the occupants of the chosen target, and some of our instructors were good dogfighters. This was very rapidly obvious, and clearing off immediately was the best chance of avoiding the disciplinary trouble that might result. We were well aware of the high expectations of this first select year, and the risk of getting thrown out was very present – but we had very experienced staff who knew what we would otherwise be missing and could tell what was sensible. Nothing was ever said.

We had two kinds of Chipmunk: the original, and the modified military version with a larger rudder and anti-spin strakes. The Chipmunk's fin and rudder were fitted ahead of the tailplane, like a Mosquito. This put it in a stronger place on the slender fuselage but meant that it effectively hid behind the fuselage and tail surfaces if the wind came up from below. There had been military accidents with the original model attributed to difficult spin recovery – hence the second model. It was made clear to us that the correct recovery technique (required for the original) was always to be used, and there was no difference in the training for either machine. We had a lot of time to practise our solo general handling and I decided to try some experimental spin behaviour observations to confirm the difference. These consisted of establishing the original model in a proper spin and letting go of everything, to see what happened to the controls. The stick flopped around in an inconclusive way, but the rudder was the most interesting. It flopped about between full left and right with no particular preference; in other words it gave no direct indication of which foot would be required for recovery. This decision had to be made by the spinning pilot, who may have forgotten how he got into a spin. Having decided (by looking out of the window or at the turn needle) which foot represented opposite rudder, then applying it, the stick was pushed progressively forward down the middle (no roll applied). This was fine except that nothing happened to begin with, and it felt as if no elevator was connected, suggesting that something might be wrong. At around mid-elevator position there was indeed, as advertised, a clear resistance to further stick forward pushing, once again perhaps suggesting that things were not going well, or that this was far enough. Of course it wasn't, and continued deliberate movement forward lowered the nose, temporarily speeding up the pirouette rotation before achieving a clean and quick resumption of normal flight. The modified Chipmunk was much less sensitive to recovery technique, nor did it do such a good spin, though it was easier to make it do a sort of spin, or a low speed spiral dive.

(This is probably the last hackle-raising discussion about spinning, but many years later several experts in the sport aerobatic field exchanged vigorous debates about the foolproof method, and Darrol Stinton of the CAA wrote about his misgivings when he looked at the shapes of some American homebuilt tails. Aerobatic guru Eric Muller of Switzerland was adamant about his own definitive technique. Let go of everything, see where the rudder settles and push it to the other side. That alone should be enough. For a dedicated aerobatic aeroplane maybe, but not the original Chipmunk. Aeroplanes with (irreversible) powered controls are yet another story.)

We did a lot of instrument flying in the Chipmunk – amber screens and blue goggles. This is a much more effective way to shut out the outside world than a long bonnet you wear on your head, like an outsize baseball cap: this cheap and easy system may blank out the view upwards and straight ahead, but other daylight clues and the ability to cheat a little do not simulate the total blackness of a moonless night in cloud. Some of our amber screens had faded over the years, and, if the sun was out, it was sometimes just possible to see its image move across the field of view. But this was of little help except to show that something in the picture was moving, and in general, with nothing to see but a gloomy bluish image of the black and white simple instruments, the vintage and vital skill of blind flying had to be learned properly, together with the ability to fully outgrow the alarming sensations of the 'leans', where the head's balance system re-references itself during a long turn. Flying straight then feels like a turn, or falling over sideways, although the instruments tell the truth (more or less – the artificial horizon will have started the same process as the canals in the ears, so a slightly wing-down picture has to be initially allowed for when trying to fly straight again, etc). Of course these complications are quickly assimilated with practice, but this is basic training that should not be short changed for a professional. Money spent on sound basics is not wasted, in fact it's cheap insurance.

When 1950s aeroplanes did something dramatic a couple of the most user-friendly instruments toppled – the horizon and the direction indicator, both gyro driven. Just when you needed them they didn't work – for the time being – so, with the exception of the luxury of a vertical speed indicator, you are left with 1930s technology, the same as a Tiger Moth under the hood. 'Limited panel' this is called (very limited by modern standards), and we only practised it with an instructor. Tootling around under these restrictions was more difficult than normal service, but not impossible – we even returned overhead the field and made our radio approach procedure, with only the primitive lodestone-in-alcohol compass swinging around on the floor in the dark for heading information.

This particular procedure (VHF Direction Finder) is much harder than it sounds. The man in the tower gives you a number from his screen when you ask him on the radio. That's it. You have to do all the thinking while you drive, with a minimum of helpful gadgets. I always felt that my limited panel attempts at this were very poor, but nothing was ever said, so maybe the others were just as bad. Could I have got away with it in real conditions? I cannot say, but I would put the limited panel VDF letdown in a Chipmunk on a windy, cloudy and rainy day in my 'good pilots only' box. Of course with our full set of six black and white instruments available this procedure was still not that easy, but a breeze by comparison.

Recovery from unusual attitudes (out of control) had its moments, but usually meant recovering from the ensuing spiral dive. Once the spiralling bit had been solved the gentle (and straight) pullout required by the turn indicator (unable to cope with high g) continued to pick up speed and sometimes ended with a spectacularly steep – even vertical – zoom, though the pilot could not appreciate the view from his cocooned environment. Blindfold aerobatics: it could be confusing. We also did the stalling and spinning set piece routines (plus recovery to normal flight) with this primitive information, and I well remember the sense of satisfaction at the ease and success of my first totally blind Chipmunk takeoff from our grass. We were well briefed by Bill Anderson for this, one rainy day lecture, including the subtle errors to expect from the artificial horizon on the way into the air. Had our instructors done this sort of thing in the past in more serious taildraggers? I suspect yes, and although the concept of the totally blind takeoff is still out of order for public transport (and might not be done in many commercial schools) it may well have been a necessary way to confront the enemy on a foggy morning. I've done it again for real myself since (without the enemy). A nice grass field is a good idea – and a plan as to how and where to get down again an even better one.

During our first year we also spent a lot of time in the Link trainer. Once again this basic simulating device was used to teach procedural and approach flying using, by modern standards, simple (and old fashioned) radio guidance devices where the pilot did all the thinking: Radio Range, for example. This was the system that defined the American airways system in the days of Glen Miller and Benny Goodman. You listened to Morse code As (dot dash) or Ns (dash dot). Where the As and Ns overlapped they filled in the spaces and produced a steady tone. Hence four airway legs were transmitted by the station. By flying a suitable heading (depending on whether you started out by hearing As or Ns) you could find out which of two quadrants you were in (getting louder or softer), make your way to the appropriate centreline, then along it to the station. Logically it was possible to fly holding patterns and let downs just using the As and Ns, with, of course, a knowledge of the orientation of the particular station and its procedures. The point of this ancient exercise was, in the words of Norman 'Slippy' Slipp, the chief link man, to get (and keep) the mental picture.

(It is difficult to exaggerate the importance of a professional pilot's ability to continuously visualise where he is without the ability to see anything outside, with not even a pointer to follow; all the while, of course, steering the aeroplane, managing the height and timing as required, not forgetting the essential checks and working of those knobs and levers required, whatever the weather – easy or difficult. During a professional lifetime it is highly likely that this fundamental package of demands will be met much more than once, under unexpectedly difficult conditions; perhaps (but you can count on it). The wisdom of experience understands that beginner's luck cannot be relied on, and in the world of all-weather, worldwide aviation you usually are permitted only one crash – your last. There is seldom a second chance. Fully serviceable modern public transport aircraft still crash reasonably regularly because the crew have dropped the ball and lost the picture. Why is this? There are always extenuating circumstances quoted as contributory factors, but everyday life is a series of contributory factors – to be managed. During our first Chipmunk year we must have spent a couple of mornings or afternoons every week practising a syllabus of 'blind flying' techniques that grew out of pre-WW2 transport flying followed by wartime bomber requirements, both European and American. Old fashioned technology? Of course, but priceless training – and quite cheap. We were fortunate.)

At this early stage we also practised our own airfield direction finder approach procedure in the Link trainer. As already mentioned, our man in the tower told us a number relating to our bearing from his aerial. The pilot used this information to get overhead, go away along the correct line, go down to the right height, turn around after a suitable distance and come back along the designated approach line, descending again so as to arrive at a place where the field could be seen and a landing made. Apart from the last bit this is all without being able to see outside, and exemplifies the sort of thing that biplanes would have done to get down at Croydon and Paris with a member of the crew getting the numbers by Morse code. Our aerodrome was shared by the University Air Squadron: their Chipmunks were the same, and they spoke to the same man in our tower. They also had the same procedure for this direction finder let down business, but the system was quite different for them – the man in the tower did the thinking and told them what to do: what to steer, what height to go to, when to turn around and come back, and so on. Why should they get this easy option, and we had to do this, clearly avoidable, mental exercise ourselves – as well as drive the machine? There are some answers, though we may not have appreciated them at the time.

(Notwithstanding research and invention, aircraft in general are mainly used as a means of transport, and this includes much leisure and training flying. The commercial transport of passengers implies their safe delivery with a remarkable level of reliability, using whatever outside assistance is available. This last concept relies, in theory, on international conformity with agreed minimum standards – minimum being the operative word, accepting, in the real world, an element of local interpretation. Military flying also concerns transport, and while many of the basic skills may look similar the core business of accurate delivery of weapons to an unfriendly target is significantly different, as are the priorities and psychological elements to go with it. Our own future job would have safe delivery of people (plus aircraft), somewhere, as a fundamental priority. Should a UAS student eventually end up at the sharp end of weapons delivery flying (be it bombs or bullets) he would probably have the support of strong interest and assistance from the ground, where possible, when it came to recovering the very expensive machine and its specialist pilot. Human capacity is limited: where it is best directed is a matter of the priorities of the job in hand, and the pilot of fare-paying passengers should never be prepared to put himself at risk. Here lies the fundamental philosophical and ethical difference – and who's paying who for what.)

To supplement our vocational classroom work we had a Liberal Studies department, run by urbane and courteous Roger Hughes, once of Sandhurst, and equally friendly and unthreatening Tony Timbs, late of Fettes School. They hoped for some level of interest in their suggested extra-curricular subjects, some of them vaguely relevant to our chosen profession, and others in the Elizabethan tradition of the adequately informed and interested all-rounder. Dr Course, from Southampton University, put together lectures and visits related to the history of transport – a visit to the Eastleigh marshalling yards of a bygone age, a lecture at the university by Barnes Wallis about his Swallow supersonic transport idea and an early morning outing to the docks to see the Queen Elizabeth nudged into the dry dock by two or three tugs at slack water, inches to spare all round. On the second try it worked. Many years later I was surprised to discover that the burnt-out brown wreck I saw from my Jumbo window in Hong Kong harbour was this ship: *sic transit gloria mundi* – shame really.

We didn't have Latin lessons, but Alwyn Surplice, organist and master of the choristers at Winchester, told us about music, and there was even a visit to evensong at the cathedral one afternoon. My early school days were spent in this line of business so I didn't learn anything new, but quite how some of our intake took on board this experience of heavenly splendour (quality music thrown in) on earth, set up by the establishment of the Middle Ages to impress and inspire the common man, I cannot start to guess.

Dr Van Abbé was recruited to set up his language laboratory teaching system, and very effective it was. Two or three of my course took German – I wish I'd done more. In the college magazine Tony Timbs wrote a very entertaining prologue about the staff in the style of Geoffrey Chaucer: '*Twa clerkes ther weere, fulle schuled in wordes etc . . . of aeroplannes they hadde nat a klue . .*'. I imagined that he must have been a Middle English scholar, and very many years later asked how he did it. No professional medieval studies – 'I just taught myself to do it for fun.' I should have asked him to teach me (or just tried anyway). We could also choose subjects. Some of us agreed that the countryside seen from above was a new interest and elected for geology, resulting in fascinating lectures and the odd fossil-hunting visit to the Isle of Wight cliffs. We had the occasional talk by a visiting representative of the aviation or airline industry, but my recollection is that these were dry, dull and poorly presented, by comparison with the infinite variety of interests available outside the schoolroom or workplace.

It was becoming evident that the boys who had experience of more privileged educational backgrounds were more likely to take to extra-curricular opportunities, though not universally so; and parental attitudes or chance exposure to inspirational teaching must play a significant part in school-age personal development. A contemporary student joined the Hamble Players (the village amateur dramatic society) and persuaded me to come along to the village hall: he had been given the part of Ondersley in *Candied Peel*, and I found myself appointed as his sixtyish blustering friend and foil, Dr Wadd, the eugenics enthusiast. Quite why me I shall never know: I had never trodden the boards before, and this exposure to solo performance was way outside my comfort zone. I was all of 19, and had to pretend to be Dr Wadd; nothing could have been more ridiculous.

As the performance week approached producer Stuart Jacobs told me to wear my dinner jacket. I didn't own one so I borrowed an older cadet's. It was too big and looked it. Stuart lent me his – a bit pre-war I would guess, but maybe it captured the 30s flavour of the drawing room whodunnit. We opened, and, imitating our college MO, Doc Turner of the Royal Southern Yacht Club, I aged up forty-plus years and harrumphed my way through my lines, convinced that the audience would see a self-conscious stumbling nineteen-year-old. An amazing thing happened: nothing happened. There was no laughter of disbelief, no suppressed sniggering. The story unfolded; Dr Wadd's knowledge of poisons carried its weight, the inspector arrested the culprit at the end. All was well. Actually I can't remember the plot, but this personal proof of suspension of disbelief willingly offered by a theatre audience, difficult to accept at first, became increasingly evident as the week wore on. Incredible as it seemed to me, I must have got away with it.

The second play, *Where there's a Will*, was easier. I played Cagey Narracott, a grumpy besmocked rustic who I placed somewhere between *Cold Comfort Farm* and *Brookfield*. Within reason, and in its place, an attempt at over-the-top caricature can work well, and my first act soliloquy rant about the cost of living (as Walter Gabriel by way of Joe Grundy) drew cheers and applause from the OAPs in the house. Accepting that the first night was on special offer for OAPs the whole thing continued to go down well, and I could not believe my cadet colleague and school study-mate Phil Hogge, who told me 'I couldn't tell which one you were until I saw you in profile at half time.' This confirmation of the ability to become someone else in public is of great reassurance to the contra-phobic, and I would recommend the am-dram experience to anyone who gets the chance. I never did it again, somewhat to my regret, but the experience has been useful – and I think I could if I had to.

One visiting speaker in our college cinema was BOAC legend Captain O. P. Jones. He told us about captain-like things to do, but did not come over as the larger-than-life figure of his reputation. James Robertson Justice in his Stratocruiser played the part much better. During the summer of 1961 we had a trip to Teheran and back with BOAC, in my case via Geneva and Tel Aviv in a B707 captained by Trevor Marsden. This was more like it. Charming, confident, diplomatic and approachable Trevor, resplendent with his DFC, radiated experience and competence: this is a real pilot, I thought. Copilot Dick Dodwell drove when we left Geneva and we enjoyed a cruise along the Mediterranean, washing our lunch down with a sunlit beer – including the captain – in true Homeric style.

After a couple of days' slipping at the Teheran Palace Hotel our crew departed eastward and we returned to London in a Comet 4. So far our studies had concerned itself with light aircraft and I had no notion of the how and why of jets. I knew that my father's Mosquito reached 36,000ft (with its freight) and could, on occasion, fly back from West Germany to Bedfordshire in 45 minutes. I had expected much more from the modern airliner, but this was an interesting look at life to come, and how little flying action it would contain.

Hamble is a celebrated sailing mecca, and when the 'Who wants to do sailing?' question was raised at an early activities meeting many of the 41's hands went up. A much smaller proportion actually showed interest in the real thing by the time the three Wayfarer kits had been made and launched. This rugged and largish dinghy was an excellent choice for the job in hand, but during construction in the corner of a hangar it was discovered that the insides of the built-in buoyancy compartments should have been varnished before the decking was finished. I was small enough to get through the hatch with the paintbrush so I joined the boat-builders. In effect a handful of us eventually had three boats to choose from, and sailing became an everyday thing.

We had membership of the Hamble River Sailing Club, raced several days a week and ate as much of their Saturday and Sunday teas as we could. On non-race afternoons and evenings we explored the Solent as far as possible in the time available. This was the early sixties: Health and Safety litigation had not been thought of, and teenagers had not yet reached their fully indulged and protected status. Attitudes to nineteen and twenty-year-olds were closer to 1945 than 1975: after all, fifteen years earlier youths of our age had commanded bombers, minesweepers and gunboats. Remote creeks revealed Thomas Hardy villages and pubs, and there was the Isle of Wight across the sea. Nigel Minchin and I dropped in for tea at a Cowes establishment one wet afternoon, in the tradition of exchange hospitality. 'Where you just come from?' asked an old buffer of a member. Nigel's honest 'Hamble' was received as Hamburg, and 'an hour and a half' in answer to the next question ended the conversation – but we did get the tea.

On some day during our first year we went to Boscombe Down to take a ride in their altitude chamber. For us the exercise was their lesson one, but the experience and self-knowledge thereby gained is invaluable to anyone who is to frequently fly well above 10,000ft. In the interests of business practice this training has become a thing of history for many – but it used to be well worth the money, and still should be. We went to 25,000ft and found out what happened if you lost your supply of oxygen. We sat on either side in the tubular chamber – an even number of candidates so that each side had an opposite number. We all had an inner helmet and oxygen mask so that communication and oxygen were as normal. At 25,000ft we prepared ourselves with a clipboard and pencil; so far so good (in-practice mountaineers can live normally under these conditions), then one team disconnected their oxygen, each watched by their fully-functioning oxygenated minder opposite. They were given things to do, in our case repeatedly subtracting 9 from 1000 and writing down the answers. All went well at first – my maths was OK to start with – and then I seemed to hear my name, and woke up to see my pencil scribbling back and forth across the paper, briefly feeling somewhat cold and detached. Then suddenly I came round – my minder had reconnected me. Recovery was instant, but the deal was that you were told to reconnect yourself when things looked bad. No chance for me; after four minutes I was out of it. Then we became the minders, and watched those on the other side. This was the most astonishing part of the lesson – the variety of behaviours: most lasted more than four minutes, and could reconnect themselves when ordered, but one rangy pipe-smoking well-into-his-twenties candidate stabilised at the dizzy-and-delightful stage of anoxic drunkenness. He didn't get any worse. He continued his slurring and scribbling routine without change. Our teacher was surprised, and let the exercise continue: 10 minutes, 15, 20, nothing changed – so it was time to go down for some Boscombe tea.

This exercise indicated to me how very different is the individual response to lack of oxygen. Body shape, lifestyle, drinking habits, smoking, physical condition, psychological makeup – who can say? There are a number of popular behaviour stereotypes. Euphoria, overconfidence – but not for me; quite the opposite. Only personal experience of altitude effects can tell a pilot what to expect (and the blue fingernail check should give a hint to anyone who is smart and quick enough to look).

Twin Flying

During our first year, the new twins began arriving. These were G model (160HP a side) Piper Apaches with two modifications – a conventional trimwheel on the floor between the pilots as opposed to a window winder in the ceiling, and a pressure accumulator on each engine to assist unfeathering. Yes – we did real feathering near the ground. Much has been written by Americans about this early example of general aviation, and all of it is true – it all depends what you want for the money, and, as in all things, you get what you pay for. Here are some quotes:

'The only thing I've heard about single engine ops in the Apache is that you may as well feather the 'good' engine too so you at least crash under control.'

'What the Piper PA-23 Apache is, in reality, is the lowest common denominator in the many-motored airplane zoo. It's the cheapest, the easiest, the most obtainable, the ugliest, the most docile and, according to some, possibly the least useful. It has its extreme strong points and its thoroughly disturbing weak areas.'

The main point of agreement is that an Apache was the cheapest way to get a twin rating. Its handling shows none of the ancestry suggested by the Piper name. Having taken over a Stinson twin project, Piper made a completely different sort of Piper, and only the easy-to-make model aeroplane wing reflected the pedigree of the classic and excellent handling Piper Cub. A Chevrolet owner might disagree with the Piper Cub flying farmer, but the Apache suited the American flying-car customer who preferred the kudos of an affordable twin in which to cross the wide open spaces on a nice day. It is always possible to argue the relative merits of a reliable single with one good (big) engine (and its 50% relative chance of an engine failure – rare anyway if you look after it), and there have been times when the idea of deliberate asymmetric training in a diddy twin was considered not worth the risk. But the Apache was cheap to buy, cheap to run, and something like the future Cherokee to drive (fly if you like) when both engines ran and the air was smooth.

These are the strong points. But the single-engined go-around handling and performance could indeed be disturbingly weak. We benefited from sea level and English temperatures, and the two callow youths who accompanied their instructor on a normal two-header detail didn't weigh that much (we were only a year or so out of the 1950s). A senior Canadian Air Force officer visited us. He made the valid point that, when compared to us, his students were intended to be hired assassins (he was a realist at least), and when asked what he thought of the Apache as a trainer, said 'It's a dandy little airplane'. This Air Commodore was right; it was dandy and little.

Our instructors were experienced and brave, and having generally learned their survival skills in machines with ten times the performance they probably continued the tradition. I was teamed up with Bruce Squirrell on the Apache and our instructor was 'Tapps' Tappin. Having first instructed on the pre-war Hawker biplane fighters Tapps went on to fly the Hurricane, and became a celebrated night fighter squadron commander, flying the Beaufighter and Mosquito. By coincidence he had been my father's Tiger Moth instructor, but this elicited no special sympathy whatsoever. We feathered with alacrity if given an engine failure after takeoff (Control, Power, Feather, Trim), and struggled round the circuit, but if the approach (probably including pumping of wheels and flaps if the appropriate engine was chosen) was not suitably accurate it was the real single-engined go-around for sure, until a satisfactory approach permitted the end of this torture by a landing.

Even after the type's second (at least) power upgrade our Apache model had marginal single-engine landing configuration climb (three on board). To go up at all the required speed was close to minimum control speed. The rudder load was high, the rudder pedals inconveniently close together, and the manual gear and flap pumping an awkward physical distraction – this is dangerous territory for an instructor (not to mention the luckless learners), and very hard work. We got away with it, but after-takeoff feathering seems to have now become a thing of the past.

Not long after we started to fly the Apache, and were making leisurely solo trundles to the Isle of Wight, an entertaining thing happened one morning. Cadet Paul Grenet was making an early if not first solo cruise over the island and noticed some oil creeping out of a cowling, but no oil pressure problem was indicated. We had already done the initial up-in-the-air feathering so clearly feathering was what twin flying was all about. He duly announced that he had feathered an engine and was returning. The approach control man pressed his red button in the tower and the siren went off in the hangar. How exciting – this would be our first crash. After Paul's uneventful landing the CFI was driven out and joined him, trying to look relaxed and reassuring. He started the offending engine and they taxied in. 'Well done Grenet,' he said, and left it at that. I've no idea what might have been discussed at staff level.

Our grass did not seem to give the Apache serious problems, even though the undercarriage complained with sharp banging and thumping during takeoff. On a bumpy day the Apache airborne ride was not great, and the short-coupled podgy little machine bucked, rolled and yawed back and forth rapidly, not possible to damp with the crude controls. This would make our future instrument rating exercises taxing, particularly on days when our altitude took us below or through the cumulus cloud layer, but solo cross countries in glassy smooth conditions were a different story, and here the little flying Chevy came into its own. In addition to our map and compass skills we now had two VORs* and an ADF* to help us out and, particularly at night, to cruise from one side of the country to the other, watching the lights of towns pass and the needles move as planned, was a relaxed, comfortable and satisfying experience – a foretaste of how well-ordered transport aviating could sometimes be.

(*The Automatic Direction Finder is the earliest of these radio aids to navigation; the VHF Omni (directional) Range is a post-WW2 device, more sophisticated in concept, but similarly universal. If you notice a round object surrounded by a circle of poles on an airfield it's one of these.)

Accommodation

When we had arrived at the college in 1960 our accommodation was well pre-war primitive, and this rather combined with the damp autumn weather, the smell of the Fawley refinery and the mournful sounds of the buoys in Southampton Water to create an unforgettable feel of a Hamble past – both village and airfield. The room I shared with Dave Gilson had divots in the lino and holes in the fibreboard walls where previous inmates had entertained themselves by seeing how many rooms they could drive a golfball through. But building work was in progress and we soon moved into brand new blocks, with our own rooms. Our old single-storey huts had to go, as did the pistol-range between the police gatehouse and the squash courts. An instructor from TS Mercury (a Victory-like hulk accommodation for a nautical school) had taught a few of us .22 pistol shooting. To a precision rifleman this was enlightening to say the least – another tiny tick in the experience box (and a new perspective on barn doors and Hollywood marksmanship), but by the time our second year started new cadets began to arrive and college life progressively grew to its planned size.

End in sight

My logbook tells me that on June 9th and 10th 1962 I made the Commercial Pilot's Licence day and night tests with Geoff Gurr of the Ministry of Aviation (now Civil Aviation Authority). On the following 19th of September the same examiner, pleasant, realistic and fair, (of course – I passed) conducted my instrument rating test from Gatwick to Hamble. This must have covered the holding and approaching first, followed by the airways on the way home. No matter. I see that five days later I made the return half of the boys' Jersey treat via Eastleigh (no wine with lunch for me). That was my last Hamble flight as a student.

Before leaving the subject of the college, a couple more things deserve a mention. During 1962, our Apache year, I apparently spent 60 hours in our new Flight Procedures Trainer. This was a basic, non-moving sort of simulator, based on Comet-like performance – something like a four jet Link trainer, without the hissing and lurching. 'Apparently' means that I remember little of the details – the evidence comes from the logbook. I think the idea was that we should get a feel for airliner speeds and heights, and we must have flown around from A to B doing instrument rating things, but a parallel function might have been crew cooperation (whatever that means). Thus far, all of our training had been as single pilot, and although Mike Kemp did his best to put over the principles of co-piloting (as of 1962), I can't remember taking away much of how it really should work, and, though my logbook times cover captain and co-pilot there's much more captain in there, so what was the other stooge doing? I'm not sure. Mike was originally a Meteor pilot who had been invalided out of BOAC due to failing hearing. This was a sad thing, as he would have made an exemplary captain (especially considering the variety of quality at the time), and I regret that I never had the chance to fly with him for real in due course. I may have learnt a lot about flying in this machine – but I have no recollection of what it was.

Instead of flying in and out of cloud and fog at low altitude it should be one or the other – either in continuous sight of the ground (as low as it takes) or the full blind flying Monty. Similarly a pilot is best either completely self contained (single seat), or as part of an agreed job-sharing process, with laid down functions and associated understandings of status etc. This has (or should have) become a fundamental principle of transport flying, but was not universally understood at this time (or perhaps had been forgotten).

A couple of weeks before our first intake were due to leave the college and go to BOAC, a man came down and announced that BOAC (the only state airline interested to date) did not need pilots, and the 35 remaining cadets (six having fallen by the wayside – but no loss by accident) would go to BEA instead. This was a surprise, and not universally accepted, so a new deal was presented a week later. Those who really wanted to go to BOAC could do so, but should understand that there would be no piloting for a while; those who had rethought their futures and were happy to commit themselves to shorthaul would be gratefully received; and there was a third compromise offer – two years in BEA with the option to then change to BOAC. A handful opted for options one and three, and around a half chose permanent BEA, starting with life in Glasgow. I elected for option three, with its prospect of hands-on flying followed by a change of scene. A number of the BOAC choosers would have preferred to do this, but after this drop-of-a-hat-with-no-warning change of plan felt uneasy about whether they could trust the promises made. Welcome to the world of work.

CHAPTER 6

BRITISH EUROPEAN AIRWAYS 1962–1964

I joined BEA on 29/10/62 (#16774): I was posted to the Vickers Vanguard (London based), and our small group soon began the classroom work at Heston. This was the necessary, well delivered ARB (Air Registration Board) nuts and bolts syllabus, but the general company ambience was not as glamorous as one might have expected (our experience of airlines so far had been BOAC). However, a job is a job, and the opportunity for a barely-out-of-his-teens trainee pilot with minimal experience to sit in the pilot's seat of a large, 4 x 14 ft propeller (4,500 HP each) monster was better than nothing (let's be honest – much better than nothing). There was a sort of simulator; by modern standards it was a systems trainer with instrument flying capabilities. I'm prepared to think I was quite good at flying it, and could do you a lovely ILS (Instrument Landing System) approach – that was a BEA co-pilot's job) but there would be more to real life outside.

My first attempt to fly the real Vanguard was on the 26th February, 1963. I had flown nothing since the previous September, and had a grand total of 287 flying hours, almost 80 of them on the little Apache. But any resemblance should be discounted – in fact there was none that you would notice.

I wrote about this experience for the Sideways Look feature of the Log in 1995 (32 years later, of course). Here's a trimmed version:

The day we hit the fence: a cautionary tale of base training

The road to the new Stansted terminal goes under the approach to runway 05, a little further out than the old one that used to take us from our hotel in Bishop's Stortford to the airfield proper. This runway was in use on the day when I first tried to guide a large four-engined airliner both to and from that position in the circuit from which an approach and landing can be made (as we 1179 people understand these things (form 1179 concerns the test items for a professional aircraft type rating).

This story happened in the middle of that winter in the early 'sixties when snow lay on the ground for many weeks, and for days the Bedford Varsity had Heathrow all to itself because of the fog – you could hear it trundling round, but never saw it. The day in question on which our collateral damage was to take place dawned overcast and remained as grey and bleak as is only possible east of the A1 in January; in fact, while the old snow on the ground tried to brighten things up a bit the end result weatherwise was a gloomy off-whiteout under a relentless grey sky.

My two colleagues on this detail had both come off the Viscount, and, while our new machine was much larger, they both coped well enough. Chalky, a captain, turned out to be a bit of a wag and remarked that the ailerons felt much like those of the Mark 3 Halifax – I expect he was right – and I admired the confident way that Roger, a self-improver, twiddled the rudder trim to go with his careful power changes; pretty much master of the machine already. Both these pilots were adapting to a change in both momentum and kinetic energy levels of, maybe, a factor of two – no problem. In my case this figure was more like a hundred. I was experientially challenged on this occasion and, while this situation doesn't have to be a problem, it can be if the man in charge isn't ready for it – in fact the combination of visual conditions and the training system put my mentor in a bad place.

My training captain was a pleasant chap, who wore his hat at the maximum jaunty angle permitted by an ear – in the style of the Bomber Command forage cap. He must have been perplexed at my inability to respond to the evidence coming through the windows.

(Why can't he stay lined up with the runway?)

(He's getting too low – why doesn't he do something about it?)

(He's getting high – why doesn't he do something about it?)

Direct assistance seemed the obvious answer. 'Have some more power.' Or, 'I'll take some power off.' 'Stay on the centreline' – easy to say; not so easy to sort out. 'I'll show you how it's done' was not in the script.

These were strictly visual circuits, no lighting or radio assistance whatever, so the new learning requirements were maximal.

On about the third or fourth approach I must have chanced upon approximately the throttle position that could take us from here to there (almost). Clearly Jim (a good enough name) thought that he might have been about to witness the instructor's goal; a non-interventional approach (if he gets away with this I've taught him how to do it – wonderful). Certainly the line-up was better, and, even though things remained soft and wavery, this attempt had a better chance of unassisted success.

At shouting distance from the runway there wasn't much to look at except the grey airstrip set in its dull white background. With a hundred yards to go a dark line shot under the nose (where did that come from?) some distance below. Then there was a sharp bang that set the machine juddering. This was a surprise, because I was flying level at the time, even climbing a bit: where did the heavy landing come from? With some delicate poling we landed gently a couple of thousand feet down the runway; nice touchdown, but it was obvious that something had happened.

The tower said nothing – nobody had seen. Initially an atmosphere of minor shellshock pervaded the cockpit, and although this was partially relieved when Jim said 'I think you've done enough for today, perhaps we'll change round' things felt tense as I taxied gingerly off the runway. As we made our way slowly back down the parallel taxiway one of the others got into the seat – and the tower still said nothing. Nor did Jim.

At the holding point the evidence was obvious. Short of the threshold the snow had drifted up into a bank against the hefty post and rail fence that ran alongside the road, just leaving the top forty-five degree element visible; visible, that is, except for the two sections either side of the centreline. These were plainly absent and a few bucketsful of freshly splintered kindling lay strewn down the snowbank towards us.

Before we climbed into our sturdy mount the next day to return to London Jim had a quiet word. 'Best not to say anything about the fence – bit difficult to explain away that sort of thing.' I agreed – and it was almost two years later that I heard about the percussive event from a stewardess, in the context of reported shortcomings of the new teenaged (almost) tyros (not me, of course – a two year old hand with a battered hat). Obviously the careless talk time limit had passed.

So whose fault was it? Not mine really; I was a learner with no idea of what I was doing, and Jim's job was to stop me hitting things other than the runway; but, as I've already suggested, he was poorly placed. Base training is a building block process where weaknesses in the structure may reveal themselves in an unpredictable way. The purpose of this training should be to identify gaps in the wall and build a sound structure as well as tick 1179 items. This is best done from the bottom up, and in my case, I couldn't have had fewer bricks to start with. I doubt if Jim had ever supervised anyone with as little experience as myself – on that day.

We do some base training on my present fleet, the Concorde. With any luck our learners already have experience in the visual approaching of the multi-jet transport. During the seventy-plus hour simulator course they make many ILS approaches, and can do them well early on in the syllabus. Our first session at base finishes with an approach and landing without radio or lighting guidance; but we start by making use of the aids with which our students are familiar so that the transition to this new environment (real world) is suitably progressive. (We also demonstrate personally the first approach and landing; 'I've got it, just sit back and see what it looks like'.) This isn't a waste of base time, it continues building where we left off in the simulator, and reduces the risk of a fall off the stepping stones because they are too far apart: pretty obvious really, but not the case when I made my USCE (unplanned structure contact event). It was nobody's fault really; let's put it down to experience – a dicey do, but a few decibels short of a prang.

It wasn't until my next conversion course that I discovered that my assumption that base training captains must have had hands-on instructing experience was flawed – stupid boy. This explained a lot, and brings me to my final point (for base training captains).

Do not hesitate to intervene/take the machine off your student (however clever he or she appears to be)/open up and go around if you sense that acceptable limits are being challenged and your own experience is about to be extended – you could be right. You will not be charged (personally) for the 'wasted' circuit, you grab a bit of driving for yourself, and why wait to find out the cost of the alternative? (in our case a couple of lengths of 4x4 – but we got away with it; well, Jim got away with it).

Better and cheaper training

I went back to Stansted a number of times after the fence-busting mission to continue coming to terms with this large and powerful machine, usually with two or three of my ex-Hamble colleagues. We flew with a variety of training captains: progress was better, and our mentors generally more at home. On March 13 1963 I flew with Ron Gillman, our training manager. Ron could not be mistaken for anyone but Ron, and he played the black and white screen hero perfectly. The precisely chiselled and suspiciously black Ronald Colman moustache, slicked-down black hair and breezy confidence were reassuring. During our first circuit session Ron professed some effects of the previous evening (wherever that had been). 'I must have eaten a dead rat,' he complained, 'fly around the local area for a while,' and left us boys to cruise around, unsupervised. Ron was not acting (much). He really was playing himself. He really had been a celebrated ship-buster – *The Scourge of the Mediterranean*, perhaps? – then instructed on heavy twins: and make films about it, specialising in low level cross countries – *Mosquito* and *633 Squadron* – the original B&W versions? The special thing about Ron was his enthusiasm for flying aeroplanes per se, and this included teaching others – the true amateur who makes his hobby his job. Ron was quite unfazed by the prospect of teaching inexperienced youths – after all, he had done it before – and our further handling training was comprehensive and effective. By my last detail on April 3rd I think I could fly the Vanguard quite well; partly, I would guess, thanks to Ron's understanding that there needed to be more to airline training than the in-house examiner qualification it was widely assumed to be. And why not? Like many things it's not difficult if you know how; or, from a management point of view, have the breadth of view to realistically assess the job in hand.

Before he slid off to a dinner engagement one Stansted evening, Ron told me about his airborne head-on crash. This event was not in the '*when sex was fun and flying was dangerous*' days – quite the opposite. This happened in the fifties, with air traffic control. Ron had been driving his Elizabethan to Paris in the cloud, approaching the Aumale beacon in northern France. Suddenly something big loomed out of the gloom and roared over the cockpit. There was a thump and a shudder, then normality. 'What the hell was that?' On the ground the damage was obvious – a wingtip missing, and the top of one fin (the Elizabethan had three) sawn off. The opposing DC4 had passed the beacon and was in a turn. Both were very much on track. The two aircraft had collided wingtip to wingtip, the top one banked (a bit), and a DC4 propeller had gone through the top of the relevant fin. Only Hollywood could make it up, but it did happen to Ron. I believe Le Bourget owned up to the mistake, and both crews were following orders, but three weeks after finishing base training I almost witnessed a nose to nose, Vanguard to Vanguard disaster – from the cockpit.

A miss is as good as a mile

The first part of our route training was exclusively riding shotgun. The Vanguard, though large, could be operated by two pilots; in fact the Trans Canada Airlines 952 models only carried two, but the Vanguard was twice the size of a Viscount, so maybe an extra crew member was considered to make sense. It could have done, but our Hamble training (and pilot training in general historically), had concentrated on individual pilot self-sufficiency, and two pilot crews had been the shorthaul norm for some years. In the past, extra crew members such as radio officers had other jobs to do: two pilots at the front became the culture.

On this day I had already completed at least twenty sectors in the forward-facing middle seat, all with experienced captains and co-pilots. Settling in, getting a feel for the job, seeing what pilots do – no problems. The P3 seat was rather grand, actually; between and a bit behind the pilots, and raised up somewhat, so that one sat at socialising height with standup visitors and cabin crew, with a splendid view from this VC10-width cockpit and its large windows. This job consisted of reading the checks (or some of them, as it turned out), getting the weather, adding up the fuel, sorting the paperwork, doing the company radio; but it was not usually overtaxing. On this particular run of duty our commander had been one of our base training captains – pleasant to fly with, laid back, competent, experienced and familiar with training; it was obvious.

The three of us had already done a few sectors together and a couple of nightstops, and we set off again from London to join the A1 as usual. The pilots chatted happily as we climbed up and headed north, and at 10,000ft one of them cancelled the 10,000ft flashing green light (doing this with a toe was quite cool). Our cruising height was FL 170 (17,000ft on standard pressure) and one thousand feet to go was duly noted as we approached it.

Then I saw it – the altimeters were still on QFE, height above Heathrow. It was a low-pressure day – in the 980s, 30 millibars difference – a thousand feet's worth! Whoever was flying started levelling off as the altimeters were frantically wound up! We topped out at maybe five or six hundred feet too high as the southbound Vanguard (flight level 180) sailed overhead going the other way. The potential news coverage does not bear thinking about – two machines' worth of blazing wreckage all over Watford High Street and environs, no survivors (definitely not), freak accident – no clues (until they find the altimeters: nothing else wrong, an extremely simple accident investigation).

Nothing was said and we continued. I looked at my check list. There it was, a Climb Check, all of which, one can only assume, would have been done by the dashing pilots (with the flashing green 10,000ft light, although this light was mainly of interest coming down). The thing that amazed me as I looked at this checklist, which included altimeter setting, was that I had been unaware of its presence. It had never been mentioned or asked for. I was interested in aeroplanes – how they worked, pressing the buttons and fiddling with the levers, adjusting the nose up and down – but it was not in my nature to take the books to bed unless necessary. And why was no one else interested in the climb check? This was a Swiss cheese hole if ever there was one (although we got away with it – to everyone else it was a normal flight). This machine was being operated as a two-pilot aeroplane with office junior, and they had missed something important, perhaps assuming they could rely on my automatic back-up, but I don't think so. They could after that.

On April 27th I went to Palma and back with Wily Wakelin, still in my shotgun seat. I never stayed in Palma because this was 1 Flight territory and I was 2 Flight (and we overnighted in Malta), but I remember this brief visit well because this upscale resort wasn't what I expected – even then. We set off with our blazered and flannelled or cavalry-twilled home counties passengers, complete with regimental ties (real and fake) and their ladies, arrived at a very quiet rural Mediterranean airfield, looking much as the war had left it, and taxied up to a large Nissen hut. This was the place. When the man with the bats said we should stop, a couple of other rustic-looking Spaniards came up and congratulated him – handshakes all round. I've no idea why. We appeared to be the only live aircraft on the field. Maybe it was his first go with the bats (or he really was the Palma table tennis champion). The last time I visited this airfield was with a BOAC bucket-and-spade, kiss-me-quick 747 night charter, about 12 years later. We parked in one of several long rows of wide body jets. The Nissen hut was gone – I didn't recognize anything.

On April 28th 1963 I had been cleared to take the right-hand seat and did a two-day trip with Angus Caesar-Gordon, another nice man. I see my first real takeoffs and landings were on this tour, both to London from Glasgow and Paris respectively. Once into the swing of the rostering system flights thereafter came thick and fast, most of them to Glasgow, Edinburgh, Belfast and Manchester, with occasional forays into Europe. Three-sector days with night stops in between were common, and the Central Hotel Glasgow became familiar. This is a large piece of Victorian history, forming one side of the Central station, then still fully in the steam era. The rooms, though divided into half their original size, were high and atmospheric, and a walk down a Buckingham Palace corridor took one to a large and similarly high-windowed bathroom where a huge bath (with two-handed Clydeside ringbolts for taps) stood in the centre of a red tiled floor. This certainly took one back to pre-ensuite, pre-shower days. I remember something similar at the Galle Face hotel in Colombo about three years later, warmer, more tropical and open to the atmosphere; no buckets of water in Glasgow, but the same bath on the clay tiles. The Central breakfast was good, as was the fish at Roganos down the road – reasonably affordable then on our allowances (and these were the days of the £1230 a year second officer's salary).

I cannot remember the exact system for who was supposed to do what in the Vanguard, though the basic principle for let-downs and approaches was that the co-pilot flew and the captain took over and landed. This could be reversed if it was the co-pilot's sector, but my recollection is that the co-pilot usually flew the whole flight if it was his go – unless the weather was bad. Co-pilots were unquestionably regarded as the instrument approach specialists and the hand-held monitored approach was the system for low visibility success. It worked pretty well, but in normal weather there seemed to be some flexibility at the captain's discretion. On a normal descent he would take over and continue when he felt like it, often early on to get his share of handling. Takeoffs were very clear cut. The non-flying pilot set the power and watched the dials (the third man must have called speeds). If anything went wrong with an engine, he throttled the whole lot back and went into ground idle. The takeoff was definitely over. I don't remember if or what he should say (maybe 'stop') – but everyone was going to stop anyway. This gave the newest learner total stop/go control the first time he got into the co-pilot's seat. I never experienced a takeoff problem, but there are various possibilities which were not discussed.

To begin with, the other co-pilot was, naturally, always more senior and older than me. Most were ex-national service military or thereabouts, and almost always helpful, unlike some captains. Accepting that some older co-pilots might have felt persuaded to temporarily side with a captain who chose to take a disparaging attitude towards a new co-pilot, I think it's fair to say that the 1950s military pilots, many from two years' national service, were better selected and trained, and had survived the military and early airline experience with fewer misconceptions and illogical prejudices than some of our socially and professionally sensitive commanders. Basically, these post-war co-pilots had less problem as to who they were and how to conduct themselves at work and interact with their fellows (though some did like to recount the dangerous asymmetric qualities of the Meteor and its nostalgic effect on their training recollections – 'They died like flies': maybe, but this may have been rite of passage bravado for our wet-behind-the-ears benefit). Collectively, however, they had a more realistic take on the demands of the airline job.

Personalities and styles of captaincy varied, as I recall. Complete beginners, like us, naturally do not know what to expect from new employment, but while a significant proportion of captains seemed unfazed by our appearance in their midst, there was a tangible groundswell of disapproval from some at our lack of 'background': we were not like them (no military service, let alone the war, therefore of no use). 'Humble Hamble lads', became a description. On a return visit to Hamble I mentioned this to Tony Timbs. 'What do they want? Do they expect you to break up the furniture?' he asked.

Before we get on to the subject of life-changing wartime service it must be said that many of our well-behaved and easy-to-get-on-with captains had survived this experience apparently unscathed as far as could be seen in everyday and relatively unthreatening up-the-road-and-back operation. But some elements of the airline itself, its shorthaul and parochial lifestyle, the history of its beginnings and the lack of a cohesive sense of identity and mythical status all added up to an airline which was to continue its busy but troubled progress into the jet age, while determinedly maintaining notions of poor-relation disadvantage, envy, resentment and a strong sense of *campanilismo* – call it whatever you like.

Danny Gray constantly reminded his crew of one of the reasons. He was an agreeable and entertaining but perceptive and realistic Vanguard captain who never failed to describe his BOAC neighbours each time he arrived from Pinner. 'You should see their gardens; immaculate – the man next door's outside doing his crazy paving; beautiful: they're always at home, decorating or gardening – and look at their houses and cars – talk about salary!'

However much Danny might have envied their apparent time off and Atlantic baron money and status, he enjoyed making a joke of the resentment that pervaded BEA, but the reason for this had happened in 1946 (when I was four years old). Was this perception just to do with money and imagined free time? BEA was founded as an offshoot of BOAC, with elements of transport command. Was there a flood of volunteers? Who might have been posted to this local flying organisation? Who would you like to get rid of? Would your experienced, DFC'd four-engined senior people jump at the chance to fly a Dragon Rapide, a DC3 perhaps, or even the Ju-52 up the road and back to a rainy Croydon or Northolt? (Maybe some of them did.) I cannot start to answer these questions, but, to a great extent, the end of WW2 defined the last knockings of a relatively brief (in evolutionary terms) but well-defined social structure that has underpinned British society since those who had lived off the land moved to industrial cities and became something else. Advancement by putdown is a well-tried emotional refuge for those under perceived social threat, and is a useful team-building ploy as well – a difficult habit to grow out of when the threats have gone. Anyone outside the circle is a target. We were the first few from Hamble, but snide comments aimed in our direction were not totally absent, along with disparaging comments about any other operators' qualities and nationalities. Of course a joke is a joke, and to be welcomed in the course of a routine day's work, but there's a thin line defining the boundary between a desire for self-expression within an environment where standardised performance and integrated behaviour has become the sine qua non of safe, reliable, and, very importantly, personality-neutral air transport for hire and reward. There was clear evidence within BEA of an awareness of the importance of standard operating and organised monitoring, but could it be that an intangible background wash of dissatisfaction chronically undermined it, eventually encouraging this airline to make a big thing of these concepts? To repeat: a majority of captains were content with a routine and trouble-free flight, but this was not universal.

I remember returning empty one night from say Cologne or Düsseldorf – somewhere like that. In the cruise the captain decided to brush up his feathering. Quite why is not certain as this was not discussed with the other two of us, nor were any books referred to. Was this a walk down Memory Lane – from the days when one went to Frankfurt but did not land? Possibly not. Or was he unsure of the correct technique for this new machine and wanted to experiment? Of course everyone had to know how to feather an engine; the ARB exam system required this knowledge. We did it in the simulator, and our base training captains did it on the runway as we took off. It worked a treat. Two things were required: HP (immediate fuel to engine) cock to feather, pull fire handle (to feather the propeller). But there were more complications to the propellering system of this large turboprop, and our captain had failed to grasp them, so it seems. If in doubt he could have read it up first, but this did not seem to have been the case. His version was to close the HP cock, thus cutting the fuel supply, and pull the fire handle (or did he push it [unfeather]? I cannot be sure). Without 'feather' (a final HP notch behind cut-off) selected, the propeller was confused as to what to do. The auto-coarsen system leapt into action and drove the propeller towards feather (as it is supposed to do if torque is less than expected), then let it go, starting the cycle again. The auto-coarsen light flashed on and off, the rpm whazzed up and down, the machine swung about, and the autopilot coped well. A nice clear day is the best time for experimental off-design test flying, but this was a very dark night on the way back from the Ruhr. He relit the engine, then tried it again a couple of times, with the same result. Why did we not offer unrequested advice; or even throw a mutiny? One didn't in those days. He could have asked his assistants how to do it, but I don't think it occurred to him to do so. Large propellers call for the greatest respect. Is deliberate feathering a hazardous action? Certainly not, but playing with heavy machinery that you don't understand is foolish. Was he a bit dim, and lacking imagination? Looked like it, but who can say?

One day one particular man told a couple of us Hamsters what we should do when we went to see the Flight Manager: 'March in, stand to attention and give him a smart salute.' Jolly good stuff, of course, but is this appropriate for the Hounslow-based Amber One bus? Aren't salutes specifically related to the sovereign's commission (Elizabeth I and before)? Saluting is not supposed to be personal, I thought, nor does saluting feature in the company standing orders (and would there even be an officer on parade?) If this was an essential part of the BEA job, why were we not taught it when we first joined (along with '*March you over, save you walking*')? More confusion in the syllabus perhaps – or confusion as to how to run an airline? Not only do I know how to do this stuff, but the Cert A pt. 2 chitty somewhere in my attic hints that I know how to teach it as well; including the correct salute – not like Benny Hill's doorman, among others who should know better. We had two flight managers; mild and polite Dingle Dell and old quiet Captain Mac. I didn't go to see them often, but neither seemed to notice the lack of salute (or lack of hat indoors). This was all rather silly, and perhaps it's better to leave the subject of non-standard behaviour there.

There were many others of a sane and agreeable nature, and it would take a trawl through the logbook to recall them, but Bill Caldwell deserves a mention. Older than most (with a special contract, I believe), he was a true Scot (and I can only summarise by including all that might go with this qualification – I have a Scottish grandmother). In every weather, summer and winter, he drove to Heathrow in his open green Bentley, scarf flying in the wind. When he started flying I've no idea, but he was in the Navy during the war, and seemed none the worse for that. But as for giving his co-pilots maximum crack of the whip, he was almost unequalled. What a nice and generously-spirited man. There are many others.

The Vanguard itself was a reassuringly solid, powerful and very mechanical aircraft, and fast for a propeller-driven transport. Ron Gillman told us the wing loading was the same as a Scimitar. Maybe he was close – although one has to bear in mind the Reynolds Number advantage of size. Manual controls, DC generated electrics with alternators for AC gadgets, hydraulics for flaps and undercarriage, and trouble-free gas turbine engines: not much to go wrong, and in my recollection it didn't. Nowadays small multi-blade propellers, fans almost, are the thing for fast (and high) turboprops, but this was the last of a tradition of big propellers that had to go round slowly. A chunky (short range) kind of Britannia, DC7, Connie, Stratocruiser or B29 with shorter wings and another 1000hp per engine.

The controls were not super light, but reasonable for the nature of the beast: engine failure after V1 was different, but considerably easier to manage than an immediately-after-takeoff feather on the dreaded Apache (and a damned sight safer). There had been some minor problems to sort out initially with the aeroplane. The propellers and tailplane resonated in the climb, giving the girls standing in the front galley an 800 rpm vibro-massage via the feet. Some enjoyed it but others complained about the distractive effects, so a special climb flap position was included; finally some weights under the tailplane solved it. Then there was the 'cracking of the splines'. The highly-geared drive train between engine and propeller included a splined sliding joint in the drive shaft, and the continuous load at climb power prevented oil getting through – risk of drying out and seizure. The fix was easy. Once we had levelled off and let the machine accelerate to a good speed all engines were smoothly throttled back to idle, then opened back up to cruise power. At cruise airspeed but idle power the propellers briefly drove the engines: the splines relaxed and oil got in for the rest of the flight – problem sorted.

There wasn't much all-night flying, though we did fly in the dark quite a lot; in fact if you go to Scotland in the winter it's unavoidable. The last flights to Belfast, Glasgow and Edinburgh each evening were called the night mail, for obvious reasons, and arrived near midnight, usually followed by a nightstop. I remember heading for Edinburgh one such dark and quiet evening. As we cruised in contemplative silence over the Peak District towards the end of a three-sector day our very nice and ladylike stewardess appeared silently in the darkened cockpit with a tray and three glasses, each fizzing discreetly with tiny bubbles. She handed one to the captain, who received it with a smile of contented domesticity; the shotgun man took the other two and passed one over to me. Nothing was said and she floated out as she had arrived, leaving us to our dark and restfully droning office.

'It's my birthday,' said the captain. He and the shotgun man sipped theirs quietly. Did they realise I would have to do the descent and approach in the dark? No concern was evident, so I tried mine. The champagne cocktail was excellent. Sugar lump, bitters, brandy; everything in perfect proportion: worthy of a BOAC crew bus (or perhaps the BEA Comet fleet, but I don't know). A disgraceful breaking of the rules, of course, but rather cool, on this special occasion. Was it really his birthday? Could it really have been his wife?

The Mediterranean

We did have the occasional overnight foray to the Mediterranean and back. The young need more sleep than the old, but staying awake all night needs getting used to, and we did not have the keep-awake pills issued in the past. The degree of flying difficulty was now quite different, of course, but you cannot store up sleep in advance. I remember a Palma/Barcelona and back one summer night. What I had done during the previous day I don't remember, but the weather was good, so it would have been something. We arrived back at London at about 6 am after our three sectors, and I went home to bed. I awoke at dusk, and thought about what my flatmates might be doing; something to eat, the pub. Then something strange happened: it got lighter. I had been asleep for 24 hours.

But most Mediterranean trips were flown during the day, and afforded a welcome, sunny and scenic day or two away. Gibraltar was an interesting place to land, and its wind problems, short runway and sea walls have historically demanded pilots' attention, but Palermo is another scenic seaside place with its own wind problems, somewhere before landing. I called in there both ways in January 1964 on a Malta nightstop captained by Joe Reay with 'Oakey' Oakford as the other co-pilot. The airfield is on the north coast of Sicily just along from the town, but it's also sheltered from the south by its own very large rock, and wind strength and direction are critical if an approach is to be attempted, even if the weather looks very nice. Captains would usually do the landing at problematic places, but on the way back Joe, surprisingly, gave this one to Oakey – an ex Treble One Squadron Black Arrow pilot who had retained his own special dynamic handling technique, even for the hefty Vanguard. Joe was on the small and spare side, and I remember him having quite a struggle with the controls one day when the right-hand seat man gave him reverse on one side after landing, by mistake. It should have been inners only – inners produced confused air over the tail, but the control thrashing was worse from the outers whose airflow also got hold of the ailerons, and full reverse was quite something, needing the help of both pilots to limit the controls' bouncing off their stops. On the two on one side occasion Joe was flipped around his half of the cockpit like a rag doll and soon called for cancel. Neither of them realised what had happened, and there was no point in mentioning it after the event – it hadn't been on purpose.

On this Palermo afternoon the air was clear and the wind within its variety of limits, but was from the critical African direction. All was smooth until Oakey was turning finals at maybe three miles, then all hell let loose, as they say. Oakey battled away like his formation loop on a rough day with a new leader and we weathered the barrage, emerging to a normal landing, but it was an impressive display of lee side mountain turbulence, and the figures in the Palermo letdown book should be read carefully; they're not wrong.

The reader may be wondering why there are not more descriptions of the cultural and historic jewels of Europe. The answer is simple, and we also lived in some degree of isolation from the more exotic fleets who quietly came and went through Heathrow less frequently than us. The occasional Comet floated off to distant Europe and the Mediterranean. The two-pilot Viscounts disappeared to more remote or smaller destinations than ourselves, and, of course, they also had the sometimes second-home option of the Berlin-centred German internals. The German girls did not usually range over the border, but I did hear the story of one unsuspecting victim who made a surprise visit to England on her days off, and arrived at the front door of the kind and sympathetic Engländer of her dreams, eager to start the promised new life. She was invited in by his wife, who pointed out the kitchen, car, dog and washing machine, announced that the kids would be home at five o'clock and left.

Even our Hamble colleagues who had joined the airline a few weeks before us had all gone to Glasgow to do a different sort of Scottish flying in the Herald. The Vanguard was very much London based – virtually every other sector returned to London, the Queen's Building, the FSDO (flying staff duty officer) desk and the tea room upstairs – and our typical flight time was one hour fifteen minutes (in other words our world was a 1hr 15min radius hamster wheel centred on Heathrow). Such a parochial routine suits some, and those who want to make the most of what their current circumstances have to offer may look to their employer or their union for additional responsibility and status, such as it is. Someone has to do it, of course, but this frequency of visit and time spent at the place of work compromises the opportunity to spend useful time on other interests and tends to restrict conversation to the lowest common denominator – company policy and industrial politics. It did not suit me altogether, and, although I had no illusion about the privilege of an agreeable (and predominantly enjoyable) non-nine-to-five, non-Monday-to-Friday job, I started to look elsewhere for other things to do, flying included. My logbook tells me that on July 10th 1963, after a morning Glasgow and back with Pete Griffin, I went to the Airways Flying Club at White Waltham and a quick circuit with CFI Archie Cole checked me out in their Chipmunk.

A couple of days later I happened to set out on a two three-sector-day Irish tour with Denis Clifton; two Belfasts with nightstop, finishing with a Dublin and back. Denis was a fleet hero, having successfully managed an extremely serious incident the previous November...

The Battle of Turnhouse (1962)

> I've just (2014) read his 2006 resume of this 1962 event of a Scottish November night (while I was grappling with the Vanguard ARB stuff – but never had seen a real one). Knowing what I know now this was an exceptionally dangerous and demanding set of circumstances. It doesn't get worse. Night, low cloud, rain, wind 20kts across. Everyday Scottish stuff, but then there are the seagulls; a lot of them. This wasn't your routine engine failure after takeoff: at 11pm the approaching engines and lights disturbed the seagulls roosting on the warm runway, who may not have had time to assess the situation, the crosswind and what to do in the dark. Against Corporal Jones' advice they panicked and took off en masse. Denis recalls that forward vision was obscured by a snow-like whiteout, and seagulls went into all the slim engine intakes, restricting vital airflow and causing damage to the rotating assemblies. All engines showed distress. Two soon failed and were feathered (correctly this time), and neither of the other two worked normally. One produced normalish power with dangerously high turbine temperature and the other also ran, but only so-so. Basically the situation developed into flight with one and a half failing engines, assorted warnings signifying their distress, and a dark and stormy night with time running out. The co-pilot flew a 1½ engine ILS procedure (a simulator first?) and they saw the lights at 350ft, for Denis to take over and land – prepared for the 20kts across and the after-landing propeller jiggery-pokery with the two still struggling engines. Denis attributed the passengers' and

crew's survival to simple and rugged equipment, and a good crew. He's right. (My – how things have changed in 50 years, especially the style of equipment and crew.)

On this less eventful routine trip we got to the Belfast Royal Avenue Hotel at about 2 pm, in time to see the 12th of July loyalist parade transit this main thoroughfare, well up to steam, bowler hats, banners and bands included. This was a year or so before the troubles officially resumed, and, despite my name, I have no Irish connections or sectarian sympathies, so this display of earnestness and commitment was something colourful, bizarre, strange and somehow disquieting for someone used to the best of Anglican establishment behaviour. There were joyful revellers in our bar that evening, not a suggestion of aggression anywhere, but jocular comments about visiting the poorer parts of the city to find Catholics to beat up were not just for our benefit – worth a laugh, maybe, but real. This was a glimpse into an alien world, but normality for someone else.

The next day we went to London and then to Dublin. This return was also uneventful except for a hold-up prior to engine start. A pale young man was sympathetically escorted off the aeroplane. 'I've changed my mind. I've decided not to run away to England; perhaps I'll go home,' he announced as he walked along the gangway to the door.

Weeks or months later I did a simulator check with Denis. He told me off for being too fast and superficial with an emergency. 'It's not a game,' he said. I get his point; he's absolutely right, but no one can pretend that the simulator is real – a rehearsal, perhaps. But what will they do on the night? His concern came from his experience of reality, and the simulator is the only way to observe possible behaviour. Might he have to fly with a little prat like me tomorrow and have a million seagulls zap him again? Makes you think. My wonderful ILS and snappy feathering may not be quite enough.

Stan Key

I flew with Stan Key a couple of times – to Copenhagen and back on April the 3rd 1964, and then an Edinburgh nightstop 18/19 of the same month. I had already been warned of Stan's potential prickliness, but, the no joking apart, all went well and there were no problems; in fact Stan gave me (a 22-year-old novice, with a mere solid year's daily Vanguarding behind him) the first sector to Copenhagen – unfamiliar terrain. The atmosphere during these two trips was quiet and formal, but not theatrically so; and my own assessment, 50 years down the road (and also at the time, I remember), would be efficient, competent and professional, and, especially significant considering our age and experience gap, socially neutral. I would have been happy to fly with Stan again – but never did.

Something I did know at the time (though it seems seldom discussed) was the reason for Stan's difficult relationship with a number of his brother officers of the Queen's Building Tearoom (on the first floor – with its squawk box: 'Captain Blenkinsop, your aircraft is ready for the 1725 Glasgow, stand 27'). I believe that it all started with the Munich winter takeoff crash with the Manchester United football team on February 8th 1958 (two years of school to go for me, but 14 years before Stan's demise).

Stan was an Elizabethan captain in 1958, involved with union affairs, and was detailed to be the BALPA (British Airline Pilots Association) rep at the Munich hearing. It was assumed, therefore, that he would stalwartly defend the unfortunate Captain Thane. That may well have been the intention, and Stan did explain his experience of Elizabethan brakes freezing in similar conditions, but the real reason (the fatal effect of a mere quarter inch of slush on the runway) was not understood at the time, and the verdict was undealt-with ice on the wings. How much ice was there on the wings, and what effect would it have had? How much weight should this verdict carry? Was there a credible defence at the time? Not really. All very difficult.

Months, weeks, maybe years later the research results came out – it was the slush; a new discovery. It wasn't the captain's fault at all. The Munich people didn't tell him about the runway and its effect on his quite fast aeroplane – well of course not, nobody knew. But that didn't deter the Queen's Building tearoom hindsight experts, and Stan was denigrated for his failure to stick up for the unfortunate Thane (What are BALPA reps for, for God's sake?) Stan continued to be hounded by an element of this Hounslow primary school playground cruelty until his death in the Papa India Trident mega-disaster on June 18th 1972. Something wrong somewhere in this state of Denmark, I fancy, but I never got to understand it, except to realise that airlines, by their very nature of safe (enough) transport of the unsuspecting but paying public by the worst people you've got, have to operate a bottom-based system.

Do not be fooled by the traditional-looking (if a bit cheap) uniforms with lavish gold barring and much scrambled egg. Any resemblance to authoritarian structures like armies, navies or air forces, for example, is highly illusory. Individual power, respect and responsibility are not how it works. There are two types of pilot – captains and helpers. All differentiation within these groups is a function of date of joining and indicated by pay scale. This extreme industrial democracy, aided by union politics, but demanded by the minimum standard system of the licensing authority, means that all members of a particular job description stratum are equally free to express their not-too-well informed and frivolous opinions as and when they wish. If they spend a lot of time together they do it a lot – what else is there to talk about? I wonder if Stan (not alone) was not able to understand this sea change of job requirement, and took it all too seriously? *(Captain Thane was exonerated by the German authorities ten years after the accident).*

Some historical trivia and coincidence

On July 3rd 1968, while I was occupied with the BOAC B707, the ex-BEA Elizabethan on the left above, G-AMAD (Sir Francis Drake), now owned by BKS and used for racehorse ferrying, was about to land at 28R, Heathrow, when the left hand flap torque tube failed. The machine insisted on rolling to the left. The crew tried to go around but the roll persisted, even with the flaps raised to the correct 10 (for a serviceable Elizabethan) on the good side. The machine ended up in the central area, its left wing having cut off the tail and engines of Trident 1 G-ARPT and the fin part of G-ARPI. PT was a write off, but PI could be repaired using the tail of PT. A good insurance job, but PI is, of course, the ill-fated Trident 1 of the Stan Key story mentioned above (June 1972). This day and its distracting weather will get a mention when we get to 1972, and a Zlin positioning cross country.

CHAPTER 7

MORE SMALL AEROPLANES

Some of our BEA Glasgow colleagues decided that they needed a means of boosting the real command piloting time needed for cranking up their licences. We had completed the airline pilot's exam paper stuff at Hamble, but to upgrade to Senior Commercial, then Airline Transport, sufficient flying hours were required. I can't remember the reason for this, but a group of them bought a Druine Turbulent so that they could putt-putt around the Scottish countryside getting the required experience. There's nothing wrong with this, and it does mean something – real flying after all – but others have achieved the same result with P51 time; not the famous Mustang, but the Parker 51 – elegant, stylish, easy to handle and cheap on fuel: and you can drive it comfortably while sitting at your writing desk. Not for our honest colleagues however; but by the autumn of 1963 the Turbulent had served its purpose and was bought by Nigel Minchin and myself, and found a new home at Fairoaks. I see that I first flew it on November 1 before going to Glasgow and back (in a Vanguard). Nigel was one of the few initial Hamsters who went direct from Hamble to BOAC, and was currently navigating the Britannia 312, so he decided that a share in the little machine would get him in a pilot's seat quite economically.

The Turbulent is a French single-seat homebuilt design, of which a number were manufactured by Rollasons of Croydon, all powered by VW Beetle engines. This flat-four air-cooled engine works well for little aeroplanes as well as the people's car, and ours was a 1200, suitably modified for dual ignition flying requirements. The aeroplane itself demonstrates the best of simple design, and does not try to imitate something else, or achieve more than is sensible for such a small and simple device. It's a small, open cockpit low-wing monoplane. What more can you say? But it has brakes for steering, and built-in slots along the outer leading edges. What for, you may ask? Very small aeroplanes like this look like toys, but should not be regarded as such. However benign their characters they have limited inertia (can do things quickly) and their controls are light and relatively short throw. They therefore can respond aggressively when subjected to overenthusiastic driving. The slots are there to delay and ameliorate the effects of wingtip stalling, but do not prevent it. If treated appropriately the Turbulent is an excellent design and can provide hours of tootling pleasure with impressive economy.

Like our Scottish-based colleagues we used it for trundling around the south of England this time – and just that: there was no ulterior motive, and I had no recollection of a need to build up hours. What's the point of a toy aeroplane, many will ask, but it quickly occurred to me that this was the first time I had flown anything without the supervision or authorisation of someone else – an employer or training organisation, for example. There was an element of special satisfaction about this true aeronautical self-sufficiency, and it is something that a significant proportion of professional pilots, civil and military, never actually experience. Maybe that is why the concepts of responsibility, decision making, commander-like behaviour and so on are so bandied about in these professional but institutionally structured fields. They are essential, of course, and the illusion needs to be fostered. But it was obvious: I was an amateur who was also paid for flying.

More than once I have come across a pilot who makes the proud boast 'I have never flown an aeroplane I was not paid to fly'. What do they expect the listener to take from this statement? Does it mean that they are of irreplaceable value to an employer, or that they could not function or be trusted without the support of others and a set of orders? The jury must remain out on this one. Of course there is nothing wrong in the concept of the professional who is happy to remain just that, and, apart from the occasional and very rich wannabe pilot celebrity, only a business or government can afford to own and operate large or high performing machines.

Apart from the essential legalities I do not remember any guiding paperwork coming with our tiny aeroplane, but it gave us no problem – except on warm days. As the summer of 1964 developed I noticed that sometimes, the Turbulent became increasingly reluctant to climb after takeoff, and the engine sounded subtly different – more of a harsh ringing element to it. By two or three hundred feet level flight was as good as full throttle would achieve, and a careful and small circuit was called for, ending that day's flying. Next day the machine might well fly well, and I took to the judicious initial circuit as the day's decider – to go or not to go (anywhere). This always worked, except once. A new Vanguard co-pilot, a year behind us at Hamble with a Scottish name – Macbeth, Macduff, something like that – expressed an interest in flying it; he had done a year on the Chipmunk not so long ago so why not? I did my 'to climb or not to climb' test flight and the little machine flew well – today was on. I started him up, he taxied out and I went inside to read the paper. After about half an hour I thought it time to check on his progress and was amazed to see him walk in through the airfield entrance.

'Where is it?' I asked.

'It's all right,' he stammered, 'it wouldn't climb. I had to land straight ahead.'

Immediately to the east of Fairoaks is Ottershaw School, a large Victorian building in extensive grounds, liberally shaded by Capability Brown arranged and sized trees. To land there is not possible, yet there was the aeroplane in front of the building, unscathed. He had done a fantastic and mysterious job. This was school holidays and the place was deserted, but the problem of how to return the machine to its home remained. There didn't seem to be an easy way to push it to the road, so we left it for further thought. I went back in the cool of the evening to survey the possibilities. A reflective stroll among the trees revealed a straight enough avenue for a takeoff run, perhaps, and once the last tree before the boundary fence had been passed the air would be free of branches; but was there enough distance for the 1.2 litres of engine (a Tiger Moth has 6)? Maybe. Charles Lindbergh led the way when it came to saving weight – he didn't even take a toothbrush to Paris – and the same policy worked here, just. My logbook tells me that this was August 14th 1964, and the problem, of course, was the wrong sort of petrol. This was a time of different octanes, low lead, modified valves and the use of motor car fuel, so there must have been a choice, when a choice was available. This story points up the limitations of an institutional background: excellent as far as it goes, but none the less directed at a specific job. Professional training creates part of the good foundation needed for the comprehensive pilot, but there's plenty more to learn. Confident pilots should beware when they step outside their box.

Why not try instructing?

By March 1964 I had decided that an Assistant Instructor's Rating would be a useful way of trying something new and would make a change from Vanguard co-piloting and avoid pay-to-fly, so I signed up for the course at the Oxford Aeroplane Club, as it then was. We flew the Beagle Terrier. This is a useful machine, developed from the Auster into the Army's AOP 7, therefore simple, rugged enough, and with a much better flap system. But this instructor training was not about the refinements of aircraft handling and the ability to demonstrate them beautifully. There was much more to learn, quite new to me in fact, and, to begin with, considerably more difficult than I expected. I think I had assumed that my own convenient Tiger Moth experience at the Christchurch Aero Club would be breezily repeated, but the official system does not assume aeroplane-mad teenagers. It is based on a detailed and progressive teaching process, historically much discussed and argued about, painstakingly hammered out and refined since WW1, and suited to a student who may have never heard of an aeroplane (if necessary – and possibly very successfully). It's How to Fly carved from the solid, instructors for the use of. In fact it covers the building of the complete beginner's wall – with no bricks missing.

On day one Mr Scott explained how the system worked: 'I give you the blackboard briefing for lesson one' (three As – Aim: to teach you Effects of Controls – Airmanship: Lookout, don't get hit – Air Exercise: Up, down, left and right etc..) 'Then we fly and I will demonstrate it as if you were the student. Next time you give lesson one to me and I will show you lesson two' – and so on.

I see we made two flights on day one, 30 minutes and one hour. I had no problem with flight one – I only had to observe the lecture and play the student, but how would I remember enough of the routine to make an adequate attempt at giving it back? This was a daunting prospect, and the hour-long second flight suggests my stumbling attempt to go through the tedious minutiae of the E of C (basic) exercise: talking, showing, handing over, taking it back (always with the right words, of course), what comes next? How can one make such a ridiculously detailed affair of what had become second nature? The preflight halting and tongue-tied blackboard attempt had been no more reassuring, and I made my way to nightstop at my grandmother's house in Oxford with the distinct impression that this plan for future cheapskate flying could be a big mistake. This was way outside my comfort zone – not me at all.

Next day I had a couple of sessions with Mr Thomas, the CFI, possibly as a result of the previous day's feedback that might have reported an unconvincing and unsuitable youth. He was more laid back and less pernickety than my first instructor, and getting chopped was not discussed, so I went home resolved to continue; after all, they could only throw me out – so what? There was nothing for it but to learn the lines and moves like a boring play. Someone has to do it, somewhere, and culture shocks can be an incentive to learning, sometimes.

I'm pleased to say I soldiered on, visiting Kidlington for a day or two every week or so, and, as usually happens, things started to fall into place: the script became easier to remember, the unfamiliar technique of doing things correctly enough while fitting the action to the words (the words to the action) slowly acquired.

Fortunately for me, John Scott was a stickler for accuracy and the comprehensive and correct coverage of the syllabus. He understood that this was not easy and suggested that I could mentally rehearse the words and imagine the business that went with them while driving the car and looking at the scenery beyond the bonnet (or commuting in the Turbulent). A good idea; while struggling through the course himself as a self-improver he had spent hours doing just this on the tractor at home while ploughing the family fields, he told me, and I do not share the institutional pilot's disdain of those who come up the difficult way. Before I finished at Oxford the first Piper Cherokee arrived, and John Scott took me for a ride in it. I have to admit that I was not totally besotted, and much preferred my XK150's handling, but this was to be the convenient general aviation future.

On July 27 1964 I made a final revision/brush up flight with CFI Thomas before taking a Terrier to Hamble for the instructor's test. I had had no hesitation in arranging to do this with George Webb as he was the only examiner I knew, but, much more important, he would be the only one who knew anything about me. Like Ron Gillman, George was very experienced and fair – very fair – and would probably not be fazed by the lack of gravitas displayed by a 22-year-old (this was 20 years after the war – 22-year-olds then would be all of 42 now, at least). We flew for an hour, did this and that, and George flew so perfectly when required that I was at a loss to find a single deliberate mistake to comment on. Of course there were none: he believed that instruction was a positive process and fooling around with pretend mistakes uncalled for in reputable circles. Quite so (in fact I have only encountered it in my two airlines). He duly signed my piece of paper and there was no debriefing that I can remember. Good examiner. I was now qualified to teach the private pilot's syllabus under the auspices of a full instructor, but not permitted to send a student on a first solo or first solo cross country. I started part-timing at the Airways Flying Club at White Waltham in August 1964.

Perhaps the Tiger Club

During the instructor's course at Kidlington it had occurred to me that while this intricate syllabus dissected the bare bones of aircraft handling for the beginner, it did nothing else. No doubt the qualification would make it easier to go to an airfield and do something with aeroplanes for free, but even when added to my job – going to a big airport frequently and repeating the transport experience in a highly repetitive fashion – was this really why I had wanted to fly? The totally experimental school glider flights, the three Sundays on the winch and the almost vertical learning curve of the mostly-solo Tiger Moth course had been more like it. I knew little about the Redhill-based Tiger Club, but saw their 1964 display at Fairoaks. The variety of machines – definitely not just Tiger Moths – and quality of aerobatics and formation flying was impressive, though clearly for experts only. Maybe I could join.

On July 19th of that year I made a Tiger Moth flight at Redhill with Bunny Bramson – my membership check. This required an unassisted demonstration of the complete but standard self-sufficient general handling routine for this along with many other single-engined aeroplanes of the day (and for the previous 45 years), but specifically in a Tiger Moth. I had not flown a Tiger for five years but felt quite at home in it, and the modus operandi (grass, windsock, no radio, do this and that) was familiar. Basic aerobatics was an optional box tick. My loop and stall turn were good, but I had only tried a Tiger Moth slow roll once before and this attempt was not good – success here is much more difficult than in a Chipmunk, for example – so 'not really' was Bunny's assessment (mine too – but the experience defined an agenda for the future).

My last flight in the Vanguard was a return from Belfast on Nov 11th 1964, with Captain Clark; and he let me drive. I had taken part in 716 Vanguard commercial flights and acquired 1000-odd hours in it. I was 22 (still) and could not have chosen a better start to a four-engined career, with its concentration on the nuts and bolts of getting a large, traditional, somewhat demanding, but reliable and essentially friendly workhorse up, down and around. Could I have got into the left-hand seat at this stage? Absolutely yes, but, with hindsight, I'm not so sure about the dealing with difficult people.

The next job was with BOAC, and it was made clear to those of us making this move that we would have to continue the five-year payments towards our original Hamble training, 'Because of our disloyalty to BEA.' This requirement had been dropped for those remaining in BEA (presumably as a reward for their loyalty in making this original choice), but our move was in accordance with the original agreement. Something of a mean gesture, I thought, but also a bit BEA, maybe. Who can say? (All right – a bit cheap and nasty, if you want an old-fashioned opinion.)

CHAPTER 8

BOAC 1964-1965 – REAL NAVIGATING, ACROSS THE EMPIRE

The move to BOAC was without unpaid holiday, the place of work not in the Queen's Building, the uniform more comprehensive and a little nicer (but only worn for flying, not to the office or the simulator – nor was saluting mentioned); and, to go with the Senior Mess (including bar and waitress service) which replaced the central area tearoom-with-squawk-box, my number changed from 16774 to 80620, perhaps reflecting the much longer history, tradition and (dare I say it) standards (in a variety of areas) of an organisation that had started as British Airways and eventually rejoined it. The first job was to learn to navigate on the Comet 4, which then shared the traditional British 'London to Australia via all points east' route structure with the Boeing 707.

Twenty-first-century readers might ask 'Why did you not just follow the GPS?' Until 1970 or thereabouts, and the advent of inertial navigation *gratis* the Apollo moon landing programme, the methods of navigating long-distances over ocean or uninhabited desert owed more to da Gama than Garmin. Despite some electronic assistance the basic principles had remained the same, and though concepts of speed, time and distance came to include air travel, the basic idea was little changed: you pointed where you meant to go, and waited till your destination appeared. A knowledge of your speed through the chosen medium (a string paid out by a floating piece of wood – or an airspeed indicator) and the expected distance helps with the timing, but both water and air themselves move – to the side as well as fore and aft – so the same navigator's problem remained; how do I keep a check on our real progress: where are we really (using the evidence available – if there is any), and what shall I do about it?

As well as that which pilots need to know (just on paper) our final exams at the College of Air Training had also adequately covered the Navigator's Licence syllabus, but there would be plenty more to learn to actually do the job, in a real aircraft – professionally alone. As a pilot you have to spend years as a pilot's helper before the pilot's licence qualification is fully wielded (and that only on specific aeroplane types), but the red navigator's licence has no such limitation. The job description page is virtually blank: 'Flight Navigator in any aircraft' is all it says. No specified region, equipment, machine or national registration. When, as one of the last of the BOAC PIN (pilot initially navigating) boys, I received my licence in September 1965 and read this economical phrase, the full implication of this solo responsibility and the history behind it took shape. I'd quite expected it to say 'Comet 4C only', but it implies much more than that, and it's the aircraft operator who has the duty of seeing that its unsuspecting passengers are competently navigated and not lost, whatever the licence appears to allow.

The introduction of this PIN boy system to replace specialist navigators heralded the day when airliners, the world over, would be operated by pilots only. The BOAC Comet 4C always needed two pilots and a flight engineer, and a navigator; also became essential where conventional navigating was necessary. BEA, on the other hand, operated the quite similar Comet 4B model with three pilots, and one of them looked after the engineer's panel. A proper navigator was not called for, there being few vast and trackless oceans, deserts or jungles in the Beirut, Bedfont and Barcelona triangle, and because pressing a button and saying something is easier than talking Morse or swinging the loop, this airline had recently dispensed with the last of its Radio Officers. Our straight (naturally) navigators had almost disappeared by the end of 1964, and the few that remained on the Comet would be our instructors in the air.

But before starting on classroom navigating I got my first and only experience of a nine to five job – for two or three weeks. The Comet fleet navigation manager needed help in completing his pre-computed fuel flight plan project for the Comet route structure, so myself, Pete Roberts and Dave Biltcliffe were detailed to appear each working day and beaver away working out the figures. We had our own office in the Kremlin (company HQ) third floor (no outside windows), the tea trolley lady came round twice a day, and we could go to the senior mess for a pre-lunch gin and tonic. In those days there was an element of computer assistance, but it was only the circular slide rule on the back of a navigator's Dalton computer: other mathematical short cuts were achieved by carbon paper for copying the common figures that set the base for the three-way framework of each sector's calculations. The work got done, and many would envy such a traditional working environment, but I was glad to look around outside in the daylight again – during the week.

Probably the most significant element of the relevant box of navigating techniques to be learned at the Cranebank training centre was astro, the most ancient and fundamental means of checking how a journey was going. It all boils down to measuring how high something in the sky appears to be above the earth horizon. Provided you know how high a star, planet, sun or moon ought to be (at a particular time and place) the difference between your measurement and the known value gives you, at least, one line to draw on the map. Ancient mariners of the northern hemisphere found the Pole Star useful because, being almost above the north pole, it doesn't move much up and down or side to side; the rest of the sky just goes round it once a day. A visual measuring device (a couple of sticks to look along, or a water-filled coconut shell with holes to look through at night) set to your destination latitude would get you to the right bit of coast so long as you could see the unobstructed sky now and again (this could be more difficult in the monsoon season). Suffice it to say that measuring this angle is what astro is all about, but there's much more to it in a fast-moving and high-flying aircraft.

Nick Hoy's dramatic lectures about the splendour of the heavens (including star recognition) were all very well, but things had moved on since the 1940s, and this knowledge, though nice to know, was not totally relevant to civilian jet age astro. The system had become slicker and faster, and did not need comprehensive knowledge of the constellations. Of course the same useful stars were out there – and still in use – but only the first one of three needed identifying, and that only by the look of its immediate neighbours: the view through the little window at the top of the periscopic sextant was small. Subsonic airliners fly at 8 miles a minute, and a responsible navigating convention settled for a fix every twenty minutes. To replace the visual horizon a bubble indicated the horizontal – like a spirit level – and to average out the effects of the aircraft movements a two-minute measuring run was required for each star. Another two minutes after shots one and two allowed time for zeroing the sextant's averaging gismo, writing down and plotting the answer, setting up the sextant for the next star (which should be near enough the middle of the new picture to be the correct one); taking ten minutes in all. This leaves ten minutes in which to plot the resulting position (already left behind), decide on a new heading (tell the man at the helm), draw a line to represent the next 20 minutes of flight, guess the next (assumed) position and do the new sums for the next three stars – could be the same ones, maybe not – but in any case there are plenty of new numbers to be found from a couple of books, and a fair amount of arithmetic to complete. It goes without saying that one mistake will probably ruin the whole venture – 160 miles wasted, and nothing useful learned.

My first Comet navigating session took off from Singapore on Feb 7th 1965 and finished there on the 18th of that month. The first six sectors were with the same Sydney-based crew, and while six sectors means a couple of days work in Hounslow terms, this was something completely different; in fact we never got near to or heard anything from Hounslow. These were two-sector days/nights and each flight took between four and five hours, consisting of Singapore – Darwin – Melbourne, nightstop, back again to Singapore, then Darwin – Melbourne again, with a couple of days off there for me. I'm sure my instructor Charlie Fawcett eased me into the new routine progressively (was it Charlie, or Harry? Or was that Fogg? After 50 years my memory's letting me down). The Comet had a long navigator's table, enough for two. I think he did the astro at first, allowing me to get used to systematic airplotting, recording the positional evidence and deducing the wind, planning ahead, reporting wind and temperature for the global meteo system, and so on. It wasn't all astro, and a navigator can use his judgment as to what can be used as reliable evidence, but the ethics of reputable navigation are similar to that of law.

A logical process that only considers testable evidence is fundamental to good navigating. Where there are islands or distinctive coastlines, the weather radar can provide an easy position. A distant radio beacon passing to the side can be useful, especially if track and groundspeed (circumstantial but helpful) are confidently enough known. The Comet had Doppler, an aeroplane-based 'how-the-ground-is-going-past' system designed for V-bombers who might have to fly large distances with a minimum of information voluntarily provided from the ground. The Doppler drift and groundspeed could be useful, especially if reliable, but ours did not work too well over a flat sea – just when you needed it – and public transport navigation demanded external evidence in those days.

To a lone visitor Melbourne was a quiet place, especially after dark. The six o'clock swill was over and the workforce had retreated to Mooney Ponds as one. The streets were empty and, away from the streetlights, a moonless night was dark, as you've never seen it before – except for the stars. The clarity of the air and an unfamiliar night sky packed with more of them than you could possibly imagine made an unusual sight for a European. A warm breeze off the Pacific added to the sense of remoteness, and Captain Cook immediately came to mind. Good astro conditions – but a long way from home. The first impressions of Singapore had been different.

This starting point for a new life had been originally reached after passengering from London, nightstopping in Kuala Lumpur then travelling the last few miles in the cockpit of a Malaysian F27, driven by two oriental cool dudes. Crowded, steamy, relentlessly hot and smelly (Stinkypore, a navy friend called it), Singapore would take a little getting used to. Overlaid by hot coconut oil tinged with coriander, the hydrogen sulphide base notes seemed to come from the stagnant black seawater that surrounded the town. Elsewhere about the island the water looked like murky seawater, and moved around a little, but this stuff looked like solid black mud or non-see-through black glass, yet the trading sampans came and went up and down the river as normal. It must have had water in it somewhere.

On this first visit Ed Hatfield and I stayed at the Raffles, still very Somerset Maugham – unobtrusive staff padding silently around, high, open and airy public spaces with quiet ceiling fans, Singapore slings and gin pahits; and there was the large wood-panelled cool and silent bedroom with its large comfortable bed and no window. No evidence of the outside world disturbed this welcome refuge from the bustling tropical life outside, and the more senior Japanese officers would have found it most agreeable after their hot and sweaty rush through the Malayan jungle. The Raffles bedroom represented the ideal environment for the jet-lagged traveller, and made it possible to sleep totally undisturbed, reassured by the knowledge that a telephone call would produce the perfect and unchallenging tropical breakfast for one (now only encountered in novels), without reference to local time. Someone said 'it's so dark and quiet in there you could be dead'. Exactly.

The Singapore Swimming Club was one attraction mentioned on the crew briefing sheet and Ed and I paid a visit our first afternoon. Remarkably, he won the fruit machine jackpot twice in about five minutes. We were not asked to leave exactly, but he was, discreetly, invited not to play again. How did he do it? I'm prepared to believe he didn't know either. Historically, captains had stayed in one hotel and the rest of the crew somewhere else a notch down the hostelry scale, but emerging notions of increasing integration had added the first officer to those sharing this privilege. As trainee navigators we joined the players, however, and starting with the first return from Australia the Ocean

Park Hotel became the Singapore home, shared with our navigating mentor, the flight engineer and four cabin crew. The Ocean Park was a taxi ride out of town to the east on the road to the airport and, so I'm told, had provided home comforts for the middle order Japanese military, and all that that implies – not the Raffles, but better than a tent and a bike in the jungle.

Further along the road one came to the coast, and here, as we sat on the pavement in the welcome cool after nightfall, came a first revelation of the major plus for the Far Eastern visitor – fast food as it should be. The term implies something quite different today, and globally-directed Western health & safety practice appears to have largely swept away such local and pragmatic tradition, but for quality and variety (not to mention value for money), no shopping centre food hall or expensive foodie restaurant comes close. I'll start with the crab claws – and leave this sad subject there.

On February 15th another Melbourne via Darwin bought me back again to the Ocean Park, to continue this first trip in a new direction with a Karachi via Calcutta, 24 hours at the BOAC Karachi resthouse (near the airport but dating from flying boat days) and a return to Singapore via Colombo and Kuala Lumpur on the 18th. I had now completed 12 trainee navigator sectors and flown with four crews, two of them Sydney based and two from London, then returned home a couple of days later on a Qantas 707.

The logbook shows a two-week gap following the three weeks away from London. 'Two weeks holiday!' This is the reaction of a Monday to Friday nine to fiver. 'And you've just been away on holiday, anyway.' Kuala Lumpur, Singapore, Darwin, Melbourne, Darwin, Singapore, Darwin, Melbourne, Darwin, Singapore, Calcutta, Karachi, Colombo, Kuala Lumpur, Singapore.

To most people travel means holiday, but this was a busy one – half of it nights out of bed, sometimes as the only one in the cockpit awake. It was not only Danny Gray who expressed his comrades' not too well-informed envy of this sybaritic lifestyle. 'The only time I see you is in the pub,' is a frequent commuter neighbour comment to the long-haul professional. The fact that 'Touché' would be a quite valid response is seldom grasped, and the uninterrupted nights and weekends at home which add up to the same (at least) proportion of time in the house count for nought. In fact this two weeks contained only one Tiger Club Stampe flight, and no instructing, so it is certain that much of the time was spent in a Cranebank classroom. There were still aspects of the navigating syllabus to be learned and understood, both for present and future practice, and to satisfy an aviation employer's responsibility to turn only competent flyers loose. This pattern (longish Comet trip, separated by some free time – some classroom) was to continue until the end of October 1965.

The Tiger Club Stampe flight on March the 3rd 1965 is interesting in that it was my first in this type, but also my only acquaintance with G-AROZ, which met its end not long afterwards at a display at Biggin Hill, in the hands of Neil Williams. This event is famous for John Blake's unrivalled commentating skills. The final, as it turned out, aerobatic manoeuvre was the spectacular outside (negative) flick roll: newly, and partly, mastered. Instead of finishing abruptly in a more or less horizontal attitude, with just about enough airspeed to continue level flight, this attempt was overcooked (for a number of well-understood sense-of-occasion reasons) and finished pointing straight down, with no speed. There was almost enough height remaining to convert the available potential energy into the required kinetic kind, and the machine dived out of sight, engine and aerodynamics doing their best to complete the required pullout manoeuvre.

'He's taken it behind the hangar,' said John's fruity and confident tones. A shower of bits and pieces exploded into the sky. 'And he's left it there,' John concluded. Tiger Club owner Norman Jones would have to buy another Stampe to join the remaining two or three, I imagine. And Neil, who had nearly achieved level flight in the time and space available, escaped with a broken collar bone – to live to continue the challenge with the ultimate limits as befits (as he saw it) an RAE Farnborough experimental test pilot, irrespective of who might pay for this personal quest.

The next Comet trip lasted 10 days or so and covered much of the original ground between Singapore and either Melbourne or Sydney. During these eight navigation sectors I came across another three of our instructors – Fogg, Hodges and Lyons. The previous twelve adventures had been overseen by Fawcett, Hawkins, Richards and Jones, and I regret that murky recollection omits first names, but I do remember them all as quietly helpful, academically rigorous and personally unjudgmental. Navigation is a responsible and cerebral job. It requires a cool head and an unflappable application of logic. These qualities are also an advantage for a pilot with good life expectancy, but while navigators seldom present themselves as dashing and devil-may-care or neurotic and volatile, this is not always the case with pilots. Interesting. Of course, sitting at the sharp end does make a difference, as does the route by which you got there.

The next six-week spell at home (end of March and April 1965) contained a lot of light aircraft flying, the first of which was a tryout of a Tiger Club Super Tiger. This interesting machine, of which I think there remained two, maybe three, was a modified single-seat version of the Tiger Moth intended for aerobatics, with considerable lightening, a Chipmunk engine and propeller, a kind of inverted fuel system (which I couldn't get to work on this first attempt, even by following the instructions on the side of the cockpit) with the fuel tank in the fuselage ahead of the pilot (more in keeping with this virtually WW1 design's manoeuvrable fighter forbears). It was a light and airy Tiger Moth: fun to fly compared with the cooking version, no doubt a good glider tug, and capable of satisfactory precision aerobatics at a basic level, but had been retired from its appearances on the world scene.

Flying club instructing

The rest of the time was spent instructing at White Waltham on Terrier, Chipmunk and Jodel. The Airways Flying Club customer base, supplied by employees of the two national airlines, provided considerable student variety – office workers, mechanics and fitters (aeroplane), drivers (vehicle), loaders (baggage of course – but a bit of this or that as well), a few cabin crew, flight engineers, pilots (even). Some were learners hoping for a licence (but not necessarily). Licence holders sometimes needed checking out on type or refreshing, and others required the practice and experience needed for a commercial licence. Many of our younger flight engineers had started out as apprentices in the hangar (five years at least as man and boy [beast, if you like]), and some of these now had an eye on a pilot's seat. Specialist flight engineering would continue to the turn of the century, but the signs of change were already somewhere on the horizon. My assistant instructor's course had covered the standardised way of delivering the basic information, but provided no guidance or experience whatsoever in actually dealing with another human being and their relationship with an aeroplane or an instructor. Prior to taking the instructor's test with George Webb I had only been involved in institutional aviating, where one expected to meet suitably-selected pilots and the expectation of logical progress.

One might assume that private aviation would proceed along the same lines, but it soon became apparent that this was not always so. Of course it wasn't. Anyone who could pay could join. Who decided if they were suitable (to do what)? No one, of course. How do you teach an unknown prospect to fly to the required standard? Good question. Of course the word 'Club' gives a hint, and motivations for membership are entitled to be varied; in fact, looked at rationally, does the club student actually have to want to achieve a licence? Could some of them in fact be closet Walter Mittys? Might they enjoy the Lindbergh or Amy Johnson experience as fantasy, but privately harbour an unspoken but chronic terror of real-life solo flying? Maybe: sometimes definitely, but if this state of affairs were to be addressed up front, calling for courage, realism and self-knowledge (I like coming here, the outdoors and the weather, the grass, the smell of hot oil, leather and petrol, the courage and confidence – even the dressing up: in fact I like everything about flying, but only with someone else in charge) the club/school modus operandi might feel inconvenienced and its time and usefulness challenged. Business common sense says take the money anyway, but many long-term instructors do not take readily to demonstrating the remorseless patience required for dealing with an incomprehensible mindset that turns logic on its head when in the air. Such a thing is sometimes possible, but it requires intellect, experience, understanding, wisdom and luck, in that order, except that a lot of time comes a good first. This is remedial work. I was a good but 23-year-old pilot. The Airways Flying Club was to be part of the start of a lifelong learning process.

Which students would you prefer to give to a new and none-too-experienced instructor, and which keep for yourself? The keen young good (easy) ones – or the much-dual/hardly-any-solo non-improvers? After, let us say, 50 or more total hours, these second option candidates may have technically covered most of the dual syllabus (borne of a CFI's desperation to progress beyond the repeated recency pre-solo check hiatus) but will have acquired remarkably little solo time. I remember one such student who worked somewhere behind the airline operational scenery, routinely meeting the easy-going, socially relaxed and uniformed aviators who, from time to time, breezed up to the counter with a friendly greeting to collect and glance at the carefully prepared paperwork, casually order a monumental number of gallons and depart for their huge, powerful, monstrously expensive, fast and glamorous flying machine. It would be nice to be like them (in your dreams, petal).

Dual check then solo circuits was my detail this day. The weather was perfect, and three or four dual circuits to start with showed reasonable approach consistency (of course there was the odd hint about too high, too low, but 50 hours! – what are we dealing with here? – and the airfield was big), just the conditions for a nice, confidence-boosting solo flight. 'Three solo circuits and come in' – no possible reason to anticipate a problem. I sat outside with my tea. The first approach was OK; a bit high maybe, but physically acceptable for this large field. Contrary to logical expectation, the second was higher. Why? What could prompt a closer turn on to base leg, or an increasing reluctance to throttle back faced with the evidence of the first attempt? Would the long taxi back to the takeoff point provide time for reflection and rational thought?

The final attempt appeared over the clubhouse even higher. The cautiously-descending machine became a dot in the western sky well before it reached the ground. A go-around – must be: but no. Eventually the now very small and attention-getting machine appeared after a taxi back that could have qualified as a cross country in itself (and must have contributed 20 minutes to the bill). This airfield had been suitable for the largest, heaviest or hottest of aeroplanes that had ever landed on grass in 1945, or later – with ease (fortunately).

The report of this counter-intuitive and logic-defying behaviour raised no eyebrows in the office, and no enthusiasm to personally take on yet again this unrewarding teaching challenge. The part time assistants would continue to be given, on an ad hoc basis, these supervised ersatz-solo and largely unproductive details, thus avoiding the fundamental problem. There are two possible reasons – either the student is no good (unteachable), or basic techniques had not been adequately assimilated. Today I vote for (b), but this was not my real job then.

The club had two instructing regulars, certainly not without their own considerable experience. The CFI (Chief Flying Instructor) tended to change from time to time; and then there was Joan Hughes. Joan had started flying as a bright young thing in the Gypsy Moth thirties, and, still in her early twenties, managed to cope with all of the one, two and four-engined military machines of the wartime forties as a much respected ATA (Air Transport Auxiliary) delivery pilot. She had no problem in recognising the limitations of flying club instruction, but generally kept her council. I only flew with Joan once, when we made a circuit for my Jodel instructor check. She had said nothing, and as we turned crosswind, she peered intently ahead around the turn as if concerned with a potential target. I looked for it also, and suddenly the engine stopped. This conjurer's diversionary tactic was an effective way of generating a surprise failure to see what an unknown quantity would do: old school, I would say.

Joan sometimes gave me a lift to the pub at lunchtime. Her reticent black Scottie dog came in the car too and sat on my lap of its own accord. 'It's never done that with anyone else' she said, impressed. I was honoured: cats and dogs sometimes like people who understand them and don't mess them about. She also told me about her Meteor flight. Not a delivery, but at the invitation of a station commander who had just acquired this new toy. She had one worrying moment when she found the undercarriage difficult to select down. 'I could only think of what would be said about this stupid woman who landed wheels up.' Success was achieved, however, and she declared it nice to fly.

When it comes to beginners' approaches, the reader may well be tempted to cite my own Stansted oak-splintering event of a couple of years earlier, but I would argue that was not the same. When I nearly missed the fence after 25 minutes on type I was learning something (even though there was no instruction). The next circuit (the next week) was better. I never hit anything again with a Vanguard, and after 50 hours of personal handling in it (equivalent to some of our dodgy AFC learners' many check circuits) I could manage it to the required standard without problem. This doesn't make me especially good, but it provides a routine contrast with the negative progress that flags up complications which can only be unravelled by a fresh start with insightful and inspired training – and probably indicates something wrong in the first place.

My next Comet trip back and forth between Singapore and Cairo variously via Colombo, Bombay, K.L. and Karachi was preceded by a couple of flightless weeks so there was, no doubt, more classroom at Cranebank; I think concerning more astro wrinkles and techniques. The sub-zenith fix was one of these and I managed to spot one coming and make use of this easy option over the Bay of Bengal. This quick and easy fix requires that the celestial object passes close over your actual position, and I had noticed that the sun would do just that. All that's needed are the sun's earth positions for your three planned shooting times. This is easily looked up in the books (almanac – horoscopes included!) and none of the usual arithmetic is required. The measured difference from 90° (a degree is 60 miles) is plotted with your compasses as an arc from the sun's position and you have one of your position lines. Three of these and you have a very nice cocked hat position (unusually looking like clever spherical trigonometry). It's not really, but, hey presto, it works, and months later the same figures from my log were presented as a question in the periodic navigator's check exam. I wasn't credited with this feat, but maybe it was a reminder to all of something to look out for.

From this trip on I have an increasing memory of having been the lone navigator: my logbook does not record an instructor, but I see I continued to record all but the last Comet outing in October 1965 as N2 (learner), so there must have been an unobtrusive mentor present somewhere; usually enjoying a well-earned career twilight in the first class, ready to exercise the privileges of the only navigator's licence on board if necessary.

There were, naturally, other aspects of tropical life to be learnt about and assimilated, as well as navigating. One afternoon I joined a Badminton knock-about in the Ocean Park Hotel's leafy but equatorial garden, prior to a couple of hours' rest before our evening pickup. It wasn't until after takeoff that I started to feel distinctly strange – lightheaded, cold and struggling not to pass out. 'Don't worry, go and lie down in the dark' was the advice, and I gladly drank the cup of Bovril – it tasted delicious. At top of descent I arose, completely cured, and felt surprisingly refreshed after my mentor's gruelling four-hour night navigating sector across the Bay of Bengal on my behalf. Heat stroke, of course, and there seemed to be some truth in the salt theory, but this was a salutary lesson. This would have been embarrassing had I been on my own, and a dereliction of duty in other circles, but, without a solar topee in sight my fellow sportsmen were unaffected. Clearly they were much more acclimatised to the lifestyle, or drank the water anyway, thirsty or not, if that was the whole story.

Then there's the sunburn. The conversation round the swimming pool in Bombay one eastward progress had been intriguing (though the Nataraj Hotel not), and I sat protected by the large towel over my head – but not the tops of my knees and feet. They didn't seem to complain, and looked normal and white as usual when I went to my room. The redness and blistering developed thereafter: careful sleeping was required that night, and the inconvenience of second-degree burns was obvious next day. But what to do; how long for significant recovery? Would there be recovery? I got some soothing yellow gunge from somewhere, and suitable bandaging material to protect the feet for the following day's aerial journey, but a test that morning proved that shoes were not possible – socks only. The inner thighs could look after themselves under the trousers, but what about the feet? Can I survive the whole day in just our uniform black socks without detection? Fortunately the bandaging bulked out the socks a little, suggesting shoes to the impressionable, and a low profile got me to the airport without problem. Then there was the 50-metre silent panther-pawed walk out to the aircraft across the gleaming apron, fiercely lit by the 10 am Indian sun. I arranged to do this alone and made it unrumbled to the flight deck.

The day's navigating work was uneventful, and after the evening arrival at Singapore the crew's normal contra-phobic's sense of satisfaction and joy at another successful mission, bolstered by taxiing-in brown cows (brandy and milk) all round, and fuelled by another prospect of cocktails and hors d'oeuvres while sitting along the Satay Alley storm drain kerb (otherwise a big gutter) followed by the most delicious and convivial roadside dinner in Bugis (Thieves or Pirates) Street, meant that not even flipflops would have been noticed. The feet did recover – though, even today, they show a slightly browner and longer-lasting colour than the rest of my surface after long visits to sun and sand places.

Exposure to the tropical sun for white skin, unaccustomed to it for countless generations, is a serious, potentially life-threatening affair – and the damage doesn't take long. Those who know better should watch out for their novice colleagues, but sometimes they don't in an egalitarian arena of liberal employment. Nairobi, along with much of Africa, is at 5700ft – nearer to the thinning top of the protective atmosphere than any of Great Britain, or many other hot places – and it's on the equator; and the air is splendidly clear. There's a special danger for the unwary visitor – the climate here is not especially hot, frequently in the very pleasant seventies by mid afternoon (seventies F as was), and comfortably unhumid. During the early 1970s our southbound daily Johannesburg 747 called at Nairobi where the crew got off and stayed for 24 hours. The new and huge jumbo cabin had bolstered crew recruitment and many of the 15 strong cabin crew were new to this kind of travel. We got to the hotel about 10ish in the morning, the flyers to remain under cover, drink a couple of beers and retire for a while; and the boys and girls to the pool and its welcome grass, some eager to benefit from this free sun-bed. A tired new one fell asleep and remained so for a number or hours over midday (sun vertical). None of her colleagues did anything and by that evening she was feeling bad, and was taken to hospital. 'What's the latest?' 'Doctor says 50% burns – there's nothing much they can do but wait: either she'll get better or she will die'. Wow! Dramatic stuff, but apparently true. Makes you think. She did recover, but I believe she has the outline of that day's long hair permanently visible on her back.)

Next we have what I learnt during my Comet days about gippy tummy, Delhi belly, (Montezuma's revenge for Central and South America), the Cairo Quickstep or whatever you would like to call it. There was plenty of advice (delivered from the safe distance of Heathrow) available for the traveller but, short of a trip into space, this is not possible to follow with the theoretically essential total rigour, and doesn't work anyway because the culprits are far too small and reside everywhere – abroad is where they live. This temporarily life-dominating affliction is unavoidable for the unseasoned oriental traveller, and can only be managed by adopting an ascetic's lifestyle combined with ongoing strategic planning for even the shortest personal journey.

From these early travels to and from the Far East the likelihood and seriousness of attacks appears to rise then fall progressively in a region starting roughly at the Suez Canal, and reaching the far coasts of Asia, therefore peaking abeam Mount Everest. Usually, recovery was instant when returning through one's own front door – remarkable. This was not always the case, but the lingering and curious symptoms that might last for weeks tended not to be of the sort requiring frequent and immediate action. The good news is that repeated exposure to these unfamiliar organisms does generate resistance or acceptance, and by the time of my last and genuinely solo and licensed navigating appearance, life had become closer to normal. This took place in the second half of October 1965, ranging navigationally between Cairo, Singapore and Abadan. My Cometing days were over, and I had taken part in 36 dual and five solo statutory navigation sectors.

A surprising and slightly disconcerting thing happened during this final trip. Following normal, friendly and mostly distant interaction with all previous Comet captains, and with no signs of distress from the subject one over the past three days and many miles of travel, I was somewhat taken aback at his unexpected attack on my non-navigating demeanour on the way home, during our post-flight bedroom drink in Bombay. I had got us elegantly from Singapore to Colombo, and the last sector to Bombay had been routine airways, straight up the coast following the odd radio beacon – no navigator required. It might have been nice to look at some passing scenery, though such a thing was only possible from the Comet's pilots' seats, but it was 10 o'clock at night – pitch black, so I read something at my expansive table for two, partly curtained off and equipped with its dinky Anglepoise reading lights.

'I'd have expected you to have taken more interest in the flying. Do you know anything about airline flying?' he said. Taken aback, I started to summon up some sort of defence.

'How many hours have you got anyway?' he continued.

My '1,250, most of it two years' worth of flying up and down the airways in a four-engined airliner' had something of a deflating effect. My reply had been unexpected, and he grudgingly backed down with 'I suppose 1200 hours is all right for 23.' Regrettably he did not have the good grace to say 'Oh, I see; then you're not a complete beginner. Perhaps a keen lad like you would you like to try the wheel tomorrow, see what this splendid British machine feels like.' I would dearly like to have done just that in this patently steady-flying and now reliable and strong first-generation historic jet with what, to me, looked like classic De Havilland handling, but I had never had the offer, and now, suspecting that our captains assumed that we were from the same background as the earlier Hamble Britannia navigating beginners – not pilots really – I can see why such a thing was never informally considered.

During the previous summer I'd continued instructing at the Airways Flying Club. CFI Archie Cole left to join the staff at Hamble and was replaced by the unmistakeable Viv Bellamy, once a Navy Spitfire pilot, and a catholic enthusiast for the interesting, novel and historic – mainly aeroplanes, but not only. Not long after he'd arrived at White Waltham he asked me to take him round the peri track in my XK 150 (3.8 version) because he was looking for a car for his son. There was no other agenda to this demo and I assumed he would like the performance, so I blasted off like the Stig. 'That's enough!' he cried, 'My God – he'll kill himself in this.' I was not altogether disappointed. Though a joy to drive and a pleasure to ride in it had been cheap, particularly because the engine had become an oil-burning, fuel-cooled Wright cum Pratt and Whitney device, and this sort of car deserved a full restoration anyway to counter the secret rust. He could have had it for a bit less than the 300 quid I'd paid for it – but you shouldn't do this to a friend.

I see that it was on September 21st that I had flown to Booker (now Wycombe Air Park) for a mini cross-country with student Tony Bianchi, son of Doug and Edna of Personal Plane Services. The Bianchi family's versatile firm had been based at White Waltham for many years, in fact I believe Doug had been looking after the aircraft that passed through during the wartime ATA days ('We had 50 serviceable Harvards lined up outside'). Tony had wanted to check out the future PPS hangars, and the Airways club moved there a few days later. Our little Turbulent now resided at Redhill and I took it to Booker for Viv to try. The 1200cc engine seemed to have now lost its pre-ignition tendencies, so I did not foresee problems. In fact there weren't any, but I had not considered that Viv's extra stone or three would make as much difference as it did. His takeoff roll down the hard runway was lengthy, and the one circuit wary and flat (not high). I did not hear any throttling back, even on final approach, and on returning he summed up the miniature aeroplane as 'charming'; another type in the logbook, and I suspected that Viv's considerable experience had made him a very careful pilot – as well as assessor of family drivers.

CHAPTER 9

THE TIGER CLUB 1964

This was a real club, not a flying school. Membership required a licence, 100 hrs, the ability to carry out the Tiger Moth general handling flight satisfactorily, and personal acceptability to the committee. In all matters owner Norman Jones' decision was invariably final, and the rules were few, but made it clear that the aeroplanes were to be used with care and consideration, and never for a disreputable purpose. Apart from that you could do what you liked, but every cockpit had a cautionary placard – *All Aircraft Bite Fools*. Very true. The intention was to provide enjoyable (and affordable) flying in a variety of aeroplanes that could provide it for those who were so inclined, and suitable to exercise such freedoms. My second Stampe flight was on August 4th 1965 at Redhill, and annotated as 'aerobatics' in the logbook. A removable front windscreen and quick-fit front cockpit cover turned the machine into a better single seat biplane, and while it might have looked like a Tiger Moth to the layman it was significantly different.

The Belgian SV4B Stampe was also a basic biplane but of a relatively modern design – in real terms, a more advanced trainer. Slightly smaller, it had a less cambered/more symmetrical wing section, equally swept top and bottom wings, four ailerons, much better fin, rudder and fuselage disposition, an elevator trim tab, and a sprung tail wheel and mainwheel brakes, making it suitable for runways as well as grass. Ours had Chipmunk Gypsy Major engines with an inverted fuel system which worked well, especially at its intended full throttle. Everyday flying used the normal carburettor float chamber to supply fuel. When sustained inverted power was required an upside-down mixture-type lever under the throttle quadrant isolated this supply, and put the normal mixture lever in charge of direct fuel flow – separate levers for air and fuel, much in the style of the WW1 rotary engine. During inverted use there was no idle system as per carburettor, and delicate throttle and fuel juggling was necessary to obtain good running at middling to low power settings, but familiarity soon solved the one engine/two lever problem. This was for airborne use only, but the float chamber filled very quickly on the return to normal fuel. The reverse procedure took a bit longer as one had to wait for the float chamber to empty, indicated by the engine cutting dead, before zapping the little fuel lever up to join the throttle. Thereafter both levers were moved approximately together, like flying a twin, and the ears did the rest; but, in keeping with training cultures whose focus is fighters as a first priority, and aerobatics as a legitimate sport, they usually lived at the front when both were in use.

The personal agenda for this first Stampe aerobatic flight was simple, and immediately took advantage of the inverted running engine and a serious aerobatic strapping system (5-point harness plus an extra waist strap secured to the fuselage. This last provides additional and reassuring negative g support, and prevents inadvertent ejection should the seat come adrift). Halfway round a slow roll an aircraft passes through level inverted flight. Mastery of this situation, getting to it and leaving it while flying level is a fundamental building block of this manoeuvre, and the ability to revise the straight and level exercise, including beginners' turning, at one's leisure while flying upside down is much more effective than the 'this is how you do the whole thing (not well) in one go' (by numbers) tradition; and I put a couple more bricks in my wall in the half hour.

I see that I made three half-hour Turbulent flights at Redhill a couple of days later, annotated 'formation', and in three different aircraft as it happens. The Tiger Club possessed a gaggle of these little machines, all different colours, all with a 1600cc Beetle engine. Whilst a bit heavier this extra 400cc made a difference, and the increased wing loading and more forward centre of gravity made the machine a tad more solid in the air. The good and straightforward handling, fresh air visibility and the fact that the Turbulent was only good for normal flying made it perfect for formation practice (and it was cheap to rent). Formal training this was (not the wary agenda-free approaching of another in flight). Where two or three are gathered together and there are similar single-seaters waiting, what else is there to do? There were plenty of members with professional formation experience, mainly past but some present, but for jobs where the aeroplanes frequently do things as a team it becomes a way of life, like games at school. Everyone has to learn something of the skills, and those who enjoy it and/or show promise have the ever-present opportunity to learn from their betters, as well as each other, and both maintain and pass on the traditions and disciplines. The important things is the discipline borne of the tradition, the whole bag of which the Romans might have called Modus Operandi Formationem, and which can work well without a chain of command, manual or standing order in sight. Some of my previous Redhill flights would have involved one-to-one formation practice, but these three half-hour sorties in different machines on one afternoon suggests filling in for some sort of communal practice, be it three or four aeroplanes. The routines of proper formation changes need practice, with perhaps a safe enough stand-in, even a less-than-polished one. There was to be much more formation flying.

I've just googled the date, to check if 8/8/65 was a Sunday, as expected. Yes it was, but what a memory-jogging exercise! The computer tells me that new films *Help* and *The Ipcress File* were in the cinemas. The 45 rpm *Help* (I need somebody) was also top of the UK hit parade top, followed by *I Got You Babe* (she's still going strong – what a star), *We Gotta Get Out Of This Place* (if it's the last thing we ever do), *You've Got Your Troubles* (I've got mine), and *Mr Tambourine Man* (play a song for me). I also see that America was intrigued by Herman's Hermits and *I'm Henry VIII, I Am* ('enery the eighth I am, I am), at their #5. Anyone else remember all the words? At a time when the names of close friends escape me on a daily basis and I have to look up everyday German words for the hundredth time it is astonishing what still sleeps in the memory banks. There must be more somewhere, but what I also spotted was that Singapore left the Malaysian Federation on Aug 8th 1965. This would have repercussions on life in this area, including for the crew of a Qantas 707 one evening arrival – to feature in due course.

The next day I took a Terrier to Eastleigh for my annual instructor's rating renewal test. I'd chosen George Webb again for my initial reason, and having picked him up we flew to Hamble for his briefing and the flight over our familiar landscape, including landing back there for the wash-up. George had retired from the College of Air Training, but – I'm guessing – only felt himself to be in CFI/examiner mode when based at the field where he'd spent forty years. Understandable. Anyway, it worked again – only another 150 instructing hours needed to add to my 50 and I could run my own school.

CHAPTER 10

BOEING 707 – 1966

Boeing have made a number of classic aircraft, and this was one of them. The fact that 60 years later its layout is still the shape of choice for long-range transport aircraft – they all look much the same – is testament to the original groundbreaking work done between 1945 and 1951, a result of German research and a new world preparedness to break with tradition – It looks crazy but give it a try anyway.

During WW2 (1943) it was decided that better bombers would be still be needed for the foreseeable future. A jet-powered B29 was tried – not good enough, too draggy. Next was something with a number of jet engines in the forward fuselage and a couple at the back – too funky, and potentially hot inside. Then in 1945 the U.S. Army Air Corps brass visited the secret German aeronautical institute at Braunschweig. The sophistication of what they found was a revelation. George Schairer of Boeing Aerodynamics looked at the wind tunnel figures, and texted the firm immediately – 'Stp bmbr; mst hv swpt wngs'. So the B47 was thought of in 1946, and a finished one flew in 1947.

Dangling the engines under the front of the wings spreads the load (but especially can provide automatic gust load relief by twisting a wing under vertical acceleration loads), saves structural weight, reduces total frontal area and minimises awkward shapes (surprising to some, but not Concorde designers). The cruise performance was fantastic – faster than any fighter currently on the drawing board (Starfighter design started in 1952) – even though it flew so high that manual flying and constant attention were required to stay in the 5 Kt wide coffin corner, but it worked, and the machine was such a good glider that a drogue parachute was needed to get a reasonable descent angle, and require a controllable power setting on finals (20 secs spool up from idle!) What about a transport aeroplane based on the same ideas? So the design of the famous Dash 80 (B367-80) was started in 1952 and it flew in 1954, encouraging the development of the KC-135 tanker and B707 in parallel. At first the airlines were not convinced and were happy to stay with familiar straight wings and four propellers, but the disconcerting-looking jets soon caught on, and BOAC got their first one in 1960.

For us 1966 began with the classroom at Cranebank. Jet engines were easy to understand, but fixed frequency AC generators on four independent engines was a new concept. Even with their constant speed drives, how did they always stay in step? Our teacher enthusiastically explained it by horse and whiffletree. Of course – my Pembrokeshire farming great uncle and his three horses (no tractor), Duke, Daemon and Grey. The grey one was younger and stronger than the two brown ones – so that's what those wooden things and the chains were for – now I get it. This use of simple imagery is good teaching – and you remember it.

The logbook tells me that the 707 simulator took up some of March 1966. Did it move? Don't think so, maybe a bit, but it had no visual, and keeping the compass straight during takeoff gave only a rough idea of engine failure control. For enthusiasts the advantage of simulators that only sang and danced slightly meant more base flying, and this we did during a week or so in Shannon during the following May. The observant and industrially sensitive reader may have spotted that April is missing. A whole month's holiday? Call it what you will, I did a lot of AFC instructing and a little glider towing that month; maybe some gliding as well, but this apparently relaxed lifestyle goes with the problems of a large and long-range organisation where a trip may take people away for weeks at a time, and you need enough staff and machinery to cover all eventualities, including training as well as holidays. Setting an aircraft aside just for a whole week's flying school junket cannot be arranged at a drop of the training manager's hat. Some staff claim to get used to the long-distance way of life, including the chronic tiredness, disrupted eating and sleeping, social instability and personality readjustment, but it is a considerable improvement on previous lengthy travel (barely a hundred years before), the Golden Age of Sail. How did they manage, with not a counsellor in sight?

Many years later in Mauritius I was involved with some examining on behalf of the French authority. An Air France training captain came along as my shadow and signer, and he told me about his start in Air France. 'When I joined straight out of the National Airline Pilots' School I was posted to UTA and the DC4 in Tahiti. I was very upset, I did not want to leave home... Actually it was Paradise.'

But there was time to slip in a first Atlantic navigating lesson at the end of March. The 707 schedule included a daily London to Toronto, calling at Prestwick and Montreal, the aircraft returning via the same places that night (with yesterday's crew). A 707 crew included two co-pilots, both of whom were qualified to navigate, and a few of them also had the responsibility of nav instructing, so a trip or two as extra crew with one of these was required to get the hang of the additional skills. The weather, latitude and available aids put North Atlantic navigating into the advanced category when compared with the intermediate demands of our eastbound-only Comet, and there were new things to learn.

Leaving tropical thunderstorms aside for the moment (and they get – or should get – the pilots' primary attention) the Atlantic navigator frequently used to find himself in the source of the sort of weather that gives Britain its reputation, which can produce the perfect storm at the surface from time to time. The northern hemisphere polar front snakes its way around the globe, guiding its alternating cloudy wet and windy, or quiet and fine weather up and down the coasts of Europe, before reaching the sea again somewhere near Tokyo; considerably drier, looking different, but there all the same.

It was during the 707 simulator course that the news of Bernard Dobson's Mount Fuji disaster broke. A mystery at first. Beautiful weather, no warning, what could it be? I will spare the reader a lecture about strong wind, very stable air and lee or shear rotor turbulence, but it's the worst kind. From out of nowhere the first bump snapped the fin off. The rest is history, but it does remind me of a Comet approaching Tokyo. I imagine their Doppler showed standby over a calm sea, but during the initial approach they were required to make a 1½ minute holding pattern while descending to, shall we say, 10,000 ft (at the correct conservative speed). The inbound leg back to the beacon took a puzzling 20 minutes because they had slid, unawares, into the jetstream on the way down.

This trendy word is applied to the strong west-east wind that occurs along the front itself at altitude – strongest at the top, and just at the height that jet transports like to fly for range. For the North Atlantic navigator the basic questions remained to be solved: where are we, what has the wind been doing to us, what will it do in the near future, where will I point the craft to stay somewhere near our allotted track (and not tangle with someone else, or get lost)? This ocean was and still is a popular part of the globe for airliners, but, prior to automatic navigation devices the degree of navigating difficulty could be further raised by the first question above: how to find out where you are. On a clear night astro is fine, and the sun (moon and Venus – to mention all three) better than nothing in the day, but it's often cloudy above cruising height – nothing to see. The 707 didn't have the handy Doppler that could sometimes tip you off as to how things were going, and Loran, kindly supplied by Uncle Sam to help B17s and Liberators find their way to Britain, was our prime means of finding a position beyond reasonable doubt.

Loran is one of a number of wartime systems using the time difference between the arrival of radio pings from two stations. A specific time difference puts you on a particular line on the map. Two lines from different stations give you a position, and in good conditions lining up the blips on your cathode ray tube and reading the answer could not be easier. In the right place on a nice sunny day you looked at clean and clear copybook examples, child's play to superimpose and line up, but as night fell these ground waves dwindled and a variety of sky waves took their place, ricocheting off their choice of a livening ionosphere, swallowed up in a background of growing grass interference. On a clear night first hop E-waves, second hop E-waves, similar F waves and the like stood up plainly on the screen, and picking the correct pair to measure was almost as easy as day, but this was by no means always the case, and sometimes Loran coverage and reception dwindled to nothing. There were places, particular hours in the 24, sunspots and weather where there was no evidence available, and this is where a cool head, a cup of tea, and a sense of quiet resignation is best – and the hope that something will turn up, all the while ignoring the insistent, relentless and unstoppable evidence of 8 miles a minute progress; to somewhere.

This was a not infrequent pre-dawn situation going east between mid-Atlantic and Europe, but there was one further wartime navigation system that could help a bit as the invisible continent was blindly approached, thanks to the Kriegsmarine U-boat division. This was called Sonne and consisted of a number of axis stations on the coasts of occupied Europe, including one at Bushmills in Ireland. Each station transmits a sweep of dashes which change into dots. You count the dashes and dots and the changeover number represents a choice of bearings from the station, printed on the chart. Coastal Command knew about

Sonne but only found out how it worked when the manual was captured along with a U-boat, and they called it by the secret name of Consol (Sonne/sun/sol, con for with – it's uncrackable, so it is). Bushmills was especially useful if you were headed that way and the Consol stations in general certainly helped us out. Thanks, Ireland – a clever double bluff.

A first piloting grapple with the legendary B707 came at the beginning of May at Shannon. For me, among others, these sessions of local flying and circuits in a hugely expensive aeroplane, usually based in scenic countryside with an agreeably small number of colleagues and convivial accommodation, were a private joy – whether as learner or teacher. Computer game training has made these residential local flying and circuits and bumps extravaganzas a thing of the past, and though teaching learners in little aeroplanes may appeal to those with no alternatives, the same sort of thing in a complex and sophisticated machine, with all-found support, is something of a privileged experience for those whose interest lies in the wonder of flight rather than the suspended animation of travel per se.

My first two-hour detail included a medium level intro with Peter Mains-Smith, finishing with three circuits. What a luxury! Cruising around in the sunshine just for me – to find out what the test pilots had settled for. 'Get the feel of the new ship. Go out over the sea, take her up to between fifteen and twenty-five thousand feet and have a play. Try the lift and pitching response to power and speed, and the elevator and stabiliser relationship – that's a bit different, roll rates with and without spoilers. Definitely check out the Dutch roll; this sweepback/dihedral thing is a compromise – we settled for a low wing for structure, and it's great for on-your-feet servicing, but we had to give it some dihedral to keep the engines and wingtips off the ground. This flying feature's not great but it shouldn't be a marketing problem, and you can kill the Dutch roll stone dead by jumping on the roll mid-cycle when the sideslip is zero – it's easiest. Don't forget to try pitch control with split spoilers – it's neat. And another thing: don't be high and fast when you come back... and if you get low, pull the nose up as well. Have fun.'

Mainspring did not use these actual words, nor did he explain the Dutch roll science or business policy, but he explained and demonstrated all these relevant things and there was plenty of time to try them. This was good training. Acceptably competent pilots do not need to be badgered about speeds, heights or staying on track, they can read these for themselves, but these are the topics of choice for the less-than-insightful check pilot, however misguidedly well-intentioned this kind of schooling may be. A new aeroplane is different.

That's the point; it's the differences from the previous machine that should be identified, explained and taught, and Mainspring (only slightly bouncy as a training captain) did it well. After my first three circuits he wrote that my approach speeds and touchdowns varied. I had not flown a large aircraft for 18 months, and the highlighted differences had straight wing propeller students in mind, for good reason. Mick Rogers, an older PIN boy a few years ahead of me, had his first go next. Mick sort of grinned anyway, and when I asked him afterwards 'What do you think?' he grinned and said 'It's just like the Hunter.' Well, a bit maybe; but this was good news. The Hunter is a special case of the guaranteed smile.

I had the impression that this enlightened transfer of helpful knowledge will have been initially inherited from the manufacturer's pilots, who naturally were interested in handling behaviour; it's what they do – 'Any damn fool can watch an autopilot fly straight and level for hours on end then take the money' – and they will have been acutely aware of the challenges represented by something significantly different – not to themselves but to the dyed-in-the-wool professional who needs to have important but unfamiliar concepts emphasised, maybe more than once, if not to be caught out when habit replaces thought.

Charles Bodimeade told me about learning with Boeing. After the customer's extensive checklist had reached the before takeoff check, the test pilot summarised: 'BOAC horseshit! Let's check the killers – GIFFTS: – Guards, Instruments, Flaps, Flags and Trims.' That should do it (and worth keeping in mind) like my Tiger Moth trims, throttle friction etc, and this single-seat approach to flying leaves maximum time for looking and thinking, but is not routinely suitable for every airline employee. Charles told me off on my final detail after he had given me an approach under the hood (training file on the windscreen), which he whipped off at a couple of hundred feet. We were not that far off the centreline and it was do-able so I went for the S turn. It worked out, but was not what he had expected. 'We don't do that sort of thing here; we don't like people who have a go!' I explained that the BEA Vanguard (and Air France 707 as I later discovered) had exactly this manoeuvre in their base training syllabus, but would not disagree that it should not be encouraged for all, especially not in this early 707 model.

Three trips under supervision to the east and back followed. These each lasted almost two weeks and involved just co-piloting – no handling. During my first trip with Paul Dane he suggested, after consultation with the real P2, that I could be more pro-active in monitoring and mentioning things that were not in order. I can't remember whether I'd had the opportunity to see the other co-pilot in action. Of course I'd done the usual things – reading the checks, talking on the radio, wheels and flaps up and down, writing on my clipboard and all the rest of it – but, while sitting at the front and therefore taking an interest in how the flight was going, had not noticed anything sufficiently amiss to be worth mentioning. I had the impression that this topic might have become recently fashionable, but rather unspecified. During the next Singapore trip with Paddy Bell I decided that I should find something to say on the way back so that this supposed box could be ticked, and pointed out an overstepping of the company's 30 bank limit as he struggled to avoid the worst parts of a thunderstorm during the climb out of Kuala Lumpur on a routine dark and stormy tropical night. He didn't say anything, but his look of pitying exasperation, added to the strain of avoiding disaster as a matter of priority, told me to stick with my own judgment and ignore the previous advice. I quite understood.

There were then a couple more navigating Torontos to get signed off for the first and second hop sky waves, followed by a further Singapore, again with the affable Paul. 707 flight deck accommodation now included the Raffles, close to town, and on arrival Paul told us that the station manager had asked if we would care to attend a meeting of staff the next morning to hear an address given by our chairman, Sir Giles Guthrie, who was making a round-the-world tour to promote confidence in our (politically appointed) board's fiscal policies. It didn't seem politic to say no, and what might such a social gathering lead to?

O.P. Jones had told us to make the acquaintance of local management, to oil the company wheels. The event was held in a large room in the financial district, somewhere behind Change Alley – a boardroom, courtroom even? There were about three or four town office staff there, and the same number of us, and Sir Giles explained policies and prospects in City Banker's board level opaque jargon: I didn't recognise anything that could be understood by the financial layman, except, in part, the conclusion that something had risen 20 points. But what kind of points? Percentage, pennies, hundredths of pennies? Perhaps it was decimals of the share price, but shares were not for sale then. Maybe there was coffee afterwards, but not a party exactly, and no further invitations into the local set. I'm not sure if the manager was actually there, and as temporary locals we certainly boosted the audience, and it would be Satay Alley and Bugis Street yet again for us tonight. But Paul had done his O.P. Jones bit.

A few days after returning from this final supervision trip I went to Prestwick with Dizzy Neville and two or three others for an aircraft circuit session. This occasion, on July 25th 1966, was 10 weeks after my last touch of the controls at Shannon, and would have been four months after whatever had been signed off in the simulator, so it was a convenient beginner's refresher and six-monthly licence sign. Because of the 707's handling demands, asymmetric in particular, and the limitations of the simulator, the statutory six-monthly type rating checks alternated between aircraft and simulator, so these awaydays for a spot of poling became an annual 436 jolly, or not as the case may be. Dizzy had a certain style about him, in fact he reminded me of Frank Muir – a hint of humour without laughs as such – but gave the impression of the easy-going competence that comes of experience, training included. I have no special recollection of my hour at Prestwick so I'm sure it was a nice day out. I don't think I flew with Dizzy again, but I remember seeing him fly the 707 a year later, from the outside.

During this following summer the Airways Flying Club arranged an air display at Booker, and, though it was not on the programme, I knew that a surprise 707 appearance had been planned, tacked on to one of these one-day non-residential base flying outings, to be flown by Dizzy. The weather was beautiful and the show progressed satisfactorily, commentated by John Blake (did we see Charles Masefield and his Mustang on this occasion? Lots of noise, large-scale figures, high energy, beautifully coordinated, accurate and elegant. Magnificent, a perfect example of the Tiger Club's reputable use of an aircraft in peacetime).

I mentioned the possible airliner arrival to the odd acquaintance, who invariably said surely not; then John informed us there would be an interlude because Heathrow was very busy and a 707 had been diverted to High Wycombe. Sure enough the silver and blue monster appeared from the east, wheels and flaps down, majestically approaching the tiny runway. It was an arresting sight. So was the opening up at a low height, turning away, cleaning up and repositioning with an expanding reversal to make a clean run from the other direction – accelerating all the while. A very light long-range airliner has uncommon powers of acceleration at low level, and this demo was clearly going to take in all of the normal speed range, let's say 130 to 380kts. Well in sight, the jet made its long turn back towards the field, bank increasing to maintain the turn radius as the speed built, and, rolling out on the display centreline, it continued a shallow descent for the last half mile to the field boundary. All beautifully judged and smoothly flown, especially considering the absence of prior practice (a helpful luxury). As the machine settled on its display run – perfectly positioned, bottoming out at a couple of hundred feet and barreling along at an impressive speed – the nose suddenly pitched sharply up and down a couple of times, in a cycle fast enough not to disturb the flight path, but surprising enough to disturb one of the watchers, at least, and raise a few mystified oohs and aahs from some of the others. The aircraft then continued smoothly past to disappear homeward.

What had happened? As a junior co-pilot it was not for me to make enquiries in the training office, nor was it then in my nature to do so, and I never had the chance to quietly float the subject over a beer, so any conclusion must be interested conjecture only, but my money would be on an attempt to correct an out-of-trim situation under the constraints of speed and proximity to the ground. Or could a fight have broken out in the cockpit? Somebody knows, but I can't guess.

A few days after the July 1966 Prestwick visit I set out on my first 707 flight as a bona fide crew member. It had taken 18 months in BOAC to reach this position – quite a long time compared with my two year stay in BEA – but frequent routine landings were not considered to be the be-all and end-all of this job; there had been plenty more to learn, but only evident to those who knew. This trip was captained by Ken King, by coincidence similarly pleasant company and as generous with handling sectors as his Vanguard namesake. This Hong Kong and back contained 11 sectors so my two were very fair at the time. The variety of the eastern route structure continued, and on this trip we called at Zürich, Rome, Delhi, Rangoon, Hong Kong, Calcutta and Frankfurt, getting off and staying in Zürich, Delhi, Hong Kong and Karachi. The first landing for me was at Rangoon. As I recall, radio aids here were thin on the ground and the weather of the monsoon persuasion. After a number of hopeful miles of jungle the runway finally appeared through the cloud and rain – a black and tatty-looking affair, no lighting to speak of, and the first one I'd seen with green patio mould on the less trodden parts. Not a problem, but different. I then navigated to Hong Kong and was able to get a first look at the famous low-level base leg harbour approach towards the mountains with the 90 descending turn to the runway. On the way home Ken gave me Calcutta – Karachi to fly.

Another five similar eastern trips and one New York-Caribbean took me to the end of 1966, a total of 69 sectors and six landings in five months. By comparison my last 69 Vanguard flights took two months and had delivered 13 landings, but I was a two-year veteran by then. However, my first 69 Vanguard qualified sectors had produced only 12, so this looks something like consistency. In the 2+ pilot world it all depends on the individual captain, a wide variety of strenuously acquired opinion about the demands of the job, and how to go about it. At this time flying backgrounds, personalities and attitudes to fellow crew members varied widely, and an assortment of a captain's expectations of co-pilots, what they are for and how much to share with them varies to this day, no doubt. But the early 707 came with a reputation, and a wariness handed down though the training system, starting with the manufacturer, aided and abetted (for the best of reasons, no doubt) by the UK Air Registration Board.

More CFIs

In the weeks between the 1966 BOAC trips I made a few more Stampe aerobatic practices, but mostly busied myself at the Airways Flying Club, continuing the part-timers' ad hoc instructing with a variety of students. Viv Bellamy had been replaced by Stuart Craft as CFI. Stu told me about an occasion when a 20mm (enemy version, one would hope) shell had gone through the thin walls of his Spitfire cockpit from one side to the other, just above both forearms as his hands grasped stick and throttle, leaving a clean 20 mm hole each side. A lucky escape: I think we had been discussing rear view mirrors because the Tiger Moth glider tug had one and I had explained that some of the glider club pilots' station-keeping was so bad that you saw them only occasionally as they flashed though the picture in the mirror (much worse than Roger Neaves' attempts to give me a hard time on my tugging checkout – he broke the string, eventually). Stuart explained that the Spitfire mirror was a waste of time – 'If you saw anything in it, it was the last thing you saw'. Fair enough. I see that on October 31st I flew with yet another CFI, Captain John 'Ginger Tom' Varley, who familiarised me with the Piper Cherokee for a whole hour. John had started out as a Halton apprentice and finished a BOAC career in the O.P. Jones mould, last seen on the 707. He told me that now, in his twilight years, he wanted to give back some of his experience to aviation. An hour in a Cherokee was plenty, but, like O.P. Jones, he turned out to be unlike the goatee-bearded image of the stern commander, and we continued to jog along agreeably in the flying club/school scene. And he seemed to like my BOAC connection with his past captain life.

Parachute flying

During my summer leave the previous month, Carl Schofield had asked if I would like to do some Dragon Rapide parachute flying for the army in Germany.

Why not (and he wouldn't have asked just anyone), so I went to Hanover to be picked up and taken to the British Army somewhere near Paderborn. Next day I went to Detmold where the aeroplane lived, to be checked out and start the parachute flying. This was sport parachuting, but within the support, assumed self-sufficiency and the get-the-job-done attitude of an established army. Great.

Two army pilots usually flew the British-registered Rapide, but pressure of work and a full beginner jumping programme meant that suitable volunteers were welcome. Staff Sergeant Barber showed me round and flew me over to the large sports field at Bad Lippspringe. We changed seats (only the one seat) and I had a go, making a circuit and then taking us back across the Teutoberger hills to the little runway on top of the hill at Detmold. This, in training circles, is traditionally a brave and seldom done thing in a single pilot aircraft; especially one with two engines. A reassuring pat on the back and 'off you go' as you jump out was usually the routine for sending someone solo in something like the single pilot Hampden, Mosquito, or a Rapide for that matter. However, it all depends on the circumstances, and I found the Rapide to be a total delight, including the asymmetric steering with engines to start the takeoff, and a reasonably slow tail-down wheeler landing (unless you are brave or foolish enough to try a three-pointer).

This machine has elegant and slender elliptical wings, four ailerons and, would you believe it for a 1934 design, the B707's movable stabiliser. Rothmans sponsored three of these aircraft for army sport parachuting, one each for the Red Devils, the 1st Army and RAPA, the Rhine Army Parachute Association. They were given Wagner Ring Cycle names: Siegfried (Sick Fred), Valkyrie (Valerie) and Rheingold (Ringo), ours. The job in hand was a course of 30 novice students who would do 20 jumps each, starting with the static line (dope rope) and progressing to as long a free fall as their progress would allow. The man in charge, Mick Turner (the Chef) of the RASC, spent much of his time running this operation, and I found the whole thing well organised and impressive. The students had unmodified round paratroop canopies and therefore no tracking control – they went where you put them. This makes life simple, but requires excellent spotting from the jumpmaster. The large sports field alongside the Wehrmacht's huge sand and pine tree training range served as airfield and drop zone, and only Thursday afternoon horse hockey (polo for the cavalry) curtailed our round canopy dropping.

This 1946 vintage Rapide was like two Chipmunks. Gypsy Queen engines instead of Majors, similar fuel systems (on or off, but with additional in-cockpit primers), brakes and flaps; the same checks worked well. What struck me immediately about the way life worked here was the expectation that everyone could do his job until proved otherwise. This saves a lot of wasted training time, and makes it easy to slot into a team; in our case the Chef and his 3 instructors, two English and a Canadian – all from different walks of army life, but spending this summer teaching skydiving (as it has become). The 30 students, from similarly eclectic trades, and with a variety of reasons for signing up to this course, had already learned the basics of packing their parachutes staked out on the grass, the importance of lining up their feet across track as the ground approached, and how to make a landing fall by jumping off the back of a moving Land Rover, so the most intensive part could start immediately: static lines at 2,500 ft. The theory of flying for intentional parachuting is not new – a streamer run first to simulate the flight of a descending parachute, the transposition of this vector to arrive at a jumping-out point, or line of them, the ruddered flat turns in response to the jumpmaster's left/right instructions, the slow flying with minimum engine slipstream for parachuting beginners – but it was all new to me. However, a clear briefing and no other distractions help, and it was soon possible to complete a full course-worth of passes and pickups without anything said except the 'two at two-five, one at three-five and two at five' as we taxied out. Students' progress varied, as one would expect, from a mixture of keen ones and those who had taken the chance to escape their day jobs for a while. Over the twenty jumps some never got off the rope, but many progressed up the ladder to the stable position, dummy ripcords, free fall control with turns, going unstable and sorting it out, and one got as far as nine thousand feet – 45 seconds freefall; yet all 600 beginner jumps landed in the field, just inside either end sometimes: and there were no injuries. I wasn't expecting anything so efficient, and safe, and if asked whether I would be happy to learn parachuting with these people – a definite yes.

CHAPTER 11

JANUARY-MARCH 1967 – SYDNEY POSTING, AND THE REST OF THE YEAR

In previous years 707 crews had been based in Hong Kong, Honolulu and Sydney, but by 1967 only the Sydney posting remained. Compared with the diurnal turmoil and tedium of halfway-round-the-world-and-back travel in one go, this division of route structure was like a holiday with a bit of flying thrown in, even though the use of crews and schedules was unchanged. The social stability of the small group and the limited degree of local time change made all the human difference, but airlines are businesses and agreeable working conditions are not the only priority, so the posting days were almost over.

I went to Sydney at the beginning of January 1967, got a flat in Manly with Dave Biltcliffe, and, after a couple of days getting the local bearings, positioned to Auckland with Air NZ for a couple of Nadis (Fiji) and back. First class on the DC8 was pleasant and I remember choosing a Tasmanian Devil from the list of exotic pre-lunch drinks, just because of the name: the real thing is a smallish animal with a pointy nose and sparkly teeth. The steward thought this choice quite original, and the drink turned out to be a bit on the green side, over-chillied perhaps, but not at all bad. The sun shone outside as we followed Francis Chichester's route past Norfolk Island, and following the friendly acceptance we'd had from those we'd come across in Sydney, I had the feeling that this wouldn't be a bad part of the world to be for three months. By and large I was not wrong.

This first double Auckland-Nadi was with two captains X – who did not get on; in fact I was not present at, but was party to, a blazing row next door in a thin-walled NZ motel room one evening, so I wondered how the trip would progress. In fact they had each refused to have the other in the right hand seat for takeoff and landing, but I was the only legal navigator, and every sector was a statutory navigation flight so how could this work? Easy: I would be co-pilot for the takeoff, go back to my table before we ran out of DME and do my clever Vasco da Gama stuff as far as top of descent, then return to the front to co-pilot for the important approach and landing. For me this was perfect: I liked navigating; the intellectual challenge, the satisfaction of an elegant use of the information available, the neatly presented evidence (and so on). On the final sector of the trip the captain of the day, being the more sensitive of the two and feeling some sense of guilt about this unconventional arrangement, let me take off and land as well. A real Chichester solo flight – drive and navigate across the Pacific in a 707. Is this a record? Possibly not, but it was fun, of a sort.

I see that I then flew with a normal crew from January 25th to the end of February. Slim Gregory was our captain and he was both sensible about flying and reasonable about sharing the handling. We covered the routes as far as Singapore to the north and Nadi to the north east, calling variously at Perth, Brisbane and Darwin for Singapore, or Auckland nightstop for the Nadi visits. During one Brisbane transit we had a message from the police. 'There's this idiot that phones up with a bomb threat each time a plane goes over his house. We want to catch him red-handed.' They explained where his bungalow was – in an estate just a bit off the takeoff centreline – and asked us to make sure we got him low and loud. I think it worked; there were no more similar requests.

Then something else happened during this agreeable Gregory/Meadows/Riley piloting partnership. Not a big deal, nothing like as dangerous as my nose-to-nose Watford affair, but still a height bust (if you want to be pedantic). Is there anyone out there who has never, ever, been involved in such a thing? Who knows? This was an early morning Perth to Sydney red-eye descent at the end of a Singapore flight. Apart from us the radio was silent, and Australia is a big place. These were the days when you wrote down your cleared height or dialled it in the HF frequency selector, our standard procedure, but nothing got your attention if you forgot. And this was Australia – rules are rules rather than guidance, despite Crocodile Dundee's freewheeling celluloid approach to life. Any freewheeling is just blokeish theatre, and Slim turned himself in as captain to do some grovelling at the DCA so that face-losing jail was avoided. Fortunately (I think) British Airways has never actively encouraged crew members to sneak on their fellows, captains included, and in this case it was not necessary anyway – perish the thought.

Life in Manly was pleasant: friends, sea and sun nearby, oysters from the fish shop up the road, one of the Doyles famous restaurants just down the road. Some have said that Doyles is just glorified fish and chips, but it was much better than that. Glorious fish and chips and a drinkable bottle of wine, certainly. Then there was the ferry ride to work. The Sydney-based away-to-days-off ratio was a little more efficient than the longer out-of-London equivalent, and it felt much better because of the limited time change, known as jet lag – frequently misunderstood. But the 45-minute ferry ride to get to town for pickup, for us as for north shore commuters, was a lifestyle lesson in stress dissipation. 45 minutes of compulsory calm in which to wait and watch the scenery change and the water go by relaxes and resets the mind from home to work – perfect. This twice-daily ride during the working week must have extended the useful lives of many Sydney residents, and I am far from the first to realise this: no one disagreed. Our trips averaged four or five days in length, separated by the same or maybe longer stays at home; but one felt less tired, and reacclimatising to normal life was considerably more convenient than the genuine long-range version, due in equal measure to reduced time change and the greater sense of community living in an identifiable group. In fact the Sydney base was squadron sized, a traditionally proven effective grouping. It may not appear to make business sense to an airline accountant, but it makes human sense, and, despite continued education (called Cockpit Resource Management) to enable strangers to interact instantly like an Apollo crew, the real thing works better within small pre-socialised communities (my captains X example providing the statistical exception).

And so Australian life continued. I had left my violin at home but took a few organ books along in case I could find somewhere suitable to practise. This only works when you have the time to pay attention with few other preoccupations on your mind, and a suitable instrument helps (a lot); but I had little confidence in how a visiting amateur pom might be received. A good instrument is in fact essential if you have a rough idea of what you are doing so I tried the cathedral first, with little optimism and little expectation of success, but the reception was more than positive. The Oxford experience and music scholarship CV worked well. 'Come here when you like and play the organ when there's nothing going on, and you must sing in the choir. There's only one real tenor and he sometimes doesn't turn up because he plays cricket.' 'But I was a cathedral treble, I'm no Caruso.' 'Doesn't matter, you know how it works, it's only on Sundays, we'd be glad of your help, and you get free supper at the boys' school after choir practice on Thursdays.' Who could resist such a deal?

My first attempt at water-skiing – a trivial and recreational experience as it might seem – turned out to be a small object lesson in enlightened teaching (to be filed for later use). Captain Reggie Langtry was a keen water skier and encouraged me to come along and give it a go at his Australian friend's training lake. The friend was well-up on the current international scene – barefoot being the latest fad; but I was not to do barefoot. This was basic get-you-going teaching at its best, much like my teenage Tiger Moth experience in 1959. Reggie was experienced enough in this school's system to be entrusted with the all-important first briefing, and this consisted of the starting position to adopt in the water, or on the beach, or on top of the water – it made no difference. 'Arms straight, legs bent, skis parallel, look ahead, stay like that until instructed otherwise.' 'Don't try to pull yourself up, let the horse do the work,' said Jeff, the bronzed Aussie teacher. They were absolutely right, and I cannot recall the number of times I have seen unsuccessful holiday beach beginner blastoffs instantly end in the immediate and confidence-denting crash, with a learning score well into the negative zone.

First physical contact with something new is seized by the memory, and instantly acquired instinctive mistakes take a lot of getting rid of.

Having covered the static beach stuff and floated similarly in the shallows, I was hooked up to the boat. 'Just watch me, not the water,' said Jeff, with a reverse version of Crocodile Dundee's dog-quieting gesture as a reminder. Off we went, slowly, trundling though the water like a hippopotamus, but with the degree of progression controlled by Jeff's speed. This is the secret – start at the beginning, make sure only the necessary basics are clearly understood and control progress thereafter with positive experience only. The clever stuff can come later – but you get to it much sooner following a good beginning. I don't think I fell in until around my fifth sortie, trying some aggressive wake crossing. Fantastic student? Definitely not. Excellent teaching? Certainly.

Reggie was the ultimate diplomat, and the perfect right-hand-seat captain X co-pilot. A socially empathetic and, needless to say, highly competent captain (these two qualities often go together) he could also be the ideal, uncontentious, seamlessly supportive co-pilot, invariably managing sensitive egos with charm and invisible discretion, while also quietly managing everything else. I sat behind for a trip with one of our prickly and darkly formal commanders. 'What a pleasure to fly with you, xyz. Why don't you do the whole trip, I'll be co-pilot, why not?' After a couple of days the change in the captain was remarkable; what a psychological massaging job was done by Reggie. Captain Queeg could have passed the CRM exam by the time we finished – until the next time. But Reggie was not in training – nothing to prove, and preferred his own flying and family life.

To some extent the Greek teaching joke is true (and examining can't be left out). Similarly, those who could teach and examine well often do not want the airline checking job (as it was), especially if they have previous similar experience in a more creative environment. The situation has improved in recent years, but it has occurred to me that if you want the best and respected training within an airline the right people may have to be identified and invited, flattered and persuaded into the job. Financial incentive alone is not enough – and may encourage unsuitable individuals. Those who are tempted by notions of status may not be ideal, nor may surviving heroes of dangerous incidents – necessarily. As we in Concorde training were once reminded, an airline with thousands of pilots contains a large number of eminently capable individuals. Quite so – and it is also true to say that a number of these would also make excellent training staff, but many of them, for this very reason, have more rewarding ways of occupying their time, both at work and at home. An industrially democratic airline is constrained by its core values: the passenger pays for a standard product. Could be better, but why? Sad but true.

CHAPTER 12

MORE 707ING, AND MORE FLYING

Based in London again, 707 trips continued much as before. Having got the general hang of it by now this work would consist of repeating the same thing over and over again – with different people, mostly total strangers – and gaining experience, but experience doing what? Doing the same thing over and over again – with repeated success! This is what airline customers pay for, or hope they pay for, and statistically it works unless you are particularly unlucky, but it did occur to me to ask myself why tens of thousands of airline piloting hours are quoted with such pride. I'm still not sure of the answer, except that it proves an extended ability to avoid the employee's ultimate badge of shame – getting the sack, or getting it seriously wrong. But, seriously, it does prove this very ability to keep doing the same thing, and keep avoiding the fatal mistakes, or the luck to have others help you spot them. One cannot but argue that the 20,000 airline hours proves a certain statistical survivability, but what else?

There was a certain consistency about the working pattern at this time. Trips lasted about 10 or 11 days, and contained approximately the same number of sectors. Two sector days with 24 hr nightstops were typical (shall we say three and a half hours average sector length), and the time at home averaged something like the same as the time away. But the variety of destinations was considerable, and very different from the layman's assumption that one is specifically tied to the Timbuktu run for example, on the assumption, I suppose, that local knowledge is everything. It's not like that at all. To give the rostering people their due I notice that in 1967 I continued to be given a mix of east and west, generally Singapore or Hong Kong to the east, and various ways to get to Toronto or New York to the west, and once an excursion to Bogota calling at many places in the Caribbean and Venezuela. But not the Pacific. Who were the people who went across America to California – and beyond? What was round the back of the world? What about the Hawaiian Islands? How did you get there, and who went to Japan – was it just a favoured few?

There was no bidline then, or invitation to express preferences – at my level anyway. Maybe there was an in-office approval system, clearing people to additional parts of the world as considered appropriate, but I have no knowledge of such a thing. My best guess is indeed that the rostering lady in the control centre used her own interpretation of experience and practice to send crew members where she thought they would be best suited, but I think it possible, aided by hearsay, that social visits upstairs, friendly conversation and the odd duty-avoided present from abroad may have helped secure popular destinations. I notice that it was a year after the Sydney posting that I did break new ground on a westerly trip with Eric Langmead in April 1968 – New York to Sydney and back staying at San Francisco, Honolulu and Nadi on the way, so the system did appear to roll around.

By the mid-sixties the world had changed since the end of WW2, but the contrast between east and west was more marked than today. Today's observant traveller would feel reasonably at home in the North America of 1967, but might find all points east rather quaint – still living in the past. Take Delhi, for example. Once the last engine was started and the clear to go wave was imminent the apron station staff assembled in right dress abeam the cockpit left hand window; load sheet wallah, ground power unit wallah, steps wallah, headset wallah, and finally, at the double, the chocks wallah – at their head the turbaned (resplendent with company badge) station engineer. His pristine salute was answered by a laconic wave from our captain, and we sidled casually away. Great stuff. Were these cowering victims of British oppression? Not completely.

Calcutta airport (Dum Dum) was renowned for its immense community of survivalist dogs. These were thinner than pets, but were not all pathetic cringing strays, and had plenty of lean, toned and streetwise athletes among them. The fastest get to eat and breed, I suppose. There's a good (true) story about a Qantas 707 crew in transit. The boys (only one sheila for the first class) felt some sympathy for the prize racing greyhound in the hold, on its way from Haringey to the Sydney tracks. It would appreciate some fresh air, something to eat and a nice drink; maybe stretch its legs, perhaps. It did just that, at racing speed, and, accompanied by a bunch of Indian street racers – inspired by real class in their midst – disappeared across the grass, runway, the rest of the grass, and into the distance, heading for town. There's no chance of catching it. What to do? A local substitute athlete, still dozing on the concrete, was put in the box and sent the rest of the way to Sydney.

I remember a memorable fishing trip at Karachi. A popular outing during a free day at the rest house was bunder-boating in the harbour. A bunder boat is a mini dhow, and the tourists cruised about, driven by their three-man crew. Lines thrown overboard might catch some swimming crabs which were boiled up in an aluminium washing up bowl on board. These, like all straight-out-of-the-sea creatures, were quite tasty, but, bearing in mind the little crabs' hydrodynamic swimming qualities, were short of substantial meat. However, the bunder boat trip was better than spending all day by the pool – but the great fishing trip was something else. Our captain, Bill Bailey, seemed to know much more about fishing in Karachi than most. I did a number of trips with Bill, and can tell you nothing more about him, but he gave the impression of old school experience, and whatever that means.

BOAC had the Flying Staff Recreation Club, which distributed an assortment of appropriate sporting equipment here and there at the places we stayed. In olden propeller days with, perhaps, one aeroplane a week, there had been plenty of recreational time: but although jets, their speed, frequency and shorter holiday time may have reduced the use of this stuff, the equipment still sat around in almost-abandoned cupboards in many of our slip stations. Some members never made use of this facility; others might sign out the scrabble set, or try a burst of table tennis, but I got the feeling that Bill was familiar with whatever might be available when he organised a proper fishing trip. We (virtually the whole crew) collected the rods, lines etc and set off for the harbour, hiring a proper fishing boat and crew for the day. There was no plan, except that we would go out of the harbour and down the coast towards the west – how far and for how long we did not know. Bill briefed us on the rods, reels, spinners, tactics if you got a bite, playing/winching/gaffing technique, and so on. This system clearly had little in common with catching minnows or swimming crabs.

Eagerly we threw the lines overboard and waited for serious action as we slowly motored west along the coast towards Kuwait. Nothing. The boat crew (three or four of them) looked listless. They knew this was a waste of time. When can we take these tourists back? Then Bill negotiated with the captain. A bit of Urdu and the aura of experience seemed to work. We have to go further west, around the corner and off the village and river estuary – Chota Chalna it was called – that's where we have to be. This seemed to work. Forget the day out for the moment, this man isn't a regular tourist – seems to know what's what and is prepared to pay for it. An hour or so later we have rounded this corner, approached abeam the said estuary, slowed to tick-over and thrown the lines in the sea again. During the transit there has been more time to brief us about game fishing etiquette – we're going to be good.

Nothing happened for twenty minutes, then the first strike. It's not called strike for nothing. A shout of 'Strike!' signals throttle back and the playing, winching and struggling is on. That's for one fish, and the real fishermen are suddenly galvanised with gaffing enthusiasm. When did they last see such fishing? After the first couple of landings a fishing frenzy ensued. I think we had four rods over the side, and no sooner had power been applied than 'Strike, strike, strike!' sounded in as many seconds. Engine to idle and the battle was on. 'By Jove, we're really getting stuck into those Surmai,' said Bill as the boys frantically gaffed and threw the hefty fish into the boat – transformed from bored guides into enthusiastic fishing professionals.

There were two kinds of victim who took our plastic dayglo squid, quite different in character, but caught in the same place. The first was a giant mackerel – the Surmai. Built for speed, it was indeed a giant mackerel, not a kind of mackerel, just a very big one; fast, vigorous, but reasonably soon winched into gaffing range. Then there was the Kokon. Nothing like the Surmai, this was a chunky silver miniature coelacanth, slow, hefty, strong, and very resistant to being winched to the surface. The crew cooked one of these (fried in the washing up bowl over an open fire in a wooden petrol driven boat: not a lifejacket in sight – no H&S here) – and very tasty it was as a teatime snackette.

The afternoon wore on and the novelty of winching, gaffing and piling ever more fish in the bottom of the boat wore off, so it was time to return. At the dockside we were surrounded by a swarm of kids eager to carry our catch to the boots of a few waiting taxis, so enthused were they at such a catch. I had the impression that this was not everyday stuff. We sold our catch to the rest house, and at dinner that night enjoyed one of our Surmai, baked by the chef – and even the accompanying fiery chilli sauce could not disguise the excellence of caught-by-yourself fresh fish, washed down by a flagon or two of wine from Rome. The money we got for the fish paid for the day out, and there was some left over to update the tired FSRC gear that had given us so much satisfaction. In fact, at the start of the Chota Chalna feeding frenzy Bill had berated me for questioning his instruction to hold the rod upside down – rings uppermost. What for? Where's the science? Why should this be a stronger option. My second fish broke the rod – was he right? 'Stupid boy, think you know best' was the comment. Fair enough. We bought a load more fishing stuff on behalf of the FSRC at Singapore and tried another heavy hit on the way back, but only caught a few. News of our previous success had spread and others wanted to come along with Bill's crack fishing crew. These were quite excited to see the few reasonable fish we caught, but we were disappointed; it wasn't the same – that's fishing, of course.

The post-independence Singapore story is simple. The politics is hazy, but the neighbouring territories were disgruntled at Singapore's breakaway, and communist freedom fighters were also active in the surrounding jungles. We always seemed to arrive in the early evening, just after dark as the routine teatime thunderstorms started to subside; and the approach procedure usually meant joining the hold over the approach NDB to the south, lined up with the Paya Lebar ILS. This beacon was in Indonesian (or was it Malayan?) jungle and as Qantas racetracked below us and descended to the glideslope intercept height, waiting their turn one ahead, pinpoints of light floated up out of the pitch dark below. The Qantas captain's concerned voice came over the airwaves: 'Jeez! The bastards are firing at us, we've got to get out of here,' and he was duly cleared. Our suave captain pressed his button: 'Thanks for drawing the fire, old boy'. Whether he was also the Frankfurt 'Yes, several times, but we didn't land' pilot I don't know.

At the end of October I did a Toronto by way of Manchester, Prestwick and Montreal with a similarly colourful and brave captain, Jimmy Linton. It turned out that Jimmy had also been at Upper Heyford in 1943. My mother had told me about seeing a cloud of black smoke arise from across the Cherwell valley one afternoon, as she returned to Deddington on the Oxford bus. My father had been noncommittal when she asked him what had happened, but Jimmy was happy to summarise OTU life and death. 'Night flying was much worse. You could tell where the circuit was from the fires'. With a one-year-old and another on the way it probably would have been better had she remained in Oxford, with my grandparents, and one can understand her jaded view of aviation thereafter.

On November the 14th 1967 I see I spent an hour's flying at Stansted with Peter Mains-Smith and G-ASZG, one of our new 707-336 models. The suffix number relates to both the machine and the customer, so the similar South African Airways version was a -338, for example; but why our first 707 was a 436 I'm not sure. There will be a simple answer for those who are interested in these details, but the 336 model was sufficiently different for a few circuits to be thought worthwhile, and our very good 336 simulator was yet to appear. To the casual observer the 336 was another 707, but to the owner it was a much-improved transport vehicle. The main difference was full span leading edge flaps; not beautifully sculptured elegant affairs like the VC10's slats, but a line of underwing panels that hinged out from under the leading edge, leaving a gaping hole and a view of green painted internal structure inside – not particularly cool-looking, but underneath was not important: this device was a means of increasing lift coefficient at speeds where efficiency didn't matter. Lowering the leading edge to meet a new stagnation point is what this is all about (and it added to the wing upper surface area), and the ability to safely fly at increased angles of attack with a marginally larger wing meant that the same aeroplane could lift greater weights at the usual takeoff and landing speeds. More powerful and fuel efficient engines helped, and, to BOAC, the twin spool Pratt and Whitneys with a fan at the front were the first indications of things to come – a more efficient use of fuel and investment, even considering our sturdy Avons and Conways which had carried the Rolls Royce tradition. Straight and bypass jets produce air that goes too fast for best cruise efficiency. Traditional big propellers do not like high airspeeds at height, so something in between has become the subsonic answer – a large fan driven by a small, hard-working jet.

While on the subject of training circuits I remember my father telling me about the original Gloster Whittle E28/39 that flew from Barford St John (Oxfordshire) in 1943, where the Upper Heyford school (16 OTU) went to do circuits in their Wellingtons and Hampdens. The Gloster pilot's concern about the few minutes of fuel remaining when he returned to a circuit occupied by struggling learners is understandable now, but, even though this jet programme represented vital research, the battle-hardened OTU staff sometimes resented the inconvenience of getting out of his way. 'What's the use of such a silly little thing anyway? And it has to suck itself along like a Hoover.'

The 336's extensive leading edge flappery gave this 707 a new character. It didn't need the ARB-demanded tail bumper, and a harder working wing gave this new version a presence and sense of steadiness on the approach that was lacking in its lighter, more floaty and wallowy predecessor – slightly sporty as the 436 was. On the approach, and a degree or so more nose up, the 336 was definitely more 'collected' (and proper horsemen will know exactly what I mean), and the series yaw damper system – which could be allowed to do its own thing with the rudder all the time – transformed this model into a stately-flying transport system. The engines were not so 'start and forget' as before. On a steady approach the throttle response was quite adequate, but it was important not to throttle back completely; the wind-up time from idle could then cause problems near the ground. Engine start also required some attention, but this call for care was not in the same league as the first 747 big brother.

For me, 1967 professional flying finished with a marathon eastern trip with the affable Pete Moffatt. We left London on December 8th and returned two days before Christmas. During this tour we took our various 436s to Zurich, Beirut, Karachi, Bangkok, Hong Kong, Darwin, Sydney, Darwin, Hong Kong, Tokyo, Hong Kong, Rangoon, Delhi and Beirut.

'There but for the grace...' A navigating story – starting WW3 and so on

In 1967 the Vietnam war was in full swing, and the Americans were doing their best not to allow it to disrupt normal high-altitude air traffic. Further north, B52s filled the air at our altitude, and night-time tracer and napalm displays were clearly visible from public airliners where the heavy-duty action was restricted to ground attack. In the daytime one of our 707s, heading east to Hong Kong, was surprised to see a flight of four F4 Phantoms fly very close past them in what was supposed to be an airway, and reported the fact as a dangerous infringement of public flight safety. But, hey, let's be reasonable: this was a nice day, they do look where they are going with great interest, and there's a war on. In theory, everyday life in tourist destinations from Bangkok to Hong Kong and Sydney continued unaffected by the many battle-scarred warriors shipped in for a couple of days R&R and, remarkably, so it was; and though new business opportunities made the most of it, R&R must have been run as something of a tight ship. What was the psychological effect of these instant transfers from battlefield to peacetime holiday and back? It must have worked – in the short term anyway.

This was a busy time for cold war diplomacy all round. Summits and exchange visits between US, UK, USSR and French premiers were frequent, and Comrade Kosygin came to see Harold Wilson. During the ice-breaking chat on the way from Heathrow to Downing Street Alexei nudged Harold and said (via his interpreter) with a grin: 'That was a clever intelligence gesture at our Turkmenistan border by your airliner the other night. We did have four MiG 21s heading for it before it turned away.' Harold was nonplussed. Why hadn't he been told? Was this Eton and Oxford Foreign Office establishment getting too big for its boots – setting up an airliner intrusion exercise off its own bat like the South Koreans? His enquiries led to BOAC, to the 707 fleet where nothing amiss had been reported – let alone secretly planned by capitalist zealots, and finally to the flight navigation office, where nothing had been spotted on the paperwork. But closer inspection revealed the story.

The navigator had made one arithmetic mistake. Usually one error will be obvious, but in this case the three astro position lines – measured from three separate stars – produced a perfect-looking fix. One mistake cannot do this; but on this flight it did. A tiny triangle of position lines has to be the right place, and in this case it suggested that the expected westerly jet stream had not yet been encountered during the last twenty minutes; but it had, and the aeroplane was actually on track for Teheran, not miles to the west of where it should be. He had done everything right, except add instead of subtract, or subtract instead of add the adjustments you can make to move the first and second star results up the track to where they would be eight and four minutes later, to join final shot three. This system just saves a few moments when it comes to drawing on the map.

The last turn point had been Zahedan, several hundred miles behind on the south west corner of Afghanistan, and the straight line from there to the Iranian capital goes over desert – nothing else. On a winter's night the sky is clear, but there's nothing to see except stars. At altitude the flying can be completely smooth, even if the subtle transition into polar air involves a wind increase of 100kts – from the side. An independent observer might have been suspicious of a changing temperature, were this to have been the case, but the two captains X at the front assumed all was well and carried out the requested turn to the right to get back on track; anyway, the radio signals from Teheran should be picked up in a few minutes, when only 200 miles would remain. But the needles and distance counters remained dead. Given the copybook stargazing conditions and the most beautiful-looking fix this suddenly becomes a timewarp situation, a parallel but radio-less world in the dark. What to do?

The captains did what instinct persuades: dogs and cats sometimes do it when in doubt, humans as well – go round in circles. If you are lost, this technique arrests the sense of getting more lost, but does it help? In this case it did, because during the first turn a clear coastline slid into view on the little radar screen. It was the bottom right hand corner of the Caspian Sea, and they were somewhere in the region of the Khar Touran National Park – way to the east of the correct track. Now it was obvious which way was Teheran, and when the next crew pointed out their 20-minutes wait on a cold apron a brief 'wind was a bit strong' seemed to explain it, and nothing more was said or written. Without the informed aside from Mr Kosygin nothing more would have been said in the BOAC Kremlin, and maybe the rogue fix would have remained a secret mystery to all. But I'm glad it wasn't me. He had bowled himself a googly for sure, and this rather suggests that you shouldn't trust anything in aviation, especially yourself. This is partly true.

Formation

In 1967 the Airways Aero Club arranged an air display at Wycombe Air Park for September and planned a Cherokee 4 ship routine as their own participation. The team was led by Hamish Hamilton and I was invited to take the left wing position; the other two slots were filled by people I didn't know and there were a couple of practice sessions during the week before the show – yes, all of two! And all this without the traditional work-up starting with a pair who do more than just fly along like station-keeping in the car on the motorway. The spare capacity of a team requires more proof than the ability to stay in place on a good day. Of course the routine was not as complex as a Red Arrows outing and consisted of gentle manoeuvring in a box formation, with little intentional changing of position, but even though nothing happened and the show took place without incident I felt uneasy about the whole exercise. After the first practice I had told Hamish that I did not think my formation was good enough, in the hope that he might replace me, but he disagreed and we proceeded as planned.

Formation is possible in most if not all aircraft types, but some are more suited to it than others; in fact the level of difficulty is related to handling characteristics as much as performance and repertoire. I have seen some very good formation flying from the Burda Staffel and their four Piper Cubs, but the Cherokee is a modern general aviation Piper, and even the vic set-up chosen by Pussy Galore's death-dealing playsuited Cherokee ladies was more of a strung out, low level battle proximity-averse demonstration. (Of course, the filming for the James Bond picture might have been done by willing extras and not the real cat-suited Pussy Cat Dolls.) I had not done this kind of ad hoc club formation before, and much preferred the Tiger Club's more structured, if apparently informal, environment (though there was actually nothing informal about it). Like school sports and its availability, those who wished to participate at Redhill could be sure of frequent, good and widespread mentoring – more a way of life really; and, like many other quality pursuits, 'good enough or not at all' would be useful advice to teachers and learners alike. However, one must remember that the Airways Aero Club (as it was then) bore the cost of this non-revenue flying, so getting-away-with-it-on-a-shoestring can work, in fact the tradition continued.

Tiger club formation

I would assess myself this 1967 summer as having been an 'improver' within the Tiger Club's 'organised sports' formation flying tradition. This was a club, not a flying school, and there were many members with past and present military experience. Apart from official leadership of the display team the organisation of practice flights was ad hoc and informal, no training records were kept and there were no instructions to read, but the syllabus was far from spontaneous. There were ways to do things, and all Turbulent formation flying followed the same procedures, be it two, three or four aircraft. Briefing as appropriate, of course, then a workout of 25 minutes on average. Formation takeoff (always), normal station keeping (mostly while turning), and efficient changes of position. A routine covered the box four change to echelon, then line astern, then back to box, during which some vital safety confirmations were essential, with everyone in agreement as to what should happen.

After takeoff in finger four the box man, out on one wing, ducked underneath his closest colleague when there was enough distance from the ground, and popped up in his box position, behind the leader. The basic box four is now set. Radio was not carried, hand signals from the leader indicated formation changes, eye contact and a nod established the essential agreement where two moved together and the leader's aileron waggle signalled back to original positions. As the team fly around, these formation changes (interspersed with the odd tailchase) would be repeated either side, sometimes while turning, so that the necessary skills, convention, disciplines and attention to detail could be practised and, as you might expect – certainly hope for – become second nature. It worked, and although team sports were not my thing at school, this was more like it.

These are the basics, and when sufficiently familiar they allow the lead to be changed during a session – it would be incorrect to assume that a leader does not have to be able to do formation flying himself. In this way the traditions of this specialised trade were passed down, learned and practised among the variety of pilots who were attracted to this team sport. Team cross country was a less concentrated practice platform, of necessity based on straight flight.

Arnold Green was an Essex farmer with his own Turbulent and airstrip. As a TC member he had become an accomplished formation flyer, and I see that on two autumn Sundays he took a group of us to the farmhouse for tea, while honing our skills on the way.

Many readers will be familiar with this way to fly, but, as a way of life, it is normally the exclusive preserve of tactical fighter flying. For this reason the basics are included in any military pilot's training – but the subject is completely absent from the experience of a private or commercial pilot. The opportunity provided by these cheap to hire but eminently suitable Turbulent formation toys, and the experience that characterised a significant section of Tiger Club membership, were priceless advantages to one keen on learning new aviating things. These tiny aeroplanes flew very close, were responsive and sensitive, and non-radio pilot communication direct and intuitive.

I continued practising aerobatics at Redhill, mostly in the Stampe. It was only during the early 1960s that the international aerobatic competition scene had developed a formalised scoring system for precision manoeuvres so as to provide some sort of level playing field for a world championship. Since the early post WW1 days the competition format had been entertainment rather than disciplined rigour: good fun to watch of course, but how does one judge a five-minute do-what-you-like airshow – to the satisfaction of the competitors? The Lockheed Trophy had continued this tradition, and the appearance of a variety of machines from trainers to fighters added interest, but the judges had more fun with the scores than the pilots. The abstemious Neil Williams told me of how he had witnessed a central European star pull a flask out of his jacket and take a huge swig as he mounted his charger for the forthcoming battle between himself, his machine and the judges. 'I go better with fire in my belly,' he had said. Perhaps; but I wouldn't recommend it for an FAI-sanctioned event. Now an intricate system developed by Spanish Jungmann maestro Colonel Aresti had been adopted, and what you had to do became more defined – up to a point.

But the British aerobatic scene was still very much find out for yourself in 1967. Those few who had entered world events came back with a rough idea of the international curriculum, but had been hopelessly outclassed. A combination of Eton playing fields tradition leavened with a dash of gentlemen and players on the same team still proved ineffective – in fact, aerobatics at this level and complexity had never been a British thing. A Russian once told me the simple reason. 'The air is our sea.' The French agree. Of course – the British are seafaring people: in Britain flying has never had the same universal status as dominating the world by sea power, or messing about in boats by association, and recreational flying has historically been regarded as a fringe pursuit for the privileged and none too academically inclined, so British flying enthusiasts had a lot to learn. In fact, apart from landing your Moth in stately homes' grounds, messing about with aeroplanes has always been just a bit infra dig in Britain. There's something socially tainted about this specialisation and it has the feeling of consenting adults behind closed doors.

During this summer I beavered away putting the basic pieces together – loops, parts of loops, verticals, 45s, Cubans, up and down, accurate rolls and parts thereof, flick rolls and spins to order, all the above upside down as well – and so on. There was no dual as such, unless you asked someone suitable, but I do remember a Stampe flight with Carl Schofield. I had struggled with the rolling circle. To get the nose progressing round the horizon in tune with the rolling while keeping a level attitude seemed impossible. 'Come with me, I'll show you what it looks like,' he volunteered.

Carl was a year behind me at Hamble, but had a considerable head start at aerobatics, and his enthusiasm, progress and success had given him access to those who knew – and were prepared to tell. 'Keep a constant rate of roll going, and push and pull the nose round the horizon in series of arcs' he said, as he demonstrated. Simple when you've seen it, and indicated the necessary compromise between what is possible and theoretical perfection. 'How about a flick roll?' I asked. ZAP! 'Thanks, now I see it.' I said. A lot learned in 10 minutes, but generally you worked it out for yourself.

The British Aerobatic Association had not yet been thought of, and international participation was arranged through the Royal Aero Club. It is safe to say that the Tiger Club was the crucible of UK competition progress, and it was they who organised the few aerobatic contests suitable for the domestic standards of the day. 'You should enter something,' people said, despite my reservations about not being good enough. I've since come to realise that expectations and concern about personal status should not be considered in this sport. Success cannot be achieved without competition experience, and a novice cannot possibly win, even if demonstrating world champion quality. The reasons for this concern judging and its difficulty, and a judge's fear of being out of step. It's easier to make a decision about something familiar, or according to expectation. A first-time competitor should be content not to come last. Things will improve, and the ice has been broken.

On October 1st I entered the Esso Tiger Trophy contest at Rochester. This event requires a sequence of simple aerobatic manoeuvres without the use of an inverted fuel system. After the aerobatics the pilot glides down for a three-point spot landing. I took the Super Tiger, hoping for sympathy votes, content with the slow roll rate, coughing and spluttering sound effects and the advantages of low wing loading. I came fifth, but got the novice's prize.

Some months earlier the Airways Aero Club CFI, John Varley (affectionately known as Ginger Tom in BOAC – possibly associated with the ginger goatee; but maybe other interests) had approached me about something of an adventure. A man from British Insulated Callender's Cables, based in Teheran, was due to take delivery of a new Beagle Husky – it would help him visit the various construction sites in that large and arid country, and take a look at the cables on the way. Captain Varley described the conditions he was about to demand from Beagle for the brave ferry pilot – letters of credit, guarantees of diplomatic immunity, Bills of Exchange... actually I can't remember the details, but it all sounded very 1930s. What about the goolie chits? How valid was all this empire stuff to the actual problem of getting the little Taylorcraft successor there? The basic idea appealed, but did I really want to, or have the time to do, an Amy Johnson? I'd flown to Teheran before and knew what the countryside past Istanbul looked like. The NE Mediterranean coast looks inhospitable, but a more direct route goes over high and arid mountains, Mount Ararat to name but one. Van, Lake Van, Tatvan, Yerevan, Batman – I'd seen them all from a great height – but would I want to be down there in a little machine, engaged in a monster solo cross country?

On a Teheran stopover I met up with the BICC man (whose name I can't remember) and we went to see a senior Iranian Air Force staff officer. After a coffee and some friendly interview chat he said 'You can do it'. That was reassuring – but did I want to do it? I flew to Rearsby (in a Beagle Terrier) to see the Beagle chief test pilot who had the job of arranging the delivery. Next to his desk was some sort of oxygen gadget. 'I don't think this will work,' he started, 'it doesn't have enough power to fly at 14,000ft' (Mount Ararat is as good as 17,000ft). I got the impression that my agent had been busy negotiating the details of this special mission, and debating my reservations about the long low-level options without landing possibilities. I felt that grass roots enthusiasm and the right kind of chaps with time on their hands might be more relevant. I chickened out and gave the job to a couple of Tiger Club friends, James Baring and Tom Storey. They succeeded, in the fashion of the Tiger Club extreme touring discipline, and stuck to the inhospitable Turkish coast without oxygen or supercharging, before crossing the many miles of desert to Teheran.

In the August I renewed my instructor's rating once again with George Webb, this time restricted to Eastleigh, and with more than 200 hours instructing time I was eligible for a full rating: I could run my own school in fact, though I had no plans to do so. But the logbook tells me that, though not directly related, I had been appointed as a Tiger Club check pilot by the end of this summer. This job turned out to be less straightforward than I had imagined, and I had little enthusiasm for the remedial work sometimes expected by prospective members, or by the club hierarchy on occasion. A test, check, checkout – whatever you want to call it – is supposed to be just that, and the classic routine in a Tiger Moth a well-established indication of self-sufficient ability as traditionally required by a PPL holder (of its day). I was not alone in feeling that, if necessary, candidates should learn the traditional skills somewhere else before they attempted to join – but, as something of an elsewhere-employed purist, I had no interest in the club's private concerns. However, this task was sometimes a pleasure to conduct, and one of my first customers, Don Henry, proved to be a most welcome example of the easiest of candidates. Don, an American who had brought his family to England for business reasons, had been a WW2 marine pilot. What else had he done? I had no idea. He was a businessman, not a professional pilot. Had he seen a Tiger Moth before? I didn't know. The briefing was straightforward, but not instructional – 'Take me for a ride, do what you would normally do as pilot, and we will do engine failure after takeoff, normal flying, simulated forced landing, stalling and spinning, then return to the field and land.' All basic stuff, but for whom? He's an American, for God's sake.

The result was stunningly good. After the stalling and spinning our intercom failed so I pointed down over the side and admired the view. Don took us back to the field and landed in exemplary fashion. There was nothing to say except 'very good', and I was sufficiently impressed to crank Don up a rank and make him a full Colonel in my report. The only flying event Don mentioned was a high speed, low level flypast in line abreast at some ceremonial function, of 15 or so Corsairs. Abeam the saluting base he was surprised by a large bird meeting the windscreen at all of 350 mph. What happened after that I do not know, but it does occur to me that the quality of a pilot's initial training at a young age probably has a lasting effect. Once this seminal opportunity has passed, the die seems to have been cast – later experience is unlikely to fully remedy shortcomings in understanding, composure, priorities or reliably rational decision-making.

To briefly jump again into this narrative's future, I will mention one other candidate's exemplary demonstration of suitable training history, and that was

Phillip Meeson. I had come across Phil some time before at Little Rissington. He and another couple of students, stuck there on a Saturday, had come out to see what was going on at an aerobatic competition. Some time later he appeared at Redhill for his Tiger Club membership check, while currently training on the Varsity, but the Chipmunk training showed, and his whole Tiger Moth routine was perfect. I suspect that he had already decided that the military Hercules or Britannia as a job did not appeal, so he had left the service and went on to other entrepreneurial things including competition aerobatic flying, running a display team and a garage (not to mention an airline). I believe Phil came from a Northampton shoemaking family. When he joined the Tiger Club the Red Arrows were flying the teeny Gnat, and I often wondered where their adoption of non-standard desert (Meeson) boots came from. These were cheap, light, comfortable and more suitable for delicate footwork, and I, along with others, bought a couple of pairs at a good price. (What are contacts for? Selling, of course.)

CHAPTER 13

1968 – MORE OF THE SAME, WITH SOME EXCEPTIONS

On the third of March 1968 there was a meeting at Redhill to revise and reassess the makeup of the various official display teams. The full TC display was a cornucopia of assorted acts, from the big opening formation to crazy flying comedy routines, streamer cutting, balloon bursting, flour bombing, standing on the wing, limbo, serious aerobatics, formation aerobatics, tied together formation aerobatics and air racing (for those who did not fancy aerobatics or formation). A full display was all immaculately planned by the second, and the absence of radio greatly assisted its timing – it all worked like clockwork, there being no other option. The time had come to restructure the official team memberships, and likely newcomers were invited to put themselves forward. I was up for the Turbulent team. James Baring was the current leader and had assembled the list of possibles. I was detailed to fly with Clive Francis (ex Turb leader, Hunter squadron commander, famous for flying through an emptied hangar in his Turbulent, to the great delight of his engineering staff (all good morale-boosting and team-building stuff) and currently something in London, I think). Arnold Green, the Essex farmer, was our no.3 stooge. We only flew for 20 minutes, but this was non-stop turning, formation changing (definitely no throttling back and dropping behind), combinations of contra-intuitive power changes while manoeuvring and so on. Clive was very complimentary, and explained that anticipation was everything. He was right of course; the followers have to be one step ahead of the leader to make the moves look seamless, and so on. Anyway, I became an official team possible.

In Feb 1968 I had come across 707 G-ARWE for the last time, during a two-week Singapore and back with Bill Bainbridge; in fact the logbook records that I, unusually again, both flew and navigated the Delhi/Singapore sector where this technique was required across the Bay of Bengal. I have no recollections as to why this should have been, but the absence of another qualified navigator on board may have been the case, or it might have just been Bill's most convenient chance to give me a drive. However, this aircraft was to become the subject of a well-publicised accident the following April, and this event, and the conclusions that followed it, give another opportunity to step out of this 'then I did...' diary. Some subjects do not have a convenient time slot.

Accidents – what really happened to WE, who got blamed and what the official report may not tell you

Jet engines are very reliable by reputation, but if they do come apart, unexpectedly, at takeoff energy, the effect can be equivalent to a missile hit – in fact one can say that a jet has the ability to shoot itself down if an engine disc flies apart: it's not supposed to happen. The relatively recent 'QANTAS A380 after takeoff at Singapore' (2010) and the 'BA B777 on the runway at Las Vegas' (2015) incidents are two cases in point. The Whisky Echo event does not need detailed reporting, and everyone knows that closing the #2 engine LP cock (in the wing, not on the engine) would have shut off the fuel supply to the external blaze while the aircraft was flying, and it's easy to blame the engineer for not pulling the fire handle (which would have closed it) or operated the LP cock switch. But there are reasons why he didn't.

Captain Cliff Taylor did a great job of getting on the ground as quickly as possible, given the available information, and being able to see that fire was streaming from the wing. Influenced by the route check captain's urgent encouragement he revised his initial plan of a visual circuit of the field and abbreviated this to the landing on runway 05. Had the wing structure actually been burning this time saved might have avoided total disaster, but it wasn't; the fuel streaming from the ruptured supply pipe was burning, not the wing, but any wing streaming flame is a very bad thing. Cliff Taylor became a training captain after this incident, and I flew with him number of times, both before and after. Some years later on the 747, and knowing that I had spent time teaching students, he told me that he didn't mind dealing with experienced pilots within the airline training job, but did not enjoy flying with airline beginners. I never raised the WE incident with him, but an Airways Flying Club student who was a BOAC driver had told me that he had picked up Captain Taylor from the confusion around the burning wreck and driven him to the headquarters building. 'He was obviously a bit shaken up by what had happened. In the transport he told me that he had landed on two engines – another had failed, he said.'

But what actually did happen in the cockpit? A couple of years afterwards I did a long trip with the right-hand seat man, Frank Kirkland, and during a stroll around some foreign city he described his recollections in some detail. At the initial bang and lurch it was obvious that the #2 engine had failed dramatically, and the engine shutdown was called for. (This was correct at the time: had the engine fire warning been lit with bell sounding the fire drill would have been appropriate.) The first action was to close the throttle, which sounded the normal descent configuration warning horn – normally cancelled as a matter of course by the flight engineer when he throttles back at top of descent, but you seldom hear this warning soon after takeoff. Naturally teed up by sense of occasion, and expecting a simulator follow up fire warning, Frank pressed this same aural warning cancel button at the surprise horn, at the very instant the fire light came on, and immediately went out – when the engine and its warnings fell off. No bell, no light, no engine. This button on the coaming between the engine fire handles cancels both types of aural warning. The short flight continued based on reports of what could be seen through the side windows. There is no 'Wing on Fire' warning in the cockpit. There were no further emergency indications inside. John Hutchinson, tucked away at the navigator's table, could not easily tell what was going on up front, and would concur that it was difficult to be sure what else was happening. A commonly taught principle is not to rush: 'Fly around for a bit, make sure you've sorted everything out before rushing to land'. If you believe the wing is about to burn through, this advice is unlikely to be heeded.

Here it is important to appreciate BOAC's policy regarding emergency drills. Improvisation is strongly discouraged in the civilian world. The system, intended to support the least experienced or capable crew in an airline, is based on the manufacturer's checklist, as modified and approved by the owner's national regulatory authority. The drills are set piece performances, assembled to cover the most significant foreseeable failures. Do what it says, based on the indications in the cockpit, and nothing else. In this case a more experienced engineer might well have pulled a fire handle, knowing that it could not make matters worse, or he might have closed the LP cock directly on his panel; but doing this is part of the engine shutdown clean-up drill, and BOAC crews were taught not to do this checklist item until there was 'nothing else to do' spare time available – otherwise do not bother with it; it's insignificant following an engine shutdown. And so it usually is – unless an engine has blown up, destroyed its pylon mounting, and made its own smoking way to the Staines reservoir, taking its wires and fire warnings with it – but was a fire handle pulled, or an engine LP cock closed, temporarily, on an adjacent engine? Why did the captain think he had approached with only two engines giving power?

Discussion seems to indicate that after the landing there was something of a scramble to get out of the cockpit windows, suggesting that a pulled fire handle could well have been pushed back in by hands (or feet?) eager to help their owners make this claustrophobic exit. The AAIB report is confident that no fire handles were pulled or LP cocks closed.

Before leaving the subject of what the crew did or didn't do, it is important to understand what the word 'crew' means in large airline terms. An integrated team of close-knit bosom buddies? Not a bit of it, especially on a first sector out of London. There is no reason why these five, fresh from home, should ever have met before, let alone heard of each other. And the extra member present was a Route Check Captain, there exclusively to assess the captain's performance, but also note that standard procedures were employed throughout – definitely no making it up as you went along. Five strangers thrown together at random, and confronted with a serious surprise emergency which did not conform to the checklist. They were poorly placed; but anything more than standard procedures, which assume (very rare) set piece emergencies, would likely produce more problems than it would solve. That's how it is – but the sometimes; quixotic machinery does not know this.

The 707 engine (surprise=serious) failure drill was changed after this incident, to include pulling the handle, whether it indicated engine fire or not. The original B707 had been considerably improved upon by the UK airworthiness authority who regarded the initial model as unsatisfactory (dangerous?) from a handling point of view. As a government-owned carrier BOAC could naturally be also regarded as having a duty to support British manufacture, wherever convenient, and a number of stock American items were replaced by British equivalents, including the Rolls Royce engines. Until British transport aircraft became things of history, a sense of rivalry between 'British is best' and 'American aircraft make more commercial sense' was a long term internal feature of BOAC, then BA employee attitudes, and there's always the 'We know better' temptation, coupled with the 'Change something – anything' motivation – especially for those making their way up the office ladder. Operating procedures and training syllabi get adapted, improved if you like, but it is difficult to say whether for the best, except with hindsight – and new ideas can work both ways. I have no knowledge of the differences between the original FAA approved 707 Flying Manual and that of the BOAC 436 version, or, more significantly, the emergency procedures – and training syllabus. But it was not until the 1980s that I discovered that the BA 707 manual contained a 'Flying without indicated airspeed' paragraph (from the manufacturer's literature). This subject, in my 707 experience, had never been mooted, in training or discussion, even though this very situation had already occurred to one of our SVC10s on its way into Bahrain. A vulture destroyed the Fibreglass radome on the nose, and the disturbed airflow leaving the new flat front end made the airspeed indicators useless (and possibly also confused the angle of attack sensors. My VC10 memory does not cover this procedure, but in this case a convenient Hunter chase helped them out).

In 1984 in Mauritius I was involved in some 707 base training on behalf of the French Authority. Our Air France examiner called for an approach and landing without indicated airspeed – he had told me in advance, but not the rest of the crew. He was surprised that it was a surprise to me, but it was more of a surprise to them. We also carried out a number of useful exercises that did not feature in the BA syllabus (too difficult, will never happen, we don't go to places like that etc.). Capt. Goujon explained: 'In Air France we do everything that is in the Boeing manual, and nothing that is not.' Of course, even simulator training is expensive (especially if the government is not settling the accounts). Maybe some of a manufacturer's recommendations are surplus to requirements, but how can you be sure?

No self-loading freight

On March the 9th 1968 I see that I made my first 707-336 commercial flight, with 'Sergeant' George Lace, the flight manager, as our captain. George was a no-nonsense practical man who could make his own decisions without concern at the above soubriquet that some of his more suave DFC'd colleagues had given him. This trip was in one of our first two freighter versions, newly busy freightshed-hopping across the North Atlantic. George demonstrated his officer qualities immediately following this ungodly hour London departure for

Manchester and other points north and west. We took off at 2.40 am. To leave home at this inconvenient hour is much worse for fighting the urge to sleep than doing the same elsewhere. We had hardly taken off when George listened to the Manchester weather and its reducing visibility in fog. 'This is no good. We'll go to a hotel and do this tomorrow.' I see that we took off again at 1045 the same day after the rest of the night in bed near Heathrow, and handed the aircraft to the next crew in Prestwick at 1335, to continue to Montreal and New York at civilised hours the next day in the other freighter. Good show, George.

London, Manchester, Prestwick, New York starting at 3 am with an hour at each stop to shuffle the pallets became the regular Atlantic freighter trip, and it was quiet, tedious and not glamorous, especially in the winter. To begin with we had a steward to look after us, and some captains brought a sleeping bag for the corridor alongside the pallets. Despite discrimination the girls were not allowed to do this catering job, and later the steward was dispensed with for economic reasons, supposedly. Some crew then brought an electric frying pan along and we had a proper breakfast – a great improvement – and I discovered that if you followed the instructions for cooking the official food it was often not at all bad. That extra half hour or fifty degrees in the oven isn't always an improvement.

Back at Redhill, Tiger Club activity continued to be varied and interesting. My personal priority was competition aerobatic practice, and in these halcyon days this was permitted over the field during the week. The short concise flights that this privilege permitted were effective and relatively cheap, and the Stampe's very good handling qualities – upside down as well as right way up – made it perfect for the improver, right up to international level (almost). Since the first modern world championships in the early 1960s, aircraft better suited to the now more structured sport had appeared; mostly monoplane trainers converted to single seat versions. More power and less weight usually helps, and probably the most successful example at this time was the YAK 18 PS – single seat, converted back to taildragger with not much dihedral. A 360 HP mini Wright Cyclone at the front was a great help, and its confident growling made these red starred Russian aeroplanes look and sound the part; but versions of the Czech Zlin were acquitting themselves well, and the British 1968 contingent, who had taken their Z226 variant (the normal fixed-gear trainer fitted with the automatic propeller) to Moscow in 1966, now had a purpose built single seat Z526 Akrobat (the 226 had spun in at Redhill). But a couple of UK pilots took a Stampe along as well. Pete Jarvis, the British judge, told me afterwards that the Stampe's performance at Magdeburg had been brave, but not really state-of-the-art, to put it kindly. A mention of the 1968 world championships could not pass by without including the Twisty incident – a true miracle. This story has been told before, but cannot be left out of this narrative, even though I was not there.

The Twisty Miracle, World Championships, Magdeburg 1968

Twisty Winternitz was a South African, sharing his small team's standard (cooking) Zlin of the day. I know nothing more about Twisty, but I got to know his mentor of the time, Nick Turvey, quite well. Nick learned to fly in the South African Air Force – Tiger Moth, Harvard, Vampire, DC3, a useful start – and had also spent some time in England, was a member of the Tiger club and had become familiar with competition aerobatics. To say that he threw himself with enthusiasm into those things that took his fancy is my deliberate British understatement: Nick was passionate about flying, an extremely good, analytical and brave fly-anything pilot, and shared the South African's deep-seated quiet heroic quality, combined with ebullient optimism and generosity. He returned home fired up with the prospect of fielding a national team; one that would put on a respectable showing at the next worlds.

Apart from the team inexperience the problem was the training altitude. Most of Africa is 5700ft above sea level, and gets quite warm, so the density altitude around Johannesburg comes out at 8000ft on a nice day. Up there there's less lift in the air and power in the engine. At sea level, with the equipment of the time, a typical sequence (programme of contest manoeuvres) used most if not all of the prescribed performance zone – a box of air with a few hundred metres between lid and floor. Air density aside, I was to find out myself two years later that the task of getting round all the manoeuvres in a Zlin, in the space available (today 900m), was physically and intellectually demanding – hard work on the arms and legs, unrelenting positive and negative g, with a huge and continuous mental workload required for coaxing and cajoling the recalcitrant beast around the show ring without a refusal. In another two years I could accomplish this feat without stopping for a break somewhere in the middle, but easy does not come into it. Nick told me that it was not possible to perform the compulsory 1968 programme ('nursery sequence' he called it – but I don't think so) at Johannesburg in less than double the height required at sea level – so the continuous run through would be a new experience at the contest; they always had to stop and climb at least once at home.

The system accepts an interruption, or break as it is known, and subtracts penalty points. Although the eventual winner is very unlikely to have been able to compensate for such a downgrade it is not the end of the world for middle-order pilots, and will make relatively little difference for novices. If you get something wrong and end up pointing in the wrong direction a break will be scored, and appropriate pilot action is to take the breather, reposition and start again where you left off, with some more height under your belt. The same penalty applies to the much more important problem of getting low. 100 metres is the bottom height limit, and each clear clang of 100m rings up on the debit side of the scoring account – but this is not common, and a disciplined approach is one reason why competition aerobatics, though complicated and difficult (PC word is 'demanding'), has proved to be creditably safe. But give 50 metres a solid thump and your score card is for the shredder. Nick was concerned that his team did not throw marks away without good reason, and emphasised the necessity of not stopping in the middle because you felt like it, or had got used to it at home. Twisty took this to heart, though he would have agreed, under normal circumstances, that getting low would not be acceptable – but going on a public stage for the first time is not normal. Ask any experienced performer.

Somewhere in the sequence Twisty was getting low, his aeroplane definitely well in sight. To the watchers he would have to stop soon and climb again: where in the programme might it be? It had to be before the half loop (to be followed by a negative spin with pushout) for sure; and the judges and their assistants prepared themselves for a brief mental relax, a stretch, a stroll around the garden recliner, a slurp of the Democratic Republic's coffee perhaps, with maybe a cautious nibble at the untried people's biscuit, left over from this morning – the Zlin does not climb fast. But no; he's doing the half loop. Ah well, it has to be at the top. Then the atmosphere at the judges' line turned to ice and all notions of military biscuit abandoned – they heard the throttle close and watched incredulously as the nose slowly rose to maintain level flight. He was preparing to do the spin.

The one turn outside spin was good, finishing in a nice vertical – pointing straight at the ground, and he started to push, following the script. In the cockpit the view of the airfield straight ahead provided a strong reality check, primeval survival instinct kicked in and he pulled, the most efficient and instinctive way of regaining level flight within the remaining height – perhaps, with engine assistance – but it would be super close. Then an amazing thing happened – he pushed again, back past the vertical and into the required quarter outside loop to finish the figure.

The mental workload is high for all competition aerobatic pilots, even while practising, but as a beginner on the world stage the stress level could reach the rational limit, particularly if things are going wrong. Decisions come thick and fast, and having decided to abandon this figure and pull for dear life – unquestionably to earn a 50-metre disqualification, but probably staying alive – the importance of not stopping mid-sequence overrode it – again! Twisty was now committed to this second push, and the extra speed acquired while dithering in the vertical might be a good or bad thing, but the two-handed push was now the only option. The watchers expected the worst, but he missed the ground – just. Afterwards it was revealed that his barograph – in those days used for retrospective policing of height limits – said one metre. Observers accepted that the top of his fin might have been that high off the ground, but probably not. US judge and veteran hotdogging legend Mike Murphy pronounced 'Ground effect saved that boy'. UK team manager James Baring emerged from the team tent after an after-lunch nap and viewed an empty sky: 'Then a Zlin roared out of the grass, upside down – amazing'. A Berlin-based Pan Am pilot had just driven over to watch the flying. It was the first thing he saw as he approached the field: 'Wild action! What a crazy sport – I don't want to miss any of this,' he thought as he gunned the Beetle towards the main gate.

As he left the cockpit a shocked Twisty could only mumble about everything going green. History shows that he continued flying the Zlin at home, but this escape had been a miracle – however they work.

It wasn't all Olympic aerobatics at the Tiger Club. I see that manager Michael Jones had invited me to try the original Rollason Beta during the previous autumn. This little machine was designed for formula racing, limited by a 90 HP engine, and this miniature version of heavy metal aircraft racing each other round the pylons at Reno (Unlimited class) provided a relatively cheap way to provide competitive fun for the pilots and entertainment for the spectators. Low flying with steep turns in close proximity to and in competition with others did not appeal to me, but these little machines were fun in their own right because they manoeuvred nicely in the conventional sense, and, despite the 90 HP, could acquire good energy because of their low drag designs and adequate wing loading. Swooping, diving, turning, looping, rolling and combinations thereof are the stuff of tactical flying, and, provided it is strong enough, the midget racer makes a fun mini-fighter – always accepting the proviso of pilot discretion in small aeroplanes.

A couple of years earlier the Tiger Club owner had acquired legendary Lockheed test pilot Tony Levier's Cosmic Wind (Ballerina). Lockheed have a reputation for original and enterprising designs, and this little sport plane – amongst Shooting Star, Starfighter, U2 and Hercules – was no exception. All metal, laminar flow wings, streamlined, and tightly cowled and canopied, it looked the part, and the shiny scimitar-bladed propeller added an exotic touch. Neil Williams and Peter Phillips both flew it at airshows in an unspoken head to head stage contest, something like Norman Granz's Buddy Rich vs. Gene Krupa drum battles. Who can achieve the highest airspeed for the kickoff, do the fastest rolls, put in the maximum number of hesitation points? The high-speed arrival was impressive, and to see such a tiny machine approach in completely un-light-aircraft character, with howling engine and propeller, gave a distinctly hardcore feel to the experience. Its small size made it look much faster than a Mustang run in, for example. It received an inverted fuel system in an attempt to compete in competition aerobatics, and despite its unsuitability for this discipline, Neil Williams flew the flag with it in Spain 1964. He did not win, but beat 14 others, all flying aerobatic aeroplanes (not surprising at a world aerobatic championship). This somewhat bizarre achievement did indicate that energy retention and roll rate helped. It would not do correct flick rolls, but this is a difficult figure to judge, and Williams told me that its stunning aileron power enabled him to cheat and score a perfect ten on one occasion. He also told me that each requirement for inverted fuel needed specific changeover action from the pilot – let's say 27 times in one programme. The Spanish called it 'La Rannita' – the little frog – because of the way it hopped about on its fast landing roll. I do remember that the tailwheel was mounted half inside the bottom of the rudder. I never got to fly it because it crashed at the first turn in an air race (to be restored elsewhere and some years later). I did read that Lockheed considered making a ground attack ordnance dropping version for use in Vietnam.

The Tiger Club had many well-connected members. On the White Waltham clubhouse wall there's a photograph of Turbulent G-APNZ (the white one) about to make an accomplished-looking three-pointer on the grass outside, piloted by a helmetless (but sunglassed) H.R.H. the Duke of Edinburgh. He had expressed an interest in trying one and the Hon. James Baring (later Lord Revelstoke) took PNZ there, I suspect because of the field's closeness to Windsor. The Duke took off and trundled immediately over to the castle, flagrantly infringing the London Control Zone. I'm sure he retained his common sense approach to life, confident that a flyby at Round Tower height would pose no threat to an airliner. Of course a purple airway may have been prearranged, but I don't think so. I have heard that during James' return to Redhill the engine stopped. I have no more details about this – perhaps it was a For Your Eyes Only case.

James Baring had been an early member of the Tiger Club and joined in 1959. He was 21, had just finished his two years' National Service during which he learned to fly the piston Provost and Vampire, and had been given a little Turbulent by his mother as a 21st birthday present. An accomplished but original pilot, his projects and exploits indicated to me the eccentric creativity of the imaginative and independent schoolboy of days long gone, a traditional experience shared by a number of his contemporaries. The stories are many. There were the Turbulent underwing rocket tubes, firing the Guy Fawkes model on a stick. This would make an excellent addition to the display team's repertoire, but predictable launching was a problem. The hot-wired blue touchpaper system worked in principle, but the exact timing of the rocket firing was a problem, and late-burners could not be ruled out, reminding one of the well-known couplet: 'I shot an arrow in the air, it fell to earth somewhere unspecified outside the display area', or words to that effect. James once told me that he had dived his Vampire vertically with full power to see how fast it would go. Even though numbers were not quoted, a certain reckless disregard for life and limb might be assumed; but this was not his character, and quiet consideration, thoughtfulness and astuteness of an idiosyncratic nature would describe the James Baring I knew. In fact the greatest and most reassuring compliment I ever received was during a Saturday evening at Biaggi's (Edgeware Road) with James and Nini. During a discussion about life and its complications James made a simple assertion: 'but you're not an ordinary airline pilot'. Thanks, James. I agree.

Sometimes things tend to happen to good pilots, as well as to the others, and James always managed to surmount them. It was decided that a nine Tiger Moth flypast would make a satisfactory tribute at the De Havilland founder's funeral service at St Alban's Cathedral. The Tiger club could arrange such a thing, with James taking his normal box 4 Turbulent leader's position – in the middle of the diamond. The weather was almost good enough but not good – cold, damp, miserable, and a bit bumpy? The ad hoc crew became a team on the way to the Hatfield staging post and arrived there in good time – and then the problem arose. As the gaggle landed on the grass beside the runway Tony Haig-Thomas somehow managed to collect the glideslope aerial (or part thereof) with a Tiger Moth wing. What to do? A diamond with a space somewhere might make a novel missing man gesture, but this would be an American import – yet to infect the future British warbird scene. To change the back 4 to a 3 vic would look like a B2 stealth bomber tribute – something well into the future, and equally unsuitable. It had to be nine. A Hatfield air traffic controller owned a Tiger Moth not far away, and someone flew him over to get it, but time was running out for making the ceremonial flypast time. The controller's Tiger Moth arrived as the others were about to taxi out, engines running. Reshuffling meant that James would take his centre diamond spot in this replacement biplane. There wasn't time to swop seats, and the story goes that the owner insisted in staying put anyway, so James would have fly from the front (instructor or passenger position). This feels different, and the view is very different – in fact you can hardly see more than your own wings, boxing you in. To be confronted with an immediate performance while also boxed in by eight bucking and lurching biplanes and their hyped-up drivers, keen to stay in close formation while on stage come what may, is not fun. But it worked. I have reread Tony Haig-Thomas' excellent book *Fall Out Roman Catholics and Jews*, and he describes collecting the glideslope aerial. One of the others following him in told me of his amazement that Tony managed to turn off so quickly. The whole eventful day is a good story, with difficult weather throughout. A senior RAF officer who came along to watch the departure volunteered to take the place of one member marooned by weather; showing what can be done with the right people.

James was also an initial member of the Air Squadron. This organisation of like-minded City-based supporters of aviation, founded in 1966, gave a name to a collection of people of quality who, like traditional yachtsmen, enjoyed the common interest of ownership, preservation, and the social activities that went with them. This does not mean that British attitudes to the science of aeronautics and its academic legitimacy had changed, but the Air Squadron's active gesture in supporting military cadet training and civilian aerobatic competition achievement, even at intermediate level, seemed, to me, to acknowledge the shortcomings of the English establishment's continuing attachment to dwindling Edwardian values, and the resulting drastic unpreparedness for two 20th century world wars: the second something of an aviating surprise, and both ultimately fatal had it not have been for the help of our technologically-accepting and less anachronistically entrenched American cousins.

The logbook (once again) tells me that on May 25th 1968 I took Rapide G-AJGS from Booker to Blackbushe for five parachuting lifts – civilian club members this time, and exactly where they landed in Aldershot is not recorded. This machine had been recently restored by Doug Bianchi of Personal Plane Services, and very nice it looked. It flew to Blackbushe like a new aircraft, but the first takeoff there raised a potential, but not serious (as it happened) problem. During my previous Rapide session two years earlier with the army in Germany we had discussed what would happen if an engine failed after takeoff. The stripped-out Ringo would fly well enough with 12 heftily equipped students plus jumpmaster, but experience and a test showed that if an engine failed the only way was down – slowly, but still down. The staff agreed that, if necessary, they could throw the static line learners out at 800 (or was it 600?) feet over the trees, such was their confidence in the basic static line tradition, and would jump out themselves if necessary at 200 feet, facing astern with reserve already pulled and held as a bundle. This did not happen in 1966, but during the first takeoff on the Blackbushe short southerly runway a cylinder of the left engine ceased firing. The other five on that side struggled on, the stopping possibility had passed, our lightly equipped civvy jumpers did not weigh that much, so I could continue into the air and successfully across the A30 – even slowing the 100% engine to match the stuttering struggler while on the way to Aldershot. After a while the sixth cylinder rejoined us and all continued well for the rest of the day. But why did this happen? Everything was newly reconditioned, and the proud restorers showed little interest in the reported mystery. During the next weeks or months I made a few more parachuting flights with this aircraft, and the same thing happened again on the odd occasion. The engines had been overhauled by a Shoreham company and were as new – supposedly. Then I heard that the wrong piston rings (or maybe only one) had been fitted. Easy mistake? I wouldn't know.

The next month I went back to Detmold for some more RAPA flying. Ringo was still going strong, but parachute flying can be punishing for air-cooled engines: hot, slow climbs, fast, cold descents, the worst combination for cylinder head fatigue. Staff Sgt. Barber had reminded of me of the careful descent consideration in 1966, but parachuting chief 'The Chef' Turner had encouraged me to make the most of the good weather and the time available. Don't worry about the engines – get on the ground as quickly as possible for the next training lift. If an engine fails we can get a man over to fix it. No engine failed in 1966, but now in 1968 an engine went bang the first Sunday morning during a club jump – friends, family, civilian staff free fallers, no static lines. We had reached about 2000 ft and I explained that we could climb no further, that I would make a pass over the field so they could jump out if they wished, or choose to remain aboard for an uneventful landing. As one they crowded round the door and piled out when the position looked right, congratulating each other after landing on their first emergency jump. All rather exciting. An empty Rapide flies well on one engine, and the next day I discovered that a single engine ferry was possible, back over the woods to Detmold. A man did come from England with a new cylinder head and Ringo was soon fixed.

This was a busy two-week session: the weather was good with a full course to get through, resulting one day in 7hrs 40 minutes in the seat, engines running pickups until more fuel was needed, and takeaway chicken and chips on the lap for in-flight catering. A Photo Reconnaissance Hunter pilot, Roger Wilkins, helped out with the Rapide sometimes, and one day he arranged to come over with the Hunter and take some airborne pictures. Our two machines had something of a gap in the speed window. Door on would have been best for Rapide speed, but our instructors were keen to get in the picture – hanging out of the crowded doorway grinning like wind-blown dogs, the increased turbulence worth a few knots by the feel of it – but, with our fixed pitch engines howling and the Hunter with a bit of flap sidling past on the outside of a discreet turn, Roger got his snaps. Compared with real PR – low, fast and one pass – this photo-opportunity did not tax the camera, but I was still surprised at our stock-still propellers. A bit grainy, but seriously fast film, and some shutter speed!

One afternoon the Rapide and its daredevil free-falling staff went to an air display nearby where a solo Hunter performed. The Hunter finished its display with an all of sixty-degree steep continuous climbing roll in the direction of its base, a few miles away, starting from a slow speed and accelerating as it went. It must have been light to do this, but it had clearly started the show with enough fuel for five minutes of full power, and what impressed me was the variety of aerobatic manoeuvring, both positive and negative, that could be beautifully presented and positioned within a relatively small space at undoubtedly critical speeds, without arousing the misgiving of the suspicious spectator, or squandering time, space and interest in long pauses for excess energy. This said a lot about this machine's handling qualities, but this was the Hunter as Stampe – presented by a true master. We went back that evening to the Bier und Bratwurst post show celebration in the tent, and I was astonished to discover that the quiet and ordinary looking bloke (like my dad) sitting across the trestle table was the very pilot. The name escapes me (although Shepherd – but not the Navy Pete Shepherd – rings a bell). But where was the flying suit, the Warbird jacket with badges, the edgy talk with the jousting of experience and ersatz knowledge? Nowhere to be seen or heard.

The subject of air display piloting, both good and bad, will feature again in this narrative, including an essay describing the reasons for, and disastrous results of, a mismatch between personality and piloting skill that continues to blight the display scene, fifty years later. The fighter-type aircraft is intended to carry some weight, climb high, go fast and corner as well as can be expected, depending on its specialisation. It is never designed for aerobatic displays as such, nor does personal qualification to carry out its intended function alone remotely suggest the level of skill, familiarity, understanding and downright time in the seat – using those few spare pre-landing gallons remaining over the field to practise a few manoeuvres – that is required for what is described above.

If my memory serves me right this vintage flying holiday was permitted by a session of BOAC pilot industrial action. A BAOR Forces Broadcasting man came over to get an inside interview and, though I had no particular views on our industrial politics, being a lowly rank and file co-pilot who valued the time off rather than the money (or kudos?), I was happy to spin a yarn for the fighting listeners, describing our long and unsociable hours, days and nights without sleep, years of reliable service with little recognition, dramatically rapid changes of climate and culture, and so on. It was easier than I thought, and, once started, the facts about our rigorous and poorly paid lifestyle came thick and fast. When the interview aired next day the sport parachuting staff gathered round the riggers' room radio set and listened intently. Men who, to my certain knowledge, might disappear to wreak silent and murderous havoc in the Malayan jungle, then return to family and day job as if from a trip to the shops, said it was interesting. I do not know what the nearby Iron-Curtain-watching flyers thought, or whether any changed their future career plans, but 707 life continued after my return, industrial negotiations solved or shelved, with never a mention of my talking to (making things up for) the BBC without company permission. Just a very small cog in a large machine – that's how airline life works.

I see that on July 27th 1968 I took a Stampe to Little Rissington to take part in the Air Squadron Trophy aerobatic competition, and the following feature is yet another cautionary and anecdotal tale, but, again, with no damaging outcome. This annual contest is set at improver encouragement level – nothing hardcore – with a minimum altitude of 1000ft above ground. The airfield is on a hill, and when I arrived and got out the altimeter read 800ft. The first competitor set off in the Stampe, and it occurred to me that they got pretty low during their flight, but nothing was said or penalties awarded. I'd have said 500 feet at best, but when I mentioned this observation to the pilot, interested to know about the lowness, they felt that everything had gone according to plan; 'I never went below 1200 ft,' was the remarkable reply. The next pilot had the answer, 'When I got in the altimeter said 1000 ft – X had just wound the big hand up to the nearest zero.'

Two hundred feet above ground is outrageously low in a 1000 ft limit aerobatic contest, so why was nobody particularly concerned? This event retained the tradition that a contest provided a good lunch for the judges and organisers, or at least a convivial picnic to include friends and family, followed by flying entertainment for all. Looking upwards at this hilltop venue it was difficult to guess heights with no distant horizon behind to give perspective, and the subject pilot must have chosen not to be disconcerted by the unusually large Little Rissington hangars and neighbouring giant cows. Everything else fitted perfectly, so why spoil a good run?

The focus of my piloting activities (as an amateur) – aerobatics, formation flying, parachute dropping and now rather less PPL instructing – were perforce interrupted by sessions of 707ing. I've no recollection of the results of our recent collective industrial action, but life on the airways did not appear to be getting more leisurely, and the logbook showed that we had more aircraft and routes, both passenger and freight, and no postings. Here is a typical two-week trip with Captain RAE Jones and Mike Dikes, a new ex-Navy co-pilot, covering some familiar territory, but no piloting for me, just some navigating:

It starts at Singapore on a 15th of the month (we must have passengered there already); then Perth, Sydney, Perth, Singapore, Darwin, Sydney, Fiji, Honolulu, San Francisco, ending in New York on the 25th. Then I can tell that we passengered back from New York on the night of the 26th because of the 10-minute aerobatic flight over Redhill the following evening, as a last-minute refresher for the next day's successful Esso Tiger Trophy and a return to another way of life. This voyage had been round the world, with toing and froing included, in a whole lot less than 80 days, though agreeably sociable, and the few Navy pilots who were now joining the 707 fleet all turned out to be jolly good chaps.

There now appeared to be no rostering preference for east or west, and many trips started and/or finished with long passenger flights. In effect our route structure circled the globe, but all the way round with one crew would have taken too long, so one passengered some of the way, spent the relevant night or day (whose night or day?) somewhere, picked up the nomadic system and proceeded in stages halfway round the back of the world, maybe changing direction, maybe not, and either ended up at London, or passengered there from somewhere far away. Some of the public still view long rides on aeroplanes as privileges to be desired, but this depends on how you wish to spend your time, and how you would prefer to feel, and best function, as a living creature. I would hazard a guess that the BOAC worldwide system, VC10 and B707, was in a state of flux at this time, grappling with an expanding and more competitive market, many destinations and a desire to maximise crew productivity within a complicated chess game. This enormous task requires flair in the office, and results indicated that times were changing, and that new planning skills might be needed.

It had been decided, quite sensibly, that a fresh rostering timetable would be a good idea, rather than repeated additions and tweaks of the many-faceted traditional one – a clean start in fact. Planning for crew movements uses a slip chart. This has a timescale along the bottom and places to stay up the side. The line starts at the bottom left-hand corner, rises at a time and distance angle, levels off at the first stopping place, proceeds horizontally to represent the time spent there, then climbs up again to the next place, and so on. Eventually the timeline comes back down in steps to home level – trip over. The aeroplanes do the same thing, though they are much busier, but the same planning system applies.

The day for the new worldwide rostering master plan approached. All the places and all the routes were included. What would our new trips be like? Then it went strangely quiet and the news broke. The rostering head man had failed to consider that, like the aeroplanes, everyone was not at home on day one, in fact they were never all at home together, unlike the Hounslow bus crews each night. Ours were all over the place all the time, and there could never be a Monday morning mass clock in at the depot, so the complex edifice could not start. It would appear that no one else had thought of this either – or had decided not to say anything; so, although the flying boat days were regrettably over, the existing planning system continued on as best it could.

Captain Satchwell had retired from BOAC long before I joined, and must once have been on flying boats. I believe his last airliner had been the Britannia, but whether the 102 or the later 312 I don't know. An old-school gentleman captain, he suffered from something of a stammer, by repute, but whether this had developed during the later stage of his career I can't say. In the real old days the captain would seldom have to talk on the radio himself, but, later, with only two pilots, a navigator and no radio officer (although the Britannia carried two flight engineers) there is a story of a latterday Satch oceanic position report to Gander, and its acknowledgement. Satch ended the lengthy struggle. 'Did you get that, Gander?' 'I got it; chiselled in stone' was the laconic reply. This anecdote is solely intended to add to the list of entertaining radio exchanges at which North Americans are so good – witty, ironic, apt, not just silly. It's the choice of words that's funny, not the cause.

At the beginning of June 1968 a quiet and rather frail Satch and a charming Mrs Satch were both members of an Airways Flying Club visit to Germany at the invitation of the Lufthansa equivalent. Nine aircraft, some AFC, some borrowed, set off as a touring gaggle, and on the way out I found myself at the front, with a couple of club members to do most of the flying and claim the time. I see that I kicked off to Gatwick (for customs), then used the rest of the outward journey as cross-country training experience. Before the final leg to the Lufthansa reception at Egelsbach a suitably straightforward but snappy arrival was discussed, and three echelons of three right (for the left-hand circuit), following each other at say 50 yards spacing might work. Fortunately the landing direction lined up with our track, so no manoeuvring was required prior to the run-in, and I set up a shallow descent along the centreline as the runway approached, picking up some speed – but nothing unsuitable for the equipment and the dramatis personae. From the aeroplane on my right Peter Newberry's red and demonically grinning face was mildly unsettling as he lived the dream, and next to him sat an ashen and rigid Satch – even more unsettling. Was all this such a good Idea?

A third of the way down the runway I broke left for landing, relieved that I had got rid of them, and confident none would catch me while in the air. As my turn finished and revealed the view from the threshold, I could not believe my eyes. Eight evenly-spaced club aircraft followed around the circle, the last one having just broken, and outside them a solitary and no doubt bemused Cessna 150 proceeded downwind. I hoped it was not a first solo. The impromptu routine had worked perfectly – and our hosts were impressed. 'That arriving at the field – it was amazing – just like a fighter squadron.' Of course, we could not have done it again, and left them mystified at such Red Arrow aplomb, and anything more, even a turn, would have required real formation flying. The closely-knit team run in, break and landing had been an illusion, though there was a smattering of varied experience among the 30-odd members of the, once again, motley crew. Later Mrs Satch told me that Satch felt ill at ease with any but straightforward flying, especially with strangers. My sentiments entirely.

On the way back we discovered that fog in the Channel had cut us and the rest of the continent off, and we stayed an extra night in Calais – a dismal, deserted and damp airfield. The nearby Café de l'Aviation was similarly dark and deserted, and a bit damp – worthy of a de Maupassant short story – but Mrs Satch's charm and elegant French encouraged the landlady to rustle up an excellent three-course dinner from what she had in the house, so we fared much better than first expected.

On the day after we had arrived back at Wycombe Air Park I was asked to take a borrowed Cherokee back to Oxford. 'The Red Arrows are doing something there so you'd better check the times.' I read the notice that referred to Oxford's half-hour closure while the Red Arrows did their thing somewhere nearby, perhaps Brize Norton. The date, June 6th, did not ring any bells and I set off so as to arrive outside this time slot; but this was far from the whole story. On cresting the Chinnor Ridge I was intrigued to see several groups of large fires across the fields in the Oxfordshire plain below. What are they burning down there, and why in these strange lines? Can this be another alien mystical message? Then it became obvious: from the east a large number of large aircraft were approaching, trailing black smoke and flying at about 1000ft. The fires were visual track markers for what must be a major D-Day Balbo gig somewhere close by. Now the Red Arrow show opener made sense, and I thought it best to keep going, duck down, scoot across the invasion bomber track before they arrived and make myself scarce, detouring round Oxford and arriving from the north to disguise my route. Nothing happened, there were no phone calls, and a read of the Notams (assuming the rest of the story had been available at Wycombe) or a more comprehensive tip off would have been a good idea. But I did get to see some of the massed V force show from below.

In the following August I was again prevailed upon to take the no. 3 position in a Cherokee formation for the Club airshow. There were others who could have done this, so why me? There is a difference between volunteering and getting volunteered, and the initial glow of recognition that accompanies an invitation should be tempered with an analysis of this question, particularly when significant responsibility for others' safety is concerned – but more of this later.

Our leader was a Mr Burnett, someone from airline accounts or some such, with, I think, military flying experience. At the back was Sqd Ldr Kerridge, virtually my father's age and an outside member of the club, who had also flown the Hampden and been at 16 OTU during the war – though whether student or instructor I don't know – and on the right wing Peter Newberry. Peter worked in BOAC ground ops and his voice would come over the tannoy in the Heathrow control centre 'Foxtrot Charlie is in the circuit,' to alert those interested that one of our birds was returning after several days and many miles away, and was about to become an individual rather than a flight number. Peter had a schoolboy's enthusiasm for flying, but he was killed in 1991 while hitting the ground during an impromptu display at a small airfield (or was it practice?) in a piston Provost. Anyway, we had several practices this time and the show went ahead without incident. I did no more Cherokee formation, but the tradition continued with the 'Haggis' name. Some years later I saw them do their party piece, the Formation Stall (approach to). Novel, anyway.

1968 continued to its close with the same mix of assorted light aircraft flying and 707ing, with the proportion of 336 flying gaining ground over the 436 – freighter and passenger trips now combined for a crew. In December I went back and forth between New York and Kingston (Jamaica) with Capt 'Pandit' Williams on a couple of eastern seaboard bucket and spade outings, having got to New York via Prestwick in a freighter. Replacing him for our final Kingston New York was yet another new flight manager – they seemed to change a lot – 'Big Jim' Fordham. Jim was known for his taciturnity and brusqueness so, forearmed, I used my future Cockpit Resource Management skills and got on fine with him. He said nothing to me and I said nothing to him. Nothing happened, so no small talk was called for, and this voyage from the exotic, voodoo-and-calypso-ridden Caribbean to megapolis Gotham City would have made a very boring five-hour Bermuda Triangle drama – life is not always as portrayed on the screen. I never saw him again; where did he go?

CHAPTER 14

1969-1970 - LIFE GOES ON – MORE CHALLENGES, MORE INTERESTING PEOPLE

Instant CFI

In March 1969 I started a course of PPL instructing on the Tiger Moth with a young lad called Brian Smith. Brian, and his other half Steve Thompson, both lived close to Redhill and had been enthusiastic schoolboy helpers not long after the Tiger Club was founded. They soon became known as Smith Thomson – a virtually ever-present multi-faceted service industry. Theirs is the classic story of the aeroplane-struck kids who spend their every spare moment at an old-fashioned aerodrome getting involved in any way they can. Of course they learn a lot on the way, especially if in contact with a great deal of skill and experience – in fact, not being in contact with a flying school club can be an advantage.

When he was old enough, and could afford it, Brian arranged to have the use of the associated company Rollason's staff Tiger Moth to cover the syllabus for a pilot's licence with me. Redhill was not then a suitably licensed airfield, so we had to take G-APMX to Rochester to record flying that would count, although the flights there and back were used for various exercises, and a few of these trips sneaked into the recorded course record – without quibble. Compared with my Airways Flying Club instructing this was a pleasant experience, because there was not much Brian couldn't already do, having spent much time riding with an assortment of good pilots, and this ad hoc flying school proceeded from time to time over the next few months. We called ourselves, informally, the Ace Flying School, and the only interruption in the training programme occurred one morning when I was disturbed from my leather armchair, *Daily Telegraph* and coffee in the Rochester clubhouse by the local CFI, who pointed out that my student was making smaller and smaller circuits. I went outside as Brian glided round the end of the hangar and landed. I was not concerned by this but thought it politic to wave him in for advice: it all depends on the circumstances, and we did need the use of this licensed field.

But this narrative of my student's Tiger Moth experience would be lacking if an earlier, long pre-Ace Flying School teenaged passenger flight with Dick Emery were to be omitted, as one of those occasional but inevitable exceptions that make life more interesting (if expensive), and sometimes educational. This occurred during the Smith Thompson schoolboy helper days, and involved an attempted return from a Tiger Club full display at Wisley.

Dick Emery may be thought of by many television viewers as a comedian, but this is not correct. Dick was a fine comic actor, with his own take on the variety of characters he portrayed in his television sketches. This skill requires the quiet person's powers of observation, empathy and imagination, as well as a sense of theatre when appropriate, and I would guess it was the traditional black and white portrayal of pilots as dashing heroes that would have appealed. It's not so much the caricature in the Flynn, Niven and Colman moulds, more the all-enveloping celluloid ambience that sets the stage for a fifty-year taildragging history, from Bleriot to Blenheim. The understated bravery, the irony, the quiet charm, a throw-away humour as dark as the narrow moustaches – it's all been sent up many times, and, at the time of writing, I just wonder if Dick had had anything to do with Ron Gillman at Denham.

I first came across Dick Emery in a Vanguard cockpit when he appeared as a passenger on the way back to London, but I knew nothing about his piloting history, except that he became a Tiger Club member who shared a Turbulent with theatre-specialising lawyer Barry Griffiths. Did they share the subject Tiger Moth at the time of its demise? Very possibly.

The trouble was the crosswind. Aeroplanes like to feel the wind in their faces. Up in the air this is not usually a problem, but making the transition from ground to air or vice versa can require an element of legerdemain when takeoff and landings could not be made conveniently facing into wind. Compared with its earlier forebears the Tiger Moth can take off in a moderate crosswind, but the correct things have to be done by the pilot. If left to its own devices with, shall we say, the wind coming from the right, this benign trainer of its day will do three simultaneous things when asked to take off: turn to the right, raise its right wings (roll to the left) and try to leave the ground before it can fly properly. These three things can be countered satisfactorily by the pilot, but each one requires its own positive and possibly confusing action – foot to the left, hand to the right, same hand forward, each by the correct amount. This is three-channel multi-tasking, and, while a basic old-timer skill, it is more difficult than steering a car with a steering wheel. There is nothing instinctively reassuring about hands to the right, feet to the left, with the machine going straight down the road, and many of today's professional pilots never come to terms with this type of handling situation. When the picture looks correct, instinct says put some or all of the controls back in the middle, and in Dick's case each brief kangaroo hop had the machine gaining momentum to the side (towards the carpark), instead of groundspeed (and airspeed) to the front. Finally the Tiger made a knight's move over the boundary rope, where it removed the wood-framed rear end of a club member's Mini Countryman, to the great surprise of the wife and baby inside. Though the Tiger Moth then rolled itself into a ball (as Brian describes it), no one was hurt, and I have seen the same sort of thing happen to much more professionally-trained pilots whose influential training environment left them with an impression of universal competence, but with no more understanding than that required for their specific military task. The ability to play the gramophone is of little help to the saxophone student, even if listening to the improvisations of Lester Young and Coleman Hawkins encourages the dream – but dream it will remain if the necessary tiresome learning work is never addressed, preferably at an early career stage.

Helping out

About two weeks after the inauguration of the Ace Flying School, a contemporary BOAC colleague asked if I would send his student on a first solo. Why not, I thought? The airline had already decided that some instructional experience would be useful for producing future training captains with some facility for dealing with learners – better than nothing, at least. Consequently they sponsored successful candidates for the assistant instructor's course at the Airways Aero Club. How much actual instructing my friend had done I didn't know, nor did I question under which umbrella his student's training to date had taken place, but maybe my new-found CFI status encouraged me to agree to this locum post. But who and where was the real CFI, and why should I be asked to replace him? I didn't bother to ask.

I met the prospective first soloer at Blackbushe with his Cherokee. Was it his own? Might have been, and reassured by his optimistic instructor I anticipated a couple of circuits and off he goes – by himself. Making assumptions about anything in the air is not wise, especially an unknown learner's capabilities, and it became rapidly apparent that, although this candidate's flying was not bad, exactly, it was the lack of consistency that made me uneasy about this ready-for-solo expectation. It was the same problem as the very-experienced dual fliers with very little solo time. The basic handling techniques and the logical structure that put them together had not been adequately and separately assimilated, and this business of learning to drive an aeroplane around had assumed the similar collection of convenient habits employed by the everyday car driver. Popular general aviation products have been designed with this in mind, and while all certified aircraft are easy to fly if flown well, many appear misleadingly easy to fly when flown less than well. It's all to do with market forces, of course.

I see that, over a week, we made four flights totalling 3hrs 15min during which we revised climbing, straight and level, descending, turning associated with the all the foregoing, spinning (you never know) and the ubiquitous circuits, of course. And when the level of variation had settled to its own relatively predictable consistency I sent him solo, relieved when the circuit finished with a successful landing (somewhere) on the long Blackbushe runway, and resolved not to put myself in this position again. It's worth repeating the analogy that learning anything should be a building block process, starting the wall from its foundation course, and leaving no bricks out. This is the easiest and fastest way in the long run: filling in the holes at a later stage is difficult, wastefully expensive and is unlikely to ever result in the uniformly sound structure originally imagined. I'd fallen for the formally-trained pilot's assumption of some consistency of standards among friends, regardless of additional catholic experience. I never did do it again.

Dick Emery's friend Barry Griffiths was an enthusiastic and sociable Tiger Club member, a great raconteur with a fund of stories about theatrical folk, acquired from the inside, and a regular feature of after-flying weekend gatherings in the tea room as autumnal dusk fell outside. He had certainly raided the wardrobe mistress' cupboard to achieve a Margaret Rutherford look for his crazy flying act – the full set of a well-provided-for widow's weeds, especially the hat. To achieve truth and conviction he throttled back at one stage and glided past in the Tiger issuing well-projected falsetto but imperious cries of 'Help! Help!' – the pilot as Lady Bracknell, uncharacteristically not in full control. I was able to suspend my disbelief, just a bit.

Crazy flyers usually crash – some sooner, some later – and Barry was no exception. I don't remember the details, but this might be a good place to mention an astonishing photograph of James Baring's Super Tiger just prior to his ground contact event whilst pursuing the same vocation. The camera has frozen the machine in a very steep diving attitude, its spinner barely a metre from the grass. He walked away, rather disgusted at having overcooked things, but, looking at the picture, it's difficult to believe that the remaining metre did not end in total high energy disintegration of all participating components. In fact, the machine was engaged in some kind of horizontal flicking (autorotational) version of losing the plot, and was travelling fairly horizontally at the time.

Shared responsibility – CRM?

Barry Griffiths was both a keen photographer and a Turbulent formation pilot. One spring Saturday I found myself as one of four to feature in an appearance at a local village event. Barry was our leader and keen to go on. I was not because of the wind, and expressed my concern about it. On a sunny day at that time of year, a Siberian high produces an east wind over southern Britain, and the nature of a whole continent's worth of stable air trapped underneath the large scale inversion somewhere above produces particularly energetic and turbulent air. This wind has rolled and tumbled past every building and hill since leaving eastern Russia, and the strong little thermals produced by the hot spring sun push air temporarily upwards, with nowhere else to go but down again. I remember flying a Super Tiger in a five-biplane formation once in such conditions. This was normal flying to all intents and purposes, without inverted fuel, but when asked to fly as level as the adjacent Stampe the lightly loaded SE5 era cambered wing reacted to the turbulence like a bucking bronco, with bursts of negative g, including repeated engine cutting. This sound effect is a popular film-maker's means of signalling aeronautical distress. In this case it was not intended, but it did call for additional attention-getting throttle jazzing to stay in place (when float chamber petrol was available).

On the ground this air is characterised by strong basic wind in which there are interludes of even stronger long-term gusts. I was lighter than the others, and seem to remember that my mount, the yellow SAM, was a tad nose-heavy for some reason. Quite simply I did not think we (I) ought to go – but this is a team of four: who decides the communal fate? If I mutiny, what happens to the four ship routine? I was hoping for the leader's decision to settle for a three-ship display and leave me to wimp out, but no. Barry seemed not to consider my unilateral view and urgently led us out to the machines, a bit preoccupied. Who was this show for anyway, and who had fixed it? I had no idea.

We started up and the first three taxied hastily out: I think I was box man anyway. The first section of taxiing tracked south, across wind, and sure enough, the strongest interludes insisted on turning my machine to the left, despite my best efforts to counter it. If the crosswind is strong enough the propeller slipstream can be blown to the side before it reaches the tail, reducing steering ability. The right brake was not particularly strong, and more power against still didn't help. The only way to return to the correct direction and attempt to continue was a complete circle to the left (gusts permitting). This wasn't a good idea because the wheels bumped over a couple of shallow wheel tracks as the machine swing through the downwind heading and the nose bobbed up and down, but mostly down, and a combination of idle power, no steering brake and reverse elevator was not enough to allow the machine to run forward and counter the wind's taking control. The little machine tipped gracefully on to its nose, and ever more deliberately on to its back. There wasn't much room left in the cockpit, but just enough for me to squeeze out between the turtle deck and the slightly crunched windscreen. The four-ship show was off, the others taxied back in, and interested observers wandered from the hangar to retrieve the machine. Flying was off for the day; in fact I do not remember there having been any before or after this bold sortie.

This was my only Tiger Club incident in twenty years, and the committee fined me £100 for bad airmanship in that I hadn't turned the ignition switches off before I got out. Their indictment did not mention handling problems or the decision to fly in unsuitable weather – but did make the point that the damage caused by my bad airmanship would cost £300 to mend. This court of enquiry and its judgment was a completely one-sided affair, and gave one an early feeling for the complicated business of apportioning blame as the inexact science that it can be. I felt somewhat miffed and replied to the letter with a cheque for the whole £300, adding that I would not like my fellow members to bear the cost of my bad airmanship. Acknowledgment of receipt was accompanied by a note of thanks for my generosity. So whose fault was it? Who was to blame? It all depends on from where you look at it, and the style of the management, and I would not argue that sometimes, strictly undemocratic draconian judgment is the quickest and ultimately cheapest way – like it or lump it.

Given time, would I have returned to inspect the machine and turn off the switches? Very possibly yes, but the situation of this machine was rapidly out of my hands. Some years later I found myself in the same upside-down-in-a-field situation after a puzzling total loss of thrust in flight, in fact somewhat worse even though the engine had not stopped. Now I had time to give the cockpit a careful look over and double check for evidence of my mistake, but there was none. This wreckage was left squeaky clean from a piloting, or investigator's point of view, and I had been an unwitting victim of this machinery's past hard life – of which more to come. But the question of responsibility for formation decisions is an interesting one. There is no doubt that I alone was responsible for my aircraft (in theory), and could have either refused point blank to go, or stopped into wind and switched off; but it didn't seem as easy as that, and I now wonder whether taxiing unusually fast had helped the others. I've never heard this recommended or discussed.

Discussing this blown-over accident reminds me of something I saw a few years earlier while sitting in the 1200 Turbulent I had shared with Minchin. I had taxied out to the SW facing runway at Fairoaks behind a local student in a Piper Colt. This was, I think, a sort of stripped-out Tripacer, looking like build-it-yourself. It sat up high on its three wheels, and, from what I saw, was usually easy to taxi with its steerable nosewheel. For some reason this pilot stopped while facing downwind to do his before-takeoff checks. All credit to him for at least stopping to do this important if boring litany, but it was quite windy – SW frontal conditions, nothing like as gusty and inconsistent as the Siberian High spring weather already blamed, but a steady blow all the same. Checks completed, he let off the brakes, gave it a bit of power and booted his right rudder to achieve the 180 turn to line up for takeoff – full of enthusiasm. Wind? Who said anything about wind? Once away from the downwind heading the directional stability obliged, and the chunky little machine eagerly turned from NE to SW, right about. At the same time the centre of gravity leant over to the left, supported by the left wheel and nosewheel. This then became the axis of action and, with geometric precision, the dumpy machine tipped until the left wingtip touched the ground, then continued tipping over wingtip and nose, until it rested upside down, but exactly aligned in the desired takeoff direction. The bemused pilot got out, obviously unhurt, and I manoeuvred my terrifying taildragger into position and took off – so it can be done.

The Turbulent's display history is not without its accidents. In August 1968

Arnold Green, the Essex farmer, was killed at Shoreham after he collected a limbo pole which folded over his leading edge. Like crazy flying this particular item did not particularly appeal to me and I never did it, but flying through a goal with bunting for its top had become a popular display entertainment, and the fiery version was an early attraction of Barry Tempest's Barnstormers organisation. The Tiger club's miniature Turbulent system used uprights of frangible cardboard frames, and, although I believe Arnold's Turbulent could fly with the extra drag, he lost control while attempting to shake the bent pole off while still flying near the ground.

Balloon bursting, streamer cutting and tied together formation were all parts of the display syllabus, and it was following the latter that Barry Griffiths was killed on May 25th 1970 during a display at Sleap. My logbook is without comment for this sad, mysterious and rather long day, but I remember that Robin Voice was our leader, and the name Philip Meeson rings a bell as the other wingman, but I can't be sure. It took three sectors totalling two and a half hours in the air to get there from Redhill, but I can't remember why. Perhaps headwind, but maybe fuel supply problems because I see that three days before, on the 22nd, I had made seven Zlin flights: the first a test flight, two of them aerobatic practice, but the others shuttling to and fro between airfields – my guess is for fuel. The two intervening days consisted of first a 707 check flight at Stansted with Jack Atkins, then 4 aerobatic Zlin sorties at Hullavington. On the way to Sleap Barry took his usual #4 position and would do so for the routine with four aircraft, but the first item for us would be a three – tied together. I felt a bit tired and inclined to take things easy if the chance came up, and I elected to be the one that stayed behind, attach the strings with their coloured little flags, help with the start up, and so on, but, though it sounds like hindsight after the fact, I well remember that Barry (much senior to me in the Turb formation world) had seemed tense and preoccupied that day, starting from our meeting at Redhill – and particularly so as I tied his connecting wool loop and started him up.

To be successful, tied together requires an adequate standard of station-keeping, but is not as difficult as it looks, and it's the tied together bit that gives this popular feature of the 1930s Hendon displays its frisson of uncertainty. The followers' ends of the strings are attached with a weak link (one loop of wool for Turbs, two loops for the biplanes) which will break if things get out of hand, or deliberately when required for the routine, and leave the leader trailing two strings of bunting. I remember once arriving as a tied-together three at Biggin Hill prior to their show, landing in formation and taxiing in without breaking the links, to the perplexity of the marshallers. (To some readers it might help if I explain that we had taken off like this as well.) Such a flight can be made, but there is, understandably, something a little more potentially nervous-making about being tied together (unless you did it every day): after all, no one wants to suffer the shame of breaking the string prematurely even though the tensioned string helps the formation flying, slightly. Actually, the string at full stretch helps pull you back into position (a tiny bit, but there's a limit, and this should not be relied on). I see that Barry had been the other wingman for this tied-together cross-country trip to Biggin Hill, also with leader Voice.

On the way back from this display, along the Ashford railway line, (not tied together) I noticed from my #2 position a green shape closing up on Barry's other side. It was Tiger Club member Dave Morgan in the Dunsfold Hurricane. He flew along with us for a while, looking very big, but flew off, no doubt conscious of his coolant temperature. I didn't have a camera.

Today's Sleap routine consisted of flying around in simple vic formation, maybe with some line abreast, but without aerobatics there's not much more that you can do – and this initial part of the show would finish with an ersatz Prince of Wales' Feathers break (only a little up and down possible), thus leaving the strings with the leader and the followers circling round to join up in line astern. These three duly flew down the display centreline at 600 ft, pulled up (a little) in formation and then made their micro bomb burst. The first 90 degrees was more or less symmetrical from the wingmen, then the one on the right's turn tightened and abruptly entered a more rapid skidding rotation through another 180 , which paused while facing the original track.

'That was bold,' my mind's eye's instant analysis told me, 'he'll definitely be the first (as #2) to make it back into line astern.' I wasn't expecting what happened next, nor the words spoken by John Taylor, standing next to me. John was familiar with aerobatics and formation, and certainly spent much time, among other things, as one half of an RF4 display duo, led by an excellent pilot, Dave Perrin. At the instant that Barry's machine changed from turning to incipient autorotating John said 'Oh, no!' It wasn't what he said that surprised me, but, to my mind, the early point at which he said it, and the sense of deliberation and resignation that went with it. What did he know that I didn't? I never got to ask him because the next part of this tragedy followed immediately and unexpectedly.

Having paused briefly at this 270 point Barry's Turbulent then continued into a fully developed flattish spin. The rate of descent was not particularly high in that the Turbulent completed 3¼ steady turns in the available 600 ft with no sign of recovery action – and then it hit the runway with the boxy sound of a crane-load of tea chests falling to the dockside. All forward of the turtle deck bulkhead was unrecognisable. From the start of this incident there was no evidence of less than full power, or stick otherwise than fully back. Arguments about rudder and aileron would require more science, but these would be somewhat academic. I have no experience of Turbulent spinning behaviour myself, having never tried it, then or since, but am fairly confident that appropriate opposite rudder, stick otherwise than back, and power reduction if necessary would have immediately resumed the diving and accelerating flight you would expect as an initial response to this departure from normal flight in the tiny aeroplane.

Standing the other side of John Taylor was Barry's wife, who set off across the grass, screaming hysterically, towards the accident site. John followed in pursuit and quickly restrained her. She could not have helped. The rest of the show was cancelled and we hung around as safety services went into action, and waited a decent time for hospital news. There was little illusion about an optimistic outcome, but why this had happened in such a conclusive and, to the observer, passively committed way was a mystery. I knew nothing about Barry Griffith's handling skills other than his Turbulent formation and crazy flying. It would be wrong of me to do any guessing – and putting together a few numbers, adding a few of one's own and coming out with an interesting story is not how formal accident investigation works. The bare bones tell you little of the cause (in this case absent). Later, post-mortem heart attack evidence was mooted. This could be; but I suspect we'll never know the whole story – whatever it was. This event was quite a mystery, though I suspect that others know more – but not me.

The previous August (1969) I had flown to the annual Shoreham show with Barry, team leader Mike Channing and John Williams. Mike Channing had led the team for some time, and both he and Williams were ex-Navy BEA pilots. John was a regular team member, quiet, courteous and thoughtful, and I was fascinated by a snippet of his experience of the fearsome Westland Wyvern. He described both the colourful social life encouraged by his squadron commander (a gin and tonic tucked into his top pocket on social occasions), and his own partaking in a box four Wyvern firepower demo at the range – a tight formation simultaneous rocket firing exercise. (In case you're asking, the box man's rockets will go under the leader – just.) The logbook tells me that I was not part of the Shoreham display so this and the return flights were as a stand-in ferry pilot, but I do remember a couple of interesting incidents at this sunny show. The standing-on-the-wing Tiger Moth's engine stopped immediately it had left the ground (who can guess why?), and the standing-on-the-wing star, already strapped in place, but well acquainted with the pilot and aware of the extreme danger of this very occurrence, immediately unclipped and bailed out. She fell through the back of the bottom wing just as the wheels touched the ground in a normal landing – but better safe than sorry. This sort of thing can lead to a temporary cooling of domestic relations, but something else unfortunate happened to another Tiger Moth pilot. David Hamilton was flying for a mass parachute drop. A D-Day reenactment? Not quite – but three Tiger Moths with three jumpers might give you a rough idea.

At the exit point David's parachutist climbed out of the front cockpit and unwittingly switched off the front magneto switches in the process. To add injury to insult he then leaped off the wing in the astern direction, arms spread, and whacked David in the face in passing, breaking his goggles and sending glass splinters into his eye. It was only after David landed but proceeded no further that his plight became evident. This is jolly bad luck in anybody's book, but shows that you can't be too careful in choosing who you fly with if there is a choice – pilots or anyone else. After this entertaining afternoon I returned to Redhill with the original three, and then had another 15-minute formation checkout flight with Channing in the lead. I think I passed.

Earlier in the year (May 1969) a group of us set off to Europe to fulfil a display fixture at Osnabrück. The booking was for the Turbulent four and Tiger standing-on-the-wing routines. This means six people, but not all doing the same things at the same time, because the four-ship leader was also the SOW pilot. All went well from Redhill to Lympne, then Calais, although I remember that our SOW lady's French was of use to explain that someone had left their passport at home. *Pas de problème, mes amis*. The prochain day the flotilla set off for Mönchengladbach. On the way, somewhere over the Belgian part of the western front, John Williams sidled up to Voice, our leader, and pointed at his fuel tank, and its remaining few cms of wire. It's remarkable how good this no radio, mimed communication can be. Even from 50 metres away you can get the complete picture. Voice waved the rest of us to continue, stuck his nose down and conducted Williams to a suitable field not far ahead.

Mönchengladbach was a large expanse of grass, perfect for a squadron or two of Me 109s, even big enough for night fighters. I made a mental note of it – this would be somewhere for future reference, (but it wouldn't be the same – a surprise). Our depleted but motley group of curious aeroplanes immediately attracted attention. 'Ah, ze famous Tiger Club' was the first and correct local's assessment. We sat around waiting for our stragglers to appear, and after all had refuelled set off for Osnabrück. It was now evening, getting dark, cloudy – not good. After half an hour we were flying low over trees in light drizzle, visibility getting worse. A clearing in the forest went past. Voice decided and pointed down. We landed at Borkenberg, where a few club members were still drinking beer in the wooden hut that served as clubhouse. We were received with enthusiasm and hospitality, and a painting on the wall of a stern-looking Luftwaffe high scorer rather suggested that he may have commanded the place once. Nothing had changed, except the absence of Me 109s and FW 190s in the hangar. Our hosts reinstated the barbecue in the gathering dusk, offered us their bunk room and checked us out on the kitchen and fridge. Perfect.

The show at Osnabrück went satisfactorily, I think, and my formation colleagues were Robin Voice, John Williams and Mike Holtby, an ex-Hunter BOAC 707 co-pilot, but any coordinated teamwork rapidly evaporated next day on the way home, due to unhelpful weather and different levels of urgency to reappear at the day job. Once again this was typical summer holiday Atlantic frontal depression weather. Having waited all day for the rain and wind to abate we took off from Osnabrück at 18:40 local time. Voice and his SOW assistant had already left in the Super Tiger – not to be seen again this trip. An hour and 40 minutes later the three airline Turbulents arrived at M. Gladbach, and were pleased to nightstop here. We had made 50kts groundspeed into the wind. Four had taken off together, but the fourth, driven by our ferry pilot and helpful mechanic, never caught up. I remember seeing him first a couple of 100 metres behind, but then slowly slipping further away, and showing little desire to follow our track. What's going on? Why doesn't he want to fly with us? This was no Blue Angels macho formation exercise, just following whoever was at the front. It's easier than navigating yourself.

I next saw him a few days later at Redhill. 'Why didn't you come along with us? Why did you just wander off and get left behind?'

'I couldn't keep up, and then lost sight of you completely. I seemed to be losing power.'

He landed in a field somewhere and sought shelter at the nearby mansion, complete with courtyard, stables – quite stately. The solitary lady of the great house, rather taken with the romantic notion of the downed aviator, alone in a strange land, callously deserted by his cruel colleagues, insisted that he stay the night with her. And so he did. 'It was amazing,' he said. Next day he looked for a possible engine problem, removed the little glass fuel filter bowl – and dropped it on the shed floor, where it shattered. Eventually a small medicine bottle of the right size was found and he was on his way. You couldn't make it up. Maybe he had suffered from carburettor icing – not unknown with the type, in fact a few years previously, Robin D'Erlanger, son of BOAC chairman Sir Gerard, had this problem while crossing the Channel in his own birthday Turbulent. There is a good helicopter photograph of him sitting astride the turtle deck, awaiting a winch up.

The airline team of three flew to Calais via Ghent this next day and there I stayed the night, as more wind and rain threatened. I cannot remember what the other two did, although I think our ways parted further to some extent at this point.

It was now the 17th, four days since we had left England, and my next 707 trip was a 3 am freighter departure on the 21st. On the 18th, I left Calais to cross the Channel, but I see it was with a different Turbulent. Why? No idea, but I expect the pilot whose next reporting engagement was closest must have wanted to swap his machine for mine. Did mine go better – or further? Was it John Williams whose thirsty machine had required the surprise top-up on the western front? Had he left for Blighty immediately after our arrival at Calais the day before? I vaguely remember whitecaps in the Channel for the 50 minutes over the sea that it took to get to Lydd – 50 landless nm, 60kts. Arrival back at Redhill was a full five days after we had left. How long ago had it taken that long to get to the Ruhr (just past to be fair) and back? My father's 1944 Mosquito 2:40 looked pretty good. Along with air racing, formula racing, aerobatics, formation, formation aerobatics, tied-together formation aerobatics, balloon bursting, flour bombing – and other Tiger Club attractions that I may have missed – comes touring. I never did voluntary touring – I don't think I would have had the nerve for it.

A month later, in mid-June, I made a four day Bermuda-Nassau-Miami and back with the easy-going Jimmy Pink. He gave me the second two sectors as my fair share of the flying, and after co-piloting the Bermuda-London overnight return I see that I went to Redhill that evening of the 19th for a short aerobatic blast over the field in the Stampe. A couple more practices followed on the 20th, and on the 1969 longest day I flew the same machine to Sywell via Booker in company with Neil Williams and Philip Meeson to take part in the annual De Havilland Trophy contest. Anything annotated 'Formation' including the name N. Williams means a workout somewhere, even if the flight appears to be only an A to B ferry.

A lot of people say 'I knew Neil Williams'. I had a lot to do with this Celtic hero, but would not make this claim. This is also too early in this narrative to comment on this iconic character, but I would never dispute that it was his single-minded determination to achieve high-ranking world level recognition in international aerobatic competition that dragged British participation from non-starter status to a position of respect. But this is leading from the front – par excellence. Some time after Williams' death editor James Gilbert wrote to me: 'every time I flew with Williams I thought he was trying to kill me'. Dramatic words, but I know what he meant. Most of us do not become heroes, and living with them can be challenging, for both friends and family.

The De Havilland contest was along the lines of the old-fashioned Lockheed five-minute do what you like system, and decided the national championship. Simple but not easy to judge; and on this occasion I came third in my vintage biplane – probably following Williams and Black in their racy single-seat Zlin 526 Akrobat. This aeroplane had one more year to live before it dramatically demonstrated the hard life it had lived – but more of this later.

CHAPTER 15

POLAR NAVIGATION – SOMETHING A BIT DIFFERENT

On June 25th 1969 I went to Anchorage in a 707-336 with Captain (Jumping) Jack Hasell. The range of this machine enabled BOAC to open this polar means of getting to Japan, and a number of new things had to be learned – both survival and navigational. When I joined BOAC in 1964 we spent days in the classroom learning about the safety equipment provided in the Comet, and the various principles of survival if having to force-land somewhere remote – deserts or jungles for example – or ditch in the sea. These subjects were covered in some detail, and much of the information assumed a survivable landing of sorts (of course), and explained the tactics required while waiting to be found (and rescued – which could take some time).

Assessing the sea surface for choosing your ditching direction, and the perfect spot (on a good day) was an interesting but complex subject. Into wind? Possibly, but not into the primary swell, that would be like hitting a brick wall. Along the primary and across wind? Better, but the local wind may not have produced the primary. What about the secondary? Across the primary and down the secondary, or into the secondary if the wind was stronger and favoured that choice? This would be like hitting a small wall at low speed – take your pick. What if there were three swells and no wind? What a nightmare – and don't forget to loosen your tie before going in the drink. The water can shrink it and throttle you before you get the chance to command a raft. Every crew member got this privilege in order of crew pecking order, and the responsibilities run deep. Keeping up morale – instilling the will to live, rationing the water, keeping the punters in order, and busy – bailing can be useful – and so on. Jungle information would have been familiar to Scouts and Guides though more comprehensive, and the desert instructions did not include the QANTAS crew advice to commandeer a passing camel and ride it to safety, captain at the front etc. This is not true, but there is an Australian joke based on this idea. Actually, walking across the desert is probably the worst choice, and staying put, lighting a fire at night to ward off dangerous animals, or keeping out of the sun during the day all assumed eventual rescue, so we come to the transmitter. Somewhere in the Comet was a hefty yellow Gibson Girl manually cranked emergency beacon. Someone had to sit with it between their knees and wind the handle – and a good aerial set-up helped, although I don't think we had the very nice box kite to fly it in a steady wind, but perhaps it was in there somewhere.

Of course, all this equipment and these detailed practices came from military experience since the dawn of aerial transport, but, by far, most of it emanated from WW2 experience with piston engine aircraft – whether single-seat or long range. The reliable jet era and much improved communications made much of it too old fashioned to be worth continuing (but 'you-never-know' still seems surprisingly valid). However, polar survival was now on in our case, and this new subject was tackled.

The Royal Canadian Air Force, as was, were the experts, and they produced the films, and probably the little book to go in the equipment packs. Of course the people in the films do all the right things and get happily rescued at the end – so it does work. We had some interesting five-person silver paper communal sleeping bags. Shared bodily warmth is a very important means of delaying the freezing to death, but who do you get to share with? It's best if your passengers stay in the bags all day, but the crew got some very fetching super lightweight but very generously insulated trouser suits, hoody puffer jackets, gloves and trendy moon boots – all items in complementary pastel colours. Warm as toast – feeling naked. I've never seen such cool stuff in the shops – nor on the snow, fortunately. Where can you get some? We should be told.

Navigation raised a new subject – no magnetic compass. The magnetic north pole is currently somewhere in the very north of Canada and this kind of steering doesn't work in this area, so we went to gyro steering. This sounds easy but there are some new concepts that need to be well understood if the cheerful 'Man is not lost' motto is not to be completely rubbished. Foucault's pendulum demonstrates that objects allowed their own freedom of movement are creatures of the limitless universe – not of the earth. Newton understood this; Einstein took the concept much further. It's not rocket science, it's much more basic than that, but we are still creatures tied to this planet so this gyro direction in space has to be slowly eased around in order to conform to the earth's personal rotation. A Korean Airlines 707 got this very wrong one day, and having left the north of Scotland either gave their gyro steering system its head and allowed it to go straight in space, or set it to turn right instead of left – the appropriate offset for the northern hemisphere. When the north coast of Russia appeared they thought (hoped, please) it was, perhaps, the north coast of Alaska. When two MiG 15s with stars on their tails appeared they chose to believe that they might be American (that would be nice). The element leader's wing rocking – 'Hi, it's me, Sergei; is anybody going to look at me?' formation language was pointedly ignored. Looking away is an oriental way of dealing with problems. Is this a good way to deal with the immutable laws of physics? Confucius he say get some in – or do not venture outside the Imchi boundary.

What had happened in the cockpit during the several hours between Scotland and Russia? Was any factual evidence garnered at the nav table at all? (Looks cold down there – that's a good sign). Difficult to guess, except that loss of face, admission of mistakes (anyone know where we are – because I don't), informed questioning (what's going on back there?) can be a difficult feature of oriental life. A MiG fired a missile, it went straight into an engine, and the 707 force landed successfully on a frozen lake. No one hurt. Nice flight – landing not at all bad – wrong country. It could have been worse.

This grid navigation business, using the gyro-in-space system, works well, but the magnetic tradition has to be juggled in the background. It can be confusing – especially the plus/minus, east/west means of dealing with the same things – and a couple of classroom days were required before one was allowed to be the real polar navigator. Then two or three trips as extra crew were required to make sure you had got the hang of it. Earth-independent heading checks were required on a regular basis and only something in space was suitable. The sun, of course, in the daytime: for daytime read all summer at the north pole. To explain this gyro/grid system simply, your gyro map-in-space has north at the top, and you drive up it as the journey progresses. Then a coastline comes into view, the north coast of Alaska. The drivers (with their lodestone compasses) are going south by now. Is this what they did in Star Trek?

On July 14th 1969 at Redhill Michael Jones invited me to try a cute little prototype tricycle single seat aeroplane called a Kittiwake. I knew nothing about this private venture, but duly took the simple machine for a tootle. I can only describe it, like Viv Bellamy and the Turbulent, as charming. It was very nice – nothing too exciting, very comfortable soft undercarriage, completely straightforward handling, but what was it for? I was then astonished when an old buffer (maybe he had proudly brought it along) told me that it reminded him of the Mustang! I've never flown the Mustang, but this comment was a surprise. On the other hand I suspect that the Mustang, despite its serious purpose, is a masterpiece of user-friendly character. Many famous certified aeroplanes are.

Later in July I did a longish freighter trip between Dubai and the far east with Keith Myers. Keith was a recently promoted captain, and I had come across him some time previously as a training first officer on the 707; in fact he had told me off for my quick-with-the-handles emergency actions in the simulator – the fastest gun in the west. 'If you're too snappy it will snap you', he said. Quite so, and on this trip, while wandering around the grounds of the Emperor's palace in Tokyo, he described, in some detail, the Hurn Britannia crash in which he was co-pilot.

This had happened on Christmas Eve 1958 at the end of a C of A test flight from London involving repeated climbing and descending activities, not under air traffic instructions but as required by the various systems and performance tests. Compared with a transport flight there was much to do for the flying crew, with a complicated flight profile to follow and readings to be recorded. The nature of a handling test flight is very different from the normal hours-long A to B airliner cruise, and although the individual crew actions required could be described as familiar, the priorities may feel different when you are not doing your normal job. The airspace was theirs, and above the cloud all had been clear air and sunshine. (The south of England below was swathed in a blanket of Christmas fog, and an additional preoccupation as to where to land would have been a concern for the captain). London was still out; Hurn must have been the landing decision, and after finishing the test programme with its various climbs and descents they levelled out at what they took to be, felt and looked like 12,000ft or thereabouts, and were then cleared by Hurn to descend to an initial approach height of 3,000ft.

They throttled back and set off down at normal descent speed, and soon left the sunshine and entered the top of the cloud layer, anticipating another few thousand feet in the fog before reaching their cleared height. The captain was flying and Keith happened to be looking forward into nothingness when, to his amazement and horror, trees, hedges and fields rushed towards them out of the greyness. He grabbed the stick and pulled, reducing the rate of descent, but they were too close to the ground to avoid it and the Britannia hit it at speed – flying almost level. Keith said the aircraft initially tobogganed along the ground, bumping through hedge and over ditch as it broke up. Radio boxes broke from the racks behind the captain and flew forward, killing him. Then the forward fuselage broke off and the cockpit rolled and bounced along before stopping. Keith was badly injured but conscious as he lay in the wreckage. When help arrived he remembers his reaction in his state of shock: 'Give me a couple of minutes and I'll give you a hand.' Keith, one of the two flight engineers and one of the hangar party survived – nine others were killed.

The reason for this accident is a simple one of 10,000ft altimeter-reading error. There is little in the way of official extenuating circumstances – but the unusual nature of the flight, for an airline crew, and the notorious altimeter of the day with its tiny 10,000ft third hand, all add up to something. It is easy to apportion blame, even ignoring the official findings, but Keith's honest and clear description of this dramatic event, unusually agreeing with the official report, told what a good captain and teacher he had become – and I felt privileged that he had chosen to describe it to me, unasked. Such cautionary tales have a salutary effect on the thoughtful listener as well as the participant, and I would not discuss such serious affairs myself with others unless they might benefit in the wisdom department.

There can be little doubt that this was a monumental accident, bearing in mind that nothing was wrong with machinery or legalities. The media would consider it relatively insignificant because it did not involve a multitude of innocent passengers (fare-paying – this makes a difference to the press, licensing authorities and insurance) – but this makes no difference from a professional point of view. And, for the times, one cannot but suggest that the pilots alone were directly responsible – after all, what else did they have to do but to drive the plane? Real life is more complicated than this, and one could say that my own near nose-to-nose Vanguard collision was my fault – I was the one with the checklist hidden down the side of my shotgun seat. But what effect had this life-changing event had on Keith, who was the one who had told Hurn approach that they were at 11,500 ft before the whole thing started?

Serious accidents change people; in different ways, it is true, and one cannot generalise as to who they become afterwards. 'Mistakes are good – people learn from them.' I wouldn't for one moment recommend this as a training principle, in fact I have no time for negative training, but when one considers the self-questioning knock to the confidence that such an event must have had to a well-trained military (as far as it goes) and competent pilot who had found himself in the 'there-but-for...' situation that can apply to most of us, I can only conclude that Keith emerged as the strong-minded, sympathetic, fair and insightful captain and trainer he became.

It is worth mentioning that crew dynamics were very different in those days – an autocratic captain with obedient helpers – and, as already suggested, a British-is-best tradition extended to crewing style as well as manufacturer, although this may not have applied to the mighty Stratocruiser (an American GI-friendly B29 workhorse bomber by another name). But when I consider Keith's fairness, sense of priority, mature (serious but neutral) approach to others, coupled with unfailing good nature, I would say he had risen above these unhelpful and rather childish sentiments. He was Concorde training manager when I looked into his office 15 years after this Dubai trip to ask if they wanted more pilots. 'Not at the moment, but when we do we'd love to have you.' I think he meant it (I hope so). Definitely one of my airline heroes.

At this time of the 1969 Dubai freighter trip Keith had not acquired enough captain sectors to give takeoffs and landings away, but invited me to fly the descent and approach when we returned to Dubai. The air was as clear and smooth as seems only possible over a windless and starlit desert night, and we swept along in the dark in silence. Then at 300 feet on finals he said 'I'm sorry to do this to you Mike, but I have control.' More than forty years later (in his eighties) we met again and he reminded of this occasion, adding 'Do you remember what you said?' I didn't, and he added; 'You said, I think you should be able to get in from here.' Cheeky or what? Maybe, but I would rather choose comradely.

Dubai has changed a lot since 1969. Then there was only one two-storey building, the Carlton Hotel, and the old town and ancient harbour stone wall with a couple of dhows alongside was a few minutes' walk away. Lamb kebab with salad in pitta bread, prepared and eaten by the roadside, was the best food – maybe the only thing for tourists to eat (though I never came across a tourist). We picked up very flat pallets there – ingots of melted Indian silver coins, on their way to the London bullion exchange, I believe. I didn't go to the UAE much after this, but know a few people who have had flying jobs in Arabia.

Graham Rutson was one of these, and he told me something interesting about the locals' sense of position and direction. An RAF Canberra pilot, then flying instructor, he had been a Rothmans team pilot for some years, both Stampe and Pitts S2. I have no illusions about the handling skills required for this display work, and would cite the three axis multi-tasking involved in propeller-powered fancy formation as evidence; in fact I believe I saw him in the ultimate four-ship tour-de-force manoeuvre, in my opinion: the true straight and level flat formation slow roll with the two-seat Pitts. (Was this a Kelly, Finlay, Rutson and Weston lineup?) Try that, Blue Angels! But Graham was a normal person – no badges, fancy hats; none of that. A quietly competent type (does he work in a bank – or is he a schoolteacher?), he then went to work as an instructor for the UAE Air Force, teaching on the Aeromacchi trainer, a friendly machine as used by the flamboyant I Frecche Tricolore. The aeroplane is irrelevant, but he told me of his training sorties over the empty quarter. After a session of everywhichway handling practice over the featureless desert landscape there would be the inevitable instructor's request, 'Take me home'. They always set off in the right direction. Graham would ask the appropriate question: 'How have you come to this conclusion?' 'It is the way home.' 'But where is the evidence – landmarks (the sand changes every day), sun, dead reckoning, radio information?' 'No, we all know which way is home.' Statistically this would appear to have been true, but how did they do it? Does it matter? Go on Graham, tick the box. They could be right. It seems they always were right.

While we're in the Middle East I should mention another amazing action story told to me by Rhodesian Peter Hay (when a 707 first officer). As an RAF fast-jet instructor he had been an initial member of the Valley Gnat four-ship Yellowjack team, led by the enthusiastic Lee Jones (later to manage Jordanian Air Force training – ('When it comes to purchasing forget the face, I'm King Hussain'). Before joining BOAC Peter had signed up for the Royal Saudi Air Force contract, where he flew the Hunter and Lightning. Jets don't go so well when it's hot, and Riyadh is hot, and opinions are divided as to the reason for the dramatic event which follows. The Ruler had arranged a demo of his air force in front of some visiting dignitaries. A light Lightning's ability (in cold England) to continue raising its nose after takeoff and accelerate away in the vertical is a surefire showstopper. What happened here stopped the show, but not for the same reason. Peter was halfway through his 'rotation' takeoff when his aeroplane flicked unceremoniously and fell into a spin. This is not a good place to be in such a machine, even at full power, so he immediately reached for his eject handle. As his hands found it the machine paused in a horizontal attitude. 'I'm back in business' he thought for a nanosecond, but no; the nose then dropped determinedly and the rotation resumed. He pulled the handle and the seat actually fired as the attitude passed though one of level pitch and 90 of bank. He saw the aeroplane leave him in a horizontal direction and heard it explode immediately.

He had left the aircraft at a height of hardly more than half a wingspan. The seat fell away immediately and the parachute lines unravelled, pulling him into a reclining, feet and backside first position as he went into the sand, still travelling fast but at only a shallow descent angle. He had ejected from an out of control Lightning and landed before the parachute canopy had even thought of opening, and he was more or less OK – good enough to limply wave to the crowd, perhaps: follow that. Actually there may have been some who were excited to see such spectacular and fiery action, but the King was not amused. This had not been the impressive display of military effectiveness he had hoped to show his guests. Ejecting with old-style seats is one thing and landing without the parachute is another, and Peter had to spend some time at the Royal Air Force rehabilitation place at Headley Court. But the staff there were confident they could sort him out. Weeks of relentlessly gruelling exercises in the gym followed. 'When you leave here your back will be so strong you'll never have back trouble again.' Apparently this was correct.

On March 25th 1970 I set off from London on my last 707-436 trip with Captain Brook, towards the east, getting as far as Honolulu and back – around the world by another name. We arrived back at London on April 6th having landed and variously stayed at (wait for it) Beirut, Delhi, Rangoon, Hong Kong, Tokyo, Honolulu, Wake Island, Tokyo, Hong Kong, Calcutta, Karachi, Beirut, Rome and Zürich.

I had not been to Wake Island before. This remote atoll used to be a regular fuel stop in the propeller days, and helped us out on the way back from Honolulu to Tokyo – into wind. The airfield was almost as long (and as large) as the coral island and we parked near one end of the runway, a few yards from the sea, on tarmac that sloped gently in that direction. Our engineer told me about a previous visit where the aeroplane had started to push its chocks out from under the wheels during refuelling, as the fuel load increased and the tyres squashed. Before he could rush upstairs and stand on the brakes the steps no longer lined up with the front door and the machine started moving backwards towards the sea, but was arrested by the two bowser fuel hoses. They were strong enough, so serious embarrassment was avoided.

The story of the Japanese invasion of this tiny place on the same day as Pearl Harbour, and what subsequently happened to the American servicemen there when the tiny island was finally overrun, is interesting. Read it and reflect:

we are talking 70 years ago, but that's not long in evolutionary terms – humans don't change much in 70 years. Of course they can pretend to.

Navigating over the Pacific was a pleasure. It was mostly daylight for some reason – smooth flying, not much if any cloud. There was plenty of satisfactory astro, and otherwise the Loran was excellent, thanks to the special American effort to make sure they won in their own backyard. It always seemed to be lunchtime an hour of two after we set out, and first-class lunch usually started with (mock, I trust) turtle consommé, amply flavoured with sherry. What an excellent naval midday tradition, and something that could be enjoyed by the navigator at his private table, courtesy of his special relationship with the front galley crew – yet another outrageous flaunting of company regulations (and the law, of course – disgraceful). The Pacific is a big place, the distances considerably longer than Atlantic equivalents, yet I do not associate these long flights with the tiredness that Atlantic navigating could create; in fact, home and its preoccupations was a long way away, and my recollection is that this was indeed peaceful work.

CHAPTER 16

INTERNATIONAL COMPETITION AEROBATICS

During the winter of 69/70 I appeared to have been shortlisted for the use of the Gold Leaf Zlin. This statement sounds rather vague, but that is how the management of Britain's contribution to competition aerobatics at international level worked. International participation came under the umbrella of the Royal Aero Club, but this body organised the diplomatic formalities only. The practicalities of this fringe sport remained very much do-it-yourself in the English (a more relevant word than British) tradition of relatively expensive ways of passing one's leisure time. Two years previously the Players tobacco company had been prevailed upon to sponsor (pay for) a standard Zlin 526 to assist those who did not own their own machine in gaining experience, to be managed by those who already knew something of the sport at world level, on behalf of the R.Ae.C.

From the 1950s the between-wars tradition of aerobatic competition, as far as Britain was concerned, had been reinvigorated by the annual Lockheed five minutes do-what-you-like Trophy event traditionally held at Coventry, in whatever machine you cared to bring. During the heydays of this discipline anything from ancient biplane trainers to jet fighters took part. Of course it was a great spectacle and fun for the participants – the watchers and judges had no idea what might happen, in fact the absence of anything that resembled a level playing field would also aid the equal-status socialising that must have accompanied the junket. How could you tell why the winner won? Did this matter? Not really; it's impossible to judge, but although this particular event was well supported internationally, many increasingly experienced practitioners the world over began to feel that something more specific and accountable might enable more pilots to compete on a universally agreed basis, particularly from those countries who encouraged amateur (quasi free) aerobatic training for all as an effective (super cheap) means of creating future fighter pilots – much like the German aero club system of the 30s. Once again one has to ask oneself what all this continuing daredevil competition action was trying to prove – the boldest, most creatively-inclined personality at the controls – or the best pilot? This is a good question. The Lockheed was to continue until 1965, but in 1960 the first FAI sanctioned world championship was held, with a more structured judging system, so the far-flung competitors started to get the same idea of what was required. In 1962 the complex analytical system devised by Spanish Jungmeister maestro Colonel Aresti was adopted, so everyone knew what the rules were. Of course, life is never as easy as that, but it became a little clearer as to what the judges were actually required to judge.

It is interesting to look at the British participation in these two consecutive contests in 1960. The Lockheed took place at Coventry on a couple of days in July. By now the Spitfires and Meteors had fallen by the wayside, and an assortment of modified trainers more or less made up the field. There were 16 competitors: a Frenchman won in a Stampe, and the next six places were taken by French and Czech pilots flying either Stampes or Zlins, with the exception of French star Leo Biancotto (3rd) who flew a Nord 3202, another military trainer. Among the remaining nine competitors were five Brits – a good turnout to fly the flag – and my records do not reveal these final placings, but they were accompanied by another Frenchman, a Czech, a German and a Swiss. Apart from a little homebuilt Currie Wot (designed by Mr Currie, chief engineer at Christchurch Aero Club), the other concerted British challenge was mounted on the Nepean Bishop Super Tiger, a stripped-out version of an aerodynamically ancient design, with a loser's roll rate and WW1 upside down manoeuvre capability. However, I'm sure the chaps put up a jolly good show. This, of course, is what the British do.

Three weeks later the first FAI world contest was held at Bratislava. The required syllabus and scoring system was not as sophisticated as the future Aresti version, but it was more prescribed than simple 'show-us-what-you've-got'. There were two compulsory sequences to start with. Various figures and manoeuvre combinations had to be attempted, or would surely score a zero whether you or your machine liked them or not – and the 1960 results indicated that the Czech home team had done their homework. However, before looking at the Brits' brave efforts it is appropriate to say something of the Leon Biancotto disaster. During the initial practice flights Biancotto conducted a tail slide. This manoeuvre requires that the machine climbs vertically, stops, then descends backwards in the vertical attitude before flipping around the specified way, (theoretically decided by reverse elevator), into a vertical dive. Which way it flips is important, and the effect of even an idling engine and propeller complicate the aerodynamics considerably, in fact perfection is difficult – no tens here. The major problem back then was that conventional, right-way-up, normal-flying aeroplanes are not designed for such off-design behaviour, and this includes military trainers. Even at the slowest reverse airspeed the control surfaces become liable to abruptly hit their stops; backwards isn't what they normally do. Despite a pilot's determined efforts to hold everything in the middle the rudder in particular can insist on being blown to full deflection – in an instant. This appears to be what happened to Biancotto's Nord 3202, and his elevator and rudder became jammed together. The accident report says a spin – of course – but this was caused by unsuitable aerobatic demands, and, probably the pilot's attempt at a good tail slide rather than the six out of ten safer compromise.

In the 1960 Worlds all the aircraft taking part were historic or existing trainers, most of them modified to some extent to improve aerobatic performance, but they retained their original character. The Bucker Jungmeisters were a specific 1930s single seat development of the Jungmann trainer, with greatly improved aerobatic handling, an excellent club improvers' solo machine – another aeroplane in fact – and Frank Price's Great Lakes had been a popular American aerobatic trainer originating in the thirties. The first 12 places went to Czechs and USSR pilots, with only one non-Czech, flying a Yak 18P, dividing the leading eight, who all flew the single-seat aerobatic version of the Zlin 226. Another three Soviet Republics pilots flying a Z326 acrobat followed these nine. Remaining places showed a satisfyingly mixed bunch of nationalities and types, except for the final three placings which displayed a unified Union Jack, flying their Super Tiger G-ANZZ. There's nowhere else to go from here but up.

In 1970 the sport was still dominated by Iron Curtain countries who agreed, to varying degrees, on the continuing potential importance of state support for this game, perhaps, but a game that would continue the tradition of airmindedness and achievement among their young citizens. However, determined individuals from elsewhere were making progress up the leader boards of each biennial world contest, sometimes quite surprisingly. The first such anomaly was Lindsey Parson's 5th place (of 32) in 1962 flying a Great Lakes for the USA. This event was held in Hungary, and Hungarians, Russians and Czechs filled most of the first 25 places, although it is essential to mention 13th place Rod Jocelyn, USA, also flying the Great Lakes – surrounded by Zlins and Yaks. I have no special knowledge of this event, and is true that the sophisticated Aresti analytical system had just been adopted, but these performances deserve note. Nick Pocock, the only UK entrant, finished 30th, flying a Tiger Club Stampe.

The Gold Leaf Zlin represented an awareness that, by international standards, better and more training was required in Britain, but apart from the opportunity to practise in this machine there was little of the structured training employed by the European rivals – after all, the air was their sea, wasn't it, so maybe one could understand their rather unsporting and businesslike attitude? I remember a couple of rides at Redhill with Pete Jarvis, during which he encouraged me to use a more decisive approach to initiating manoeuvres than the economical style required by the Stampe. He was not wrong, and his appearance at the 1968 Worlds as British judge would have given him an idea of how this academic and difficult discipline worked – but there would be much more to it. Having been accepted as a member of the 1970 squad I joined Frances Macrae, David Gaster, Tony Haig-Thomas, and Pete Jarvis' air force friend Mike Sparrow in the same position at Hullavington; but it all seemed a bit informal – an elusive extension of the Tiger Club, with a different leadership style.

Frances had put up a brave show in a Stampe at the 1968 worlds, but her scores were not recorded. Tony had flown the British consortium's 226 Zlin at Moscow in 1966 and come 31st, ahead of many good pilots, one of whom, at 45th, was Walter Wolfrum, future German judge and a celebrated high-scoring WW2 fighter pilot, with most of his victories achieved on the Russian front. Walter flew a Bucker biplane in 1966. He said that his favourite wartime mount had been the uprated (was it 2000HP?) Me 109 – leaving the easier-to-fly FW 190 to the beginners – but light aviation had not been available to German citizens after his previous Kiev posting so he was at something of a disadvantage at this Russian run show. Hullavington was to be the site of the 1970 summer's world championships, and the home team had always done well. This airfield, now a parachuting barrage balloon maintenance base, was available for our practice from the beginning of the year and I started practising in the free Zlin.

This was hard work. If you were lucky someone else might watch and comment with a mini tape recorder, which you listened to afterwards, but this remained DIY training – quite unlike the organised system operated by the European air-minded nations. They tended to have an identified coach who had no personal sense of rivalry with the pilots – done it already – and they used radio, in-the-moment corrections only. Nothing said means correct. It works.

The 1966 event had been won by Soviet pilots, closely merging into a selection of Eastern Bloc members, then a handful of Spanish (from 1964 worlds momentum), then Neil Williams. He had done well, having 'carved it from the solid' – so to speak. Tony Haig-Thomas also flew well but missed the cut for the final; nonetheless he finished creditably among a large contingent of closely-packed names. At the previous April flyoff for the team Tony had finished a close second to Williams, followed by the third member of the Zlin group, Taff Taylor. Another eight flew the Tiger Club Stampe, the best of whom was Barry Tempest, whose final score looks impressive to me considering the equipment. Of the remainder Robin D'Erlanger and James Black took the Stampe to Moscow. Despite his result and aircraft, Taff Taylor did not go to Moscow because the Foreign Office demanded that he did not. What kind of black had he put up? He hadn't, exactly, but Taff was a serving RAF officer – a single and experienced fighter pilot who had spent some time flying a single-seat civilian jet which required these pilot qualifications. I can say no more, except that his sparse logbook entries would not have met the stringent requirements of the CAA, had it been a British-registered aircraft.

(Once again I can recommend Tony Haig-Thomas' account of his own military career *Fall out Catholics and Jews*. The title alone indicates the wry sense of the observation and insight that characterises this engaging and revealing personal pilgrimage, where determination and charm achieves a lot, but not seniority or a desk job. He reveals Taff's unmentionable four-year civilian job.)

After a few weeks of my struggling in the Zlin at Hullavington Tony came up and sportingly shook my hand. 'Congratulations, you're in the team.' What team? It transpired that we Gold Leafers had been pared down to a final squad – Jarvis, Gaster and Riley. The definites at the top were the three members of the current Zlin Group – Williams, James Black and Carl Schofield, now a company called Aerobatics International run by James, a business executive by profession. It wasn't the same Zlin – the previous one was no more – but this

526 Akrobat was single seat (saving weight), had a retractable undercarriage (more weight less drag), and was of superior performance, but I doubt any stronger.

As the sixth FAI world championships approached it was announced that I would be the reserve pilot. I could get round the compulsory programme, sometimes, but could not guarantee it – it was a step too far in the practice time available. Taff Taylor had been appointed chief judge and, recently returned from his Bahrain Hunter squadron commander position, he took on the business of single-handedly setting up the judging requirements, starting with defining and marking the FAI performance zones on the airfield and its environs. In 1970 this was 1000m long by 800m wide, so, to accommodate different wind directions, one box was clearly not suitable: the more convenient 1000m square version, and less restrictive wind limits, was yet to come. Compared with the more established aerobatic countries we were distinctly short of any permanent infrastructure, including organised training and logistical help. However, the use of a 1930s live military airfield with no aircraft of its own was a godsend, and accommodation in the comfortable ivy-clad officers' mess, a large hangar for our aircraft and completely free use of the airfield and its airspace an unaccustomed luxury. Heretofore the home team had always done well, in fact they always won. Could this tradition continue?

With a few weeks to go the Aerobatics International single seater lost its struggle with metal fatigue and broke over Hullavington, and Neil Williams was remarkably lucky to survive the incident. That he used consummate judgment for the final – and difficult to repeat – landing manoeuvre is unquestionable, but the frequently vaunted military 'to its limits' tradition has its own limits. Numbers are one thing, but finding an ultimate limit, either personal or mechanical, is quite another. Neil's Wales-for-ever quest for success – and I would not stop short of calling it obsession – had materially raised the status of British participation in this sport but, over the years, there would be prices to pay. He had been impressed by the Czech Zlins he had seen perform in previous competitions, and had done surprisingly well at Moscow in 1966 with the Z226 – but why were they so good? How did they do it?

Intended as a basic military trainer, the Zlin Trener series had official manoeuvre limits of +6 and -3 g, and a never-exceed speed of near 300kph. In my experience -4g was considered universally acceptable, but the other numbers were not disputed in conventional society. It was believed that the Czech competition circle took a private and pragmatic attitude to fatigue life and gave their competition machines away to their clubs after a specified number of hours (100, was it?) Neil had told me that his observations (backed up by indiscreet revelations, or perhaps mischievous Bohemian humour?) suggested that they flew their machines to +8/-6, and Vne+100. They clearly understood the limited future of this policy. Privately courageous copying of central European strong-arm determination had already encouraged the Biggin Hill 'taken it behind the hangar (and left it there)' Stampe destruction. What, or who, might be next? The Zlin manufacturers, Morovan, took a paternalistic and sympathetic attitude towards the brave and somewhat disadvantaged British efforts and lent or rented a 526F to our top three contenders for the duration of these worlds. This was the current trainer with a supercharged engine. Quite what level of aerobatics this model was designed for I'm not sure, but Williams showed it no mercy.

The 526F supercharger was connected to the engine by an alloy casting, and it was not long before this part cracked – for the first time. A replacement arrived, was fitted, and that one cracked after a few days' flying. Another ultimate structural limit was clearly being rediscovered on a routine basis by the repeated performance of manoeuvre 2 in the first programme (a vertical upwards three-quarter flick roll), and quite how many times this part was replaced I don't know, but the contest was a couple of weeks away. A sense of desperation overlaid one of discretion. Could the home team still win?

Interestingly enough I heard that this manoeuvre had been chosen because it was thought by some that the American Pitts would be sure to overshoot. Actually three-quarters are a Pitts natural, and offensive figure choice is a risky business, especially if you are not the most experienced and accomplished factor in the international scene. Anyway, the nations arrived and the contest assembled itself while the several days of settling in/training flights took place. On the second day a request was made for the return of the serving officers' hats that had been stolen from the mess facilities on the first day. Clearly the assumption that elite pilots of many nations would conform to officer-like conduct was flawed.

As the various management functions assembled themselves from a motley collection of bemused volunteers, some unforeseen administrative essentials appeared. This always happens when novices take on a sophisticated version of what they might take for granted, and, as well as my duties as judges' warm up pilot and minimum height demonstrator Taff suddenly asked me to check the free sequences. I'd cobbled up one of these for myself, but the rules were complex – so many from this and that group, negatives, positives, roll combinations and so on. An understanding of this protocol could be expected from those who'd taken part in this level of contest already, but there was no training for outsiders as such. Are you an insider or not? That's how it worked.

Let's say there were 60 pilots who had submitted their 20-figure programme (although I remember the state-of-the-art being more extensive than this), each figure consisting of two, three or more manoeuvre combinations. The whole lot had to add up to not more than the maximum points, and then did the choice of figures agree with the rules? Flying the current two programmes would take at least four days of good weather, but this checking is a big job: how to do it? A home-made proforma to start with – ticks in boxes and so on. I had a little office in the control tower, a pile of my check proformas, 60 or more sequences and I started. It was obvious that I would not see much flying (hear it perhaps), and progress was slow. It soon became obvious that I could not do it all by myself, so I recruited a spectator, Dave Allan, to help. Dave had flown the Tiger Club Stampe for Australia in the 1966 Moscow Worlds. He hadn't won exactly, but he'd been there and had a go (the published results showed him as representing Bulgaria!). He was the only visitor I'd come across who knew something (anything) about the international system, and, very sportingly, he agreed to help. This was a particularly magnanimous southern hemisphere gesture because he had come from Australia just to watch the contest.

My fellow Gold Leaf hopeful, Mike Sparrow, a Valley fast jet flight commander, took on the job of runway control, assisted by Brian Smith, my Tiger Moth student. They amused themselves in their red and white chequered runway van by leering at the girl pilots waiting at the holding point, and played with their Aldis lamp. They raised a few eyebrows by driving their non road-qualified vehicle around to the OM carpark for lunch each day. Not quite the thing, but nothing happened.

Politics and gamesmanship play their part in all international events. It's interesting to see it – or maybe imagine it if you don't actually see it. How do you establish the truth? Usually it's difficult. That's why spy stories are so popular. I was sitting at the judging position one day (having finished the programme checking) and Bob Herendeen's propeller stopped during a spin. There was no chance of diving to start the engine in the height available and Bob made an elegant dive at the field, landed on a convenient runway and stopped right in front of us. Bob had been a P51 pilot in Korea, and was now an airline captain. He and his machine sat there while everyone wondered what to do next. I took a drink over. 'Thanks, I guess my mouth is a little dry.' Bob was a leading contender for the US, but there are no marks for landing in the middle of a programme. If a technical reason can be found for the interruption a repeat attempt may be allowed, continuing the scoring from where one broke off, otherwise this performance is over. By all accounts Bob's slow running was tweaked pretty low because the Pitts' idling metal propeller produces significant and disadvantageous precessional effects in some manoeuvres, but, on the face of it, his engine might have stopped for some other reason. For a re-fly something had to be found.

A day went by while the technical commission made exhaustive investigations of his pristine machine – expertly looked after by a determined and proficient American team support. Then, surprise surprise, some dirt was found in the fuel system. A re-fly was allowed and Bob did well in the rest of the contest. He did not win, but came a very close second to Igor Egorov of the USSR. Would the interrupted flight have made a difference? Probably yes, and this world championship near miss from a talented part-timer showed that it was possible to challenge the state supported Iron Curtain teams. Bob's result showed that he had acquired an excellent understanding of how the sport and its scoring worked. He had realised that a quest for unachievable perfection as seen from the cockpit was an irrelevant distraction. It was all about flying for the judges – clarity where it mattered, easy to read style – straightforward to downgrade – and consistency. Bob used his brain to maximum effect, not his emotions. A good pilot in any aircraft.

The next five places were also taken by pilots from the west. Williams came 5th as the top Zlin pilot, but with the exception of this trainer, second to seventh went to purpose -built competition aerobatic aircraft; four American Pitts S1s, third place Charlie Hillard in a special Spinks Akromaster metal monoplane, and Arnold Wagner for Switzerland who managed fourth with a completely new and revolutionary Akrostar – developed thanks to his experience of the modified KZ8, featuring wing flaps interconnected with the pitch control system. With the exceptions of Frenchman J-C Ordoux and a Spaniard all the next places down to 26th were taken by a mixture of the usual suspects from the Eastern Bloc. Research and development does work, and the days of the modified military trainer were numbered, but it was the Pitts with its noise, agility and apparent disregard for g which most ruffled feathers throughout the aerobatic community. The unspoken words outrageous, unfair (dare we say dangerous?), bubbled beneath the surface, but worried comments such as 'too aggressive, too much g, is this how aerobatics should be?' were clear indications of the sense of insecurity evident when comfort zones change their shape.

James Black and Carl Schofield, both denied the use of their partly-owned Zlin when it had fallen apart a few weeks earlier, finished in the 30s, and my

Gold Leaf colleagues, Jarvis and Gaster, brought up the rear. Carl had been a fellow witness to the wing-folding incident, and, though I have not discussed it with him, he must have given his competition future some thought. After this catastrophic structural failure, the subsequent eerie minutes of last-resort upside down flight, and the dramatic, spectacular and desperate but fortunate crash landing we wandered over to look at the remains, the only sounds being those of the Wiltshire skylarks. The machine was definitely dead, and after lunch Williams said to me 'Are you going for a practice? You've got the place to yourself.' Much as I admire the Biggles spirit I declined, saying that maybe some thought should be given to the cause of his breakup – it's only a game, after all, but I don't suppose there was any doubt.

Williams had left his Farnborough military test pilot job some years before in the interests of family life, and now flew for Manx Kelly's Rothmans team as well as Handley Page. As he prepared to leave Hullavington for Booker in a Rothmans Stampe he asked me whether BOAC would be looking for pilots to fly the Concorde. The Bristol prototype had made its maiden flight the year before (1969) and now lived at Fairford for an extensive test programme. I was noncommittal, not wishing to dash hopes, but I knew the answer already – BOAC pilots like me.

Before leaving this account of the 1970 Worlds it is worth mentioning an engine failure I experienced in the Gold Leaf Zlin during the days of the training squad. I'd taken off on the same runway as would be used by Bob Herendeen for his dead stick demo (an irrelevant coincidence) and, at maybe two hundred feet, the engine stopped firing totally and without warning – there was no fuel pressure. I stuffed the nose down, closed the throttle, lowered the undercarriage and made a 270 on to the main runway (all at the same time). This is far from the recommended procedure, but sometimes it's possible. What surprised me was that the engine was idling normally as I slowed to taxi speed, so I taxied in. We looked at the fuel filter – half full of sand. It let enough fuel through for slow running, but the system soon emptied of fuel at full power: and here it is relevant to mention that aerobatic aeroplanes tend to live at full power. Power limits – what are they?

Chronic high engine temperatures and continuous full power caused the Zlin engine to leak oil from the cylinder head bases. If untreated this symptom got steadily worse, and Ken Flack, the voluntary RAE Farnborough engine man, eventually developed his own cure by dispensing with the official paper gaskets and using his own gasket gunge on nicely-cleaned metal. This worked fairly well with the Aerobatics International Akrobat, but the Gold Leaf Zlin had not had this advantage, nor had it yet been used as intensively as now, and after a 10-minute aerobatic flight it returned with a lot of sticky oil over most of it. Oil wiping between flights became a tedious necessity – but where had the sand in the engine come from? There was nothing wrong with the fuel supply – fresh barrels brought by BP – and it only took a second's observation to come up with the answer. One of the enthusiastic wipers found that a petrol-soaked rag worked best, and had been dipping theirs straight into a full tank – repeatedly, during an oil-and-dust-wiping session. Were the British enthusiasts ready to take on a world of substantial and well supported teams? Not really.

The contest finished and I returned to normal work and play, the first flight being a 707 check at Stansted with Peter Mains-Smith (Mainspring – still going strong). This would have consisted of a few circuits with engine failures and the essential three-engined approach and go-around under the hood. I see that my session started at 9:30 pm and finished at 10:30. It must have been dark, more or less. When did we get back to London, and home? I see that I won the Air Squadron Trophy on August 15th in a Stampe. I don't see this entry as unfair because my world championship experience was limited at this stage – non-existent actually, and I had now seen what good means to foreigners at the world championships.

On the 22nd of August 1970 I entered the De Havilland Contest again, which took place at Little Rissington, and finished 4th (officially). I flew the Zlin, and actually my performance was not that bad, but I remember this event clearly because of a circumstance which typified the uniquely English (Edwardian really) sporting approach to management at staff level, be it of a military service, managing the empire or a school. This contest required a nostalgic do-what-you-like time-constrained performance of the old tradition. The aerobatics had to last five minutes – exactly. The total timing started before takeoff, based on a time-to-climb declared by the pilot. I had said four minutes climb, and the performance should start on the second – indicated by a Verey flare. On the four minutes I started my routine, but saw no evidence of the stage effects from below. OK, GB's got it wrong: keep going. After one minute of my precisely-arranged routine (there's no other way), I happened to see a likely-looking smoke trail drifting across the field. A cock-up in the organisation, for sure. Never mind. My definitive final figure finished right on the five minutes and, to my satisfaction, there was the finishing shot arcing, once again, into the sky. All was well. Imagine my surprise when my mark sheet showed 60 seconds worth (not 61 or 59) of starting time penalty. How could I have compressed my to-the-second five-minute routine into exactly four minutes, off the cuff, to make the nine total minutes? It's not possible.

GB (Wing Commander Arthur Golding-Barrett) was a founder member of the Tiger Club, responsible for check pilots and initial checks, for which he originated a very simple and useful pro forma. The only personal detail required was a name, and, on a single side, a series of common sense yes/no questions covered all you needed to know about the required behaviour and skills in one flight. Pass or fail at the end. I liked this system. A between-the-wars pilot, he had been called back to do the sort of operations control management jobs you see in the Battle of Britain films. He once told me about something that happened while he was flying upside down in a Fairey Flycatcher in the Hendon air display. The straps came apart. 'That finished me for aerobatics' – quite understandable. Still of senior staff officer demeanour in 1970, he had recently remarried, had a young son and lived close to Fairford. With about 70 years between them he would walk the small boy along the lanes to the perimeter fence to see the prototype Concorde take off. 'The noise, the flames – it leaves the runway smoking when it's gone. Stupendous.' I wondered if the child liked it as well. I remember he'd also described to me some hiatus in the judging routine at Hullavington. For some procedural reason Taff decided that he needed to stop the proceedings mid-flight, and had either fired a Verey light or thrown a smoke bomb. It went among the judges' tables. 'Absolute pandemonium,' said GB. 'If we'd have had the second coming no one would have noticed.' I only saw him in the air once, and that was his landing at Redhill in a Super Tiger one Sunday. As the machine turned off the grass strip and headed for the hangar an elegant, superbly-brushed Crufts-worthy dog of the Afghan persuasion bounded out from the bystanders, mane flying in the wind, and bounced enthusiastically around the Tiger and its propeller. 'What bloody idiot's dog is this?' roared GB from the cockpit. It belonged to recently-joined Darrol Stinton, Neil Williams' test pilot's course buddy, and now of the CAA, responsible for light aircraft handling standards.

The 707 had recently started calling at Moscow on the way to Japan, as an eastabout join up with the Anchorage route. I was intrigued to see the bundled-up babushka-type ladies chipping the packed snow off the aprons and taxiways. Similarly novel was the pensioned-off Nene engine on a flatbed truck, pointed over the side. The Nene at full chat blasted the apron and sent sheets of ice cartwheeling through the air, to shatter ready for the babushki's shovels. Thc road to town goes past the steel girder memorial marking the end of the German advance, and I went there in December 1970 with captain Mervyn-

Smith (Mervyn-Smooth). On a previous trip he'd asked the station manager to get him a couple of tickets for the Bolshoi Theatre – whatever was on. It was Boris Godunov tonight and would I like to go? Why not? A free show should always be attended. This opera is a massive and dark historical work but the Bolshoi do things pretty well. The giant theatre has been glammed up a lot since then, maybe back to its pre-revolutionary bling, but this dark and dreary 1970 soviet interior was packed with fans, looking somewhat similar to each other, many still with their headscarves and shopping bags. At half time we had some very good value caviar (choice of black or orange) butties and fizzy drink, but this is a tough show – not a single laugh in it. The many players and singers did an excellent job, as did an imposing basso Boris, heavily costumed – but Mervyn Smooth slept through much of it, and I was relieved when it was over. As the massive curtain finally fell we woke up and clapped, and as one man the rest of the audience rose to their feet, but not to applaud the gallant cast and orchestra. They grabbed their shopping bags and scrambled for the exit – to get a good place in the queue for the last tram home. Surely, I thought, these wonderful artists at various levels deserve some recognition of their stupendous efforts, but no: everyone's an equal-status worker here – in theory.

My last 707 trip as a co-pilot/navigator (we shouldn't forget that specialist and soon-to-be defunct part of the job) was a Miami-Nassau with Pete Davis in February 1971. I then went to the nascent 747 fleet.

CHAPTER 17

THE THREE 747S

Our first three 747s had arrived quite a few months before, but they sat outside the hangar because their size, I imagine, suggested that pay-packets should be similarly enlarged. This concept led to extensive industrial negotiations, during which the 12 BOAC engines were progressively lent to Pan Am, who often arrived at London after trouble with theirs. The problem was that the round fan casing tended to change shape a bit en route, so the whirling fan blades touched the sides. Touching the rotating assembly is never a good thing so, in a way, Pan Am's courageous research programme was a convenient time to have industrial discussions – at no extra cost to the employer – and arrange for the next engine version.

I think my course was the third BOAC one, following the training that the initial management people had received at Seattle before they brought the first three outside-the-hangar queens over. I remember seeing one of these machines doing circuits at Prestwick quite a few months before, as the first training managers, both piloting and engineering, taught each other how to do it. The aircraft looked huge and stately in the air, and this made it look easy. Either it was, or they had been well taught. It was both, of course.

This being a new toy with little time for airline input our classroom course was the manufacturer's – logical and comprehensive, everything you needed to know, presented in easy-to-learn progression. The basic philosophy of the aircraft was that of a double-sized 707, but with a completely fresh look at flying controls and other moving systems, the way to power them, and the most efficient way to make use of the luxury of size and space to create a conveniently shared responsibility between hydraulics, electrics and pneumatics. A masterpiece of its day? Of course.

Prior to the simulator we had a few lessons in the cardboard bomber, running through the checklists with pictures of lights and switches. Something rather quaint struck me about our engineering mentors who had clearly spent some time with the Boeing people the previous year. Winston Churchill (half American) made the 'divided by a common language' comment, but it's true. The checks were divided into normal, non-normal, alternate and emergency. Plain enough, but I was puzzled that even this new subdivision of unsettling possibilities was not the whole story. Thus far, flying life had consisted of normal and 'I'm in serious trouble' classifications. But our otherwise British engineering mentors had even brought a fifth one back from the west coast – 'nun-normal'. What have nuns got to do with it? I reasoned that there must be none-normal checks hidden in there somewhere, implying that these secret events could be peculiar in the extreme, but no, it soon became clear that this was how their Boeing teacher(s) had pronounced non-normal (from 'unnormal'?)

Fortunately this virus quickly died out. The Pilgrim Fathers had taken Shakespeare's English with them, but central European influence has rationalised this erstwhile official language in the meantime. Sometimes it's we English who have changed without noticing. The Bajan 'What is this foolishness?' no longer has its serious connotation to us today, and the American industry is not happy with inflammable. *Enter Romeo, stage left, flamed with passion* would suggest to us that his tights are on fire. Bernard Levin could do a lot with this subject – maybe he did. On a previous safety equipment course, cabin crew led, I was intrigued by the references to portable water when the subject was the kind that came out of the drinking water tap, as in hippopotamus or a reviving potation. Of course you could fill special takeaway containers with it for emergencies, but we hadn't got to that part yet. Maybe this was more Hounslow than Pacific coast.

The systems were much more complicated than those in the 707, but logical and easy to understand – just a lot of them. The 1970 state-of-the-art simulator worked pretty well, as I remember, and base training at Shannon was an interesting and pleasant experience, as usual. I see that I did three sessions with Reg Tibble, and three with Norman Todd, the training manager. In many ways the new machine was like a giant 707 to fly, but inherently more stately, with more flying control authority (totally powered, of course) and, by and large, the handling was more straightforward. The view of the ground from such a cockpit height was something quite new. Taking off was easy because you start in an easy place, but rotate was called at what looked like taxiing speed. Naturally the same applied in reverse as the ground approached before landing, and here the astonishing sense of height off the ground was a new experience to be assimilated. But the new use of radio altimeter height calls, 50 and 30 feet, and the simple things to be done in response to them helped a lot.

I was walking around the Shannon countryside one soft and overcast day when the airborne crew decided to do some mini circuits at 500ft, instead of the usual 1500. This is a quite legitimate, but the sight got your attention. This height off the ground is 2½ wingspans only, and to see the large fin proceeding behind the trees gave the impression of some outrageous low flying – worth a phone call for sure.

It's easy to be a good instructor when you have a good student. Norman Todd was a forceful and decisive character, and one of my colleagues did not fare so well. There was one handling difference which was not identified at the time. Natural airspeed feedback was less than flying a 707, by both sound and feel. The 747 cockpit air condition noise was greater, masking changes in the already noisy airstream; there was (naturally) no natural feedback through the powered flying controls, and less seat of the pants from the machine in the circuit. That is not to say that static stability was lacking, but the 707 seemed to have had more of it at low speed. Did the 747 also operate at a more efficient and aft C of G, because it could? Larger and more modern machines tend to distance and insulate their occupants from the aerology outside, and the 747 beginner had to keep a close eye on the airspeed indicator, otherwise speed could drift surreptitiously away from the desired number. On an early route flight I (we) discovered that the same caution applied in the cruise, and a passengering colleague just happened to come to the cockpit as a fair amount to power was squeezed on. 'Aha, I thought I could feel it starting to tremble down the back.'

My first trip was to New York and Bermuda with captain Peter Sleight, leaving London on May 11th 1971. To begin with this single daily outing was the only 747 route, and the London-New York part of it definitely the airline's new prestige sector. The most revolutionary feature of the experience, for me, was our total dependence on inertial navigation (INS) where there were no alternatives. These small devices in their boxes somewhere downstairs had taken the astronauts to the moon and back a number of times. The principle is simple

– the gyro-stabilised box of tricks knows two things before you release it: where it is, and the fact that it is not moving (on the earth's surface anyway). Once it's up and running it is released to do its feeling and calculating. Accelerometers continuously measure rates of movement (accelerations), and arithmetic transforms this into speeds, directions, distances, times, position – everything you need to know – without looking outside. The three wise men would have been as amazed as the dhow captain or Vasco da Gama. I was amazed at the pinpoint accuracy of our landfall on the Labrador coast. Incredible: a doubting Thomas no more. How could you create such unassisted precision in such a small device? The Luddites' and Levellers' worst fears had been realised. No more navigating. One less in the cockpit. Millenia of skills redundant.

Like other computerised devices INS is also slavishly obedient – it goes exactly where you tell it, and the importance of a fool-proof loading and cross-checking routine is vital. A few flights later I was astonished to hear our captain tell a passenger that this machine knew where we were by measuring the earth's magnetic field. Not really – but does this matter? How it worked was not important – how to work it more so, and some simple imagery in the classroom stressed the necessity of keeping it topped up with a list of places to go. If it ran off the end of its stock of nine it would head for the original no. 1 again if topping up had been forgotten, and if there were less than 9 in the playlist, default zeroes is the next place. To a computerised navigator this is a position in the sea off west Africa; where the equator and the Greenwich Meridian cross. 'If a jumbo disappears this is the first place they will look', said our teacher. We remembered.

Before the first New York awayday to Bermuda and back someone told me not to be disturbed by the narrow look of the Bermuda runway. 'It will look like a garden path – listen to the height calls'. They were right. This airfield is run by the US Navy, and navies like to paint things – the runway was in tarmac black anyway, but it looked especially black against the pristine markings in easy-to-see dazzling white. It must have been officially wide enough, although narrower than large civil runways, but the garden path business was uncannily correct. I'm not sure how our wheels fitted. My fourth trip was a second 747 outing with Les Ward and he gave me the NY-Bermuda sector. It was nice to have seen someone else have a go first.

A test flight with the top test pilot

So far only three registrations had featured, aircraft NC, ND and NE, I imagine because we still only had three at the time. A couple of days after this fourth route trip Les Ward and myself were detailed to accompany the great Dai Davies on an ARB test flight in ND, on May 28th 1971. We met up in the office and he introduced himself. 'My name's Dave,' he started, rather pointedly. The Welshness was clear, and he reminded me a bit of actor Hugh Griffith, but soon became Dai the test as he briefed us about what we were going to do. I was unsure whether this introduction was an invitation or a warning. Maybe Mr Davies would be appropriate. He was already celebrated for his scepticism of optimistic, can-do, thick pencilling by the Americans, and one of his main topics for this flight was the two-engine climb performance (for real, of course). He had arranged a suitably long track along Boscombe Down's centreline, starting at circuit height, more or less, and proceeding overhead and away to the west for as far as it took. There were a number of other registration checks and renewals to complete thereafter. Les would co-pilot in the right-hand seat, the flight engineering manager would observe and record adjacent to the panel, driven by another, and Davies' couple of acolytes would sit behind him with their clipboards and charts. There wasn't much room left in the flight deck, but there was plenty of space elsewhere. Davies did make the point that if anything broke, and an emergency was indicated, there would be an immediate musical chairs session, and the owner's licensed crew would be on their own.

We left London, descended after passing Newbury, shut down engines 3 and 4, wound the other two up to go-around thrust, and Dai the Stick + Rudder practised his craft – his two spotters behind eagerly taking notes. We growled along the A303, over Boscombe Down as planned, and on into the republican west country. This was going to take some time, and a casual observer might call it a good attempt at straight and level, so having no function (except to be one of the few licence-holders aboard) unless there were to be an emergency, and there being no room in the cockpit anyway, I wandered around down the back to enjoy the better view, check the galleys for anything of interest left there, and so on.

I took a look at the struggling left-hand engines. The intakes had spring-loaded suck-in doors in front of the fan to let more air in under this low speed/high power condition. There was no doubt about it; one of these at the bottom of the No. 2 intake was coming apart. Its inside surface had come unstuck/unriveted at the front and was bending up into the ferocious airflow. Would it come off and go into the fan at max continuous power? Very possibly. Apart from the instant drama this would cause we would then be flying on one engine, none too high and over Shaftesbury. Experience of our second flight was to prove, two hours later, that starting an engine without a fair bit of speed and legerdemain could take time: I didn't know this then, but still thought it a good idea to go up front and tell a licensed member of the crew about my observations. The flight engineering manager strolled back with me, mildly interested in what this newly-qualified and perhaps over-sensitive co-pilot thought he had seen. The current exercise was quickly abandoned and we returned to London.

During our wait I asked Mr Davies about the change in rudder gearing at about half rudder, noticeable during two engine flight in the simulator, its illogicality suggesting a last-minute tweak, but never mentioned. 'I'm on to that,' he declared, and drew me a diagram of the unusual rudder law. An hour and a half later we were off again to continue the in-service research. Quite what our pit stop men had done to repair the intake I don't know – speed tape, Araldite (quick-setting), a few rivets perhaps. Maybe they'd found a spare door. I don't remember the remaining details of the second flight (apart from protracted efforts to relight an engine – paraffin streaming for miles before success, or not), having accepted my place down the back, except the opportunity to once again observe the effects of a rapid reduction of oxygen partial pressure. Only to 14,000ft from sea level this time, but the previous Boscombe Down training was confirmed – without the loss of consciousness. The general sense of unease was evident, but in particular there was a noticeable loss of colour in the vision – a normal picture except a sort of greying out in the colour of everything familiar. The pale blue fingernail syndrome was as expected, and, as I went around counting dropped-out masks a kind of normality slowly reasserted itself. Acclimatisation, I suppose (though this may have been a cabin descent to something normal). Everest base camp is at 17,000 ft – but this is a start.

On the way back to London the ARB disciples had finished their ministrations, and I went upstairs to have a look. All was normal; straight flight, all engines equal power, and the great man fine-tuning the rudder trim. He ended up with exactly one division of rudder, but this looked very like the zero on the winder. The ball was in the middle, the ailerons were in the middle – a picture of perfect straight flight. I wondered if he thought he had zeroed the rudder trim. I'd had nothing to do so far; could I contribute? I mentioned discreetly that he had one degree of rudder trim applied. 'I know that!' he barked back, affronted that an outsider, a common or garden commercial pilot, had deigned to offer information: he sounded like Utah Watkins, *Under Milk Wood's* angry farmer, the Llareggub accent suddenly exaggerated. Sorry I spoke, I thought, and slunk away.

One way and another it had been quite a long afternoon. I came across him a few weeks later in the upper deck bar on the way to New York, champagne in hand, one of the boys, going to Seattle perhaps, to help them out. The test pilot as Squire Western? Funny how quickly things can change.

In the interests of a brutally honest autobiography I have to declare that, after 45 years, I was not certain that the two dead engines were actually shut down for the performance climb, but a management colleague tells me it would have been yes (which makes this single engine probability look precarious – but it was not a public transport flight). This confirms the story above, and leaves the old question in the air: is even more rudder required with engines 2, 3 and 4 shut down? Answer no: Only one outer running has the same asymmetry as only one shut down.

747 household arrangements

Our flight deck shared the top floor with the first-class lounge bar, for that was what it was. Upstairs was not a large area – more like a wide executive jet – but although this floor was our own little home the first class did not share it as such – they lived downstairs for takeoff and landing. David Frost was a frequent New York passenger, currently gaining fame and status with London and New York Frost Reports on the go at the same time. There was some trouble one evening NY departure. Frost went straight upstairs to doss down on the sofa. Good idea; but this is not allowed for takeoff. We all know that, but it was 2 am in London, we all felt knackered, the risk of a life-terminating event relatively small, and if the worst should happen, who cared? Absolutely to all of this, but rules are rules, designed for the ordinary people, and, after much start-up-delaying protests, he had to go downstairs and wait through the interminable taxi out in the Kennedy evening traffic jam until we had climbed away, the seatbelt lights went out and one could rush upstairs to bag a sofa, hoping that other first classers weren't planning a party up there – you never know (why not buy your own jet?).

It was very quickly evident that this large new aircraft was having a significant sociological effect on crew dynamics. Many new cabin crew had been recruited for the new flagship – at 15 a throw, not four or six – and to command this many, and reflect the commercial significance of each jumbo flight, a new job title arose – Cabin Service Director. Two and a half times the number of cabin crew required, two and a half times the revenue per flight. What about the flight deck's contribution? Only three of them now instead of four, and dilute that by the two and a half factor; how significant are the flight deck crew? I'm not suggesting that this was openly discussed, but it suggests the underlying reasons for a burgeoning awareness of a direct relationship between catering and financial success, and the perceived status to go with it. The physical separation of flight deck from the action below did not help, and CSDs took to making captain-like announcements (the captain may be busy, I'll do as well, anyway). As time went by first class customers were not encouraged to venture upstairs because their presence required a bartender, and the CSD became known as the Fiddler on the Roof – the upper deck lounge being regarded as a nice and quiet office where he could privately complete his paperwork, undisturbed.

One particular feature of this numerically-unbalanced new status was the scrum at the hotel desk to get the money and key. Fifteen big and strong boys and girls, especially the girls, won hands down. It was best to wait to one side, captain included, until those at the cutting edge of customer service had felt suitably serviced. Was this the way of the future? Could be; I didn't like it much, and privately pondered my own view of things to come: many others would not have noticed the changes.

For the three undeserving and inconspicuous flyers upstairs the seclusion, automatic navigation and reliable and plentiful systems made for a relaxed flight. There really wasn't much to do, apart from keep track of progress, make sure there were a few future positions in the navigation system, and make the odd radio call. One novelty was the requirement to grab the control wheel when an upcoming change of track was indicated, otherwise the auto pilot would call for sudden roll in an aggressive manner, almost throwing you out of your seat and spilling drinks (especially upstairs, above the roll centre). This was not addressed during my four years on the Jumbo, and, 40 years later, I mentioned this behaviour to a retired Toulouse engineer who had worked on Concorde development. He specialised in the autopilot; I mentioned how beautifully smoothly the Concorde autopilot flew, including the same inertial change of track. 'We had the same problem, but I fixed it. I soldered a capacitor and a resistor into the roll circuit.' As easy as that.

An interesting thing happened during an early takeoff at London. The 747 cockpit windows did not open, but there was a hatch in the flight deck roof as an alternative means of escape. It hinged down inside when opened and, if you stood on the flight engineer's seat, you could get a good look outside. Shut and locked was a before-start check. On this occasion Cyril Earthrowl was a new captain and off we set down the runway. I had the distinct impression that I could hear the engines more clearly than usual, almost as if I was standing outside, watching the machine go by, but why? I looked behind. The flight deck door was closed, nothing unusual: am I imagining this? But the airspeed noise was now adding to the effect. I had to shout the V1 call at Cyril as he concentrated on driving. I looked round again and the engineer looked at me with a what-are-you-looking-at-me-for expression. Then I saw it. A square ring of daylight around the hatch. Dynamic pressure was pushing it in, air conditioning was balancing it. The FE followed my gaze, saw the daylight and leapt out of his seat as I shouted rotate at Cyril. Our F/E desperately grabbed the handle, turned it to 'open', the hatch snapped shut and he turned the handle the 90° to 'lock', swinging from the ceiling in the process like a Titanic chandelier in a heavy swell.

By comparison it was then surprisingly quiet as we climbed away. There was nothing to discuss. Was it Cyril's first trip on his own? Of course he didn't know what to expect from a non-training crew. We looked at the hatch after arrival in New York. It was possible to turn the handle to 'lock', then push the hatch into position. The rubber seal round the outside held it in its hole, and it looked closed. The only way to be sure was to swing on it. There was no warning light – not necessary, this thing was part of the cockpit.

But the official in-flight entertainment downstairs was a delightful, diverting and high-quality novelty. Air-driven earphones provided surprisingly good sound, far better than what was to come, and the tasteful and well-chosen musical selection much to my liking. Then there was the film: a real celluloid one with a proper projector at the back of the cabin. The early seventies saw a flowering of the UK film industry, and a succession of well-written, well-directed and well-acted films became available. Improbable petrol-fired explosions were few and far between, and multiple car crashes a rarity. There was always a story, and the relaxed workload in the flight deck meant that two of the three crew could easily cope. Who would like to see the film – have lunch as well? A couple of hours, perhaps. There was no doubt that the steadiness, comfort, sense of space and relative quiet in first class was a huge improvement on what had gone before. I found the experience a completely absorbing way to accrue time in the logbook. The comfortable, darkened cinema environment and a sharing of the lives portrayed by John Mills, Lionel Jeffries, Julie Christie, Alan Bates etc required a certain mental re-referencing as the credits rolled. 'I wonder if it will be dark outside? Where did I leave the car? Which way shall I go back to the hotel?' were the initial thought processes. Then an awareness of the background flying noise slowly intervened and one could return to the real world upstairs, to the sunshine of an Atlantic summer's day, the blue sea with icebergs; relaxed, mentally refreshed – definitely worth the money.

By third millennium standards this early B747-136 model (since called the 'Classic') has become an old-fashioned part of history, but the large and divided crew, self-contained area navigation system and new features of the autopilot all represented fundamental changes in the flight crew job. It was the start of the future – light years from the Wright brothers, but only 68 real years. The autopilot system would do a good approach and autoland, but for success the pilot had to carefully settle the machine on to the approach path before engaging the autoland mode, and this last had to be done at the right moment. This was a sufficiently demanding task, within the constraints of air traffic control instructions, that it might be easier not to bother unless the area was quiet and a nice long approach could be arranged. This situation identifies the question of manual or automatic. Sometimes fiddling with the autopilot system could be more difficult than normal (now old-fashioned) manual flying. This weakness gave the distinct impression of low development priority, like the omission of something (cheap) to smooth the INS track change demand. 'Not fully finished' is a popular term.

But, to me, the game-changing autopilot feature was the altitude-acquire novelty. The aircraft would actually level off by itself at the height selected in the window. Pointing the machine in the required direction and not flying at the wrong height are fundamentals of safe transport flying, and heretofore both of these priorities had required on-going pilot attention. I remembered the Gregory/Meadows height bust on that quiet morning into Sydney, and the pommie grovelling required to make obeisance. A bit of fun for the relevant authorities, perhaps, but it didn't happen often (and traditional respect for the long-respected flying traditions in various nations was not damaged). Even though awareness would still remain valid it was clear that the compulsory level of scanning and monitoring required of a pilot could be relaxed by these helpful devices. And better autopilots meant a reduced need for universally good and ever-current handling skills. Many airline pilot professionals would welcome this look into the future, especially those who saw the job as free travel from one major city to the next (with pocket money), a welcome interruption in the routine of home life, the perceived status of special respect from an uninformed public, and an agreeably sociable if not too sophisticated working environment. But, while this jumboing was an agreeable way to get about, did it have anything to do with my original boy's obsession with piloting a flying machine? I thought about it. We are all different in our interests and motivations and the priorities that go with them. There's nothing wrong with horses for courses – more important is that they enter the right race. After four years, the answer was to be no.

CHAPTER 18

MORE FLYING FOR ENTHUSIASTS, AND A RED OCTOBER MISSION

A week or so before the B747 Air Registration Board test flights, Michael Jones suggested that I should try the Arrow Active. This was the survivor of the two examples built in 1932 – Alex Henshaw had bailed out of the Mk 1 when it caught fire. This G-ABVE Mk 2 was a perky-looking silver and red single seat biplane, of all-metal basic structure, designed as a well-heeled gentleman's sporty runabout of its day. A locker behind the cockpit was long enough for the golf clubs, tennis racket and evening dress basics, and its compact look was consistent with the story I heard, but have not read, that its developers hoped that the Royal Air Force would be interested in a cheap way for the chaps to keep their hands in while not flying their larger and thirstier biplane fighters. It sat on the ground in a significant nose-up attitude, the top wing low to the fuselage, and forward visibility limited; but the view to either side of the nose was not bad. 'Neil will tell you about it,' said Michael.

Neil Williams, another Welsh test pilot of course, briefed me on what I should know, and nothing else. This is how it should be, and he explained the reliable landing technique. The correct final approach speed – enough for a tail-down wheeler, but not too fast, then once on the ground raise the tail to a horizontal attitude and keep it there until no longer possible, so that the final bit at the three point attitude is as short as possible. This worked perfectly, and the nicely-damped long undercarriage gave a good ride across the Redhill turf. Though nothing like a Tiger Moth in character it had the same Cold Comfort Farm cum Woburn grass-only tail skid, which provides helpful drag and restraint when the tail is on the ground, but in intermediate ground attitudes without power the limited vertical surfaces behind the pilot hide behind the chunky nose. A three-pointer is the best way to land a tail dragger when it makes sense, and may be a satisfying morale-booster for the enthusiast, but there are a number of characteristics – wing loading and sneaky wing-dropping being two, and unhelpful C of G positions and running out of control could be added – where a suitable compromise is more reliable. Sometimes you can get a good idea of what to expect just by looking first.

The Active was good fun to fly. Relatively fast, it had a nice solid feel in the air, well-suited to the coordinated swooping, diving and barreling manoeuvres that Americans call military aerobatics. I had a couple of flights in it that day, then made a 30 minute C of A test flight in a Stampe. All boxes ticked and numbers recorded – no hassle, no problems, Cockpit Resource Management to a high standard.

The De Havilland Fox Moth was another example of a 30s machine – something like a flying Hansom cab, and rather pleasant to ride in as a passenger. The performance and handling made for a stately flight, and its gentle but rather vague notions of stability discouraged anything but sedate flying. It too was not always ideal for the Tiger Moth three-pointer. Here in Switzerland in 2016 a Junkers F13 true-to-life replica is being built. The original single-engined passenger aircraft flew in 1919. It looks like a miniature Ju52, has the same corrugated dural skin, the passengers sit in an enclosed cabin and the two side by side pilots outside, but in front – behind the engine. This relatively modern machine beat the old-fashioned Fox Moth into the air by 13 years.

The 1971 summer was busy with an assortment of light aircraft action – Rapide parachute flying at Netheravon, aerobatic practice and competition, and Turbulent team displays. As well as four-ship formation, flying the Turbulent routine usually included other fun things to do with these little aeroplanes, and the list evolved as time went by. Some ideas had fallen out of favour because of their logistical demands or problematic history. The limbo event was one of these, as was James Baring's air-to-ground rocket firing idea, but streamer cutting, balloon bursting and flour bombing were still on the list. Streamer cutting did not require ground support during the show although, without the overnight slow roasting, the streamers themselves tended to disappoint by not unravelling properly, descending too fast and not locally shattering into confetti when cut. The correct procedure required old-fashioned shiny paper toilet rolls – two per pilot – bone dry, and primed before takeoff by unrolling and gathering a foot or so to ensure an immediate clean unroll when thrown. They were stowed somewhere secure but convenient because accurate ordnance deployment was important, and it goes without saying that too much, badly stowed priming leader could cause an escalating problem in an open and windy cockpit.

A break from line astern would lead to a suitably-distanced procession along the display line (allowing for wind). The leader grabbed his first primed roll and held it above his head, a signal for the followers to prepare likewise, then all threw first and second rolls over the side at the leader's throw. If all went well this produced an impressive giant curtain across the site, and a tail chase back and forth along this line, cutting up the wall of streamers, provided the action. Ideally the streamers not only broke where hit, but the shock should encourage many adjacent perforations to fail, producing the partial confetti effect, intermingled with some helplessly swirling and tangling sections, to be mopped up and further shattered by increasingly agile passes.

Balloon bursting was something I only did once, at Elstree on August 15th. I had witnessed it from the air during my Tiger Moth course in 1959, but only as a gratuitous demo by my instructor, dashing the hopes of holidaymakers a few miles to the west. Another one that won't make the Dutch coast. I see that my Elstree machine was the white one, PNZ, flown round Windsor Castle by Prince Phillip, but this has nothing to do with this event. Balloon bursting requires a ground crew to inflate and release the balloons, so putting a ground party together just for training would be a lot of trouble, and, as Flanders and Swann pointed out, practising beforehand spoils the fun: it's the sort of thing unsporting foreigners do.

Unlike the streamer cutting act, balloon bursting was not a team sport, as such. I've no doubt this had been tried before, but four enthusiastic marksmen chasing the same balloons at the same time has a hysterical and random feel to it, so it had been abandoned. Our performance was an individual scoring contest – one after the other in arranged time slots, more like a penalty shoot-out. The tactics soon became clear. The balloons climb faster than the Turbulent so a struggle to pursue one at the same height from any distance would fail, ending up in hanging on the propeller with no speed, and a triumphant balloon soaring disdainfully upwards. The trick was to pick one below, soon after it had been released, and dive at where it would be when you got to it – obvious. The featherlight balloon jinked about in the naturally turbulent air, so some theatrical precision manoeuvring was required to achieve the necessary accuracy. A near miss might well leave the balloon spinning helplessly in one of the vortices left by the aeroplane. Until this dissipated and the balloon escaped, the aeroplane energy could be used to quickly wheel around and pop it on a second pass. Wild excitement from the crowd.

I soon got the hang of it and was doing rather well. Then I beaded up a dead centre hit – great. But instead of the expected audible pop there was a muffled 'Whumpff', and a broad wash of an all-enveloping ethereal halo of baby-blue warmth swept past. I'd seen this colour before, it's unmistakeable, and my O and A level chemistry qualifications both confirmed that this was the colour of burning hydrogen; and, compared with the squeaky test tube demo, plenty of it. Did this happen all the time, or was it a rarity? A member of the crowd reported that enthusiastic commentator Benjy (Lewis Benjamin) became temporarily lost for words; and subdued oohs and aahs were heard from the unified spectators. His erstwhile namesake Benjamin Franklin would have been interested. It was overcast and humid (thundery even?), and whirling propellers create plenty of static. A voltaic discharge usually goes for the most pointy thing on the front of an aircraft, and the locking wire on the front of the Turbulent's spinner was the most pointy thing available. I'm not sure what I did with the last two targets – closely missed them, probably. I returned home not much older, but slightly wiser, and definitely more experienced.

From the summer of 1971 BOAC B747 operations expanded, first to Canada, then, in December, tentatively to Africa, followed by exploratory trips to the end of the all-points-east routes. New crew members continued to appear, and by May 1972 the registration alphabet had reached K, and A, B and C having now appeared, this meant 11 747s. That's roughly a new one each month – someone had done a lot of shopping. In January 1972 I went all the way to Sydney via Hong Kong and back with Terry Brand, 13 sectors in three weeks. This was very similar to the old Comet and 707 eastern route days, and the flying times were no different, but the unusually long trip had a pioneering feel to it. Our roster seemed to bear little relationship to that of the various cabin crews, and this independent and quiet upstairs life made the three weeks feel more like a freighter posting. We stayed in Darwin for a few days each way – at a German lady's B&B. When Terry politely brought some deficiency to our landlady's notice she took exception to his use of 'high' English, as she called it.

During the first stay at the Darwin *Gasthaus* we visited the Glomar (Global Marine) Challenger deep-drilling ship which was currently tied up alongside in the harbour. This vessel was engaged in a worldwide geological study and did indeed collect samples providing evidence of seabed and tectonic plate histories. To a newcomer to automatic navigation the positioning readouts on the bridge looked interesting, but were not explained. There are a number of ways that a ship can keep itself in the same position over a deep ocean floor, and dynamic positioning has developed since then into a large and complex industry.

During the second stay at the B&B of *ziemlich Gemütlichkeit* we again made our way to the harbour. The Challenger had gone, but in the same place at the dockside was an oldish Russian ship of similar size, a Baltic ferry by the look of it, unmodified except for a few aerials on top. This was not a coincidence, and the highly secret CIA project, funded by Howard Hughes to raise a complete sunken Russian submarine, was well under way. The Hughes Glomar Explorer would be ready in two years, and was partially successful in raising the submarine from 5 kms down in the Pacific, together with its missiles, of 3 megaton calibre, their guidance systems and programmed Silicone Valley targets, code books, everything you could think of. K-129 had sunk in 1968, and all of it left the seabed, but it broke on the way up and only a small part was recovered. The Russians would have dearly liked to get their own submarine back, but how to do it was looking difficult: the secret shadow (and it's not every day you see an Estonian ferry alongside in Darwin) might pick up some useful ideas. This top secret project was not that secret – clearly our own part in this unobtrusive intelligence gathering had been much more professional than that of the major players, and the B&B cover a masterstroke.

First flight, 1958. Same glider – different school. *Photo P. Benest, Epsom College.*

First ideas for a career/hobby, 1943.

First job: signed up member of Christ Church
Cathedral Choir, Jan 1951

Place of daily part-time work, 1951-1955.
Where can you find builders of this quality today?

Self-explanatory

Last term at school, 1960, end of staff row left. Phil Hogge, future General Manager BA 747 fleet, same row, 3rd from right. One of us seems to have anticipated NASA's advice for stressed space students: Take the subject seriously – but not yourself.

Pre-break echelon after the opening ceremony flypast. Instructor Alan Smith (3rd in the picture) wonders what Tapps Tappin is doing. Bill Anderson and Pete Stanwell look happy. The 5 vic flypast had been good.

Instrument flying practice could be tedious. Jackson and Riley coming down – action is west of Newport, IOM.

Vanguard EI safe and sound after surviving the Palermo barrage. Sister ship EE happened to be my fence-busting example (it was later totally destroyed when it dived into the Heathrow runway one foggy night. Something of a mystery.)

Our Palermo hero Oakie relaxes in the shotgun seat on the return leg to London.

Singapore 1965. Rowing the captain ashore. On the left the huge
Anjong on the bow of an Indonesian Pinisi.

Tiger Club Stampe, 1960s vehicle of UK aerobatic progress.

XB47 prototype, 1946: the forerunner of the 707 – today's standard shape for transport aircraft. The US took the German idea and ran with it.

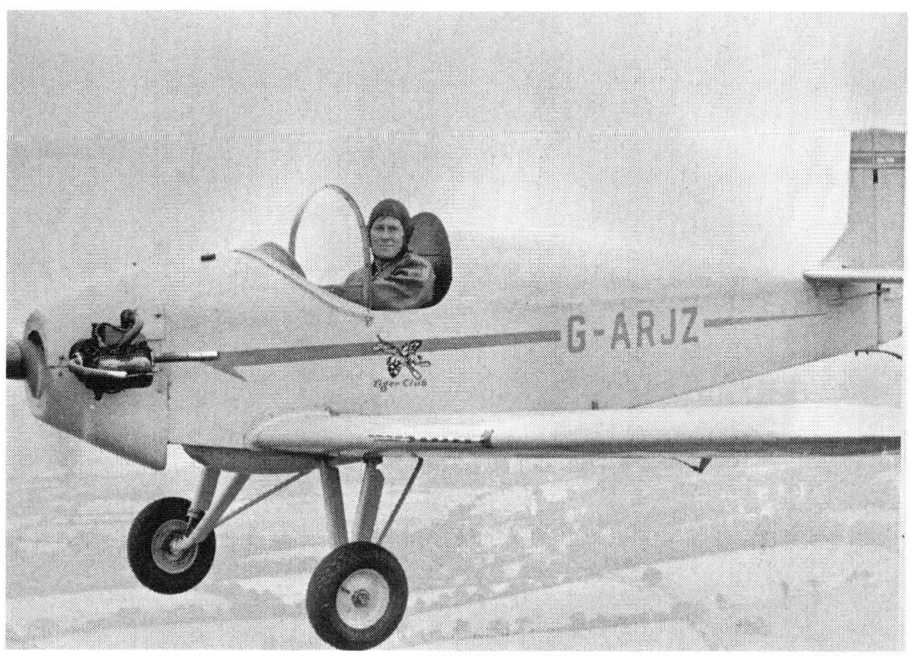

Formation practice (wearing father's 1939 Tiger Moth helmet).

Retrieving a lost Airways Aero Club student (not mine). A couple of counties adrift, but the right country – just. Nigel Minchin (B312s and Jodel ferry pilot) looks professional with his tie. The Terrier is facing into wind, unscathed – quite a good school.

A Conway-powered B707-436 at Heathrow in 1964. An agreeable machine of character. FK was destroyed in March 1977 by the British Airtours training department. What had happened to the Boeing test office advice – to be handed down over the generations?

Ringo's captain reassures two jumpers prior to the unexpected engine-failure emergency baleout over the horse hockey field. Such informality could cause distress (or worse) today.

A happy couple with the Tiger Club Fox Moth at an Old Warden.

Airways Aero Club formation.

1970. Carl Schofield shows the Gold Leaf Zlin, high in the sky.

Hullavington 1970. The end of a hard life for the Aerobatics International single-seater. Our hero bids farewell to his fallen mount. (Black and Schofield regret the damage to their competition hopes.)

UK team at Salon de Provence, 1972 Worlds. L to R: Riley, Black, Williams and Mitchell. Only Black made it to the final 4 minute free. The Salon newsletter had no trouble with his name, but reported the other three as Villimas, Mitchkill and Relay.

Official photo at Salon. Champion Charlie Hillard 3rd from right, back row. 7th from rt. is 1970 winner Igor Egorov; at his 6:30 is careful Swiss pilot Michel Brandt – later something big in Airbus. On his right are the Swiss 'terrible twins' Christian Schweizer and Eric Müller. Female champion Mary Gaffney is 2nd lady from left, front row.

1974 Biancotto team winners at Rochefort-sur-Mer.

All that's left of the training VC10 VM – a great flying club for the staff, tribulation for the learners.

The chocolate bomber doing something in North Africa.

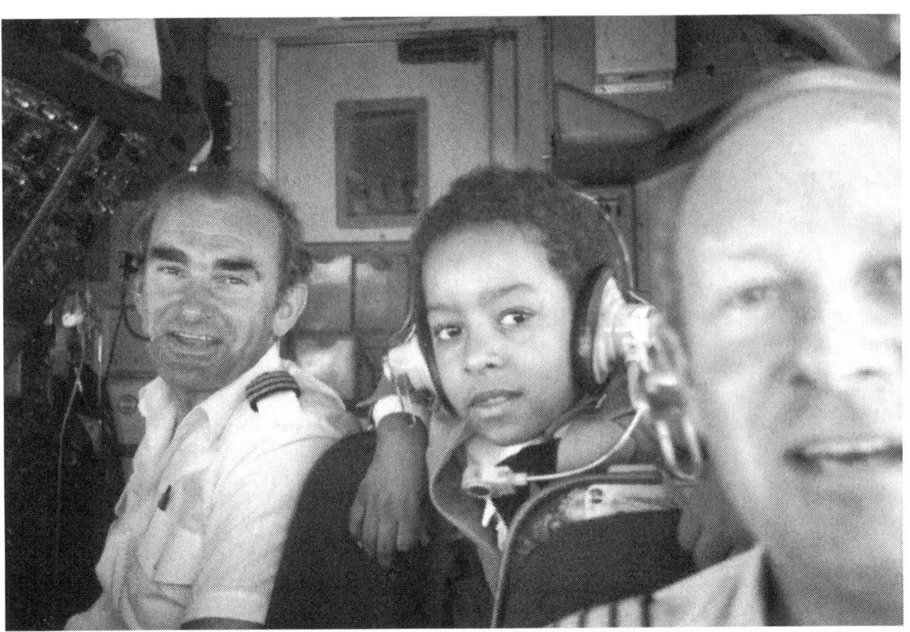

The first selfie. Olympic yachtsman John Neale at the panel assisted by a young Al Thani family member.

Air Mauritius team. Engineering manager Ranjit Appa 2nd left.
Chief Pilot Dominique (Luke Skywalker) Paturau 4 from right. Neale and Riley imposing London formality on the right.

A Concorde raising its nose at Barbados, the only sector in the repertoire where the correct flight profile was possible – throttles wide/barber's pole until Devon, 20 minutes to Mach 2 and 50,000ft (not bad for an airliner), and direct climb to 60,000ft here (tropical stratosphere).

Competing aircraft at a Lelystad contest. John Blake (judge) has the splendid moustache: with cap is Ian Groom (BIPO), next is Hendrik van Overvest. The contest director has the red jumper – irrepressible and multi-talented Frank Versteegh. Silver hair and scarf is Diana Britten (BLZZ).

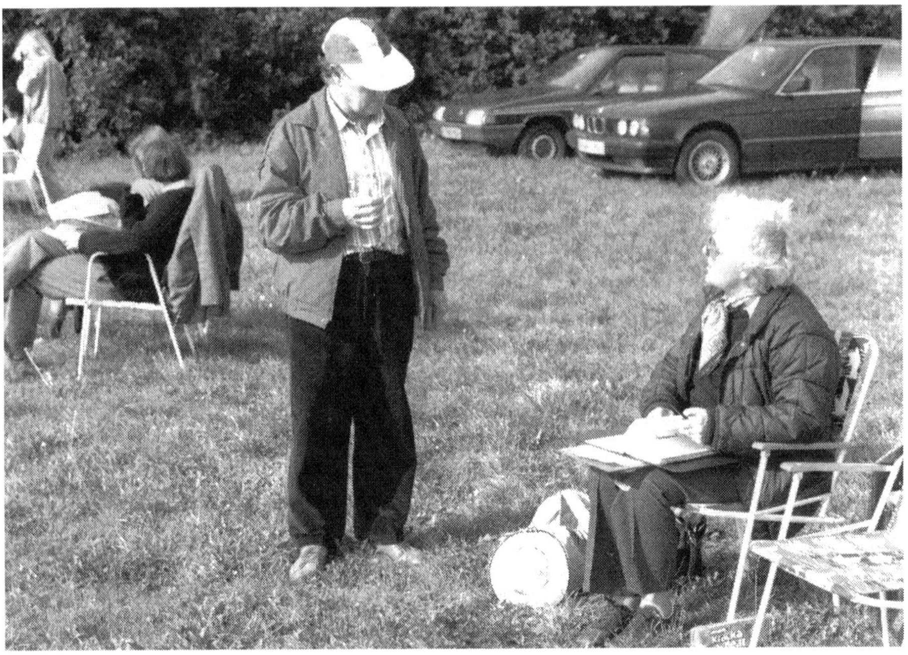

Judging setup somewhere in UK. Chief judge compares notes with assistant Iona Radice of GCHQ.

Concorde live training. Adopting an encouraging demeanour while watching Keith Barton turn finals at Machrihanish. All looks good in G-BOAG, but it was the very next day that my most dangerous flying situation occurred. Undercarriage downlock failure in a Mach 2 shape aircraft with no ejector seat. Picture *Tony Yule.*

Silver thing at top is the up/down hydraulic jack. Bigger device below has the downlock inside the grey thing (with red flag). It is not powered; when locked it provides all side bracing for the leg, but when unlocked it is not a rigid structure. A trigger warning explanation is not needed.

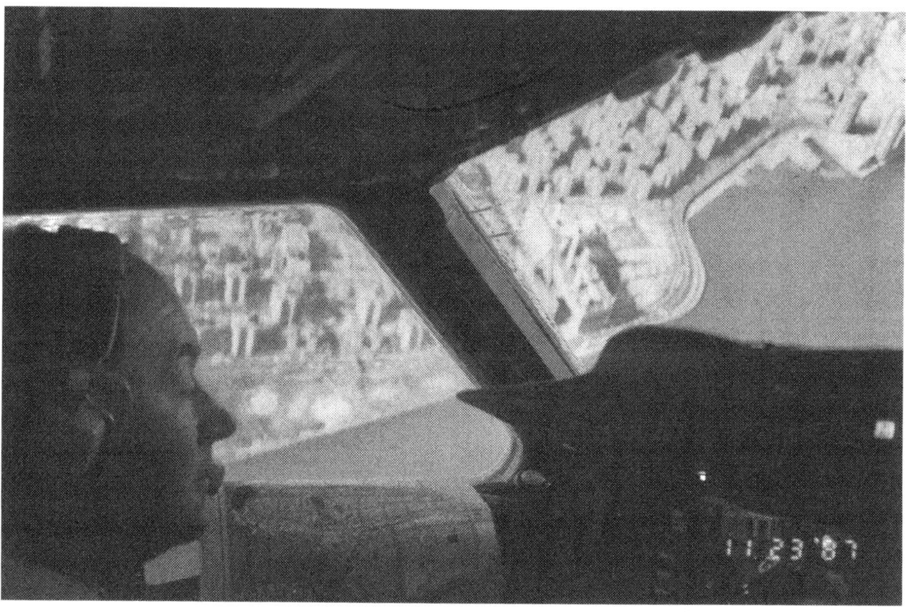

Hanging a left around the end of E11th Street. Con Ed power station just in front of window frame. United Nations coming up. Heading for a flypast of BA HQ USA party in Queens, further up the East River.

Cabin chief Peter Parmenter with his girls (ladies). Co-pilot Neil Rendall on right. The seafaring man is Captain Norman Britton, who retained his Scimitar *joie de vol* for the Concorde. This day he is the PR man, informing and enthusing our young student passengers.

A traditional Russian scene. A Sukhoi 26 landing at the team training base, Borki, near the Volga.

Maintenance day at Borki.

A visit to historic monastery town Zagorsk. now restored to Orthodox worshippers after 75 years. Nicolai Timofeev (nearest) and the Viktor Schmal family.

Irish pit stop. Louisa's Extra 300 at Abbeyshrule.

After her flight in Richard Goode's SU26. Louisa says Wow!

Flying for Randy Gagne's camera in Florida.

A bit of a devil to fly? No, that's the big silver one in the distance.

This is a unique picture. Never to be repeated. Vulcan pilot is Sqn Ldr David Thomas of the CFS. You can see the back of my Concorde seat. *Picture by Tony Yule, ex Vulcan pilot.*

Long time Concorde captain Colin Morris, at the controls with chart, looks across the Antonov bridge with a look of nautical authority, here in southern Germany. A well-known Sea Vixen pilot, Colin's clarity of explanation has made him a familiar television Concorde pundit.

Perfect crew coordination and versatility: captain (on the bonnet) checks the oil, first officer does the captain's checks. This is called CRM (cockpit resource management). In Bavaria, at Straubing on the Danube.

Squaring up for the Estergom grass, Hungary. Slovakian hills beyond, across the Danube.

This is a real picture. A Concorde on short finals at Barbados.

Co-pilot's panel at the moment of touchdown on 31L at New York (captain under supervision flying). Attitude similar to that for the approach (good), incidence has reduced to 11½ degrees at the nose (during ground effect). Up elevon has reached 5°. Perfect – what a good school!
Picture Tony Yule

Les Brodie demonstrates the above at the last Concorde landing – ever. Only 30 centimetres to go.

Zlin rebuilt

Still wearing its Czech registration OK-XRH Zlin Z-526 G-AWSH sits in the sun at White Waltham following its return from the Czech Republic.

My 1972 world championship Zlin, a quarter century later.

CHAPTER 19

1972 - THE NEXT WORLD CHAMPIONSHIP SCENE

By the beginning of 1972 I had bought some shares in Aerobatics International and was permitted to fly the cooking Zlin 526, WSH, albeit no longer competitive at world level. The previous owner had driven it into a Pennine stone wall, but, suitably written back on, it was a good machine. The company now purchased US champion Gene Soucy's custom-built Pitts S1-S, and it arrived in a large wooden box. This little machine, G-AZPH, was to have a varied and interesting life. It now hangs in the Science Museum, but was the closest to state-of-the-art aerobatic aeroplanes available at the time. It was also made clear that only two pilots, Neil Williams and James Black, would fly it, until the 1972 season was over.

The compact wire-braced biplane layout makes for a strong structure, and its ear-splitting practice sessions soon showed its potential in bone-crunching cornering, fast roll rate, vertical penetration and dazzling flick-rolling characteristics. I remembered Bob Herendeen's 1970 Pitts style. Not restrained exactly, but well-judged, cool and collected, and very successful at scoring points. When interviewed about his machine's performance he said 'If I need more power I just advance the throttle another inch'. Later this 1972 summer I was mesmerised when I happened to see a Pitts flying a small but perfectly flown and positioned routine at the Salon world championships. It was Bill

Thomas' first international appearance, and he flew exactly as he practised at home. I was astonished that he did not get the marks he deserved, but that's international judging for you – in many sports. But once the competitive spirit takes hold flying styles can change, especially if previous experience suggests to you that others give it loads of welly. Might as well practise like that.

This fixed-pitch Pitts would achieve maximum rpm in level flight – quite easily. Of course revs mean power, stored energy, and acceleration when you need it. I heard James mention to Neil 'If you don't throttle back it goes really well.' This was true, and to add to the sonic propeller tips was the sound of the howling wires. When the Pitts manoeuvres, the sharing of the flying loads on wing and tail bracing wires varies a lot, and the set of relaxed ones can be free to flutter. One could call it vibrate, and this effect can be reduced by tighter bracing; although, while this reduces the number of screams per minute, it raises the pitch of the notes and sense of drama. For hardcore aerobatic use, inordinately high tensions are required, very much like a Wimbledon competitor's racket. As in tennis, aerobatic points can be deducted if airborne misuse of equipment is adjudged. The term 'racket abuse' came to mind.

During the six months up to the July championships – between sessions of 747ing – I practised in the Zlin, starting where I had left off in 1970. The people at Shobdon airfield very obligingly allowed me and Bob Mitchell to fly over their field and this proved an excellent arrangement. Finding suitable airfield practice sites in Britain was turning out to be a big problem, especially when the neighbours realise that a single showoff flight is far from the agenda. 'You mean you're going to do it again? What for?' The motivations behind competition and display flying can be very different, and an Olympic quest for unattainable perfection has no end. This Herefordshire field's wide runway, built in WW2 for military glider training, had apple orchards on its south side, neatly aligned parallel to the runway, helping the relative beginners to refine their orientation and positioning. There were rural B&Bs nearby, and the agricultural hilly land on the Welsh Borders felt far from the home counties.

Ferry flights to and from the south-east took an hour or so, and, as I'd already found out with scheduled transits to and from air displays, the British summer weather seldom plays ball – in fact if you stick a pin in the calendar and fly 100 miles to somewhere in a simple VFR aeroplane at 8 on that morning, then back at 5pm the same day, it is seldom that weather will not become a problem somewhere along the route: you go as low as it takes, following line features when possible. This is such an individual pursuit that limits and techniques cannot be set, and there come times when flying in company becomes impractical, and the day's exploit may well have evaporated into every man for himself, in complete contrast to the team performance on stage. On a number of occasions, more often than not, I seem to remember, I have set off on the return to encounter the variety of effects of the inevitable Atlantic frontal depression crossing the country, and after miles of low visibility, living 'in the moment', have felt a sense of relieved achievement as the Redhill airfield boundary appeared and quickly went under the nose. I'll be the only one here, for sure – never again. But no, they're all there. How did they do it?

On Sunday June 18th I took the Zlin from Farnborough to Shobdon. There was no rush to start – low cloud and rain, wait for an improvement. This was slow in coming, and it never looked particularly promising, but after midday the rain stopped and a cloudbase of a few hundred feet was discernible. I'll give it a go, at least it's good enough to get back and land. At, let us say 500 ft, the visibility was not bad – under low cloud, but with very little rain – and I considered my chances. This will be a Bradshaw's trip until it clears up – Basingstoke, Reading, Oxford then the Worcester line. The rain increased towards Moreton-in-Marsh and increasingly close contact flying was required. The railway line is straight here, and the ground slowly rises as far as the west-facing Cotswold escarpment. There can come a time when salvation is a few miles ahead, and to leave the lifeline difficult. The rain got heavier, the cloud lower, and the rails, telegraph poles and bridges closer. This was not English rain – it had to stop soon. Fortunately the Zlin is a steady flyer, but, for maybe 30 seconds, the rain became tropical, deafening and all enveloping. This is bad, but don't flinch, let the Zlin do the flying. Then, in an instant, the rain stopped and moments later I emerged into clear air; the Vale of Evesham was spread out comfortably below, and a towering wall of sunlit cloud behind, reaching the ground. I'd flown through the cold front as it hesitated at the ridge. Phew, plain sailing to Shobdon. When I landed, one magneto was stone dead. Despite the various baffles and covers inside the cowling the rain had been strong enough to get to it and short it out, wires burnt. Don't they get rain in Czechoslovakia?

I remember this flight well because Trident PI crashed soon after take off at London a couple of hours later. It immediately occurred to me that they may well have met the same conditions that had continued further east. The sound of this rain, so heavy, immediately after takeoff, can be very distracting in an airliner cockpit. You may not be able to hear yourself think.

The UK team for the 7th FAI world championships consisted of Neil Williams and James Black with the Pitts, Bob Mitchell and his KZ8, and myself with the Zlin. Me and our engineering support, Trevor Davies, would lead, navigate etc. on the way to Salon. At the end of a long day we stopped at Lyon where my unfamiliarity (then) with daily mountain wind effects nearly assisted some damage to the Pitts and one or two of a choice of Dassault Mystères parked alongside the runway. The actual Lyon weather, checked before we left Dijon, was light from the south, and I considered it likely that it would be much the same when we got there. Lyon doesn't appear to be in the Alps, though they are not far away, and a straight in to the south looked inviting in what seemed and felt like a flat calm. It was getting late, the runway large, and the two followers had time and space to organise themselves behind on their respective sides of the generous runway. I landed in the middle and let the Zlin roll.

When we had parked I heard about the drama behind. It is true that mountain wind had just set in – tailwind – but this was not totally to blame. Williams, the second to land, had temporarily lost it after touchdown, swung to the side, straight for the Mystères. Brake and rudder contained the swing and, with squealing wheels, he scythed back to his own side to be overtaken by a flash of white – Bob's KZ8.

When we arrived at Salon the next day Curtis (Pa) Pitts ambled over to look over his creation. His first words were 'You boys must be faahn pilots to fly thet thung.' He was looking at the mini tailwheel and its slack bath plug chains hanging in generous loops. This was how it had come out of its box, but the spring-and-chain connections between rudder and tailwheel are supposed to be more direct than this, otherwise the demanding little beast could be considered uncontrollable on concrete. This feature was adjusted straight away, and both Pitts and Gene Soucy watched the high energy and noise practice flights with silent interest. After Williams' run Gene turned away and laconically said 'Some ace,' and Curtis Pitts declared 'He sure yoooses that airplane,' as the two walked off. It hadn't been quite what they expected, and it is difficult to say whether the attempt to unsettle the opposition had quite worked.

Charlie Hillard won the championship with a Pitts, and the next ten places were taken by a mixture of Pitts, Yaks, Akrostars and the top scoring Zlin Akrobat flown by Jiri Kobrle (9th). James Black did well to come 12th, and Neil Williams was 6th in known and unknown programmes, but for some reason the Aresti free let him down (45th) and he just failed to make the cut for the final four-minute free, finishing 23rd overall. I had the only off-the-shelf trainer there, and the lowest power to weight ratio, giving rise to comments like 'small pilot, small engine' and 'he used to be six foot before he did aerobatics'. My default ambition was not to come last, but 43rd out of 59 overall was not too bad for a first go, though it felt disappointing at the time, but the Swiss Akrostar twins Schweizer and Müller, both top ten finishers, were complimentary about my careful coaxing and cajoling. One of them flew the cooking Zlin in 1970 – 'We know how difficult it is'.

Nick Turvey of South Africa came last, but not through want of skill or trying. The Soviet Union was courting African countries at the time under the guise of support for downtrodden proletarian peoples, and were building world support for sanction of the South African National Party government. This had not come into effect yet, but as the 1972 worlds approached there did not appear to be a competitive aircraft available in South Africa. Then, with not much time left, Nick got an unexpected phone call from Professor Reid: 'The Rooivalk (Red Falcon) is finished, come and try it.' Since the late 1960s the engineering faculty of Natal University had been working on their own project to design and build an original South African aerobatic biplane, and Nick rushed down to the coast to check it out. Preparation time for the worlds was pressing and he took off with a simple agenda. 'If I can get it round the known compulsory, we'll take it.'

It could, just, with some difficulties and a lot of strength. During the sequence, a good height over the sea, he was pushing round a negative manoeuvre with both hands when the stick shook violently and became immovable. He pushed harder and it freed with a bang. After landing it was evident that the trim tab had first fluttered, then broken off. He told me of other built-in problems. The professor had given the wheels a tad of toe in, like a car. A taildragger usually needs some toe out. Nick said it was very difficult to taxi. There was another interesting novelty. The design team had included the electrically controlled reverse pitch propeller available with its Continental engine, with the idea that reverse thrust while descending might give more time to fit in the manoeuvre components. Nick soon found a serious problem. When throttled back the propeller would sometimes go into reverse pitch of its own accord, and start freewheeling backwards. There was no way out of this, so the flight was over, with not even flight idle available to help the runout slalom. The Lycoming engine has proved popular for aerobatic aircraft, and one of the South Africans wrote that using a Continental for industrial-strength sport was like wearing your treasured gold Rolex while slugging it out with Mike Tyson.

I saw the Rooivalk prior to its trip to France. It looked a bit like a Stampe, with round section cables for flying wires, as opposed to other biplanes' streamlined rods, and bicycle cranks and pedals for the rudder. I don't remember seeing anything in the way of brakes. Like a Harvard there was no floor under the pilot, as such, but there was the luxury of see-through perspex on the bottom of the fuselage. Some of the sheet metal work had a tinsnip DIY look to it, but the professor had not skimped on strength – or drag. It needed its largeish engine, and the reversing system was not required.

A few members of the South African aerobatic community flew it in anticipation of the upcoming worlds, but only Nick and Scully Levin could get it round the figures. It was finally decided that Nick alone would fly it at Salon. Scully was part of the support team who helped manhandle it out into open country. It certainly got some interest initially, and there was no mistaking the strange Whoo, Whooing noise it made, mainly, I think, caused by the drag of the wires. It sort of got round the figures, but could not achieve the speeds to create long enough lines, and the scores suffered accordingly. The work required by its pilot became recognised, and American 30s hot dogger Mike Murphy was heard to shout 'Ma arm's achin' for ya, boy!' from the judging area.

However, when one considers that unlimited aerobatic aircraft have very specialised requirements, and many of the handling features assumed to be desirable for conventional machines are in fact a hindrance, the fact that a university faculty with little experience of the sport could make an aeroplane which would get round the manoeuvres and not come apart was a significant achievement, and much of the ribaldry it attracted was from the same people who were afraid to be the first to stop applauding their political leaders – so what did they really think? We shall never know; nor did they.

After the contest Joe Hössl asked me if I would like to try his Akrostar. Of course I would. Joe was a tall, thin, aristocratic-looking German who had flown a Zlin at Hullavington in 1970 and was something to do with the vintage Klemm flown by Manfred Strössenreuther. (Curtis Pitts had trouble with Manfred's name, and when I visited Homestead next year Pa Pitts was puzzling over a fax from Manfred who had ordered an aircraft. 'This Roto-Rooter fellow...') Nick Turvey also told of an airshow act done by Joe and the elegant slender Klemm. 'He had a wire on a wing tip, would pick a handkerchief up off the grass with it, pull up into a stall turn (towards the hanky) so it fell off, then zap it with the prop.'

Joe had a sophisticated German's wry sense of humour. One hot afternoon I was due to fly soon, but there were holdups. I strapped in inside the hangar, to be pushed out ready to start; then there was a hold up: back into the shade again. Joe shouted across the concrete 'That is why we lost the war – always into the hangar, out of the hangar!' Almost Monty Python.

I'm not sure if he was joking when he told me how to do the vertical S with the Akrostar. This was the final figure in the first sequence and only possible with state-of-the-art machines; In the Zlin I could only go for broke with what height was left after the penultimate manoeuvre, and then do what was possible. Vne and 6g enabled a brave gesture at the figure, and my early change of direction in the middle, 20 short of the horizontal, was obvious but rewarded by a generous 6 out of 10. 'You came booming over the top' said the South Africans, very supportive of courageous Zlin underdogs. As a dedicated unlimited competition machine the Akrostar would manoeuvre positive and negative with equal ability, helped considerably by the linked elevator and flap system. Joe said go to Vne and pull 11g. I didn't pull all of the 11g, but he was right, the aerobatic machine was good at manoeuvring, and the S was not a problem. Above 2g, or thereabouts, the stick force per g levelled off, giving the impression of being in a cunning reality simulator.

The flight back to England was another long day. We landed at Reims for fuel, and set off again, conscious of the inevitable deteriorating weather to the north. A few minutes after takeoff the Reims controller said something. What did he mean? Then he asked 'How many aircraft do you have in your formation?' Three, I said. '*Pas vrai!*' I looked around, no KZ8. 'One has come back.' I started to turn and Williams continued north in disgust. Bob's KZ8 engine was a Gypsy Major with a Zlin carburettor for negative flight, but a somewhat modified one with a history of soldering, drilling, tweaking, to get it to work. During the contest it had given increasing trouble, faltering especially in vertical climbs, just when you need it. 'It's had it,' said Bob. 'I'll leave it here, can you take me to Le Bourget?' Two hours later I picked up Trevor from Reims and we set off again for Ashford by ourselves. Low cloudbase, drizzle again, getting dark. It was night when we left Ashford, and even more night when we got to a totally unlighted Farnborough. Local knowledge helps when it comes to estimating where the runways are. No more touring for me. Too bad for the nerves!

A couple of aerobatic firsts in September punctuated the routine of 747 trips. On the 7th I was asked to do a display in a RF4 aeroplane at a fete at Bucks Green, a village near Gatwick. This was a late request, probably a phone call the night before. I had never flown an RF4, but the task was simple. 'Just do some basic stuff, it's easy to fly.' The RF4 is a single-seat powered glider type of thing, capable of hill soaring or thermalling on a good day, powered by the familiar Beetle engine. I had a practice flight on the Saturday morning at Redhill. It was nice to fly, did simple manoeuvres well enough and the slender wings used little height if flown with discretion. Of course it had no inverted fuel system and it was clear the small propeller had little momentum, so I practised a few almost stall turning manoeuvres to find what avoided the float chamber limit. On the right was a handle to pull the engine over a compression to get it going in the air after deliberate dead-stick soaring.

I cobbled up a suitable sequence and set off for the venue that afternoon. It was a smallish field in the woods, and landing was not part of the show. The first few manoeuvres went well and I got to the stall turn, and forgot all about my preparations; I was a competition pilot on show now. The instant the fuselage reached the vertical the engine stopped dead, and I was looking at a stationary propeller. Too low to find out how much dive it would need, but there's the handle. I reached for it, but my arm was not long enough – I was strapped in for aerobatics, and this Scandinavian machine made for lanky pilots. Fortunately the right shoulder strap was easy to loosen: the first pull turned the engine over a compression but it did not fire – the second a millisecond later was successful. To hell with the shoulder straps, the show must go on – maybe no one noticed, or thought the stopping and starting was a part of it. There are some simple messages in here about familiarity with everything in the cockpit, and the scout's motto. I'd looked at this handle, but was not inclined to play with it because I did not expect it to feature in the mission. But you never know.

Another limit found

September 30th 1972 was my first chance to fly the Pitts, after the end of the airshow and contest season. It was a Sunday morning and I was rostered to go to Nairobi in a 747 that night, so a reasonably short getting-to-know-you flight would be sensible. It turned out to be shorter than planned – but that was nothing to do with me. Strapped in tight for aerobatics, I took off towards the east at Farnborough, and made a lazy left turn to pick up the Basingstoke railway line that would take me a few miles west to open country. Performance and operating figures were strictly classified, privy to our two senior pilots who had flown the aeroplane that summer, but I wasn't expecting a problem that would have challenged a Tiger Moth on this flight of discovery. After perhaps 4 minutes, and agreeably impressed with the briskness and ease of the three-point takeoff and preciseness of the controls, I had just reached the edge of open country and, encouraged by the little aeroplane's manoeuvrability and obvious reserves of power, decided to advance the throttle an inch, cool as Herendeen, and pull up into a lazy loop so as to look around and decide where to go for further investigations. Coming round the back of the loop I returned the throttle to a modest position and rolled a few degrees to the left, towards the best-looking area; all very gentle stuff. Then, twenty or so degrees short of level flight, something gave a jolt, and the engine made a completely different sound. After having followed an exceptionally smooth-running Lycoming I found myself sat behind an erratic two-stroke lawnmower, two and four stroking in a random manner. Something had happened – but what?

Altitude 2500ft. Fuel and oil pressures good. RPM needle vibrating wildly. A modest nose down gliding attitude produced 110mph (published stall +50) and the flying behavioiur felt good. Below me were two small grass fields. A five-barred gate looked to be the weakest link between them if the landing got that far. I turned left to set up a circuit. Ahead of me passed the airfield, about five miles away. Surely the engine would help me reach it? A couple of seconds could be spared to fiddle with the engine controls. Left or right magneto – no change. Throttle open – no change. Throttle closed – instant silence from the front. The gliding performance remained obvious and quite serious, and I was now committed to my first field, thankful it was underneath to start with. After 180 degrees of turn I was over my 1000ft point, close in and abeam the touchdown area, looking down at about 35 degrees.

We teach students to land one third of the way into the field. This one wasn't big enough for that – it would have to be down in the first few feet, and then through the (closed) five bar gate at the opposite side, maybe, if the landing got that far. Slicing diagonally across the bottom corner of the field was a line of high-tension cables and pylons – these were large and I would have to turn inside them. This was not really a problem because the angle and rate of descent were becoming increasingly apparent; it was obvious that the little plummeting beast in which I was confined had only one diving 180 left in it – more like an attack than an approach to land. I was glad I'd tried to teach this stuff – it really works. Even so, the last bit seemed tremendously fast, especially sideslipping inside the wires. No seeing things in slow motion today.

As I crossed the wooded hedge with inches to spare, straightened up and started to flare in response to the grass coming up, things couldn't have looked better, and I could now see that the field went gently uphill – I was going to get away with it; hurrah. But the grass never stopped coming up. Stick all the way back just raised the nose to horizontal – the last speed I saw was 90 mph – and the aeroplane pressed itself on to the field as if leant on by a giant hand. I felt no sensation of touching down; just saw plenty of green between the nose and the top wing as the landing slide went from belly to nose to top wing and fin.

I was completely unhurt, and the aeroplane was rocking gently on its uppermost surface. It was six minutes since I had taken off and one minute since something broke – if something did break. I was in no rush to get out – all in good time. I was more interested in getting my story straight. What did I do? Can it be that I'd assumed that this machine was so simple that I had overlooked something basic and vital?

I looked around the cockpit for the mystery control. A self-destruct button, perhaps. I couldn't find one so I slid gracefully out (I'd done this before) and surveyed the damage. Top of the fin bent; fuselage a bit bent around the undercarriage; cowlings a bit bent; no propeller. I spotted it 100 feet downrange beyond the tail. It was almost unbent and was still bolted to the crankshaft flange. The inside of what was left of this part was chamfered and smeared, 'graunched' would cover it. Back to the aeroplane and I saw that where the propeller flange used to be the metalwork there was also chamfered and smeared.

I went to Nairobi that night but didn't mention the Pitts to my airline colleagues – no common ground. The next day we went to Johannesburg and that evening I was at a party for some visiting American fly-yourself clients of AVEXAIR at Mike and Jeanette Van Ginkel's house. After two drinks I suddenly threw up, fortunately not over anyone, but unexpected, even so.

'Delayed shock,' said Nick Turvey, a veteran of many exciting flights. I'm sure he was right. In my mind I had already run through a number of alternative possibilities. What if the propeller had gone forward in flight and then hit me? No parachute. What if I had landed successfully and the propeller had gone underneath the aeroplane? Could have been nasty. All in all the details of the landing could not have been more fortunate, and the aircraft was not seriously damaged. I had been extremely lucky.

The Lycoming crankshaft flange that drives the propeller has lightening holes in it, suitable for a Cherokee, but the rapid cyclic overloading of this part caused by certain popular Pitts manoeuvres combined with over-the-limit rpm wears the metal out: cracks develop, and eventually the propeller will come off. This was known about at the time, and you could look for the first signs of cracking – grey dust on an exploratory finger – but we were not aware of this, or any history of Pitts behaviour with a free propeller. Apparently this accessory had previously flown away in America – a much better gliding option. I think this was the first time a propeller had stayed on the front – freewheeling. This provides extra drag, blanks some of the wings and the tailplane, thus reducing lift and control power. A different crankshaft and periodic checks for cracks were instigated by the EAA (Experimental Aircraft Association), but, as we had little truck with colonial cowboys this intelligence had not filtered across the

Atlantic yet. I can assure readers that a free or runaway fine pitch propeller (not an engine failure) on any aircraft can be a major problem, but even your simple fixed pitch treasure could suddenly resemble a brick more than usual.

The only comment I could get out of Neil Williams was 'I'm glad it didn't happen to me.' I think he meant it. After all, it so nearly did – but not after only five minutes on type. He also said 'too slow'. Easy to say after someone else has done the research. Another 20 mph might have done it, but that's quite fast for a teenie biplane spot landing in a small farmer's field (Vref = stall x 2)

If you are determined to seek the ultimate limit, you are sure to find it sooner or later. It was by chance that I found this one, though that was not my intention, and the Accident Investigations man who phoned me sometime later and pointed out the fatigue problems of repeated overstress was wasting his breath. I didn't point out that I had only flown this machine for six minutes, but the problem of sharing aeroplanes with other people is well understood, and many high energy circles take special care to preempt disaster before the ultimate limits are found. Williams had already demonstrated the Zlin mainspar limit in the presence of others, despite the common knowledge that the Czechs usually gave their used machines to lower order clubs before this happened. There would be more structural failures with something in common, but Williams was to find his own ultimate limit in 1977 – a touring one, of all things. As low as it takes has its own ground rules.

CHAPTER 20

1972-1975 – THE FINAL YEARS AS A CO-PILOT

By the end of 1972 the 747 had satisfactorily taken over a significant proportion of much of BOAC's worldwide route structure, first establishing itself between major destinations, leaving the 707 and VC10 to continue with less frequent and lower capacity services. To start with, the level of flight deck 747 experience varied greatly, in relative terms, and the few early course members became the old hands after a whole year's operating, but the aircraft's practicality and user-friendliness enabled a steady flow of crew members from both traditional fleets to make a seamless transition on to the 747, and a number of new ex-military flight engineers slotted in as if to the manner born. The few PXs (brand new cruise-only co-pilots) also seemed to cope without problem.

Perhaps one could attribute this problem-free transition to a magical improvement in the airline's training, supervising, mentoring etc., but I think there were other reasons. After 15 years of the real jet age BOAC was experiencing, eventually, something of a post-war coming-of-age. The 747 represented better equipment for the job, and it came with a comprehensive set of instructions which were difficult to argue with. The assumption that 'British is best' per se, was reluctantly fading, as was the enthusiasm for ordering non-standard (nun-standard, perhaps) British parts as a little flag-waving gesture – and a politically motivated fillip to the home industry. It was fairly obvious that buying an off-the-shelf machine, such as a 747, to participate in the world's airline structure in the 1970s made financial sense, and the crew's task was not as challenging as getting a B17 from America to Prestwick in 1943, nor, indeed, conducting a bomber from Norfolk to Germany and back on a frequent night-time roster (without considering the additional challenge of German attempts to interrupt the service). Times had changed a lot in 20 years. Some individuals had difficulty in acknowledging this, but most of our 747 captains of this time, whether battle-scarred (only slightly sometimes) or national service Meteor survivors, suddenly became relaxed and easy-going commanders of our three-man crew. It was obvious that a standard way to do things was the easiest. Why make it more difficult for yourself? Good communications, automatic navigation and tons of fuel lower the worry factor.

Once the fleet build-up had quieted down the single co-pilot got a very good share of the flying, and, if my memory serves me right, oddball captaining seemed to be becoming a thing of the past, in general. If asked to comment on technical problems in these early days, engines, and sometimes takeoff performance, are the subjects that come to mind. An ideal engine produces a lot of power for takeoff, and also cruises very economically. These are the same conflicting requirements that apply to a car with tyre-smoking acceleration, but impressive mpg: higher compression ratios and a comprehensive gear box work for the car – and the jet engine, another internal combustion engine, is similar. The ubiquitous Avon engine's automatic 2 position inlet guide vanes was an early example of a gear-changing principle, then came the twin-spool idea which allowed the two parts of the engine to find their own speeds to suit the required conditions. But the notion of including a propeller in there somewhere was not long in coming – first with a compressor bypass stage or the turbine turbofan, but then came the fan at the front: a kind of fast, fixed-pitch propeller, as first seen in BOAC as an oversize compressor stage on the 707-336 Pratt & Whitney JT3D engine. The 747's much larger JT9 concept was a relatively small but harder-working jet driving a much bigger visible fan at the very front. The harder-working jet idea means more compression and a more critical airflow behaviour inside the engine, and to enable this device to cover all power settings a number of bleed valves were required to spill undigestible air when required. The touching-the-sides problem had been solved, but these bleeds sometimes got out of kilter and this would lead to unexpected thumps, or give rise to the wrong relationship between the two freely rotating parts of the engine, without any other sign of distress. In this case a shutdown was called for. Odd things related to the fuel control unit could also happen, but by the time I left the fleet in 1975 747 technical problems were few and far between.

Takeoff performance was sometimes puzzling. All multi-engined commercial aircraft are supposed to be able to leave the ground and fly away if an engine fails approximately halfway down the runway. Not as well as with everything working, of course, but well enough. But some of the 747 takeoffs, with everything working, did not give the impression that one could have relied upon this fundamental assumption. Nairobi was a case in point. The return flight to London took off in pitch dark, with only the runway lights and the machine's own headlamps, such as they were, to indicate how much runway was left. When the spiky long grass appeared you knew the end was very nigh. Sometimes, with all evidence correct, the wheels appeared to leave the ground just as the end of the runway zoomed underneath. On other occasions, with similar statistics, things looked more comfortable. How could this be? Did our flight engineers always give us exactly the correct thrust? It always looked like it. Did the tower man help us with optimistic weather numbers? Maybe, maybe not. Was the total weight what the load sheet said? This is an interesting one, and is my vote for the not infrequent dodgy-looking takeoffs. I've since heard that traffic staff found it difficult to believe that the load mattered much to such a large aircraft – of course it can fly; it's so big. Fill it up. And what about all those people of all shapes and sizes, wardrobe suitcases and comprehensive carry-ons? The equatorial world has nomadic traditions and travelling with everything you own is often assumed – of course you need the kitchen sink. Was there plenty of thick-pencilling with the freight weights? I've no idea, but there were some variables in there somewhere. I've since made critical takeoffs with the P&W 707. They had grown older than in the 1960s, but the non-critical attempts stayed non-critical.

These four 747 years were generally busier than the Comet/707 days, or they seemed like it, but there was still time for continued assorted sporting flying. I see that on June 18th 1974 I next flew the Pitts after its fairly lengthy repair (cosmetic enough for light aircraft standards). One specially reassuring factor was the new crankshaft, without lightening holes, and I see that I made a couple of 30-minute aerobatic practices on that day – more than one loop anyway. But a few days earlier I had accepted a day out that was informative and not totally easy. James Black, our Aerobatics International boss, had phoned and said 'You like flying the Zlin – would you like to do a show at Humberside in a 326?' I said all right, and though I had not flown one before, I knew that it was the same as a 526 – except that it had a wooden propeller and the pilot sat in the front instead of the back, the latter machine's metal propeller making sufficient difference to the weight distribution.

Before continuing the story it is worth mentioning that the later Zlins' self-managing variable pitch propeller made a huge difference to this aeroplane's performance, as I was soon to find out. It is a clever idea, a simple bolt-on fit with no pilot control. It senses airspeed and sets the pitch accordingly, so that, once in the air, full throttle will achieve maximum revs or thereabouts; in other words, it behaves like the ideal fixed-pitch propeller at any speed. But this 326 didn't have one. I went to pick the machine up from Thruxton on the day of the display, and discovered that the owner was coming along too. Off we set and got to Kirmington in 1hr 30. Like the RF4 sortie I planned an easy and progressive routine which would be on-the-hoof familiarisation as well as an elegant if boring performance. The owner wanted to come along for this ride as well. I said no, and wondered what (if anything) had been agreed with our management. After a few simple manoeuvres to get started, and somehow get the measure of the wooden paddles in front, I could understand where the Czech Vne+100 tradition might have come from (Vne – never exceed). At least the engine kept going all the time, but this historic and craftsmanlike propeller should have been gracing a pub wall. A Chipmunk would have given this Zlin a run for its money at subsonic speeds. One can safely say that the toughest Czech learner would have been unlikely to overspeed the engine. Could he have done a Williams with the wings? Given time, yes.

The logbook tells me that I also took part in a Stampe formation aerobatic routine at this display. I have no recollection of this, and assume that all went well for this reason. On the way back to Thruxton we encountered the routine summer frontal progress – lowering cloud and rain. The cloud got low enough by Oxford that I landed to wait. It must have been six in the evening. There was no improvement, so I suggested that today's flying was over, at which the owner was disappointed – however he was reluctant to take his pride and joy onwards by himself, so we got a taxi to the station and continued by rail. A long day, but one lives and learns. Never again – again.

CHAPTER 21

THE 1974 EUROPEAN CHAMPIONSHIPS

There was to be no two year world championships in 1974 – the Poles had elected to host it, but couldn't manage to do so – so the Biancotto Trophy as a European Championships became a sort of ersatz FAI world event – all the major players would be there except the Americans, but on a reduced scale: three pilots total per team instead of five each of men and women. There were six weeks in which to practise and, between 747 trips, I flew the Pitts over the Buckinghamshire countryside, and at Enstone airfield. At the end of July we set off for Rochefort-sur-Mer, Williams flying the Pitts and James Black and me in his Citroen – and very fast it was in its home country with a pilot at the wheel.

Rochefort is a historic shipbuilding town not far from La Rochelle, and its large grass airfield had been in use since 1916, when the authorities decided that airships were too dangerous to fly over land and restricted them to the navy. This military base was now the engineering trades school along with the usual aviation facilities, but what made it even better for a large competition was the food in the NCOs' mess. Every lunch and dinner was quite delicious, without fail, accompanied, of course, by the huge flagons of water and wine in a minimum of three colours (not the water). This was not haute cuisine, as such – not silly menus – it was the standard of ingredients, preparation and cooking that exemplified what French (and Italian) grandmothers used to do:

totally delicious every time, whatever it was. Was Rochefort home to the air force cheffing school as well? If you want to look forward to every meal join the French Air Force – as a mechanic.

Though the teams were small there were plenty of big names in evidence, in fact the list of starters could have been a world contest minus the non-European Americans. This gave us something of an advantage, because our one Pitts was the only example there. Two years previously the USA had done spectacularly well at Salon-de-Provence with this type, so judging expectations were already primed. Compared with elegant and easily critiqued monoplanes the Pitts' impression of energy, bounciness and enthusiasm, combined with its compact appearance, fast roll rate and dazzling flick rolling behaviour suggested confident competence, and the fact that it was not so easy to see the detail was an advantage to a middle order pilot. This Pitts halo effect served us well, and though my two colleagues were much more experienced than me, both in world level contests, and flying the Pitts (as I had found out two years before), a good apprenticeship helps, and the flying tennis racket was much easier to get round the standard stuff than in the Zlin.

I think I had a bit of judging luck in the third programme, the Aresti free. A wall-to-wall line of purple cloud had started to form offshore in the Bay of Biscay on this humid afternoon, and by the time of my group 3 flight it had appeared to grow as it moved steadily closer. Lightning became clearly visible and I wondered how close it would get as I climbed into position. It was clear that I would not be enveloped during the few minutes the 20 or so figures would take, so I fired in and pressed on regardless. I was the last flight that afternoon, and observers commented on the dramatic theatre of this little aeroplane battling gamely against nature's ever more threatening black and purple backdrop, with impressive and growing special effects, the retina-searing lightning flashes. 'There was something of destiny about the occasion, something primeval, portentous (and so on)' someone said.

Were the judges able to tot up all my 5 errors, and other misdemeanours? Not as well as usual, I suspect, and this visual drama of man and his puny machine set against the approaching and ineffable forces of nature writ large might have encouraged them to give me the odd benefit of doubt. After this third programme had been completed a competitor said 'Congratulations, you've won'. The contest had not finished yet, there was another programme to go, how could we have won? 'You're the only team with all three in the final'. What had happened to the others?

The home team had started at a great disadvantage because of current problems with their CAP 20 single-seat contest machines. All that was available to them was the CAP 10 trainer and they did their best with equipment that was uncompetitive at this level. The Russians had a similar team makeup to ourselves with two experienced stars, Viktor Letsko and Liubov Nemkova, plus a newcomer whose name I don't remember. I seem to remember that he started well enough, but got things wrong as the contest progressed. I am not aware of what happened next but his name and scores are not recorded. The Swiss started with a strong team – Eric Müller, Christian Schweizer and Michel Brandt, household names. I was once present when Christian made an unfortunate mistake, and I think this was the event.

Each formal programme must be flown in a specified direction related to that of the wind. This applies even if there is no wind – an into-wind direction is declared. For some reason Christian and his Akrostar stormed through the known compulsory (first) sequence in great style, but in the wrong direction. Everyone could see this error, and there was no doubt. There are no sympathy marks – any figure flown in the wrong direction scores badly – *null point* in fact. After landing and discovering the disaster Christian headed for the billet, collected his stuff, tanked up the Akrostar and immediately took off for Switzerland in a state of disgust, anger, embarrassment, shame, high dudgeon (write your own list if you wish). Which combination of these we'll never know, but there was no pilot there who did not privately sympathise: it only takes one teeny mistake to spoil your whole day – sometimes rules have to be rules.

A number of nations were represented by only two pilots. There were five from all-Germany, two from the West, and three from the East, including a world champion, Erwin Bläske, good pilot Manfred Jürk, and another Zlin 526 Akrobat pilot. I asked Manfred how their system worked, how much did it cost to fly in East Berlin? 'It's the same as joining the football club. You pay 12s 6d (60p) a year to belong, then you can practise as much as you like, over the field, just outside town – free of charge.'

The final consisted of the current four-minute do-what-you-like show. Like some of the others, I'm sure, I had nothing prepared for this flight because of the limited training time available, and the relative importance of the formal manoeuvring that was required in order to reach it. I cobbled up a simple programme that would fill out the time, and could be cast-iron safe; in fact, excepting my conservative Pitts additions, Barry Tempest would have made it look better in a Tiger Moth. I started with something different, intriguing, and very time-consuming. I pottered in and made a vanilla loop. This is so banal and unusual a figure at this level that I hoped that the questioning mind might wonder what was coming next – how creative. The first loop continued into a second with a flick roll at the top – an avalanche. Then I continued on the same theme: yes, you've guessed it – two flick rolls at the top of the next one. Did I do three? Very possibly, although these were not the punishing, flange-melting affairs that had challenged the previous crankshaft; in the fact the low-airspeed tumbly things that could be achieved during a zero g, top-of-the-loop parabola might be rather attractive, I thought. I have no recollection of what else I included to pad out the four minutes, but returned to earth without punishing the equipment or attracting the risk of disqualification – and with some more marks; however few didn't matter.

As I prepared to leave our machine for the next challenger, Manfred Jürk's protégé approached and asked Manfred about my performance. 'Dolles Program', said Manfred. He was not wrong, even though he would have suspected that I did not understand German. As dolles as I could make it, I thought – but it's not my day job, and I'm still in.

The cut for this final had included the top 10 scorers, and James Black was leading we three UK qualifiers. Something had let Williams down (by his own standards) during one of the foregoing flights, and he was keen to rectify the situation with this last chance air display flight. Neil's name was already engraved on the Biancotto trophy which he had won in 1967. He had a spectacular and ambitious programme planned, but seemed rather preoccupied on the day. Lack of practice due to the Pitts rebuild time since 1972 may have been one reason, and the presence of a BBC team keen to feature us in a film called *Plane Crazy* may have been another, especially for a celebrity. As individuals the TV team had no intention of making a nuisance of themselves, and were unobtrusive, diplomatic and polite, but filmmaking does require some proximity to the action, and some inclusion of banal and trivial detail for a balanced picture of this difficult way of life. As I had lifted off for my first contest flight a few days before, something blue hove up alongside, rather in the manner of an already airborne Edwards chase observing the maiden flight of an unpredictable prototype. It was the French Aerobatic Association's Max Holste Broussard carrying the BBC team, aided and abetted by the enthusiastic retired French general who was a figurehead of this Association. As a good citizen patriot he not only supported his own nation, but was keen to foster friendly relations with the many friends of France – and give a good impression of French preparedness to accommodate requests where possible. He even surprised the younger members of the Russian delegation one evening at a major event by starting a community rendition of a Russian patriotic song. Had he learnt his Russian as a Free French pilot flying the Yak 3?

But tradition assumes that a contest pilot has the aerobatic performance zone to himself and his thoughts. The runway ran close alongside the side of this box, so this camera ship may technically been outside it, but a brief word of warning might have been nice – the billion cubic metre arena does not have chicken wire around it like a giant tennis court – but I'm sure the general was doing his best to help out with some *entente cordiale*. I got some speed up and pulled pointedly upwards and away. This disapproving gesture made it to the film.

Neil's five-minute free programme flight (Group 4 it might be called) took place several after mine, because he gave me the task of repeated checks on the local wind information, up to 1000 metres. Rochefort is by the sea, so some sea breeze effect may likely develop during the daytime, perhaps differing in direction with the wind above. Positioning the performance as it went along might clearly be an issue, but it is usually not possible to see the wind up there from the ground, just by looking. You find this out when in the air. I did my best, and made several visits to the organising office to find out the latest figures, but requests for extra weather balloon launches over and above the two-a-day norm were not sympathetically received, especially on a nice summer's day on the Biscay coast. There was not much wind, especially if 200 mph airspeed was well on the cards. Why was he so preoccupied with this distraction?

Elizabethan Britons were familiar with the 'All's well that ends well' concept, and orchestral professionals also have a 'start together, finish together – what happens in the middle doesn't matter' saying. This is not always true, but it will do for the general public. Williams' plan started with a monumental up and down vertical figure, and finished with a snappy Pitts-only manoeuvre directed straight at the judges. I had a rough idea of what was supposed to happen in the middle, though I do not remember it now, but I remember the end well. The opening attention-getter he called Idi Amin, in honour of the Ugandan president, the man who would be King of Wales (or was it Scotland?). It started with a maximum energy vertical ascent, with a variety of things on it, and then a similar extensive downward return, with more attachments. He also called it a totem pole. Did it go well? I can't be sure of this, and had the impression that the exit energy was taking the machine in the wrong direction. I certainly remember sensing that the remaining minutes were a frantic effort to keep the action going while regaining position for the finish, and somehow the expected impression of structure and precision were missing. The final figure was correctly timed and lined up, however: straight across the box towards the judges – a bit low maybe. The machine rolled smartly to its straight and level knife edge position as it raced towards us, then made its snap roll, but not exactly by the planned one and a half rotations – more like one and three eighths, finishing betwixt wings level and the required opposing knife edge. Held for a second, the novel one eighth position returned briskly to the wings level at the four-minute point as the angry bumblebee sped over our heads and out of the performance zone.

Joe Hössl was German judge. The last item of this performance, heading straight for him – and going a bit wrong – was the last straw. He jumped out of his chair, pointed at the machine as it roared past, and declared 'That pilot should be disqualified' (in English). I heard later that he thought it had been me.

My flying had already finished, and the BBC crew, our friends, had wired me for sound in order to capture some dialogue from our elusive and camera-shy star. A few days before, after the first programme, they had attempted to set up a clip of Williams doing something other than in the air. The unknown programme had been assembled and published, but I had not seen it. 'Why don't you explain the sequence to Mike, and we can film you telling him about it?' GB, one of our elder statesmen, would refer to this cryptographic picture as a wiring diagram; to the American hot-dogging legend Mike Murphy it was a 'complex', but it looked like a wiring diagram, and alone explains everything a pilot needs to know about the manoeuvres. Williams reluctantly agreed, and we sat down either side of a long dining table corner, Williams with paper and pencil. I hoped for some tactical advice about heights, positioning, speeds etc, but nothing would be given away – to me or the camera. Neil hunched over the table, head down and protective arm around the A4 sheet, like a Swiss farmer eating his muesli or macaroni with apple sauce. He drew the sequence and described each figure in muffled tones. The KGB would not have learned much, and the footage did not appear in *Plane Crazy*. But they hoped for better when filming the four-minute action from the touchline. I approached the machine with the mini chocks as he taxied in and switched off. When the propeller stopped he asked 'What do you think of that, then?' ironically and a bit crestfallen. 'It was all right,' I said, 'the crowd loved it, look at that,' pointing to a couple of Frenchmen sat on the apron fence, applauding and cheering enthusiastically. The camera panned accordingly and this was in the film: Tony Bianchi liked it.

We won the team prize: James was 3rd, Williams 6th and myself 10th. I see I scored 95% of winner Eric Müller's result, sandwiched between a couple of international stars. I can claim little responsibility for this. Judging at this level is difficult, and this shows what can happen if you are associated with well-known pilots and fly an aeroplane that is kind to average flying, when other better pilots fly more revealing shapes and sizes. *Flight* magazine was gracious and said I did well for my 10 hours on type. They did not mention the first six-minute tryout and its difficult content.

More touring

At the end of September 1974 I took the Pitts to an airshow at Bergneustadt (New Town on the Hill), in Germany. The airfield is called Auf den Dümpel (on the dimple), and this describes it quite well – on top of a little hill, shortish, surrounded by trees, and quite an up and down place. You could land a Pitts there, but I did not fancy it; nor did many others, and I would fly out of nearby and conventional Meinerzhagen. The Pitts carried 17 gallons of fuel which would last, say, 2½ hrs at a reasonable cruise speed, but the only time you had any indication was when there was not much left. A see-through tube at the bottom of the tank started to reveal the level with maybe three gallons remaining. Yet again this trip indicated that the complete pilot leaves nothing to chance, and reduces the sense of adventure and discovery to the absolute minimum – to the level required by public transport. As a passenger I appreciate this, but the airline pilot has assistants and a research department to do the considerable and intellectually boring donkey work.

The show was no problem, and the accommodation, transport and big tent party afterwards a success. But then there's the touring, and touring weather. As usual, summer Atlantic conditions prevailed west of the Rhine, and although the outbound cross channel leg from Biggin Hill was into wind and on the slow side, a left turn at Cap Gris Nez, heading for the Ruhr, improved groundspeed and it looked as if I would reach Mönchengladbach successfully. France, Belgium and Holland passed underneath, and as the German border was crossed it was just possible to make out the fuel level bobbing up and down in the clouded neoprene tube above the pilot's feet. Dutch and German trees agreed that the wind was now SW and the night fighter grass expanse was assured. Unlike the previous Turbulent visit I now had a battery-powered radio, and the conversation indicated a straight in on 13. Perhaps that was the longest stretch of grass, but an into wind modification of that should not be a problem – but where was the field? Could this be the wrong town? It was definitely the correct place but no sign of the grass. Where it had been a mere five years before was now housing estates, roads, trees and autobahn: the German economic miracle was no joke.

Not far away was a full-size new runway, with buildings and a line of poplar trees along its south side. No grass to speak of. This was now the place, and the fresh wind was straight across. Some delicate geometry with the stated wind direction favoured 31 by a couple of degrees so here I would land with my two gallons.

The Pitts had lost 50 kgs on the way and now felt much lighter – landing would be slower. This may sound nice, but gusts would find the jumpy little machine easier to blow around: an unnecessarily long runway is of little help for a critical crosswind landing, and just prolongs the agony for a nervous tail dragger. It is also a mistake to think that extra speed will help you under these circumstances, although many professional pilots reassure themselves with these faulty notions. I remember a talk by Phil Brentnall, 747 training manager in the early days, where he pointed out that it had come to his notice that some pilots had invented a new rule of thumb for using Inertial navigation information when landing: your newly-revealed groundspeed should not be less than the calculated approach airspeed. 'This idea is to be discouraged immediately.' He was right, even if the 'a few knots for mum' battle-scarred warriors felt encouraged by a new electronic excuse for fast approaches, over and above the one third of wind addition generally accepted as reasonable for the airliner.

The initial landing with the light Pitts went better than I expected, and the line of uniform trees to windward combed and slowed the wind to a manageable character, but the buildings and hangars further along had the opposite effect, both blocking and accelerating it – like a walk down Broadway on a windy day. All was well – but only just.

Then we have to consider the restart after customs, coffee and fuelling. Starter motors are heavy, and require a heavy battery so the purpose-built competition machine had neither. The art of prop swinging had dwindled dramatically in the world at large, even by 1974, and the safest, and usually only solution was to do it oneself, with a helper to hang on to the aeroplane proper, just in case. This worked well with a cold, fuel-injected Lycoming, and required no interference in the cockpit, but a hot or even warm one was different. It demanded a fully competent person in the cockpit and a reliable ambidextrous prop swinger, because this was an American engine. Once away from aerobatic or vintage circles a mention of this last job turned eager, helpful experts into shrugging, shuffling and downcast passers-by; eye contact would be avoided and a pressing engagement might be remembered. The sure-fire hot engine technique required the idle cutoff to remain cut off, but full throttle selected, nothing less. Even after the time required for booking in, passport stamping, paying for fuel, statutory cross border flight plan, coffee and cake etc had elapsed there was still enough fuel vapour hanging around in the system to create too rich a mixture for start – except with the throttle wide. The engine would then fire at the first blade and consider making its way to max power before the vapour ran out. But the correct technique made it much less dramatic than this suggests: the 34-pound metal propeller took a few Otto cycles to accelerate, and if the pilot (hand on full throttle) immediately snapped the throttle closed at the first sign of life, then opened the fuel cut off (same hand) the engine would be idling sedately with hardly a roar. But no mistakes were permitted. Without suitable help engine cooling time dictated the transit schedule.

The way back from the Ruhr on the day after the show was, as usual, not without its weather and technical problems. First was a one-hour thirty flight from Meinerzhagen, into the headwind, the lowering cloud then the rain that made Ghent my destination for the night. Sint Denijs-Westrum was then still a large grass airfield with customs, just outside town; it's another field with a long history in both world wars, starting out with two Gotha squadrons for London bombing trips. After reoccupation in 1940 it was enlarged, became a fighter base then repair unit, and also helped out as a handy liaison field for servicing the Luftwaffe HQ at the Palace Hotel down the road. After (allied) liberation in 1944 it became a British forward base, and the nearby hospital encouraged USAAF B17s and B24s to land and drop off their wounded there. Three Polish Spitfire squadrons arrived, and while they were doing something over Holland on Jan 1st 1945 the Germans set about the field with a massive aerial attack and destroyed a lot of aircraft on the ground. They were about to leave when the Poles returned and a huge battle took place overhead on what Polish fuel was left. 32 Polish and 21 German aircraft were destroyed, killing 11 Germans, 2 Poles, 1 Canadian and 3 hapless ground support members. My guess is that the unbalanced figures indicate that the Poles had fought fiercely until their fuel ran out, then glided down to make the best of whatever landing spot presented itself. The convenient Don Bosco bus stop made this field a good bolthole for small aircraft in less strenuous times, and when the rain abated next day I duly got off the bus at the Don Bosco stop and set off for the Channel and home.

Though the Pitts has a small steerable tailwheel, brakes are also an important part of the ground control system, especially if it's windy. As I got to the Ghent holding point, struggling with a strongish wind from the west, the right brake pedal suddenly went to the floor and the Pitts turned itself into wind, brake fluid squirting here and there about the floor and bilges. Normally this simple and direct brake system has virtually no travel – the fluid is incompressible. One can consider the brake as part of the rudder pedal in flight, and the weapons grade flick rolls were popular to the right – so it was obvious what had happened.

What to do now? The John (Don) Bosco already mentioned was a poor Italian boy who found his way into the catholic system at a young age and decided to help other no-hopers do something other than hang around by village pumps being cool. He founded a trade training system (a bit like Halton) so that its students would leave with the possibility of doing something useful rather than nothing. One of these institutions in Belgium was near the bus stop, hence the name. Was it worth taxiing back in case a qualified master cylinder seal crafter could be found there? Possibly not, so I took off, pondering my tactics to ensure that the next landings had to have any crosswind coming from the right. The slow and lonely hour's flight over a windswept sea and the landings at Lympne and finally a deserted Farnborough were uneventful, but when it comes to touring, include me out – again.

CHAPTER 22

VC10 COMMAND COURSE: THE GOOD AND THE NOT SO GOOD

A year later it was my turn to be a real captain (as the airline system knows it). My last 747 trip was on September 18th and 19th 1975 to NY and back with Captain English, and he gave me the last sector. I had signed up for the VC10 because this would be a new type. My ten years with Boeing-influenced pragmatism (not to mention the two on the here and there Vanguard) had given me the impression that I could do the job much the same as everyone else, not counting the taxing single-seat touring adventures, but the transition to VC10 captain highlighted some personal deficiencies on my part. I'm still not sure what they were, or who was out of step.

The BOAC VC10 technical and simulator courses went smoothly enough to start with. As usual we swopped seats in the simulator, the only difference being that we drove from the left and co-piloted for each other from the right – otherwise the conversion details were along the lines of previous airliner types; nothing had changed. The first hint of trouble after detail 5 was an unwelcome surprise. Instructors 1 to 4 had written 'Good progress – Good performance – Very good – A high standard, no problems', in that order; then came number 5.

This detail contained a knockabout session of technical items; some relatively trivial and others required for the type rating qualification – for example high speed run to limiting speed, emergency descent, approach to the stall in various configurations, various electrical failures, landing with partial flying controls – nothing much resembling an everyday passenger flight. Trainer number 5 signed all the items off, writing 'Very good technical knowledge and flying to a good standard', but he then noted that 'control of the exercise was not as polished as might have been expected – I would like to see more anticipation and authority'. The skids had been greased, and even though subsequent details 6, 7, 8 and 9 earned 'Very good throughout, no problems observed – A very good detail – High standard – Highly competent,' number 5's debriefing, in the middle of what I had taken to be an aircraft conversion course, was a surprising and disturbing 16-year career first – including the initial two years' professional training.

Military organisations, which usually have the economic luxury of taking a professional view of training when not engaged in national survival, make distinctions in their conversion training policy. It follows the well-tried and respected step-by-step building-block process. First you learn to fly your new aeroplane, then you learn to fight it: this concept may sound melodramatic when applied to the flying Woolwich ferry, but the same principle applies.

The bare 'anticipation' and 'authority' comments did not have 'ofs' after them, and, as a takeover instructor I might be puzzled. What was not anticipated during this briefed technical exercise with good knowledge and flying? Were the crew unruly during this nuts and bolts lesson? I don't think so. I can hear experienced readers suggesting 'You had a new and keen training person with zero previous instructing experience and only the government examiner's course to go on, and who had never conducted conversion training.' It happens: why didn't you ignore it? And were the others all wrong about the other eight details? What had they missed? Who's out of step here? Is this training organisation properly managed? 8:1 says not really.

The final elements of the training captain's observations look general and unspecific on the page, but his critical debriefing left me accepting the likelihood that a final attainment of the overall required standard for a change of seat was far from assured. How could such an industry's on-going assessment system have failed to recognise and point up even the suspicion of such future inadequacies and, above all, areas where it would be imperative that improvement should be necessary and worked on? No doubt he had given his honest but individual opinion, but leopards don't tend to change their spots overnight, and I was privately at a loss as to where to begin.

Then came the simulator final check to confirm that fourteen years of worldwide transport under the mentorship of a great many role-model-worthy captains, within two great and reputable airlines, had inculcated at least a beginner's idea of the real rather than pretend commander's job. I have no intention of sounding presumptuous when I say that, to my surprise and private dismay, I failed – twice in succession. It was like discovering that John Humphrys had someone else's Mastermind paperwork.

Some years ago the BBC made a film for television about the Royal Navy's submarine captain course; it was called *The Perisher.* Our VC10 captain's simulator passing out check was something similar, and already had a reputation as a game rather than a training exercise, but the similarity ends there. The Perisher candidates were already qualified and experienced on type, their five-month course was specifically about captaincy and final suitability, bearing in mind that a mistake could start World War Three, and much of it was in real ships, not playing games in a simulator. There is a difference.

There was no special briefing before this exercise – jump in and go, ordinary flight from A to B. 'Things might happen' had to be assumed, but just what and how many a complete unknown. Based on my career to date I did not anticipate a significant problem, but experience of real life is irrelevant when one considers the possibilities of recreating it in a simulator, especially as number 5's bolt from the blue had softened me up – no doubt about it. It is an obvious *sine qua non* that the official objective was to assess the candidate's suitability for attaining a captaincy on this new machine (but it's an airliner – the philosophy is supposed to be remarkably consistent), and this first attempt kind of petered out in suspended animation as my putative crew members became less and less communicative, as did air traffic, and I appeared to have become less and less captain-like. Of course it was a disaster. We finished doing nothing in mid-air, and left the hovering electronic marvel for a not particularly informative de-briefing, in the training sense (if we consider the accepted meaning of the word), except the advice that I should use my crew more. With a real crew in a real aeroplane this is not difficult and works well, but was I discovering a VC10 game-playing failure culture that, unbeknown to me, had already been applied to many of my VC10 contemporaries the year before? They seem to have expected it, and passed eventually. The word 'Kafkaesque' comes to mind. My checker/trainer announced that my performance was not good enough and I would have to do it again. To give him his due he had used the correct and euphemistic terminology and did not say the amateur's 'I'm failing you because'. This is lesson one at the state examiner's course, and I imagine that my supervisor, not long out of the right-hand seat himself, was well aware of this checker's required etiquette, but, if and when we did it again what had to be different? I took little of use away from this debriefing – another throw at the coconut, perhaps, but how could my next tormentor then know that this was not a fluke? This sounds a dodgy way to qualify someone who has now proved themselves deficient.

The next final check was similar but not the same. I had decided I must spend more time communicating with the crew, and the accuracy of my otherwise good flying (failed autopilot) appears to have suffered – if one considers the instrument rating parameters used to justify the decision on paper – although I do not think control was lost or mountains hit (yes, I have used this I.R. examiner's ammunition myself, but not much, and it is seldom applied in in-house examining). Different people, same result: not good enough, do it again, little in the way of useful advice about fundamental personality change; in fact, although the written reports in my training file may have made suggestions, I have no recollection of taking any improving wisdom away with me – I was too busy considering where a change of career might take me. Given the chance again, older and wiser, less concerned with job security, I would have gone then and there. The second final check training captain who observed me fail for the third time (my memory had already filed detail 5 as a fail), did acknowledge that I had the skills and potential to soar to the heights of eminent captaincy, but did not tell me how to do it.

For the final attempt I had an older, nicer, suave and DFC'd real pilot who helped me out by pretending to be other aeroplanes on the radio. OK, I get it, there's a game plan somewhere here; thanks for the tip (I've never been on this fleet before). He passed me (to use politically incorrect grammar) – wonderful: hit the coconut on the fourth throw. Is this a reasonable way to expose the public to risk – 3:1 odds against? Was I a better person, had I learned life-changing stuff? Not a bit of it. This bizarre waste of time confirmed that my lack of interest in becoming involved with airline 'training' as a first officer had been justified. I had better hobbies to pursue.

There may be readers who agree with the much-loved VC10 system, with its nostalgic tradition of individual assessments, personality-based training and reliance on a splendid British aeroplane that was easy to fly, but I was at a loss to understand what was going on, or how to make the instant chameleon change of hue that appeared to be required. The aeroplane base flying was enjoyable, without problem, but then there's another final check. Once again suspension of disbelief suffered, even though this was a real flying machine engaged on a pretend passenger-carrying flight, and the in-house jiggery-pokery employed by the training club to simulate failures undermined the credibility of the performance. For example, as our wheels left the ground my co-pilot gave a quick and conspiratorial nod towards the centre console and then I saw the engineer's hand come forward to the #1 HP cock (fuel shut-off) and close it to the extent that power reduced to idle or thereabouts. A real captain would have said 'What the hell are you doing!?' When keeping straight had been demonstrated, another nod reinstated the power with a cancel-emergency 'engine's come back' statement of magic. This only confirmed the obvious flaws in this three-handed game with two not-so-good card sharpers, and any illusion of a real flight went further out of the window. This had been my statutory engine failure, but such a trivial dismissal and assumption of normality would not be acceptable on a normal flight, let alone the formal requirements – in fact, treating any real aeroplane as a toy could be extremely dangerous. In principle this also applies to flight test and development, and some professionals have caught themselves out, but, to give him his due, ARB chief test pilot D. P. Davies (Dai the Test, of the 747 test flights already described) understands this very well.

It's worth mentioning the consternation caused by my contemporary Tom Weller (incidentally with 10 years VC10 experience already) on his first VC10 aeroplane command check attempt. A hydraulic system had 'failed', so part of the undercarriage had to be freefalled. This leaves the doors swinging and at risk of getting dinged on the ground if the touchdown is less than quite good. Once all the simulated (this is not the simulator) emergencies had been dealt with and the 'realistic' flight was due to land, the training engineer reinstated the hydraulics but the undercarriage doors did not close because he had failed to reposition the freefall lever while downstairs. He announced an urgent (another pretend) need to leave the cockpit but Tom, enforcing his pretend captain authority, insisted that he stay in his seat until after landing. A point for the defence, I think, and the door, fortunately, did not require repair or replacement. But Tom required another throw at the captain coconut (meaning still failed).

Our cross country with surprises continued with the nice DFC'd captain and when we landed I was disappointed at his summary. 'Too many mistakes', he said. That's it, I thought. Maybe I can go back to being a 747 co-pilot while deciding what to do next.

However, this setback was quickly remedied. We took off again, flew round the local area for five minutes and he announced success. Amazing, a miracle in fact. Miracles are real – escapes from certain death and so on – but extremely rare in my experience; and, after numerous demonstrations of unsuitability for this job – Shazam! – my failings had been corrected by a wave of the VC10 training wand, courtesy of the trusty Victor Mike. You didn't have to make it up.

A recent conversation with a contemporary who had come up the Britain's finest, Britannia and VC10 route, revealed that the year before, only one member of his VC10 captains' course passed this aeroplane hurdle on the first attempt. Was this normal? It looks like it, and I can see a certain logic of insisting on a pedantic conformity with every jot and tittle of the instrument rating limits satisfied in order to take personal discretion out of this test when it comes to a final judgment – in theory. This policy makes life easier for the system, and provides one cast-iron entry on the squeaky-clean paperwork that gives the employer an element of future indemnity: we saw him hit the coconut fair and square (once) — it's not our problem. Every nationally-qualified examiner knows that the parameters are a guide, and that 'they are your ammunition – if you need it,' but there's more to driving a coach than possession of a driving licence.

Back on the road

The next pre-solo phase consisted of 40-odd route sectors pretending to be captain, with a variety of supervisory captains in the right hand seat. All these routine flights took place without incident that I can remember, and these mentors were particularly helpful in giving advice borne of practical experience. The usual strolls around far flung cities provided useful ideas and strategies; not particularly about flying, but mainly dealing with people, namely staff, including the boys and girls.

There's a saying that when you get your command the pay goes up and the weather gets worse. This is true, but you repeatedly find yourself in situations that had never seemed significant to a co-pilot. Not long after I had been released from the system, and just before engine start, a stewardess burst into the cockpit declaring a unilateral mutiny. 'The chief steward's been very rude to me and I refuse to work with him,' followed by the chief, anxious to get his story in. This is not the sort of thing a teenaged Biggles wants to get involved in, and my unreconstructed self would have felt flummoxed at such an unwelcome people problem, but one of my supervisory advisors had already explained the simple logic of such a situation. It clicked into place perfectly.

I took the chief into the front galley. 'How many passengers?' Answer 'X'. 'Can you manage that number with one short?' 'Yes', he said. Wonderful, problem solved, and I returned, told the girl she could stay in the jump seat and said 'start #3'. The flight proceeded as normal, we cruised upwards in the velvety smooth air of a desert dusk, comfortably and silently sat in our spacious Vickers cockpit, and after about 20 minutes a voice behind me said 'I think I'll go back now, captain,' and that was an end to the problem. What a masterstroke of captain-like anticipation and authority, with diplomacy thrown in. Hadn't I learned a lot! But not much from the authorised core training system, except to be wary of status without judgment or experience. Personally, I have found that competence and rationality earn more respect, and work much better than an authoritarian disguise: it's not as if the job requires inducing hesitant subordinates to go over the top. On the Buses (flying version) requires something different.

Pip Hadden was pleasant and helpful. I did a couple of supervisory trips with him, and he gave me a useful nudge in a sensible direction, against the natural airline flyer's assumption of routine and the instinct to go with the flow until compelled to do otherwise. We nightstopped in Kuwait, to take next day's VC10 eastward via Calcutta. It was a time of year when early morning fog was highly likely at Calcutta, and sure to burn off during the morning. What would normally happen? Machine proceeds as planned with extra fuel, hopes for the best, but more than very probably flies round in circles for an hour or more over the top waiting for acceptable landing conditions. Nothing wrong with that – that's weather for you, but Pip phoned me up the evening before, said the forecast was as usual, and that the fog and its clearance was 99% assured. Why not delay the flight here, and go a couple of hours late? Good idea – I'm not the real captain so I'll do it – why not? The BA man at the airport was disconcerted, and ummed and aahed: 'All right, I'll phone London and ask permission to delay the departure', he concluded. 'Not quite, but you've got the idea,' I said.

We got a couple more hours in bed, left at a slightly more godly hour, and the passengers had to doss down around the airport building as an alternative to two nail-biting hours above an invisible Calcutta. But the plan worked perfectly. We arrived over the top as the visibility rapidly approached our limits, into the hold and straight out on the approach procedure – first landing of the day – and finally arrived at Change Alley, Satay Alley and Bugis Street less tired than otherwise. To throw a spanner in the works and stop the momentum and routine of a large number of people is sometimes a good idea, but it's easier not to. This was positive training, as opposed to the other, regrettably popular kind for amateurs.

All training should include on-going assessment, ideally with feedback and advice. Records should report relevant details, and indicate to the next mentor where there is room for progress. Our assistant training manager had written of this 34-year-old: 'He is a quietly-spoken young man who will have to work to exercise his authority.' I was, in fact, Sergeant Wilson in the body of Captain Mainwaring. Would the other combination have given the staff more reassurance? Maybe that would have been an answer, but I don't remember this metamorphosis happening. He had also written 'He appears to be a natural pilot.' There's no such thing as a natural anything – it's the result of intelligence and hard work.

I remind myself of my father in a number of respects. Though a bit taller than me, he was similarly quiet and undemonstrative, but this had been of no disadvantage in terms of competence and crew leadership during six years of military flying, with challenges. It would seem that elements within this airline might have wanted something different, but I don't think they got it, and having been given the all-clear by tall, lean and sociable Pete Tebbit I was free to roam the world with a real crew. It was a relief to be rid of this training system, or so I thought, but not long after I had achieved the scrambled egg hat Douglas Wilkins, now training manager, asked if I would care to be a route supervisory captain, then raised the subject of training captain shortly after that. This was a surprise, and I was not inclined to jump at this opportunity, which would encroach on my valued free time, but he was diplomatic. 'You're an enthusiast' he said. 'You don't have to do it, but it's nice to be asked. Think about it.' This was a politely urbane man with insight, and base flying had been a civilised pleasure with Dougie. I thought about it and accepted, and was soon on my way to Stansted with Steve Deakin for the Authority's examiner's course – an independent qualification eminently valid in its own right, but a possible cause of problems within an airline if not tempered with other suitable experience or judgment.

Some time later, courtesy of the training job, I was whiling away a quiet, customer-free afternoon in the VC10 training office and came across my own archived pre-VC10 file, dating back seventeen years to Hamble. Progress at the College of Air Training had been assessed in three areas – flying, classroom and personal qualities. Although Roger Hughes had tried to encourage me out of my repressed introspective reticence halfway through the course – 'You're not such a bad chap, Riley' (the only personal qualities feedback event I remember) – Nick Hoy had written the final overall appraisal of a cadet's status at the end of the two years. I had done well in all three respects, and then he finished with the following observation: 'If he had been 6 foot tall he would be an impressive character.' I couldn't disagree with this bald statement of instinctive anthropological sociology, but felt a little sad at having discovered it in writing, and it occurs to me that he might have written it in a mood of reflection on his own blighted career: a school nav teacher instead of the gaunt, imposing and somewhat imperious figure of high office with the thick bars on the sleeves, large RAF pilot's wings and plenty of gongs to go with them. I understand – maybe it was intended to help me on my way, despite everything – but at least I had the wings, of a sort, and one each side. Such an official comment as his might be considered politically incorrect today – even actionable in the European Court of Human Rights – and we students were not aware of these handover notes. Who they helped or hindered must remain a mystery, and I should apologise to any who suffered from an inappropriate assessment or emotionally judgmental attitude on my part, as a result of the stunted and warped personality that could be inferred. Nobody gets it right all the time, including Nick, though he wasn't completely wrong.

The VC10 was designed with traditional values in mind. Good hot and high takeoff and landing performance, to service an empire on which memory suggested that the sun might never set, and handling that suited the BOAC captain of the old school. To achieve these requirements the uninterrupted wing had sophisticated full span slats – much more aerodynamically fancy than a bit of bent tin that hinged down at the front à la 707 (or 747 for that matter). The engines at the tail reduced noise in the cabin, were less likely to pick up stones, and would provide less asymmetric affect. Their weight at the back required a long nose at the front, and the relative shortness of the tail for the same reason meant a large fin to counter the long nose. The tailplane, also close behind the centre of gravity, needed to be large, and the fin that supported it had to be strong. This high tail flew far above the influence of the airflow behind the wing, and, so long as suicidally high angles of attack were avoided, there was no trim change for anything except airspeed itself. Such an absence of pitching moments was difficult to believe, but it was true.

There was a minor handling downside to this long nose/short tail/swept wing set up – Dutch roll – but this was looked after by three rudder sections, each with their own yaw damper taking a keen and permanent interest in this subject, so normal handling of this machine was straightforward in the extreme, just what was ordered. All aircraft are a collection of compromises, of course, and the weight in various inconvenient places required a strong structure to support it, calling for plenty of metal. Detractors called it the iron duck, and powerful engines and lots of fuel were also part of the equation, but the Conways provided the power, and fuel was cheap when this aeroplane for traditional pilots was thought of. As time went by the hot and high became less of a priority, and competitive machines increasingly less thirsty.

A 707 engineers' joke went: 'How do you make a 707 fly like a VC10? Fill the reserve tanks (wing tips) with concrete.' More weight and less range in one go. I heard of one serious VC10 incident when divergent Dutch roll became alarming at altitude (as it may). Due to an oversight in the cruise, all the engines stopped on a dark night. This is not only an unwelcome surprise but leaves the machine with very limited primary flying controls (all electrically powered) with not much else working either. To provide emergency electrical generation there was a dropout air-driven generator which would restore some flying control and fuel pumps to get the engines going again. All was well eventually, but the little propeller that drove the emergency generator (ELRAT – known as the Spanish Mouse) soon fell off. Following complaints the manufacturers pointed out that this was the only time this had happened. The flight engineering office responded with the news that the gadget had only been called on twice: they were not impressed by the 50% failure rate of a last-ditch lifesaving device.

The VC10 training establishment was an impressive structure. The fleet was large and originally expected to grow, so two simulators were acquired. When the Standard aircraft was progressively replaced by the Super it was argued that a pensioned-off standard would be an excellent training aircraft, one argument being that the two-for-one bargain simulators were not particularly good, and a real aeroplane to practise on would considerably enhance the learning process. Training Manager Tony Smith pointed out that while a training aircraft might look like an expensive luxury it would represent the cheapest insurance you could buy. This meant lots of fun base flying for the staff, especially as trainee flight engineers got a lot of individual experience on this machine.

The relative complexity of the VC10 systems compared with the straightforward nature of the pilot's handling rather skewed the training content and priorities. The flight engineering department were a law unto themselves, and a large syllabus of possible problems-to-be-solved had to be demonstrated or practised. Could it be that their equivalent pilot training fellows, having to justify their input with a straightforward flying machine, established a tradition of extra challenges for their students – improv rather than rehearsal? Sometimes flight engineer training was required when there were no learner pilots, so the piloting staff flew around as required by the engineering department, or just flew around as they liked, if an airborne VC10 was adequate for the numerous items on the list of engineering things to do: pleasant low level sightseeing tours of the Atlantic coast for the drivers. Visitors came to stay at Prestwick. If the training syllabus was not too pilot-heavy they might well get a little touch of the controls. I remember a relatively young and preppy flying instructor from Hamble, with only light aircraft experience. I gave him a few night circuits, which he flew beautifully. I heard later that he had resigned his Hamble job asap and gone for an airline pilot (as they used to say). I suspect they had lost a good instructor, but perhaps he would come to add value to an airline in due course.

CHAPTER 23

1976 WORLD AEROBATIC CHAMPIONSHIPS, KIEV

The UK team for the 1976 aerobatic championships consisted of Neil Williams, James Black, myself and Brian Smith, all members of Aerobatics International, and Philip Meeson with his Marlboro Pitts. The VC10 pilgrimage had occupied much of my time in 1976, so, as usual, practice for the event had been limited, but A.I. had recently bought a second S1-S Pitts from the United States, reg G-BDXZ. It looked similar to our original custom-built Soucy example, but was not quite the same. The engine cowling was a bit higher and wider at the front – not the close-fitting tailored affair of ZPH – and was it my imagination, or did the top wing have a touch more positive (or less negative) incidence? Perhaps it was parallel to the bottom wing, something logical enough, but ZPH's top wing didn't seem so high at the front. This new machine's wing profile with its routered ribs certainly looked symmetrical, and the ribs came from a plywood Sparkraft kit; and the stiff, garish and shiny paint job made the little machine look new, strong and in good condition. It had a wooden propeller – lighter, less taxing for the engine, and resulting in less nose-heaviness. 'I think you'll like it,' said Neil Williams. Now why should he say that?

I first gave it a try on July 10th with a couple of fights at Booker, barely two weeks before the worlds. At the first pull up it was obvious that it was not the same aeroplane. Above a modest (say 4) positive gs it shuddered, and after the 90 corner required to achieve a vertical climb, a very common element for much competition aerobatics, the remaining speed was less impressive. Tests with differing parameters (to stay just clear of this buffeting) showed no real solution. A side by side pull up with the other Pitts would leave the latter disappearing vertically into orbit, apparently. Where did this disturbance and drag come from? Was it the cowling shape? Could it be the undercarriage fairings producing detached airflow? Could it be the wing section? Curtis Pitts had told me of the critical nature of S1-S Pitts' wing sections (and the top version should be a little thinner than the lower); something was different about this machine, and I was not immediately gruntled with it, nor was anyone else. There was nothing unsafe about it, and was a bit easier to fly as a normal aircraft or for a lower order contest. It would have served as a teenager's gymkhana mount, but to enter the Derby or Olympic dressage something would have to change – but what?

The next day I took this machine to an airshow at Koksijde on the Belgian coast. There must have been others involved because the logbook shows formation as well as a solo aerobatic display at this military base, but I do remember the venue and some details of the day. All operations were assumed from the main runway. The weather was good with the potential to get a bit breezy, as befits a North Sea seaside resort, but I had no radio. This is not a disadvantage, but it concerned the air traffic man who gave the pre-show briefing. 'How will you know when to take off?' My slot was directly after the Belgian air force instructors' aerobatic team in their Fouga Magisters. I asked the leader what was his final figure. 'Downward bomb burst, then we circle around and land.' I said that after I saw the bomb burst I would take off, accelerate along the runway then pull to the vertical up the centre of where they had been. 'Are you happy with that?' asked the air traffic man. 'Perfectly' said the chef. Then there was the landing problem. I told our briefer that if the wind had got up I would land on the more into wind grass runway. 'If you have no radio how will you know what the wind is?' he asked. 'Don't worry, I'll be able to tell', I said. The instructors' team smirked. CRM sometimes just happens.

After another VC10 trip to the sunny Gulf states there followed a week of assorted ferrying and aerobatics as this 1976 world championships approached. A final team selection flyoff took place at Wickenby (or it may have been a last minute organised training session), and although I see that I took BDXZ along, all four Aerobatics International pilots chose to fly the better ZPH. Williams had not been successful in persuading any wet-behind-the-ears contender to change horses, despite his optimistic recommendation, but the new Pitts did come along to the Ukraine as an emergency standby. The assembled team set off for the iron curtain on July 21st and reached Nuremberg for a first nightstop with its motley collection of aircraft – 3 single seat Pitts specials, a good Cherokee and an oldish 5 seater Jodel 140.

The modus operandi and team makeup is worth a few words. An FAI world contest allows for quite a number of official team helpers in addition to the contestants and a judge. For this Kiev event we had a manager, doctor, engineer, judge's assistant and a couple of others, but I do remember Walter from the Coventry Aero Club. He was not an aerobatic aficionado but had a Polish mother and was familiar with the Russian language so Bob Mitchell thought he would be useful as a communicator. His interesting contribution to politics in the Ukraine will get a mention in due course. Ian Senior, an accomplished aerobatic pilot himself, was our manager and flew the Cherokee, complete with assorted radios, retractable wheels and engine with constant speed propeller, so this would be our cross country lead aircraft. Aerobatics International had fielded four pilots and two Pitts, so Williams and Black would alternate by the day with our good one, and myself and Brian Smith shared ferrying BDXZ. As transport professionals we last two also alternated days in the Cherokee right hand seat as commodore of the flotilla, and radio man. The first day to Nuremberg went well enough, and the nightstop in the old and perfectly restored historic town enjoyable enough as a relaxing start to the trip. Then it started to get a bit more difficult.

Next day it was my turn to fly a Pitts, a single-seat radio-less day off just following. We set off for Kiev, first landing at Prague, across the iron curtain and its electrified double fence with ploughed and mine-sown strip in between. From here Jiri Kobrle accompanied us to Brno in the Czech aviation institute's Morava twin, wished us well and sent us eastwards, towards Kosice in the far end of what is now Slovakia. But the complication of the transit stops was slowing our progress, which, restricted by the slowest aircraft in the party, was not fast anyway. Even though this was a Moscow-approved incursion into cold war territory the coordination, communications, clearances and permissions kept the locals busy: no one wanted to get it wrong – you could tell; a bureaucrat's dream, or nightmare, depending on an individual's take on the system. High ground and the weather did not help us either, and we ended up in Bratislava, a literal stone's throw from Austria – but having officially crossed the curtain ordinary citizens did not recross it willy nilly in those days, so here we would nightstop (we thought), but Bratislava was not on our official plan of campaign. We had no people's clearance to stay there, and the border police were at a loss as to the suitable procedure. Our administration and coordination team of Williams, Black and Radice arranged a compromise: you keep our passports until we go, cease phoning for advice from elsewhere, get us a nice hotel and pretend we're not here. Smiles all round – problem solved.

Iona Radice

Iona had been involved with the aerobatic scene as a helper since 1970, and she deserves a few words here as a personality who brought many estimable qualities to competition life; qualities which exemplify those quietly respected for what made Britain great, but which are dwindling as fast as a disenchanted, envious and emancipated majority can demolish them: today's international value of the pound is not a good sign.

Father: ex-Indian Army archetypal Cheltenham retiree and expert cryptographer. Mother: editor of the Times Educational Supplement. Iona, a member of the Gloucestershire Aero Club, presented herself as a volunteer at the 1970 Hullavington worlds and became a touch judge, a box corner-watcher; she was a private watcher of humans as well. Who would have guessed that she worked at Cheltenham's famous intelligence gathering hub? How were her language and inherited code-breaking skills employed at work? You can guess. In 1972 she drove her MGB to France and volunteered at the Salon worlds. As a result of her past competition admin experience she got just the job – to assist German Democratic Republic's Professor Pilz and his research with the Pilz machine, a mechanical/electronic device for recording an aircraft's position relative to the contest zone. Who knows how many of those tiny and apparently irrelevant snippets of the intelligence jigsaw were gleaned from two weeks of social chat with the East Berlin research professor? As a past intelligence-gathering pilot Taff Taylor had not been allowed to go to Moscow in 1966, although he would not have been much of an intelligence risk. As a four-year U2 pilot there would have been little he could tell them they did not already know – intelligence gatherers do not know more than the intelligence creators – but he could have been a diplomatic risk. At home, Iona had established her place as part of the aerobatic furniture, nominally coordinating the scoring paperwork and procedure, but offering wise judgment and cultured friendship in many areas. As an official observer at Kiev, she could do no more than any observant tourist, and the sports-car-driving Miss Marple from Cheltenham looked like a good cover, except that it was not a cover. That's who she was.

The following day, July 23rd, it was my turn to conduct operations from the lead Cherokee with the repeated objective of reaching Kosice. The official route was direct in this quasi-controlled airspace, over the Tatra Mountains National Park, but the weather was not looking good for a VMC flight (good visibility) – low cloud on the mountains with drizzle. Maybe we would be able to approximate to the required track and play the reporting point game, might as well go and look, so we set off from Bratislava. Initially it was possible to head in the right direction, but as the ground rose and the cloudbase became closer, deviating along lower ground became necessary. This was predominately to the south, and our distance from the formal track increased as Ian obediently followed my directions, over the border into Hungary. The invisible Tatras on the left did not relent and continued to push us south, and as the distance from cloud and hillside reduced so did the spacing of the formation: there was going to be no way through today so we turned back, crept along the side of the hills until into the correct country, and arrived back at Bratislava after an hour or two of fruitless optimism. We'll stay another night, better weather tomorrow.

The Jodel with five up and baggage was the slowest of our group and dictated our speed, but a new cruise problem was emerging. The Jodel's propeller, wood with plastic covering, had been routinely maintained by its owner, who had lovingly DIY'd the dings it regularly collected from the stones of its home runway – Hucknall, Rolls Royce's airfield. What's the best stuff to fix this damage? Polyfilla, Halfords' pink and white resin body filler, Araldite? You name it. After wet and dry sanding and some varnish these repairs don't look too bad, and gentle flying in fine weather retains most of the propeller's laminar flow, but after our cruising in the rain the fillings began to fall out, and cracks in the plastic began to grow. Neil, one of its two pilots, was concerned, and propeller testing to destruction, experimental test pilot style, looked to be quite on the cards even while the Jodel was nursed all the way to the Great Gate of Kiev and back to Blighty. Trevor Davies, our engineer, did what he could, but he could not magic a new propeller from out of thin air, and the concern at what might be happening to it while it whirled relentlessly around in flight, in rain especially, was a continuous source of worry for our two senior sportsmen. From here on plaintive radio requests to slow down were common; 'Slow down a bit – just give me two miles an hour – please,' and the worried looks on the passengers' faces showed that this concern was shared by all on board. Clearly one cannot criticise these two captains for not keeping their passengers informed – but a certain degree of discretion is customary in the business.

The relatively slow team speed thus required was not good for a Pitts whose engine tended to oil up a bit. A brief session of full power with a pull away to the side, up, around and back would clear the plugs, but BDXZ suffered another problem – the people's petrol. This was of low octane, souped up with much lead which turned to real lead at the low power setting. The tiny grey globules so formed would dance around behind the spark plug electrodes, shorting them out in a disconcerting way, and the full power blast didn't really work; they seemed happy to hide in the core of the plug, to return to the contacts at will – only on the ground could the plugs be taken out and these offending mini ball bearings shaken and poked out.

After this second Bratislava nightstop it was my turn to take BDXZ across the forested Tatra Mountains. As the only experienced Pitts forced lander present, I was under no illusion about what would happen if one tried it on less than a billiard table, but fate came to my aid. Another Pitts had joined us – Pam representing New Zealand. She had struggled around in the same low cloud and rain and also ended up in Bratislava the day before. She was not happy with solo touring in a strange continent with bad weather, and gladly accepted the invitation to passenger with us while someone else flew her Pitts. This would be our doctor, John Firth, and she was the only one with a parachute. Despite Neil Williams' assurance that he would unquestionably have bailed out of his upside-down Zlin in 1970, had he had one, the British aerobatic community still did not carry parachutes – useless weight (and not very sporting really, especially as enemy action was not now expected). This attitude towards parachuting takes one immediately back to the First World War, and the British approach to brave piloting had not completely changed, but I had no hesitation in requesting the use of Pam's parachute, swopping it with BDXZ's seat back, and would have eagerly jumped over the side had this machine's engine required it. To use Mrs Thatcher's TINA phrase – There is no alternative – perhaps we could have bought a more competitive Pitts with the insurance money.

I was familiar with John Firth's aerobatic Stampe career, and he had recently been flying the Gold Leaf Zlin for his neuro-physiological research into the effects of high g on the human organism. Having first read classics at Oxford he turned to medicine and was now an eminent neurosurgeon in London. Part of the research involved flying a programme of g-loaded (up and down) manoeuvres in the Zlin, with a neurocolleague, then taking a significant quantity of blood from one or the other for scientific analysis. The sample clearly had to be taken as soon as practical and the bloodletting usually occurred on the grass outside the Tiger club hangar, at weekend teatime – disconcerting for the squeamish?

Just a bit, but that's professional doctoring for you. I did not know whether John had flown a Pitts before, or done much formation flying, but, by Jove, he made a good job of it that day, and we now had a very presentable super tight 4-Pitts box for arrivals at Kosice and Lvov. Now I had the parachute my engine ran well, and I could see the formation quality, where it mattered, equally well from my box position; great stuff. (Williams 1, Firth 2, Meeson 3, Self 4.)

We nightstopped at Lvov and they put us up in the Aeroflot co-pilots' bunkhouse on the airfield: pretty spartan it was – backpackers, scouts, that sort of sybarite's level – but we were now in proper Soviet territory – the basics of life provided for all ordinary citizens, and that's it – but who actually needs (not would like) more than the basics – if they have a good mind? I'm immediately reminded of what the Greeks said about a classical education: it enables you to live without the money you're not going to make – some philosophical food for thought here.

Next day was Kiev via Rovno for lunch. The Ukraine is a large place, and at Lvov we picked up the Antonov 2 that would lead us to Kiev. The rules about this escorting business seemed to vary according to how close you were to major centres of USSR politics and tradition, but in 1976 a training solo cross country usually meant following an Antonov 2 which flew airways, NDB to NDB, even at 1000ft or less in perfect weather. (Future experience would tell me that Antonov 2s have three traditional local flying heights – 100, 200 and 300 metres).

After lunch (good home cooking again) at a sunny Rovno we set off for Kiev. Senior could follow the Antonov as well as anyone, so I volunteered to ride in it. We took off first on the bone-dry grass runway that had not a blade of grass on it, such was the regular traffic. Our new leader pilot, of the tractor-driver (promoted to the leather jacket) persuasion must have firewalled it for this special and very unusual mission, and we blasted off from the strip leaving an atomic quality ball of red dust behind us, climbing at the spectacular angle that a light AN2 can achieve. I watched this impenetrable sandstorm from my cabin window to see what, if anything, would happen next. While I was pondering a longish wait, tiny bees shot out of this cloud at various places, far below: our boys were on the road.

On the way the captain was captain-like but, understandably, influenced by this once in lifetime sense of occasion. When Philip Meeson came up alongside on the left, upside down, in his red Marlboro Pitts, waved, closed in, waved etc. just outside our window, the captain grinned nervously due to the new experience, stared ahead and gripped the controls in a vice-like grip, as if he could influence Meeson's flying. I felt a bit sorry for our co-pilot. He was thinner, older and quieter than the captain, and his job was to follow the ADF track required. He seemed to manage well enough, but the captain would occasionally point out some inaccuracy, grab the stick and make a correction. An indication of professionalism for a Westerner's benefit? Not sure. Our engineer, who combined maintenance with all other helpful duties, would occasionally lean into the flight deck and make some adjustment to the engine controls, to the irritation of the captain, who might slap his hand out of the way. The fine tuning of cylinder head temperature, mixture, air intake and oil temperatures could all warrant minor tweaking as an excuse for something to fiddle with, and no two crew members, given the chance to do something, will agree completely when it comes to setting up a large petrol engine.

Out of the right-hand windows I was surprised to see Williams in the Jodel flying unreasonably close to our right upper wingtip. Was he trying to compete with Meeson for silly things to do? Under the circumstances I felt this would be uncharacteristic, and then it occurred to me that he was desperately trying to find the upwash sweet spot to surf, as popularised by long range geese. This was not for fun, and it was obvious that our speed was too fast, and his rpm too great for his propeller, or did he expect to run out of fuel? I indicated this to the captain, requesting slow down a bit, just a few clicks, but he refused to compromise. 200 kph was the official speed of the day, and that was it – no concession.

Once things had settled down the engineer opened the large wooden toolbox and distributed bottles of beer and dried salty fish – sprat-sized. Not bad, and the 300-metre altitude gave a good opportunity to study the flat collective farm countryside. That had been the intention, but there was little evidence of farming activity, and most of this late-summer prairie looked like uncut grassland. Where was everyone, and what were they doing? What was interesting was the odd MiG 15 or 17, sometimes two or three, standing outside isolated farm buildings, miles from anywhere. If a field were to be mown and rolled they clearly could have been started and flown off the grass: were they actually ready to go now? Probably not, though it is unlikely that they formed an enthusiast's private collection – they just sat there.

Eventually signs of civilisation appeared and having descended, we crossed the boundary of what looked like a large and gently-rolling village common, with structures, vehicles and people scattered about; only the cows were missing. At a few metres height our captain steered gently between the obstacles, then landed on the first likely-looking open space, and we taxied in.

Had he been here before? Who can say? This was Kiev West, I think familiar to the German team's judge, Walter Wolfrum, who had already done considerable damage in the area with his overpowered experienced-level Messerschmidt (we old hands kept these and left the FW190 to the new boys'). I imagine that our six following aircraft flew around for a look before carefully choosing their touchdown spots because all arrived safely.

Our big and old hotel in town was more agreeable than my Moscow experiences, and the street-level ambience less obviously Soviet. This town had less of a hard-faced people's revolutionary aspect to it, and the bustling fruit and veg market made a big contrast to the vast uncultivated prairie outside. So this is what the invisible collective farm worker had been doing – growing stuff at home for money in the pocket. The daily contest packed lunch ('Warsaw Pact lunch,' said judge John Blake) did have its country character, and I thought the blitzed-plum thick drink rather nice once one got used to it – a pleasant drinkable meal in itself – but my flying performance was undistinguished, very middle of the road. I would put this down to lack of practice and the focused commitment required for success, but I would argue that there was more to it than that, and the requirement for a USSR win come what may did not make life easy for the Soviet home team, or the amenable-by-nature chief judge, Juri Tarasov.

I had a very early draw for the first programme, single figures I think. This is the reopening of a show that has not happened for two years, so interest is high and judging not quite settled down at this point. Joining me as openers were the 1970 and 1974 champions to name but two. Igor Egorov (the 1970 guitar-playing aerobatic champion) was very early on stage, if not first up, and I remember his performance as I prepared because the nerves showed from the very start. He failed to get his Yak 50 undercarriage up fully and didn't notice (or check) so one main gear neither up nor down degraded his machine's performance and handling, and didn't look too stylish either. He struggled round, but neither he nor the distracted judges could expect a top of the leader board performance. A relatively straightforward spin featured in the programme and my cheeky Pitts beat me to the finish, and the figure overrotated by 35° (I would argue) – 7 points theoretically deducted – max score 3 out of 10. But a clear angular error of this clarity gives the judges the easy option of declaring 'more than 45°, we need tot up downgrades no further, it's a zero score for this figure'. If they are not unanimous the majority's average score replaces the minority's zeroes when the scores are compared afterwards. Later that day our Judge John Blake gave me the sad news – majority zero for the spin: well that's how it goes, and it wasn't as if I expected to win.

A couple of days later, probably after programme 2, James Black told me to go and check my score sheets for the first programme. He had just checked his last flight and found an incorrect zero decision – the majority had scored the figure, and their average mark should have replaced the zeroes. As a well-known pilot, and a member of the 1974 winning team was he, among others, being targeted as a potential threat to the shaky USSR domination plans? Was something going on with the scoring? I was also in the 1974 winning team. I went through my prog. 1 scores – he was right; I should have got the majority score. He had got his protest money back and his scores: I put in my protest, but it was not upheld despite its clarity because the protest time limit had run out: no corrected marks, but I got the money back as a consolation prize (and tacit acknowledgement that the mistake was not in my favour).

Half the judges were from Warsaw Pact countries, and it became fairly obvious that they were favouring the Russians, within the judge throwout limits, of course – not that they specially wanted to, but had little choice under the circumstances; to do otherwise might have had career and social consequences; who knows – and then there was the drawing of lots debacle. The fully-manned Russian team (five men and five women) had battled manfully but a bit desperately. Some were much more experienced than others, and Egorov's shaky start had rattled the whole organisation, I think. They all flew the unknown programme (no practice allowed) with a machine-like stereotyped urgency. I remember watching a young Yevgeny Frolov (to become a celebrated Su 27 demo pilot). He was good for a 20-year-old, and in this apparently preprogrammed unknown was just as good as the much more experienced others. We never saw any of them around the site. Where did they go, what were they doing? I would not suggest that they all went somewhere else and secretly practised this programme, but it certainly looked as if others had done so elsewhere, and provided a well-drilled tactical plan – heights, speeds, positioning; everything you needed to know but normally had to decide on the hoof. The unknown sequence is normally where experience can be clearly seen.

The FAI system accepts a maximum of 10 judges. If there are more than 10 available a draw decides who stands down for the upcoming programme. Before the final programme it was not certain that the Russians would win. This put the chief judge in an unpleasant position: on their home turf, they had to. Yuri Tarasov was a mathematical genius who held a significant position at the historic Samara aerospace centre. Who better to deal with the numbers? But his problem now was very simple, and politically pressing. There were eleven judges, and one had to be stood down. To aid success it was imperative that the Russian judge scored the final flight, and an exclusion draw had to be held among the eleven. Guess what, the Russian judge got the short straw – on the first attempt. After some thought Yuri declared an invalid draw because they had drawn in Latin alphabet country order; 'but we're in the Soviet Union, we should have drawn in order of the Cyrillic alphabet – we must do it again.' This put the Russian judge nearer the front of the queue, but John Blake also noticed that one card had a corner turned down – the Russian took it and stayed in. Uproar, but that was that.

The daily pilots' briefing was held in a rather stern atmosphere – like the people's court. There was a dark and humourless admonishment one day, and I felt rather sorry for the recipient. The large grass all-purpose sports field had no special markings, and one took off and landed wherever looked best. It was not completely billiard-table smooth, and this choice needed some care for our small and delicate capitalist private sector sporting machines. On one side was the circular parachuting sand pit, and Monika Lack, a Swissair stewardess, ran into it at the end of her landing run. She was flying Eric Müller's Akrostar. The Akrostar landing is not a problem, but needs care; it's not like a Cessna (in fact Joe Hössl sold his Akrostar to a man who had just got his PPL. The purchaser made eight flights in it, and after the eight ground loops had asked for his money back). The day after Monika's mishap (no damage) the magistrate announced 'Yesterday the Swiss pilot Lack landed in the parachuting sandpit. Landing in the sandpit is not permitted and is against the regulations. Pilots will not land in the sandpit.' It wasn't as if Monika meant to do it, but we had been told, and I was reminded of the draconian story of the wartime Russian pilot and the Hurricanes delivered to Russia. He landed wheels up on his first flight with this novel machine, and was shot by an officer on the spot for damaging Soviet property.

Another evening James landed on a reasonable looking area, but the bumps were too much for the undercarriage bungees and one side gave out. The Pitts sat with a lower wingtip on the ground, the fabric a bit wrinkled from the structural bending. When picked up the wing looked correct, and Trevor Davies had brought a couple of spare bungee loops and the special tool so the bungee was fixed – but what about inside the wing? Word had got around that our good Pitts was out of action. American journalist Don Berliner asked me what had happened. 'Wheel fell off,' I said. 'Oh yeah, happens all the time,' said Don. The scores at this stage indicated that Brian Smith would not fly again, so Neil briefed him for the permitted test flight. 'Dive it to Vne, pull six g and then give it full aileron, each side, holding the 6g. If it doesn't break it's OK.'

I'm sure Brian borrowed a parachute, Pam's maybe, but nothing happened and Neil went on to finish fifth after three Russians and a Czech.

Considering the political pressures and expectations our team did very well to come third, after Russia and Czechoslovakia, in other words first of the free world (if you like simplistic politics) thanks to the efforts of Williams, Meeson and Black. The Americans were disappointed and suspicious of their fourth position, and what had gone on behind the scenes at this FAI sanctioned event we will never know – but it's only a game. There were 68 pilots in all, with many well-known names among them, and had I been more concerned with results, and less trusting of the local management, I might have regained my stolen marks, which would have made a small improvement on my 31st place, but, if my suspicions agree with James' pragmatic realism, it was an honour to be targeted: and, perhaps, also quietly favoured by some old friends of Britain. Who can say? The Russians always had a very well-established aerobatic system, and the Czechs have taken their aerobatics seriously for many years.

John Firth, our doctor and part-time Pitts formation pilot, started with a bit of doctoring advice: nothing wrong with this, but there was nothing wrong with us. Fortunately he was rapidly distracted by the organisation's official English language interpreter, Marina. Marina was something in the university, and a lady of character, charm, intellect, erudition and perceptive judgment. 'There is no escape, Mr Bond' might have covered it, but she really was very nice with that combination of instinctive warmth and exoticism that is irresistible to those from north-western presbyterian longitudes. Firth became the celebrated visiting neurosurgeon and received privileged access to the university's top medical facilities and their experts. We saw little of our doctor during the contest, but he found a wife. We also saw little of our Coventry-based Russian language specialist either, and I found out what he had been doing after we crossed the Polish border on the way home.

Our flotilla left Kiev on August 5th, again following an Antonov for the first three hours' worth to Lvov. It was my turn to fly Pitts BDXZ. Fortunately a young Russian military pilot hitched a ride in the Antonov, and his presence and status on board helped us out on the first sector to Rovno. He looked like a lecturer at an established university – obligatory off duty cover of sports jacket and tie (like the students in our 'how to present yourself as an officer' Cranwell film, but less schoolboy-like), and the thin leather document case, in case something happened on his days off (I met Frolov again many years later at Oshkosh – he looked the same as this officer then).

As we proceeded west the usual summer holiday weather approached: a lowering overcast, wisps of low cloud, rain. The Antonov continued on its 300m ADF track and I wondered what to do if and when, as was sure to happen, we became totally enveloped in thick cloud. A very mixed bag (now 7) tight formation on the instrument equipped Antonov, or descend as low as necessary to keep the ground in sight, with no map or knowledge of the area – and hope for the best. Fortunately our airforce pilot understood the predicament and encouraged the Antonov captain to forget the airways stuff, and descend. This worked, and we followed the main road in the rain, as low as it takes; the traffic below with its headlights on. Fortunately this part of the Ukraine is very flat.

We were soon through the front, and continued with the plan: lunch at Rovno, continuing west via Lvov and onward to Poland, this time without the Antonov. Led by our Cherokee we cruised serene and relaxed into a perfect glassy-smooth evening. Between Lvov and the Polish border the lakes dotted about in front reflected the evening sun. I was flying in a second out on the left position, about 80 yards from Meeson, who was similarly distanced from our leader. I became aware that Meeson was staring back at me instead of looking generally forward and to his right. A glance around is good idea in high-level cross country formation, but why the fixed stare, what so interesting about me? Then I saw them; a pair of large storks at one o'clock going south, same level, constant bearing, one above the other, both heads looking towards me with detached curiosity. It takes much longer to read this than do the thinking in real time, and the 'what will they do? what shall I do?' process had not had time to leave the brain when they shot past, one just over my top wing, the other just under a bottom wing, at about 150 mph closure speed, that's 220 feet per second.

Poland is very popular with the white stork, and maybe these had started the journey to South Africa for next winter via the Adriatic coast, or Spain, perhaps, making the most of their leisurely power-assisted final glide of the day. They have no airborne predators, so they don't get out of your way, and at 4½ kilos each could have done me some damage – a lucky near miss. We landed at Krakow and were settling our machines for the night in a quiet corner of the apron when Neil took me aside and told me his story. 'I've only told James, but we were lucky to get out of there'.

Neil's experience of Moscow 1966 had sharpened his sense of international intrigue and the ways people get information, however trivial. The Foreign Office had not permitted Taff Taylor to go to Russia then because of some content of his international flying experience, and the possible newsworthiness of what could be revealed about an erstwhile sportsman. At the time, Neil's current work as a home grown military experimental test pilot did not warrant this travel ban, but he would have been well aware of the Official Secrets Act, even if there were fewer secrets than the signers might imagine: however, every little helps. At an official getting-to-know-you social event at the beginning of that contest a convivial Russian with perfect English singled Neil out and asked 'How's it going?' in one-of-the-boys mode. Neil started off about competition aerobatic trials and tribulations. 'No, not that!' said the enthusiast, 'What about your experimental stuff at Farnborough?' Neil was taken aback, shocked at such daring effrontery. 'I made my excuses and my departure, straightaway' said Neil. He later told me that this opening shock tactic was a fencing ploy, as explained to him by fellow Welsh test pilot and swordsman John Lewis. Start with a blatant foul – it will unsettle them and might get results.

Ten years later, at Kiev, there was no such interest expressed, but one day Neil, our senior and most famous pilot, was discreetly asked to visit the control tower office block. He had no idea why.

A man conducted him upstairs, through the drab corridors to an office that astonished him. Behind its door was sudden film set plush. The lighting, decor, furniture, carpets, pictures – one could while away the *Telegraph* crossword here with pleasure and satisfaction. Nice coffee as well. The well-dressed man sat him down and sent the other away.

'One of your team has been doing bad things,' he started. It's Firth and the girl, thought Williams.

'Have you seen much of your team assistant, Walter?'

'Hardly at all.'

'Do you know where he is now?'

'No idea.'

'He is in prison down town. He has been going to the city centre each day and haranguing the crowd about the bad things in the Soviet system. This does not go down well here, so he was arrested. He will be released if you guarantee that there will be no more trouble. When all your group have crossed the Polish frontier successfully the case will be dropped. I'm sure you understand the seriousness of our position. Let me top up your coffee.'

Few captains relish extra-curricular hassle like this and, to give him his due, Williams had showed no sign of this disturbing knowledge before he told me in the relative safety of Polish territory. Some diplomatic stories are not all made up. Our travel group now contained the two Canadians and their aircraft, and

Jay Hunt's blog makes a point of Williams' careful planning and briefings for the three communal flights to Poland, now containing five Pitts, the Cherokee and the Jodel. Williams was keen that the day went according to plan.

Next day it was the Cherokee right-hand seat for me again, cloud on the hills, rain threatening, first leg SW down a long valley to Bratislava, then along a brown and swollen Danube to Nuremberg: more Jodel pleas to reduce speed – this was not a quick journey. The final day home reads like 1930s airline work: Nuremberg – Saarbrücken – Lille – Shoreham – Wycombe Air Park; a long day, but only 4hrs 20 in the air. No meal allowances, no sector payments etc., but also no crew, no radio, no decisions, no CRM – just following and enjoying the view. That's the kind of touring I like.

This arrival home was on Aug 7 and it was back to VC10ing for a couple of weeks. I see that I took the Jodel back home to Derby on August the 27th. I called at Nottingham to top it up as a goodwill gesture, but what had it been doing in the meantime? Getting its propeller fixed at Farnborough I suppose. It certainly looked sound, and with only a pilot on board the machine flew like a box of birds – 'One careful owner, as new condition, no cowboy pilots'. Of course not.

More structural evidence of a hard life

The next day I went with James Black and A. N. Other to Bad Neuenahr, south of Cologne, via Shoreham, Ghent and Dahlemer Binz. These were still the days when one had to land at a customs airfield either side of a border, and my guess is that is why Dahlemer Binz might have featured. I had the Zlin, James our ZPH Pitts and the friend flew James' CAP10. As an Aerobatics International commercial venture you can put together quite a lot of acts with which to mystify and amaze the unsuspecting locals – solo aerobatics with each machine, two and three-ship formation, mirror formation, to mention only a few possibilities. It was with such entrepreneurial skills that James ran A.I. and generated income for it. When we arrived at Bad N. he decided to impress any onlookers with a spectacular Pitts knife-edge run past the tower. The Pitts' deep and aerodynamically shaped fuselage and the 180 HP up front can support the machine for quite a distance, in true straight and level knife-edge flight. You can even do a bit of a climb to end the run if starting it with enough steam. As James made his crisp 90° roll to knife-edge and tweaked some top rudder he chanced to see the fuel tank above his knees move. This is not normal, so the run changed to a sedate circuit and landing.

The top left fuselage longeron had failed at a weld cluster. Like WW1 biplane fighters all the heavy bits – engine, fuel, pilot, guns etc are gathered round the centre of gravity. This makes for good manoeuvrability as well as efficient use of structure, and partly accounts for the Pitts' rapid flick rolling rate, but, in addition to the propeller and crankshaft problem that I had already discovered, this manoeuvre requires a very aggressive initial transverse loading to start the figure. It doesn't matter how quick this abuse is, the peak loading goes somewhere. Despite what is accepted as the logic for left or right, virtually all single-seat pilots have to steer with the right hand, and most pilots are right handed and footed, so most flick rolls are performed to the right, whatever the machine or engine, whether positive or negative. A local man did a temporary weld – enough to get home, but the airshow punters had to make do with whatever can be done with a Zlin and a Cap10.

The 1976 World Championships was to be my last involvement in serious aerobatic competition as a not very competitive pilot; slightly perhaps, but not to excess. I liked the learning process and the interest of the technical challenge, but this is a personal affair – man and machine seeking individual understanding and refinement – and competitive success requires other motivations that demand too single-minded and exclusive a focus. Aerobatic colleagues had drifted away from the piloting side of this sport for reasons of family commitment, an awareness of the diminishing returns relative to time and effort, the very limited kudos of the sport as a source of acclaim, and, not discussed much, our history of serious technical failures. Sharing aeroplanes with others can increase personal risk, and we were not alone in this respect. The large state-supported teams, with on-going organised training and full-time technical support, also had their problems – with the machinery as well as the people. At Kiev I remember going to look at Viktor Letsko's Yak 50, which was rumoured to be needing repair. Viktor was a small package of dynamic energy – certainly capable of turning on the 110% Russian performance when required. Yak 50 construction was still based on old training aircraft tradition. I spotted the problem easily. The elevators were intended to be attached to the tailplane by none-too-hefty piano hinges and small brass wood screws. Viktor had managed to pull a few screws out. And then there's the limitation of the human frame and its working parts. Stories of permanent neurological damage were to increase.

Autobiographer's note

It's acknowledged that autobiographical writing is considered to reveal more about the writer than others he writes about. In some cases it can be assumed that the whole narrative is skewed – in the writer's favour. But America's greatest writer Samuel Clemens – pen name Mark Twain – who wrote much perceptive, conversational and easy-to-read biographical entertainment from life, concluded, towards the end of his life, that the writer's real character will seep out from the lines, whatever the attempt to conceal it. Is a narrator of (true) flying stories the only one who has never got things wrong? Do such people exist? Have I ever met one? It is possible, but it would have been in the airline environment and I would not have noticed.

Alan Curtis supported our aerobatic efforts for the 1976 worlds in Kiev. A charming, energetic, multi-talented entrepreneur with interests in property development (I think) and other things, no doubt: I do not have a clue about what he or his family do or did, now or then. I do know that he is a good entertainer at the piano. After this contest he created a trophy to replace the now defunct Lockheed, with something similar – the five minutes free for all – called the Alan Curtis Trophy (not surprisingly). He had his own business aeroplane and employed a retired naval officer to manage and fly it. Some time after the Kiev visit a photo flight was arranged and I flew the Gold Leaf Zlin. Was this the day when a lunch had also been arranged at British Car Auctions, Blackbushe? It might have been, but I also remember an awareness of distractions prior to takeoff. Unaccustomed jacket and tie might have been one of them. I also remember interrupting my walk round for some reason, and remember the point at which I did it. However I returned to the machine, continued, got in, started up, took off from Wycombe (Booker) and headed for the rendezvous Basingstoke way.

The first bit of formation was straightforward. 'Can you do some upside down?' was requested. I half rolled and continued to fly along. OK, that'll do – I rolled back right way up: the left-hand half of the canopy was covered in oil, and there was no oil pressure. Something has happened. I throttled back, looked for a good field, then saw Odiham down wind. Should be able to make it. Fortunately this field had finished with jets and now dealt with helicopters, so a downwind straight in on the runway was not an inconvenience. The station commander drove out to the turn off as I was looking for/at the evidence. As I have always found, meetings with senior military officers exemplify charm, discretion, sympathy and understanding personified. 'You can leave it here. Someone can come and fetch it, just give us a call', and so on. No asking what happened.

The Alan Curtis car auction lunch was surprisingly good, not what I'd expected by the look of the place and the one-time forlorn Blackbushe ambience.

Phillip Cartwright (I think), his pilot said 'it's a good place to come when you have your emergencies,' and left it at that. No one mentioned it or asked what the hell did you do. There comes a time when one doesn't.

I know exactly what I didn't do. What I did do was check the oil and put the dipstick/filler thing back in its place and under its lugs. When I returned to it and saw it looked correct I shut the little hatch on the wing – without twiddling the spring-loaded twiddler that locks it. Enough said. Though it is nice to have a flight engineer who checks these things on your behalf.

CHAPTER 24

THE LAST YEARS OF THE BRITISH AIRWAYS VC10, 1976-1980

The remainder of 1976 was quite busy by airline standards of the day; a minority of two or three day trips interspersed with sessions of 10 or so days away: in fact a browse through the logbook leaves the impression of roughly half the days of a month spent at work. That doesn't sound much to the layman, but one has to consider that it includes the nights as well. Our 747s had been in action for six years now, but the variety of VC10 destinations was still impressive, featuring many of the traditional venues of the middle east, central Africa, the far east, and some last outposts to the west – New York, Montreal and Toronto.

On Dec 6th 1976 I did a few right hand seat circuits at Prestwick in VM, the training VC10, so I became a supervisory captain. New pilots continued to join the VC10 fleet, and there was a regular supply of trainee captains to accompany on their numerous sectors under 'suspicion'. Hong Kong now had its 45° offset instrument approach, but it was still acceptable to make the famous 90° low level visual harbour circuit arrival, weather permitting. Would such a thing be acceptable today? The procedure required a well set up long base leg, which headed straight for the hillsides, and a clear idea of the landmarks that defined the 90 descending turn of the final approach, and the heights to go with it. The trick was to do this part carefully, and not be distracted by the inability to see the runway until a late stage of the turn. It's all to do with following the correct geometry and a clear plan as to how to achieve it. Supervising others in flight can be more than the bare word suggests, and well-chosen preemptive advice or suggestion can make life easier for all. A few salient tips prior to an attempt can lead to the elegant performance that would bolster confidence, and the experience might make all the difference one day – you never know.

Tourism opportunities

People often ask 'What's your favourite place?' 'Where would you live if you could choose anywhere?' and so on. A modern, post-nomadic city-dwelling public tend to assume an airline job to be serial holidaymaking, with pay instead of cost, and these enquiries are based on the would-be tourist's notion that somewhere else must be better than where they live: it's obvious, otherwise why would holidays be for sale? This is not an easy question. 'Where would you not like to live?' might be easier to answer, but there is no doubt that ad hoc travel does throw up visitor opportunities that might be difficult to arrange by package tour. Sometimes, accidental tourism – minus the accidents – can be more rewarding than the deliberate kind: there are no expectations and subsequent disappointment. The VC10 took me to places that were worth the visit for this reason, and I had never heard of the Rocket when I stayed at Dhaka. We had a free day, and this town did not appear to be a popular tourist destination in 1977. The weather was overcast and humid with only occasional light rain, so a river trip to Chandpur was arranged, a few hours downstream and about a third of the way to Chittagong and the open sea.

Built in 1929 on the Clyde, the Rocket paddle steamer was the fastest water transport in Bengal, and though the East India Company had been dissolved 50 years before its launch, much had not changed; in fact the condition of the 50-year-old Rocket reflected much of this history, although the details now showed its age and changing times. From the bustling ghats we made our way up the gangplank. On the port flying bridge stood an incongruous-looking tall, spare and gaunt man overseeing the departure proceedings, swathed in floor-length off-white sheeting that paid out in the wind, his head somewhat informally swathed in the several useful metres of similarly off-white cloth required by custom and practice. Who was this distinctive figure? The captain as prophet? Indeed it was, and, strangely enough, this get-up gave him rather more kudos than our own rather more stereotyped apology to the merchant marine. I had the impression that he would be actively assisting the will of Allah.

We were the only tourists in this bustling town, it appeared, and had the first class to ourselves, the whole top deck. A look over the rails revealed something quite different below, where the below-deck passengers and their possessions seemed to be constrained by chicken wire in what looked like a dark and bare hold. Much cheaper for sure, but better not for us to tarry here. After an hour or so out we were summoned to lunch, served in the saloon, and sat either side of a long bare table along the centreline of the ship. This cool and dark space is walled by the doors of the inward-looking windowless first class cabins, and our bearer dished out the mulligatawny soup into well-used monogrammed plates that must have come with the ship. Meat and two veg followed, and we finished with a bread and butter pudding worthy of Mrs Bridges, baked in a chipped enamel baking dish that had also come with the ferry's delivery. Plain, tasty, easy-to-digest and satisfying food; nothing grand or first-classy about this by modern standards – not a single burger, pizza or tandoori chicken wrap on offer, no menu either – but traditional fare for the admin classes, unchanged for a century, at least. Not one single detail had altered since 1929, and this was no attempt to recreate the old days. They were still here. The scene would have made a disappointing film set – not enough colour or 'authentic' props – but it was real; and the voyage continued its time capsule course.

The river widened as we proceeded south towards the sea, and other more substantial craft appeared. Smaller, local wooden trading boats were replaced by larger, square-rigged sampans, if that's what they're called, making their way northwards in the south west wind. We seemed to be the only powered vessel in evidence, and a square-rigged boat under sail was a rarity in the 1970s. Where the river direction was favourable a fleet of square sails confronted us, the sails made up of a variety of materials, but where else could you get a live impression of the Spanish Armada – even Trafalgar perhaps – in relative miniature may be, but alive? These were working boats; all of them. They favoured the west bank, and where the direction was too close to the wind the handful of crew would be dropped ashore, each with the end of a long rope attached to the mast, to trudge up the path in single file, towing the vessel until the river turned right again. Warping it's called. As we neared our destination our river joined the combination of Ganges and Brahmaputra – now so wide that you could barely see the other side – and as we waited for the modern diesel ferry back to town a wander round the adjacent railway sidings revealed the forged iron track fittings made in Cardiff. They're either still there today, or a part of industrial chic furniture, a worthy reprieve.

Current Google research reveals that there are four Rockets, but this was not evident on this day. The experience, like the next one, cannot be the same as part of a globalised tourist industry.

Political unrest and local strife used to have a larger effect on tourism in general. Accidental tourists are now less likely find themselves alone in notable places while communication, freedoms of information and access, and unstoppable by-the-minute visual news coverage of daily violence (to balance all the trivia) cuts a fear of the unknown down to size – sometimes at a price. Like invasive migration, tourism too has become unstoppable in the twenty-tens. It used to be tritely said that travel broadens the mind; but whose mind? Travel reinforces prejudice and encourages cultural strife, envy and greed: but it can (should) put historical cultures and the achievements we take for granted into a new perspective.

The VC10 also took me to Amman for the first time in 1977. We went to Petra, famous since its European rediscovery in 1812 by a studious Swiss lad. Another site to knock off on a free day down the routes – but it was more special than that.

'It's upside-down mountains,' someone said. Sounds novel, I thought, I will look for them with interest. The three-hour drive south revealed only flat desert, and little changed as our destination approached. At the visitor sign-up centre there was no sign of ancient monuments; the scenery had become vaguely hilly to the east, but upside-down mountains? Not as far as the eye could see. The word went around that the main place was a couple of kilometres away, and one rode on a slender animal to get there. Duly mounted on an assortment of generally mouse-coloured (to borrow Mark Twain's Cairo description) small horses we set off. Comprehensive horsemanship was not required as each was led by its walking owner, and, in any case, the Bedouin system is different – a single rope round the neck, held in the left hand, leaving the right for flamboyant waving of weapons. We set off into a nondescript gulley.

The sides soon became vertical and got progressively higher – in fact we were descending, and the narrow ravine meandered a little, so it was impossible to see where this was leading. After 20 minutes or so the limestone sides, mouse-coloured like the horses, had risen far above us, a hundred feet at least, leaving only a narrow glimpse of sky far above. A couple of the animals side by side filled the gulch – Indiana Jones country, but where were we heading?

Then we rounded a bend and there it was, mere yards ahead; initially the thinnest vertical sliver of brilliant orange light. Another few feet and the main feature of our quest was dramatically revealed: the famous red sandstone facade of what they call the Treasury, brilliantly lit by the morning sun, directly facing us across a wide vertical sided deserted canyon. We'd stepped out of the narrowest slot in our side of the upside-down mountains, but there was no one else here. Which way did Burkhardt arrive? Along the canyon from the south? He was amazed at what he saw, and nothing can equal the visual surprise of our dramatic eastern entrance on to this stage – the curtains pulled apart. Only the King of Jordan could arrange a private visit like this, and this chance circumstance is my answer to the 'What's the most impressive tourist experience of your career?' No question.

The real thing is much more impressive than its pictures. The size, the perfectly proportioned design can only be appreciated for real, and it's the precision, the accuracy of the triangles and circles, brightly exposed in the sun, that take your breath away. Surely it must be new – it's too good to be so old. Classical; Greeks or Romans, must be. These shapes have been copied for public buildings the world over, but the tradition long predates the Latin and Greek tradition we assume. Did pre-biblical desert people really come up with this stylistic sophistication? Where did they get the ideas? Makes you think – or should do.

During the same summer I went to Compton Abbas, a grass airfield on top of a hill in rural Wiltshire, for their air display. As an airshow visitor it is difficult to predict whether the journey will have been worthwhile – it all depends on the quality, of course, but not just of the flying. The commentator is vital, and on this occasion the combination of story-telling, straight man and comic genius produced something rare and unique in terms of aerial entertainment, in my experience. Wartime Tiger Moth instructor David Tomlinson took the part of the commentator, and his easy-going brilliance as a raconteur between acts was worth an Oscar by itself. There are qualities of the black and white film genre that are lost when colour is added, just as the stage does not translate directly to the screen. *Gone with the Wind* might have survived without Cinemascope, and David Tomlinson is probably best known by the public for his part as the father in *Mary Poppins*, but it's his old-school charm, perceptiveness, humour and generosity of nature that will be remembered.

He announced a demonstration of a new kind of flying instruction. The instructor demonstrates the exercises, and the student follows and copies – in a separate machine. This might have been an old gag, but it was new to me, and I wondered what flying surprises might be in store. However, the routine was one of lengthy and elegant preparation for the punchline, and the wearisome continuous struggle of the student might have become boring had not have been for its contrast with the correct, sedate and flawless behaviour of the instructor in front. There were no special manoeuvres, the whole routine was based on a couple of standard training circuits – a succession of the elements of basic flying training – but it was the relentless tedium of this awkward, lurching 57 knot progress of the hapless student, played by Barry Tempest, that both expressed the idea that learning to fly is not usually an overnight affair, and made it very funny because of the contrast with the effortless suavity of the instructor's flight. David Tomlinson's informed (naturally) commentary was not deadpan exactly, but it sounded totally credible – what you would expect of a 1940s documentary; simply informative with undertones of optimism.

At the start of the second approach we were informed that the loop would be next. The instructor picked up speed (90kts) and performed the small round figure that so eminently suits the low wing loading biplane trainer. The student followed a couple of hundred yards behind and similarly picked up speed, a bit uncertainly perhaps: a bit steep? A bit low? Not necessarily, but the nervous student was still at the controls, clenched his teeth and pulled up. The Tiger Moth soared into the sky, hesitated, fell over the top and dived decisively out of sight into the steep valley alongside the field. Afterwards I told Barry Tempest how it was the mundane but relentless contrast of the two Tigers that kept the attention and was so funny. 'Yes,' he said, 'Neil [Williams] is a good straight man.'

Training the trainers – a Hamble project

At the end of October 1977 I went to a course for commercial training pilots, cobbled up at Hamble. This dismissive analysis is in no way intended to involve the staff there, who continued to do their job as best they could, and it might have been that this scheme was a part of British Airways' plans to address what clearly had been identified as a need for development in the understanding of what the word 'training' should mean in the workplace. It could also be that the college currently had spare capacity, but I'm guessing. I see that our session lasted three weeks. It is possible to learn a lot in three weeks, but this was traditional instructor stuff – briefing, pattering and so on – the one-sided bare bones of teaching learners, without any of the people-handling interaction and flexibility that should go with it, especially relevant for dealing with experienced employees. But, in its defence, I will say it introduced or refreshed elements of principles of flight, briefing and explaining, in-flight demonstrating and so on, which are subjects missing from the basic examiner's qualification.

This course had also been offered to the world's commercial trainers, and we BA candidates were joined by a couple of Americans. They turned out to be a breath of fresh air; on first acquaintance rough diamonds indeed, but sociable, quietly experienced, with an American pragmatic approach to flying – of anything. Both were Vietnam veterans, one navy and the other army. Dismayed by our Hamble boy formality they confessed to having been highly unimpressed at our two blazer and tie wearers. 'We thought you must be snobs' they said. Exasperated by having to sit through Effect of Controls part one in a Cherokee, the army pilot took the controls from Bernie Sercombe and said 'Here's the American version,' then he booted the rudder, tipped the wings the other way and asked, 'Hey Bernie, you feel your ass hangin' out the door?'

For my part I did manage to get the CFI to renew my instructor's rating – free – and the three-week visit down memory lane, all in, was pleasant and relaxing enough. One afternoon I knocked on the door of an acquaintance from my Hamble Players days. She had been an accomplished, versatile and charismatic actress, and I expected a sunny rekindling of old enthusiasms. 'I'm sorry,' she said, 'I've no recollection of you at all [my character acting must have been better than I thought] but come in and have some tea anyway'. A teenaged daughter eyed me suspiciously as the mother explained 'I've given up all that – completely'. Best not to pursue the inquiries, I decided, and left after sufficient and totally insignificant small talk. Sometimes one can't start to guess.

It was during a dank and quiet December 1977 that I had a phone call from Peter Woodham, the Rothmans team manager. 'Have you heard from Neil recently?' This request was unusual in that I had no direct dealings with Rothmans, and there was no current competition aerobatic activity at all. 'He seems to have disappeared,' he continued, 'I wondered if he'd been in touch.' A couple of days later the news percolated around: the Spanish Heinkel 111 wreck had been found in the mountains north of Madrid. There were no survivors. It had been the last of many difficult cross-countries.

Sheikh's runabout

On Feb 1st 1978 I signed my namesake and flight manager Pete Riley's licence after a simulator session. That evening he phoned me and asked if I would like to go to Doha tomorrow. This is an unusual way for the roster system to work, but why not? 'The first officer knows all about it; and if you want to know anything ask the chief steward.' Definitely unusual, but I turned up, met the crew and discovered that this would be empty positioning for Qatar's private contract operation, part of which was G-ARVJ, a standard VC10 masquerading as Gulf Air. A few months earlier I'd come across a similar-looking A40-VG and taken it to Tehran, but, apart from VM, the training aircraft, the standard machines were now thin on the ground, and rarely seen in action. VJ was operated by relatively dedicated crew and a couple of office captains, as far as I could tell, but as a new joiner and therefore hardly part of the VC10 furniture I knew nothing about this fringe operation.

This invitation turned out to be an introduction to an interesting and enjoyable extra-curricular job, starting with the first evening. We'd arrived over Doha after dark, and it was foggy – below limits. We flew around for a while but there was no improvement, nor likely to be one, so a nightstop at Bahrain, just up the road, seemed the answer. No one disagreed, and we made seamless progress to a very nice hotel, and excellent dinner – this was a well-oiled team at work; I could tell.

When I'd got to my room John Willett, the manager of this quiet VIP operation, had phoned from Doha: 'Hello Pete,' he started. 'It's Mike Riley, not Pete,' I said. A slight pause – this had been a surprise – then 'OK – I've got a little job for you tomorrow; come over here after breakfast, go to Geneva, 1030, then come back the next day,' said John, the subtle tones of London unmistakable.

We'd not met as such, but John, now retired from the airline, had been VC10 technical flight manager during the command course, and had given us a lecture about saving taxi-out fuel – takeoff downwind if it's quicker, go from an intermediate turnoff if you can – shorter taxi etc., don't leave your engine running on the cab rank – not exactly, but he was financially correct. All these details make a difference to what's left in the till at the end of the day, in the manager's favour.

Next day Ray Jacques, chief steward – in fact manager diplomacy and catering might be a better job description – gave me a quick rundown on the Amiri Flight system. 'No cabin address, nice landings, idle reverse only – they don't bother with strapping in or sitting down necessarily – if you go in the cabin don't look at the women, and shake hands with the men; Arabic first names are more important so you are Captain Mike.'

Our hotel in Geneva was again very upscale, and all the crew, including Ray Daley, our flying spanner, met in the posh bar for nice drinks before another fine dinner. There's a special reason for this – no allowances, but a step up in accommodation plus signing for the food and drink as you wish, within reason. I discovered that Dom Perignon is an easier-drinking aperitiv than first class champagne, that real fine food is tasty, and they give you just enough – not too much – and that real wine is pleasantly restorative without the intrusive assault of burnt chocolate, roasted woodland fruits, tanned oak bark, mid-term notes of petrol-marinated smoky pineapple with ethylene glycol at the finish. If you really wanted to taste these you could make up the concoction yourself, and without them you sleep better and wake up feeling fresh as a daisy.

Music, tropical medicine and the NHS

Airline crews tend not to eat and drink in the hotels they stay in, even though industrial politics used to require that their local eating allowance (cash in hand) was defined by this assumption. Frequently, elsewhere in the relevant town offered cheaper prices and more variety and local ambience, but it all depended on which town, and the exchange value of the local currency, and eating in was sometimes a good option – even if you paid with what now seemed like your own money.

At the beginning of May 1978 I did a trip which started with positioning to Nairobi, then pick up a VC10 service and proceed via the Seychelles to Colombo and stay there for nearly a week (that's what the logbook says). Colombo was somewhere I'd scarcely visited since my Comet days – Galle Face or Mount Lavinia hotels then – but now we stayed at the new Oberoi, a splendid affair in the current multi-storey atrium style, and their food was great (Muscat had a similar one with flying lifts – very modern). One evening at dinner the expansive and palm-treed ground floor space was treated to some music from a local string quartet, led by a saried lady who can only have been an established Colombo violin teacher, and they weren't bad at all – not the Amadeus or Allegri teams exactly, but good – 'Competent in all respects'. Then they were joined by an earnest-looking and slight young Sri Lankan man, bearing no instrument; the leader's son, perhaps, he's going to sing. Without further ado they launched into the 1914 '*Wien, Wien, nur du allein, etc (Vienna, city of my dreams)*,' made famous by Richard Tauber, and now sung (in the original) and accompanied with accuracy, simplicity and sincerity, with no expressive posturing; just standing and singing the song like an eight-year-old at the school concert. To say I was enchanted sounds arch, but it's the best word. It was as charming as it was unexpected. A little incongruous, perhaps, but a flickering reminder of something from days long gone, and definitely far away.

We left Colombo to go via Dubai to nightstop in Dhahran. That night I didn't sleep much because my head was ringing for some unknown reason, and I felt cold. May is not a cold time of year here and, believe it or not,

Saudi Arabia is an abstemious place, and next morning we were to continue to London in tomorrow's aircraft, so there had been little active winding down and team building following the day of sunlit cruising. Neither had I been sitting in the sun because this was yet another supervision trip – and I sat on the right. To drink some water and wait for the feeling to go away seemed the most sensible plan – any deciding can wait until tomorrow. The cold and somewhat distant sensation had not gone away, but enough life remained for a carefully judged spear-carrying part (the real alabaster captain, for those who remember our Comet flight manager), and I was confident that the two boys plus trusty flight engineer could easily get us home without my help, should that become necessary. However, the 7hr flight went normally with its quiet and non-controversial co-pilot.

Readers may have opinions about the outrageous recklessness of choosing to operate a long-range commercial passenger-carrying transport when you have a suspicion that you may not be your usual 100%, and have the power to interrupt the everyday lives of many people in an instant. This, in fact, is not as easy a decision as a majority of Twitter or a naive minority of PPRuNe commentators may suggest. It's a matter of experience and judgment, and it has been gratifying to once read the comments of a respected American pilot in defence of a technical decision to fly which was bureaucratically criticised as putting people at risk. 'I put my passengers at risk every time I take off. If you want to avoid all flying risk stay, on the ground.' Of course, it's all a matter of degree – assessing the odds, and knowing which way to bet, and these were still the days before universal electronic communication had had time to undermine respect for all tradition established outside the jungle.

Next day I went into the training office with the boy-captain's file and the two ladies who did our work for us were immediately unanimous. 'You look terrible. Go home and don't come back until you're all right.' There were no other symptoms, but that seemed to clinch it – I'd got something, but what?

There was no doubt that my temperature alternated between too high and too low; the several degrees too low was novel, but there it was. A neighbour thumbed through a weighty nursing book from distant days. Malaria? No, not enough symptoms. Dengue fever looked more like it, but all the possibles had multiple choice symptoms, and I had none except for the thermometer and a sense of distance and fragility. If I did nothing I felt almost normal, but after ten minutes of easy gardening I was exhausted. With no supplementary symptoms I felt a fraud, but what was interesting was the change of preference in food and drink. I could not countenance the idea of anything except water or fruit juice to drink; didn't fancy the idea of tea, coffee, beer, wine and so on, and was only interested in fruit to eat – not much either, but a nice fry up? Forget it.

'It's probably best if you stay in bed,' said my wife, who contacted the village doctor practice, a husband and wife team who could alternate when attending profitable NHS courses without shutting up shop. We'd usually seen the wife, who was a local violin-playing acquaintance of mine, but the report of my lack of obvious symptoms did not tick any of the routine kids and family boxes, so she sent her husband (women's problems and serious stuff) round. This was Doctor Cameron to her Finlay, and he felt around for an enlarged or solidified liver, but failed to find one, and was noncommittal. What about a blood test?

The district nurse came round the next day and took some, but what was the result? To this day I've no idea, except that a weekly repeat would be prudent. Ten miles away there was a major and world-renowned ancient university town, with its variety of hospitals swarming with teaching and research, in fact I have the scars to prove it – 1949 radiation burns on a hand from an experimental wart-removal procedure. The warts were tiny anyway, and any others soon went away of their own accord, out of fright, I would guess (but where did this idea come from?) Even so, there was no diagnosis, recommendation or prognostication. I didn't cost the National Health System much, and doing nothing worked. I got progressively used to feeling lighter, weaker and clearer-headed, and around the fifth week got up one morning feeling surprisingly normal (apart from lighter), went to the bathroom as usual and, my God! dark brown urine – now it's serious. But I was cured, I knew it. I reported this down the village. 'You'd better go to the Churchill and have another blood test,' said the doctor/violinist neighbour. This result was clear, I heard a few days later – no sedimentation: so the others had sedimentation, had they? I can only guess.

The M word had never been mentioned, nor had anything else. The suspicion is that nobody had a clue. My next door neighbour had been a practising doctor, and was now part of Wellcome Institute management. I asked him where the risk extended. 'Anywhere south of Rome,' he said. When I'd started out in BOAC Lapudrine and Paludrine tablets were an indispensable way of life for Eastern travellers, along with assorted jabs and a yellow passport-sized record book, but this custom seemed to progressively die out as the world became more global. Does this principle mean safer? Only if you're trying to sell something, and I do remember the phrase 'only a mild attack' having featured somewhere in the paperwork so maybe I had benefited from this pill-popping tradition. Of course the Hippocratic oath does not exclude 'Do nothing', and bearing in mind that life itself is not a good risk, invariably fatal of course, and that there was no desperate pilot shortage, I cannot complain about my treatment. It worked.

Continued life on a declining fleet – more training the trainers

My return to work was met with no special interest whatever: no enquiries, no doctor certificates, no company fitness for work check, signing on or off. Had I made up the story in order to give myself a month in Benidorm or Hawaii? No one asked. Landing recency? Way outside, but not even the office ladies raised the subject.

I resumed work with ten days of Atlantic trips at the end of June. This is how it should be in an organisation where individual responsibility is assumed, and thereby encouraged – quite unlike the no doubt well-intentioned but soft-minded, naive and ill-informed, politically correct but totalitarian snowflake bureaucracy that has eventually replaced a way of life over the intervening 40 years. The concise-sounding 1984 was an Orwellian guess as to date, reversing the current year's digits, but the author was correct about the advent of the internet, it's influence and the beginning of 'interesting' times.

However, during this second half of the '70s life for British Airways flyers was to change, for the better in general, represented by changes of attitude and new understandings about how they should deal with each other at work, in a manner best suited to peaceful transport in well-equipped, generally user-friendly machines, supported by a legion of unsung, unseen and, by and large, unrecognised but faithful non-flying helpers. This narrative has already suggested that the 'training' among flight deck members had not always been ideal in either BEA or BOAC who, perforce, had started to join forces in 1974. Each organisation had their opinion of the other – resentfully critical from the parochials, disdainfully dismissive from the worldly-wise – but now the long/short specialisation was slowly beginning to lose some of its character, and it was elements of the parochial zealots, of approximately my generation, who determined to wield the new broom. Were we to experience a mini Reformation?

There is nothing worse than the new convert, they say, but, with an historical foot in both camps, I can say that this move for change was a good thing (the exchanges of trivia aside). It became evident that homespun psychology (common sense by another name) had become a saleable product in commerce and industry, and week-long courses in human communication and behaviour and the best way to go about them began to appear – nothing to do with Aim,

Airmanship and Air Exercise, but how to best transfer and receive information; about anything, for anyone.

The first course that I remember presented simple concepts – nothing too Freudian, Jungian, or tacky new-age therapeutic. Why not start by considering what your student does or does not already know? How do you check whether they are taking your information on board? Ask, of course; but these helpful ideas, which make life easier for both sides (which includes you, the man with the concealed stick), would have been quite revolutionary for some case-hardened examiner/trainers. The CAA response to complaints about the conduct and result of their own tests on the public had been to require a candidate to sign that they had understood the briefing, for subsequent use in court. Why not ask the candidate to explain the bare bones back to you before leaving the briefing room? Aha! That would be cheating! This is not the full story of the CAA examiner training by any means, but, along with 'Make sure you have your fail points clearly noted' it can suggest what some will have taken away from the course as the whole story. And I might repeat my theory that many suitable airline people with real instructing experience don't want to do the job for various reasons.

We heard about matching personal one-to-one communicating style; adult/child, adult/adult (sometimes applying to husband/wife), and so on. It's a bit of acting, but everyone does it to some extent, and you should be aware of it – adjust your game to the student, make it adult/adult, create a level classroom, even a level cockpit. It works best.

I found this classroom invitation to a logical analysis of one's identity when communicating with others quietly therapeutic, and a welcome opportunity to step back from the emotionally-charged environment whenever training/checking is mentioned. A retreat, a cloistered session of meditation and mental clarification? Definitely, and I've no idea what anyone else thought.

This Age of Enlightenment in the workplace was to continue, but it may have got a little above itself in due course, particularly when the idea was spread to large areas of unsuspecting staff, both flying and non-flying. Tinkering with the minds of others, however well-intentioned, has long been known to have the potential for damage if not handled with care and, historically, this practice has only been made available to those with adequate judgment and understanding. By virtue of staying on minor fleets I happened to miss the Putting People First course ('Kiss the Customer'), but Cockpit 2000 and Breakthrough (renamed Breakdown by cabin staff), upset some people. The ability of such introspection to undermine the sense of self was not worth the risk, in my view. If it ain't broke don't fix it (much) is not always wrong. The original versions of these transatlantic invitations to self-revelation were intended for the higher echelons of business life, with the essential assumption that individuals had actively put themselves forward in the bid for career advance. But a growing enthusiasm for DIY psychotherapy and the questionable legitimacy of those who peddled it seems to have encouraged a filtering down through the employee pyramid – perhaps an end-of-line cheap sell-off of their premium products, not to forget the street-level consumer's eagerness to buy. We may get to this subject later in this story, 15 years down this road.

Early on in my captaining career it had long become obvious that much more was to be gained if potential captains (co-pilots) acquired as much hands-on experience as possible; after all, I might well be their unwitting passenger one day. What is to be gained by a captain selfishly practising what he considers himself to be good at anyway – unless this is genuinely needed? He may well have his private reasons – it takes all sorts – but this war baby's quest for Biggles excellence had dwindled somewhat over fifteen years of commercial transport. How difficult is it really? Even so, one lives and learns: never assume, is one good rule, and keep a weather eye out is another, especially if your crew are total strangers to start with. In the case which follows we had already spent a week flying our VC10s all over the place up and down Africa and three places in India. Now, this last day was to take us all the way home from Delhi, calling at Tehran and Dusseldorf on the way. It was mid January.

We had a few Cat C first officers in those days. These were co-pilots who had been deemed not suitable for command, generally older ones from distant days who had failed years back; but there were chances of reprieve. At the start of this trip the Cat C co-pilot explained that his case was to be reviewed and could he have some flying, and my subsequent report. 'Absolutely,' I said, 'Delighted to be of help.' I cannot remember how many, but certainly he had flown most if not all of the ten sectors we had already done, and things had jogged along without problem, and years of even non-captain experience must mean something.

We had not long left Delhi when we got the latest weather for Tehran. Snowing again and likely to continue, still open but on our approach limits. Not good: even if we got in would we get out again in 45 minutes? Very unlikely, maybe stuck for days, who can say? (I've been there before.) So the decision was made to call at Kuwait instead, and get rid of our Tehran passengers. Good idea; so, like a good co-pilot, I went to the nav table to rustle up some suitable paperwork for the reroute. When I returned to my seat and looked at my inertial box it showed many miles off track. The autopilot was still following our initial heading, and we had long gone beyond the range of the Delhi VOR. No one else was driving, and the putative captain was already fretting over charts depicting a problem-free Kuwait, hours ahead. Inertial navigation is a wonderful labour-saving device and a simple press of the 'go straight to the next legitimate place' button reestablished order, but the ball had been well and truly dropped and the first priority of keeping the show on the road overlooked, for no credible reason except preoccupation with trivia.

Back at London I discussed this problem with the training manager, not wishing to appear too judgmental on paper. 'Write it down' he urged. But that was not all. A couple of weeks later flight manager Peter Riley called me in as I passed his office. He gave me a letter from the Indian authorities. 'It's probably rubbish, but does this mean anything to you?' The letter pointed out that our flight had left its intended track and strayed close to the Pakistan border, a very dangerous thing to do – you could have been shot down. Kashmir tensions were high at this time, with much military attention directed at the area. I explained the truth and wrote a suitably grovelling and apologetic reply for the Indians. Problem solved, but another lesson – for me.

I flew with another of these co-pilots, but his problem was more social than technical. After his command course he had become a 'captain' to the neighbours, his children, his wife? Difficult to say, but he had acquired a captain's jacket and hat and left the house as such, to stop at a pre-airport alternative-universe telephone box, do the Superman trick in reverse, and then run this film backwards on the way home. Stay in the real world and keep the stress level down, I would have advised. 'It's unlikely your wife hasn't guessed anyway. Fess up and avoid the telephone box nonsense.'

We had some retread co-pilots as well – retired officers from all three services who had joined to make use of the few years that remained before our retirement age of 55. Like the Cat Cs they were older than me, and invariably demonstrated the easy-going and unruffled demeanour one associates with long, varied and responsible military life of around the three-ring level, at a guess, though I might have underestimated this in some cases. I can't remember names, but, just to give balance, I remember that one had flown the Sea Fury, another had been responsible for a squadron of Beavers, and a third was an enthusiast for black powder, muzzle-loading weapons.

The latter (with Royal Air Force experience) suggested that he and I should take a windsurfing lesson in the Seychelles. This was a whirlwind sweaty and sandy run through of the basics on the beach, followed by an attempt to put them into practice in the shallows. What our instructor demonstrated was all correct, but the compressed time scale meant that our waterborne struggles were supremely unrewarding. His own scooting around the bay proved that it can be done. If he could do it it was possible, and I resolved to pursue this sport at a later date, in my own time. Like the decision not to return to mainline modern BA fleets this turned out to be worthwhile, again from a personal rather than financial perspective.

Display at Denham

On June 4th 1978 there was a Tiger Club full display at Denham. This wasn't quite the multi-facetted event that it had been in the early 1960s, but over the Thursday, Friday and Saturday I see that I made nine biplane flights, two Super Tiger and the rest Stampe, totalling 3 hrs, all formation. I remember the Super Tiger participation because the light wing loading combined with a historical wing section gave a bucking bronco ride in the sunny early summer east wind turbulence, sufficient to create peaks of negative g which temporarily starved the engine of fuel (during non-aerobatic mode station-keeping), but all the flying on the previous two days had been a work up with Pete Jarvis for his duo routine – formation and synchro aerobatics in the Stampe. Ten years previously Manx Kelly had asked me if I would care to join him in the Stampe mirror formation act he was working up, but being of a cautious disposition and a wary learner I declined. Since then the ten years had passed, Pete was one of nature's team players, and enjoyed nothing more than formation management – for its own sake. This was the first time I had taken part in this duo performance, the basics of which had been in place for a number of years with Stampe and Zlin, and his special qualities of confident leadership and well-chosen advice on the finer points rapidly produced a good enough result. My evidence for this claim comes from the remarks of Peter Phillips, who specifically asked who was doing the formating. 'It was very good,' he commented after the show. Praise indeed.

Formation aerobatics in low performance light aircraft has its challenges; the manoeuvres are small, happen quickly and require very good station-keeping because of limited spare power for catching up. The leader is restricted by the ultimate performance of a wingman, but is able to make the most of what's available if the latter calls 'Power' when on his limit, and 'Go' when the lead has given you a brief catch-up bonus. This luxury is still not always possible, especially in looping, where any individual increase in radius means more distance to cover, and inevitable falling behind – not possible to recover except by pulling inside the circle and cutting the corner. A box man, behind, a bit below and virtually under the tail of the leader does not have this ability. I remember being very impressed by a military 4-ship Chipmunk team display at around this time. When I saw a loop in box formation coming up I wondered what would happen. To work, the loop itself had to be small, started with plenty of Chipmunk speed, and no hanging around over the top, and to keep everyone's radius small enough the wingmen had to stay well forward, almost line abreast thus making a squashed diamond shape. The box man was bound to drop back somewhere, I thought, but this brief loop was impressive. He got himself some extra speed on the pre pull-up dive, used this to slide virtually underneath the leader as they proceeded up to the top, propeller tips close below the leader's seat, and the inevitable slide back on the way down as geometry took its toll only ended up in the right place at the end. Many years later I discovered that this had been Concorde copilot Ken Snell's dad Dick, one-time Hamble instructor. Kid's stuff for beginner's aeroplanes? Not a bit of it. Much easier than Hunter and Hawk? Not entirely.

The remaining two VC10 years passed with an agreeable mix of assorted route flying and useful time at home, but the last time VM, the training aircraft, appears in the logbook seems to be the end of August 1978. I believe it then went to the Cosford Museum, and the last time I saw some of it, 30 years later, the bits were at Brooklands. But at least it escaped the fate of some of its standard model colleagues.

Approaching the company car park one day in 1979 I saw a surprising sight behind the hangars. Had there been a monumental accident? In a corner of the hardstand area, a bit to the left of, and not far short of the 28R threshold was a huge pile of wreckage strewn around. There was too much of it for one airliner, definitely something bad, but I'd heard nothing on the news. There were no obvious signs of fire, and on closer view it was obvious that these were pieces of VC10, dismantled by wrecking ball , chainsaw and the thermic lance for the strong bits. Whether the site was guarded by mean junkyard dogs at night I don't know, but, encountered unawares, this was something of an apocalyptic sight. And though I cannot claim an attack of distressing sentiment, a sudden doubt in the assumption of secure future employment was understandable. What am I to discover upstairs? Has the whole company actually gone bust overnight?

But the reason was more business-like than that. A recent deal had been struck up with Boeing for new aircraft, and one condition was the on-the-spot destruction of a number of old but usable ones, these being they. No sentiment please, this is business, and British Airways was now a sink-or-swim public company, responsible to its shareholders – 'Our price for you requires no selling off your second hand stuff to those who might otherwise buy our new ones' Boeing had contracted. The old days were going, but our continued agreeable working pattern allowed for plenty of assorted light aircraft flying, with some interesting teaching, all unpaid, but rewarding none the less. It's nice to help out – give something back, as Captain Varley explained – and charitable work gives a freedom not found in paid employment. It can also represent useful experience and learning.

The RAE Flying Club at Farnborough replaced their Tiger Moth with a Chipmunk so there were members who needed converting, plus a number still on the way to their licence, or keen to learn new things. There were aerobatic lessons in the Zlin to give, and displays in both Zlin and Pitts, and the last two VC10 years continued with some extended periods of home-based life which did include some simulator and base flying, but gave the eating and sleeping system a chance to resume diurnal normality. Many airline staff tend to claim that they become accustomed to changes of time zone, and the modifications this calls for when combined with what amounts to random shift changes. As creatures we are also psychologically sensitive to unusual temperatures and light levels, and there is something disturbing about standing in a freezing American winter street with a blue sky and midsummer light level at a time when the interior clock says it should be dark and one should be preparing for bed.

'A night's sleep and I'm on local time' is a frequent claim, but it does not reflect my own experience. I had long assessed that one hour per 24 is the fastest one can genuinely adapt to changes of local time, and chronic shortage of regular sleep on top changes the personality, thinking and priorities – just a bit for some, perhaps – but I also came to the conclusion that six weeks of living in the same place was needed to restore the original person, and three months even better. Many frequent distance flyer readers may disagree, but the private opinions of close family members might contribute to a valid study. These were the days of 28-day recency for captains, but we all know what rules are for, and training staff were expected to decide these things for themselves in this slightly old-fashioned fleet. Quite right too. 1984 was still a few years ahead, and the soft Orwellian world of the twenty teens not even thought about.

At the beginning of April 1979 I made my second and last Amiri trip in the Gulf Air lookalike VJ. A few weeks later Pete Riley was coming back from Doha in this machine when, somewhere over Yugoslavia, there was suddenly a thump and a shuddering, and some loss of performance. Inspection showed that some of the engine cowling on one side had come adrift and was acting as a speed brake. It didn't look too good either. They went into Vienna, jury-rigged it in place with rope and took off for London. It's wonderful what can be done when an airliner is operated as a private aircraft with a resourceful crew. This VC10 escaped the crusher and went on to be a military tanker, as did a number of the supers, but between my last VJ encounter and my last SVC10 flight exactly one year later I see that 13 SVC10 registrations feature in the logbook. These cover A to R, missing out O, N and Q. Two of the missing ones had been hijacked and destroyed by the Palestine Liberation Organisation.

Two South African air display accidents

In December 1979 I took a Zlin to Goodwood to renew my instructor's rating with Peter Phillips. The test includes the full briefing and airborne lesson of one of the classic exercises. 'Why don't you teach me inverted spinning?' he said. This request was unusual but not a problem. The routine spinning patter is quite adequate, except that it starts with the upside down straight and level stall, stick forward and a choice of rudder for the spin, then the appropriate decision of rudder direction for recovery followed by stick back instead of forward. The Zlin, of course, is designed for right way up flying, and therefore does a convincing inverted spin, and the upside-down scenery passing the nose from one side to the other clear to see, albeit opposite to the roll element as observed from inside. This all went well, and he then asked to fly himself around upside down for a while, a few turns this way and that to achieve more negative g. 'It relieves my back, quite a lot,' he said.

The Trilander crash at Lanseria near Johannesburg had occurred two years earlier, probably a result of African density altitude, a trap for visitors. This performance problem has already been mentioned in the Twisty Winternitz aerobatic affair of 1968, but the central plain of Africa is so large and the coast so far away that the 5700 ft altitude seems to have no significance to a visitor, and ISA + 20 feels pleasantly warm, but not hot.

A few years before, Nick Turvey had taken me for a ride in a Wittman Tailwind, also near Johannesburg. The Tailwind was designed as a home-builder's fast and economical two-seat cruiser. These requirements suggest simplicity, relative ease of handing, adequate strength and manoeuvrability, combined with low weight and low drag at cruising speed. Like all successful designs this is quite a balancing act between many interrelated parameters, and formula-racer designer Steve Wittman's high-wing, low-aspect ratio side-by-side little machine bowled along at a very respectable clip for its small engine. It was straightforward and pleasant to fly as well, but its secret was its wing section, and the complications of this black art will not be covered here (I recently bought the 1940s bible by Abbott and Von Dönhoff. Pages one and two were promising, but I was lost in the mathematics thereafter). What surprised me, following the eager if fast takeoff, good climb and handy cruise was Nick's advice before we approached to land, and this was similar to that for a high-performance jet with limited power available. Until arrival on the runway was guaranteed, the speed required (to be able to climb away and escape) was a good bit faster than touchdown speed; in other words, the difference between minimum drag and minimum flying speed was considerable. Wing profile and low aspect ratio (ease of building, good rolling, strength and hangar width being four reasons) and a propeller carved for high-speed cruise might have had something to do with this, but density altitude (about 8000 ft in the Transvaal) was significant. As a sea level flier, given an unbriefed solo flight in this innocuous looking toy, I would have made a stall check, added a few knots and felt confident that all would have been well, but it might not have been if this low density environment had not been carefully considered.

Peter Phillips did not mention his accident in connection with the upside-down Zlin pretend lesson, and I had taken little interest in it, but I heard more about it later, especially after Nick Turvey's Pitts accident at the same airshow a year or so later. The Pitts in question had wings of the normal S1 shape but increased in area to compensate (a little) for the Johannesburg density altitude problem. This has never been mentioned as a cause of his crash – but it seems that the final gyroscopic manoeuvre finished with inadequate height remaining to achieve level flight. The final Trilander wingover (also reported as a stall turn) also found itself without enough of the thin air below it for the intended orderly landing which should have followed. Though injured and briefly stunned by the first bounce off the ground (which removed one undercarriage leg with its engine, and nodded the centre engine, bending the tail and jamming the elevator position), Phillips had the presence of mind on the subsequent second descent to wind the trim forward for more pitch up to alleviate the final ground contact. However, none of this alters the fact that this was yet another airshow accident that should not have happened – it was supposed to be a marketing demonstration of a transport aircraft.

Both these public accidents were reported with the suggestion of the heroism society seeks for the reassurance it needs in times of trouble. This is a kinder way of interpreting the event for posterity, and undoubtedly takes into account the great experience and skills of these two pilots. After writing chapter 22, noting my last piloting involvement with world aerobatic championships, it occurred to me to write an essay comparing the motivations of the competition discipline with those of display flying. The former is surprisingly safe because as a technical discipline there are no marks for theatre and no public acclaim; the latter enthusiasm can be fraught with risk, as is demonstrated worldwide on a regular basis, because it gives pilots of inadequate skill, experience, maturity and judgment (pick-and-mix, as you wish) the opportunity to indulge a mistaken delusion of ability in front of an uninformed, uncritical but expectant crowd. I have no hesitation in describing an attempt to do something you know you cannot do, justified by the theatrical environment, as a kind of criminal insanity, but I would not include the two Lanseria accidents in the same category: their backgrounds contain more of the genuinely heroic, plus adequate experience. Mistaken judgments were made in both events, and there are common factors.

Both pilots were born within a year of 1930, so both were 15 years old, give or take, at the end of WW2, a time when military aviation was to the forefront of national consciousness. Nick Turvey joined the South African Air Force in 1953, trained on the Harvard and the Vampire – aerobatics, formation and low level included – got his wings in 1955 and began teaching in the civilian world in 1958. In 1963 he founded Avex Air with likeminded Mike van Ginkel, and this company went on to engage in many ventures – assorted training, charter, from crop spraying to magnetometer survey with the Beaver and DC3. Aerobatics continued alongside and Nick became national champion in 1964, also taking part in that year's worlds in Spain where he shared a Tiger Club Stampe with Peter Phillips. Nick won his national championship another 7 times, and also took part in the 1968 and 1972 world championships, this last in the challenging Rooivalk as already described. In total this all represents a lot of hands on flying experience.

Peter Phillips joined the RAF in 1950, and was first posted to a fighter squadron in north Germany, flying the Vampire, then the Sabre. Next came instructing, and more Vampire formation display aerobatics in the CFS team. The Hunter was next, with many solo display appearances – in all, ten years of the swooping, looping, wingovering, Cubaning, rolling and combinations thereof that make up High Flight's dancing on laughter-silvered wings, popular for fighters and advanced trainers. This is a kind of flying plus agreeable institutional lifestyle, only available to those with access to the right machinery and support. The Tiger Club came next – some aerobatic competition tried, and the tiny Cosmic Wind replaced the Hunter display, just a bit: but, for young boys imprinted with manoeuvring flight, the change to a completely different life is not possible thereafter. One has to make do with whatever version is available. So why did they both get it wrong at Lanseria?

I've read overconfidence presented as a reason. Maybe one could rephrase this as lack of attention to detail – inadequate consideration of all the relevant factors at play. There certainly was a reason, there always is, but why did two very experienced and eminently capable pilots forget what Nick had told me years before – an aerobatic sequence uses twice the height at Johannesburg? These words would suggest that, on average, each height-burning figure is not only larger, but uses twice the height – this means the loss of height during a manoeuvre required to achieve enough energy for the next one. This will become very evident when near the ground, but by then it may be too late to observe the warning. Any analytical pundit can throw in a few more factors: the machine handles differently, there's less aerodynamic damping, behaviour is more dynamic, and so on. Anyone who can spell 'pilot error' can make the final judgment, and he would not be wrong; but I think there's more to understand than this would suggest. What is the real reason? Of course it's the pilot, and pilots change, all through life, whether they like the idea or not. Some build on their experience and go on to achieve command and management responsibility and status: others just want to be pilots (I am one of these).

A judgment of overconfidence does not tell us much, and confidence itself mellows with maturity and experience. A problem for maturing enthusiasts can be the changes of focus and priorities that come with life experience. Life tends to get more complicated as time goes by: the mind routinely reboots, reprograms, readapts itself to current situations and demands, taking on board more unavoidable baggage, more distraction. People currently say things like '50 is the new 30'. In your dreams, maybe – why not 70 the new 40? It's a mistake to believe these encouraging but misguided statements, especially for the maturing Biggles and Algy, and one should remember that limitless experience does not alter the 50/50 odds of each heads or tails throw, or a chance encounter with the unexpected – which, by definition, cannot be predicted. Something unexpected happened to both of these pilots: I cannot say what it was, but mention the events as a caution to those who would rush to judgment, and also to any pilot who is reluctant to acknowledge the difference between the fully focused and clear brained youth, and the more experienced, knowledgeable and analytical, but mentally cluttered sage they will become.

At the time of writing (2017) I happened to be reading – quite by chance – a book by Deneys Reitz, a celebrated and influential South African soldier, lawyer and politician. This is what he says about a flight in a DH84 (September 1933):

> *My family and I had a narrow escape about this time. There was a well-known pilot in Johannesburg, Mr Cochran-Patrick. He had assembled a new Dragon plane and he invited my wife and boys and myself on a test flight. We sat on empty petrol boxes and as he had several thousand flying hours to his credit I felt no anxiety, though I did not like the careless manner in which he banked and turned, and when we landed I noticed that the plane keeled over until one wing was practically skimming the ground.*
>
> *I think that this was a case of familiarity breeding contempt as he did things a less experienced flyer would never have attempted. He shut off one engine to prove that he could fly on the other alone and he slowed down to almost stalling point before revving up again.*
>
> *When we landed I heard one of the mechanics say, 'We don't like that kind of flying here, it gives the club a bad name.'*
>
> *Next morning he went up with Sir Bernard Oppenheimer and stalled the machine. It fell like a stone and when the two men were dragged out they were both dead.*

William Kennedy-Cochran-Patrick (18 in 1914) was a much-decorated WW1 fighter pilot who continued to fly for the rest of his life. This accident happened at Baragwanath, the Johannesburg field where Nick Turvey took me for the Tailwind ride. Wikipedia reports a stall following a steep turn at 250 feet.

CHAPTER 25

1980 – THE 707 AGAIN

As a BA airliner the VC10's day were numbered by 1980, and my school colleague Phil Hogge was making his way up the management ladder, now 707 training manager. Flight Ops management in general was changing shape and style with the blurring of the boundaries of long and short, and the concept included combined management for different aeroplane types. The days of a utopian uniformity for airline affairs was visible on the horizon, encouraged by modern technology, especially in communication, computerisation and automation – simpler and cheaper, until it goes wrong, or something unexpected happens.

Following my last VC10 flight on April 5th 1980, I started a mini-707 course together with Mike Emmett. As we were already licensed on this machine, a couple of circuits could have provided the necessary signatures for us, but a reputable airline should take its responsibilities more seriously than this so it was decided that we should do the full simulator course, well-conducted I'm happy to say. The new 707-336 simulator was a good one, quite different from our original 1960 example, and this refresher was useful. All good stuff, and before continuing to a few real circuits Phil Hogge asked me to come along on a maintenance test flight. After ten years with the 747 and VC10 the thing that struck me about the 707 was the beautifully progressive and natural feel of the manual flying controls for pitch and roll in normal gentle manoeuvring flight.

VC10 enthusiasts will regard this judgment as deliberate heresy, but it was true, and, in contrast with the concern and consternation the early machine created, and the cautions acquired by the early trainers, one can only repeat the plaudits for those who created the original many years before.

A circuit session with John Suckling at Stansted and another with Denzil Beard at Prestwick covered the base flying, and a Beirut Baghdad and back, followed by a New York Prestwick made six supervision sectors; then it was a London Istanbul with Phil for a route check on June 26th. The street food in this town had a lot going for it – especially the fried (tempura) oysters washed down with a glass of cold, clean-tasting EFES draught. Plenty of history there. I wonder if Paul and Silas had downed a few glasses in Ephesus, in between prison and speaking engagements: I normally prefer oysters as they come, but these were special, and the correct batter, very fresh cool seafood contents and exactly the right dunk in the right oil, hot enough, is the answer. Thin and crunchy on the outside, as-opened oyster inside. I was reminded of the Singapore crab claws et al of the 1960s.

More amateur stuff

The mainline 707 route structure was similar to the VC10's without most of the African part, and life proceeded as before; 707ing east and west, Chipmunk instructing at Farnborough, and a little parachute flying there for the Red Devils in their Islander, but this was like flying a left-hand-drive white van, and the novelty soon wore off – it bore little resemblance to the delightful and charismatic DH89a Dragon Rapide, and I drifted away, like other piloting volunteers. Finally the soldier team manager got himself a pilot's licence and twin rating and flew the Islander himself until a day or two before the SBAC show. He landed on the NW runway but ran into the recently-assembled crowd retaining fence, doing some damage to the aerial Transit. Had they finished this east end of the fence since he had taken off to drop the chaps at Aldershot? Quite possibly. There was also plenty of Pitts and Zlin flying to do, mostly aerobatic displays here and there.

Another minor Pitts problem arose at about this time, and again this was to do with the current recipe for aircraft petrol. When used for transits the Pitts sometimes began to misfire, but lead additive had long since been banned. This time the cause was found to be the formation of varnish-like deposits in the injectors. The fix was to take the little brass injectors out, soak them in a suitable solvent, swill them around and blow them out until no evidence remained, although there was no guarantee that the odd flake of this amber wafer-thin petrol enamel might not still be stuck inside, waiting to get free and interrupt the fuel flow. Microns thick, you could see pieces sparkling in the washing liquid. The basic problem seemed to develop if the machine was left unused for a few days, but the symptoms did not appear immediately. It took some running time for this coating to break off and create impromptu butterfly valves in the injector exit.

I remember going to the Isle of Man a couple of times, once for a show at Jurby, and then for the British Nationals at the same place. The first trip required an initial landing at Ronaldsway, with prior security clearance at Blackpool: Irish Sea crossings for small aircraft were sensitive at this time. The engine ran perfectly from Farnborough to Blackpool, but guess what? It's a good 60 miles from Blackpool to the island and, sure enough, halfway across a cylinder or two started to falter. Would the problem clear itself or get worse? Had anyone ditched an S1 Pitts? I didn't know, and the engine dithered the rest of the way, keeping the attention but not giving up. I recall going to Ronaldsway the second time in a Cambrian Viscount, my only flight in this type, and pleasantly smooth running it was, with a reassuring 'together' feeling to its behaviour in the air. A younger and braver person took ZPH across the Irish Sea: I think it was Brian Smith, Dick Emery's youthful rolled-into-a-ball Tiger Moth passenger of 15 years before, now flying for Tradewinds.

Before leaving the subject of the Isle of Man it is worth mentioning that the airfield at Jurby borders on the famous motorbike racing circuit. On the first of these visits you could hear bikes passing by. This is where they takeoff at Ballagh Bridge, near the Raven pub. The road is narrow and windy, and the corners of the stone buildings obvious. What was quaint but astonishing were the optimistic bags of straw tied to likely obstacles. Go, see, and be astonished. See real gladiators at work.

Aerobatic and Artistic Flying Club (A&A)

In October 1980 Tony Bianchi at Booker asked if I would care to teach aerobatics in a CAP10 he had sold. The new owner had decided it should earn its keep and the two of them had formed a somewhat informal circle which they called the Aerobatic and Artistic Flying Club; initially a teach-each-other-and-have-some-fun arrangement, it seemed to me. But something a bit more structured might be better, and Tony had a high-profile student lined up. Perhaps the have-a-go for fun approach might not be good enough, so I started.

I was not familiar with the student's name, though I sensed that it was assumed I would be because many others were. 'He's a genius,' said one of Tony's warbird owners, himself well up to speed with the world of bling level flying, and a previous CAP10 owner. And so I met a quiet and very private glider and helicopter flying architect who proved to be a rewarding learner – punctual, attentive, demonstrating clear progress and (I think) receptive to my step-by-step, build the structure from its component parts principle, extending elements of the basic handling syllabus where relevant. Today he continues to create worldwide masterpieces using cutting edge technology, as appropriate, but always combined with good taste: this is something superstars do not always get right.

The CAP10 is an excellent aerobatic trainer. It's a modified and beefed-up development of the French homebuilder's Piel Emeraude, powered by the fuel injected 180 HP Lycoming, and has been used by the French Air Force for years. There's nothing military about it, except that it's an easy, agile, natural, straightforward and capable aerobatic classroom for two. What more do you want? First things first – they can come to terms with the heavy metal later; start with just the good handling training – much better value for money (if you can spare the time).

Years down the AAFC road I took Moshe Benshemesh for his first CAP 10 ride. Moshe had been a very experienced Israeli fighter pilot, with much action under his belt, mostly flying the little A-4 Skyhawk. He immediately set about his accustomed diving, wingovering, barrelling, looping etc, and his reaction was one of delight. 'He is the friendliest little aeroplane,' he said: unmistakeable accent and central European grammar. That must be why the French liked the cheap trainer.

It's easy to recognise a real pilot (if you know what this means), but they are reasonably thin on the civilian ground, and maybe I will leave more mention of Moshe until the timeline fits; but for starters it's worth mentioning his two dead stick Skyhawk landings (shot down, ejector seat serviceable but not pulled!) and when I told him that the Chivenor weapons school wished to invite him to talk to their students about his air-to-air combat and ground attack experiences he replied 'Absolutely not, I'll turn them into pacifists!' He does now choose to live in London, it has to be said, preferring the more sympathetic politics.

The CAP 10 takes off in the 3-point attitude, and easily reaches 120kts in level flight. All basic manoeuvres can be comfortably achieved from this speed, and it also happens to be the 6g stall speed – manoeuvring speed. This speed is also the one that gives max rpm at full throttle, so there's an easy rule: up to 120 you can have full throttle, faster than this something less is appropriate –

let's say two thirds as a safe position, minimum looking inside, one ballpark speed and one middling throttle position to get used to. It worked.

The side by side seat positions meant that the view over the nose was a bit lopsided, but I found that a convenient cowling screw immediately in front of the student was an effective straight ahead and pitch reference. I also found this training set-up much better than one behind the other (separated really), because there is more to communication than electrically conveyed words. Indicating, gesturing, pointing can sometimes replace a thousand words, and the pure sense of human communication from visual clues invaluable. All in all the side-by-side set up was vastly superior to one behind the other for the specific task – proper aerobatics for all-comers. Transport aircraft pilot seating is similar, and later I found the same advantage in encouraging the Concorde turn off the ground that would get us some more circuits per tank, and imply the fun to be gained from flying a machine with an outrageous excess of performance at landing weight. One doesn't discuss these things in formal airline circles.

There was a satisfying element to this personal aerobatic job. There was no formal agenda; this was to be bespoke training for those with little in common except a licence and a desire to learn something – they knew not what, generally. No gaining of licence or rating was involved – no training qualification needed either. This was private flying between consenting adults and so long as one pilot had a private pilot's licence everything was above board – especially as I did not get paid. Whether the club members paid or how much I've no idea: but it was an opportunity to put my aerobatic construction theories into practice, with completely personal responsibility. Some things you cannot put a price on.

There was no set course, as such. Aerobatics is a big subject. My principle was to establish an individual's starting point, and take it from there – what do you want to learn? Usually they don't know – of course not, that's why they've joined. I've come across aerobatic 'training' operatives with a fixed and somewhat robust agenda who propose a fixed-time course consisting of remedial emergency survival techniques – without much reference to previous experience, skill or understanding. 'How to get out of a…?' This is like the 'Recovery from unusual attitudes' syllabus for instrument flying, taken in isolation. It's an idea, and may be considered appropriate in some circles, but it does pose questions? Should you be doing this? Would you not rather learn some reliable and logical technique first, and reduce your fright factor? I disagree with this negative training – unless time is pressing, and one needs to send partially trained heroes into battle with a certain element of stress inoculation already built in.

A couple of years before, I'd decided to do something about my violin technique. Why did the good players all look the same, make it look so easy and produce a nice sound? Why had I never been able to approach this easy, relaxed and accurate technique?

Learning the hard way or the easy way. Constructive teaching and the other popular kind

What has this got to do with a flying story, you may well ask? Whether recognised or not, teaching others is, or should be, a massive part of life as we know it, regardless of subject, and the difference between good and bad is enormous in its effect – the bad frequently a damaging and wasteful influence on the lives of young people. Hard words indeed, but in my thirties, and as a 'useful' long-term contributor to amateur music at a reasonable level I plucked up the courage to ask a professional acquaintance of mine for remedial violin lessons. The useful tips and tricks she had put over during orchestra sectional rehearsals (like a good briefing, often sadly lacking) had always been relevant and helpful, and my instinct said 'good teacher'. She had never told me I was rubbish – far from it within these circles. Nobody had told me I was rubbish – you have to ask: this suggests that you are ready for the truth.

The first lesson was a surprise, and clearly set the scene. 'Stop there: forget everything you know,' was the starting point after less than eight notes, and so began the process of a detailed, logical and step by step approach to the physical handling of this equipment – nothing to do with playing tunes, or even notes to begin with. It took some time. 'Come back when you have taken this on board,' was the summary of each lesson, but the process was transforming – quite revolutionary to me, and it eventually raised my game a lot, opening new doors, and turning a tiresome and unsatisfactory chore into a relatively effortless affair of precision and fluency.

The primitive, get-you-going, 'grasp it firmly and press hard with the fingers' basics I had received as an eight-year-old in Europe's land without music had not been helpful, and the fact that, at that age, I already had a good appreciation of how music worked, and therefore did not need to be taught the meaning of a dotted crotchet or the difference between B sharp and C, was a further disadvantage. This facility with the science of music is irrelevant to violin technique, but might have suggested that there is less to teach about handling the equipment.

In addition, the beating I received four years later from a totally non-musical and socially misshapen headmaster did not help. It was recommended by a stern music teacher of the day to encourage greater efforts towards the music scholarship that would pay for future school (not musical) advancement. As a frivolous aside I might add that this lady had something of the Hausfrau style to her with the married name of Bl*wf*ld (as in white cat and sharks). But effort and practice were not the problem. How to do it would have been more useful, and sometimes it is a mistake to imagine that children will just pick things up. Good teaching works better, and if anyone's interested, a beating from a strong man with a proper stick hurts like hell – ask the Singapore bad boys – and dents the self-image of those who are not intentionally wicked enough to deserve it. Strangely enough, the experience neither improves violin technique nor enhances enthusiasm for the instrument; and, in any case, the scholarship was gained by my cathedral singing experience and grade 7 piano. I was then aged twelve.

As a brief interlude in this extensive description of flying things as perceived by an emotionally-crushed schoolboy obsessed with the escape of flying, a few words about this headmaster might provide some Thomas Hardy observation and critical entertainment. I will enjoy it anyway.

This was a man of the cloth. The headmaster position required this, as the job went with a junior post of cathedral chaplain. He was a son of a wine merchant in a relatively major western city with docks, who had clearly capitalised on a burgeoning middle class social preference for wine over Dylan Thomas' 'warm Welsh bitter beer', and this son will have been one of many whose parents wanted a better education and hence position in society for their children. Whether other siblings went into the army, the law or became explorers I don't know, but doubt it. A MA from a major university, the ability to teach Latin topped off by holy orders, then a job at Oxford; what more could an aspiring father want for a son? Better than the pit, boyo!

But this lost-the-Welsh-accent success story was not comfortable in the rarefied, intellectually suave atmosphere of Oxford's senior college and its miniature but historically well-connected cathedral. Religious commitment and belief has nothing to do with it: that's for the simple people – Chapel, Lutherans, Wesleyans, Baptists and all the rest. Oxford's highest circles inherited the traditions of Roman splendour, without the Rome, or some of the conspicuous excess, but retained the tradition of effortless erudition, social ease and charm, and ability in many areas. Unfortunately our luckless headmaster had none of these qualities, and worst of all, he had to sing the responses in the daily services when it was his rostered week.

Charles Aznavour was rather cruelly and variously known as 'Az-no-voice' or 'Az-no-talent' but this does him a slight injustice – and the French citizens rather like this naturalistic singing-in-the-bathroom man-or-woman-of-the-people's style of quavery and thin voice production – but our man was no Aznavour, and suffered agonies of distress about it; you could tell. The Responses require a straight man/harmonised music response double act between priest and choir: the sound of monastic history, for sure, reaching back through the original European Gregorian plainsong to, believe it or not, as far as the more elaborate calling of Islam's muezzin in the minaret. Our man definitely could not have managed that (or the funny notes), and the standard one-note samba from his side of the dialogue was demanding enough. The pitch (frequency) itself was adequately correct and consistent, but the croaky sound far from ideal, and conveyed the stress behind it – physical and mental. The worst event occurred towards the end of the seldom intoned Litany one Sunday morning. This monotonous and interminable repetition of plaintive requests (well it's a litany, isn't it?) calls for the straight man to intone his phrases on one note, so it's not of coloratura difficulty level; it's just lots more one-note samba (first couple of bars thereof). He gets a break after each phrase when the choir come back with the repeated up and down and harmonised backup request for a heavenly hearing, but then he's off on the next one. He almost made it to the end, then, at about 25 minutes of one note samba, with two or three phrases to go he lost it – vocal and mental exhaustion; and croaked these in a pathetic and very un-Cathedral-like death rattle, much lower in pitch, and bearing no relationship to the rest of the set. Professor Higgins is Pavarotti by comparison. This was a shocking and bad fail – a one-off in my five cathedral years. Once again we silently cringed but were delighted – out of your depth, and in the wrong place boyo? (you mental cripple. Some people can be so cruel, can't they?)

He and his ailing wife were childless, and she died soon afterwards. Shortly after this (to my, for one, amazement) he married the perfectly nice assistant matron and left the school, the cathedral staff, Oxford and all that goes with it (in unseemly haste?) to become vicar of a tiny Gloucestershire village which shall be nameless called Bledington. At least it was halfway back to Caerdydd. (Christminster attracts a lot of superior people – call them snobs if you like, but many of them have good reason to justify the status.)

The current occasional but productive lessons for a 30+ student finished when this real violin teacher said, 'I've told you all I know, what you do now is up to you.'

'Did you learn all this at the Royal Academy?' I asked. The answer was unexpected and revealed something about institutional tradition.

'None of it; I worked it out myself,' she said. This was an object lesson about teaching and the individual approach, based on personal analysis and practical experience. There are other examples of easy violin playing, but these involve Rumanian gypsy children and the like – not British at all – so perhaps I'll leave this there.

The logbook suggests that my Aerobatic and Artistic experience continued for ten years, during which a large number and variety of members came and went, on whom I could try out my ideas for introducing unusual and potentially alarming human experiences in the progressive, understandable and logical way which is best for effective learning, very much tailored to each student. An opposite approach can also be popular in some circles, but only with the intention of frightening, thrilling, cautioning or a combination of these three. There may be justifications of expediency and economy in the rough and ready approach where a rough and ready result is required, but, in my view, fear and the sick bag have no place in the well-ordered peaceable learning process. But personalities and human emotional response and desires are varied, and for light relief I will recount here an experience (some years down the road) of someone I first met as an A&A pilot.

Completely different in personality to me, Ian Groom went on to become a competition pilot and teach aerobatics in America with his S2B Pitts. Of social, gregarious and Hollywood-based nature Ian also gave rides in it and told of one such occasion at a regional airport where a husband had booked an aerobatic ride for the wife. They were a quiet couple; he tall, restrained, bespectacled and serious. Better take this carefully, Ian thought.

'What shall we do?' he asked after takeoff. 'I don't mind – everything', she said, so he set off with some easy stuff. 'More, more!' she shouted. I'd never come across anything like it, he told me. Whatever I did she screamed for more – outside manoeuvres, inside and outside flick rolls, tons of positive and negative g, big verticals – the full unlimited stuff. The reader may guess where this is going, but after landing and the canopy opened she screamed ecstatically across 100 yards of apron at husband, staff and onlookers, 'I HAD AN ORGASM!!!'

Whether this is an old chestnut I'm not sure – but in this case I'm prepared to believe it. Clearly the sense of powerlessness and complete abandonment to primeval and unimagined forces had worked. I'd not heard the story before.

New jobs – the significance of 'differences' training

Because the VC10 was disappearing, and the 707 fleet was dwindling, there were First Officers to spare, so the question was: what could they do before more flying became available? In addition the Concorde fleet needed some remedial hydraulic work because the original seals suffered under the high temperatures they experienced in flight – became hardened and leaked on the ground. Some co-pilots accepted the offer to temporarily become cabin staff, one of which was SFO (Lt. Cdr.) Roy Withey who I was to meet later on the Concorde. Others helped out below stairs in baggage handling, some left to fly elsewhere, to come back or not as the case may be.

So that these fleetless pilots could keep their hand in to a basic extent, Phil Hogge asked me to devise notes for VC10 pilots to provide adequate guidance for them to fly the 707 simulator; well enough to cover the ubiquitous instrument rating requirements, with enough three-engine base check bits thrown in. This was interesting but not difficult, and, as well as a few numbers, it focused on the basic handling differences and similarities that, ideally, should also be made use of in a conversion course. Unfortunately the one-licence-fits-all British airways system does not run to such helpful sophistication, but it was fun to do in this case. My future 'Concorde Stick and Rudder Book' was to continue the idea. This radical machine was to be an example par excellence of the value of this 'differences up front' teaching – but more of this later. Concorde Training Manager Tony Meadows and Training Engineer Bill ('Chopper') Johnston also came for some practice in the 707 simulator to find out if they remembered enough about this machine to manage the same exercises themselves for Concorde crew members currently gardening.

The Chocolate Bomber, the Green-Eyed Brown Envelope Monster, and Dibley's Air Force

In May 1981 I was asked to set the ball rolling for crewing the new Amiri 3. The Doha palace had already purchased a brand spanking new 707 as their #1 machine, and very splendid this was, though the floor up the walls to the ceiling carpeting, dark wood panelling, furniture, gold taps and so on were relatively sober compared to the tastes of other parts of this sandy region. This regal transport was flown by a Doha-based crew of ours, and its care included a couple of Indian cowling polishers. The cowlings shone like silver, and the Doha royal hangar floor was as pristine as a proud American homebuilder's. The fleet also included a Boeing 727 for short and medium range, fastish runarounds, crewed by a Dan Air crew also based in Qatar, and our own BA 707 XGX had just been recruited as a full time #3 to replace the VC10, and garaged at London. This time, GX had the full Al Thani paint job, the only difference being the background colour of the palm tree motif on the fin, white instead of gold. It also looked splendid, but there was another minor outside difference – the cowlings were not so shiny, or their rivets quite so tight. The main fuselage colour was a warm chocolate brown, hence it became the chocolate bomber. When it stayed in Doha for a day or two it also got the hand-polished engine treatment, and looked quite nice at first.

From the VC10 Amiri 3 I had taken away the opinion that a dedicated first officer was a lynchpin of this pseudo-private operation. As well as co-piloting he had to be able to arrange diplomatic clearances, flight plans, loadsheets etc, plus a number of other administrative affairs that are best done by such an informed subordinate, and he had the briefcase with all the special gen in it. His liaising with manager John Willett on these essential but specialised admin details left the captain to conduct the basics, usually introduced by the 'I've got a little job for you,' phone call.

I first sought around for a couple of junior (but not beginner) co-pilots who might show interest in this work, and wrote a description of the nature of the operation and captaining style desired, circulated to the current 707 training captains. I did not expect, or wish for, many takers, but almost all of them expressed interest – surprisingly enough. Experience was to show that enthusiasm rapidly dwindled after just one trip. Why could that have been? Where did the enthusiasm for something different go? I had pointed out that independent, mature, competent, quiet and diplomatic captaining was the style. Right up their streets, I would have said.

The recounting of stories used to be a traditional entertainment skill, all done from memory, passed down the generations by telling and listening under the starlit night sky. *A Thousand and One Nights* is a collection, but are they all true? Not really, but the same tradition continues today, especially when the stories conjure up images of exotic adventure, cruelty, romance, glamour and, significantly, more riches concealed in a neat, pristine, slim but solid-feeling fresh-off-the-press-smelling brown envelope than you can shake a stick at. Did my full-career Heathrow-based colleagues suspect that I had discovered a source of untold riches during my VC10 special exploits, or were they just smitten by the romantic spell of the entrancing Sheherazade? One such hopeful misfit had his hopes raised by the cabin crew who assembled a collection of everyone's worthless paper remnants from many eastern and southern destinations. The fat envelope was discreetly passed up during the descent of the final working sector. It was not immediately ripped open, but discreetly trousered. He did not come back either; in fact very few did.

Fresh off its check, with rearranged interior and new chocolate colours, Amiri 3 was detailed for its first trip on June 6th 1981. 'Go to Orly, pick some people up and come over here'. I set off with Jan Sitkowski, Geoff Coyle, flight engineer, Ray Daley, the VJ flying spanner who had done a quick 707 hanger conversion and Brian Horn, one of the two regular Doha VC10 co-pilots. I thought his considerable experience might be invaluable for the new 707 replacements, especially when dealing with the Doha management. Normally the system would be for the co-pilot to fly all empty sectors and the captain all customer-carrying flights, but on this occasion I thought I would start out myself with this out-of-the-hangar revamped machine. During the takeoff roll at London the nose gently but deliberately set off to one side – easily controlled with rudder but uncharacteristic. Not a problem, but I could also see that the yaw damper indicator had made its way to one side of the gauge. Normality resumed when it was switched off. The autopilot cannot be used without yaw damper, but Orly was close, and Air France still had 707s.

At Orly Geoff rushed off round the back of the Air France hangars to rustle up a likely spare part, whatever appeared off the shelves was changed, the black Mercedes convoy arrived together with lorry full of Louis Vuitton stuff bags, and our unspecified group of privileged servants, nannies, assorted relatives – who can say? – came aboard after their Paris visit (Paris stands for shopping – serious shopping). During the takeoff at Orly the same thing happened, but the weather was nice, we had three pilots aboard with nothing much to do so we shared the drive to sunny Doha and our luxury hotel – now with a difference: no drink, and bacon made of beef (that's what they said, we weren't convinced; it was difficult to tell). First job done.

John Willett decided that it would be best if we personally drove our 'new' 707 back to London two days later to actually get it fixed, which we did, but there was a minor hiccup before we had gone 10 metres, which could have created some embarrassment, but didn't. As the captain I can blame no one but myself – but you can only go on the evidence.

We started up and started to taxi. The co-pilot tried to turn but nothing happened, so he stopped; 'There's no steering' he said. 'O, God, sorry!' said Ray the flying spanner, who leapt out of the jump seat and scampered down the hatch underneath the navigator's table to the nosewheel bay to jump out and put the relevant pin back in. The 707 is towed with nose leg link disconnected, but this is not done for a VC10. In a couple of minutes he returned, apologising for this omission, and took his seat. 'All these differences, I'm not sure if I'm going to get it.' The co-pilot released the brakes and we resumed taxiing, and immediately my eye was caught by the unusual sight of the ground support combi shooting out from under the fuselage below us, to a safe distance: we had nearly run it over like a monster truck car crushing show. The occupants jumped out and waved cheerily. They had guessed the problem and rushed under to help. I don't think this potentially embarrassing incident appeared in the BA incident reports; I certainly reported nothing, but much worse would have been John Willett's reaction to having to ask the Ruler for another new second-hand tarmac car, or pay for one himself – even worse.

This month of June continued with a couple more short Amiri 3 trips, interspersed with a typical assortment of other flying – an Instrument Rating renewal test in a Cessna 340, a Cairo and back for BA, a Chipmunk C of A test and 3 type famils for Farnborough club members, some more aerobatic lessons in the Aerobatic and Artistic CAP10, and then 5 Pitts S2A instructional/famil flights with 2 A&A leading lights, one of whom was Jeanne Frazer. I think Jeanne was Rothmans Team manager at this time, and my guess is that she wanted to be able to fly herself around in a team aircraft, but the enigmatic thing about my logbook is the RKSF registration (Rothmans King Size Filter).

Recent research indicates that this belonged to a removable-wing, ground-only S1 mock up, but as well as local flights it got us to Old Warden and back. Either I've got something wrong, or it was an outstanding cardboard creation. Later that summer I see that I collected BGSD from Teesside and flew with Jeanne in it at Booker, but the mystery RKSF crops up again a year later when Hoof Proudfoot wanted to see what the Pitts powered sideslip approach looked like (it's the only way to see the runway from close range). In fact there was a real S2A RKSF, and the little pretend one as well, but anorak internet threads can eagerly spread confusion, of a level to rival the press at this time of writing. In this case there really were two alternative facts.

Amiri 3 was permanently busy as the Arabian taste for travel to Europe and North Africa caught on. Our training captains tried this new job in their turn, but for reasons of upcoming postings to the 747, or the disappointment already mentioned, they seemed to lose interest. My five-week, 26-sector stint during September and October indicated how smoothly the operation was running, and the chocolate bomber never gave problems. This session included the odd London nightstop, so home and family were not totally abandoned, but it indicated the European pattern for this third string machine: Paris and London for shopping, Stuttgart for Mercedes orders and Geneva for United Nations business. On the final two days of this block of duty we made a final Paris pickup with a regular BA 707, temporary callsign Amiri 4. I imagine Amiri 3 needed its 100 hr check – such were the demands of heavy shopping.

My original two co-pilots, Chris Humphrey and Colin Brewer, had done a great job, and the knowledge appeared to have been handed down when others came along, although much time had gone by since the original VC10 days, and it has to be said that John Willett was now well enough organised to manage three aeroplanes, their crews and his relationship with the palace with consummate skill. From others' experience of this personal flying taxi job I can vouch for the effectiveness of John's perfect firewall between customer and product. He gave us an easy time by comparison. Within reason we enjoyed an established airline's comprehensive planning and facilities – everything done for you except get in and drive. No phone calls in the middle of the night with short notice and frivolous requests, only to be cancelled, then maybe reinstated on a whim. This is not an easy way to earn flying money. There may have been trivial circumstances where the accepted airline rules had to be bent, and 'they also serve who only lounge and wait' for their passengers' return appearance might apply. But captain's discretion and a retrospective completion of the voyage report times prevented the ruffling of the anyone's waters; and this was not a routine airline job in any case. No one was compelled to join – there were no mutinies.

The sparkling #1, Qatar reg. AAA 707, continued to be operated by its dedicated crew, but occasionally it would be seen on a locally reassuring Doha circuit session. Was this to show that the royal flight was properly managed, with training to ensure the highest standards? A change of crew member was worth a few circuits. Though just another new 707, the instrumentation was different, there were extra radios on board, it looked, felt and sounded different – BA's youngest example was well-used by comparison. And Captain Willett would sometimes arrange a detail for himself – in his office suit – when a visiting training captain was available. Though retired from BA, and not 707 qualified anyway, he flew it beautifully, and the point was tacitly made to those silently interested that the manager really was a real captain. The first time I did it he paid me with a bottle of The Famous Grouse – a generous gesture, for sure; rarer and more dangerous than the pretend-beef bacon we got at breakfast.

By 1982 Phil Hogge had moved on to be Chief Pilot 747, leaving Hugh Dibley to be 707 training manager as well as flight manager. So began a period of increasing outside work for our crews and home aircraft; and other people's aircraft as well judging by the assorted registrations that appear in the logbook. This entrepreneurial management style was quite out of monster airline character, and a breath of fresh air for those who took to it, hence Dibley's Air Force, plus more silly names to go with reducing numbers and an increasingly clubby, albeit competent, atmosphere.

In July 1982 I went to Stansted to conduct a few circuits with captain Mike Tate, with a man from the Ministry sitting behind. Whether this session was completely for my benefit or whether Tate needed getting up to speed for the Mauritius job I don't remember, but a session with the man watching is required for an examiner to get signed up for the real aeroplane. I'd done the simulator routine a couple of years before and imagined that the aeroplane event would roll my examining qualification accordingly, especially when the inspector asked me to brief and carry out a token base check on Mike.

The three-engined stuff with the fearsome 707 all went well, but afterwards he told me that my briefing (sitting in our seats in the cockpit) had been a bit 'buckshee': casual/informal I imagined this to mean. Well of course it was; this was pretend in-house training and I did not want to compromise my student's confidence and give him a hard time for no good reason – I already knew he knew what he was doing. However, I passed, and all was well, and it wasn't until a few months later that the true significance of this formality became evident. I looked in my licence one day and discovered that simulator and aeroplane were not the same – connected but different – and that my simulator qualification had been out of date for a couple of months.

What a scandalous situation! *'Bogus jet examiner sends illegal BA pilots into the world's skies to endanger the lives of innocent passengers!'* Sort of; technically correct, though 'endanger' is going a bit over the top – but this is what the tabloids say, to delight the people, and the Ministry base their democratic judicial decisions on such press reaction, representing the people's interests – as they do. I know this to be true because a CAA operations inspector told me so. This sort of oversight did not happen on the big fleets because all affairs were organised by office ladies who kept the records, arranged renewals etc., meticulously; like putting things away in the right place in the kitchen or suggesting (on a relentless basis if necessary) personal appearance improvements.

Men don't bother with these important things, being more concerned with games and amusements – typical, and indeed it is. At no stage during the examiner's course were we appraised of the minutiae of the rules (that I remember). Someone else does it, but this small multi-tasking unconventional fleet (now with hardly any training captains and one first officer instructor) had little in the way of dedicated office staff. Of course, Dibley at his adjutant's desk in the corner sorted it out without fuss. A phone call to the pragmatic Ralph Kohn of the CAA who asked for a list of my illegal checks, and then his visit to renew me in the simulator sorted it out. There was no fuss, nothing in the papers, business as usual – and another tiny lesson learnt about running a small office (or a big one, so I'm told).

CHAPTER 26

MORE VARIETY: AIR MAURITIUS 1982-1984, PART TIME

Following the Seychelles windsurf introduction with the black powder enthusiast retread in February 1981, I had worked away at this skill at the Radley gravel pit and Hayling Island beach. Frequent stays in Doha also provided warm light conditions for calmly refining the flat-water basics, without the Seychelles struggle. I looked forward to visiting Mauritius where two (I think) of our crews were flying Air Mauritius' one 707. This island is a mere 180 miles inside the Tropic of Capricorn and receives south-east trades much of the time – sort of tropical, but sometimes overcast with rain to protect one when the sun is highest. For the rest of the year the weather is generally very pleasant, excepting cyclones. Mark Twain quoted an enthusiastic local's comment about his home – much misquoted as being the tongue-in-cheek lecturer's own assessment – but it does have much of the charm and limitations of many remote islands. Eventually I got there in December 1982 to stand in for Mike Tate (Umtata), on leave. I took up residence in his bungalow on Pointe D'Esny beach, which faced the huge stretch of protected lagoon, whose live outer reef totally breaks the power of a big relentless open ocean swell: next stop Antarctica to the south – a very large distance away.

I'd already come across the chief pilot of Air Mauritius, Dominique Paturau, whose lean good looks were to get him the handle of Luke Skywalker.

Dominique was currently in London training to be a 707 first officer, and the engineering manager, Ranjit Appa, was learning to be a flight engineer. Originally a joint cooperation of BOAC, Air France and Air India, the long-range Air Mauritius aircraft and crews had, in the past, been variously wet-leased from these airlines. Air Mauritius was now creating its own identity, currently operated their own two or three Twin Otters, and had acquired their own ex-South African 707 – until recently flown by Air India crew, who were paid by the time they spent in the air. For a very small island airline every gallon counts, and, so I'm told, 20-mile finals with full flap ran up the flight times and used plenty of fuel.

The current arrangement with British Airways seemed to work well, and my first 10-day fill-in stint took in Durban, Johannesburg, Nairobi and Mombasa with Mike Tate's crew, then a Bombay and back as Ted Deacon's co-pilot. Over a routine weekend the aircraft also went to London via the Nairobi already mentioned, so there was an element of positioning via Air France for the Nairobi-London-Nairobi part of this busy schedule, and I seem to remember that the London returners stayed on board for the final sector – a long night it was, but nothing that a couple of beers, a splash in the sea and a good night's sleep could not cure; the time change was not of transatlantic significance.

The logbook becomes confusing here, by big airline standards. It says I returned from Bombay to Mauritius with Ted Deacon on December 30th, then flew as Howard Taylor's co-pilot from Rome to London on the morning of Jan 1st 1983 (having left MRU on the previous 31st?) How did I get to Rome? In the bunk perhaps. I will have gone home on the 1st, then, the next day, I co-piloted to Rome again, on the machine's Sunday return from London: end of session – positioned home on BA I suppose.

There was plenty of simulator to do in January in connection with Dominique and Ranjit's 707 training, and after an Amiri 3 London day out – to take some people from Paris to Geneva (extreme shopping again) – it was time for a couple of months of Air Mauritius route training with their chief pilot and engineering manager. I do remember, however, the chocolate bomber departure for this triangular, lightly-loaded afternoon tootle. It was a busy BA afternoon, clearly, because the load sheet person had not appeared by the time we were ready to go. An empty and obscure private charter does not take traffic office precedence over numerous BA problem departures, but we had two dates with both French and Swiss black Mercedes and Louis Vuitton lorries, so we got our clearance, started up and took off. At around 100kts our company Selcal went off, and a scandalised voice told us we had gone without our load sheet.

'We've done it ourselves,' said our engineer. They're only doing their job, of course, but this can indicate that big airline service is sometimes not as helpful as the simpler but less industrially correct do-it-yourself self-sufficiency of the small and integrated cowboy outfit – - Who said that? Not me, I must have imagined it.

Interestingly enough, I recall going to a meeting at Gatwick whose intention was to discuss future plans for those crew members currently employed in a number of fringe operations, or were temporarily stood down, and so on. This was the beginning of the combined fleet concept, under single, larger aeroplane management – the Tristar being the current large aeroplane, as I remember. Flight Operations offices were still in the throes of readjusting to the BOAC/BEA/BA amalgamation of six years ago, and the scramble to find pastures new combined with the reforming zeal of those who thought they knew best seemed not to have settled down completely. And, as often happens, those with the most limited scope of experience seem the keenest to make judgments. I could not believe my ears when the man(ager) running this conference, discussion group, fact-finding assembly – call it what you will – got to Air Mauritius in his notes and asked if these crew members would still be suitable for British Airways employment when they returned from this distant, small and presumably disreputable activity. Apart from 'yes' I could not think of another answer. 'When did you stop beating your wife?' or 'Where have you hidden the rest of our money?' are similar questions which are not possible to debate. British Airtours, famous Gatwick operators of the 707, was not discussed, as I remember.

Far from the misgivings implied by his question, and the blinkered insight it betrayed, the opposite was actually the case in the Indian Ocean. A small identifiable group of those who know what they are about often works better than a large number of strangers who meet the required standard, provided the small group respect established traditions and have good leadership. This was certainly the case with these charter and ad hoc operations, thanks to High Dibley's good sense and judgment. Hugh's apparently easy-going and patrician style upset no one, and this applied to our various customers. Most of this work was not immediately obvious, but dealing with a Kiplingesque world east and south of Cairo requires a special kind of patient and on-going diplomacy, just to keep the wheels oiled, everything under control and the show on the road. Is it in the genes or to the manner born? I couldn't say, but it worked, and demonstrated a level of people-managing skills in many areas far superior to the impression I took away from Gatwick.

On February 9th 1983 I set off from Mauritius with Dominique on the first of his 36 route sectors under supervision. He had originally trained at the French national pilots' school, and already had considerable experience in charge of the MRU Twin Otter operation to neighbouring islands, but our long-distance, experience-gaining sectors were required for his French 707 P2 qualification. 3B-NAE had previously belonged to South African Airways, and though it had plenty of mileage, had been well looked after; in fact I can safely say it was the nicest handling 707 I have come across. A 338 model, it must have dated from the middle '60s, and, South Africa being far away from anywhere, will have done many long flights – something that this airline specialised in. Someone told me that this example had been specially earmarked for the South African president's personal journeys, which may explain its good technical condition. The flying instruments looked a bit different to ours – more 1960s black and white, and the pilots' gyro compasses had one of those dot/dash plus/minus annunciators in the corner to indicate synchronising activity. The flight deck seats had the sheepskin covers that apparently come with a Boeing stock order. Was it true that BOAC paid extra not to have them? They were certainly comfortable, and warm when it's cool and vice versa, surprisingly, due to the sheep's ventilation and temperature control. The distance between flight deck and first class was longer, with a couple of good bunks. The whole thing gave you a slightly better being-looked-after feeling than our own 707s.

This route experience session lasted two months, taking in all of the network – a number of times. We started with an assortment of the shorter sectors, restricting the distance to Johannesburg, Nairobi and Bombay, but it still took four hours to get to JNB or Nairobi, and the weekly milk run to Bombay and back represented six hours each way. Towards the end of March we made our first weekend London trip, which called at Rome on the Saturday and Sunday. The French still spoke French to each other on the radio and I suggested that Dominique might prefer to join in as this was the Mauritian's natural language (despite 158 years of English rule), and his PA French was of De Gaulle clarity and perfection. On the way back from London he told me he did not want to do French over France any more, and would speak English, like all other foreigners. Why was this? Do Mauritians sound old fashioned or amusingly regional to a Parisian or Marseillais – like hearing George Formby, or Rab C. Nesbitt – or was his perfect French too posh? I never found out.

Some background history

Mauritius is a similar shape to Barbados but larger – nearly five times the area. Apart from both having been British colonies which gained their independence in 1968 and 1966 respectively, their cultural development has been different. It was the Portuguese who first managed to get to India by sea, followed by the Dutch, who made use of the island as a stopping off point between Cape Town and the East Indies. The Dutch cut down the ebony trees, ate the dodos and released goats and cattle to roam free and provide meat for the next boat. Cats, dogs and rats also went ashore and modified the island's irreplaceable ancient fauna. The Dutch also gave the island its name, then lost interest to some extent. By the eighteenth century many northern farming French had gone south and joined the Dutch in South Africa, where they similarly wished to follow a life free of excessive bureaucracy, and have since been completely assimilated into Afrikaaner life and language, except for many French names. Some of them also went to Mauritius for the same reason, and regarded it as a new home rather than a transit stop. These set up their sugar farms, stately buildings and local government as if they intended to stay, and so they did. Like the Dutch they got their slaves (workers) from Madagascar, but found their unruly behaviour an inconvenience. These Madagascans did not willingly accept their servile status, tended to escape, set up shop in the hinterland, team up with disenchanted military deserters and attack and rob those with established possessions on a regular basis – so life was not easy for the new 'Mighty Whities'. However the French farmer (and intellectual) is made of stern stuff, and, as the ruling class in a small island, they insisted on continuing to be as French as they could, even though this policy, unlike the British in Barbados, or the reformed Dutch in South Africa, did not rule out melting-pot social convenience. Voltaire's philosophy of people as people, whatever race; philosophy as the philosophy of life, and so on, seems to have applied to Mauritian life since. If you prefer your inconveniences to remain trivial it works well.

Then we come to the Napoleonic wars. The French government encouraged privateering in the Indian Ocean, in other words encouraged freelance pirates to do whatever damage they could to enemy shipping, and keep a suitable percentage of the proceeds, of course. Francis Drake was probably the most famous English example of this heroic seafaring tradition. Of course the terms you use depend on whose side you're on. Ne'er do well Corsairs from every corner of the seven seas descended on the Ile de France to grab some of the action. The Mauritian capital, Port Louis, became a party town – big time –

something like Barbados, where every second establishment in Bridgetown used to be a rum shop, and plenty of violence to go with it. To get some idea the reader should think girl's night out in Liverpool or Brighton.

By 1810 Britain had decided that something had to be done, sent a few ships along and took the place over. They set up their own people in the town offices, and abolished slavery in 1835, but changed little else. Stay as French as you like, but leave our ships alone. The established sugar farmers had little problem with the now defunct slavery tradition as they were compensated in cash, and then advertised for the same jobs, with pay. Workers came from the Far East, Africa and Madagascar, but mainly from India, who, as the largest ethnic group, became the major influence in Mauritian politics. Those of a French background are still the sugar planting, business and banking elite, and have kept their language intact – but the island has become something of a cultural and ethnic melting pot, with some success.

1983 LSO World Tour – something different

This is nothing to do with the landing safety officer who critiques every carrier landing. British Airways were at the time a sponsor of the London Symphony Orchestra, and a 707 (XXZ) had been earmarked to take them on a round-the-world performing tour. I would do the first half and Dibley the second, and a couple of weeks before the launch of this trip we were invited to a mini-reception at the Queen Elizabeth Hall following a concert, as a getting-to-know-you gesture between contractors. This was a good idea. A big orchestra has to be run like a business, and after the gig we met orchestra leader Mike Davis (called concertmaster in America), the general manager, the lady with the clipboard who looks after the operating details, and a handful of others. Most of the board of management are long-term players, and when the complete official team (signed up members) are on the results can be stunning. It's no secret that quality can vary depending on substitute freelancers, rehearsal time and, quite importantly, conductor. Change conductor for football manager and does this sound like Manchester United or Real Madrid?

The day's concert had been OK, but, as Mike was later to explain, 'so long as you start together and finish together it doesn't matter what happens in the middle'. This was supposed to be an insider's joke, but, up to a point he's right and, like British Airways, the punters get as much as they think they've paid for, and can report a seriously mismanaged flight as very good – so long as there are no bumps and the landing is good. But I'd been to a concert given by this orchestra a year or so before in Toronto, with the touring A team and our same conductor, Claudio Abbado. In Toronto the precision, ensemble and plain brio had been electrifying, so they can be good – really good. A visit to foreign major cities is certain to be critiqued by members of the local star band who will be no slouches themselves. Away games are important, in America especially.

We set off for Washington on April 26th 1983. A major symphony orchestra in full commission numbers well over 60 and the large gaggle assembled on the tarmac at a remote stand before getting aboard. There was a hold up – a second violin fill-in, recruited for the month this trip would take, had cold feet about the whole thing and didn't want to leave home for so long (maybe having met some of his future and battle-hardened campaigners for the first time). Fortunately he was cajoled into coming and all trooped up the steps – sit where you like, but this turned out to be rather like a crew bus; the most senior members at the front. Below decks was everything you need for a concert; all the instruments (except a grand piano, though there was a pianist in the team), and all the music, plus bags. During my 12-day part of the tour there were concerts in Washington, Boston, Philadelphia, New York, Chicago and San Francisco, all towns with great orchestras led by famous conductors. It was explained to me that New York was a sensitive one because of some embarrassment on the last visit. 'Claudio will relax a bit after New York, so long as nothing happens.'

However, all went well, and the days passed with agreeable socialising, concert attendances, a good atmosphere in flight, with minimum transport hassle (I would argue), and some great after-show dinners out, the best being at Bookbinders in Philadelphia. Not long after the trip started the subject of orchestral experience came up (not volunteered by myself – if you know what good really means discretion is good advice). As well as one or two tenuous connections, my Henley Symphony and BBC Concert Orchestra teacher currently taught the daughter of a second violin (and second doesn't mean no good) so the word had got around that the captain played a bit. Basically this meant that I had some idea of what their job was about, and this helped with crew/customer integration I like to think. Then leader Mike suggested 'we'll get you a play in a rehearsal somewhere'. 'But Claudio will go spare if he finds out,' I said. 'No he won't, but it'll have to be after New York'.

Was this just a laugh, or had the gauntlet been thrown down? I wasn't sure, and made the immediate condition that it would have to be a piece I'd played before. There was only one of these in the current horrendously difficult tour repertoire and that would be on the programme in San Francisco – rehearsal in the afternoon after we arrived. If people at home asked me how much I practised I would normally say 'I can't play anything by myself, but I'm good enough to play in orchestras without practising.' But this was a very different ball game – everyone could play every note, up to speed.

Terry Morton, another of the big violin gang, asked in a quiet moment 'How good are you really?' This is a difficult question to answer, and the playing in orchestras without practice remark would have been insouciant in the extreme. I tried something else – 'I can stay out of trouble.' 'Can't we all,' he agreed. I seemed to be in.

David Albermann was someone I'd come across in my Oxford Sinfonia career. A wonderful player – soloist, quartet leader and so on – what was he doing here? He was an outsider recruited to make up the numbers, and sat by himself at the back of the second violins. I told him about the rehearsal offer. 'Great,' he said, 'you can sit next to me, it'll be fun'. This offer suited me well; at maximum distance from the conductor, behind everyone else and unlikely to be noticed. I told Mike Davis I'd found a place. 'No, your place is behind me, number three.' 'But can I borrow someone's violin for some practice, I haven't played for months?' 'No need to bother about that,' and on the way between Chicago and San Francisco said 'Present yourself at the hall at 2pm and everything will be arranged.' I should have said no from the start.

The leader's desk partner Lennie Mackenzie had been given the afternoon off, Bob Clark (married to a BA stewardess as it happens, and on the LSO board) gave me his own violin ('you'll like it, it plays itself') and played Lennie's (don't give it to an amateur) and we were set. There was time for a few notes and a look at our music during the setting up session. Cyril, sitting a couple of desks behind, said 'that's quite impressive'. I wondered what he expected to happen. One or two old-stagers, not part of any management/front row gang, looked aghast and horrified to see this incongruous charade taking place. 'Can you play?' one asked, in scandalised disbelief. 'You're on, maestro,' said the front row as we trooped on to take our seats.

Nigel Broadbent – normally #3, my place this afternoon – sat on my inside: he turned the pages beautifully. Of course this position thing sounds like formation flying. To some extent it is: in fact the whole orchestra is a team – a compendium of teams who, hopefully, share a high degree of precision and coordination on stage. Three of the four sitting in the first two pairs of first violin were not sitting in their usual places, but this is not out of order – the eight, ten or even twelve of them operate as a finely-tuned team after all.

Claudio announced that we'd start with the second movement, the composer's ballroom fantasy scene. I had played the Berlioz Symphony Fantastique from roughly this position a couple of years before with the Oxford S.O., though, in theory this should be much easier – everyone played the same things, there was no internal struggle with disagreements as to how it should go, but on the other hand, if the majority were in step any inconsistencies would stand out, visually in particular. At this period of his career Claudio conducted without the music – from memory. This increases the risk of conductor confusion, and is not universally popular with players who play a large variety of music on a very frequent basis. The first violins tend to play the tune a lot – Claudio's pianist's right hand – and I noticed his eagle-eyed spotting of even a nanosecond's inconsistency in the front few desks' bowing – that's up and down – in my direction. Better be careful; follow Mike in front, and stick with the clearly marked instructions, as a priority.

We jogged along, getting the idea of how it would feel and sound in the Davies Hall tonight. Nigel mentioned under his breath 'You'll make more noise if you play closer to the bridge'. I was aware of this, as well as the suspicion that our great conducting superstar was thinking 'they've done something with the violins – what is it?'

It was 40 minutes later that our usually serious and preoccupied conductor's face broke into an uncharacteristic grin: the penny had dropped. Since we'd started I'd dreaded the inevitable moment, possibly after one bar, when he would wave his stick wildly and cry 'Che passa qua? Stoppa da musica!' but he didn't. Of course I looked familiar because our travelling show had been on the road for a week and a half, and only the context was different. In fact he didn't stoppa da musica, and we progressed through some fast and furious bits before stopping for a statutory tea break; when Mike stood up and explained my presence as a new member there was applause and bowing. Given a couple of weeks at this and I could be up to speed, sort of, I thought. It had been a great privilege and a regret-tinged glimpse of what might have been without the bad teaching of the land without music, compensated by the obsession with flying things. But you have to try to play the cards you're dealt, and I do know that when a hobby changes into a job it's not always the same.

Another pleasant evening with some of San Francisco's patrons of the arts, this time with some of the orchestra's higher management – my currency had gained in value somewhat. Principal oboe Tony Campden was also chairman of the board. The son of celebrated bassoonist Archie, he certainly had the presence of a captain of industry or commerce. 'He could be chairman of ICI' a member told me.

Next day we flew to Honolulu for a swim and nightstop. The coast of the orchestral lion's den had been left behind and the next two weeks should be fun, whatever happened on the platform. The flight was in holiday mood and Claudio said he thought I did well. 'I saw you in the fast passages – you were good,' he said.

Leader and chairman did their double act with Mike's violin. He played the notes and Tony did the bow – very good Mendelssohn – then they swapped jobs and played the same thing; amazing, especially as Anthony Campden is supposed to play the oboe. Next day Hugh Dibley took over and I positioned home. Back to the day job, but the orchestra continued to be generous and hospitable. The experience had encouraged me to continue working privately through the list of techniques Helen Cooper had explained to me; there's nothing worse than being caught with that unprepared feeling – with an aeroplane or a violin.

CHAPTER 27

B707, THE FINAL DAYS

On May 16th 1983 I delivered one of our first 1965 vintage 336 freighter/combi models G-ASZF to Manston. The days of the 3am, four-sector transatlantic freighter departure were long gone, thank goodness, and, along with many others, this machine had spent many years as a BA airliner. Three weeks later I took WHU, one of its 3am colleagues, to Paris, once again for pick up by a new owner. What happened to them thereafter I've no idea; like part-exchanging a used car. But a couple of days later I came across another second-hand 707 for the first time; it was to provide some interest.

International maintenance of public transport aircraft – previous careful owners?

On June 11th, a Saturday, Hugh phoned and asked me to go to Paris to pick up the 'new' Air Mauritius 707 and bring it to London. Its crews had had a bit of trouble with it the previous night and had left it in France, getting rid of their passengers on BA and coming home themselves by the same means. This was NAF, sister ship to NAE and it had also originally belonged to South African Airways, but its career had not been the same, exactly. Before arriving in Mauritius NAE had been registered in Luxembourg for just one month after leaving SAA. By contrast NAF had spent the previous six years under this flag of convenience, doing this and that, I know not what, before arriving on the island; there were differences, despite the fact that they looked the same, both in paint job and on paper.

Its first MRU trip was the Friday night London via Nairobi and Rome (I think). The first crew discovered that the autopilot could not fly the aircraft in the cruise. The second team had an engine fire warning while climbing out of Nairobi, so did the fire drill, dumped fuel and returned. After the fire wire problem had been fixed and fire bottles replaced they set off again, to find the same height-keeping problem in the cruise, and also had the impression that the machine was not particularly 707-like in roll. Whether they called at Rome or intended to reach London direct I don't know, but by the time they were over France the fuel used indications added up to more than it should and theoretically they could not reach London – at all. This information is supposed to take precedence over the tank gauges and they did not feel like more research, so they landed at Paris and left it there, as had been said by John Blake at Biggin Hill, twenty years earlier.

On the way across the Channel I checked out the roll control. It was agreeable, but significantly more sedate than usual, more Bianchi/Fokker Eindecker replica than 707. I tried again with spoilers isolated, and the difference was minimal – the aileron/spoiler pick up was not correct. At the landing, more up-elevator control than expected was required to arrest our downward progress. Something was wrong with the elevator system. The aeroplane looked the same as its sister ship, but it did not have the same character. By this date BA proper no longer had a 707 of their own, but those staff in the hangar who could remember were encouraged by Hugh to take a look at it.

Next day I went back to Heathrow to take it back to Mauritius. They'd corrected the spoiler problem – way out of adjustment – and also reckoned that the elevator servo tab geometry was not correctly set up, so this was also tweaked. We set off for Rome, slightly intrigued as to what we might find.

The roll control had been fixed, and it was now just like a 707. The pitch business was different, but still not quite perfect. Pitch control was now biased in favour of either up or down – it doesn't matter which. This was evident at altitude where the response to control demand had improved in one direction and reduced in the other. This gave the autopilot a better chance to maintain height, but only by a sort of default. The fact was that, somewhere between control column and elevator, something was wrong. Not long after, at another check or investigation, the servo tab geometry was returned to what had been its correct adjustment, and the cruise problem continued. Complaints on the ground only resulted in engineering representatives demonstrating that the autopilot pitch servo was correctly obeying pitch demands – 'It's working, you see,' in response to the little voltmeter's movements. This was not the point in hand. 'Unable to reproduce on the ground' is not a relevant answer to basic flight problems.

The practical problem, and a potentially serious 707 feature, was the divergent phugoid (ever more extreme switchback ('roller coaster' US) ride that would result from normal autopilot cruise behaviour in this particular aircraft – even in glassy smooth conditions where control activity is normally almost imperceptible. If the autopilot has to persist in a steady push or pull in an attempt to get the result it requires it will eventually conclude that the pitch trim needs adjusting, and run the stabiliser – in the case of this design an excessive response, so an expanding climbing and diving cycle begins in this example. Without pilot intervention this would, without fail, lead to the sort of out-of-control runaway dive experienced by early 707 pilots who did not fly the machine correctly or took liberties with it. This aircraft's elevator problem could be demonstrated on the approach. At the correct speed, trim and power for a full flap final approach at normal load it was possible to quickly (albeit briefly) pull the stick back to the max with very little effect on the flight behaviour. This was not typical for the type, and, together with the tapping the stick with a knuckle demo, could not have been in greater contrast to the NAE sister ship. I would call this undesirable difference disconcerting.

There were a few other niggles, not so fundamental as this control peculiarity, but attention-getting, nonetheless. In response to a normal choice of modest cabin rate of climb or descent the pressurisation control would sometimes instantly lose the plot, sending the cabin rocketing or plummeting at ear-popping low-level jet aerobatic proportions, and one of the two inertial navigating systems routinely developed an increasing position error during flight. The rotating principle of the Carousel self-correcting system moved this error around and through the real position in increasing wobbling swings, like the lurching of a dying gyroscope or an ever-more inebriated meander about a straight line. Raj, one of the two home-based engineers, did all he could to solve this problem. About a year later he found that the feed from the pressure instruments had not been connected on delivery. With only two relatively large aircraft Air Mauritius was a small airline which did the best it could, and bore no responsibility for the engineering state of this latest addition as it had arrived, in fact they must take credit for the excellent condition of NAE, which this non-aligned nation's airline had looked after during its busy life since 1980.

Apart from a couple of Gulf contracts Air Mauritius was now the major arena for BA 707 crewing, such as it was. This now involved quite a lot of the requalifying of ex-707 returners, both co-pilots and captains, as a transit job before their turn to proceed elsewhere, and included on-type new commands as well, so the minuscule training section had plenty to do. After my last Amiri 3 Doha session and some more CAP10 aerobatic instruction I went back to Mauritius towards the end of August. The 3B-NAF rogue machine had not improved its behaviour and while many just got on with managing it (as best they could), the original full-time crew, with a couple of years concentrated action on the good one, started to take a stronger line about NAF, quite rightly deciding its pitching behaviour (or lack thereof) was not acceptable, and insisted that more should be done to correct it, sort-of threatening mutiny. Boeing representation from Seattle actually came to Mauritius to look at it, I was told, and concluded that while all the tolerances etc were within limits, the end result was not good, but theoretically acceptable (allegedly). I'm sure they enjoyed their couple of days of Mauritian hospitality, but I was not there, and it was Dibley whose masterly diplomacy and bargaining acumen kept this contract going – to the satisfaction of customer, provider, and the provider's staff. Not easy.

My own purist's perfectionist aviating instinct apart, we have to accept that this is the world of making a living, control of financial outgoings, engineering accommodation and many other things that the small and cash-strapped airline operator has to do. The intrinsic safety nets of transport flying legislation give plenty of leeway to those who want to squeeze the lemon quite dry, with my proviso that the crews must know what they're doing. This appeared to be the case here, and indicates why the Gatwick manager who questioned whether these crew members would be suitable for legitimate employment on their return was so wrong. In fact the quality of operation was very high among the small and identifiable group, and with basic principles to adhere to but a minimum of bureaucratic impediments in the way these two uncomputerised and basically-equipped jets were operated efficiently, both in sector times and fuel used. This means fast where practical, making the most of altitude gained and choosing the most efficient method of approach. Unless the wind or night required the straight in over the island a visual approach along the south coast, from either direction, provided a scenic ride for the passengers, and an efficient and quite spectacular turn on to a short finals for those watching from below. From my windsurfer I could see what was going on and never had cause for concern.

An afternoon conversion course

Dominique Paturau asked if I would like to try the Twin Otter. Of course; and, in my captain's shirt I went with him one afternoon on the double Reunion schedule. There was no other pilot, and for the first sector I sat in the right-hand seat, read the checks and flew a bit. On the return I flew from the right-hand seat and Dominique read the checks. Then we changed seats and I flew to Réunion and back as captain. Most of the passengers seemed to be personal friends from similar long-established Mauritian families. They seemed quite happy with this one afternoon conversion course.

DIY Search & Rescue (except for the rescue)

At the end of January 1984 I heard the news that a couple of teenagers had taken a pirogue from Flic en Flac and were now missing, somewhere out to sea. A pirogue is instantly recognised as the cutter from any picture of an 18th century French man of war. They were, maybe still are, the standard local wooden transport and fishing boat. Occasionally a 707 was rostered to replace the Twotter to Reunion and back if the loads were high enough, and the next day I did one of these.

On the morning in question the airport phoned to ask if we could look for the lost boat on the way. The drift of the call was that this was not an especially serious proposition, but the authorities had asked. It did occur to me that the 707 was the only viable search aircraft short of something coming from South Africa, and I had been on the water the previous two days, with an accurate interest in the prevailing wind direction. Our endurance was not a problem, the airspace was completely empty for many miles and time was not pressing, so why not use the return leg to do some proper searching on the way?

I remembered having read somewhere about coastal command's visual search procedure. Finding something small in the sea from a large aeroplane is not as easy as it sounds. Too high and you don't see it, too low and you can't see far enough, too fast and you miss it, too slow and you can't see over the front, might fall out of the sky, or run out of fuel. To search a specific area the creeping line ahead search is best, I read. This means flying parallel tracks which advance with the diameter of the 180° turns at each end. I thought that 1,500ft, one notch of flap and 180kts would give a comfortable speed with the required flat attitude, and based the search area on the boat's start point, Flic en Flac beach on the lee side of the island. This position formed the peak of a triangle centred about the recent prevailing wind direction. I also decided on an initial (base of triangle) leg that considered the maximum distance the pirogue might have drifted in a couple of days (50 miles perhaps).

Leisure time on a tropical island is usually not a problem and the crew were happy with the idea. On the way back from Réunion I told the passengers about the plan and asked them to look for the boat. We duly descended, settled into this 1500ft search business and set off along the first and longest leg that formed the base of the triangle. Inertial navigating enables accurate true tracks to be flown and Ian Stevens (flying) duly made the first 180 at the end of the first one. Of course we had no expectation of success, but the exercise was a novelty, and gave us the feeling that we were doing something rather than nothing. It was in fact very pleasant trundling along over the sea at circuit height in good weather.

Then something remarkable happened. About halfway along this second leg Ian, looking over his side, said 'There it is!' I stood up in my seat and leant over. He was right, a pirogue was passing rapidly down the side, in a decidedly deserted sea. No sign of life; from 1500ft a small boat looks very small in a deep ocean, but clearly visible, and engineer John Neale saw it as well round the side of his panel. But the next problem was immediately apparent – we had no continuing plan; no one, myself included, had actually expected to find anything. There's a lesson here. As far as it went my planning, based on a tropical windsurfer's close attention to the recent wind and water, combined with a chance reading of an interesting article about someone else's flying, had worked – quite outside the scope of routine transport expectations. But to what end, apart from some entertainment on a Tuesday afternoon?

I said 'keep straight' and pressed my INS Hold button. Anything but an immediate and very accurately flown mini racetrack would have had little chance of taking our cumbersome craft back to the same place. A better alternative might have been the VC10 runway reversal procedure, with the precise crosswind seconds added to allow for the drift, but this was ancient history, and I was the only one who'd done it. The INS position should give us a place to return to, having made some kind of orderly reversal, but this didn't work – mine was the dodgy reeling set.

News came from the back – a number of passengers had also seen the boat and were quite excited, but this did not help. At this altitude we were sheltered from the airfield VHF, so the only thing for it was to head for the island, climb up to crossing height and tell them the position of our sighting, defined as 35 miles and the bearing from the Flic en Flac beacon. Later that evening I heard that the island helicopter had gone to look, but chickened out at their industrial limit of 30 miles offshore, and it was getting dark. The coastguard launch went out and wallowed around the general area for some of the night, but no luck. A good Inertial position would have helped a boat with GPS, but this was before the days of GPS for all.

I read about the maritime search exploit the next day in the paper. Then, four days later, the news came that the pirogue had appeared near Réunion Island, with one teenager alive; subdued, but OK. He said that his colleague had jumped overboard early on. Another lesson there about swimming into wind in the great oceans.

French training and licensing

Dominique Paturau had a French airline pilot's licence. I was not party to the exact details, but the French authorities were happy to give him the 707 co-pilot's rating on the strength of his having trained with us on this type, although they required some personal examining input when it came to an upgrade to 'pilot in charge' on the licence. Although it may take a number of years for a co-pilot in a large and reputable airline to actually become a captain, it is not uncommon for co-pilots to hold the same licensing qualification as a captain, even though this means a little more training and cost, in theory. In September 1984 captain Goujon of Air France came to Mauritius to check him (and us) out, by proxy because Air France no longer operated the 707. In fact Capt. Goujon may well have been on an Air France 747 stopover. It was he that told me about the unpopular DC4 posting to Tahiti straight from the national airline pilot's school, and the paradise reality. And, 30 years later, I heard his contemporary Edgard Chillaud, latterday AF Concorde manager, recount his same cadet experience, except to add that this beginner job had been as DC4 captain. This is in great contrast to the reception we experienced from BEA, and its battle-scarred but mainly social-scarred heroes. He pointed out that his co-pilot had been 30 years older than him and slept most of the time. A grizzled flight engineer had looked after the engines, and given helpful advice on occasion. This can be very helpful for a beginner, in fact it's CRM – so long ago and done by foreigners: can you believe it?

Our base flying detail at Mauritius would be operated by Dominique, myself and John Neale, with Goujon sitting behind me. He explained to me first the list of familiar circuit exercises – normal flying, engine failures and so on – and concluded 'then we give him a surprise (surpreez)'. Leading up to this statement he had been tearing and folding a couple of pieces of paper, initially a mystery, but the surprise turned out to be an approach and landing without indicated airspeed. 'But we don't do that,' I said. 'Ah, but you should,' was the reply. 'We do everything that is in the manufacturer's manual, and nothing that isn't'. The origami items were a cover for Dominique's instrument, and an angled one for mine so he couldn't see what it said, though I could – just to be on the safe side.

I looked it up. It was in our book, but never referred to, although this had happened to a BA VC10 already. The principle is straightforward. The desired pitch attitude combined with correct vertical profile (level flight or desired rate of descent) indicate that the speed must be correct enough. Familiarity with attitudes and powers and so on helps a lot, of course, but this was a surprise to the others, and called for flying around over the sea while John duly told us what the manual said. Dominique sort of coped, considering, but it was not easy, and the long debriefing in French also included discussion of approach speed control in general. He had taken away from his 1982 BA 707 training the impression that target speeds, based on weight, flaps etc, were minimums, but Goujon pointed out that they are intended to be exactly flown if the various geometries of slow flight manoeuvres are to work out correctly. He has a point.

A month later another 747 training captain came for a couple of days; something like the boss, I would imagine. The first session lasted two hours 35 minutes and included various exercises I remembered reading about in an Air France 707 training publication many years before, never in fashion in BOAC during my time there. There were two kinds of handover approach and landing: much too high, or way off to the side. I would fly and our examiner would direct as I skulked around the hills: 'Over here a bit, more over there, now straight; keep the height' etc, until the moment when 'Dominique continue' handed over control. In each case there is a decision to be made – can I get in, or not? – and if the answer is yes, how to do it with conviction, safety and accuracy. A 707 with full flap can descend very steeply, and the correct approach path must be recognised and adopted when the time is right, but if the threshold speed is correctly maintained one variable is not a problem. The not-lined-up approach correction is the 1963 BEA Vanguard exercise that had distressed the captain at Shannon during my original 707 base training, but now our Air France examiner advised an additional helpful manoeuvring principle. At the decision to go for it, pick a point on the correct approach track halfway between your distance out and the threshold, and head straight for that initially. Simple, but it works, gives more structure to the technique and avoids indeterminate S-turning.

The next day we did more of the same for an hour and forty minutes, this time including the low-level circling approach. This assumes conditions requiring an instrument approach where the wind favours a landing in the opposite direction, and also assumes adequate but not excessive space with limited visual clues – all likely to be found at a tropical island, of course, on a dark and none too fine night. This sort of thing implies accurate speed control, turn radius, timing and so on, not to mention careful height keeping.

We finished with some three-engine flying, including approach and landing without rudder boost (also in our book, believe it or not), followed by the surpreez again. This time the no-airspeed was not such a surprise and looked no different from a normal landing, and the conclusion was praise all round. 'Good flying, good captain, good help' (to John at the panel). The no-airspeed approach had been excellent, though John said to me afterwards 'Well, you did give it him in trim with the right power'. This may be true, but Dominique had done well, and I had learned quite a lot. My reading of these two sessions of French supervised training exercises, with ourselves as relatively unknown quantities, is that we had been given an insight into a tradition much more comprehensive than our own, conducted by those of considerable experience at both the flying, and dealing with their students. This was my last flight in a 707, on October 17th 1984.

Even at this time, much of these old fashioned techniques had become politically incorrect in British civil flying circles. They relate to the old days of small airfields, limited electronic approach aids and an absence of automatic landing devices. Air France had a number of 707 accidents in the aircraft's early days, but the traditions of Saint Exupéry and the Postale de nuit had been maintained rather than abandoned in favour of a comfortable assumption of standard jet-beginner-friendly facilities for all – the real world had not changed so fast. During my examiner's course at Stansted our teacher was surprised to hear that we were prepared to land a VC10 at night without approach slope guidance. Try Colombo in the wet season (then).

Old-fashioned training is expensive, and a modern combination of entitlement (cheap flights for all) and the globalised consumerism that has produced an across-the-board dependence on electronic intelligence appears to make sense; but at what cost? Statistically, modern commercial transport is remarkably safe, but it's the new nature of the accidents that gives rise for concern. The Air France 'wrong sort of ice' airbus loss was an extreme surprise for this airline with its history of traditional values. What can have happened? If new brooms are determined to sweep out the old they may appear to have been successful, in the short term. Goethe's story of the Sorcerer's Apprentice (and its French composer's musical version) should not be forgotten. In the end it was the old wizard who cancelled the magic and restored order.

CHAPTER 28

CONCORDE TRAINING, 1984-1985

Getting on the course

There had been no Concorde conversion course for a number of years, and to date, flying this unashamedly spectacular aircraft had been the preserve of its original airline owners. It is no secret that BOAC had paid £1 for the British half of the project – seven aeroplanes, the bits and pieces to go with them and manufacturer's support. It had become obvious that the machine could not be operated effectively while the operator was bedevilled by politics while attempting to become a government-free business, and this was the deal struck; and it was also accepted that the total development cost would never be repaid to British and French taxpayers – £11 for each man, woman and child (In 2017 it might be interesting to consider the sums the NHS spends on people in Britain who are not ill).

Ten years later, by 1984, much post-amalgamation BA flight management had been rearranged, and attitudes to training within the big airline reformed in order to improve it, and bring it into line with the operating style of the modern airliner and its multiple computer assistance (only thought of when the Concorde first flew in 1969).

Another reason for revision of training procedures was an awareness of the increasing risk of litigation in the case of accidents, which could easily lead to financial ruin for an airline, and the manufacturer – there's no end to this crumbling pyramid if the legal profession's priority of cash for crash is allowed its head. Records had to show (by default) that blame lay elsewhere than with the airline itself. Training progress reports should be correct, clear-cut and consistent across the fleets. There's nothing wrong with this as a basic principle, and the intended tacit effect is that responsibility for incidents will lie with the individuals who can be shown to have made mistakes, rather than deficiencies in the system that allowed them the opportunity to make those mistakes – in other words the system that put them in the seat and let them loose. The reality of complex work can be much more complicated than many might confidently imagine, such is the intended reliability and redundancy of routine airline operations.

Concorde has always attracted attention, for a wide variety of reasons. The early BOAC crew members who took part in much of the manufacturer's necessarily extensive development flying required by the certification authorities had few illusions about the demands and risk level of this complicated and revolutionary machine, when viewed against the perspective of subsonic tradition. When the machine first carried commercial passengers, the day before my 34th birthday in 1976, did the BOAC crew who carried this out accept that it had become just another airliner, now that all the necessary paperwork had been signed and stamped? I don't think so, and I suspect that, despite the element of marketing that goes with the test and development of a new product, manufacturer and civil aviation authority pilots, both British and French, did not think so either.

Early paperwork problems – to write or not to write

During my time on the 747, in the early 1970s, I was present at a briefing given by Capt. Phil Brentnall, our training manager. After the relevant 747 business had finished he told us a few details of Concorde progress. The five-year development and route proving process in the air was well underway, but the complications of agreeing the procedures and techniques required for certification as an everyday airliner were raising problems. There were a couple of current knotty discussion points. The first concerned the nautical equipment.

Everyone with a feeling for the physics of a Concorde agreed that successful ditching would be impossible. Weight, as always but specially for this machine, was at a premium, so why not do without lifejackets, sea-going escape sides and the rest of the paraphernalia that goes with life on the ocean wave? Agreed – but if we put this in writing everyone else will want to throw away their lifejackets as well, otherwise it's not fair, democratic or equal. True, so Concorde got the lifejackets and sea-going slides. These seldom-used accessories are still universal despite the rarity of copybook ditchings – with remarkable exceptions, it is true – but routine safety training to this day makes the point that 'Across the Airfield and into the River' events may still be on the cards. (Apologies to Ernest Hemingway and *Across the River and into the Trees,* though this has already been gently parodied as a characteristic *Across the Street and into the Bar.* There could be other versions.)

The second sticking point was undercarriage failure. The experts had all agreed that the results of a landing attempt without all three legs down and locked would be unpredictable, extremely hazardous and very likely to cause serious injury to some or all of the occupants. The projected fate of the cockpit crew in the no-nosewheel case was pointedly pessimistic. The best solution turned out to be no advice – the undercarriage has to be down and locked. The likely Eject word is not in the airliner lexicon. A copious emergency checklist with philosophical gaps where there was nothing to say was the result. I had cause to think about this later.

Early Concorde training

Prior to the final handing over of the ignition keys, manufacturer pilots had some input in decisions as to airline captain suitability. There were training failures; and there were still failures among the few in-house courses run after the pragmatic Norman Todd became manager of a self-sufficient Concorde training office. These mid-1970s courses had all consisted of long-haul (BOAC) crew members.

Between Norman Todd's retirement in 1979 and my course in late 1984 there had been three Concorde training managers, but no training as such, just routine refreshers and checks (called training). Why so many managers? Keith Myers had decided to take early retirement, Tony Meadows had stood down but continued as a training captain, and now John Cook was doing the job. What was behind these musical chairs? It is true to say that the daily routine of the machine had been disrupted for a while because of hydraulic seal problems, and Tony had been trying to set up a deal with DHL for a nightly US to Europe next day delivery arrangement that could only be done by a Concorde, but this never materialised. Was there something else going on within the airline – a new move for correction and improvement that would sweep out the old and bring this radical (make no mistake) machine into a new training and employment-friendly computerised era? I've no idea, but I can guess.

The basic system for moving to a different aircraft type is based on personal choice, arranged in company seniority (date of joining). But apparently a special rule had been made for our new course of four captains – something about age at the start of the course – but these details were not published, nor was this age idea normal industrial practice. It could be that justification for maintaining enough experience on the Concorde had been a reason, but 42½ sounded rather arbitrary and Adrian Moleish. I heard that the date of this course had been rolled by six months, altering previous plans and excluding a political appointee, but including me, the only long hauler. What was all this about, is it even true? I've no idea.

My colleagues were Dick Boas, Ian McNeilly and Trevor Phillips, all good chaps. Trevor told me that he had flown the Hunter in 63 Sqn with Tony Haig Thomas, author of my book recommendation *Fall Out Roman Catholics and Jews*. As an entertaining/cautionary tale against himself Trevor told me of an early career occasion at a medium height above Cambridgeshire when he spotted a vic of three Hunters ahead and decided to creep up on them, catch them up and slot into their box position. He applied power, and only at a late stage realised that they were coming towards him, not going away. Good story; easy to do – just the once.

Before we started work we were welcomed by general manager Brian Walpole. I knew Brian from the 707, both from the BBC film (***The Pilots***) and his 1960s training position. The Concorde hydraulic problems had been solved and the mothballed AG (once intended for Caledonian) brought into service to make seven working BA Concordes; all busy – in Concorde terms. The fleet was on a roll, Thatcherism prevailed, money was good and a base of dedicated frequent Concorde flyers was establishing itself, all paying full fare; no deals. Brian's ability to sell the product to the rich, famous and successful, aided by Jock Lowe, was without doubt a major factor in this story, much to the dismay and envy of others in the airline. Fleet managers are not supposed to take over marketing, but Brian and Jock were good at it.

I can say nothing about the Walpole family tradition, but feel inclined to mention that Brian had been a member of the 4-ship Meteor aerobatic team who had represented the Royal Air Force at some time in the 1950s, and while this has nothing to do with airline management, I have to say, from a personal point of view, that this job is something that requires more than adequate communal poling ability. Such arbitrary assessments of personality have now been consigned to the dustbins of democratic history, but one should consider that a broad view of abilities, qualities and diplomatic facility should be taken into account when standing in judgment. Without this flair and determination to make a success of this novel and specialised Concorde product, for which selling the idea to a likely section of the public is paramount, I have the feeling that the Concorde's working life might not even have reached the generally expected ten years. The word 'marketing' covers a range of subheadings, and exaggeration as a way of life is a part of it. Larger than life statements and claims do not mix with the stark realism required for safe flying – but had the front office not have done the job they did since British Airways took total control of the Concorde, I think it likely that our 1980s courses may not have had the opportunity to take issue with Concorde training and its perceived foibles, nor the chance to open the throttles and 'pour the coals to it' (southern USA), like the Braniff engineer who had scandalised his instructor Terry Quarrey by staring ahead out of the window, rising out of his seat and shouting 'Holy shit, look at the son-of-a-bitch go' instead of monitoring fuel flow, primary nozzle positions, reheat lights and a number of other things on his first takeoff.

Brian was welcoming but proprietorial in his address. 'I demand high standards on my fleet', and so on. This did not worry me, but I had the impression that my colleagues felt that his comments about high standards were out of order and slightly unsettling. Were their suspicions of long-haul elitism and discrimination confirmed there and then? Not entirely, but, as competent pilots in their own environment this suggestion that the Concorde was something special conflicted with the new British Airways public transport assumption that all men are equal, and therefore all the aircraft conform to etc. etc.. No one I've met outside the airline agreed, even though the Concorde had a public transport certificate.

The classroom work and the simulator training took place at Filton, the British Aerospace factory. This would involve six weeks of classroom followed by 76 hours of simulator so, apart from weekends and a couple of days for Christmas, weekly residence somewhere between this airfield and the M4/M32 became a way of life. Lunch at British Aerospace was included with the classroom arrangement, and John Cook had already extolled the virtues of Bristolian life, including the lunchtime sherry on tap that had been a long tradition of the city's business life, also applicable to the Bristol Aeroplane Company. After an invigorating morning's mental exercise in the classroom a bucket (his word for the generous waisted schooner or two) of Jerez's finest before and perhaps with lunch seems fun, but means that you will have to do the afternoon's work in your own time. The sherry was nice, the introductory week informative though not emotionally taxing because there was no exam directly behind it, but we got the message. In any case, this reminder of a Bristol/Cadiz trading tradition soon ceased: only water remained to wash down the crunchy sweet and sour spam fritters, chips and veg, and maybe a coffee with the tinned peaches and Bristolian custard.

Trigger warning

At the time of writing I believe that university-level establishments of the English-speaking world have become increasingly conscious of the psychological and social fragility of their students, and the duty of care that the academic staff are compelled to consider means that course work content is pruned or presented in such a way as to avoid distress or emotional challenge. This includes the knotty problem of unfamiliar technology. Text which presents concepts which might give rise to unfamiliar thoughts and ideas are now regarded as psychologically taxing or damaging, requiring safe spaces, on-hand counselling or even therapy, optimistically intended to heal. Sections of course work may be sidestepped if they are considered unsuitable for a student. 'Physics is against my religion' may well do the trick – at no detriment to the degree. 'That's all right. Run along, I'll tick the box anyway.'

I started this memoire at the request of people concerned with aviation, and, in general, the technical content would not give professionals or enthusiasts serious problems, but it is also a story, and the intention is not to include more homespun technology than is necessary to give the story some framework.

However, for those already familiar with the world of flying a background to the novel character of Concorde technological concepts is essential if the nature of Concorde flying is to be understood. So that lay readers will not lose heart and stop turning the pages I have decided to follow higher education practice and indicate challenging or alarming reading with a trigger warning (TW), and perhaps a change of font. So far, the sex and violence remain unwarned.

The Pink Book

This was a novel way to start a conversion course, taking a whole week, but it was a good idea. This slim, trade show handout-sized volume was a marketing publication produced at the aeroplane's inception, and intended to give prospective purchasers an overview of those features of the design and operating parameters that would be different from conventional subsonic transports. In its own way it was a masterpiece of clarity and succinctness. There were a surprising number of differences, and apart from the obvious similarities – engines, electrics, wheels and so on – the different concepts outnumbered the similar. This detailed but clearly written week's worth of study explained why this or that had to be, how it was achieved, and did indeed lay a foundation for the next few weeks of classroom. It's much easier to understand the nuts and bolts if you know what they're for.

Trigger warning

First we looked at the flight envelope graph. This shows the fast and slow limits, set against the intended height range. It's usually a rhomboid affair, but this one was more like a thunderstorm cloud, oddly-shaped, towering up the page and wider at the top, reaching out in the fast direction. A novel point was the conservative maximum speed at ground level – only 300kts – which soon climbed to 400kts for subsonic climb. 400 is minimum drag speed at takeoff weight, and slower than the best climbing speed for distance and economy, but there are a host of system and structural reasons why these speeds are pedestrian, even by Hawk two-seat trainer standards. The graph shows what the whole project was designed around, the thunderstorm's anvil – unprecedentedly efficient supersonic cruise, without thirsty afterburning. From the sound barrier at 30,000ft the desired indicated speed rises steadily to 530kts at 50,000ft (Mach 2, a mile every three seconds). At 60,000ft the airspeed indicator says 460kts at M2. These figures put airline flying into a very different perspective. To obtain correct performance the whole flight up to top of descent, where possible, had to be flown exactly up this right-hand side of the graph – maximum permissible speed all the time. Coming down could be more leisurely, somewhere down the centre of the page was recommended, and, generally, one could assume that the light Concorde was a comfortable glider at 350kts, a typical easy-going speed for jets.

The engines themselves were very traditional (and relatively reliable and bulletproof) — 1950s Vulcan Olympuses beefed up for the TSR2. With after-burning these give twice the thrust of the Vulcan version, and I did hear that the TSR2 was intended to be able to take its crew of two away from a hotspot, supersonically – on one engine. But the add-ons at either end of the square engine box were extensive and special. Variable geometry intakes of course, to focus the shockwaves precisely, or all hell lets loose. Then there are inlet doors for extra air at low speeds, within large spill doors underneath to dump the intake pressure if an engine is throttled back or fails at supersonic speed. The

5:1 compression ratio in the intake rolls the aircraft away from a shut-down engine when directed downwards at M2 – novel, but that's the way it is.

Then what do we have at the back of this boxed engine? Reheat inside (afterburner), of course, otherwise there would not be flames to light up an evening takeoff. This extra pressure immediately behind the engine tends to slow it down so the exit has to widen accordingly – primary nozzle. The Concorde also used these devices to achieve a gearbox effect between the two rotating assemblies, first, second, third and overdrive (flyover), for fuel efficiency and a version of whisper-like flight when climbing out over housing estates or city centres. Then we have the supersonic expanding and accelerating flow shape behind this engine action. The moveable parts to accommodate this are called secondary nozzle. These also double as thrust reversers, and mimic excavator buckets, hence their bucket name.

What else would the recreational reader like to know? Why so thin and narrow? Like a needle going through stiff fabric. Why Mach 2? This is interesting. Intake/engine/nozzle efficiency improves a lot once you have gone well supersonic. At cruise speed the Concorde behaves as if it had five engines (a free ram jet added) – best miles per gallon. As you go faster this advantage gets better. The Lockheed Blackbird went as fast as it could: Mach 3.5? (and then some). Wonderful supersonic economy (relatively speaking). The problem was that this produced 500°C+ at the Blackbird's leading edges. Seriously hot nose and wings, hence the black paint scheme to radiate the heat, and a tricky sliding titanium construction.

Flying physics becomes straightforward once fully-supersonic flow has been established. The air has no warning that the aeroplane is coming. Instead of moving aside it compresses – it really does – and tends to do things in straight line geometry, like the change to cubist painting. If you were to hold your empty baked bean can out of the Concorde window facing into the wind, 7 cans worth of air would be crammed inside, and this gets hot, like the end of your bicycle pump, but much too hot to hold, despite the fact that this is -50°C air before it is collected in the very fast tin. The designers decided that 400° Absolute (K for Kelvin) would be the limiting temperature, just because they considered this to be a reasonable figure for the specified aluminium alloy and the number of temperature cycles it might experience in its lifetime. 400°K sounds more scientific than the +127°C that it is, but each flight has a subsonic climb to 30,000ft and a cold -30°C, then up to 60,000ft cruise and +127, then down again – how many times, for how many years before the skin is worn out – temperature fatigue? Nobody knew; it was an educated, conservative guess.

As it happened, the metal showed little change at the end. How fast could the Concorde metal really have gone – for better mpg, and even faster flights?

Mach 2 gives you something approaching 400°K ram air temperature in the tin (total air temperature if you like) so M2 was decided upon as the cruising speed. As a round number, 2 is easier to remember than the more confusing decimals, and absolute zero (0°K) is -273°C – as cold as anything can get. On a warm day (ISA+10) at cruising height the +127°C TAT limit would be reached before M2, in which case 127°C became the speed to fly. The speed to fly? What sort of speed is that? Think about it. Just another airliner? Not quite.

Then we have the centre of gravity business. Everyone knows that the centre of lift moves back as compressibility effects change the airflow over the lifting parts of fast aeroplanes, so the machine might like to dive of its own accord. The simplest thing to do is to move fuel and centre of gravity towards the back, by two metres in the case of the Concorde; a situation which would tip the elegant machine on its tail on the ground. This has happened in the hangar – no serious damage though, just embarrassment and amusement. It is obvious therefore that the fuel disposition about the Concorde's 13 tanks, numbered 1-11!, had to keep pace with height and speed (tip tanks 5a and 7a were a post-numbering tweak). The machine would be impractical to fly if it descended and slowed up to land with the fuel still in the cruise position. Of course, load planning has to arrange that a centre of gravity position is feasible in theory for takeoff and landing with no fuel aboard – handling still acceptable. This just leaves us with the situation of having to descend and slow up earlier than ideal, at a range disadvantage (just when you need it), when the balance fuel in the rear tank (#11) is all that's left – it must come forward to drive the engines. Tell the passengers at the front to leave their seats, crowd the rear galley and sit on laps or the nearby floor instead? Not really.

Next question? One could go on, but these concepts were useful to know before learning the details of the machinery. There had been few volunteers for the first BOAC courses, and some left seat places were taken by very junior captains. An acquaintance of mine who was persuaded to join one of the earlier 1970s courses managed to de-volunteer himself by the first Pink Book Wednesday, day 3. The exam syllabus did not even start until the next week.

Lessons for the exams

Several years had gone by since the last technical course for Concorde pilots and flight engineers, and I wondered what our classroom teachers might have been doing in the meantime. Six or so years seemed a long holiday for these specialists, but British Aerospace was not an airline, and no longer made complete aeroplanes. I was soon to find out that they spent most of the time teaching the workforce whatever improving subjects were required – Health and Safety, Industrial Relations Theory, Human Factors: or any combination of these three plus unknown possibilities. By anybody's assessment it would have been those things which have traditionally assisted the honest Christian worker to earn his daily crust by the sweat of his brow. The building that housed the Concorde simulator, and our classroom, was also where some Airbus wings were made, along with bits for other machines. The apparent craftsmanship was impressive, but someone told me that the fact that flying parts were being made here was irrelevant. 'It would be no different if these people were making washing machines.'

On leaving the site our car would occasionally be stopped by the company police. 'Anything to declare?' What did you have in mind – 200 fags and a bottle of gin? When it became obvious that we were not drillers, riveters, gluers and screwers they always let us go with a wry smile, and maybe a perfunctory peep in the boot – to show a politically correct lack of discrimination. On the other hand the scrap metal pile outside the shed did have some very useful-looking fancy metal failed attempts, ready for the taking. You would not find the like at B&Q, or the quality tools used indoors. Elsewhere on the Filton field American F-111s from Upper Heyford were given a major overhaul – one at a time – so there was the occasional arrival or departure. Some years later I asked the American judge at the world aerobatic championships their condition when they returned. He was now an airline pilot but had flown these from Oxfordshire. I expected 'Fantastic – like new', but he said 'OK, not totally great', and left it at that. Maybe it was the language problem, or something to do with the new washing machine ethos.

Our five weeks of classroom were well-delivered; clear, logical, well-paced. This very well suited my classroom-for-employees policy. You will be told everything you need to know by your teacher, and everything you need to know is also in the books – if necessary. Why not sit back, no note-taking (what for? You could look it up later). Just pay attention and understand and absorb the information as it comes by. Above all this requires the ability to put aside all other mental distractions and involve your mind in these fascinating facts, delivered for your interest and entertainment, encouraged by the realistic suspicion that their understanding might save your life one day, as well as avoid remedial work in your own time. This is at variance with the professional's tick in the box, good enough attitude, but the extra mental effort is always worth it if you value your safety, rather than assume the passenger's 'I've bought the ticket – therefore it must be safe' opinion. It's how it is – that's how the world works, given the chance.

I think we had an in house exam at the end of each week, to check on progress, then at the end came the required Air Registration Board paper. Of course this covered the whole six weeks' worth of study, but was not more difficult in detail, and what interested me were the two or three pertinent questions about high incidence protection. This must have been an historic hot potato. These sentences gave signs of having been revised and rewritten since the last contestants had attempted the exam, and were expressed in relatively long and elaborate but unequivocally correct and cultured English. I rather liked them, for the language alone, and the fact that someone had taken this subject seriously, intellectually and somewhat academically. A traditional multi-choice question might be: The green hydraulic system is powered by a) two engines, b) five engines, c) no engines at all. Most readers will probably get it right, but this exam was a good and fair test of technical knowledge and understanding.

The whole flight manual and its associates were particularly well written, and similarly belied a creditable educational standard, much superior to many of today's Oxbridge entrants, and presumably a significant number of their graduates as well. In fact it was worthy of the machine and the quality work that had produced it, taking into account the fact that the entire certification programme had been focused on world acceptance. These two or three questions about high incidence, in my view, indicated the historical concern felt about the unconventional nature of the machine's behaviour at anything but quite a fast speed, and highlighted the fact that its basic behaviour broke a mould partly established rather before WW1, and much relished since – hands off stability.

Trigger warning

Back then, the mainstream had not thought of the possibilities of extreme speed variations and the peculiar shapes that could be made to fly in the future. Now it's accepted that a sentient pilot could easily contribute to keeping a flying machine on the straight and narrow, especially with electronic assistance. But when it came to up and down, left and right, the Concorde's active electronic assistance was remedial and defensive. The pilot kept direct control, and the auto stabilisation system only backed off the results of his efforts if these were too vigorous or things looked like exceeding certain boundaries. As such this was only a basic part of 'fly-by-wire' or 'stick steering' as various forms of artificial control were to become known. Pilot or autopilot retained full and direct control.

The popular term 'fly-by-wire' as in 'The Concorde was the first fly-by-wire airliner' is misleading to the modern reader. The reality was a novel electrical signalling of the flying controls, themselves driven hydraulically. Rods and cables (not electrical) had been the usual way for cockpit demands to be transmitted to the moving surfaces on an aircraft's wings and tail, whether for the Wright Flyer, Spitfire or B747 (powered controls included). The problem with the Concorde concept was threefold. First, the nature of the radical machine required precision for its controls; second, the distance from cockpit to control surface was long; and third, this front-to-back distance expanded and contracted by ten inches (25 centimetres) each flight. In addition, the auto stabilisation channels needed to share the elevons and rudder and these boxes produced volts, not push and pull as such (though it is true to say that there was a last ditch, desperate means of control which did not require electricity).

At the end of this six weeks of classroom, punctuated by the sweet and sour spam fritters, we successfully passed the technical exam. Actually the S&S spam fritters were not real, although they might have proved a hit, but the lunches still provided a good and enjoyable daily interlude. At this stage I judged the amount and variety of the learning content to have been three times that of a typical airliner conversion course. This factor would be maintained.

The Simulator

Prior to the course I had already been to New York in a Concorde with Jeremy Rendall, and had a bit of a drive on the way, but this does not count, so we still had not seen a real Concorde. Apart from one pre-production route flying model, now hidden away somewhere at Filton, all the birds had long since flown the nest. Unlike a course at London Airport, where it was possible to pop over to the hangars now and then to look at a real version of what you were learning about, all our Filton technical details were creations of the imagination. There was the simulator nearby, of course, and this had been very useful in putting life into the throwing of switches, seeing lights go on or off and gauges move, but the formal starting up and getting the simulator going, although still pretend, was to create something a little more realistic, if not totally so.

After a couple of days of pre-Christmas cardboard bomber (wading through the checklists in a cockpit mockup with pictures of the switches, buttons, lights and dials) the simulator proper began on January 3 1985. I was paired up with Trevor Phillips. Our first detail was conducted by John Eames, who had been trained by the test pilots and then involved in the initial task of assembling the massive set of information and instructions into recognisable subjects for airline pilots. His Concorde experience must, by now, have approached ten years full-time, but the first thing he told us, as a precursor to what similarly-experienced Tony Meadows later referred to as a 'pilgrimage', was that it took him a year of normal flying to feel 'at home' with the job. This was an interesting observation to long-term professionals, and I was interested to find out what he meant.

When I retired in 1997 the office gave me my own training file as a memento of my captaining career, starting in 1976 with the curious VC10 command course. This is not normal, but some kind soul thought I might be interested, rather than throwing the file out with an office clear-up. The Concorde era tells me that there were in fact 17 four-hour Concorde simulator details, and, as is traditional for two pilot transport aircraft, two hours' worth of action is repeated each session – in our case for two captains, swopping seats at half time and co-piloting when it was the colleague's turn to drive. Of course you learn almost as much watching and helping as doing. The pair of us therefore shared 68 hours of simulating; and the process took almost all of that January.

The content and pace of this learning process was good, with much time spent on the process of normal flying, in particular the typical London and New York departures, and the routine of arrivals and approaches. The behaviour of the machine, the speeds required and the enormous accelerating potential (for an airliner) once the minimum drag speed (400kts) had been approached required a new consciousness of priorities as well as basic handling techniques, and the instinct to be sensible and conservative if something went wrong could be unhelpful. 250 or 300kts sound like very reasonable speeds to fly if a conventional airliner finds that it cannot continue as normal, but these speeds are inconveniently slow for a heavy Concorde which only thought about relaxing above 350 and started to smile at 400. At 530kts it was content. Pilots familiar with flying heavily-loaded tactical jets may understand. Going straight up in the air is all very well if you can, but it's not always like that.

In amongst this everyday stuff was the long list of unusual and emergency things that made up the statutory failures that have to be coped with. Of course they just might happen, but a new and very radical machine has many questions asked of it before it is even accepted as a certified airliner, let alone sold to the general and possibly unsuspecting public. The answers to many of these questions find their way into the initial and recurrent training syllabus, even if some of them seldom happen, or are not a big deal to someone who has minimal but at least trained experience of the machine. One has to consider what will be questioned by airworthiness authorities who have no experience of the project. Many examples concern 'What happens if xyz happens during or immediately after takeoff?' Quite understandable, but what struck me were the lack of questions about controllability during the aerodynamically ticklish reentry regime.

Fooling around in the thick air and low speeds of Wiltshire or Gloucestershire is one thing, but soaring at great speed through the thin upper atmosphere of the planet is another, especially the coming down if something goes wrong. Ditching and wheels not properly down had already been considered and quietly forgotten, but why should a dictionary of problems only occur during or after takeoff? Maybe some questioners had not been fast and high themselves, and the potential problems of controllability while returning to half speed and height with a less than fully-functioning Concorde were covered by a simple policy: at the first sign of trouble throttle back, slow up, descend and make the transition to subsonic flight – before the next thing goes wrong and possibly confines you to remaining in orbit. Of course tootling along at Concorde cruise does not resemble space shuttle flight, but I believe the shuttle's brief regimen of maximum dynamic pressure – backing off then throttling up – occurs at the same height and speed; while going straight up, of course. This is an irrelevant coincidence, but takeoff and landing may not be the only attention-getters for the crew of a radical flying machine.

Once we step outside the familiar world of subsonic transport there would be few who know what questions to ask. There is no doubt that the test crews would have spent a lot of time practising descent through the transonic regions with flying control problems. The purpose is to prove what is possible, despite the difficulties, and then agree that this or that situation could be satisfactorily conducted by a typical airline pilot under the possible and/or agreed failure conditions. The first level calls for no auto stabilisation. Delicate precision is required here, the instinct of familiarity replaced by micro-analysis and virtuoso Dutch roll technique. It can be done, although this exercise in real flight became dropped from the airline training syllabus because, not infrequently, an impending out-of-control situation had to be rescued by restoring the 'failed' gadgets. The next stage would be an attempt using the last-ditch control method – mechanical signalling. This bucking, lurching, swinging, partially in control technique we practised for approach and landing in the simulator, and attempts to land the real aeroplane like this had been downgraded to 100 ft minimum height in the early days because of the risk of damage when the ground was encountered. The transonic business in the same configuration defies imagination. Did anyone actually do it?

Training engineer Peter Phillips had flown with the French during early training development. He was impressed with the number of practical exercises on the list. He asked about one of the many. His test pilot shrugged and smiled knowingly. 'We sign, but we don't do it,' said Jean Franchi. There were a number of French items that the British decided were unnecessary, and, in any case, the very difficult things seldom occurred, and tended to slip away from consciousness and syllabus.

However, given the official content of our training programme, the required stuff was covered at a reasonable pace with a lot of normal flying practice, especially including the important attitude flying. Equally essential was the novel technique required for maintaining the required climbing speed when flying 150kts below the minimum drag speed after takeoff, or 100kts below it for much of approach manoeuvring – despite the excellent auto throttle system when used. The term 'extreme speed instability' would cover it, and combined with static instability in pitch, neutral in roll, this was neither a hands off nor seat of the pants machine. The saving graces were excellent control precision and instrumentation and considerable steadying longitudinal inertia due to the machine's relative length. It soon became clear: the more economically and accurately you handled the controls the less difficult it became; actually, anything less than very good didn't work. After the seventeen details the required standard had theoretically been achieved, so now we were ready to grapple with the real thing.

Base flying

This means circuits and bumps with a real aeroplane, a luxury that has become a rarity due to the sophistication of the bedroom computer. If we had a modern Concorde would it be possible for a pilot to make a first flight in it with passengers, having never seen a real one? Why not? Theoretically, yes; but this is not so easy to answer. It all depends on who's paying, their take on gambling, and a personal and therefore subjective assessment of risk. No one can be correct here, but the times move with the technology.

On February 4th 1985 we collected G-BOAC from outside the hangars at London and took it to Prestwick to practise with. As the most senior of the four students I got to drive there, assisted by John Eames in the other front seat.

No one could claim that a pilot's first takeoff in a Concorde is not a special personal event. It's the assault on the senses that does it, and an awareness of what you have unleashed, aided and abetted by the machine's readiness to go straight down the runway (though this is the easy part). The crescendoing roar, the curious and unmistakeable combination of hot engine oil, hydraulic oil, fibreglass ducting and burning paraffin would never be forgotten, nor the acceleration which builds relentlessly for the first eight seconds. Circuit training had not taken place for a number of years, and this positioning flight was intended only to get to Prestwick and settle in – find our rooms, and allow for the pitstop crew to find their feet and assemble their collection of wheels, tools, manuals, tea-making equipment and pin-ups for the walls of their office. This would, in fact, be a routine airfield noise abatement departure with one difference from the normal kind seen at London, and practised in the simulator – light weight with transatlantic power.

For this trip to Scotland we would carry about 60 tons less fuel than that required to take 100 passengers to New York, and for the sake of a standard procedure and no surprises or self-made booby traps, we would follow the normal instructions as calculated for weather and weight. The correct noise abatement time was relatively short on this occasion. This interval is the number of seconds started by the pilot when he pronounces the word 'Go,' simultaneously presses his stopwatch button with one hand and opens the throttles with the other. The required initial pitch attitudes today would be more radical than usual, and the reduction of power more dramatic when 'Three, two, one, noise' was called as this countdown ended. This 'quiet' power setting was the minimum required to achieve an acceptable climb gradient above the outlying housing until a suitable height allowed more thrust to be applied.

This version of the London takeoff happened quickly, spectacularly, but without problems, thanks to what had been learned in the simulator. We reached our first cleared altitude, 3000ft or thereabouts, while still within the airfield, and the degree of sudden noise reduction in the local area might have been a surprise in Hounslow or Staines. 'I heard a Concorde taking off this afternoon, then it stopped. I don't know what happened to it; I never saw where it went.'

When we got to Prestwick John took over on final approach to do his demonstration landing, then took off again, handing over to me again for a mini circuit session with what fuel was left. For an instructor, this landing and taking off again without stopping was quite busy to conduct in a conventional airliner. Flaps to takeoff, run the trim to a suitable takeoff setting, stow the speed brakes and then arrange for the right power to be set, all the time keeping an eye on the far end of the runway. This procedure was much simpler in a Concorde. There are no flaps or speed brakes, the trim position does not change, and something less than climb power is quite enough for the touch and go at landing weight. Opening the throttles is the only action required, and normally that can be left to the student and fine-tuned by the flight engineer.

I made two touch and goes, a full stop, and taxied in. My first Concorde flight was over, 1 hr 55 mins. Of course, a simulator and the aeroplane it represents are never quite the same. The aeroplane flies more like an aeroplane, usually, and you can expect the real thing to be more natural in its behaviour. At low speeds the Concorde simulator pitch, power and flightpath response had been strange and difficult to get really right. One's most careful fine adjustments didn't seem to work as expected – the simulator is probably as good as they could get it. What surprised me about this first grapple with the real deal was the similarity with the simulator. The Concorde behaved like a strange flying machine, not completely like the intuitive, look-after-itself traditional seat-of-the-pants character that typified most conventional aircraft of decades past.

Of course the wisdom of reality had progressively changed over the years, particularly when swept-wing jets came along, and the interrelationship of nose up and down vis à vis more or less engine had become more merged; but there were still those sages who continued to advocate what had worked with an Avro 504 or Tiger Moth, despite the evidence. The Concorde blatantly reversed the ancient teachings. The truth was that the simulator had actually been very good, the only exception being the landing behaviour which is associated with large lift coefficient and pitching moment changes encountered with a very strong but low ground effect, resulting from the Concorde's unusual shape and airflow pattern. But when development time is always pressing that's the last priority: in this case the simulator must have been fully devoted to flying behaviour – up in the air.

First landings

The correct and only feasible landing technique is quite foreign to a non-Concorde pilot, but a first attempt often works well because of this very state of affairs. The student relies on the instructions because it's all he has. The look of it, the speed at which the ground approaches and the low height at which landing action must begin defies the instincts of many. The eye height at touchdown happens to be the same as for a 747, but that is of no help: and following a successful first Concorde landing the new pilot now knows where the ground is, cannot ignore this knowledge, and hopes to improve on the quality next time around, using traditional values. Wrong! With the suspicion that the wheels are as good as on the ground, and that the Concorde has patently stopped going down, a bit of refined controlling must surely improve the touchdown. This instinct does not work, for well-understood but special Concorde reasons, and my touchdown three was less good than touchdown two. The first one had been the best, but they looked identical from the cockpit – perplexing. Better luck tomorrow. For more explanation read pages 44 to 63 of *The Concorde Stick and Rudder Book*. Trubshaw liked the book, and French test piloting doyen Jean Pinet liked it even better. (Jean Pinet was the first man to take the Concorde supersonic. Mirage chase pilot Turcat said 'They left us standing'.)

Supervised route flights

On the sixth day at Prestwick and a total of 33 landings (for me) it was time to come back to London. After a final circuit session with Tony Meadows it was my turn again (no idea why – seniority perhaps) to fly the machine to London with John Eames. I seem to remember a wet and dark evening when we got there, but all went well, although if asked whether I felt ready to take a load of passengers to New York an honest answer would have been 'not sure'. Then followed 22 route sectors under the watchful eye of training or supervisory captains. For the history files these were Cook, Rendall, Linfield, Meadows, Massie, Chorley and technical manager Dave Leney for my official route check, conducted from the co-pilot's seat (just in case).

Two New Yorks a day had long been the Concorde's bread and butter, and three Washington/Miamis a week completed the regular route structure. During these 22 flights – pretending to be captain (and the pretending is significant) – I managed to abandon much long-term landing instinct (unhelpful with this machine) and achieve the correct Concorde technique. This works wonderfully well and produces the smoothest and most aeromechanically elegant touchdown you can imagine. If the runway is wet the only way to tell that the mainwheels have landed is the clicking of the reverse latches in the throttles under your right hand. One day John Cook said 'You're breaking people's hearts with your landings'. 'Oh... thanks,' I replied with a show of diffidence and modesty. After my route check Dave Leney complimented me on the ideal and virtually constant landing attitude. Strong ground effect does the rest, provided the pilot does his bit with the controls, and does not flinch. It all happens at a low height, and 850 feet a minute close to the ground looks fast, especially if you are familiar with the 747.

But this gift of providence didn't last. Actually being in charge instead of having a more experienced safety pilot in the other seat is not the same, and my subsequent solo landings varied a lot, I thought. Variable conditions tend to upset the apple cart somewhat, but this situation was unsettling; I even had the phone call from the union anonymity man about flight recorder readouts concerning one touchdown. I would not have called it potentially damaging, but not exactly polished and gleaming. But asking the others in the cockpit what happened never helped. Nobody could say, exactly; it could have been lots of things – anything. A few weeks after going it alone I passed the training office and told John Cook, 'I've been doing some terrible landings recently.' He was completely unfazed. 'Welcome to the human race,' he said. On another similar occasion he replied with what could have been reassurance, 'Nobody likes a smartarse,' but I don't remember what this was about.

The ticket price alone gave the New York flight an inclusive and clubby feel. Critics might use the word 'exclusive', but this was not the case – you only had to be able to pay, no one was excluded – and the flight always had a pleasantly informal, civilised and socially relaxed atmosphere. On sector 21, my first official not-under-supervision flight, but the Leney route check, I spotted F. Murray Abraham's name and sent the visit invitation message back during the cruise. He is an actor who does films, not a film star, and I liked his depiction of the admiring but envious Antonio Salieri in 'Amadeus', the film of the play about Mozart. I also thought the elements of musical analysis put over by Salieri (F. Murray really) were well done – true, informative, educational if one chooses, and leaving unanswered questions. He agreed about the film and mentioned the Ferrari he drives (carefully) around San Francisco, while Dave sat quietly being a co-pilot as we bombed along in the 60,000ft sunshine: the mile every three seconds cruise, 750,000 sq miles of Earth visible from the lofty vantage point, with everything working and good weather ahead.

Leney gave me a good write up, and mentioned nothing else. A couple of weeks later a general letter came from the technical office reminding captains to keep their priorities in mind. Did he mean me? I'm sure he did, and I was reminded of what someone had told me at the start of the route flying. 'Although you've finished the training, the best you can do at this stage is to cope with a normal trip. You can't manage by yourself – you'll need your crew.' This was very true, and John Eames' one year estimate for settling in would turn out to be conservative. This depends on imagination as much as experience, but after twelve years of Concording I revised my version in answer to 'how long did it take?' to 'ask me next week'. You never know: anything can happen, and sometimes did. There was always the chance that it might.

CHAPTER 29

CONCORDE BEGINNER

Normal route flying

The next few months were quite busy with the Concorde. Was this rostering intentional in order to rapidly build some necessary solo experience? Perhaps, but contrary to the Concorde decliners' excuse that the route structure was not variable enough I discovered that the work was most agreeable. I was more interested in flying than hotels and cheap beer. I'd been to many parts of the world already and had little desire to waste my life visiting most of them again, especially if someone else had chosen them for me. Though some of our passengers flew more frequently than us, the massive advantage of Concorde transatlantic flight for the human animal rapidly became apparent. We were never picked up at 8pm after trying to sleep in the afternoon. The flights were relatively short – for a passenger, enough time to read the papers, start the catering with a fizzing glass of the easy-to-drink (expensive) pedigree, and enjoy a small but nice lunch. By coffee it was top of descent, time to throw each individual sheet of the world's broadsheet press on the floor, and prepare to leave, gathering thoughts for the rest of the day's business.

But the main thing was how you felt when you got off. It was a little earlier, local time, than when you got on, and you did not feel like a piece of chewed string. In the case of the morning New York, 10:30 chocks away, take off around 10:45, you landed (after the small but nice lunch) at 9:15 same morning, feeling totally normal. The terminal was deserted, another five hours to go before the jumbos arrived in the heat of the afternoon. The short flight time was partly responsible, but the cabin environment equally so. The cabin altitude never rose above 5,000ft (compared with 8,000), the machine didn't spend enough time in the air for the cabin upholstery to dry out, and there was no ozone inside.

If you are not a mountain dweller or alpinist, exposure to altitude is tiring – you need time to acclimatise. For a sea-level person three hours at 5,000ft is much less draining than eight at 8,000ft. It used to be thought that the dryness of the air inside made your nose and eyes sore, and to some extent this is true. The original 747 came with copious humidifiers, four of them. I remember it well, and they worked well, but there were problems. First of all the amount of condensation that froze on the fuselage skin, then melted during descent and poured through the ceiling on to the passengers was unacceptable, and the devices themselves plus water weighed a lot – so they went. But then the experts discovered that it was high altitude ozone, collected (from the ozone layer), concentrated and pumped into the cabin with the rest of the air that made the eyes and nose hurt. So the second generation of improved 747s were designed with ozone extractors. But the news got out. How was it extracted – what happened to it? I don't actually know, but as a saver of the planet I would say they turned it into oxygen... or something similar, but this is a bad thing. They killed it! So this was no good, and the ozone collectors went. So what about the Concorde and ozone? This is classified, but it's no secret that the cabin air came from the engine compressor stages which received quite hot air to start with when at speed. Somehow no ozone got past them, except when you throttled back. So did the Concorde engines eat the ozone? I've no idea, I'm only a pilot.

Washington and Miami was a longer day, but we still had time to go to the beach, get a windsurfer and splash about for a while, then enjoy a drink as the sun went down before dinner. The flight there from Washington was fun because we followed the standard airline route all the way, first subsonic (overland) to Wilmington, North Carolina, then it was over the sea to the far end of Florida, and who else wanted to fly along Atlantic Route 66 at 60,000ft? We were light of course, and it didn't take long in level flight to punch through the sound barrier, reach our barber's pole and follow it up to this height very quickly.

The thing that was fun was the innate American enthusiasm for fancy flying machines, especially the powered kind. They sort of invented them after all, and it soon became clear that, as a race, they were our greatest fans. On this short offshore dash it was the other airliners below who had to say something – each one six times a week if you count both ways. To the people going the same way the white dart went over, 25,000ft above, at relatively something more than their own speed. From the opposing direction the speed difference was considerable, nearly 2000 mph. I can only imagine what it looked like because there were few Concordes nearby when I was in one. I did once see one go the other way on our standard Atlantic tracks, separated by one degree – 60 nm. I saw the dot and the trail – definitely moving.

The Washington/Miami sector always had a few passengers, but never crowding the doors. It seemed to be an add-on, but why not? The fares were expensive, and Jock Lowe told me that the first 15 people paid the basic costs of a Concorde flight; let's say another 30 was break-even, and the rest was clear profit. Given that the total Concorde package cost BOAC £1 to buy, this may make some sense. The Miami departure back to Washington was a relaxed affair, and maybe the captain would take a coffee in the punter's ritzy lounge before getting aboard and saying 'start number three'. As a workaday professional you might think this just silly and inappropriate, but where money and perceived status are involved it helps. I remember balancing my coffee and croissant as I chatted to a sharply-dressed man and his bubbly-blonde wife. (OK?) 'I'm taking her on this special treat.' 'When we take off, will we go straight up?' she asked. I hope not, I thought; but of course, Cape Canaveral is just up the road. Quite understandable.

But for the vast majority of regular passengers, kudos, image, prestige, status, conspicuously glamorous lifestyle, were not significant reasons to travel on this machine, although this was invariably the basic press comment, and therefore also the received opinion of the many who prefer to be told what to think. The time saving was of course significant, but the there-and-back business trip in a day, also quoted by those who did not do this, was not a common factor. It was the much-reduced impact that 3½ hours in a Concorde had on the traveller's sense of identity and ability to function, together with the proportion of the same day left for useful living, that was the expensive reason. The eastbound flights clearly arrived with the day shortened by the 5-hour time change, but, even so, the arrival times still meant that you could go home or wherever and have a full night's rest – the Concorde passenger had no nights out of a civilised bed. And intelligent, successful or rich people are seldom preoccupied with making an impression. They will have done it already. Only those who have crossed the Atlantic in a Concorde fully understand the difference and the benefits, and this could also apply to the crew.

Charters

By 1978 the BOAC Concordes had been operating scheduled services for two years – definitely no cheap seats. Brian Calvert was in at the beginning, in fact he was one of the two pilots on the very first commercial foray to Bahrain, with Shirley Bassey as a star passenger; I saw it on the TV. He lived near Streatley in Berkshire and frequented the Bell Inn at Aldworth, a tiny picturesque village with a cricket team, part of the very fabric of rural village life. The pub locals raised the point that the entire population had paid for Concorde development (true), but the project had dwindled into a product for a few of the unusually rich or well-supported (also true). How can we, the people, ever hope to get a ride in something we'd paid for? (good question). Being a sensitive soul, Brian thought about the logic of this, and the first Concorde charter came into being, ticket sales organised by the pub, £100 a seat, 100 passengers (plus a fiver for the bus). This was the first round-the-bay London to London, including a large turnaround circle in the Bay of Biscay with flight at 60,000ft; faster than a speeding bullet and so on: it was a PR and social success.

Anyway, it started the charter ball rolling, so that available time on the aircraft could make some cash on the side, and also enable worthy citizens to experience regimes of flight only thought of by most, in other words go faster and higher than many professionals, or certainly a vast proportion of the human race. Of course they will tell their friends about it, and bore family members and neighbours alike. But this is marketing, spreading the positive word; and it works. With increasing crew experience of managing the Concorde fight envelope this local flight, round the bay concept, developed into something more abbreviated as it became accepted that you did not have to go half the way to Africa and back to wind the machine up to speed. The normal Bristol Channel Atlantic departure route and climb could be followed until clear of Cornwall, then a left turn would end up pointing the aircraft down the English Channel, during which it could make its normal descent procedure, backing through the sound barrier off Dorset before heading for the Isle of Wight and London. The whole flight, chock to chock, took about an hour and a half.

The first time I did one of these I was astonished to see a printed note on the flight log, alongside the place where you leave the normal US route and do the left turn. It said 'max rate turn'. Wow! Where did this come from? Had it always been there? I happened to know that the planned turn at Mach 2 assumed a normal cross country 20° of bank. This creates a diameter of 114 nm and the planned 180 degrees takes 8 minutes to get round. Not much max rate there, but I did hear that Colin Morris, some years previously, assumed that the best you could do was required. He had been a Royal Navy Sea Vixen pilot, the back-seat man with the radar issuing turn instructions in this all-weather missile-launcher. Many years before, a BEA co-pilot had told me about the same sort of thing in the Javelin. They had two basic instructions from the radar man; 'turn' or 'hard turn', with subtle modifications, no doubt. The navy system might have been similar, but, in any case, pilots of combat aircraft have to be familiar with a variety of limiting turns – max rate, minimum radius, best way to keep the energy and so on: it's a way of life. Colin read the instruction on the clipboard and went for it – to an extent that seemed reasonable, given the different circumstances. The result, of course, was that the nose was soon pointing straight for Land's End, not Berck sur Mer, and many greenhouses and citizen's nerves could soon be shattered. What happened next I don't know, nor why this misleading and unspecific instruction was still on the paperwork, but the policy had always been to keep up the pretence that Concorde and the things it did were normal, and other things not discussed outside, or inside it seems. It's easier that way – part of external and internal political survival strategy – and more convenient if one found out for oneself.

My first charter was one of the other kind, where a group or organisation hired the Concorde for a conventional supersonic transatlantic journey, a fast airline flight by any other name. In this case the Detroit-based Nomads travel club arranged for two Concordes to take them to London. They were used to their own B727 so this would be something different, and incidentally the only time a Concorde would visit Detroit. There were in fact two Concordes on this job, and I do not know how much Nomading in the other direction was concerned, but I'm sure we had positioned to Detroit the day before, and, while waiting for our machines to arrive I remember the local television newsroom star asking me the simple interviewer's get-out question 'What, exactly, is it like to fly the Concorde?' Of, course, at this level of broadcasting the answer is irrelevant – anything will do – but I started to mumble a few things about this monstrous subject before Peter Horton, the co-pilot, helped me out. This was a salutary lesson, and, chastened, I later assembled a few appropriate answers in case it happened again. My favourite was 'Fast', followed by 'you get off quick', if there was a supplementary. This summarised the essence of the machine, I thought; quite adequate for the *Daily Mail.*

We waited with our excited Nomads at the front of the terminal building before the aeroplanes arrived. The first one made a nice sedate pass, clean, nose and visor up at 300kts and maybe a few hundred feet, then manoeuvred around and landed. There was no evidence of the second one until it appeared on finals and landed. The captain, John Cook, took us aside and said he didn't do anything because they'd shut down an engine on the way from NY. This turned out to be solved by a simple box re-rack (probably a secondary nozzle reverse warning), so all was well for the two returns – starting with a sector to New York.

This trip was only one logbook page after I had done my 16 personal landings and had become a normal person, allowed to give flying away, but it was starting to reveal one reason for the advice suggesting there would be plenty more to learn on the road. As we prepared to depart for New York Peter Horton explained to me that the usual thing to do on such visits was to make a circuit and normal approach to a low height, then level off and make a low pass down the runway for a while before powering up, wheels up, afterburner and so on while blasting into the sky – en route. Like the 300kt pass on arrival, this was news to me. I had flown for BA (as it became) for 23 years, but this sort of thing had never been on the syllabus, or mentioned on the six-month Concorde course. Why had we not been told? Where were the procedures in the books? Would we not get into trouble? 'OK, you'd better show me how it's done,' I said.

He took off and did exactly what he'd said; a training circuit, ILS approach with level off at 50 feet, some level flight down the runway past the building then a briefly reheated climb away – all completely within the event recording parameters. A normal airliner flight on the trace, but the Nomads liked it, the tower liked it, everybody liked it. It's not every day you get a Concorde hot-dogging at Detroit, in fact that's the only time – ever. Is this history or what? I was slowly getting the picture, and you could learn a lot from the crew. (You would not learn it anywhere else.)

A couple of months later I did my first Goodwood Travel charter. This company had specialised in Concorde charters early on, and persevered in marketing this product with commitment and enthusiasm. Excursions varied between the short RTBs already mentioned, or a two or more day trip to a venue with special attraction(s), with a bit of supersonic thrown in somewhere suitable and useful. This particular one was to Moscow, a frequent feature of the Goodwood calendar, featuring a night at the Bolshoi Ballet. The crew were technically on just another night stop, but this company was very generous in including them in dinners and attractions, where possible and appropriate, and chatting to the crew was an attraction for the passengers, or a surprise if they were unlucky – but enough said. These, unlikely if you like, Concorde passengers got the flights, the nightstop all found, maybe with gala dinner or the like thrown in, plus the special event in the good seats. All (yes all) for maybe half the price of a New York single. There were many other examples.

What struck me on this very first November Goodwood (for me) was the change in the passengers' demeanour between the start and the finish. Compared with the holiday on the Costa Lotless it was not cheap. The long coach trip from Huddersfield to make the 8:30am departure in November was not exactly glamour personified, and then, once they got aboard, what did they get – a cup of tea, same as in the caff in Morrison's. What sort of ripoff is this? You could get two weeks in Elsbels for this. But by the time we were on the way back (jetting faster than the speeding bullet across the North Sea) this was how they lived, to the manner born – champagne on tap, exotic venues, gala mealtimes, once in a lifetime shows, every detail of life organised. Cheap at the price. What a bargain! Colin Mitchell, co-director of Goodwood Travel of Canterbury, proved that it could be done.

On this occasion Swan Lake was the billboarded show, but we were one too many for the tickets so I volunteered to stay behind. As it was I spent an entertaining evening at the Mezhdunarodnaya (International) hotel. This was a very different affair from the Moscow hotels of the 1960s, and the buzz was different also, as indeed was the king's ransom value of Western currency. A couple of the blue folding ones slipped to a friend produced a rucksack of roubles, more than enough for dinner for three, and I found that, as a hotel resident, my ability to greet a fur-clad acquaintance at the door, thus clearing them past the doorman, very welcome. These were nice, intelligent and charming people (there is no escape, Mr Bond), whatever the attractions of the hotel and its exotic residents. Needs must in straitened times, I suppose.

Things were not exactly as expected for the ballet fans either. Instead of Swan Lake, with the cygnets-holding-hands-behind-the-back 4-way formation routine, there had been a late change of programme. They got Ivan the Terrible instead. I still haven't seen it – very few laughs. It might be wonderful.

On a future Goodwood Moscow I got to go to Romeo and Juliet at the Bolshoi. We sat in the royal box section, centre circle. Since my 707 Boris Godunov with Mervyn Smooth in the 1960s they really had blinged the place up no end: like Covent Garden on steroids. The reds were redder, golds goldener, seats much more plushy than before, and brighter and more glittery house lighting – a bit bigger than the Garden anyway. Not a headscarf or shopping bag in sight.

This ballet company is renowned for its tradition and classical rigour, but this does not detract one iota from the power, emotion and clarity of the storytelling. Prokofiev's punchy music was conducted marvellously by an electrified and expressive conductor – his intricate acting out of every bar of his countryman's music was inspired, he could almost have got a part on stage himself. The orchestra played with passion and sweaty conviction: it was great. The point where Juliet's father strode imperiously (very butch) up from the dark of the back of the stage carrying his apparently lifeless daughter across his two arms in front of him (like shelf brackets) as if she weighed nothing, as if to say 'look what you lot have done', was rather wonderful, if sad.

One thing that surprised me was near the beginning. We'd had the story baseline set, the boys sword fighting in the street, Juliet skipping girlishly in front of her nurse, her mother lecturing about suitable boyfriends; then the nice stewardess next to me said a surprising thing. 'It's very nice, but I'd rather have come to something with a story I recognised, like Romeo and Juliet.' Follow that, if you can.

On May 8th 1986 I took Concorde AC to Basel and back, another day trip charter. I think this is the only time, in history, for ever, that a Concorde will have been to a city in Switzerland. The Swiss have a blanket ban on such noisy machines (two F18s taking off together is OK), but there was a get-out. The field was in France. We were met on the tarmac by a local jazz band (the Swiss, Basel in particular, are keen on this kind of musicality), and good it was. I was interviewed by the Swiss radio chief, and a good interview it was. Intelligent people's questions, including an unintended curve ball. He asked me why the Concorde was white and the SR71 Blackbird black. I'd sort of heard this theory before but was initially flummoxed. 'White reflects the sun's contribution to heating the Concorde, but the Blackbird gets so hot that the sun is irrelevant. Night or day, black is best for radiating heat at 500°C.' Was I right? I've never thought of it since.

In this May I also got to try Tony Bianchi's CAP 21, and the Meeson/Lamb Extra 230. During the CAP 21 flight a large screwdriver floated up from behind the seat. 'I wondered where that had gone', said Tony when I gave it back. The CAP 21 was nice in its own French CAP way, no doubt an improvement on the CAP 20 – and I liked the Extra 230. Compact and coordinated would cover it. Enough power, but not too much, and I could see why this machine had served Phillip Meeson and Nigel Lamb so well in the British Championships that I had witnessed as a judge some time before. It was obvious the master had taught his pupil well, and their flying was difficult to distinguish. Nigel Lamb (the pupil) had flown the Vampire, then the Alouette – real ANC action (read about it: few talk about it) — in his home country (now called Zimbabwe). If asked who is the best pilot I have encountered, he gets my vote.

During this competition in Norfolk, Jiri Kobrle, a celebrated Czech team member of bygone days, visited my judging position. 'Good pilots,' he commented, 'but bad training.' He meant the absence of effective coaching directed at competition success, not piloting as such. He was right, and British aerobatics was still caught up in the mistaken obsession that attempts at perfection from the cockpit were what was required. Neil Williams' competition career demonstrated this well. As one of the 'I'm a pilot, not a judge' brigade he never fully comprehended the mental processes required of a judge. He did his best, but that's not good enough. The established national teams had the luxury of trainers who were good pilots with judging experience and long forgotten egos. British is Best or Wales Forever is sometimes not enough.

Concorde training, and a disappointment

When we had finished our training John Cook asked for feedback from the four of us. Mine was complementary about the pace and progression of the simulator details, and I had nothing special to say about the individuals who conducted our simulator and aircraft training. They did their best consistent with their examining or, perhaps, training experience, the Concorde training they themselves had received, and the fact that most of them had not flown anything else for a number of years. I had taken away the impression that some of the concerns and priorities of the manufacturer's flying specialists had been passed on and retained, 10 years down the line. But, considering the character and demands of this machine, this is very understandable. They were test crews, concerned with the difficult possibilities, compared with everyday life when everything goes well (as expected). In the light of a quarter century of successful BA Concorde flying they had done a fantastic job.

From my own point of view I had a list of handling details that I would have preferred to have been acquainted with on the course. In particular there were a number of fundamental pitch and vertical behaviour differences that required changes of traditional techniques. Many pilots do not notice these refinements, and are usually able to adapt without realising it, but others to my certain knowledge would have benefited. This inertia of tradition explains why some training words (patter) do not change while reality does, in many walks of aviation. Flying training tends to be very conservative, as a function of the people who do it, and the perceived risks of change, despite the fact that things do change.

When I entered the training office and gave John my very thin A4 file he immediately said 'So I'm going to get another bollocking, am I?' Why would he have said that? 'Absolutely not,' I said, 'It's good, with a few ideas – totally personal.' Why should a training manager say such a thing to a student? What was going on? Did he suspect that I was a member of some cabal? Or was it an ironic compliment?

Time went by fast on the Concorde. It seemed like a few weeks but must have been a number of months when he told me that they needed another training captain. 'You'll be applying?' he said. 'Of course.' So I applied. For those with previous suitable experience this was sometimes done on the nod, but it became clear that this would involve the full interview procedure, everything above board – anyone can have a go. My interview board consisted of someone I had not met before, sat in the middle, with a contemporary close acquaintance of 25 years, and John Cook – one on either side. We chatted happily, the questions were routine, superfluous in fact; there were few subjects that were not already patently obvious from company records – nothing about personal tastes, predilections or quirky traits at all.

A few days later I got the letter telling me I had failed – not got the job – extra to requirements – failed to achieve the required standard – skills and experience not needed. It did not actually say all these things, but gave no reasons for this unpreference. I wrote back to the relevant manager Tristar/Concorde/Battlestar Galactica (solar system cyberdrives only) etc, asking for some reason for this decision; after all, feedback and a list of inadequacies are the very thing of improvement in today's progressive staff encouragement. I cited my flawless 10-year career as an (invited) VC10 and 707 training captain, and wondered where I could make the necessary improvements, having received no hint of ever having challenged the required standard. He replied with the bitchy comment that I had not dated the letter (I forgot), and, in so many other words, told me that no further answer would be forthcoming – one could easily interpret its gist as 'get lost'. How confidence-inspiring is that from a world-renowned airline's senior management?

Was this one of the world's leading airlines? Not sure. Were we involved in interesting times? At this point I have to explain that the captain who did get the job was an excellent choice, with much better personal qualities than myself. But that is not the point. I quickly reconciled myself to the prospect that I could spend more Concorde time zapping about the skies, choosing the morning show and thus developing my career as a New York restaurant and performing arts critic in the afternoons (matinees are better for time zone victims), still with every night in bed.

A few days later John Cook buttonholed me. 'I was pissed off with that letter you wrote.' Why, I thought, what might he expect (he was on the failure board)? 'The reason you failed,' he continued, 'was that you looked at the picture on the wall when we asked you what airliners you had been on during your career: but I'll get you in anyway.' So that was it. It *was* interesting times.

The helpful historic poster in question included many assorted aircraft types, old and new, and, as a people's Biggles rather than an ambitious office suit, I had looked at it as a raconteur's reminder. After all, this was a chat between friends. Of course, looking at the wall is a sign of evasiveness, I guessed – not enough staring into the eyes (seven seconds is the animal limit, then it's aggression – or the simple villager's curiosity and vacant rudeness on the Swiss bus). He must be a shifty little bugger, untrustworthy and evasive; a cross in one of the psychological profiling boxes. A fail point: got him. As a long-term instrument rating examiner I'm well aware of the ethics of examining. I have never been party to pre-arranged tactical failing, but John's revelation demonstrated it loud and clear. Had he been encouraged to put a fail in his eye contact box? We'll never know, but I'll give him the benefit of the doubt.

A few days later he copied me his letter to the same small pond reformer requesting that I be posted to the Concorde training section forthwith, and stated that he had told me why I'd failed (but did not mention the requisite remedial correction that I might need). I didn't make any of this up. Piss ups in breweries? It's not as funny as that. All sorts of things were going on at office level, not particularly concerned with orderly flying. I did not envy him his job. Maybe it explained why the previous two training managers had left in short order. This one was under all sorts of pressure.

I've never had interview training, but I googled the body language and eye contact stuff. Apparently the eye contact tick box is becoming a problem with millennials – approximately early 20-somethings. They have been taught 'stranger danger' as kids and have acquired resistance to eye contact with those they do not know – it might be a creepy perv trying to gain your attention then confidence for some unseemly activity, aided by the sweets. I've recently become trendy and cool it seems, if you discount the millennials' enthusiasm for celebrity dressing up. But averting the gaze suggests a liar – the internet says so, so that's it. I shouldn't have included the HP42 and Sunderland in my experience claims. Lovely kites, of course, but I'm too young and they must have put two and two together. If only these machines hadn't been on the poster. One lives and learns.

CHAPTER 30

CONTESTS, SHOWS AND JOYRIDES

Since Neil Williams' final cross country in the Heinkel (Casa) 111 in 1977, Aerobatics International's members' enthusiasm for international competition had dwindled. Time passes; interests and priorities change. It wasn't a lack of interest in exciting flying, but it had been Neil's obsession with achievement at this sport that had led the way. The rest of us were happy to be dragged along, and James Black, the only non-professional pilot, also managed the business (as well as doing a proper job). Carl Schofield, Pete Jarvis and Brian Smith all filtered into Ray Hanna's Duxford scene, and I would cite all three as ideal examples of who should be flying old-fashioned and charismatic aircraft at flying displays.

It is not always thus, and the hurly-burly, favour-currying, irrelevant qualification and experience-claiming, plus ability to buy a historic machine, and the many other characteristics of the warbird scene – its tacky badges, sentimental associations and so on, (not to mention the unforgivable crashes) precluded me from involvement. To fly these aircraft; wonderful, of course – but I suppose my unassuming and unpretentious father is my real warbird example. Money, talk, badges and sometimes ill-judged showing off had nothing to do with it then. Safety (surprising to some today, perhaps), reliability and operational results were everything when the warbirds were doing their intended job.

The logbook shows that there was virtually no light aircraft flying until mid 1986 – John Eames' Concorde settling-down year, perhaps – and there will have been plenty of simulator time practising how to conduct current refreshers and checks, required for CAA simulator examiner qualification. The next conversion course was under way in late 1986, so then the extensive menu of simulator training exercises had to be rehearsed – practising on these learners, under supervision, of course. During our own course it was clear to me that Tony Meadows' personal briefing notes had added useful detail to the formal instructions in the official documentation. He was kind enough to give me a copy which I found useful for the next couple of years, until I didn't need to look at it, but it did encourage the idea of helpful hints and tips that I thought should accompany 'This is the routine. Have a go and I'll tell you what you did wrong' style of the usual training borne of examining. This is the wrong way round, of course, even for teaching the wife to drive.

From the middle of 1986 aerobatic instruction in the Aerobatic and Artistic Flying Club gathered pace, and Concorde appearances at air displays also feature. At our pre-course address from Brian Walpole I asked him how the airshow scene worked – how much practice is there? There is no free flying, he said. The shows are tacked on to round the bay charters. There was no practice. As a Concorde manager I would have been very careful as to who was allowed to take part. Quite how this worked within the democratic structure of airline rostering I don't know, but in this small and rather special fleet it sort of did.

On July 1st 1986 I see I did an unusual in-house flight organised by a young flight manager (Birmingham, perhaps). He came with us, full of enthusiasm for this wonderful opportunity he had arranged for a selection of older schoolchildren from a group of midland towns. A Concorde's normal job was to cruise effortlessly at great speed and height, giving the impression of being bolted to the hangar floor: that's what it feels like. This was to be a 2000ft tour around their close-knit towns. Why? Perhaps they had done well in their exams. Won a competition? This route around Birmingham looks big on the road map, even reasonable on the club pilot's half million – but it's tight and constrained for an airliner, especially a Concorde. Of course a joyride over the house in Dudley might be nice in a Cessna 172 for a pub raffle-winning couple, but this is not what a Concorde is intended to do. Had he ever been in a Concorde? Did he know what it was like? No, but he was a manager and had organised this special treat. We settled for 250kts. It wasn't a treat.

Of course the intention was to provide these unsuspecting young people with the privilege of a ride in a Concorde: and here I might add that this level of unawareness and lack of aviation insight exemplifies those who have frequently accused Concorde people of elitism. The formula 1 takeoff is fun, and 400kt magic carpet swoosh to 15,000ft takes little time – a couple of minutes. Birmingham appears very soon and it's time to come down again, and enter the Concorde slow flight regime. Of the 100 teenagers, 50 can't see anything outside, the other 50 can't see much out of their little windows, including anything of their waving relatives, washing blowing in the line, school, town, even county (I couldn't have done). At 250kts the Concorde shakes continuously. At this speed it flies at 7° nose up – not perfect for orange juice, coke and a selection of sticky buns. 30° of bank to take in the succession of progressive academies is no big deal, but adds to the sensory overload. This is a beautiful July day, and although the thermals indicated by the puffy clouds don't affect the Concorde to the extent that you'd notice, a little up and down lurching cannot but add to an already shuddery flight with plenty of turning included.

After passing Halesowen or Sutton Coldfield – it doesn't matter which – the chief steward came up, looking distinctly disenchanted, and said 'It may interest you to know that half of them have been sick already'. He seemed neither enthusiastic nor impressed with the mission. I said 'That's enough, we'll climb up, go to the south coast and make our leisurely way to London to allow the crew to clear up the mayhem as best they can'. I received no passenger feedback. Whether any of our young passengers, with their whole lives ahead of them, ever made another Concorde flight I don't know. I'm prepared to guess no. It wasn't my fault.

At the beginning of August 1986 I did a typical flypast/airshow flight. This followed the standard pattern for this routine with the appearance at the venue tacked on to the return from a round-the-bay. In this case we followed the normal RTB route until becoming subsonic during the descent off Dorset, then doubled back for a flypast at Exeter (airfield/show I imagine, but don't remember) then more off airways to the display at Cosford. Timing is important for these events, but clockwork precision something of the past for many displays because of the variety of participants and ad hoc programme changes.

Despite Concorde aficionados claiming it 'handles like a fighter' this was not the case in all respects, particularly as this is always a passenger carrying flight, so manoeuvring was necessarily a bit cumbersome. All of it would be below minimum drag speed (325kts at landing weight – max permitted speed 300 at 1000ft) and, despite auto throttle, it had to be done with care (absolutely no seat-of-the-pants, and always visual flying by instruments!) When on track for the field we would warn of our impending arrival, of course – with luck this would be as planned – and not accept off-the-cuff changes of plan at short notice because light aircraft might be doing improvisational things. With half a minute to run the message 'can you stay clear for a couple of minutes, there's a Chipmunk filling in, it hasn't finished yet' is not helpful, and 'not really' has to be the answer. A couple of quick loops or steep turns over the countryside is not practical. 'What would you suggest?' is unlikely to be helpful. Fortunately the Concorde is relatively big and you can hear it coming, so these problems seem to solve themselves. A pretend approach to land, with a power up and accelerating climb, which could disappear steeply into cloud at speed, made a nice contrast and covered the syllabus with taste and discretion (less is more). Join airways and proceed to London finished the outing.

A couple of weeks later I made an airshow flypast at South Cerney at the end of another Goodwood Travel round the bay. On this occasion a row 1 passenger was the oldest person in Britain – 106 or thereabouts. This was also the closing day of the 1986 world aerobatic championships, and the South Cerney fixture followed a flyover of the Hot Air Balloon Jamboree at Clifton, Bristol. Concorde Flight Engineer Tony Brown was a keen ballooner and could talk to us from the ground. This simplified things for us – balloons cannot get out of the way easily.

After Bristol, overhead Kemble made sense to set up an accurate track for the South Cerney downwind position, for a small Concorde circuit gesturing at the grass. This famous military field had ideal qualities for prewar aircraft. It's a large and roughly circular expanse of grass – no obstructions – with a perimeter track all the way round, so one would have been able to taxi round to any takeoff spot to suit the wind, and always land into wind. Perfect. Now, movements were more formalised, with a main grass runway marked out, and today, crowd lines etc. The Concorde is not a bad glider at 350kts, not far short of 1 in 20 I would say, but this cannot be demonstrated near the ground. The low-speed behaviour is much more interesting; 180kts looks slow and nose up, and relies totally on engines and high incidence (detached flow) aerodynamics, so a 45° banked final turn on to the westerly strip seemed a good idea. This creates 1.4g, unusual for passengers but not out of order; at landing weight and 180kts the Concorde has considerable reserves of thrust from three engines.

After landing (at London) I had a chat with the country's oldest inhabitant. She seemed none the worse for the experience, and told me this was her first flight. She had been 23 years old when the Wright brothers flew. Makes you think, and I hope makes my point of fast-moving (and disappearing) history, especially that of aviation (hence this narrative).

That evening at the WAC wind-up event at South Cerney, Eric Müller told me that he did not think the approach would work. 'You were very close downwind, I thought the turn would take you behind the hangars, but it didn't.' The airshow was managed by the Fairford air traffic specialists, now airshow organisers. Things were running late, and the final free aerobatic programme was being fitted in amongst airshow acts. They would have preferred a straight pass and clear off, but I thought some minor manoeuvring worth it. The mixing of a large competition and airshow management was to have its problems, but there had been no alternative for this competition.

1986 WAC – World Aerobatic Championships

An event of this size needs two basic things – organisation and money. The problems here were organising the infrastructure for the contest, arranging the final airshow, and getting the money. As the time approached it became clear that neither would be adequately forthcoming, and the organisers arranged for the RIAT management to sort out the event. These people do a fantastic job with the annual Fairford show, and getting money from the spectators must be a significant part of the revenue, and while money rolling in is nice, this part of the package created a conflict of interests and some awkwardness, I sensed. Until the official public display on the last day the championship is not an airshow, and, even though spectators are welcome, an airshow interface with the public can be very unhelpful, unless the judges are situated well out of earshot of the public area. My description of contest judging may make this clear.

The main problem was the commentating during the contest flights. The handful of daily aerobatic anoraks, spotters and autograph hounds may appreciate it, but as the loudspeaker words bear no relationship to the complexities of the aerobatic evaluation system they can be distracting to the judges who are not in airshow mode – in fact I would start with infuriating; debilitating actually.

Imagine a television commentary from the Olympic pool. Tom Daley's foot accidentally slips off the 50-metre board as he launches. 'What brilliance, what a novel way to convert three and a half twists into a spectacular tumble, arms and legs flying. What a huge splash as he hits the water: pure genius. Tens all round, it must be, Britain leads'. This may be fine in the privacy of the broadcast commentary box, but the judges would not appreciate such opinion echoing round the pool. They have their own complex debate with themselves to resolve, and a mark is required. The aerobatic judge has fifteen or twenty consecutive dives to assess. One follows the other, there's no time to fend off intrusive cerebral rubbish.

It's like my theatre visits in New York with a theatrical friend, now concerned with coaching, rehearsing, rewriting bad scripts and so on. If I said I liked a play we saw, thought it was good, more often than not it turned out to be bad. 'But I liked it anyway', I might say. She explained: 'if we went to an airshow I might have enjoyed a particular act, but you might point out that it was incompetent, reckless, and too low. I know nothing about flying, or aerobatics.' She had a point.

I had no official function at this event, but had helped the home team in their lead-up training, and did some dogsbody flying during the contest when available – judges' low line flights, weather checks or taking a jury member up to decide if conditions were within limits if a competitor complained. On more than one occasion I was sent to the tower to ask if spectator-commentator Sean Maffet could moderate or preferably stop his comments about the quality of the manoeuvres, these being at variance with what was required by the accepted judging criteria. These requests were unwelcome and I gave up, along with others. The RIAT attitude was clear and hard-nosed: we are helping you out of a hole, we are an air display business and will follow our normal air display business principles – even if there are only 20 paying public present. Unfortunately there was not suitable space available to put the judges on the opposite side of the box (performance zone – therefore a kilometre away). This is all one could have done in this case. The value of a competitive event can be considerably compromised if commercial pressures override, but (in 2017) this appears to be globally endemic. As with many other sports, competitors are now required to be entertainers, whether it suits them or not. The boundaries get blurred.

A first sight of the Sukhoi 26

South Cerney 1986 was the first time the world championships had seen something completely different from the Russians, the Sukhoi 26, one number after the ground attack Frogfoot and one short of the stupendous Su 27 hi-tech fighter. It looked like a mini-Focke Wulf 190, but more aerobatic – built-for-purpose. There were three, I think, looking like prototypes – unspectacular matt paint jobs (with the red stars) and slightly differently profiled leading edges.

Its vertical performance and stunning roll rate, not to mention apparent strength, clearly tempted the Russians to make the most of its wow factor. This terminology has often been used to suggest unfairness by those who have less of it, but why not flaunt it if you've got it? It may not get more marks, but it will upset those who suspect it that might. I asked one of the Russians about the airspeed achieved when they dived in for a fortissimo start. '50 kph'. This was a half-joke, and the truth later emerged. The airspeed indicator goes from 0 to 400. There's no stop, so the needle can continue on a second circuit. The aircraft has no airspeed limit, the expectation being that you would not need to go over the 400 mark, but you could. I first was able to fly one four years later. It was indeed fabulous on first acquaintance, and I was astonished at its sheer athleticism combined with good-natured friendliness; like meeting a scary Russian bear that grinned instead of growled. But I had also already concluded that the Concorde was the world's most user-friendly Mach 2 bomber.

To continue with the Russians, there was a ceremonial event one day at South Cerney – perhaps the opening function. Prince Michael of Kent arrived and walked around; tall, slim, elegantly suited, grey-bearded, chatting to the various assembled teams. The Russians were surprised, abashed, intrigued – I could tell. One of the girls said to me afterwards, eyes wide with reverential wonderment, 'He looked just like the Czar, and he spoke Russian with us.' After a lifetime under Soviet drabness and permanent caution a thoughtful Czech had said to me, quietly, as we watched, 'I think (this) is a better system.'

CHAPTER 31

TEACHING THE CONCORDE

Towards the end of 1986, two years after we had started our own course, the next group started on their month of simulator. The subject matter made the instructing task more interesting than for previous airliners because of the new and different content, and good student progress was therefore rewarding. It's easy to say that there are no bad instructors, only bad students. This is not true – an easy joke of course – but one can also claim a version of the opposite: all airline students are good enough, and if there are problems it must be due to poor training. I will be the first to claim that a slow starter can turn out to be the soundest performer in the long run, and can assure the reader that teaching the Concorde to enthusiastic and able pilots was a satisfying process – this applies to all instructing (with experience, you can tell straight away) – but I also have to say that, in some cases, I found this job quite difficult, and this view did not change during my 11 years of Concorde training. To be in a position of final judgment can be much worse if you cannot decide yes or no with an untrammelled mind. Most experienced pilots do not like the idea of risking lives – even at a distance. The no-risk-no-fun T-shirt is not appropriate for this job.

Like previous airline training experience I always had, at the back of my mind, the following simple prospect if I was not confident that I was seeing adequate progress: I might, one day, find myself as their passenger. What was the required standard for this stage? Despite box-ticking and evasive reporting ('should improve next detail') this is a personal thing, and I cannot speak for my colleagues. Your judgment may not agree with theirs, but how do you know? Does it matter? What do they really think? Do they actually write it? History proves, give or take, that the system works and it all comes out in the wash, but the Concorde demands more – could anyone seriously claim otherwise.

This fact was not disputed in problems that were to come, but achievement of the required (minimum) standard for the training exercises does not add up to what may be required on a bad day. Unexpected reality cannot be simulated in advance, and only those with experience (and imagination) can recognise in their students a reliable expectation of ability to manage this machine in real life. As a conclusion to this sermon I have to say that BA got away with it.

This course were a mixed bunch, and two of them had a tendency to apologetic banter: 'The course couldn't have come at a worse time. I'm rebuilding the house, the child's got health problems, we're living in a caravan in the garden and we're flooded out,' delivered with a smile of resignation mixed with the hope of understanding. The other feigned self-deprecation: 'Oh dear, this is all too difficult, I'm never going to get it.' Was this just a joke to encourage sociability, or was it real? (acquaintances from a past life thought it real). I had not come across this attitude before. Something had changed. Had crew room gossip and the previous course primed some of them for difficulties, or was there something more systemic? The good ones showed no such preoccupations.

Something else that struck me about this course of pilots was the amount of discussion between a pair while flying the simulator – trying to resolve operational puzzlements, no doubt; helping each other along with the difficulties of the task. A lot of relatively inconsequential chatter might be good CRM (getting on with each other) of course, a kind of bonding process, especially when time allows. Was this a cultural result of new and much more automated chummy two-pilot aircraft? Perhaps yes, but could it not get in the way of the thinking and doing required when learning to deal with this unusual and traditionally equipped aircraft, with its lack of automated technical systems and not a single flight management system in sight? There is, of course, a very important third person sitting behind to help in a Concorde – the flight engineer, but this had already become an old-fashioned concept elsewhere.

It had been ten years since amalgamation had created this new, improved and inclusive Big Airways – more than twenty since my surprise, as a 21-year-old, at hearing my captain reveal that he had two sons, older than me, who still lived at home, living the comfortable life they had come to expect, ***gratis*** a fortunate father with a good job and a house to call his own. Had he really had it lucky? Was his rapid promotion from office boy to aircraftsman to Lancaster pilot to airline captain a result of luck? Partly, you can be sure, but not entirely. Did this quite novel sense of childish entitlement based on indulgence and easier times indicate the founding of the snowflake culture? Was this current fashion for apologetic mateyness, which assumed acquiescence and accommodation (because we deserve it as employees), an indication that snowflakism had quietly started to establish itself in the workplace? Looking back forty years I think it had.

The members of my own Concorde course of 1984 showed none of these new signs of fundamental sociological adjustment (by this I mean the progressive shift of the balance of influence to student from teacher, to candidate from examiner, to employee from employer, from parent to child etc...). One member of our 1984 course did not finish, but went quietly with dignity – he had nothing to prove. (Could I have subsequently taught him to manage a Concorde satisfactorily? I'm prepared to say yes, but it wasn't my flying school, and I was not paying.) Would we have another failure on this 1986 edition? Training Manager John Cook sincerely hoped not, and did his best to encourage the well-liked but self-doubting captain, and prove to detractors that Concorde training did not have an agenda of failing people for reasons of personal prestige. We no longer were dealing with fuddy-duddy old-style BOAC pilots, but, as an integrated whole, discussion of long and short haul experience was a touchy subject. We should not be having failure problems in such a well-run airline. But one pilot failed – again!

A lunch to remember (or maybe not)

To continue with the same subject, it was not long after this course that something extraordinary happened. HTTFC (head of technical training, flight crew, aka Hotf**k to the rank and file) invited all members of the Concorde training department to a lunch in TBA (technical block A, once the BOAC main building). That's nice, I thought. The lunch was a pleasant interlude, conversation convivial, and by coffees and chocs I wondered if that was about it, and then our host rose, perhaps to wish us well and bid us goodbye. But it wasn't like that at all. He addressed us without further ado.

'Your training style is perceived as elitist. You appear to be making the syllabus up as you go along to make life difficult – randomly erecting new hurdles for your students to jump over. British Airways contains enough talent to fly the space shuttle. Your attitudes, methods and their results are unacceptable for this airline, and Concorde training will be improved. There will be changes, and I will see to it that everyone attends the current instructor courses.'

He left forthwith. This clearly was not a discussion session. It was an ambush, planned and fuelled by something long-smouldering somewhere. The lunch was apparently over, and we finished our coffees and quietly wound up our conversations. This address had certainly been a surprise. I felt a bit stunned as I processed the contents. But the remarkable thing was that nobody mentioned the topics raised by this senior manager who had arranged the gig, and signed for it on central funds. No one referred to the views expressed, nor ever mentioned the subject again in my earshot.

What immediately concerned me was the influence this address might have on end-product Concorde standards, despite the universal airline box-ticking that proves perfect training. I will be the first to declare that instructors who have little or no training experience elsewhere may not appreciate the full difference between a complete type novice and their regular customers, but is this a problem when you have an ample supply of suitable candidates? Not necessarily. Less than ideal? Could be.

Regarding the background to this unseemly demonstration of staff officer style we have to consider his problem, based on a responsibility to ensure the safety of all the airline's passengers, all the time: there is no Concorde crew selection. Where are those of (space) shuttle potential that he referred to? We don't know, and we are not allowed to find out – anyone can have a go. This is democracy personified. What did not help in the case of the previous course was the general manager's initial pep talk, designed to stir up feelings of competitive excellence. But here it sowed the seeds of doubt and confirmed suspicion among those who have become familiar with comfortable if routine employment. Times have changed: the general manager's air force had been different.

What did my colleagues think? To this day I've no idea, but I do think this use of a social occasion to give an across-the-board generalised bollocking to all and sundry an unseemly use of position. Before leaving this subject, a very competent co-pilot on this critical course told me later: 'X had to go, but the way it was done was bad.' I wouldn't disagree with this, but this situation was a result of our leader's prolonged attempt – as a result of pressure from outside to demand that we improved our training (no failures) – to continue X's training and avoid the undesired decision. And there was another thing that happened which gave rise to negative speculation from the shop floor. A chirpy co-pilot, also from the 737 or similar, had only just started his route flying following the base training, then unexpectedly dropped dead one day, just like that. What does this prove? You can put two and two together and make whatever you like of this, but it can only have ramped up the sense that something serious needed to be treated in this neck of the woods.

Part of the justification for the petulant attack on the Concorde training 'club' was some unconventional if useful public relations traditions – carried over from VC10 training practice, to my certain knowledge. The Concorde, in particular, was very noisy, and while some locals may have been enthusiastic about its presence, complaints about noise were an on-going threat to the use of Prestwick as a base training site. Would an assortment of the local community like a free and relatively exciting ride in this iconic and unaffordable airliner? Few said no, and I was surprised to climb aboard for a circuit session to find 50 seats occupied by unknown Ayrshire people. Did it matter? Were they at special risk? Not with training staff in one of the front seats. 'Surely this is in contravention to BA's flight for hire certification?' was a point raised by a member of this contentious course. As a mini-AOC person (CAP10) I don't think so. These passengers were volunteers – the flight was free.

My own disconcertion about the abrasive manner of this generalised affront to Concorde training was based on a certain amount of Concorde experience – much less than that of many of my colleagues – but I did have plenty of training/learning experience in a number of fields. The CAA training and qualification syllabus contained a substantial number of predictable situations that might be encountered, but perhaps we should realise that these were defined with the optimism that this project would actually work. It did, surprisingly well, but real-life possibilities remained of a time-pressurised and critical life-threatening nature, dramatic as this may sound to the established and perhaps complacent airline professional. What concerned me about this frontal assault on our 'bad' Concorde training was that the only experienced people present were those in the audience. A shameful episode? NASA space shuttle people were not so stupid.

Problems in observing the required standard

CRM (getting on together – being a team – helping out) has become a popular and valid subject. NASA are cited as having invented this revolutionary principle following the Gemini two crew orbital project, but they were then dealing with two competitive single-seat perfectionists flying together. You can be sure that WW2 bomber crews, of all sides, had rapidly discovered that effective teamwork was an essential survival strategy, twofold in the case of the Americans where daylight missions depended on essential station-keeping for defence; as well as vigilant on-board teamwork, good leadership and American improvisation. Airline simulator training consists of learning new skills, within the framework of normal crew integration. To some extent this is a nice idea, but whichever pilot seats are involved, one of them can effectively carry the other – just by appearing to do his normal job: call-outs, subtle suggestions, fielding those little incipient mistakes that could lead to big ones. This helpful activity may look like a good crew at work, and indeed it is, but the statutory type rating and instrument rating qualifications require a certain level of self-sufficiency. Later we did abandon this simulator teaming up/mutual-support-in-adversity system and swop them around. (One should not forget that the industrial principle requires that the two weakest, together, be able to cope. 'But all of our pilots are of a satisfactory standard and there should not be training problems'. Nice idea.)

Base training is not quite the same. Prompting and coaching may be appropriate to start with (and it is essential to fly the machine yourself while describing technique; the student cannot listen and fly a low speed Concorde at the same time – but few airline instructors do this), and though the instructor acts as co-pilot, he is required to observe the standard required by the CAA, so full-on CRM may be sometimes out of place. The student has no tactical decisions to consider anyway; just dealing with the machinery reliably is what's required.

As an afterthought I'll mention something Tony Yule (who became 'the Adj.') told me about his military instructor's course. It refers to the modern and caring way of engaging with your student.

'What does your mummy call you, Yule?'

'Tony, sir.'

'Right, Tony; you're f***ing chopped.'

I think it's a joke, perhaps an old one.

CHAPTER 32

MORE SETTLING IN

Life continued with a similar assortment of Concorde normal routes, charters and training as well as various aerobatic activities in Britain, Long Island and Florida. No two Concorde flights were ever the same because of the cruise climb procedure where height and fuel burn varied with air temperature. It made quite a difference, even though the Concorde did its best. The prevailing west wind made about 10 minutes difference in the east or west flight times, because it only applied at subsonic levels. For the two hours of cruise/climb the wind was usually insignificant. London to New York took 3 hrs 25 minutes from opening up to turning off the runway, and the opposite direction 3 hrs 15 mins, give or take a very little. An interesting feature was the westbound 2-hour point, 50 west. This was remarkably consistent. I cannot remember seeing less than 1hrs 59 for this position, and 2hrs 02 was a slow day.

The fastest easterly flights occurred around the New Year, when the jetstream may still provide 80kts of tailwind in the low fifty thousands. The record hunters could level off before climbing out of this wind, and trade a slightly more expensive lower altitude for the groundspeed advantage. Les Scott, a New York commuter captain, may well have arranged an early speed release after takeoff and convenient directs for the initial route. His record for

New York-London is 2hrs 53 minutes. I'm sure it still stands. (Anyone from the airline/executive jet scene tried it recently?) I recently read about the British Airways A318 service from London City to Newark via a stop at Shannon – 'As convenient as a Concorde'. I'm not convinced.)

Westerly times were more consistent, as shown by the 2hrs to fifty west. It has occurred to me that an increasing headwind while climbing out of London gives the Concorde a significant climb performance advantage. If this positive windshear applies below 10,000ft, as it will on a windy October day, the machine reaches its minimum drag speed (400kts) more quickly, and will then climb well, and in addition, continued increasing headwind can provide a subsonic 12,000 feet per minute instead of the steady conditions where the Concorde climbs at 4,000fpm. I've seen it, it's rather fun, especially if you shoot out of the top of the overcast into the sunshine at this rate and equivalent angle. This rapid climb to subsonic cruise height (28,000ft in this case) somewhat offset the disadvantage of the extra headwind (before it's up, up and away at Cardiff – into the quiet air of the stratosphere). The Concorde transatlantic routes were always the same; two parallel straight lines, 60 miles apart, one for east, one for west. The straight line (called a great circle for trigonometric fiends) is the shortest distance, of course.

But below the stratosphere, in the troposphere where the weather lives, this is not a convenient way to travel. It just so happens that the strongest winds occur at the height where the conventional jets like to fly, so a set of daily routes are arranged each day to take account of this wind – go round the problem going west, take advantage of it going east. This is not a new phenomenon.

In 1938 my eleven-year-old aunt saw the Hindenberg fly over the family town of Barrow-in-Furness, at maybe 1000ft. This was unusual, and many thought it was an intelligence-gathering detour to get some hi-res pictures of the ship-building layout and the steelworks. But I looked at the contemporary marketing. Barrow was exactly on one of the four or five westerly standard tracks, published in the Hindenburg schedule of 1938 – and this Hindenburg was on track to a few yards. As you might expect, the easterly tracks were straighter and further to the south. The public information in the handout looked very similar to today's daily subsonic tracks. So much for conspiracy theories... but hang on a minute, why not base some of your standard tracks on intelligence targets?

The Concorde was not concerned with daily tracks, but sometimes, when there wasn't much jetstream, the subsonic tracks were underneath – jumbos 20,000ft below going backwards at Mach 1.1. 'See you later guys, a whole lot later'. Is this fun or what? I positioned to New York once and experienced Brian Walpole's cabin address. 'I expect you would like to know how things are going – the answer is fast.' (I'd thought of this already, but only for the media). On the descent – 'Our friends you saw below will be arriving in five hours' time.' He was right, the punters loved it. This was marketing, but it was true.

Things to think about in flight

It had, or should have been, always understood that a Concorde should be fully serviceable, if possible, when it set off. The number of apparently trivial deficiencies that would not endanger slow and low flight were considerable, but for the standard two hours of Mach 2 cruise it was best if everything worked. A single failure of many things at height and speed would not generally create an immediate problem, but the 'what if' chance of something else going wrong had to be considered, and, usually, the 1,350 mph flight was over – to avoid fate's next roll of the dice.

A number of these trivialities would require a transition to the status of a fastish (M.95) and lowish (30,000ft) subsonic flying machine. In this case the range reduced by a quarter. It would take twice as long to get there, and also meant that the aircraft may have descended into a strong wind regime – not planned for. A shut-down engine meant you could go a third less far, also in the windy troposphere – further range problems, perhaps. (The Concorde could continue supersonic flight on three engines (M1.7), but this was not more economical than subsonic flight, miles per gallon, and the high windmilling speed may not have been good for the failed engine.) Better to come down and poodle along, maybe looking for somewhere else to land as necessary.

More insidious was the problem of fuel consumption at low speed. A normal flight with no weather problems and the correct amount of fuel aboard at top of descent could land you in trouble if you followed air traffic instructions – it's all to do with miles per gallon, and being an unusual animal. A busy afternoon at New York was a typical example. When President Reagan sacked the striking controllers and new ones were employed, a new one-behind-the other vectoring system was instigated: managing a single line of marching ants on the screen is easier than having them come at you from all directions. This system required early and long-distance speed control, and a fifty-mile downwind was not impossible. This, of course had to be followed by a fifty-mile final. 250kts (75kts below clean minimum drag speed) was not perfect, though acceptable for a Concorde, but the tower could request 180kts with many miles to go. It was better to request a detour, fly a much greater distance at a better speed, then come back and pick up your place in the queue later on – if you could arrange this.

On final approach at the correct speed the induced drag was high. Fuel was consumed at the same rate as required for cruising speed, but there was a major difference; three miles a minute instead of twenty three. I think it was John Chorley who, in the late '70s, highlighted the problem of a routine flight on a nice afternoon. He followed the New York vectoring system and its required speeds around the lengthy slow tour of Long Island, and during the 100-mile runaround decided that the remaining fraction of the paper 12 tons they might have landed with elsewhere was getting serious. OK, we'll steer you around for a visual on 13L. this was accepted and looking good – this runway is right in front of our terminal as well. Then on short finals he was too close to the Piper Aztec that had been slipped in front and had to go around. I don't know any more details, and all ended well but with very little fuel, and this situation was food for thought for those who had been brought up on, and believed, the principle that following instructions would ensure a trouble-free life. Up to a point this works, but the life could be shorter than complacently assumed.

Popular technical and logistical problems

If asked to contribute to this topic, based on personal experience, I would quote an engine shutdown after the first power reduction after takeoff as one thing that happened to me several times. After a couple of these you get quite good at it. It was not serious. Others will have a completely different take on their own reminiscences, so this trivial subject may be a unique answer.

The culprit was the electric box of tricks that controlled the secondary nozzle (perhaps in collusion with the throttle amplifier), the multi-purpose bucket at the back of the engine. It usually worked well, but if the little blue 'reverse' light came on when you were not interested in reverse, it meant something was wrong. There was no other information provided. This secondary nozzle had much more precise supersonic things to think about than the simple application of reverse, but the light implied that you might get uncommanded reverse at any time. Ignore it at your peril. The simple instruction was 'Shut down the engine.' Good advice for the gambler.

This always happened on the 7pm New York flight, always after the aircraft had come off a significant check and once after a first-in-a-lifetime several-month duration major check. On that occasion we asked 'Has it had a test flight?' No. 'We'll be back' – we were.

What happens is that everything works well until the '3, 2, 1, noise' call for the noise abatement cutback, round about abeam the Datchet roundabout. As reheat is cancelled and the throttles are zapped aft to the marked position a blue light comes on. The faster-than-a-speeding-bullet flight to America is off: simple as that. What to do? Go back, of course, but it's more complicated than that.

The first customer service priority is to tell the company so that plans can be made for a hasty revamp of the departure, either with the same aircraft or perhaps the one earmarked for tomorrow morning's flight. The first answer they need is a yes or no to 'Have the ovens been turned on?' This involves gaining the attention of the front galley crew at end of the twenty foot 'tunnel', the narrow passageway to the cockpit, walled by electrical and electronic boxes (no room under the floor; it's like a submarine). A yes means extra delay replacing the hot menu. A no is the welcome answer.

This subject of food temperature history became a hot potato after the March 1984 hors d'oeuvres debacle. First and club passengers (in all directions) were affected by something in the stuff they made the chicken in aspic with; quite a number became very ill and had to stay in hospital. Among that evening's Concorde passengers affected were Peter de Savary (quite a regular) and the retired Saudi Ambassador to the US – who died. Although this particular problem may not have been directly related to the reheating or undesired warming of food, the man with the Avometer and probe was frequently seen during delays thereafter. Lord King told me about it:

Our chairman was a reasonably frequent passenger. He would always come up for a chat, having found out when would be convenient. This was a diplomatic courtesy not always respected by occasional staff VIPs, and gained him some respect. He told me he didn't eat much on the aeroplane, 'Just a bread roll, piece of cheddar and a glass of claret, that's all I want.' He also told me of an experience during the aftermath of the aspic debacle. There had been plenty of substantial compensation claims, some from people who had so much access to money that it had no intrinsic value, but could provide entertainment. Unlimited payouts can take a company down – with ease – and he had been very worried about an eminent and very influential oil-state customer who had been stricken (but survived). The monumental sum demanded was a serious disturbance to the legal department, and the chairman arranged to go and meet the victim's representative in London. 'I was very worried, and wondered what I could do about it.' After some small talk around the subject the man said, 'Actually, all my friend wants is the guarantee that he can always have seat 1A.' 'Done.' What a relief. And we can be sure that another special case of non-standard booking procedure was set in place. Outrageous, of course, but a very good idea at the time.

A currently popular if simple mantra for reminding crew about dealing with reality is Fly, Navigate, Communicate. Perhaps we should add Cater, but it's now time to go back to basics with our returning Concorde. First get some speed up before shutting down the engine. More than 250kts is the first good idea. Negotiate a heading for dumping fuel (usually while continuing to the west). The proper climbing speed will help to rapidly achieve the height where dumping is allowed to start. As I recall, going over the sea was not part of this. The overboarded fuel does not fall as rain on people's washing, it just seems to vanish. The intention now is to arrange to head back so as to land at 20 tons above normal landing weight. Though not used on a regular basis, this fuel-saving heavy landing technique was planned as acceptable for 20% of Concorde landings.

One should turn back when half the required dumping figure was reached in order not to waste time after the correct figure had been reached. Approach and landing speeds were increased by 20 knots at this heavier weight, and a hundred and eighty something looked quite fast on a still night: the streetlights fairly zipped past, the Concorde felt more solid in the air, the pitch response was less lively and the landing more purposeful but very satisfactory: the extra weight, inertia and speed shrugged off a pilot's unnecessary adjustments. This shutdown, dump and return process took about an hour chock to chock. With another hour to prepare another attempt the New York arrival would be more eightish than sixish the same evening, but the result was sooner than an alternative method of travel.

Staff travel

I can think of a number of reasons why staff travel was not permitted on a Concorde, and I would not disagree with them, but hesitate to appear elitist. However, there was a private exception (not in the Staff Travel Manual). At this time, a Concorde captain's wife was granted one free trip per year, on his flight (I think it was assumed to be his own wife). My then wife's first of these was on one of these engine shutdown/return/have another go evenings. The Concorde was full, she was the only female passenger, suitably prepared for the glittering occasion, and she told me that she was seated next to a very nice and very bronzed man called George Hamilton who told her his wife had been a stewardess. This may have been true at some point in time. She had no idea who the popular and personable actor was. Many would pay for the seat next to 'Gorgeous George'.

Everyday travel

Other things happened occasionally, some that you would not notice. I recall going to Montego Bay and back from New York. This traditional winter sunshine route had long British traditions, and an offshore supersonic flight made it quite fast; the day certainly fitted in easily between a reasonable breakfast and an evening beer. As I levelled off and slowed up downwind for a visual approach at the aforementioned Mo Bay, there was some discussion at the back of the flight deck. Jim Rodger, old-school unflappable flight engineer, leant over in my direction and quietly spoke into my non-earphone ear. 'Captain, they say the cabin's on fire down the back.' This was a new experience and the possibilities of drills and instructions reeled through the brain, but this is an easy one. Only recently the policy for cabin fires had been much simplified: land as quickly as possible at the nearest suitable. The obvious dawned immediately; I'm in the process of doing that very thing, I don't even have to say anything, let alone do special captain-like things. By short finals the message came up that they had sorted the problem. It turned out that a passenger had dropped a cigarette down the back of his seat, allowed it to smoulder for a while among the upholstery then tried to dowse the resulting smoke with his glass of post-lunch brandy. Maybe a burst of soda subdued the flames – but what captaincy! Exemplary.

This must have occurred before smoking on aeroplanes was banned. Non-smoking flight deck members did not like it much, and I did hear of a couple of captains who chain-smoked on the taxi out – prior to the nerve-jangling takeoff. This was not popular. As a co-pilot years before I was not impressed by a 747 captain who finished his lunch and then pointedly lit up just as you got yours. Could put you off your food – definitely not a role model.

Famous for an eighth of a day

An eighth of one day is three hours. This is roughly the time passengers sat in the Concorde between settling down after takeoff and thinking about landing. Most of them were thoughtful people who seemed to have no illusions about the radical craft they were sitting in. Most of them also appreciated the clubby feel of the flight, its crew and its open cockpit door policy. I never was aware of cabin disturbances or the unruly behaviour of forty-year-old English lads having fun, and many passengers seemed to have a special regard for the unknown captain, whoever it was. This was nothing personal, just something encouraged by the Concorde itself, and the sensitive person's feeling that there might be something slightly precarious about this mode of travel. Some captains made use of this by striking up in-flight acquaintances which they hoped to pursue outside of working hours, and could therefore include the odd name in their circle of friends, but it was a mistake to think that a passenger's enthusiasm to come to the flight deck and chat meant that the captain had suddenly become their best friend. He's only the driver for three hours, then, having safely stepped on terra firma, the passenger becomes the special person again – back in their own world.

This became obvious to me one day, fairly early on in this Concorde world of magic, and fortunately nothing to do with the rich and famous. On board was a British Airways person, guiding a group of three commercially-useful people on a New York jolly of some sort. They came to the flight deck, looked around at the view and chatted enthusiastically, and the leader invited me to join them for lunch (central funds) at such and such a place – one o'clock. Why not? I said yes, and with an ordinary person's M&S jacket and tie went to the appointed place and looked for them. There they were, so I joined them, ready with smile and hand ready for repeated greetings. Their conversation stopped and they looked dumbfounded. Who the hell is this insignificant nobody crashing our important business lunch? The penny slowly dropped and I was invited to take my place, but they showed no interest in lift coefficients, three-into-one hydraulic systems, shockwave stability, crew allowances or afterburners at all. Actually I did not raise these subjects as they had not asked, and may have expressed the occasional invented opinion about exchange rates, the value of BA shares or the future prospects of this premium product, but I have no idea what they did, or why they were there. I was certain I shouldn't have been, but hoovered the free lunch as compensation and an allowance saver. One saves and learns. I never did it again. I might also add that the decision to accept such an invitation should depend on who's doing the inviting, and how well you know them already.

But it was not always thus. Of course encounters with celebrities was part of the job, but in those far-off, pre-millennial days they were celebrities for being good at something, not for being celebrities just like ourselves. The first I remember was Stevie Wonder – quiet, dignified and blind. He sat in the jump seat and asked me to describe the view outside. I did so, and he listened carefully, but all the time I asked myself what my words meant to him. As I spoke I wondered if he had ever seen anything? The answer is no, and how he interpreted my description of the vast area of sea visible, the curved horizon, the dark blue sky above the light part etc I can never have any idea. I could say one cool dude, but he was much more than that, and as far as courage in adversity goes – respect. Compared with what he had achieved, and the difficulties surmounted, my own progress and its trivial problems with the required standard shrivel into insignificance, and I would advise other disappointed but still employed airline employees to accept reality, or get another job.

I've made it a point not to do Concorde namedropping, as a point of respect for those many I could namedrop as a result of incidental but meaningless meetings at work. There may follow, here and there, a breaking of this principle, but the next topic will be the most dangerous incident of my flying career; and one which few noticed because of the fortunate and private circumstances.

CHAPTER 33

A LUCKY ESCAPE

In April 1987 the next course had reached their base flying phase, which we did at Prestwick, staying in the Marine Hotel, Troon; somewhere convenient, comfortable and traditional and close to Ayr, where you can get your half-stone of real fish to take home. What a treat today. On April 21st I had shared a double header detail with John Cook: he flew to Machrihanish, not far away, with Tony Yule, where they did a number of circuits then stopped for the pitstop. Then I set off with Keith Barton, did some circuits there, and returned to Prestwick when our engineer said that's enough, let's go back.

With enough fuel to make the first landing at normal Concorde maximum landing weight you could do up to ten circuits on a training tank, and achieve about an hour and a half chock-to-chock time. I would say this is enough action for a learner in this machine, but some pilots thought it good fun and were disappointed when the engineer suggested that we should land when he had ten tons of fuel left. The minimum landing fuel (incident report limit) for a passenger flight was six and a half tons (a theoretical half an hour remaining in the air), but this story might explain why training engineers were happier with something more than this – just in case.

This is also a good place to not only acknowledge the exceptionally mature and professional judgment displayed by our Concorde training engineers – in fact words fail me – but the same goes for all those they trained and released as competent as well. A number of years before there had been a general company policy change, consistent with reduced crew numbers on the flight deck, whereby flight engineers were to take on more involvement in what was going on – as well as working their panel and the complex machinery behind it. Someone told me about their lesson one: 'There are two things that can kill you – they're both sitting at the front.' Never was a truer word spoken in the classroom (and I was one of those at the front).

The next day, April 22nd 1987, we did the same thing, apart from swapping students. John went to Machrihanish with Keith Barton, and I was to repeat yesterday's routine with Tony Yule. After two or three circuits I went to the flight deck to see how things were going, just in time to see special interest in the undercarriage lights. They'd not long put the wheels down, but the left leg did not have a green (locked down) light, or a shortening lock light. There seemed no logical reason why this should be so, but something had certainly gone wrong, and the absence of the shortening lock light should mean that the leg had not reached the more or less down position, but there was a secondary problem with this system which will be mentioned later. Recyclings (more wheels up and down – though not recommended) made no difference. The fact was that the leg was going up and down as usual, more or less, but was not locking down. The only checklist instruction applied to freefall – but this was intended for a hydraulic failure, or something wrong with the uplock. Clearly we had no such failures – nothing had failed, except the left leg's refusal to lock down. Based on what I knew about the Concorde choice of emergency procedures, and some (virtual) blank pages, this was bad news.

History

I've already referred to the early discussions of two situations, ditching and unsafe wheels, both of which were considered too hazardous to write about. They did not exist and could not happen, but one had – pure and simple.

An early Bristol prototype, maybe the first one, had once landed with a swinging main leg, but not on purpose. Its downlock had functioned, but the component containing the downlock became detached from the leg during enthusiastic manoeuvring. They had returned from a test flight and were asked to make a run along the Weston-Super-Mare seafront. They did so, lowered the undercarriage in the process, then made a flashy turn seawards before it had all locked down. This is a bad thing to do with delicate retractable undercarriages, and the seaward leg was collected by the rolling (descending) left wing as the leg approached the down position. The ensuing impact broke the telescopic strut, leaving the left leg to swing in the athwartships direction. There was little they could do except pray and land at Fairford. They were in luck as, I believe, the main bogies are toed out a tad, and the left main immediately went outwards on touchdown and leant against the side of the number two engine box, which is close by, for the rest of the landing run.

What happened to us

This training flight was over and we headed to Prestwick, fortunately with, say, double the fuel on board compared with that for a typical route arrival. Roger Bricknell, our engineer, decided that the undercarriage freefall procedure was the only vaguely relevant checklist item, so he would try that. I was not convinced that this would help at all because it would isolate the leg and its jack from hydraulic pressure, and replace it with 65 psi compressor air in the empty telescopic strut to help a bit. Not quite the same as 4000+ psi hydraulics, but, granted, the geometry is different. Until the downlock was made, hydraulic pressure would continue to push the leg towards down. But there were no other ideas, so he went back to do this, I sat in the engineer's seat and Keith Barton continued to fly in the left-hand seat. John Cook also went back to consult our pitstop crew, though none of them would have encountered or heard of such a problem before. However, he returned and said they had looked through the floor and confirmed the leg was not locked.

I showed him the italic sentence under the freefall check list. This had never been mentioned or considered in our training (or anyone else's). It said: *If a locked indication cannot be achieved try to raise both main gears and land on the engines* (and presumably the freefalled nosewheel). Nice idea, but I would appreciate plenty of notice and some experiments before trying it. John just shook his head and we started the musical chairs to put me in the right-hand seat and John the left.

The wind at the field was from the south and Prestwick had cleared us to land on 13, but I chose 31 because the crosswind element would provide a left to right force on the aircraft on the runway, opposing the left wheels' freedom to move to the right (inwards); just a bit of force, maybe, but better than the opposite. We got our ground people to come out to the front of the apron and flew past, waggling the wings. They said the legs looked normal – no swinging. We flew a circuit and prepared to land. I then noticed that we now had a shortening lock light on the offending side. This was good news in that it indicated that the leg must be virtually in the down position, and that the locked-knee strut on top of the leg would resist the shortening that went with folding inwards (up direction), but how strongly is not known.

It's surprising how fast the fuel goes in a Concorde when you're faffing about with the gear down at circuit speed, and by the time we were downwind for the approach itself we were in low fuel drill territory, so Roger did that checklist as well. This allows the fuel to run to the lowest places it can find so that all can be used. In this nose-up case it goes to the back, so the aft centre of gravity warning came on. This cannot be cancelled, and has a red light and continuous sound – rather mournful under the circumstances. As John flew down the approach I felt strangely exposed and cold with only my shirt for protection, and a long way from the ground as it approached. It was too late to get my jacket.

He made a beautifully straight landing and rollout, and the Concorde's behaviour was normal; and as we approached our turnoff he said, cheerfully, 'It's all all right then, we can taxi in' and started to turn left. 'No!' I said, 'we have to stop here, straight.' So he turned back the few degrees to the right and stopped. Our ground support team told us to shut down where we were. The left gear had leant inwards as we turned right, quite visibly. Later they Dexioned the strut to prevent further folding, and as they towed the Concorde around the left turn off the runway the leg walked itself upright again – at walking speed. It was completely free to all intents and purposes. Everything had not been all right. The leg had stayed upright like a coin on its edge. Had we been lucky? I think so. It would not have withstood any loading from the left (a right turn).

Aftermath

Next day another telescopic strut (the thing with the downlock in it) was flown up and changed. There was zero publicity. No crash, no flames, no one hurt, a non-event. A training flight – what do you expect? While we waited for another Concorde I had time to pace the beach and reflect. No one had the faintest idea what was wrong. What if the same problem was waiting on other Concordes? Actually it was. I'd read Neville Shute's *No Highway* and seen the film, many years ago. Designer James Stewart knew there was something wrong, but the operators preferred to pretend that there wasn't. Surely we should cease all Concorde flying until the cause was found, especially as this situation was too dangerous to consider. Should it happen tomorrow on a passenger service, the crew would be very poorly placed. But marketing prefers to avoid this hassle and publicity if possible. I also had time to think about the landing on the engines suggestion. What if I had to do it next week? Speeds, attitudes, steering, stopping, what kind of slippery sledge would it really be? A couple of engines to in-flight reverse just before touchdown? Better than nothing. Don't worry, it'll never happen. It shouldn't, but I now know that's not true.

The offending part was dismantled and a few days later the answer was found. It had been incorrectly reassembled after a major check. Not the hangar's fault – paperwork finger trouble. The undercarriages are made by Hispano-Suiza, specialist items, light but ultra-reliable. I saw the dismantled parts – small and perfect, like a Swiss watch, except the graunched ones. There had been a recent amendment of the maintenance manual (originally in French from this manufacturer) and some of the relevant English pages – how to put the pieces together – were missing. There's an important torquing and feeler gauge check before final tightening, which confirms that the delicate collet lock bits and pieces are in the right places. This page was missing and some of them weren't. They did their best for a while, but the abuse of incorrect fit and some guillotining from the sharp edges of their sliding slots did them no good. Not a pretty sight to a precision engineer, or the people who designed these intricate pieces.

Crew relationship with maintenance

When I started on the Concorde we were met on every arrival at London by two or three Concorde-specific engineering people for a general conference about our machine: that's both pilots and flight engineer. The idea was to discuss anything about the aircraft's behaviour, however trivial, even if nothing had gone wrong at all. This was intelligence gathering at a sophisticated level, and continued the idea that there were not many Concordes, they had not been flying for that long, and, despite the development years each flight was extending a development programme. Of course, this specialness died out as the people's airline demanded the people's standards and expectations in all things. A Ferrari in a bus garage? Not quite: moving that way, perhaps. But to end this chapter, we got away with it.

CHAPTER 34

THE LAST YEARS OF THE OF THE EIGHTIES

Life continued with a mixture of Concorde training and route flying, and assorted light aircraft flying; mostly aerobatic involvement, helping others with their aerobatic activities – including coaching and competition judging.

In 1987 I made a couple of route supervisory trips with Alan Harkness, who was to become our new training manager. He was a very experienced instructor at the Airways Flying Club, and also personal pilot to David Somerset, to become the Duke of Beaufort. This would consist of flying with the Duke in his Turbo Commander to those fashionable capital cities with an interest in the serious art market, eventually returning to the grass strip in a secluded part of the Badminton acres. It's not at all smart to discuss your aristocratic acquaintances with outsiders, but, some time prior to the Turbo Commander and the creation of the Badminton airstrip, I had made a few visits with the future Duke while he was training for his licence. These were commuting flights, doubling as dual cross-country time, and we would land in the allegedly Lancelot (Capability) Brown tree-defined oval in front of the big house. 'My grandfather landed here in a Sopwith Camel during the first war,' he said.

If we look back 1000 years, his cross-country navigation technique was traditional, now unconventional, but infallible; there was no point in questioning it. There did not appear to be an area of southern England that did not belong to or was not lived in by a relative, now or some time long ago, and was immediately and correctly recognised, often accompanied by a minor anecdote or observation. More royal than the royals, I have heard it said. Much more, if one is prepared to split hairs, and there was something quietly special about this direct connection to a life long before Ivanhoe, even the school history books which started at 1066; a life now with less institutional public violence, rather comfortingly. An effortlessly gracious host, he made these trips to a leafy Gloucestershire, maybe including a swim and lunch, an interlude of calmness and elegance, in every informally tasteful detail. Style? I can't think of a better word. I was rather sad to see that he died last month, August 2017, aged 89. That's a good age: moderation in habit, active in body and mind, fit, thin, and closely involved with something of the arts. A traditional formula – sounds easy, and it does work if you can manage it. My many Gloucestershire maternal ancestors did not have these advantages, but they would not have resented this fact one bit, then.

After the eight Concorde sectors with Alan (a couple of Washington/ Miamis), nearing the end of his six-month pilgrimage, I asked him if he thought the Concorde was as safe as, for example, the 747 with its copious redundancy and traditional flying qualities. He said 'no' immediately. I was relieved; this was a good sign, and even though he had been parachuted in, it indicated that his varied experience had not been steamrollered by a 'just another airliner' doctrine.

Popping to Scotland or Europe and back can be called international travel, but there are other places that are even more international, and further away. Since the amalgamation of the two airlines which became one, could our perceived captain qualifying problems be attributed to a lack of appropriate experience? 'But our captains do lots of landings, and sometimes the weather is foggy (not so much these days) or wet and windy. They have lots of experience – far more than your people, who hardly ever land anyway.' Of course this is not the point – quite the opposite. Reliable long-range supersonic flight first needs to reach a place where this challenging landing can be made. The reactive statement above would not have been a good thing to have told Neil Armstrong. A few supervised sectors and beginner's luck may not be enough.

John Cook had asked me to design some simulator details that would present typical and credible Concorde situations with problems of weather, fuel (running out of), American air traffic system, things going wrong and so forth, that would provide ersatz replacement experience, as it applied to the possible problems of getting a Concorde around. I suspect that this was in response to those who had countered the 'Not the right experience' comment with 'Then you must provide it (on the cheap), you're supposed to do training, not failing.'

I set about this task by asking those with more Concorde experience than myself to relate real-life difficult days, and some did, but others did not respond. It's not their job after all, it's all in a day's work anyway (a good pro-experience point), and the seriousness of events will have evaporated into the mists of time for those sane professionals who are not obsessed with London Airport life. This was not an especially fruitful exercise because most of the real-life problems I did hear about would have been too unexpected and serious to present to those without the right experience. Something of a vicious circle here. In any case the real difficulties of adaptation were more to akin to managing a Formula 1 car in the London or New York traffic than blasting along the Nürburgring straight.

I started this original project, and several training people told me not to bother: 'Don't waste your time – the simulator details will never be used.' They were right, but after some time had elapsed John encouraged me to finish them – 'Where are the details? I want them', so I created four (maybe six) believable scenarios from my imagination based on some experience. I tried a couple out on a suitable in-house crew. These were a training captain of my Concorde vintage and a very good co-pilot, fairly new to the Concorde. To simulate the position of a crew who were still within the throes of the training system, and therefore create an element of fumble factor, I suggested that they change seats, and the co-pilot become the captain. They did well, and, for the first detail, agreed that the American change of clearance as the Concorde was getting into its subsonic stride, with helpful 'directs' to strange places, plus the unfamiliarity of a different air traffic system, now adjusted for twin turboprop feederliners with flight managements systems, was very realistic. The short range flight had been hard work; but credible – and a difficult detail for beginners – but so can be everyday Concorde life. Whether I included a trivial failure (perhaps affecting landing performance) and/or weather requiring a divert I do not remember. But the idea had been to make a credible exercise without attracting the accusation 'You're making it too difficult for us – on purpose.' The correct answer to this complaint is 'Not exactly, it's the Concorde that will make life difficult for you. Accuse the staff all you like. How much would you like to know – and how much time have you got?' In the contentious days of WW2 they used to say 'Get some in', I believe (not in a simulator). (Cruise climb at Mach 2 in a straight line was remarkably straightforward [so long as nothing went wrong]. This was what the sum total of the curious design had been designed for. I never came across a guest pilot who had trouble with it. All other Concorde operating environments called for a satisfactory quality of airmanship, in every respect.)

Action in Normandy – and the French democratic ideal

That 1987 summer I went to Deauville a couple of times to help Ian Groom, Nigel Lamb and Diana Britten prepare for whatever aerobatic contests they had in mind. The airport there is a proper airport – runway, radio aids, customs, control tower building with all the appropriate offices, météo, briefing, flight plans – everything. There were few passengers, pilots or airliners in evidence, maybe a few private aircraft for Deauvillites, but it's wonderful what real democracy can provide. The occasional freighter did arrive with horses for the Deauville races.

During my time in Mauritius I had come across an Air France co-pilot who used to stay with local chief pilot Dominique Paturau – for a month at a time. This wasn't holiday: it was for windsurfing, waterskiing, fishing, diving – whatever you have to do when not in the cockpit. A contemporary from the French national pilot's school, he was now on the B727, and could back up two weeks' work a month with two weeks off, making a month on and a month off. Far from a revolutionary lefty, he told me 'This is socialism – it's wonderful.' The French citizen's share in public facilities meant that Diana, who lived in Surrey but had a French house near Deauville (and spoke the language perfectly) was able to arrange for aerobatic practice (min height 100 metres) over the field, with the runway as a centreline. This worked well, and I only had to walk to a suitable place on the airfield for the correct judging alignment. If a racehorse DC10 came it could land underneath. What could be simpler?

One day, as I was walking back along the grass from my judging spot to the airport proper after Nigel had landed from another good flight, I saw him engaged in excited conversation in front of the doorstep of an aged native, not far from the apron. The house had clearly been there long before the expanding airport had included it, but it was the gesticulating, pointing into the sky in a northerly direction, and the enthusiastic shouting that had impressed me. Nigel had clearly gained a real fan. 'He must have really liked it,' I said. 'No', he said, 'it wasn't like that at all. He was complaining about the noise and disturbance, as a repeat of the 1944 invasion. All you British and Americans coming here with your aeroplanes, guns and tanks, making a hell of a mess and noise. It was much better with the Germans.' Not everyone was happy to be rescued, in fact we came across one or two more locals with similar views. Just politics, of course, nothing personal, and if you consider the enormous damage done to property and history it's understandable, to some extent.

A charter to the capital of New York, and Bob Hoover

At the end of August there was a New York-based visit to the airshow at Schenectady. To most international people New York means the area in and around Manhattan. To most Americans New York City is more like a foreign country, and they are keen to remind you of this fact. New York state is very large, and bears little in common with NYC. For all its funny name and small-town character Schenectady happens to be the NY (state) capital. This charter day out consisted of three flights, each with the supersonic round-the-bay excitement included. The airfield was small (2000m runway) and the local community had spent some money repairing the joints between the concrete slabs, just for us and our tyres. The plan was: JFK, out over the Atlantic and into Schenectady. The second an out and back with supersonic over the sea with a bit of a flyaround for the show on the return, and then a reverse repeat of flight one back to Kennedy.

It all went well – another first in the history of the world, the solar system, the universe...

When we got there it was on the cloudy/misty side and the approach glide slope was out of action. But we had INS and they had DME (distance measuring equipment) so an autopilot approach with height control based on distance could be almost as good. The Concorde autopilot vertical speed mode worked very well, and I found that fine adjustment at each miles-to-go height check produced the perfect approach. One only had to take the autopilot out and land. The television lady asked if the arrival had been problematical, because MAC (Military Airlift Command part-timers with a C5) had chickened out due weather. 'Absolutely not,' I said, 'piece of cake.' (It's what they expect, of course.)

The legendary Bob Hoover later made his way over and graciously congratulated me on the beautiful landing. Of course he was there with his Shrike Commander, to do the things Bob Hoover is good at. He was interested in the Concorde and its landing on this short runway because he had been a test pilot at Edwards and told me about the Mach 3 XB-50 Valkyrie, including its collision accident one disastrous Sunday morning when the mixed bag formation of supersonic aircraft photoshoot was arranged, led by the Valkyrie slender delta bomber. General Electric were keen to have the publicity material because all the aircraft featured GEC engines. The photo Learjet got some nice pictures, but the F104 Starfighter pilot had difficulty finding the comfortable position relative to the Valkyrie's right wingtip, which was far behind the Valkyrie's nose and difficult to see from the 104. He could only see his own wings via the rear-view mirror. In his number two position he got himself forward of the leader's wingtip but too close in, perhaps forgetting the enormous vortex flow required by this design at relatively low speed. The upwash in front of the Valkyrie wing picked the F104 up and tumbled it back over the delta, where it removed both Valkyrie fins. Both aircraft crashed, killing the Valkyrie co-pilot and the very experienced F104 pilot. The Valkyrie captain was able to eject on the way down. The Valkyrie programme suffered, and there were questions asked because this photo opportunity had no function in the research programmes at the airfield; the engine manufacturers had liked the idea of the unique marketing pictures. Things might have gone better without this disaster, perhaps.

It was only a few weeks later that Bob Hoover had gone to Moscow as manager of the US team for the 1966 World Aerobatic Championships, as a late replacement it would appear. At the end of the event the Russian hosts (and winners) offered members of other teams a flight in their YAK 18 PM, the current single seat aerobatic version of the trainer. Bob Hoover decided it was his turn to fly and took the slot. The world championships is not a good place to demonstrate your hot-dogging skills; it's the wrong audience. But, I imagine, after the frustration of two weeks watching the academic precision nonsense Bob decided to show the Ruskies a thing or two about real fancy flying. Spectators might have liked it but the authorities, and the Yak's owners, were scandalised, not only by the low flying (not difficult to do but not a good example), but also the retraction of the delicate pneumatic undercarriage while rolling, and the side loadings during his trademark one wheel landings. The inverted flight low after takeoff was not a technical problem, but the subsequent upside down ducking out of sight over the Moscow River wall was considered to be in bad taste, considering the nature of the event. It would be difficult to find an assembly of such superb but unsung aircraft handlers as at this gathering, American pilots included, some whom were not interested in hot-dogging before an uninformed public. The courtesy of visitor flights was cancelled immediately, and embarrassment reigned.

Apparently guest Yuri Gagarin could see the funny side, and put the thing into some perspective with the authorities. Whether the Russian trainer, Kazum Nazhmudinov (another MiG 15 pilot and Vostok class mate of Gagarin) also stilled the waters I don't know, but the day ended, fortunately, in vodkas all round and the telling of career stories, genuine or otherwise. Bob Hoover had been Chuck Yeager's standby for the Bell X-1 sound barrier flight. So near yet so far; perhaps there are some parallels here: in any case this sort of thing is character-forming – in one way or another. Kazum is quiet, friendly and businesslike, in my experience. He may actually have been quite relieved not to get the orbital flight, particularly after the fate of the first attempt.

After our second Schenectady flight, doubling as an item in the airshow, I was waiting around with others on the tarmac. The show had subsided, and little else was going on; the low cloud and mist had returned. A US Navy Hawk appeared through the mist, making a very low and close turn on to the runway for a landing, almost brushing the tops of the poplar trees. There are some good pilots in this country, whatever the obsession with rules. 'Where's Hoover? someone said. A mile away a fin was occasionally visible scooting past the gaps between the main street buildings. 'That's him', someone said. Who else?

Bob Hoover was a legend for a number of reasons. The flying-mad teenager's enthusiasm was unattenuated and infectious, and the southern gentlemanly charm, politeness, straw hat with suit elegance could not fail to open doors. But survivability showed the shrewdness. He concentrated at what he was good at – the looping, barrelling, energy-conserving on-design manoeuvring already defined as military-style aerobatics – and was not tempted to try anything else. Of this he created the Bob Hoover airshow persona, specifically directed, commentated and orchestrated towards a specific audience. He was good at it. I only met him this once. How do I know? Sometimes you can tell.

As a life lesson to the reader I would conclude this: if you're tall, good-looking and nice to everyone you can get away with anything. For lessons, I'm the wrong person to ask.

Filming Concorde training and its results

As part of the policy of improving flight training, each British Airways fleet was given a video camera to encourage them to make training films. Harry Linfield had custody of our Sony 8 Pro, but effective film-making is much more difficult and time consuming than family holiday stuff or outtakes for ***You've Been Framed***. It is work for either professionals or very motivated amateurs with more time than you might guess on their hands. The most effective use would have been the production of structured explanations of techniques, their reasons and results, and the effective use of the autopilot during climb and descent was a good example. Management of the considerable speed and performance changes, including the most convenient use of attitude modes during transonic phases, where static and dynamic pressure modes could not be used, gave beginners some trouble.

Flying the Concorde yourself when all was well was different though not that difficult, but it required your undivided attention. Correctly instructed, the autopilot flew better than a pilot, and its use could be very useful during the changing phases at the beginning and end of a flight. There was no 'You are required to use the automatics' policy, and it seemed easier at first to fly yourself, but the autopilot could be essential if the spare capacity among the crew of three was not to be overwhelmed by tactical problems, sometimes even without technical ones. This film was never made, however.

But the camera was taken to Prestwick for base training sessions. I thought it would be fun to record circuit action when not flying myself. We had a MELOMEL scheduling system for the three four-hour details per day, Middle, Early, Late, Off etc, so there was time to stand somewhere on the airfield and learn to play with this miniature version of News at Ten, the camera sitting on your shoulder like a parrot when not on its tripod.

For anything but wide angle, hand-held was too wobbly; the tripod worked well except when panning a touch and go and walking round the legs at the same time, so the monopod system seemed best. A commentary as well was essential to add interest, colour and analysis, and with a little practice the landing behaviour was easy to see and critique (much more revealing than from the cockpit, even when looking at the tiny viewfinder picture). The Concorde wingspan is 80 feet, so an imaginary projection of the square made when the distance from the ground equalled the span defined a height of 80 feet. Naturally 100 ft occurs just before this point, and the important 40, 30, 20-15 heights could be interpolated, with a half span of 40 ft mentally clocked as an update. A mainwheel diameter of one metre was an important height for the critiquer, and its continued behaviour vis-à-vis the ground was a good indication of correct technique, or otherwise.

Basic Concorde landing mistakes were easy to see, as were the results of inappropriate instructor assistance. Personal Concorde experience was considered adequate for instructional technique, but students are all different, and there are different ways to get it wrong. To my recollection new instructors were given no specific advice as to how to deal with incorrect landings (the 'tell them what they got wrong' afterwards was of no use – too late), apart from the go-around if you were quick enough. And the response by some to the typical mistake – student raises nose too early and therefore too much – of pushing the nose back down to its rightful position could only result in a quasi-heavy landing. 'Quasi' because the long flexible fuselage attenuated the shock and translated the centre of gravity's heavy landing to a shaking up and down of the cockpit far ahead, at the end of a bendy fuselage. But there was nothing quasi about the experience of the centre section. On one occasion the degree to which the wings and engines bent down towards the ground on impact was disturbing to witness through the viewfinder, and I gave up the day's shooting and the lightweight commentary that went with it. I really did not want to see a repeat of this abuse. It's traditional that an aeroplane breaks when some other unsuspecting soul is flying it at a later date.

At some stage of its career two structural repairs were required for all Concordes, on both sides of the Channel. First there was the cracking across the upper fuselage, then the problem of cracks in the rear spar between the engines and the fuselage. The cause was declared to be the opposing rotate moments about the mainwheels at a heavy weight takeoff – the download on the trailing edge against the mass of the rest of the machine in front. This may have been so for the top of the fuselage, but the engine weight bending the wings down on landing gave some empirical food for thought regarding the rear spars.

But I now seemed to have talked myself into recounting some bad stuff, so on to something more positive and cheerful. The airfield shooting sessions were well received in the evenings, and I thought it was therapeutic for our students to see themselves approach and land in this dramatic aircraft. From outside it looked much better than it felt inside – for a beginner. Although the Concorde answered its controls accurately it did so in its own way, and, being of a neutral nature (to be kind) it did the pilot no special favours. It went exactly where it was guided (assuming all axes were in trim), but not for ever. This constant requirement for control, albeit both discrete and discreet, ideally, gave the new pilot the feeling of constant correction and less than total control. But when you watched the grass playback the sense of presence transmitted by the approaching Concorde was confidence-inspiring. 'Look at that, that's me – doesn't it look good! Can I have a copy to take home? They won't believe it'.

The first takeoff in the dusk for a night detail was best for afterburner flames. First takeoffs of a circuit session were always done with full reheated power – enough for a 4000-mile flight. This wasn't strictly necessary, but it checked serviceability for the next flight, wherever that might be; it was theoretically best for noise outside the field (sort of), and it was frequently required for the statutory engine failure tick box at max thrust, day and night, but was it fun for simple airline pilots? No answer is necessary.

With sufficient fuel aboard so that the first circuit arrived at normal landing weight a full power takeoff gave a 1:2 thrust to weight ratio. Only half a g in the crew's backs, but unusual for an everyday airliner. But for the videoing in official twilight, at the beginning of a night detail, the video camera's special ability to open up and produce a picture almost looking like daylight transformed the full power takeoff into something visually special, creating an image that was not relayed by the naked eye. Initially the approaching machine looked normal on the screen, as in daytime, but when it drew abeam the camera the video system saw the reheat as bright orange-fringed 30-foot long conical flames, with the white and blue diamonds inside, more large and defined than you've ever seen, stretching back beyond the pointed tail: the magic of special effects, *gratis* the Sony 8.

When it got completely dark, and the second refuelled half of this detail took off, the video picture looked quite different. Only the aircraft lights could be seen, white spots in a black background, until the throttles were opened. From near the runway threshold the afterburning then appeared like two pairs of large incandescent white lights. There was no evidence of a large aeroplane, no scale indication. Two pairs of whiter-than-white searchlights accelerated away from you at an astonishing rate. Two fighters taking off? Perhaps, but the acceleration and whiteness of an extra-terrestrial power source was a better description of these videoed images against a very dark Scottish environment. Where are those tapes now? Either Harry has them or I recorded over them, after all, there's always the next course to film. I gave the camera back in 1997. Words and the imagination will have to suffice.

Recently Harry told me he does have some footage of a session when he was the instructor and I was roving the airfield with the camera, now an experienced enough cameraman to be looking for interesting and creative viewpoints. I'd made my way to the approach lights of runway 13, the Troon end. Here, inside the dual carriageway fence, the light arrays slope down towards the runway, the last one leaving a length of lawn before the actual threshold. After a few clips from the side, showing the Concorde grow larger and then fill the screen as it went overhead, then recede towards the runway, with a zoom in for the tyre-smoking touchdown (student Paul Douglas settling in with a crosswind), I decided to try a centreline position. Between the last two lights was perfect.

The shot opened looking back up the slope of the supports into an empty and white northern sky. Nothing moved. Then, slowly, a Concorde shape rose out of the top gantry, first the nose, more fuselage, widening wings and pointy tail until the whole thing sat suspended in space. No movement was apparent, except that the featureless silhouette grew steadily in size (of course it was coming straight towards us, wasn't it?) Larger and larger, louder and louder until only a small part of the underside rotated in the frame as the cameraman followed it over his head. Then the storyboard changed. The camera wobbled, shook and appeared to fall, like the James Bond title sequence; the camera looked closely at the grass, then wearily raised its groggy gaze through the shimmering heat to finally catch the touchdown as the Concorde landed a few hundred yards away – drift still on, smoke, rubber fragments flying, and so on.

I had not expected my aerodynamic theories to be demonstrated so convincingly. I was writing my handling book at this time, half of which concerns landing. It was clear that, in keeping with all swept wings, the Concorde progressively loses lift from the wingtips as incidence increases. This means that the inner parts of the wings have to work harder to carry the weight. But the Concorde is an extreme case. The resulting downwash (representing the momentum of the air that has to be pushed down to produce the lift) is concentrated significantly closer to the fuselage. Narrow and especially fast, this hard-working air includes the engines in its width, I can confirm. Let us say a 40-foot wide waterfall that has been supporting 100 tons. The downburst of heavy air mixed with industrial strength jet blast had pushed me instantly to my hands and knees as I turned for the pan, experiencing a small proportion of the 100 tons of bricks. No man can withstand it. The viewers thought I'd fallen over. Absolutely not, the camera was not dropped; it kept running, and finished the shot. My captain's hat might have come off at some stage.

When we saw the rushes that evening Harry told me he had wondered where I had gone on that approach because I was not in the previous place. 'We were a bit low actually, then I saw you below the nose, close to the runway. My God! I thought . . .'

A vintage aircraft at Prestwick

There was only one of these at a time, and it had nothing to do with me or my logbook, but to see this astonishing piece of 1956 technology do its thing – a pilot pursued by a big engine with guide vanes – was always an arresting sight. An American told me 'It doesn't fly – it bores holes in the sky.' Many in various countries liked it. Its bad reputation from those who tried to make it do jobs it was not designed for is a completely different story.

Scottish Aviation carried out major checks on Canadian F104s at Prestwick, and after the work was finished the aircraft needed checking out, and taking back home, presumably. A taciturn 'old' Canadian did the acceptance test flying, so they told me. I never saw him so I don't know how old or taciturn, but this makes sense. First there was some systems and engine testing to do, outside in a safe place, well away from the workshop. The engine was very advanced for its day, with variable-angle compressor vanes and a large primary nozzle at the back to cope with the considerable afterburner effect on the engine – like us, really. These gadgets had to work, or you could be seriously short of thrust. We have four engines, so the problem level is not quite the same; the Starfighter's one engine is a very important part of getting around. When the ground functioning was accepted the flight testing took place.

Approaching and landing speed is 180kts, no throttling back until the wheels touch, following a flat approach to keep adequate power going and avoid unsuitable manoeuvring near the ground at this relatively slow speed. Closing the throttle and gliding a little before touchdown is not a good idea. The small dart-like object looked fast, even faster when it took off, but it was the way it had of following the civilian noise abatement requirement that was both efficient and rather cool.

The Prestwick runway 31 official departure procedure was a turn to the left by about 30° at, shall we say, 1000 ft, on to a more westerly heading to avoid the town of Troon, level off soon at something like 2,000 ft, and proceed a handful of miles at this height until a set distance. To achieve this comfortably while gaining the energy for the climb to height the little dark olive object would half barrel roll the thirty degrees (to the left), pulling down on to the horizon in the process, twizzling the second half of the roll on heading and height, continue to pick up speed until the DME fix then pull up to a steep angle, and with the head of steam already acquired, rocket into the sky at an astonishing speed, to rapidly disappear: boring holes in the sky – exactly.

Recreational flying in America

Ian Groom, who I first came across with the Aerobatic and Artistic CAP 10, then lived in Germany, and appeared in England from time to time to do some business and flying. A single seat CAP 21 followed, and now, in 1987, he lived at a great height in Manhattan and pursued his aerobatic interests in Florida. In December 1987 I see that I visited Pompano Beach for a flying visit, but first

I had to get a US licence, and this involved a visit to the FAA office in Fort Lauderdale.

The FAA man was busy, not keen to deal with a transient tourist. 'OK, wait over there.' I did so, expecting this to take some time, then the word Concorde was mentioned (not by me). The change of demeanour was instant and striking. 'What a privilege it is to have your incredible talent in this room.' I'm stealing this line from Martin Jarvis. It was what they said in Los Angeles after he read for a television part – he didn't get the job. I call it metaphor-speak, older and one step up from its detuned descendent simile-speak, currently popular with younger inhabitants of the Pacific rim, but, for both communication systems, the words don't quite mean what they say. The man didn't actually use the quoted words, but you get the idea. However, the Airman's Certificate was now quickly forthcoming – but no hire and reward permitted. I discovered that you had to do the exams to get this upgrade. This was not my intention, but I looked at the syllabus later at the Pompano Air Centre.

The questions and answers are based on the democratic freedom-of-information system. All the possible questions are published, together with their multi-choice answers, and the correct answers are indicated in the back of the book. They told me that if you pay for tutoring a school will tell you how to pass without the tedium of studying the subjects. Maybe the fee includes the highlighter pen, and the technique requires the student professional aviator to highlight the correct answers. You then read through as frequently as necessary, *only looking at the highlighted answers* – this is important. It is also important not to trap yourself where the same set of answers apply to different questions. The highlighted answer must be associated with its question; then, even if the question is not understood, the correct answer will jump out at you. This method is much quicker than learning the subjects.

The British system was much sneakier. It may have changed in recent times, but listen to this: not only did they not tell you the questions in advance, but you did not get the answers either, and they changed the questions from time to time as well. What sort of exam is that? Is that fair? This kind of elitism has compelled some to buy a foreign but transferrable piloting qualification without any exam. This may have led to accidents, but accidents happen.

One unspoken reason for these Florida visits was to be my part in Ian's ambition to feature in the UK team at the next 1988 world championships. During the last ten days of 1987 I spent a number of days at Pompano flying either a Pitts S2B or S1T to Pahokee or Airglades to critique aerobatic practices, or to have the odd little practice blast myself. Pahokee is on the shores of Lake Okeechobee; Airglades is a grass field in the midst of pastures a bit further on, with a parachuting centre. Clint McHenry came along one day with his current monoplane for someone fresh to look at his manoeuvres. He told me the real definition of the hotdog pilot: 'Mike's on next, let's go get a hot dog.' He did like my Pitts flick rolls however.

The ten days mentioned actually involved local flying on four days in Florida – Dec 21/22 and 30/31. In between I did my first Rovaniemi Father Christmas trip. This outing to the Arctic Circle and back began (for the passengers) as a one-day Concorde charter idea because of the aircraft's ability to cover the distance in a reasonable time. The route was somewhat indirect to make use of the North Sea. Having left the East Anglian coast the Concorde could fly at high speed over the water until nearly abeam the top of Norway, then throttle back, make a right turn, descend and proceed to the destination from the north west. This all took two hours. The previous few Concorde flights had felt concern about the regular on-limits cloudbase forecasts for Rovaniemi, but experience was proving that the numbers actually represented nice winter weather here. The last approximately 200 ft of the approach proved to be in good visibility in very stable no-wind Arctic conditions, and so it was. As we taxied on to the sparkling frost-covered apron, Father Christmas with his real reindeer was waiting by the steps. 'We'll have a slice of that this evening,' said co-pilot Jeff Huson.

Before leaving this airfield it's worth mentioning an interesting polar discipline which we did not follow, but which I discovered was routine for the local Finnish Drakens. They take off on the left and land on the right. The reheated takeoff happens to melt the surface on the left, creating a glassy skating rink, but they land on the crispy and grippy permafrost on the right. Good idea. In the early afternoon we kitted up in Arctic survival suits and went for a skidoo tour of the frozen river and woodland environs. It was a kind of daylight but not exactly sunny, and the temperature was something like minus 40, but in the low humidity, no-wind weather it felt quite reasonable, especially while there was still a little psychological daylight – quite surprising. Even while covering the ground at a good speed there was little sensation of cold, and little feeling of a frost-bitten face. This is difficult to understand, though the suits had a lot to do with it.

In the evening there was the gala dinner; mainly 50 different kinds of pickled herring, of many different colours as well to add to the sense of variety.

I liked this, though there was meat of sorts for those so inclined – and Father Christmas and his docile reindeer turned up unscathed, reindeer padding softly between the tables with its master, to our and the children's delight.

The Concorde bang

Generally, the public was not supposed to be subjected to the Concorde primary shockwave experience. It can be quite something. Now, thirty years after this point in the narrative, supersonic nose-pointiness has become a future design project feature of optimism, but I would have to hear it before I believe it, and the Concorde nose was somewhat on the pointy side, but nothing like pointy enough it seems. In about 1976, I was in a yacht somewhere in the English Channel. The sea was flat, there was virtually no wind, we were almost becalmed and there was not another vessel in sight – unusual but true. I went below to look at the map and had not been there for a couple of minutes when there was a substantial and totally surprise single bang outside. It reminded me exactly of the experience of a 100-pounder field gun when you stand not so far behind it. This had been at a school cadet summer camp event at Castlemartin, impressive and not forgotten.

The only instant cerebral conclusion was a military ship close by, but where had it suddenly come from? Ship there was none, not even a surfaced submarine. This was briefly one of those surreal alternative universe experiences, and then I heard it: jet engines, very quiet, far away and high. It's no good looking in the direction of the noise. The machine is far out of sight already, but the immediacy of the bang! Like a lightning strike in your garden, but without a shred of additional evidence or warning.

I had experienced the Air France Concorde under the perfect conditions for a maximum-strength single bang. These are: heavy weight – just left Paris for New York. Extra wing loading in a turn – left turn to proceed down the Channel. Ideal bang Mach number combined with minimum distance – Mach 1.3 passing 30,000ft. Boom focusing for the recipient – nose and tail shock waves converge at the centre of the turn, and there's the physics of acceleration itself to consider. When an aircraft passes a fixed point, while accelerating, the tail goes past faster than the nose – so the front and back shock waves may arrive at the same time. Albert Einstein would have had no trouble with this, which is one reason why Concorde crews appeared to get progressively younger than their slower colleagues. This may or may not be true, but is yet another idea for the lecturer, or the relativity pseud.

To arrange these conditions for an observer would take some thought (and plenty of arranging), but there was a way to hear the cruise double ba-boom if someone in the sea had a radio. Our North Sea flights passed over some helipad oil rigs, and it was courteous to call then up. The Mach 2 shock wave array makes a 60-degree cone, and meets the ground at a distance of twice the aircraft's height behind it, so it's simple to calculate the time delay between Concorde overhead and the shock wave passing the sea position. You give them a few seconds warning, they hold their button down and you hear the bang in your earphones. Harmless, but entertaining and informative. Concorde First Officer John (Noj) White went on a transatlantic sailing jaunt with Robin Knox Johnston. We tried the same thing in the region of the Grand Banks of Newfoundland. It didn't work too well, if at all. We were not convinced they knew where they were – within a mile or three, of course.

Back to Florida

Both Pitts S2B and S1T were factory-made examples manufactured by the Christen company. Both were updated versions of the originals – bigger engines, bubble canopies, more bells and whistles, beefed up here and there and, of course, heavier. The single-seat version had more useful power than the original 180 HP fixed pitch motor, and the extra weight needed a lengthened fuselage and wing position, but the ability to strap in, slide the bubble shut, press the starter and depart was convenience itself. As expected it felt more solid in the air, though aerobated well enough, and the extra tailplane struts added confidence for strong arm flyers. With 260 HP and its big canopy the S2B was a far cry from the original S2 prototype that I had ridden in at Homestead with Bob Shnuerle in 1971. With the same engine as the single-seater this one had reminded me more of a nippier Stampe.

The US nationals took place in April 1988 at Sebring, one of many 3-runway B17 training fields of the south, and this one now containing the famous race track; and I was invited to judge. To have a foreign judge participate in an all-American event is unusual, and could be thought of by some as contradicting the mighty nation's fundamental raison d'étre, therefore unpatriotic and subversive; but Clint McHenry, Eastern Airlines and long term US world championship team member, expressed a more far-sighted view than some of his countrymen, and felt that an international element might 'add a little class' to the proceedings – maybe indicate different and widely-held perceptions of the rules. It is obvious that international sport raises different interpretations of what is required. But to claim that everyone else is cheating – to your disadvantage – is neither true nor helpful, however virtuous it helps you feel in the familiarity of home. An analytical and objective judge may sometimes not be popular with his own team, but will probably get more international respect. Ian Groom also hoped that, at least, I could relay first-hand witness of UK team suitability, but team selection doesn't work like that, generally.

The whole event was well-organised and enjoyable. One judge's assistant worked at the Miami Suntan Research Labs, and we were all issued with state-of-the-art sun blocker. Before the start of each session the call came from the chief Judge position 'Judges, grease up!' It did work very well. I flew the S1T back to Pompano.

Two interesting replicas

During this 1988 summer I got to fly the Bianchi Focker E-111 Eindecker, made for a 1969 film, 'Crooks and Coronets', in which it was flown by Dame Edith Evans' character (a lookalike, of course). That was as far as the replica requirement went, although it may have had a walk-on part in WW1 films as well, but from a distance it looked the part, with a small (80 HP Continental perhaps) engine hidden inside the rotary's cowling, which had a suitable-looking Spandau machine gun on top. At the back of the long skinny fuselage was the small round all-moving fin of the time, and a bungee-sprung non steerable skid underneath. Film-only replicas may or may not have the qualities of their originals, and while this machine did appear on the screen but did not do much, it still had its own appeal as applies to all ancient stick and string machines. It might have been a bit on the heavy side, is my guess, and the original had at least 20 more horsepower.

Takeoff and landing were easy, and the small engine of this bit-part film extra was not the problem; it was more the handling in flight. The trouble, or one of them, was the roll control. The wire-braced wings of this replica originally had the real thing's wing warping, but this did not work well enough for modern tastes, so the wings were converted to include ailerons, with, so they said, appropriate stiffening of the wing structure – or maybe different external bracing. Of course, ailerons rely on a wing that resists warping under their influence, but these wings still did warp a little, tending to cancel out the aileron effect. While this example was slow by nature, it had no desire to level its own wings and was unstable in pitch. This sounds like a Concorde, but here the similarity ends. I soon discovered that 45 miles an hour was a good speed for everything. As you went faster than this, the roll control reduced to not a lot. The pitching response to turbulence was what one comes to expect of a pre-WW1 Wright Brothers type thin cambered wing, but if a bump tipped the nose down and caused roll at the same time one got the feeling that the situation had to be restored to normal quite soon, or roll control would become zero, and the nose increasingly reluctant to rise – perhaps compensated for by the original's powerful one-piece elevator-cum-tailplane; a lively combination. I believe the Eindecker was known as a bit of a handful in its day (though it looked similar to Nesterov's looping machine of 1910).

I never tried anything but normal and sedate flight in it, and never heard of anyone else exploring the limits. Hoof Proudfoot flew it once, on a cross country, to be a static exhibit at an airshow. He knew it went slowly and took some sandwiches and a drink to enjoy on the way – something to pass the time anyway. Hoof had been a Harrier pilot, and Harrier pilots' skills are legendary – the ability to fly anything taken for granted – but he told me he never had the chance to grapple with the catering on this summery day because of his concern with keeping the Eindecker on the straight and narrow. Not a hands-off machine. I once took it to Leavesden for their show, in company with Jonathon Whaley who flew something similar; a Morane I think. I generally enjoyed the experience of tootling around in it, with care. It was never a problem, but somehow kept your attention, with that frisson of the unknown lurking – possibly not far away.

In historical life, fear of the Eindecker 'Scourge' dwindled once observation aircraft, its usual target, got a crewman at the back with a machine gun, or at the front in the case of the Gunbus; or real fighters appeared. The actual Waldo Pepper's Sopwith Camel was quite a different experience. This was a good replica of the real thing, and although it had a radial engine, lacking the rotary's precession effects, its behaviour was realistic. I can understand why the Red Baron liked his nippy triplane. The Camel had ailerons which worked quite well, although it was no Stampe. However, it was the dihedral on the bottom wings that could be used to good effect. Rudder plus pull made it roll well, and without the pulling the rudder slid the nose from side to side effectively. I have no experience of military things, but the natural scene ahead, looking between the two guns, and the ease with which the view past them could be moved up, down, left and right at will, gave an idea of the aircraft as an instinctively aimed gun – like a shotgun. This replica had brakes and a tailwheel for runway use, which greatly reduced the directional damping on the ground, grass included. Care was required after landing, and the original skid would have been more user-friendly in its natural habitat.

1988 World Aerobatic Championships

This running of the biennial event was held in Canada, at Red Deer, and I went to Alberta for a week or so beforehand to help a very small UK team practise at High River. This little town was far from anywhere, so we were well looked after by a couple of local families and given a practice area close to the local airport. One of the families, the farming Nelsons, had a couple of aeroplanes – Ted's spray-it-yourself AgCat, and his wife's Citabria. Above the farmhouse fireplace was a painting of patriarch Lloyd Nelson driving his four-in-hand chuckwagon at the Calgary Stampede. Lloyd won a number of times and had been world champion in 1949, but he handed the reins to other family members in 1974, unhappy about the increasing sponsorship and the money that was changing the nature of the event. Sport become paid entertainment again.

At the foothills of the Rockies, this part of Canada was quite unlike Toronto; it was much more western but with less of the wild, more *Bonanza* than *Gunsmoke*. Canadian government and its bureaucracy was still an incongruous feature of these wide open spaces, and the chore of two languages encourages legislative attention to detail, cowing the city dweller and creating resentment in the farmer. There was delight at the airfield one day when the local Transport Canada inspector flew in to check things out. This lady was known as the Wicked Witch of the West, and was at the wheel of the authority's King Air when it landed heavily on the relatively short and wind exposed prairie runway, bending part of the undercarriage. This is embarrassing for anyone of official status.

While at High River I had a go in Ted's AgCat, and gave a few basic aerobatic lessons in the Citabria. I knew nothing about the latter machine, and it was better for its purpose than I guessed. Then it was time to go and see some of the contest at Red Deer.

In 1988 there was a collection of Douglas Invaders (A/B26) at this regional field, serving as forest fire water bombers. These were all more than 40 years old then, though some would still be flying at age 70. 1988 World Champion Henry Haigh was also over 40. He had finished his B26 training as a twenty-three-year-old on VE day, was transferred to the B29 Stratofortress but before his squadron got to the Far East the Hiroshima bomb ended his B29 career. He explained that he had a lot of good and expensive training and some luck

– didn't upset the enemy and was not once shot at. He won this contest at age 64 in his own development of the aerobatic monoplane, the Haigh Superstar.

The US team eventually won the team prize, but there was a lengthy hold-up in proceedings to adjudicate a hostile protest about one pilot's flight, and the jury debate that followed. In this case it was not about aerobatics, but an academic point of procedure. I thought it quite silly, and a lesson for the future.

It was all about the wing rocking a pilot does to indicate his intention to start his routine. Clint McHenry, one of the winning team, fired in along the centreline, did the wing rocks, levelled off, decided he needed to proceed further into the performance zone, lowered his nose a bit, levelled off again then pulled up into the first figure. This is the point where the scoring starts, and few would have considered the flight so far to have been problematical, but one or several decided to protest that the second dive and level off were out of order, though quite what the charge was I forget. I can only assume an interruption penalty, or an added figure as the possibilities within the rules, although the aerobatics had not yet started, and I thought that there was something ridiculous in making the world aerobatic championships into a wing-rocking contest. Each year the rules are improved, added to and made more specific. This is international committee work at its most tedious, but still does not prevent unexpected challenges of the rules in the hope of disadvantaging others. Quite like politics, really. I think the protest was not upheld, and quite a lot of time had been lost. Clint ended up 5th overall in any case, out of a total of 40 competitors. The US won the team prize.

The Dutch aerobatic scene

The next year I was asked to chief judge the Dutch aerobatic championships at Lelystad. Quite why me, I'm not sure, but these are adventures one does not turn down, whatever their significance or status. Lelystad seems to be the capital of a large polder (reclaimed island) in a part of Holland completely below sea level – at the mercy of the coastal defences. The local sea is three metres below real sea level, as is the local land. There's a nice airport, and some extremely flat and relatively uninhabited fields close by. What more could you want?

The ebullient Frank Versteegh was contest manager and did an excellent job. What a force to be reckoned with! Diana Britten, who had been a participant in this contest the year before, told me that it had rained, so Frank took them all to his dance studio for a session of Strictly Ballroom training to pass the time. 'It was great fun'. I'm sure it was, and I sensed a general positive and informed practicality that still applied to these our British neighbours, but which may be evaporating in Britain. Apart from the odd Amsterdam transit I had never been to Holland to stay. I thought these thoughts then: many years later I'm rather convinced.

However, on to VINK – Dutch Aerobatics. There was a relatively small but varied and keen group of aerobatic enthusiasts, ranging from school beginners who flew the Fuji, through group and individual ownership of a Decathlon, the odd Pitts, one or two American home-build fibreglass high performance runabouts up to Frank himself and Hendrik van Overvest, a Transavia pilot. Hendrik flew his Cap 21 with great care and precision, to considerable success. Hendrik's father (of the same name) had the distinction of shooting down some German aircraft with his Focker 21 fixed gear (and propeller pitch, I think) fighter, when Holland was overrun in 1940. The second one was an ME109 which belly-landed on a Dutch field. Its pilot was the squadron commander who got out and asked 'Why are you Dutch bothering to put up this resistance?' Maybe he had a point, but that might not have been the best thing to say at the time.

The guiding hand at the Lelystad school was CFI Bert Huizinga. An ex-Dutch army fly-anything pilot, Bert had competed at all aerobatic levels and seemed to have taught everyone. The Fuji is a kind of strong Cherokee with a longer rear fuselage which clearly gives it better pitch control and behaviour. One enthusiastic tyro offered to take me for a ride. I was not wildly enthusiastic, but didn't like to hurt any feelings so agreed. He muscled the craft around the basic manoeuvres with decision, cranking the steering wheel to its limits while pulling, pushing and pedalling as appropriate, and pattering Bert's instructions to me at the same time. Agricultural, but effective and safe would be my assessment of the training supplied for this machine – something of an achievement, I would say.

Bert himself took me for a ride in the centre's Harvard. Quite different but delightful, demonstrating all that is appropriate for this classic for-its-purpose trainer – and nothing that isn't. To me this indicated the range of skill levels available at Lelystad, and the maturity to go with them. Is this a feature of this seafaring, diplomatic and accomplished nation, on the dividing line between Nordic and Latin Europe? More international judging experience was to indicate that perhaps it is.

These judging visits continued for several years – to 1997 in fact. On my second visit I heard that a mini flying boat had just arrived. I never saw it – only pictures in the paper. I imagine it was amphibious and the day before the aerobatic contest it took the Lelystad mayor for a ride, to make a ceremonial landing on the water by the town. The weather was nice, but all did not go according to plan. Several interested parties went to the waterside to watch and what one of them told me was intriguing: 'As soon as I saw it appear I knew it would crash.' This is a typical example of language refinement problems, and, naturally, I conjectured how he could foretell the future. Either he knew the pilot well or something looked wrong with the seaplane, but the reason was simpler than this: the water was too choppy. These little water craft can be very sensitive to even the most innocuous-looking waves, and my informant clearly knew something about this; maybe the subject had been discussed before takeoff, but the acceptable wind-generated short wavelength chop had steadily risen with the sea breeze. A centimetre too far perhaps.

Memories of 'Into the secondary, or maybe down the secondary and along the primary? Definitely not into the primary – it's like hitting a brick wall' (from the days of large propellers, overworked engines and long flights) came to mind, but on this landlocked seawater lake there was no secondary. Along the primary with a stiff crosswind was not on the cards, I would confidently guess. The single option was into the wind and into the primary (or give up). The first touch produced a bounce, the second a bigger bounce, and the third a forward somersault, perhaps with an element of cartwheel. The two occupants were rescued, the wet pilot returned to the airfield with the spectators, and the wet mayor may have cancelled the stirring quayside address to the citizens and press, intended to encourage a thriving waterborne commercial challenge to Schiphol. The local paper report ended at the rescue, and I think the bent flying machine was beyond repair.

A number of visiting pilots took part in this annual aerobatic event, including several from Britain, and various guest judges judged. Despite the variety of local pilots, some of whom knew plenty about aerobatic competition, there was never a Dutch judge. On one occasion I was asked to go a day early and conduct a judging school. I was happy to do this, and explained the logical approach to evaluating the separate components of the simplest figures to a class of volunteers. Some basic aerial manoeuvres were observed, the relevant questions asked and the numbers decided upon. This worked well, and the scores they came up with were certainly as valid as those of a typical contest, but I still never came across a Dutch judge. Is this to do with a Dutch sense of well-behaved equality?

In subsequent years the venue sometimes changed, and I can remember a couple of events at the grass airfield at Middelburg. These recollections include large ships occasionally going close past our hotel dining room windows at breakfast, and a deluge of rain which forced the judges to abandon their chairs and take cover while, incredibly, Steve Jones battled on through the sequence in his black and virtually invisible aeroplane – even though the unlimited minimum height was only 100 metres. The only fair thing to do was to allow a refly from the last evaluated figure. No one complained, but Steve's press-on (in a safe way!) spirit had been impressive, although I did not see it – nor had anyone else. Many pilots would consider 300 feet outrageously low for complicated aerobatics, even in a manoeuvrable light aircraft, but Steve was doing Olympic stuff in on-limits airliner landing weather. Something of a tour de force, I suspected; but I could only imagine. Later I was to witness something similar at an airshow in England from Nikolai Timofeev and his Sukhoi. Comments about the relationship between the Russian sport aerobatic hobby and this manufacturer's military products will follow later.

Aerobatics in the land of Poirot

Since the early 1960s, the judging and procedural principles introduced by the FAI for world championships had been adopted by many countries for their aerobatic contests – at least in a watered-down sense suitable for lower-level domestic events. This not only made it easier for everyone to understand what was required, but the structured content promoted safety (no marks for improvisation, however good: that's a different discipline) and, ideally, established ground rules for judging at least, but this was not always the case everywhere.

During the 1990s the Dutch Association arranged to team up with the Belgians for hosting an annual event (or the initiative may have been the other way round – but I can't start to guess): anyway, I went to three competitions in Belgium, during each of which there were hiccoughs. The first concerned a judge, the sociable station commander of the nearby training centre: 'Keep in touch; we'll fix a day for you to come over and I'll take you for a ride in an AlphaJet.' Nothing wrong with that, and I had no qualms about experience that would have ranged from Stampe to Mirage and Starfighter.

There was a Stampe in this contest, and it left out the flick roll in an 'avalanche' (aka Porteous loop; ref. the Farnborough Auster Aiglet with some lead in the tail), or perhaps it was a Chinese loop. These airshow manoeuvres had long been assimilated into the competition precision repertoire, within the comprehensive sub-section 'Loops plus things added somewhere specific on the way round'. It had thus become a combination of two figures, each with its own difficulty coefficient, added together to create a value for the complete manoeuvre, to be judged as a whole out of ten. In this case, one essential element was omitted by the pilot and the figure scores zero – no question. I thought no more of this until a scoresheet assistant came up and told me that the colonel would not 'correct' his mark to zero (the score of all the others). I had a word and explained the system, but he was adamant. 'Well, I liked the loop part and considered it worth eight.' This may be acceptable for the military students' end-of-course aerobatic cup where all competitors would be relieved to have reached this stage, and there is no point in arguing with high command anyway. But a more democratic worldwide system with tediously hammered out rules for all, including rival superpowers, has to prevail on the level playing field of international sport.

What to do? A shouting match is not a good diplomatic idea at any level. Can't deal with this yourself – pass it up the chain of command. So I had a word with our host, the President of the Belgian Aero Club – a quiet and polite retired air force general. He understood, from a global point of view. The problem was solved, the Colonel changed his scoresheet, but I didn't get to ride in the AlphaJet.

Confusion of the more serious kind

The next revealing incident occurred at another airfield somewhere in the flat and sandy country east of Brussels. These Belgian friends-across-the-borders meets were organised by willing Dutch Association members, but it was becoming clear that the higher-achieving Dutch pilots were not particularly interested. These allcomers-friendly Benelux, low-key contests attracted a few pilots from the UK, Germany, maybe a few Dutch, one from Jordan but not many from France, and hardly a handful from the home country.

On this occasion a confident Belgian pilot pitched up in his Yak 52. This is the updated trainer version of the historic Yak 18, recreated after experience of the single seat competition Yak 50 and 55. The 52 contained less wood and more metal than its Yak 18 predecessor, and its systems and instrumentation gave it the required business-like provenance of a military trainer. For a moderate-hefty beginner machine it flew pretty well. At this time there were approximately four accepted levels of contest activity: Standard (or Sportsman US), Intermediate, Advanced and Unlimited. A fifth (Beginners) had been recently informally adopted here and there. Every future Olympic swimmer has to put a child's first toe in the water somewhere, and it's difficult to underestimate the value of a slow but reassuring start, especially for the cautious but able. These may become very good, and will probably survive longer.

However, the demeanour of the Belgian Yak 52 pilot suggested that he was no beginner pilot, but whether of contest or display experience I had no clue. A visiting chief judge can only observe and decide safety issues based on the evidence – and his own experience. This contest was pitched at standard or intermediate level – suitable for a good aerobatic trainer, in this case positive manoeuvring only. The subject pilot started at a conservative height, and the first two or three figures gave an impression of handling confidence – perhaps without the refinement of competition experience, but this alone is not a safety problem, this concerns style and scoring only. Then some unusual things happened, which first invited interest and private conjecture, then real concern. I had not seen the like before, especially from a trainer which was fun to fly, but demanded respect, to my certain knowledge.

After the two or three problem-free figures there was a simple one-turn spin. It commenced and rotated correctly but the finish overshot by maybe 60 degrees, impossible to conceal from a judging panel. The first unusual thing then happened. The same spin was reentered from where it hovered, and the recovery attempt repeated, this time correctly on axis, after another 300 degrees of spin rotation. This had been an invalid figure, and the extra spinning thrown in with correct exit might be the tongue-in-cheek gesture of an experienced and quick-thinking master (perhaps). The next manoeuvre can then follow in an orderly fashion, without the extra penalty and hiatus of a break penalty, climbing up, repositioning and so on.

A contest spin finishes in a vertical dive and the figure ends in level (and fast) flight after the subsequent pull-out (quarter loop). In this Belgian event the next manoeuvre required was a half loop and half roll (roll off the top, Immelmann?), logically trading energy for height. But the illogical happened here. We got the next but two figure instead, its opposite – a half roll and downward half loop (pull-through, split S? (US Eng) – a height-burning downward energy-gainer par excellence following a doubled (by mistake) extra height-burner. A lot of g was employed for this inappropriate choice. This and the remaining figures were therefore all flown in the wrong direction so scored no points, but that was not significant. My decision had already been made: this hasty and impulsive airborne decision-making could not continue, whatever the reasons behind it.

Even though a lot of height had been squandered rapidly and unexpectedly I did not disagree with this pilot's claim, on hearing that he had been disqualified from further participation, that he had not infringed the 1000 ft minimum altitude for this contest. 1200 ft had been my estimate – but the rapid way he had got there from 2500+ ft, in two beginner manoeuvres (which, in total, should have used little height), was more to the point. After reading the brief report I had written for the contest director the pilot went to his aircraft, started his 360 HP miniature Wright Cyclone and left in a state of high dudgeon – but alive. Was I right? We will never know, but hasty and impulsive decision-making of this nature is unsuitable for competition as well as display flying. The difference here is that it may not be as obvious in a display before an uninformed public – until the crash occurs.

Compared with the supporting structure and accepted conduct of this sport in Holland, not to mention Britain, France, and the United States among many others, the inflexible Colonel and now the wild card Yak 52 gave me the impression that the sport had less tradition and structure in Belgium. Competition entry tacitly assumes some sort of pre-assessment and understanding; even honest self-assessment might suffice, but here participation seemed to have insufficient mentorship. The influence of the willing Dutch organisation did not seem to be channelling the Lelystad well-ordered flying tradition.

The next year I was yet again invited to judge at the Dutch/Belgian event, again in Belgium, this time near Luxembourg among the rolling fields and woods of the Ardennes. Someone told me that this rural area boasted the best traditional cuisine in the French-speaking world. The accommodation was simple and the food tasty indeed, but I had already made it clear that I was not prepared to be chief judge, on the pretext that it was time someone else (maybe Dutch) had a go. The real reason was a feeling of disquiet about the previous year's event. I had already been chief judge at a world championships (1990), but did not relish the prospect of managing the considerably more difficult situation of dealing with inexperienced and angry strangers, or a serious accident, as a visiting guest.

Tony Lloyd from Birmingham, editor of *British Aerobatic Association* magazine and an experienced judge, officiated. The first manoeuvre of the intermediate unknown programme was a crossover negative spin. As the first manoeuvre, it could be started at a generous height. This was fortunate for a Belgian pilot flying a CAP 230. He had flown very well the previous year, at this level, in his Pitts two-seater, also used for aerobatic instruction. (The 'crossover' term refers to an inverted spin commenced from normal flight, in this case, or vice versa as required.)

The manoeuvre entry of this dot in the sky was sort-of OK from this distance, and the motion a little strange, more of a power off knife edge spin, though it would certainly get some not-too-critical marks, but then something unexpected happened – again. The nose dropped correctly for the recovery after the required two rotations – but the rotation did not stop. The machine now continued spinning properly, alternating a faster, nose almost vertical, then a slower, flatter version. The modern, built-for-purpose aerobatic aircraft does not have surprise vices; the controls are powerful; the pilot has a large element of control. Something had broken, for sure, and the varying behaviour seemed to indicate the pilot's desperate attempts to find a solution.

...4, 5, 6, 7, 8, 9... we observed the descending rotations, as height ran out. Few counted, but then, with the total of rotations into double digits, the rotation stopped abruptly, as if someone had thrown a switch, and the CAP 230 pulled out at about 200 ft over the trees and headed for the runway. German Judge and veteran aerobatic instructor Heinz Klassen from Trier jumped out of his chair and waved his clipboard at the retreating machine. 'Aeiy! Aeiy! Aeiy! Aeiy! he shouted, in a state of shock. Never had he seen anything like it at a contest – nor had I. The moment the spin stopped the reason became obvious, and explained the rather strange initial spinning behaviour – wrong rudder. Wrong for an outside spin, where roll and yaw, as observed by the pilot, are in opposition.

Crossover entry can be unofficially assisted by aileron, but in this case the nimble machine's powerful roll control, joined by rudder and elevator in the same front corner of the cockpit, was able to predominate, while the drag resulting from the attempt achieved the initial, slow speed knife-edging behaviour. When rudder was reversed, preparing for the exit, the correct inverted spin came into its own. The penny had finally dropped when all other recovery ideas had been exhausted: another close-run thing in Belgium.

To me (and Klassen, I'm sure) there was an important brick missing from somewhere in this learning wall. A pilot in this situation, confronted with something he has not done before, and no opportunity to explore it, has choices. Leave it out, fudge it with something similar or accept the honourable zero (silly me, I read it wrong), or ask someone suitable to explain the technique, if he can find someone suitable in the time available. If he happens to be the best pilot in his circle this may take time, although at this contest there were others who could have explained the correct technique, but as competitors they might have been reluctant to do so. (He could have asked the chief judge to explain the basics at the briefing, but judges are not required to have specific flying experience themselves.) It is also possible that as a prospective winner with a shiny new machine he did not like to. This individual pilot did have enough experience to have benefitted from some informed advice, and this can work well enough: it's better than a major trip over the furniture during a performance.

During a couple of the Dutch-based events I came across a Royal Jordanian Air Force pilot who had also made his way into the world of light aircraft aerobatics. The previous ruler of this nation was a flying enthusiast, and a Pitts 2 ship display team had been supported in the past. That project, flown by two Americans, had met an unfortunate end during a show attended by the king, who went to the microphone and made the appropriate heroic and consoling speech.

Now, some years later, this officer was flying an Extra 300 in air displays, and also took part in selected competitions. He clearly had received some informed training for this aircraft, and presented himself with that certain disdain one associates with an elite officer of those nations that feel inclined to remember the mythical glories of days past. His flying was good, but strong-armed and mechanical. He seemed to prefer the apparent freedom of the air display and the currently popular manoeuvring while continuously rolling at max rate. He had the ability to do well in the formal sport, but I doubted he had the temperament for the painstaking and tedious practice required for success, with very little exposure to the limelight. The following year he crashed fatally At the Ostend airshow. Another hero of his country, no doubt.

CHAPTER 35

FAI WORLD AEROBATIC CHAMPIONSHIPS 1990

I was invited to be chief judge at this event, at Yverdon in Switzerland, but none of it appeared in my logbooks, so it has no real place in this historical piloting document. It was, of course, a massive collection of fantastic piloting by a great number of pilots from many nations, the largest assembly I have come across in this discipline. Was I any good? Difficult to say. The FAI president told me afterwards that I had been a popluar chief judge, and I have to say that the 400-odd competition flights got done within the time available – with no serious protests that I was aware of. That was my goal, mindful of the problems of recent years. At least Kazum Nadjmudinov did invite me to Moscow to fly, and said I was a good sportsman. The French have also said I am a good judge (I think). Maybe we should leave this dilettante sport and its opinions there; but something that happened on the final day is worth reporting as a flying enthusiast. I thought it was great.

A MiG 29 entry

During the afternoon of the final day of competition, the 4 minute airshow routine, Mike Heuer, head of the international jury and therefore supremo of the whole contest, radioed me to say there would be a break after flight 16 for a couple of Russian MiG 29s to come and look at the site for the next day's airshow. We waited a few minutes after the end of flight 16, and they duly appeared from the west, heading our way sedately, showing no sign of gaining energy for a roast around. Their track was perfectly aligned with our grass runway, and with half a box to run the leader rolled inverted and the wingman pulled alongside. The leader then pushed the line abreast pair up to the vertical, exactly on contest centre, and each then positive looped their separate ways to start a perfectly synchronised opposed intermediate difficulty routine; loops, crossovers exactly centred, half-Cubans, point rolls, perfect humpty bumps and so on. Then there were separate things – the cobra, the tailslide, how slow can you go, and so on. I cannot remember the details because this display of handling and presentation mastery was a surprise.

When they left I suggested to my fellow judges 'Do we need to watch anything else?' Well, of course we had to, but it was the clarity and precision of this most unusual display of modern heavy fighting aircraft, performing precision manoeuvres at conservative speeds and low altitudes, that had been so unexpected. Where did they learn how to do it? I did find out in due course, and the answer could not be more different to a deeply-entrenched British attitude to aviation of all kinds: in fact the not-too-sparkling Cranfield A1 was a good example of the Soviet system in reverse – a couple of RAF officers (an instructor and an engineer) getting nowhere with a sporting aircraft project that produced a flying tractor.

The air is our sea

There came a time when it was realised that straight-line missile-launching interceptors, like the MiG 21 (or Starfighter), may not be the complete answer to air superiority after all. Dogfights may not actually be a thing of the past, so maybe we need fast aircraft that will manoeuvre in extraordinary ways at slow speeds as well. Why not? We have to try. The manufacturers came up with revolutionary designs – but who was prepared to wring them out in conventionally alarming ways? Not the seasoned veterans of Angola, Vietnam and the cold war. 'No speed and everything in a corner? Forget it.' So who do we get?

Reminding one of the German sporting and airline pursuits of the thirties (Lufthansa doing formation cross countries at night?), the soviet sport flying Dosaaf (gliding, parachuting, aerobatics) had military connections (Why not? We all share the national interest). 'The people who might be best, and more importantly, prepared to throw our prototypes around in outrageous fashion, are the Dosaaf aerobatic people,' so that's how it began. Forget the square bashing, ritual violence and humiliation that make a fighting animal – we need analytically-inclined superb aircraft handlers: that's all. Who better than instructor level pilots from the Yak 18/50/52 competition aerobatic environment so, I believe, suitable youngsters got some fast track air force induction to give them the general idea of the requirements.

I heard that at the end of a day's state-of-the-art test flying, there would sometimes be an aerobatic competition: FAI rules, intermediate level, marks out of ten, difficulty coefficients etc, individual pilot rankings, Mig 29 or Sukhoi 27 (as familiar examples). Judges sat in their chairs out on the airfield, score sheets to hand, the specified programme of manoeuvres carried out and assessed for accuracy, positioning etc.. Is this what I saw at Yverdon? Who can I say? Extraordinary, and wonderful. Socialism – as it should be? A harvesting of young talent for the good of the country, wherever it may be found? Probably yes. Of course it all depends...

The German judge in 1990 was Erst Paukner, in his eighties. Walter Wolfrum, previous judge and famous Kiev high scorer had retired from judging, and a younger Paukner had taken his place. Ernst joined the Luftwaffe towards the end of WW2, and found himself flying the Me262, expecting to attack the American bomber formations, bowling in from great height and speed, but the Russian advance changed the plan and he found himself coping with an Me 262 tankbuster. Quite unsuitable, he said, but he also survived, to run the family perfume company in Munich.

WAC 1990 Postscript

Afterwards I wrote my chief judge's report for CIVA. The last world contest I had taken part in, other than as a helper, had been in 1976 (when a young Frolov, of Su 27 demonstration fame, had taken part). As well as numerous comments and suggestions about procedure and rules the report included a view of the current state of this sport. Despite a history of disagreement and probems the 1990 conclusion was positive – the volume of superb flying, advances in specialised aerobatic aircraft and the broadening of good training environments had given many access to a difficult and sophisticated flying sport, once thought of as available to a few extraordinary people. At the annual CIVA meeting a few months later mention of the circulated report got a round of applause. 'It's a novel', said Peter Celliers. It was intended, like all writing, to say something, but also be readable. Later again Mike Heuer phoned me and said I had been a popular chief judge – but they did not ask me to do it again. I didn't ask why, I'm not sure he knew; but responsible involvement in any multi-national, multi-cultural undertaking presents new problems to the plain man. There are no easy answers to the inevitable questions, and new challenges are seldom as straightforward as they might look, but the attempt is probably worth the risk to the self-image. Like the Concorde pilgrimage or the choice of life partner you will be changed by the experience – for better or worse – but will emerge older and wiser, even if the choice had turned out to be naive or foolish.

A year or two later Ken Larson wrote in Sport Aerobatics that he would have preferred more breaks and video playback conferences, and knowing who the pilots were – it's more fun. I wouldn't disagree with any of that, but there's a job to be done, and any diversions must be of good value, and not detract from judging fairness and consistency. In reply I wrote an article for Sport Aerobatics about Olympic ice skating and its judging. There are parallels, but judging a world championships is a tough job. The scores and judgments are never correct!

CHAPTER 36

THE REST OF 1990 - LEARNING AND TEACHING

I finished the Concorde Stick and Rudder Book in early 1990. It was deliberately informal and homemade in style and picture, and focused on what was different about the way a Concorde behaved in the air and answered its controls. I had long thought that the traditional way of teaching pilots the basics about how their flying machine worked was not entirely suitable for its purpose, and too academic. The problem stems from the very earliest days. Much of the science of flight had already been assembled by researchers with a mathematical bent, well before the Wright Brothers attempts. They (including the Wright Brothers) understood it well, but as early aviation grew, teachers and learners included a majority who did not have the same background of academic physics and mechanics. This applied in an English-speaking world more familiar with the wind in the sails, the effect of a boat's rudder on the water, the acceleration and speed produced by a horse and the weight of tea or sugar on the grocer's scales.

The typical pilot does not have to design the aeroplane and, assuming that has already been done satisfactorily, he can learn to fly it successfully with understandings provided by suitable, simple, everyday imagery. Many piloting professionals, to this day, manage to do their work well, despite the very scantest understanding of how the magic works. Had they not have been confronted by $\frac{1}{2}\rho V^2 S C_L$, low and high pressures in curious places, Bernoulli's principle, Giacomo Venturi's theorem, French left-wing vote-rigger Pierre Buys Ballot's activities and induced drag as a special subject (there's plenty more) they might not have responded to lesson one like a nursery child with a bad drawing teacher. If at first you don't get it, give up – it's too difficult.

Bad or inappropriate teaching loses students immediately – usually forever. Why not start with the simple basics? A wing pushes enough air downwards at a suitable rate to support the flying machine. This is true, but does not sound clever enough to a teaching establishment conscious of their own shaky knowledge. The refinements, if desired or necessary, can follow later. This is the level of explanations pitched in the *Concorde Stick and Rudder Book*, and it was well received. My intention was to present the many features of the subject that differ from those of an accustomed airliner, in easy-to-understand form – no bullshit-baffles-brains tradition. The readers could take what they wanted from the pages (it wasn't compulsory reading). The student then has a better idea of what to expect, has a credible explanation of the whys and wherefores, and is less perplexed by first acquaintance with the real thing.

It was many years later, long after the Concorde's demise, that Jean Pinet, a senior member of the original French test and certification team, looked at the *Concorde Stick and Rudder Book*. With a shrug of recognition and resignation he immediately said 'We wrote a manual this thick (1½ cms between finger and thumb), with exactly this stuff in it, for Concorde instructors. The British didn't want it.' (The British appear to have managed without it – but the training journey could have been easier for some.) Later, after he had seen more of the pictures, Pinet told me that my small book was a collector's item. That was nice; in fact one of the Russian delegation at the August 1990 aerobatic contest approached me, waving his copy. He worked at the aerospace research centre in Samara, a colleague of Russian judge Tarassov, famous mathematician. He showed me the page which indicated the Concorde's simple but powerful flying controls, compared with the complexity of a conventional jet's multiple ailerons, flaps (front and back), spoilers, elevator and stabiliser. The advice at the bottom of the page was 'Don't move them more than you have to'. It was the next caution that he liked – 'If you want a fight you will get one.' Did this ring any bells from Tu144 experience? Could be, but there wasn't time to follow this up, and it might not have been in his interests to discuss it further at this time and place.

Only one Concorde student did not like this helpful book. He said that it added extra difficulties, and made him feel that he was being set up to fail. Why,

I cannot guess, and it's best to approach a conversion course with minimum baggage and preconceived ideas. This leaves more space for learning – if learning is your only agenda.

An old Pitts S2A and a new Sukhoi 26

Concorde flying and simulator continued as usual, and Bob Mitchell asked me if I would do a couple of shows, Leicester and Staverton, in his ex-Rothmans S2A G-BADW (Bad Whisky), later in August. Why did he ask me? I don't know, but I was aware of Manx Kelly's max performance style of operation, team transits included. Full throttle, reduce the revs and weaken the mixture to enough to keep you going. Good mpg but hard work for the engine, which was far from new in this well-used example: the lemon had been well-squeezed for sure. I asked Bob how well it still went. He said 'It will give you 2,700 rpm'. Considering that the ostensibly 200HP Lycoming had a constant speed propeller, this doesn't tell you a lot. As can often happen with an unknown pre-owned example, the plan for a dazzling show progressively loses its sparkle as rehearsal progresses, but I settled for some Stampe beginner stuff, and the two shows and nine here-and-there flights got done.

The brand new Sukhoi 26 was something else. Since 1988, and the easing of Cold War borders, Russian aircraft began to be available in the West. By August 1990 Ramon Alonso of Spain had acquired his own Su26, and Randy Gagne and Guido Lepore had been to Russia to train with the Russians for the 1990 contest, representing Canada. Their deal included provision of an Su26 at the Yverdon contest, and considering the familiarity required to achieve top marks they did well; well, quite well – they were not last; in fact Guido's result was very creditable. Having practised at home, Ramon, who shared #16 with the 'Canadian' pair at Yverdon, did well to come 30th, and started to show the stately, polished and authoritative style (Ramon's address is next to the Prado, Madrid; classy or what?) that he was to develop with the Sukhoi, but said he liked his own new export example better. On the free day at the end of the contest other pilots could queue up to try the Sukhoi. Nikolai Timofeev gave a good briefing and several had a go, with tentative and sometimes slightly strange results, but as a non-pilot there was no chance for me. 'Come to Moscow' said Nazhmudinov, and I thought that perhaps I would, in due course.

But I got to fly the Su26 at the end of September 1990, at Page, Oklahoma. The Becker family Pompano Air Centre had obtained Sukhoi dealership and had two examples, pink and blue, ready for Elena Klimovich (pink, N12SU) and Nicolai Nikituik (blue, N26SU) to fly at the nearby US Nationals. I flew the blue one (both had decided they liked the pink one better). Randy told me to check the magnetos at 60% revolutions, then go. 'You'll be off the ground before you get to full power', he said. There was little else to add to Timofeev's Switzerland briefing, so off I went. Randy had been right.

Sukhois had not made a light aircraft before, so they had nothing to copy: just fit the brief of the competition aerobatic establishment – starting with a blank sheet of paper. Sukhoi recent tradition included heavy fighters, a chunky ground attack tank buster (as flown by president Yeltsin), and supersonic bombers. How this new project accorded with company tradition I have no idea, but this was the point, and given free rein in the Sukhoi conference room the aerobatic enthusiasts, old and young, could abandon all references to historic trainers, conventional stability and so on. 'Tell us what you actually want.' Light, strong, reclined seat for lots of g, powerful but light controls, similar positive and negative manoeuvring, fantastic roll rate, point it anywhere and it stays there. And as simple for the pilot as you can make it. That's what we want. (A bit military? But they'd come to the right place, especially if the state are paying.)

I wrote about the first flight experience in Pilot Magazine and Sport Aerobatics. Without wishing to repeat myself it was fantastic fun. I was expecting something of a daunting challenge, but first impressions suggested that I could not have been more wrong. This was a friendly, simple, manoeuvring machine – like nothing else. Apparently able to fly at any speed, totally controllable at all times, and this blue one just happened to have the most perfectly balanced engine/propeller combination – turbine smooth (not experienced since). The only handling problem was the attempted flick roll. I had seen Kairis' demonstration of the technique at Yverdon, following Timofeev's basics. He sat on a chair and made some lightning-fast moves with hand and feet: 'This for one, this for two (rotations),' followed by the right and left variations. Negatives were not covered, but the speed, decisiveness and millimetre accuracy of these requirements suggested that there might be plenty to learn here. It was exactly like watching the movements of those robots that assemble and weld the pieces of a new car, albeit rather faster. Surreal, but burned into the memory. Actually doing it would not be easy.

Following a beginner's reassuring experience so far of this first ride on the quirky thoroughbred I decided to give this manoeuvre a tentative try. I'll sort of do what Kairis did, as a start, and work up to the real thing – step by step. The combination of what I might normally do to impress a passenger in the CAP

10, Kairisised a bit, at around half power, had an extraordinary result. The Sukhoi gave a lurch, stopped in surprise, then continued in an unquantifiable tumbling manoeuvre, with the stick pressing itself into my reclining right hip bone. Further research can wait, I thought: first impressions can deceive.

Back at the ranch I mentioned the flick roll and the stick-in-the-corner business to Elena. She just smiled and tumbled her hands around. Aha! I was not alone. This was the start of a road all must take. Randy gave me a lift to our motel as Oklahoma dusk fell, but we set off in the wrong direction, between featureless fields. 'Got to go to the next county first to get some beers. This one is dry.' It was only a mile to the lonely post office store, but time has not moved on everywhere, and old-fashioned values may still prevail here and there.

A month later, at the end of October 1990, I went to Pompano Beach, further south than the South, for some more research for my article. Sukhoi sales here had started quietly; there was guarded interest in this exotic machine with evil empire connections, and a number of local pilots I spoke to expressed similar emotions – 'It intimidates me.' 'But you haven't even tried it yet, how can you tell?' 'When I look at it I feel intimidated.' I suppose this is avoidance-speak for afraid, but I felt this response was unjustified, especially for anyone who could fly a Pitts.

Randy had told me that four years ago he had been walking out to his aeroplane at Pompano, watched a shuttle launch trail rise into the air 200 miles to the north, then noticed the trail did something peculiar. He went back inside and told a student 'Turn on the TV; shuttle's just blown up.' He was correct, but this could have little influence on fun flying four years later, surely. Why don't I fly the Sukhoi in next weekend's Sebring contest – Sportsman level – to show how easy it is. I'm an unknown mature visitor; it should be fun, one way or another. PAC director Brian Becker said he'd have a go as well, and so did aerobatic instructor Randy, though he had recently returned from his Sukhoi adventures in Europe. Was there some reason for the impromptu enthusiasm to join my innocent marketing gesture? It occurs to me that Tom Jones' accident in June 1990 would have had a significant effect on the little Russian sport plane's reputation, but I had not thought of this then: in fact I'm not sure I knew about it.

Tom had been US Champion in 1988, and had been a US team member at Red Deer so he saw Su26s in action, but Airshow was his real interest, and as an unmistakable local he had organised the Oklahoma City show for years. He acquired an Su26 early in 1990, the first in the US, and painted it a villainous black with yellow flames. It was called *Rushin' Rage*. He also worked hard to arrange for CCCP (now Rushin) participation in the June 1990 OKC event – 2 Sukhoi 27s, another Su26 and the 6 engined Antonov 225 that brought them. Maybe you can guess who would demonstrate the Ragin' 26. There seems to have been no firm conclusion about why what happened happened, but the crash was as dramatic and tragic as such an event can be. Not a good start for the Pompano marketing campaign.

On the Thursday before the Sebring contest I had a 10-minute practice over the Airglades grass in Pink Floyd (the smooth running blue example seems to have disappeared – sold perhaps). I certainly had no intention of demonstrating the 240Kt intimidating wow factor Sukhoi opening dive. I'm not convinced that this approach always works really, and had not taken part in a proper contest since 1976. I'd never felt a vestige of the desire to intimidate anyway. I'd had a month to think about what I'd learnt from the 25-minute flight in the Oklahoma farmlands, and decided something really downscale would be more appropriate to reassure the grass roots flyer, show off this user-friendly product, and not disgrace myself too much. The Sukhoi has a similar weight to a Chipmunk, and it's approximately the same size. 360 HP, a big propeller and +/- 12g does make a difference, but full power at all times is not compulsory. As the doddering visitor I would demonstrate the Sukhoi as Chipmunk, applying some careful power management to complete the illusion, although the manoeuvring itself was much easier. It worked reasonably well.

Next Sunday was the contest. Sportsman is called Standard in the UK, but it's very similar, and, short of the new UK Beginners' class, is actually about competent aerobatic beginners in this country. Simple figures, no inverted fuel system required, no overtly upside down (negative) flying demanded. It does, however, include the simple snap (flick) roll. I'd tried this a few more times in my Airglades ten minutes' practice, and come to a slightly more approximate accommodation with the novel rotational dynamics of the Sukhoi, but halfway close is nothing like good enough. My contest attempt avoided the out-of-control tumbling, but the snap roll finish was patently on the awkward side, and caused some amusement. Apart from that, the scores were surprisingly good, so I'm told.

The second programme was the free (make it up yourself), but I discovered that if you rearranged the order of the figures already flown this would conform to the regulations – I didn't even need the book. Not a problem, but while I was arranging this, news came that Randy was having a technical problem in the air with Pink Floyd. He had lost throttle control and was stuck with middling horsepower. All assembled to watch what would happen, but he switched off and glided down to land on a Sebring runway, petrol pouring from the engine. In the meantime a body of competitors had started to complain about the unfairness of patently non-Sportsman pilots taking part with such a machine. Mutiny threatened, but the problem with the aeroplane solved the matter and we gatecrashers retired. The throttle linkage had suffered a disconnected ball joint. This involved a taper screw junction with locknut (locknut on the wrong side of the joint after shipping reassembly). Reassembly with assumption rather than the book sometimes raises these problems, but all was well after some thought.

After another six Concorde trips (4 NYs, a Barbados and a Washington/ Miami), I went back to Pompano to get some pictures for my finished article. They now had an Su26MX demonstrator and this is what we would use. The basic 26M aircraft was only conceived as a contest aerobatic aircraft, intended to take off, fly about over its home for twenty minutes and then land. Range was limited, but American owners expected to be able to fly long-distances at will, something that had not happened in Soviet private aviation circles (there were none), so more fuel was needed, and some indication as to how much there was aboard. Like the Pitts S1-S you could only see the 26M fuel quantity when there was hardly any left, and Timofeev had described this perfectly during his type briefing at Yverdon. 'Fuel is (wait for it) 'inwisible', he said, after having thought of the best word to describe this in English. The MX had a couple of additional wing tanks, and elevator trim. As a neutral pitch machine when powered no trim is needed. At full power the 26 goes wherever you point it, and stays there until instructed otherwise. After throttling back it heads for the ground – where else did you have in mind after your aerobatic flight? But the trim was now required for cruising.

The air-to-air pictures were easy enough. The S2B instructional Pitts minus canopy would be camera ship. 'Just fly a steady circle and my man will position on you, high and low, inside and outside, and I'll take the pictures. Then reverse the direction – same again. 'Father figure John Becker directed me to the photo shop in town for develop and print. 'Tell them to charge it to us'. (John Becker had been a 16-year-old daredevil free-fall airshow jumper. As well as the wing-walking stuff they had how-low-can-you-pull contests in the 1930s, developing stable free-fall in the process. He did a lot of it, and won the annual race-to-the-ground contest three times. I don't think they would allow such things these days (apart from the stable free-fall). He flew the C-46 in WW2, continuing with Far East airline work.) This last 1990 visit was just before Christmas. The Florida weather was still quite nice for pictures.

CHAPTER 37

MORE CONCORDE TOPICS

Barbados

I'd already done the odd Concorde Barbados, usually one way, because the timing required a crew change, so we night-stopped and passengered back, or vice versa. Originally a Kuoni charter, this Saturday destination proved popular enough to become a scheduled up-market bucket and spade trip. There was a Barbados every weekend for the winter season, mid-December to mid-April at least – sometimes two, even three. A visit in January 1990 had called at Shannon for fuel on the way out, and this was not unusual because the statutory planning requirements for a public transport flight sometimes could not be met from London. The direct Barbados was often close to the public transport planning limit for the Concorde as an airliner, but not quite beyond it.

The correct flight took 3 hours, 40 minutes. Add something for taxiing and the general idea was leave at 9:30am, get there at the same 9:30 local time; on the water by 11. Wind and wave permitting, this suited my windsurfing well. Stops at Shannon seemed to become less frequent as experience was gained and the ramifications of the critical part of this long flight over the sea became more familiar; but the effortless-looking sunshine morning fun cruise disguised the need for careful awareness of how the tactical situation was changing, and the importance of the what-to-do decision if there was a surprise – always on the cards, whether you chose to believe this or not. 23 miles less to go passed every Concorde minute – that also means 23 further from where you started, but it was the lack of options around the centre that was the usual planning reason for a Shannon pitstop.

All public transport flights have to be able to do something safe if an engine stops, at any time. Believe it or not this applies to single-engine aircraft as well, but the essential Concorde 3-engine planning might have a gap mid-flight between London and Barbados, so we had to look to the side – Newfoundland, the Azores, Bermuda possibly, then Antigua; almost as far ahead as Barbados but a few miles closer. These possibilities were computed for the day and its wind and temperatures aloft, and, assuming the direct flight was theoretically possible, there was a relatively brief but a few hundred miles long stretch, mid ocean, where progress against fuel on board was checked carefully against the day's 3-engine graphs as we progressed. 'Shannon has gone' would be the first observation. We now had Gander for the next eight minutes – and so on – until 'we can reach Barbados on three' seemed to satisfy the legal requirements. Two engines was of interest, but not statutory. One hoped not to be so unlucky.

Sometimes the optimistically assumed uneventful flight didn't work. I don't know the reason, but one day Dave Leney, flight technical manager, had to go into Lajes in the Azores. This airport is run by the American Air Force, and helpful they were, I'm sure. The Concorde was soon ready to continue – should do it in a couple of hours – but there was a problem. Lajes only had military JP1 fuel – lighter grade kerosene. The Concorde could fly with this fuel, but supersonic flying was not allowed. This wide-cut stuff was too volatile for extended fast flight; it would boil away en route – or worse perhaps. No choice: subsonic the rest of the way. Maybe the Concorde arrived at Barbados teatime after another leisurely four or five-hour flight (all fancy catering eaten on the London-Lajes sector); I've no idea, but this sort of thing is something every Concorde crew would wish to avoid.

Once up and running the trusty engines seldom gave problems – far from it. But a lot of trivial things could interrupt the supersonic cruise. They didn't actually change anything, except the odds on the future *if* problem. This 'if' business is fundamental to the redundancy required for public safety, but do we not also expect brave and fearless captains to look after our travel interests as well, not to forget the considerable investment represented by the ticket price? No comment.

Stack Butterley is a familiar name in various flying circles, and was known for his call of 'We're on our hols, boys!' as V1 (stop or go takeoff decision at 160kts) was successfully passed on the London runway when headed for Barbados. Something logical and ebullient about this; but he was confronted with one of those captain-like decisions when most of the way to Barbados one day. One of the Concorde's three hydraulic systems disappeared – just like that. (This is how it usually happened with this narrow, 4000 psi philosophy.) There are means of dealing with this; nothing immediate has been lost and, on the face of it, the Concorde can continue as normal – but the checklist calls for immediate slow up and descent to the low, slow and more fuel-expensive subsonic environment. Why should this be? The destination ahead continues to be the natural (if only) option, but an early descent will use 25% more fuel and take longer (longer for something else to go wrong with less fuel remaining?). At the risk of requiring another trigger warning, a few words about Half Bodies might be of interest to those wondering why Concording was different.

Trigger warning

Half Bodies

This means Concorde flying controls powered by only one hydraulic system. Two systems share the job in a kind of mirror-image, synchronised pushing and pulling at opposite ends of each narrow jack, but a single system (half bodies) can manage for all normal flying – you wouldn't notice the difference: except for the more aerodynamically difficult transonic descent. During this reentry phase the Concorde's centre of gravity has to move forward, staying in its changing and narrowing speed corridor. If the moving centre of gravity were to meet either (also moving) fore or aft limits on the way down to 40,000 ft, one hydraulic system alone doing the flying may not be strong enough to keep control – and disaster may result. That's the reality, hence the instruction to descend immediately with two systems working – before a second system fails and commits you to the hazardous descent you have elected to delay by not following the checklist immediately.

'But it's nice up here, let's not be rushed into hasty action. We'll be at our proper 200-mile throttling point in a few minutes, and there's no indication of anything else wrong.' Would I have done the same? Possibly… Does that make me dangerous (like Maverick)? This would depend on who you ask, but getting away with it is a point in your favour: and this sort of decision-making went with the realities of managing this fully certified (and therefore safe) airliner.

Keeping the Queen warm

Captain Leney also had the honour of taking our Queen to Barbados in a Concorde in 1989. She was not expecting to be paparazzoed by the *Mail on Sunday* on Sandy Lane beach enjoying a rum punch with Rihanna, Simon Cowell or Sir Cliff Richard; this was a formal gig and she stayed at the late Sir Anthony Eden's old colonial pad, surrounded by low hills, sugar fields waving in the wind and the towering royal palms that define the garden.

The flight got to Barbados as planned, but a couple of things made the trip slightly special. On the way, one of the four cabin air-conditioning units failed. Of course three can manage, but not so well as four. To take hot engine compressor air and cool it to room temperature when everything else is hot requires physics of a magical order. The domestic fridge works on the same principle – make something even hotter by compressing it – cool it with whatever's conveniently to hand, decompress it again and it will be colder than when you started. The details of how this heat-exchanging system actually worked have faded after so many years (and old style, crew-of-three captains had a special man who knew, sitting behind), but fuel also came into it. Concorde fuel was used to cool hydraulic fluid, and also acted as a heat sink for the wing lower surface. Much of the Concorde's exterior ran at about 90°C during a 2½ hour cruise, and, as one can expect, as heating time continues and the remaining fuel reduces in quantity it gets hotter, and less effective as a heat exchanger coolant. In this case it was the flight deck that suffered most, although the royal seat in row 1 was not that far behind, maybe 20 feet. Normally the flight deck window frames are too hot to touch; I heard that co-pilot Jock Lowe had reported that, by top of descent, the control columns had become too hot to touch without the wet towels. Though not amused there was not much else to do but grit the teeth and get the feel of tropical life before stepping outside into a cool 29 degrees C.

The second trivial but public event happened on arrival. Everything had been organised: prime ministerial reception committee, police band ready, red carpet leading from the carefully positioned steps – with BA manager Barbados in best suit waiting on top. The Concorde taxied expertly towards the marshaller, the fuselage side passing inches from the top of the steps. Keep going, waved the man with the bats. The front door drew alongside manager Elwyn Sealey – right forearm prepared for the welcoming handshake – and continued past as he swivelled to follow it, hand still at ninety degrees like a techno dance move.

Stop, waved the marshaller, and the Concorde duly stopped, a few feet too far forward. The front door opened, someone looked out, to left and right but especially down – confronted with a gasp-inducing 4m drop to the concrete. The captain's window opened, the captain looked astern: the door is nowhere near the steps. Something's wrong: what to do? The event was on national television.

Acquaintance and German windsurfing honcho Wolfgang Langer (The Reef Sheriff) caught it all on video. As a winter resident he had already been my guest on the Saturday Concorde visit for locals I used to arrange during the four-hour stopover. He also has some cockpit footage of local sea-going characters; Bright St John (ex-prime minister's son) and 'Heads' Marshall, two dreadlocked figures, sat in the pilots' seats, heads together over the throttles, debating the perplexities of the cockpit. Wolfgang thought the royal parking debacle would fit well in a humorous short he might put together. I don't know whether *The Rasta Pilots* ever got completed, though I think his house guests found the clips amusing.

The Barbados Week

Around this mid-point of my Concorde career the Barbados week took shape, to apply during the December to April season. Rather than having one flight deck crew passenger there and another back each weekend and surrounding days, taking valuable commercial 747 seats, why not have each Saturday crew stay the week and come back the next Saturday – no positioning seats required? A deal was struck: you can stay in the hotel for the week, but no allowances for the Tuesday, Wednesday and Thursday, and these will also count as days off. Fair enough, so that's how the system began to work. But immediately democratic cries of unfairness were raised concerning undemocratic seniority. The senior people (me, for one) will choose this trip every alternate week – few others will get a look-in. So a rationing system was arranged. All the weeks were advertised in advance – choose your one week per winter by seniority. This sort of worked until the novelty of the tropical paradise wore off, and things improved for wind, sea, sand, rum and coke enthusiasts. I believe that the logbook's December 23rd to 30th 1990 Barbados trip was my first of these, and the family came too – staff travel on the Jumbo. Copilot Tony Yule arranged the same thing. His children were younger than mine, and as I'd arranged somewhere else to stay around the coast (cheaper than the cost of an extra room for my teenagers on the west coast) he could have my room at the Paradise Beach. He told me the staff were surprised when Captain Riley's early morning Ribena was received by a seven-year-old imposter.

The only proper Concorde climb out

The return flight from Barbados to London worked well from an operating point of view. I remember it as our only regular flight where the machine could depart and climb to height as designed. I can't think of a single flight that didn't make London direct – and this has nothing to do with cruise tailwinds.

A few seconds after the clifftop liftoff the track went over the sea. No noise abatement was required and the throttles themselves could stay at the front until North Devon. Reheats off at 500 feet was the first action, climb power at 1000 ft (roof switches) – and more or less the initial rotate attitude would have the speed and rate of climb progressively making their initial way (trigger warning again?) with the barber's pole from 300 to 400kts at 4,000ft and 4,000 fpm climb thereafter. What could be simpler? Nose and visor all the way up immediately the wheels were up-and-off made it nice and quiet inside as well.

Trigger warning

(Wheels up and off sequencing, and its importance)
Many large and complex aircraft have three positions for their undercarriage selectors: down, up, and off in the middle. The off position releases the hydraulics for other things, but the Concorde's structural sensitivity at cruising speed made the off position quite important. During initial marketing publicity the Chinese asked if the Concorde could be modified as a bomber. 4000 miles at Mach 2 and 60,000ft for a 200-ton flying machine was not everyday stuff in those days, and it was a thought – quite strategically useful, maybe. But the answer was 'not really'. The problem was how to release the bombs from a bomb bay at cruising speed. The drag force on the Concorde undercarriage doors would be catastrophic if they opened at cruising speed.

For this reason it was decided that the Concorde undercarriage system should be completely isolated once the prospect of supersonic flight was on the cards. (In other words if an idiot was to select wheels down in the cruise nothing would happen.) Raising the visor was the decisive factor for isolating the Concorde undercarriage department after takeoff, both hydraulically and electrically. This only worked if the undercarriage selector was already in its middle off position when visor up was selected.

> *During a 'proper' Concorde take off the speed rises rapidly. The wheels and doors take their time to rise and close; nose up can be selected when you like, but visor up (before 300kts) must only be selected after the undercarriage selector is off, otherwise all may look normal, but the wheels and doors system may be sort of live, and potentially dangerous.*

There was another performance bonus because, for reasons of more sunlight to heat the Earth, heated equatorial air climbs higher and continues to get colder to a greater altitude as you travel upwards. Jets like cold air, and the London-bound Concorde could frequently reach its maximum permitted 60,000 ft for the first part of the cruise (cruise power selected, once again, by ganging the roof switches the other way). Mach 2 at 50,000 ft would have already been reached 20 minutes after takeoff from Barbados. By comparison, 20 minutes after leaving London one would be proceeding past Severn Beach at 28,000ft, awaiting that 30 miles from Cardiff moment when the pedal could be pressed to the metal. Too low and too slow is an expensive way to fly a jet (and fiddly for the crew).

Thereafter the London-bound Concorde would lose some altitude as tropical troposphere changed to warmer polar stratosphere – cruise climb became cruise descent for a while – but with some speed advantage, and the overall nature of this ideal return flight never gave problems as I remember. The 12:30 departure arrived at 8:30pm London time; time for a quick bonding beer before going home.

The view from a Concorde

The passengers could see quite well out of their little windows, even though most of them were sitting over the wing. Arrival at New York could sometimes be an interesting experience for some of them, who would report a bold arrival to acquaintances: a zero/zero landing in sea fog which we appeared to shoot out of as the nose was lowered after touchdown. Daredevil stuff. In fact the fog had been generated by the narrow but deep region of reduced air pressure over the wings at low speed when humidity increased as sea and mudflats were approached. The cockpit and first few seat rows ahead of this action enjoyed beautiful weather for the whole approach and landing – no grasped teeth and gritted armrests up here. But special sights from the cockpit are worth a mention.

In March 1989, I think on the 6th, our evening flight (BA#4, the late show), returning to London from New York, gave us a ringside seat to something I have not seen before or since – it was the effects of the first of an unusually strong session of solar flares. It must have been about 7pm local UK (Greenwich) time, as we approached our throttling back position, maybe 300 miles west of Ilfracombe when I noticed it. The sky had been completely dark, but to the side, to the north and east, it was becoming red, suggesting that the street lighting of northern Britain was lighting up the clouds. But we were at 58,000 feet, and there were no clouds; and the street lighting was not generally red, or that well distributed and concentrated; and could you see it from such a distance? Definitely not. Could it be a pre-sunrise effect? Not over the western approaches at 7pm in March.

I was familiar with the Aurora Borealis. In pre-inertial navigating days, years of Atlantic crossings on clear winter nights at almost polar latitudes frequently produced these ectoplasmic green shapes hanging in the sky. Sometimes low across the horizon, sometimes self-contained heavy curtains high above, always a pale laser-green; maybe a corrugated circular affair that slowly undulated its shape like a jellyfish. What will it do next? I had also, very occasionally, seen something quite different above the display: periodic (every few seconds) whooshes of light sweeping over the top – away from the invisible sun, and moving very fast. I believe these ejected particles almost reach the speed of light. If it takes a second and a half for light to reach the moon from the earth, and these waves of particles were near the top of the ionosphere (1000kms altitude), was I seeing things approaching this velocity? I imagine Einstein and the earlier physicists would have enjoyed this view of manifestations I could only guess at – and done some quick calculations. But the red sky on this Concorde night was something completely different, especially as the furthest north we got was 50 degrees. Definitely not Aurora country.

Far from fading away as we descended and approached London, it got stronger. The colours varied, with a selection of yellow and green spreading across to the east, over Europe. Below, the picture of town lights, roads, traffic looked tiny but bright and normal in their pitch black night, but above, the firmament was glowing with solid background colour – red, green and yellow; no beige, pink, magenta, turquoise, taupe or avocado. By the time we landed it had faded towards black, for us, back on the ground. The night was as dark as usual behind the streetlights. But the routine view of the sky was again different, some of the features due to speed, others to altitude.

Reverse sunset and Earth shadow

New York is five hours behind London, sun's time. It is also on the same latitude as Rome, quite a bit south of London. The evening London departure, chocks away 7pm, took off in complete darkness during autumn and spring (as well as winter, naturally), but the equinoctial flights arrived in New York at 5:30pm local in bright sunshine. On the way we experienced the sunset in reverse, which looked, understandably, like a slow sunrise, more or less ahead, so our clip-on sun screens were required despite the very sloping none-too-optically-perfect visor windows in front of our gold-plated windscreens. You could see the scenery and sky though the visor, but I often wondered whether it would be possible to spot an opposing Concorde (on the wrong track) coming at you at 46 miles a minute. Probably not.

The return flights from the western hemisphere always took off in daylight, but more than half of the transatlantic London landings were at night. Dusk occurred quite quickly because the flight now added significantly to the Earth's rotation, but the view ahead was quite novel. It didn't just get generally dark; the night rose from the distant horizon in front in a curved shape – a rising segment. It was the Earth's shadow. It contained stars, even though the sky above was still blue, and sunlight still shining on parts of the Concorde. Once, early on in my Concorde experience, the clarity of our 150 mb air made these contrasts clearer than usual, and the circular shape ahead had risen quite high and plenty of stars were visible inside it so I looked behind, at the limit of my side window, to check that the sun had set. It must have done, I thought, but the scene behind was a sensory shock. The sun had just reached the lowered horizon behind. Familiar with the reverse sunrise when travelling the other way, and normally viewed through the visor and clip-on sunshades, the exploding flashbulb was a big surprise, and not something you could look at for long – if at all. Astronauts are very familiar with this view of an even brighter sun in a black sky, in their case, but although our 20 kms altitude was not even one fifth of a lowest acceptable shuttle height I could tell that looking at this whiter than white object is not a good idea up here – without Blues Brothers shades.

CHAPTER 38

1991: NEW PROJECTS, A VARIETY OF EVENTS

Louisa Knapp

On March 1st 1991 I made my first flight with Louisa Knapp in her Extra 300. I first came across, but hardly met, Louisa at an airshow some time before. She looked perky and business-like in her Richard Goode flying suit, and I discovered she was a part of his organization; doing what I could not make out, except that I came away with the impression that, apart from helping out, she was going to take part in airshows. Then a few days later I had a phone call – or was it a letter? – from her father, asking if I would get her started in whatever was needed in terms of experience and qualification. He explained that she had learned aerobatics at Pompano with Randy Gagne, and had been bought the Extra 300 'to grow into'. I didn't know what to expect, and had no illusions about the responsibility that went with this job. Why me, I thought, privately acknowledging that I would have considered the options carefully in his position, and made discreetly judged enquiries. I accepted, and Louisa, her Extra and myself met at Wycombe Air Park to establish a plan and a starting point. We went for a flight in the Extra. She flew it very well. I was impressed – and relieved.

Louisa had learned a lot in Florida. During her travels she'd found her way to this state and got a job looking after the parrots at Parrot Jungle, and teaching them their routines (aerobatics, perhaps?), then came the interest in aerobatic flying, the journeys to Pompano Beach and the aerobatic lessons in the Pitts S2B. I have no idea, even now, of what other flying experience she had, apart from the private licence at Bourne with the Cessna 150. What had happened since then, except for the Pitts dual flying, I do not know. However, this first meeting and the Extra flight indicated that Louisa was a well-organised owner, manager and very competent pilot. I use the word manager because ownership and care of a 300 HP aerobatic aircraft, capable of respectable world championship performance, requires these skills. An Extra 300 is not a beginner's machine, but bearing in mind the Extra's viceless nature and relatively easy takeoff and landing behavior, it was a good choice, if the price is not an issue.

I was not presented with a fixed agenda or goals, but a CAA Display Authorisation would be the only obvious paper requirement. However I was firmly of the opinion that some competition achievement would be a good idea as well, especially if a state-of-the-art competition machine were to be displayed, so I decided on an intermediate contest as a first experience project. Louisa's current aerobatic handling skills were more than adequate for this level, but actually performing a set programme in front of a critical audience tests the ability to keep the driving and thinking going at the same time, in a revealing way that cannot be simulated.

The Kernow Trophy at Bodmin, April 20th, was what we had in mind. Arranging competition practice sites had always been a problem in crowded, sensitive and proprietorial Britain. I did hear that the residents of Nutfield village, bordering the Tiger Club's Redhill airfield, used to complain about the noise of the Spitfires taking off in 1940. Patriotic habits die hard, but Louisa was very good at arranging agreeable airfields. Her engaging personality and confident manner seemed to pay dividends, especially with the military, and I see we went to both Swanton Morley and Netheravon to practise.

On April 20 1991 we flew to Bodmin for the Kernow contest. There were to be two programmes flown, known and unknown. Well-flown aerobatics are likely to be well scored if the judges can easily see a well-positioned performance, right in front of them. Not-so-good flying might benefit a little if it is high and far away, but the quality would not be in question here, I hoped. Provided she flew as well as usual I knew Louisa would do well, and the performance of the Extra was such that a desperate, propeller-howling dive-in prior to starting was quite unnecessary for the easy manoeuvres; rather undignified too. 300 HP would be more than enough for a straight and level entry – at the bottom of the box. Like a proper coach (something of a luxury outside international team circles – rare in Britain) I ran through the suggested positioning tactics over this unfamiliar airfield, and also advised a bold gamesmanship ploy worthy of Williams and the opening fencing foul that would both surprise and privately impress with its audacity.

A thousand feet was the minimum height for intermediate level, so I suggested that Louisa should motor in confidently in level flight at 800ft for the opening pull up to the vertical. 800ft does not look much different from 1000, and beginners do not do this sort of thing. Of course she flew this whole first sequence accurately and confidently – easily the best – and when the results came out guess what? She was not first. I was a little surprised, but understood perfectly. I did overhear one judge's assistant mention that she did think that Louisa might have been low, but quality of the flying is the decider when it comes to calling low, and nobody did. All the other flights had started much higher, and nobody starts at bottom limit from straight and level. The scores had nothing to do with height. But these are not seasoned and disinterested international judges, and this is the personable and chatty blonde's first competition. No one gets high marks on their first try; 'we don't know what to expect. If I score what I see I might be wrong; the odd man out,' is the concern of the uncertain.

'Don't worry about the scores. It always happens to a complete unknown,' I said, and we worked through the unknown sequence, walking through the positioning over an imaginary airfield on the car park. The low start was not repeated, but Louisa's flying was equally good, especially so for an unrehearsed performance, usually with some scrappy moments. It wasn't luck, and the second set of marks were realistic. Did the judges compensate for their indecisive miserly initial scoring? Possibly, but the confident and audacious start had paid off: she really was good, and won the trophy easily. Unfair to the others? Not really; you have to start somewhere. But it was a fun day out, and I rather enjoyed the Svengali experience, though it wasn't really like that. Randy had done 99% of the work.

The next milestone would be the display authorisation. There are some essential features of this test, observed from the ground by the authorising official. Give the impression that you know what you're doing, don't fall out of anything, get low or lose control of the positioning. Louisa put together a suitable sequence of competition type manoeuvres, with a couple of additional dynamic auto rotational figures (flick roll/tumbling things), at a more than safe height – and reliably repeatable. Then, for an element of variety – often not well, if at all, done by competition-only pilots – I suggested she wind down the engine revs and change the noise (less angry bee) and style completely; some elegant loopy and swoopy, traditional coordinated 'military style' manoeuvring. Who knows, somebody might invite her to fly their Spitfire.

A few weeks after the Kernow Trophy triumph we flew to Duxford to meet Brian Smith, my Ace Flying School student, also the examiner. Louisa did her routine and we watched. She passed, and listened to his advice, partly based on his heavy metal experience, no doubt. The first show came soon after – not an easy one because it was not an airfield event. This would be a town fete, county show or something similar near Farnham, I think. First you have to find the place without making it too obvious, and be sure of the permitted performance zone, plus your real height above the ground. Then there's the wind to assess before you start, plus the correct time slot; all without informed contact from below. It is a totally self-contained performance, and I had no doubt that a certain CAA official would be sure to be there, rumpled mac with knotted belt and folded copy of the *Aldershot Advertiser*, but with an eagle eye watching carefully for any infringement of the published conditions. I think it went well – I was not there – and had asked Louisa to make a small detour on the way home to overfly the annual Concorde cricket match at the remote Berkshire village of Aldworth – already mentioned as the source of the first Concorde charter – to make a couple of manoeuvres overhead before proceeding to base. This Bell Inn event was a front for a splendid families-included picnic that only works for a close-knit community. I wasn't there either, but heard that Louisa's day had been a success, and to the best of my knowledge there was no official feedback. My display input was finished.

Abbeyshrule

Three days later we went to Abbeyshrule, in the centre of Ireland, where Louisa had arranged to continue with competition practice. This was a good place to fly – a quiet airfield surrounded by moorland and pasture, 15 miles from the nearest town. Much of the *Blue Max* film had been made west of Dublin in 1966, and Sammy Bruton, then of Weston, had been instrumental in looking after the gaggle of assorted aircraft, mostly replicas or biplanes in disguise. He now ran his family maintenance business at Abbeyshrule. It was a family affair, with emphasis on saving aircraft parts that might be useful, and inside the hangar the walls, ceiling and most of the floor were occupied by a spotter's Mastermind specialist subject cornucopia. Small spaces were made, as required, for on-going floor work, and bargain second-hand imports from America could be assembled outside, alongside their arrival crate. This was a place of positive, helpful energy, ready to improvise at a moment's notice.

Leaning against the wall were some pieces of a written-off Mooney; they might come in useful one day. A visitor's aircraft, it had landed somewhat hot, run off the end of the runway, across the grass and into the Inny river, just before it runs under the stone viaduct of the historic canal. Mrs Bruton left the office to help Sammy and sons retrieve the occupants and machine, then back to work and cooking the dinner. All in a day's work? The locals told us no, things like this were unusual, life proceeds in an orderly fashion like anywhere else, they said. But after a few days here – sometimes flying but mostly watching the Extra respectively, or finding other things to do when it rained – I got the impression that little things did occur, and were dealt with as an accepted part of a rural and pragmatic way of life that long predated William of Normandy.

For instance, a couple of days after our arrival a recently-licensed pilot took the Rallye for a local flight and did not return, and the news quickly came that he had collected a telephone wire about the propeller and nose leg, and forced landed in the field by his house. When the Rallye returned by flatbed farm trailer the effects of the wire and the hasty landing were clear to see, but easily repaired – there's a propeller and nose leg hiding somewhere in the hangar. Then there was the example of Irish secondary radar. We were sitting in the hut where the radio lived. This was not manned on a permanent basis, but the radio was on and, though the weather was not aerobatible, the solid stratus and light drizzle would have been acceptable for quality Bradshaw cross countrying, but nothing less.

Out of the silent ether came a radio call addressed to us; unexpected – a British-registered aircraft on its way to us (international flight?) Louisa, sympathetic by nature and always keen to help, took the initiative and answered. It was a Christen Eagle from the North, requesting navigational assistance. There was a half-million topo map on the table, our total equipment. She asked the logical questions: 'When and where did you start from? Heading?' etc. The answers were not particularly helpful, and 'What can you see?' was answered by 'A lake, there's another lake, there are lots of small lakes everywhere.' No distinguishing features. This is a common problem in some flying schools. This pilot/navigator only feels reassured if he can put a name to a ground feature, like driving the country by the names on motorway signs or, even better, turnoff numbers. This flying technique soon ignores distance, time, mountain ranges, giant river crossings – and heading – and searches this way and that for a likely looking place that may have a familiar name. The logic is irretrievably lost.

Our map showed a wide area of small lakes, some distance to our north – no names. 'Just steer south', advised Louisa, 'and tell us when you see something useful.'

We are not locals, and only have the map. This situation has the potential for turning into quite a complicated game, and we are joined by a local flyer who also sits at the spread-out map. The best tactic, we decide, is to use the east/west running 18th century canal, which passes us on its way between the Shannon and Dublin, but which direction to follow, if they spot it? A radar return is received: 'We're passing a town with a big grey church with a green roof.' Sounds promising, but our local says there are three towns with big churches and green roofs. These were the county towns of Athlone, Longford and Mullingar. They make an equilateral triangle, 40 km sides, and we are exactly in the centre. It all worked out in the end, and the Eagle arrived, one occupant emerging on crutches and a leg in plaster. Irrelevant, perhaps, but not unusual in this land of small but frequent surprises.

Civil Aviation Authority Operations Inspectorate

In 1991 our Concorde ops inspector, John Oliver, was soon to retire. He had trained on the Concorde in the initial manufacturer's course, 15 years before, and had already joined the Ministry of Aviation after a varied military career, dating from the times when a quick briefing from a colleague and a couple of speeds to remember might constitute a conversion. A couple of days after my first flight with Louisa in March, John Oliver and I (plus training F/E) went to Prestwick for some (Concorde) circuits, then back to London after refuelling. I imagine John had some unused Concorde time to use up before he left the now CAA, and this was a chance. The total flying time for G-BOAC was three hours, including the hour on the circuit doing this and that – all of this and that, in fact. Was it fun? Of course – what are expensive aeroplanes for? Especially if this goes with the job.

Around the same time James Black decided that his Avia Special company should use his CAP10 for proper aerobatic joy rides for the public, not just cost share lessons for licensed pilots. My type rating examiner qualification (courtesy BA) would be useful – I could be the necessary training manager. Charging off-the-street passengers for a ride in a light aircraft has to be covered by something legally acceptable. In essence, handing over a pound, even 'buy you a drink', constitutes flying for hire and reward – something taken seriously by reputable governments on behalf of the world's unsuspecting citizens. Much UK light aircraft joy ride business is covered by the 'trial lesson' scam.

The word 'scam' will doubtless raise howls of protest from its worthy protagonists, but we're now entering the complex world of understanding, intent, meaning, and so on; that which can be argued in a court of law if necessary; certainly in a legal professional's office (aka chambers if the money's right). In reality, this trial lesson business works and is a relatively harmless accommodation to suit the aspirations of the simple citizen. It requires two things, apart from the suitable aeroplane and site: the pilot must have an instructor's rating (a good thing) and an assumption that the passenger has expressed curiosity about learning to fly. My case rests. Without the instructor's rating and the passenger's tacit intentions, the next step up is a giant leap for mankind.

The true hire and reward requirements are the same for British Airways as for James and the little wooden two-seat CAP10. The relevant books are thick and heavy, assembled over nearly a century – whether applied to a couple of warriors and their London to Paris biplane, or the modern monster airline and all it does – in great detail. The task of compiling your own operations manual – a complete story of everything – is a daunting prospect. Fortunately we had a good friend who actually had done this for his two-seat Pitts; it was his day job, after all. For a suitable consideration we borrowed the book and changed the words, graphs and numbers where necessary. It took a little time, but made the impossible possible. What are friends for? Thanks Alan.

The next stage was the official approval of the Avia Special CAP10B Operations Manual. I was summoned to the Civil Aviation Authority at Gatwick to discuss our submission. I feared the worst. Things to change, things wrong with it, who knows? This whole process could take a long time: more work, more visits. But it wasn't like that at all. I met our man in his office. The book was on the table. He told me it was OK. 'Let's go and have lunch.' Today the cafeteria had chicken curry – with poppadoms (not unlike the excellent BA Compass Centre Tandoori Tearooms). We carried our trays to a table and chatted about this and that. What's the Concorde like? He told me his current ops inspecting field was a twin turbo-prop, as well as the small aeroplanes; he had been a self-improver. Nothing wrong with that, and after more inconsequential chat and a coffee we returned to the office. That was it then, but before we said our goodbyes he told me about John Oliver's pending retirement, and that he had his eye on this job. I could say little other than good luck, hope you get it. Was there the hope of 'I'll put a word in'? It wouldn't have worked anyway. I've an airline pilot's rough idea about the seriousness with which this sort of responsibility (and people-handling diplomacy) is regarded in official circles, even if exact previous experience is not available.

In the real world, we got Gwyn Williams. A quiet, considerate, diplomatic examiner and agreeable flying companion, now that our CAA representative made periodic route flights with us as a pilot. It is often the way with the right people. You could not possibly tell their history from routine acquaintance. I was astonished one day when Gwyn told me that he had flown the McDonnell Voodoo during a Canadian posting. Unlike Harrier tradition, he would not have told me unless I had asked. The job sounded fascinating and exciting, especially so. A head-on supersonic attack against a flock of opposing bombers, loose off a nuclear missile (on loan from the US) towards their midst, and make a (giant) half-Cuban to go back the other way, hoping to put enough distance between yourself and the effects of the bang when the nuke went off. Maybe the considerable altitude and thin air initially gained in the looping part would have softened the blow. (Gwyn has since corrected this to roll and pull in the general downward direction – whatever.) Clearly a man of some experience anyway. I googled up a photo of him leading a formation flypast of nine of these impressive aircraft, a limey in charge of Canadians flying heavy-duty American aircraft. Like the Hunter maestro I mentioned from the 1967 German beer tent, you would never guess.

CAA test pilot Jock Reid (ex Boscombe Down staff) was a Concorde conversion course member in 1989, and similarly flew as captain or co-pilot on route flights. During his military career Jock flew the Lightning, was dragged off to be an instructor and then became a test pilot, also teaching others how to do it at Boscombe Down. The Concorde is not a big Lightning (or a complex Voodoo), but readers may notice some common operating features, probably taken into account by the Authority when making appointments. But there's more to the sharp end of setting standards than that. I would happily have sent Jock and Gwyn solo as the real Concorde captain without prior employment in our company, or claims of airline experience. Perhaps it's time to run the Greek academic joke again: What's old so-and-so doing? Don't know – he's either dead, teaching somewhere, or examining'. It's not always true.

A clash of cultures, without the clash:

The Guild of Air Pilots and Air Navigators have a garden party at an aerial event every summer, and In June 1991, well-known Concorde pilot and long-term Guild member John Hutchinson asked if I would arrange and carry out a flypast at this 1991 event at North Weald – in company with the last flying Vulcan XH558. That was the complete brief. Sometimes it's nice to organise something on your own. I've written up an account elsewhere, but as a unique experience (no one else, ever etc.) it deserves a mention in this story-behind-the-logbooks.

First I went to meet the Vulcan pilot, David Thomas (Sqn Ldr) at Scampton where he was on the staff of the Central Flying School – in between formation practices with three sweating prospective instructors. I explained my plan – pick him up over Honington, then we would proceed together overhead Stansted to the venue, followed by a break and go our separate ways. What speed would he like? '200kts, no faster – fatigue life'. Slow for us, but possible. Join up? 'You fly a 30-degree banked circle and I will join you, on your left because I will sit in the co-pilot's seat – throttles in the left hand.' Positions? 'Not a problem. I'll try them out on the way. I'm quite happy with all of this; now I have some more training to do – one of my staff will give you a ride in a Tucano.' So far so good.

This arrangement, between the pilots only, had been SAS (short and sweet), and my next move was to write to Barry Tempest, of Barnstormers and CAA display authorisation fame. The 'no free Concorde shows' policy was unchanged, so appearances at air displays had always been an addition to a charter flight, paid for by the passengers, who remained entitled to the provisions of the pay-for-a-flight bible – the Air Operator's Certificate part of the Air Navigation Order. On a personal basis I was happy to take part in Concorde airshow flights, and, under the right circumstances, regarded the real risk factor as no different from those inherent in some aspects of normal Concorde long range flight, but civilian participation in airshows normally required a number of conditions to be met in each case, including the pilot's display authorisation, which includes type of aircraft, type of manoeuvres, minimum height etc. Some things in life are conveniently done on the nod, so long as nothing amiss happens and nobody gets hurt.

This was the case with Concorde appearances – theoretically just part of a normal public transport flight which happens to be seen by an assemblage of people. Like the trial lesson business, a very grey area, in my view, if one wants to be pedantic, but normally organised and done with no special agreements or conditions. But this sedate flypast would be different; it would involve proper, if easy, formation. To say nothing, and just do it, would probably not have worked. Word would unquestionably have got around, and a hornet's nest of enquiries provoked. Big aircraft, with no display authorisation, was not Barry's field, exactly, but I estimated that he would appreciate the recognition, and bat on my behalf. Two days later John Oliver phoned me and asked me what I planned; I explained the detail of what I had arranged with Dave Thomas. 'I'm completely happy with everything you've told me,' John said. 'Write it down, give yourself some weather limits and send it to me.' This was good news, and I felt that all would be plain sailing from here.

A couple of days later Peter Horton, now Concorde fleet manager, called and told me there had been a restriction placed on the spacing: no closer than 100 metres. This was a retrograde step in a number of ways, but a clear Concorde wingspan (25 metres) between wingtip tracks and 100 meters could be within the same estimation ballpark. Then, with two days to go, inflation had really started to take effect and the requirement for 300 metres came through, from somewhere in the Authority. This was now a huge compromise between the 'proper formation or not at all' principle and the few miles separation generally accepted for public transport near airports. Clearly this was intended to triple the contribution to flight safety – separation numbers proportional to office floor levels – but an attempt to guess 300 metres could look more like a dogfight, or the mistimed arrival of separate acts. The anticipated line abreast, equal status appearance of these two, distantly related but visually arresting large deltas would not happen. I telephoned the Squadron Leader and told him the news, and the conditions. However I said we would do the whole thing as originally planned, except that after passing Stansted I would call him out to his judgment of the required spacing. Then after passing overhead the site would call him back up, start to pull up as he drew abeam then call the break. 'OK' he said.

June 23rd was the day. The bargain subsonic-only charter was offered to the Vulcan supporters' club, and seats were also eagerly snapped up by Scampton and Waddington staff and families. Louisa came along on the jump seat, an informed extra pair of eyes, and a jolly champagne Saturday outing atmosphere prevailed in the cabin as we made our way to Honington, descended to 1500 feet and slowed to 200kts as we approached the closed airfield. The weather was not good: overcast, light drizzle on and off with wisps of lower cloud, but it was not bumpy, and the Vulcan was there, a camouflaged shape banking towards us against the dull green and brown fields below. I set up my turn to the right, he slid underneath then out and up on the left as I rolled out on track to Stansted.

Except for co-pilot Tony Yule, this was an unaccustomed view of a Vulcan to an outsider; for most of our passengers also. The news came up that some of them thought it looked very big, and the crew were waving at them. Our

PR man, training engineer Ian (Mc)Smith, told them that the little Concorde windows have a magnifying effect; and there was something rather stately and splendid as we proceeded along together, the Concorde distinctly nose up and shaking gently, while the green and grey shape alongside cruised smoothly through the scud, vapour streaming back from its airbrakes. Stansted told us we made a magnificent sight as we passed overhead, and as North Weald approached I told the Vulcan to move out to the required spacing. Once having passed the Guild marquee we raised our noses and peeled off with lots of noise, ourselves to the right, afterburner flames disappearing smartly into cloud, the Vulcan to the left and into some of its routine over North Weald.

I heard later that garden party opinion had decided that the weather must surely be too bad and the flyover would not occur. Of course it was entirely for their benefit, but clearly little communication had been thought of. Granted that conversation level would have been high in the tent, eight Olympus engines approaching (on time) must have given some warning, and members who were not preoccupied with bonding and networking inside thought the sight highly evocative, as, I hope, did the spectators who remained at the field. Unfortunately I have no knowledge of a photograph in existence, nor does John Hutchinson.

There was more communication from the Authority, so someone didn't assume the show was off; a letter to our office asking whether I considered the aircraft spacing and the weather to have accorded with the laid-down conditions. I replied that my wingman, an experienced professional formation teacher, no less, had been well briefed by myself and was well aware of the required spacing; I was the leader, and therefore had no direct control of where he chose to put his machine. The actual weather at Stansted at the time of the flypast was quoted. It coincided with my limits. The historic and unrepeatable event had turned out to be an example of an exemplary stealth mission, it seems. But thanks all round anyway.

Admiral Topgun: a flying visit to the US Navy, the work of the adj

Our 1991 guest speaker at the Concorde Dining Society annual dinner in March was Vice Admiral Jack Ready (Stinger), currently commander of the Atlantic Fleet, US Naval Air Force – that's one half of the American carrier fleet. You can see his Stinger mug on the Commander Air's desk in Topgun, the movie ('Goddammit! Launch Maverick and Iceman…') The idea had been to invite someone with a special and interesting flying background – an early astronaut, a Blackbird crew member who'd ejected, the Russian general who'd ordered the Korean Air shootdown, and so on. How did we get them?

Tony Yule became a self-volunteered sort of PR and social secretary for the Concorde fleet, hence the adjutant title, and he routinely set out on his networking tour of the streets of Manhattan within 20 minutes of first entering his hotel room. I never joined him, but others reported the day as rigorous; like a beginner's job in sales. Tony once came across a large and rather splendid pharmacy in the mid-town fashionable shopping area, and was amazed to see an S1 Pitts special aeroplane hanging from the ceiling. He went in to enquire, and discovered it belonged to the successful apothecary himself – also a flying enthusiast (or enthusiast for flying people). Americans were our greatest Concorde fans – no doubt about it – and the mention of close connection with a Concorde guaranteed free-flowing conversation. Jack Ready was an acquaintance of this magic potion purveyor, and it was Jack's reputed wide-ranging schoolboy's obsession with flying of all kinds (another 15-year-old Biggles really) which qualified him for the after-dinner job. I think the local connection might have been Jack's current membership of a part-time 5 Harvard formation sky-writing team, in between carrier fleet management. Not quite worthy of another trigger warning is a brief explanation that these sky-writing aircraft hold line abreast formation and the words are created by computer-controlled smoke generators, by radio link of course. It's like a printer.

Guest speakers from North America were offered a Concorde ride each way, and London accommodation etc. It was arranged for me, the adj and Dave MacDonald to do the collecting flight, and I sent the text of my handling book, which was well received. In London Mrs Ready and the admiral's secretary had seats for *Miss Saigon,* and enjoyed the show, I believe, though what memories of Nam days were rekindled I don't know.

Following the dinner and return flight to the USA the upshot was that we three plus Mrs Yule were invited for a week at the admiral's house in Norfolk VA, with an aircraft carrier visit. Very few outsiders get this experience and I wrote about it for the Pilots' Union ***Log*** and ***Pilot*** magazine. On land we played around with the simulators, and went to the test pilots' school at Patuxent River for lunch and to give a Concorde talk to the students – Jack felt that they should take an interest in efficient supersonic cruise as a future military necessity. Some were interested and others feigned pointed disinterest or boredom. They had many other things on their mind, no doubt, but this Norfolk visit, and other flights and conversations, gave some insight into the stresses and tensions that modern social politics can bring into the lives of those with responsibility for national security, balanced against the safety of many individuals. The safety of passengers in a single airliner is one thing, but Jack's job was very different.

Jack was the same age as me, and was about to 'take' early retirement – early 50s. It is wrong for someone with no military experience to express opinions about military life and the degree to which its demands conflict with a media-driven outside world of post nuclear (?) comfortable entitlement and expectation; those inside are forbidden from doing so, yet are expected to present an image of exemplary behaviour, as assessed from the cosy civilian terms of reference. But it is we content, democratic and increasingly liberal civilians who expect intelligent and able people to live a sometimes very unpleasant life on our behalf, and do very unpleasant things to other people, if required – behind a screen of unknowing, of course. Do we really expect the strains not to show, especially if peacetime social advancement policies create extra tensions?

Our Norfolk visit occurred shortly after the notorious Tailhook affair. My Going to Sea (See) article about the carrier visit concerned itself solely with the fun and challenge of flying (wearing my 15-year-old Biggles hat), and did not reflect my take on the underlying concerns about who gets to take part. One clear principle I took away from the US Navy is a determination to be as good as possible as a credible fighting force – this is the most successful (and cheapest in the long run) way of avoiding conflict, bearing in mind that the last thing you want to do is to get into a nuclear-throwing fight. Recent equal opportunity initiatives have given increased selection consideration to an individual's desire to join, contrary to the traditional opinion of many who have experience of the real job. Who's right?

Jack Ready's Concorde dinner talk concentrated on his command heyday, the first Gulf War. He had told us nothing about his early 'just a kid from Boston' navy beginner days, Vietnam, getting checked out as a carrier captain, commanding the Top Gun school, and the test pilot's school – or the current tensions between politically correct Washington and Navy tradition. At the conclusion of one evening's conversation in the Atlantic air force commander's splendid *Gone With The Wind* transported house in Norfolk, he asked me a final question: did I think it was a good idea to have women on an aircraft carrier? We'd already discussed my experience of very talented lady aerobatic pilots from various nations (skill levels far in excess of the required airline standard), but there's more behind this question than technical ability. I believe that there is a fundamental hard-wired difference in male and female response to physical risk (and many females would agree). I had a simple answer: do you want the best fighting force?

CHAPTER 39

AEROBATICS IN RUSSIA

At Yverdon in 1990 Kazum Nazhmudinov had said 'Flying the Sukhoi? – Moscow.' So in July 1991 I spent 10 days at Borki, the national squad's training airfield about 100 kms north, in the woods and fields outside Dubna, a town created in the 1940s to house a major nuclear research centre. Building the original proton accelerator started in 1946 and was completed in 1949 – big bang catchup, perhaps, or was it domestic energy? The airfield had been a single long runway military defence base is my guess: one accommodation block, no hangars, but a storage and workshop area, now with no signs of life. Aircraft, now sporting, lived outside, alongside the taxiway, and maintenance was also carried out in the open, with the grass as working surface. An old runway control van served as informal ATC, phone contact and timekeeping centre, with a couple of briefing huts as protection from the weather. Diagrams of the Yak 52 pneumatic and fuel systems decorated the walls. This airfield was a place to sleep and fly.

I got a nice room, on the third floor, opposite the floor's primitive shower and toilet. The Russian aerobatic elite had to double up in rooms half the size – some of them, anyway. Downstairs you could make yourself tea or instant coffee, and the girls (pilots) made the breakfast here at weekends. Otherwise everyone piled into the old, asthmatic and environmentally-damaging bus that took us a mile or so towards the town and a community eating centre for three meals a day. The food was good, traditional institution, with daily variety of a sort, and, like school, no choice, but for a sense of functional well-being without the distraction of indigestion or between-meal snacks (there being none) I would recommend this system, old-fashioned as it is, even though diametrically opposed to a certain capitalist religion: relentless marketing of unhelpful products to populations who cannot resist it. You sleep and work better as well (again).

On my first day I made a first flight in Yak 55 #96. then two in Sukhoi 26 #31. This was the numbering system for these sport machines; red stars and just a number. I said I'd already had three flights in a Sukhoi, but I was not the first western visitor, and maybe Kazum had learnt something from the others. It's surprising what the deluded may say about their own flying experience before they demonstrate the lie. A number of people have told me about Concorde pilots who live in their village – I must know them? Very seldom: perhaps they worked for someone else, but this was frequently unlikely.

As well as the overhead box there were three practice areas within sight of the Borki field. 'Mike taxi, Mike takeoff and Mike returning' were my own radio calls. 'Mike takeoff, area A, B, or C' were my clearances, and I've no doubt the wily trainer/manager had someone watch my cavorting in the Yak, next to the Volga, for this first checkout. With the same responsibility for state property I would also have done so, although just taxiing, take off, arrival and landing tell you most of what you need to know. The Yak 55 was friendly fun to fly; something of a physical workout, and nothing like as skittish on the ground as the Sukhoi. Able Russian aerobatic students made their first taildragger flight solo in this ultimate successor to the Yak 18 single-seater. This is not comparable to a training first solo, and, assuming a good enough standard reached in the Yak 52 trainer, pilots first practised flapless landings in that machine, from the back seat, to get used to addressing the ground in the three-point attitude. They told me this works without problem.

One of the girls had the caravan/office job of recording takeoff and landing times in the book, to the minute, and my first day totalled approx. one hour – US$35. This is good value by our standards, and I think a visitor's payment for everything else came to about the same daily sum, maybe less. No cash was required during the all-found stay, and you got your bill in dollars when you went home. The exchange rate for Western currency was still very unrealistic and the $35 represented a lot of roubles, much needed because government support for this large Dosaaf sport flying and parachuting organisation was dwindling. Knowledge of the outside world was spreading, and an understanding of values becoming less misinformed, even than in the year before when there seemed to be widespread belief that our monumental salaries (by informal exchange rates) represented pocket money. The notion that wicked Westerners had to pay for their houses or accommodation, heating, school fees and all other costs of living was not believed. But the institutional propaganda had not all been true.

In August 1990, at the end of the world aerobatics (after the MiG 29s, and a beautifully smooth Red Arrows routine led by Tim Miller – it looked too easy!), sponsors Breitling had presented all the various trophy winners with a Breitling watch – entry level quartz it has to be said, although nice ones – at a few hundred pounds a throw equivalent to a year's pay for some Russian pilots, so I heard. Several fancied the money instead, and Randy Gagne quickly set up a backyard trading system to help them out. He had acquired enough pidgin Ruski-yazook minus grammar during his spell at Borki to construct an instant market, and scouted around for investors with dollars or suitably recognised currency, but collecting the cash to settle the initial trade was a first priority because the original watch owners would be going home tomorrow.

The days went by in a predictable way at Borki – three on, then a day off. This plan rolled along without concern for the weather or its forecast. In good weather you flew, or walked in the woods to gather berries to make jam on the day off. Bad weather precluded either of these pursuits, and it was only a few of the girls who picked the woodland fruits and made the jam anyway: swimming in the Volga between the bulrushes was another possibility. Slow and steady is a good way to train for difficult things, and, in the old days with only one world championship every two years, there seemed to be plenty of time to prepare a ten-person team (five men, five women) to demonstrate core Soviet sporting supremacy. The Borki sessions were arranged on a regular basis: let's say two weeks every month or so. Some team members taught aerobatics at various schools, and others came and went as suited their other job. For a visitor however, life consisted of quiet nights, a lack of distraction and for the three days out of four flying, everything taken care of: get in, fly, get out, walk away. The simple life.

John (Colonel John) Morrisey from America had already been to Borki with his son, and I read what he wrote about the experience. It had taken him straight back to his air force days, specifically his time in Vietnam a quarter century ago, flying the hefty single seat F-105 Thunderchief. For him Borki was a distinctly nostalgic reminder of a lifestyle, courtesy of the opposing empire's 'sport' air force.

There were a few Antonov 2s at Borki, used to lift the many young people who enjoyed state-supported parachuting – in between aerobatic box sessions. I was due to accompany James Black on an Antonov course in the Czech Republic the very next week, so an advance look-see flight might be helpful. Kazum arranged it: same flying rate; 'You can have a lesson with Vladimir,' or Russian words to that effect. I climbed aboard for a parachute dropping flight before my lesson. Vladimir sat in the right-hand seat. In the captain's seat was his teenage son, learning, clearly: at no extra cost to anyone. Well, why not? Vladimir knew what he was doing, and Soviet property belongs to the people. This works well so long as damage is not done, state equipment is not used for an unworthy purpose, and the people's law is not brought into play.

I stand in the doorway between the pilots and watch how they do it. We taxi across the field to the parachuting centre and a bunch of late teens and young twenty-somethings troop out. Apart from the parachutes on their backs they do not look like parachutists – no special suits, fancy high-speed relative work helmets; any helmets at all? Not sure. Just a bunch of assorted young '90s people who happen to have picked up a parachute, one might assume. They file aboard and we proceed out to the grass to take off. Where's the jumpmaster? Which one of these kids is the jumpmaster? There isn't one. There's also no evidence of static lines, so this appears to be jump number-building for self-sufficient plain round canopy jumpers.

We take off, climb up around the field and cruise generally overhead, the kid directed by dad in the right-hand seat. Vladimir must be jumpmaster/spotter as well as base training captain. He presses the green light button and our passengers pile out of the doorway. Job done. We then descend and do a couple of training circuits, which the lad manages quite well, although he has trouble remembering to go to fully fine on finals. Did Vladimir write 'Good progress for experience, should be good next detail?' Probably not. 'Excellent progress; my son will make a valuable addition to the fleet' more likely – if at all!

What fun, and it was. When we taxied in to our aerobatic north side I was intrigued to see a number of our passengers variously walking out of the trees with their bundled rigs. They usually landed on the airfield grass. Though interspersed with fields, Russia is mostly forest, but here we are talking about spindly trees about fifteen feet high. All in a day's jumping it seemed. Then it was my turn. Get it going, taxi out, take off and fly round for a couple of circuits, taxi in, switch it off. 25 minutes. I see that I then did two 15-minute blasts in Sukhoi #24. Almost an hour for the day. Let's say $30; good value.

Expensive coffee

A few days later it was time to go to Moscow to catch British Airways home. Nicolai Timofeev drove me to the airport in his Russian-built Fiat 1100 pride and joy, and was able to come through the passport check to airside with me. I thought it was my turn to buy us a coffee – with a couple of dollars (foreign currency only). The effect of such a trivial demonstration of different values to a national who lived in the rouble and kopek world, but had been to Britain and Switzerland as a team member (no cash required), was striking. The same cup of coffee as served landside suddenly became the equivalent of a priceless Fabergé treasure. A cup of coffee kind of drives the point home. He had already told me of a friend who now 'owned' a titanium factory. 'He's asked me to tell visitors that they will make anything in titanium for the price of aluminium.' I did hear from elsewhere that some Swiss climbers sent a steel piton to copy with the request for a few bucketsful. The bag on the belt became much lighter to carry, and you don't always take the pitons home.

Timofeev also told me about something closer to home. A particular piece of new Russian aviation machinery currently selling for, shall we say, two hundred export dollars, could be bought by a Russian for the rouble equivalent of 12 dollars – a sixteen and two-thirds factor. If we reverse engineer this in emerging Soviet-into-capitalist changeover bizniz terms, my $35 an hour Sukhoi flying looked more like $584 to them. This also had put my modest all-inclusive daily rate into a new perspective, and explained Randy's Breitling pop-up stall at Yverdon.

This was not the only reason why I was well looked after at Borki. The stay there indicated inherent qualities of consideration for others that are a feature of societies with a history of communal survival under reduced circumstances. This observation is about Russians, not politics, and the quiet, firm but fair style of Kazum's management has more to do with post WW2 reconstruction of national identity (and the importance of a strong air force) than the 1917 revolution per se. He did, however, take to pulling rank and bending the breakfast rules on my behalf. Eggs were not everyday things. One morning in the people's cafeteria queue he asked if I would like one, being now familiar with American visitors and their expectations, perhaps. I expected him to shovel one on to my plate, but there weren't any. A word to the dinner ladies produced one almost immediately. 'What about the others?' I said, not wishing to be singled out; after all, some of them were bigger and stronger than me, and certainly worked harder at their aerobatics. Shrugs and rueful grins were answer enough.

The following April (1992) I went back for a week. In the previous summer Louisa had made a flight In Richard Goode's Sukhoi at White Waltham. She returned with a wobbly smile and just said 'Wow!' No further comment. I thought she would enjoy a session in Russia and set about arranging the visas. She would certainly be popular with the team, well looked after and encouraged sympathetically but effectively by these able and inclusive people. But with a few weeks to go she told me she had decided not to go. Was it the James Bond depiction of Rosa Klebb management style, or the overall impression of severity and harshness spread by propaganda and film industries? The reality of life for a visitor without a Walther PPK under the jacket could not have been more different, but she stayed at home with her familiar Extra. As an amateur sporting tourist, of course, I cannot make a more comprehensive assessment of post-Soviet life, but being a tourist with connections helps.

During my first visit to Borki I had met Sergei Rakhmanin. At a prior world championships when the Russians had done well, as usual, and were a subject of interest, one of them said 'there's someone even better than us, but he's not allowed to come abroad.' This was Rakhmanin, but I don't know the reason. Well-educated, with perfect English, his pragmatic Sukhoi advice was useful, and he and Timofeev had a ferrying job to Leningrad (St Petersburg) to arrange. Would I like to take a Yak 52? Why not? I think I could manage the cross country, especially with someone else to follow. But then they thought better of it. Timofeev told me about a mystery problem he had recently experienced with this type during a normal instructional flight: it would not recover from a simple spin. Eventually it did, but he cannot say what achieved this. None of the obvious questions had answers and there was some kind of restriction in place. Letting a foreign visitor fly one might have caused trouble so my ferry didn't come off.

On this second Borki visit I did have a Yak 52 flight with Viktor Smolin. Viktor, sitting in the back, now weighed a good bit more than me, and this did affect the manoeuvring at high speed (some care required not to exceed +6g) but this had not applied to Timofeev, who was strong but wiry, and sat in the back anyway – and was very experienced at spinning. An American Cessna on a round-the-world trip turned up for a nightstop. Viktor used their HF radio to call up a friend currently in the Mir space station – entertaining, anyway.

This second visit had more working content, and the dreaded clearance 'Mike takeoff; box,' began. During the 1991 messing about in the practice areas, coming to some sort of arrangement with the Sukhoi, I'd decided it was time to practise something representative and chose Elena Klimovich's free sequence. I liked the look of this one because it followed my own conservative policy – the least physically punishing and most reliably achievable way to put together 700 difficulty points: minimum wow factor. I asked her if she minded. 'Not at all, I'm very pleased if someone flies my sequence' she said. After practising parts of it I asked her about one place requiring a push-out from a vertical downline which had contained some rolling activity. Within reason a general consistency of radii is preferable during a sequence, and this place could not be an exception. I asked her how much negative g she pushed here. She was too experienced an instructor to tell me, but asked what I thought. I ventured our official – and my personal – negative g limit of the 1970s, and added one, maybe two: 5, 6, perhaps, I suggested. She smiled sympathetically, not dismissive exactly, but said nothing: just a what-planet-are-you-on look. I knew this particular corner would stay a large and leisurely airline pilot's version.

But it was not all stay-in-your-own-league. 'Is gooood: you should compete' a couple of the girls said encouragingly, in that cooing mumsyspeak common to the languages of many European females. One day I was asked to join Kazum and his permanent coach as a judge in a judged practice competition session; all present and future maestros flying the current compulsory programme. The results were eagerly seized upon by some of the newer members, who may have suspected discriminatory try-harder assessments (and dare I say a touch of gender preference) – just a bit? Kazum had been interested in the international criticism of Russian competition spin entry technique. For years they had adopted the convenient policy of cranking into the spin before the speed had reached the minimum required by the rules. This ploy saves distance and reduces the risk of a touchline infringement, and is routinely defended by a standard 'aircraft characteristics' defence, but my first Sukhoi flight in Oklahoma revealed otherwise. One evening, soon after, a lone Sukhoi returned to the field in an elegant curved approach and touchdown. It was Gagarin's brave (no doubt about it) friend of long bygone days. 'Does Kazum often fly?' I asked, as we watched this arrival. 'It is never known,' said Elena.

Then they decided it was time I had some coaching – correct some of the basics. Of course the pilot is the only one who cannot see his manoeuvres, and the system here gave real-time, brief error feedback by radio. Judging is exclusively concerned with error, so this is logical. It is not a flying lesson. We started with verticals.

'Positive' means on your front. 'Negative' means on your back. Silence indicates correct. It works. You get the idea very quickly. Round shapes are corrected by 'push, push' or 'pull, pull' as required to modify and correct the observed circular shape. Equal or well-judged line lengths can be indicated by a simple go, roll, or similar command. 'Zak!' is a popular trans-language term to indicate a point of action. (It's half of 'zig-zag'.) The instant, error-feedback system may have become universal by the time of writing, but it's much more effective than the tape-recorded commentary of olden days; or flying instruction by radio to replace tried and trusted step by step teaching. There are no shortcuts, but the best way is quickest in the long run.

Timofeev's next exercise for me was the tailslide; not in the airfield box, but alongside it, where he could see me, and I would not interrupt the national practice going on at the same time. I pointed out that I would be over the suburban blocks of flats. 'Don't worry,' he said, 'they don't complain here.'

This was not to be the reliable and rather pathetic tailslide approximation of days gone by, in the hope of scoring 6 for the correct fall-over direction. This would be the real thing – over the particle physicists' rooftops as well. To make progress in changing circumstances, a pilot sometimes has to abandon what has become tradition and habit, and learn something different. The Concorde was a good example, whether realised by its crew members or not. Traditionally the tailslide had its structural risks (flying backwards tended to be outside the design intentions) and the rotating engine and propeller assembly, however slow you could get it to go round, inevitably added an unhelpful sideways and mark-punishing package of squirrelly moments. We used to zoom vertically, cut the power, cheat a bit by tipping the nose in the desired fall-over direction at the last moment, hold everything in the middle (as best one could), and hope for an acceptable result.

The correct technique, requiring both bravery and confidence in the equipment, was easily taught and understood. It required the perfect vertical (standard, as already mastered), to start with. Close the throttle shut, continue with the perfect vertical, and watch the string on the wingtip. When it falters as the flight direction changes, full rudder and elevator in the appropriate directions. Hang on and wait. The reverse airflow on the full rudder should counteract the unhelpful effects of propeller and engine rotation, and after a pause the Sukhoi flips violently around, but straight. The longer the pause the better the result, and a blink-of-an-eye pitching through 270 degrees, ending in a brief period of parachutal, flat descent, proves that the figure was a good one. This brief pancaking float can be extended slightly with elevator, prior to the finishing vertical dive, and my last attempt scored 8.5 from Timofeev. It was unusually good: 'Perfect – you can come down now.'

Good training requires the right environment. A clear mind, simple instructions; concerns about structural risk or the academic atom smashers preparing their tea and homemade jam in the flats below all banished. Timofeev and Rakhmanin both demonstrated the clarity of understanding that defines exceptional teaching, and the ability to reduce information to the appropriate bare essentials. I'd asked Sergei how he fine-tuned his rudder position during negative looping manoeuvres. 'There are only three rudder positions,' he said, 'left, right and centre.' This is not literally true, but overthinking may be an unhelpful habit, and the good tailslide works provided you follow the instructions, start with a correct vertical, and apply the full reverse rudder at the correct instant – in the tradition of the successful triple Salchow, I would imagine.

The next essential figure was the vertical upwards negative flick roll. This is a very physical affair, and the entry requires speed (aircraft and pilot), precision and strength – all at the same instant. I'm not sure I possessed all three, and attempts were not 100% successful, the finish overshooting and leaning to the side. But I also did a stupid thing, and failed to tuck my shoulder strap ends away. At one of the forehand smashes the right-hand strap flipped up and hit my right eyeball, fair and square. Russian straps are hefty woven cotton affairs, unchanged from Yak 3 to Sukhoi 27. Some weeks later an eye surgeon friend in New York checked me out and found no damage, but logic and symptoms tell me that the muscles that flatten the lens were overstressed. The long-distance focus in this eye is not as good as it was, but the resulting short-sightedness compensates for the longer arm requirement with age. Both eyes together still work well.

The MI 2 and General Mikoyan

Further, but temporary, sensory damage occurred during this visit – on the way home. Our Kiev 1976 flying doctor and his wife Marina had got to know General Mikoyan, who had visited them in England. They said I should see him in Moscow, and Kazum managed to arrange this via military connections and the ancient arts and crafts Bakelite phone in the Borki control and timekeeping caravan. (I'd seen exactly the same model with its plaited flex in Lvov in 1976 when an official had a long and shouted conversation with Moscow to get our permission to leave. My grandmother had the same 1930s model in 1944.) After our goodbyes and his 'you are a good sportsman' compliment (I think), he also put me on the MI 2 Dubna milk run flight to Moscow. I sat next to the pilot, who had a flimsy leather helmet, but the rest of us occupants had no ear protection. During the flight I found the gearbox whine above our heads loud and excessively pervasive. Fingers in the ears helped a bit, but the others did not seem concerned. They must be used to it; and deaf, I supposed. My ears were ringing after we landed and I was met by the retired general, but all extraneous sound, including speech, was unpleasant.

We had an interesting lunch somewhere in the city. He was interested in Concorde things, and told me about the tailless MiG 21 with Concordski shaped wings. 'The pilots liked it,' he said. I think he had been in charge of the national experimental test flying programme and recounted the story of the Buran space shuttle, intended to be boosted all the way into orbit by its external rockets – no engines of its own. But a test version was powered by a couple of Sukhoi 27 engines, and could take off and fly around like an aeroplane; particularly useful for practising the dead stick landings. It was primarily a military project and the shortage of friendly and suitable worldwide landing spots might be a problem, and so the project acquired suitably shielded jet engines for atmospheric flight after reentry, to reach somewhere to land, as a function of reentry accuracy and last-minute changes of friends. All getting rather complicated.

He also told me of his enjoyment of the visit(s) he had made to John and Marina Firth in Derby. It is common knowledge that a new freedom to travel for some, and concern for the future of a disintegrating soviet system, had made the cultivation of outside acquaintances a priority for those with imagination and talent. His most abiding and favourable impression of middle English life was the local pub. The idea of an old building which attracted a cross section of the community to meet and discuss every subject under the sun of an evening, but not get as drunk as quickly as possible, he recognised as a feature of socialisation as it should be – I could tell.

This is, of course, the teenage General Mikoyan who was shot down by a squadron colleague after having collected a new Yak 1 from the factory – wrong colour, factory green instead of snow white. I was impressed by his perfect English – self-taught from books – and regretted declining his invitation to stay the night, but the ears worried me rather, so having made my excuses I was soon on the teatime BA flight. The ear sensitivity and sound distortion lasted a few weeks, but finally went away.

CHAPTER 40

ANTONOV 2 COURSE IN THE CZECH REPUBLIC, A CLOSE SHAVE WITH THE FAA, MORE TOURING

James Black had decided that Avia Special should try operating an AN2. The B17 technology, carrying capacity and impressive short-field performance, would be fun anyway, so a couple of days after my previous return from Moscow at the end of July 1991 the two of us were on our way to Prague. Unimax chairman John Fuchs drove us south, past the high-grade uranium mine (now quiet), to a tiny village and grass airfield, Strunkovice. In Iron Curtain days the uranium ore was dug by political prisoners and convicts. If these men returned home they glowed in the dark, so locals said, but generally they did not return.

Our plan gave us three days in Bohemia (towards the Austrian border), and although one might have imagined that a couple of circuits in this overgrown Tiger Moth would do the trick the whole handling course was required, especially as we intended to take an Antonov away with us in due course. This aircraft of character is not regarded as a flying club device for private pilots, in fact the cockpit has the ambience of a 1946 transport – for that's what it is. The engine is the B17's nine-cylinder Wright Cyclone, with just the built-in supercharger – no troublesome additional turbocharger – so this engine produced 1000 trouble-free horsepowers. High altitude was not envisaged for the AN2.

We started the 10-exercise course on the arrival afternoon with Ex.1 – switching on, starting up, taxiing around the field this way and that, and parking with pinpoint accuracy by steering your own mainwheel up to its chock, then shutting down. Actually this represents quite a lot learned in 25 minutes, and includes the tradition of the accurate parking required for permanent tie downs. Since the return of private enterprise many of the locals seemed to be building their own houses – very well, it seemed. DIY was alive and well in these small villages in the rolling hills (what's B&Q in Czech?), and we stayed in such a residence.

Our hosts had thoughtfully made some stick-on labels for the more important cockpit indications (all produced in ubiquitous Russian). The complex Nordic/Saxon/Latin background of English, uncorrected by invasion or revolution, gives we Rosbifs the advantage of a nuance and colour privately envied by other wordsmiths, but is the bane of dictionary translators – there's such a choice. Were our Antonov fire bottle test lights 'Squib 1 and Squib 2'? Perhaps they have fireworks at Christmas – come to think of it wasn't good King Wencelas Czech? Then there was the reduction gear chip detector warning light: 'Splinterinoil light'. A splinter in the oil? Sounds correct to me – 'Feather No.1 Tovarich'. Then there's the fuel priming pump (Ki-Gas?): eight pumps for a true cold start, with one up the spout for initial coughing and spluttering assistance. I prefer the bucolic village pump tradition. Look up things for medieval water supply. We had a choice of reference – spring pump, or splash pump. Who needs international technology?

It would be wrong to take away the impression that this language fun is intended to belittle our hosts. Quite the opposite: the insular English-speaking world are the losers when it comes to appreciating the cultural richness of history and the advantages of our long-established neighbours – especially those who have survived social turmoil and emerged quietly stronger, without the benefit of 22 miles of sea.

The next day continued with exercises 2, 3 and 4 (test, it says). These all took place in the circuit, of which there were three kinds, 100, 200 and 300 metres. The 200m version featured different sorts of takeoffs and landings – from 0 flap to full flap, long and short etc. Interestingly enough, the short takeoff calls for full power on the brakes and full flap. This works well, though, having lifted off after a few metres run the initial airborne stage requires the careful flap and speed tweaking of a heavy VC10 which loses two engines after takeoff. Obviously the 100 m Antonov circuit is the smallest of the three, and is closely associated with the local topography, but these three variants are obviously based on ancient soviet tradition; 300 metres altitude being the Antonov 2's airways height. Unless the Urals are to be crossed there is little advantage in going higher, and fast aeroplanes above 300m do not have to look for pottering Antonovs. Ex.3 involved precautionary landings with and without power, and after an all-of-the-above 50 minutes base check the monster biplane basics had been covered, now with four attempts at arriving on the chocks to the nearest centimetre.

Our instructor was Pavel Landa, another quiet, courteous and self-effacing, curtain-defending MiG 15 pilot of old. 'I quite liked the MiG 15' he said, but suggested that getting too slow could encourage a problematic behaviour mode. There were a couple of other experienced Antonov 2 pilots on the staff, but Pal was the only authorised signer, maybe because of historical experience.

Our final intensive day of seven flights started with a couple of 'in charge' flights – circuits, then a tour of the local area. Much like captaining a Concorde this was not actually solo, but another knowledgeable person sat in the right-hand seat, and showed us our first look around the Bohemian countryside. Pal then returned for the second phase, after lunch. This involved all the previous handling stuff, at maximum weight.

A fully-loaded Antonov 2 weighs exactly the maximum permitted for a single-engined private licence, 12,500 lbs, something more than 5½ tons. Quite hefty as biplanes go; and during lunch the tanks had been filled and a bunch of teenagers and/or volunteer grown-ups collected from the local school to fill the passenger seats. They were all sitting quietly and perfectly behaved as we climbed aboard. Either they had done this before, or were terrified. Ex.7 was covered in two flights and covered the closed throttle forced landing, slow flight and stalling. This aircraft has very sophisticated slow flying qualities – designed for the actual landing manoeuvre (not the approach) – and it was possible to fly under control, at heavy weight, at virtually 50 kph – at a safe altitude with some power. John Fuchs, not a pilot, came with us on one of these sorties. 'He's a Concorde pilot, this is a joke' – but it wasn't. Then followed another couple of local and circuit 'solo' sign-off flights and we were done.

Something interesting happened during one of these circuit landings. It was a damp and cloudy day, the field had been recently mown, and damp hay still lay where it had been cut. There was no wind, the landing direction was a bit downhill, and with all the kids and plenty of fuel still aboard some braking was required to avoid a very long taxi back. After a few judicious squeezes of air all braking and steering effect ceased. We just swept along the grass like a swan landing on ice. The AN2 finally slid gracefully sideways and stopped. Without a word, whoever was in the right-hand seat immediately went aft, jumped out of the door, went round the front and pulled a wet hay chock from in front of each mainwheel. Not aquaplaning, but a very good simulation – vegiplaning? Something new.

Patty Wagstaffe and the FAA man

After a one-way Concorde flight to Washington a couple of days later I see that I was in Hartford, Michigan, watching Patty Wagstaff practice aerobatics at the small rural airfield there. She wanted to know if her verticals were vertical, and also my opinion about the merits of a Sukhoi 26. (So far I have only described this machine's fun factor, but there is more to this purchase decision.)

What else was going on in Michigan? Nothing I can remember, and the logbook gives no clue, but it does record a flight in Patty's Extra 260. I remember this well, and I liked it, especially the 260 HP in the little symmetrical single-seater. She had flown her manoeuvres over the runway, and I did something similar, maybe adjacent to the other end, away from the buildings, but over the field, well within the circuit. It was very quiet, I remember no other flying, and when I taxied in was met by someone who announced himself as the local FAA man, and told me I had been flying in an airway. Personal details, name, address, passport, licence – no breath test, but this was a bizarre experience. I've seen airways before; they often contain airliners, but here there were none in sight, nor had there been any all day, certainly not cruising past the airfield in the circuit. Having taken down my particulars and informed me of the misdemeanor, he left. Patty was concerned. 'It's best if we get you out of here: these bastards can be pretty mean.' So we checked out of the Super 8 and hightailed it out of town to somewhere. I heard no more.

The Federal Aviation Authority (Feds) do the same sort of job as our CAA, and I have little experience of the former, but have no doubt that they do their best to rein in the enthusiastic excesses of their own nation's frontier spirit – in the interests of public safety, as interpreted by the legal industry. This attention to detail – crossing every I and dotting every T – is as important when certifying the machinery as allowing the pilots to do their thing. This brief FAA encounter reminded me of something Curtis Pitts showed me on a Homestead visit in the early 70's. He had employed an enterprising and personable aerodynamics/engineering man to do all the stress analysis for the two-seat Pitts full certification. The laptop work had been sophisticated and extensive, and probably made a welcome but pay-poor break from the computer-rich offices of Boeing, Douglas, et al. Pa Pitts proudly showed me the latest technical reply. It was a valid page of science and explanation, but if you took the first letter of each line downwards it read 'F**k the feds'. Very clever, very likely not noticed, certainly the result of careful editing and format-juggling, but indicating the frustration felt by the conscientious small-time operator when compelled to conform to nation-sized bureaucracy.

A vintage week

More Abbeyshrule with Louisa followed in August, then in September 1991 Sammy Bruton asked if I would collect a Luscombe from a man in England and bring it to Ireland. 'Tis a lovely little ting' he assured me. I'd not seen one of these before, let alone flown one, and phoned the grass strip in Hampshire where the current restorer of vintage craft cum dealer had his business. I spoke to his son, who was curiously uncertain of his father's whereabouts.' I'm not sure where he is, in fact I think he's flying it at the moment.' That was reassuring news, so I arranged to collect it a couple of days later.

It was tied down and the grass had been cut round it, but the area underneath lay undisturbed and there were plenty of cobwebs in the front of the engine. The logbook recorded no recent flights, but I could see nothing amiss. Its original condition, simplicity and round monocoque design were quite appealing – no electrics of any kind. If the engine runs, what could go wrong? Someone swung it, the little 65 HP Continental ran nicely, the heel brakes worked reasonably, I taxied to the end of the grass strip and could find no reason to take it back.

Acceleration was good on this short runway; better than I expected – the engine uses its 65 horsepowers well, or the all-metal design is impressively light, or both. As it was about to leave the ground I noticed that the airspeed indicator had not moved. It didn't work. It was too late to stop; the trees were approaching fast and I had very little experience of the Luscombe's behaviour – stopping included – so I continued to White Waltham, its intended transit base. There appeared to be no blockage in the pitot system and blowing into it had no result: this instrument was dead. Unlike the rest of the retro indicators it was not original, and the oriental place of origin suggested a budget homebuilder's mail order supplier.

The next day, a timed out-and-back M4 motorway space/time performance check was initially not promising in that many of the commuters below were travelling noticeably faster than me. This situation improved on the way back with the wind behind. Careful arithmetic revealed 84 mph airspeed at my chosen rpm, and the fuel consumption rate was agreeably modest. Before I had done the maths I was assured that my daredevil Concorde captain's personal motorway 70 mph red line was far behind the times. 'You mean they'll be doing eighty?' 'No, much more than that!' Has the breakdown in respect for law and order started already, preparing the way for the future – imported corruption as normality?

It's not a bad little aeroplane for a side by side two-seater, 45 years old, with its roots in 1930. My handheld radio was rendered mute by the all metal fuselage, but the correct length of rod outside, some coaxial cable for inside, the right aerial connection plug from Maplins and some snipping and soldering in my garage gave me airliner quality VHF, essential when calling at security- and customs-sensitive airports, and a good idea for an oceanic crossing.

The first attempt at the passage to the republic on October 8th was abandoned after reaching the Black Country – weather becoming too light black (dark grey), plus a touch of LMF, or a faltering of the Lindbergh spirit, call it what you will (what's the rush, anyway?) Three days later looked quieter and more hopeful during England's equinoctial gale season. Liverpool's John Lennon Airport was initially reluctant to let me enter their control zone. A little unannounced aeroplane with only one radio device? Whatever next! Maybe this cavalier discriminatory air traffic policing could learn something from the Americas (was Little Britain still ruling the waves?). At least my registration was British, and I was eventually admitted to this international hub. By contrast the ground level minions were perfectly accommodating, and after the usual affidavits were signed and no offensive ordnance found aboard I was under way again; desired track more or less west.

The little machine had little in the way of blind flying equipment – none actually. There was an understated 1930s art deco compass in the panel, and maybe a balance ball, but apart from engine revs, oil pressure and altitude nothing else that I can recall. The uncommunicative airspeed indicator remained as disinterested as before. To follow the Lancashire coast as far as Calder Hall put off the moment when a decision would have to be made about committing to the water with no further positioning aids for some distance, but the only way of progress was now west and into a globe of horizonless haze. A sun was vaguely visible above and to the left, and this provided an element of vertical and directional reference, but apart from a murky impression of a sea surface directly below there was nothing else to look at.

Fortunately the little craft's coordinated stability and no turbulence meant that a quiet hand and mind were enough to keep on the straight and narrow.

Sit still and wait for evidence. I settled for a slow climb in the hope that the air might clear and suggest a horizon – none appeared, but at least the sun got a little brighter as the haze density reduced. The northern tip of the Isle of Man passed vaguely underneath as hoped for, and indicated that the lines and numbers visible through the small piece of glass on the compass were correct. During the next half-hour the descending sun disappeared behind the overcast ahead, greying the view but improving forward visibility, and the northern Irish coast appeared, with Strangford Lough behind it. A brief low level explore southwards along the coast revealed cloud cover on the hills and drizzle. The next depression was on its way, as was night, so my bolthole of Newtownards would end this delivery trip – my presence was required at BA the day after next. At least the Luscombe was on the correct Island, even if in the wrong country, and Sammy would have no trouble rustling up a suitable airspeed Indicator from the Abbeyshrule stores, or the means of driving the roads of Ireland to collect the lovely little ting. Actually it was just that, speed or no speed.

The Perfect Storm

Logbook 6 starts on October the 13th 1991. It's the last one that guides this narrative, so the struggling reader can look forward to a glimmer of light on the horizon and a metaphorical calming of the wind, rain and sea that confront the literary air traveller. The Luscombe adventure had lasted a week, and now it was back to something more routine, orderly, and mostly predictable, restoring the rationality and communal sanity represented by the world of work. A couple of routine New Yorks followed, and other sessions of back-to-back Concorde trips were interspersed with conversion course simulator training.

The actual Perfect Storm of the book and the film occurred on the night of October 28th 1991, but the general weather situation that caused it continued its effects for many days. A Concorde New York and a Miami in the second week of November gave a good look at the western Atlantic where the depression was still active. From a height of 20 kilometres, objects on the surface are tiny. Spotting a ship in the open ocean is difficult, but you can see a large one from 58,000 feet if you look carefully, and a supertanker has the appearance of the minutest toy. The mind's memory of this image does give a sense of scale to the scene from altitude, and the first of these early November return flights revealed a sea south of Newfoundland that arrested the attention. A casual unthinking glance gave an impression of a rough sea – plenty of wind down there, and long breaking white waves. Good hardcore windsurfing weather? But it was the scale effect that boggled the mind when you considered our height. The tiny ant that is the supertanker could be 1,500 feet long; the QE2 is virtually 1,000 feet. These individual miles-long breaking wave fronts would have dwarfed them. Coastal buoys had recently recorded waves of over 100 ft, one tenth of a large ship's length, but this offshore scene was of a different magnitude again.

Cunard had established a QE2/chartered Concorde New York package, one way by ship, the other with ourselves. Surprisingly enough the returning passengers were often complimentary about the short Concorde ride, and had not much liked the five days at sea, not always because of the weather. But there were occasions when the swell had got the better of the stabilisers and our smooth ride provided much less torture. Three hours of physical tranquillity (for the same distance). Walking wounded with arms and legs in plaster sometimes came aboard at New York. Apart from simple nautical stumbles there had been runaway grand pianos, crashing chandeliers and escaped furniture to contend with. As I studied the water below and tried to compare the giant (and fast) heavily-breaking waves with the 170 foot QE2 tiny ant's height, there could have been no contest. Could the luxury cruise liner possibly be down there somewhere in these mega-gnarly conditions? I doubt it. The southern route, definitely.

A perfect storm spinoff

A mention of this weather resulted in something else of interest – at this time everyday stuff in the privacy of Captain Riley's Oxford kitchen, but bizarre to the many sane inheritors of the Age of Enlightenment who take reason and logic for granted in their daily lives. To those I say 'Everyone is not the same as you or me – you could be surprised beyond your most fanciful imaginings.'

On my New York hotel television I had seen the news helicopter footage of a well-established swell sending regular and very large rollers down the New England coast from right to left of the screen, across the lawns, through the front and side doorways and windows of the presidential Walker's Point residence, out of the side and back doors and windows on the other side, across the back garden and presumedly back into the sea on today's lee side of this promontory. This sea state would be bad news for any coastal householder, and at home that evening I told my wife about it. The Storming Norman Gulf War had finished eight months before, but the US Navy was still flying precautionary peace-keeping missions in that area. 'Our brave boys, doing the Lord's work' the president had told the nation; a WW2 navy flyer himself, and a supporter of the Republican party at prayer, no doubt. She, with acquaintances, had developed a comprehensive relationship with supernatural powers, and immediately interpreted nature's trashing of this misguided Christian's official residence as a sign and wonder. I was to hear the truth.

'That's very interesting,' she started. 'We had an Israeli student (another Jewish conversion success story?) at our last prayer meeting, and it was revealed to him (by hard-wired divine communication, and confirmed by the unanimous group of needy sheep who shared the gifts) that President Bush's recent attempts to negotiate peace agreements in the Middle East are not the Lord's Will; the president's got it wrong. The Lord's Will currently requires Israel (with outside help, perhaps) to attack all the area's Islamic states with all available weaponry, including nuclear ordnance, and nuke them out of existence.

A bit drastic – over the top, you might think, but you can't argue with certainty (with any prospect of success, take it from me). What has this situation got to do with a narrative of a life's work happily playing with flying toys and other diverting amusements? Nothing directly, but home and family often form a significant part of an aviator's life, sometimes throwing up extra problems, it is true. The level of severity varies, I'm sure.

I recently saw a television interview with an ageing Winkle Brown. He was repeating the subjects of his talk I had already heard at an annual Concorde dinner, and interesting it was, particularly because he came over as an educated, careful, thoughtful human being: quite the opposite of a daredevil, macho, status-seeking (and maybe dangerous on the quiet) risk-hungry hero. But during this television programme he also added that the family of such an enthusiastic pilot as himself can suffer terrible distress – I don't remember the exact words. Why should he share such thoughts with us? Was he considering only the layperson's inherent fear of flying per se, or was there something else? His statement was a surprise and remains a mystery.

I will leave this irrelevant subject here, but take the opportunity to apologise to and thank those many colleagues and friends who may be reading these words for their uncomprehending but patient forbearance in listening to my obsessive reporting of a struggle with real live madness – not my own, I hasten to add. Useful communication with others is essential for retaining a sane balance of mind under difficult circumstances. Friends who understood, to some extent, would ask 'Who's supporting you?' Or, 'How can you be so strong as to cope with this situation?' Life is a solo trip, there is no real support when it matters, but the interchange with a challenging job you enjoy, and the opportunity to work with a close-knit society of rational people can be an invaluably restorative and stabilising experience on a daily basis. This isn't a core intention of big airlines, but the smallness and demanding nature of the Concorde community was something rather special in this respect.

CHAPTER 41

FIVE YEARS TO GO

The logbook shows that I did the Barbados Christmas week in 1991, but until a supervisory New York with Peter Sinclair on Jan 31st 1992 there had been some large Concorde gaps up to this date – in fact almost four weeks prior to this trip. My guess is partly windsurfing leave to study the January trade wind and Atlantic secondary swell over the reef, while the gaps in the previous October and November (perfect storm) would have meant simulator for the current conversion course. Due to my having stepped on the first rung of this airline's ladder at age 20 in 1962 I had been top of the seniority for some years, in fact the last certificate of test I signed for someone more senior is for David Leney on Feb 2nd 1988. Normal retirement age was still 55, and he must have been one of the last national service joiners in the middle 1950s, with management extension perhaps? These statistics have little meaning, except to indicate how time flies, and how much had changed on this fleet since Dick Boas, Ian McNeilly and I joined it in 1985.

The five years remaining to my 55th birthday were to continue with an eclectic mixture of routine Concorde (the one paid hobby), assorted Antonov 2 projects and adventures, and the CAP10 aerobatic joyride operation (fully kosher), where the same checks, competency tests and training standards were equivalent – on a teeny scale – to those of British Airways. It worked because I was cheap by airline standards: free actually, because of an historic type rating examiner's qualification courtesy of the airline. My position as an Avia Special company director was 'pro bona', but I would not quibble about this arrangement because, from my own point of view, the experience of both Antonov 2 and CAP10 responsibilities and variety of flying challenges was invaluable as part of a personal flying story. Whether others in British Airways benefitted from this experience I cannot say – within the machinery of a large airline, probably not – but I've already questioned in these pages the value of the boast: 'I've never flown an aeroplane I was not paid to fly.' Big deal. Varied personal experience, individual responsibility and an open and enquiring mind are everything.

Louisa and Besenyei

You learn as you go along, especially from your students. With a display authorisation and a couple of contests on her CV, Louisa moved on to a much more charismatic and heroic aerobatic teacher, Peter Besenyei. I've just googled him and was amazed to see he's 14 years younger than me. I first came across him in international action when he was less than 20, and even then there was something definitely Hungarian about him, similar, if not the same, to the man who Neil Williams told me about from the Lockheed old days. But not the big swig from the flask in the leather jacket – 'I go better with fire in my belly' (works for some; don't count on it). Besenyei is leaner, sharper, smarter than this. He must have been born looking weather-beaten, rangy and experienced, but at one world contest, 1986 or 1988 I would guess, I happened to see him practise his virtuoso mastery of Zlin 50 (low energy) autorotational control. World championship parameters have moved on to favour vertical performance and roll rate – they're easier to judge – and the Zlin 50 was the last of a development which represented comprehensive values of handling and control that have effectively been discarded by the FAI scene in the interest of long verticals and fast aileron roll rates.

This practice flight consisted of a series of autorotational flicking and tumbling manoeuvres which defied normal definitions of 'departures (out of control)' manoeuvring, and should warrant a rewriting of the aeronautical dictionary. Virtuosity always requires a redefining of the possible. This is always achieved by skill and practice, never luck. What I saw was not wild manoeuvres performed at a great height, with non-specific recoveries – very popular at airshows. This was a continuous sequence of precision 'departed' manoeuvres, positive and negative, all finishing accurately in a clear attitude, all started from a low speed, without losing height, making use of engine characteristics and perfect flying control technique. I can honestly say that I have never seen anything approaching this level of off-design aircraft control and mastery – a new art form in itself. You might guess that he was a full-time instructor at the national sport flying centre (part of the Soviet system). A Hungarian student told me that he would routinely hear an engine open up before breakfast, and watch the show from his bedroom window. It was Besenyei grabbing a pre-school flight, practising this mastery, straight off the ground.

Back to Louisa. What a delightful, able, generous and communicative student. During one of our British Airways instructors' improvement courses we had learned that students have different thinking styles (not the same as you or me), take information on board differently, and that we should take account of this. All good enlightened stuff of course, and during conversations with Louisa the lack of Pitts solo experience came up. She had learned a substantial part of the Olympic repertoire in this machine with Randy in Florida, but had only gone solo near the end. She now flew her Extra very well; brilliant landings, every time. Why not more Pitts solo, maybe a local beginners' competition or two?

'I couldn't land it.'

The Pitts, both small and larger versions, is not a beginner's taildragger, and very unlike a Cessna 150, but she had no trouble at all with the Extra. What had been the problem? Didn't Randy explain how to do it? 'Many times – I just knew I couldn't do it.'

Clearly, something must have changed at some stage, and the answer was revealing. Eventually, I asked the obvious question. 'How did you finally learn how to do it?'

'I overheard Randy, in the next room, telling someone else how to land the Pitts. I thought, of course I can do that, and next flight I could, it was easy.'

The secret of this postponed success was the different environment in which the information was received. This represents a psychological fresh start. Sports psychologists like to talk about mental blocking, in a variety of versions. In my view, this is a function of over-thinking, it's the opposite of stupidity: in fact it's too many mental processes going on at the same time, most of them irrelevant, but intrusive, and especially unhelpful. After an initial difficulty and the doubt that goes with it the brain says: 'too difficult, I can't do this, maybe we can sort it out later' each time the same circumstances are repeated. This problem does not indicate lack of ability or potential; quite the opposite – It's a result of intelligence combined with an overactive concern for self-preservation acquired at an early age by a wary child who grows up in the emotional isolation of boarding school. That's my excuse anyway.

I had a similar problem with the Morse code test at Hamble. The slow three-letter groups were ridiculously easy to interpret and write down. That was the problem – too much empty time waiting for the next letter – double check, was that correct? Do we need a second opinion? Spend the spare time running through the alphabet. If I get this wrong I might fail the whole two-year course. An initial difficulty can precipitate this brain runaway, and bring the shutter of doubt down each time this challenge arises. When the same information is received from a different source – in a new and unprimed way – it may be easily assimilated before the shutter comes down. The problem disappears.

I did not discuss my theory for this miraculous occurrence with Louisa, but we had discussed school. We partly shared experiences with the Prince of Wales. Louisa was at Gordonstoun, Kurt Hahn's character-building experience. I rest my case (again). Louisa had German family connections on her mother's side, in fact I think it was a grandfather who commanded the first Zeppelin to bomb England – the dastardly attack on Great Yarmouth, I think. Not a deep intrusion mission, but the damage to the unsuspecting and not particularly strategic town was a considerable if not fatal shock to national morale.

Cockpit 2000: clumsy work in the watchmaker's workshop

During these early nineties I attended a personality awareness and improvement course foisted on the well-intended workers of my employer. These ordinary people (I am one of them) tend to live their daily lives based on a working image of themselves, acquired over many generations of survival-based experience (of which they are mostly unaware – but it represents a lot of inheritance!).

Chimps do very well on their 94% (human experts now think) of the genetic qualities we share. Additional human brain function represents one major difference. The sensitivity and complexity of exceptional human reasoning ability has historically been treated with respect by those with imagination, erudition and concern for the mental welfare of their fellow men for many centuries – sensitivity being the critical word. Meddle with it at your peril. Here I leave out the subject of nefarious mind control, yet British Airways thought fit to import bargain basement American personality adjustment psychology to improve their employees' means of relating to each other. How nice: better safety, fewer problems, cheaper operation. Of course it makes sense – if it works – but cheap psychoanalysis has risk.

The lynchpin of this project was called Cockpit 2000, another name for an ageing business product designed for ambitious company partners, associates etc – actually salesmen and reps to you or me – who had an eye on company promotion, and therefore had put themselves forward for the treatment. It consisted of a thinking-style analysis based on two questionnaires, one for the subject to complete, the other for a handful of their working colleagues. It works very well, and the large variety of simplistic and apparently irrelevant questions produces a good picture of the individual and the personality they present – at work, at home, anywhere: it's you, more or less. I looked forward to my results, and was impressed at how perceptive they were – relatively kind, detuned, perhaps, but correct where critical suggestions were due.

What surprised me was the reaction of some of my fellow course members on reading theirs. Much worthier, jollier good chaps, family fathers, experienced training people etc. than myself were dismayed at the extremely mild (from my point of view) suggestions that their dealings with their fellow men might be defective. 'I feel as if I've been kicked in the balls,' said a very reasonable and sensible training man in my class. 'Hey, that's nothing; look at mine,' I offered, but he was too preoccupied with the worrying revelations of his own printout. It's official and impartial, can the computer be wrong? He's a flawed human being.

Before opening our envelopes, we had been reassured that those suffering distress after reading their reports could receive 'counselling' from members of staff – the relatively junior amateurs, like ourselves, conducting this travesty of the principles of psychoanalysis. First of all, the very idea of this Cockpit 2000 questionnaire, sent to California, processed by their computer (good as I think it was) and then presented to unsuspecting and, above all, undiagnosed patients, directly contravenes the Hippocratic principle. You do not treat people who are not ill, and, in particular, those who have not asked for help. This last feature indicates the inappropriateness of BA's judgment in purchasing a crass business tool that should have remained in its own, less sophisticated culture.

Of course, the great majority of our 'patients' will have ignored the whole thing, and regarded it as the nonsense that it was, but I suspect that some will have found the experience unsettling, especially when their current state of mind and preoccupations are included.

The cabin crew's equivalent – Breakout (from what?) – was rapidly renamed Breakdown, informally, and many stories of distressed behaviour emerged. Can we assume that flight deck heroes are universally made of more robust stuff? Not necessarily, and it did occur to me that more rumours of flight deck suicides were doing the rounds. Was this a coincidence? Maybe, but I asked a parachuted-in Concorde management person about the statistics. He agreed that the numbers had recently gone up, and now equalled the national average. I was amazed. I would have guessed far below the national average (even allowing for recent enthusiasms for suicide/murder from flyers of other nations). I wrote a Sideways Look article for the Log about the inappropriateness of this psychological meddling with sane people, and its dangers. I asked if the BALPA people had had thoughts about recent BA suicides (Did you hear about so and so? Shot himself in his garage etc), and expected a non-committal answer, but felt vindicated when I got a yes.

Antonov 2 operations: an introduction

Avia Special was still operating an Antonov when I retired from BA in 1997, and it had been an interesting few years with these characterful machines, although the project had not worked out quite as rewardingly as we hoped. Our AOC operation with the CAP10 proved that such things can be done on a minute scale, and public transport specifically for aerobatic rides is not run-of-the mill stuff – and it certainly shouldn't be – but it was the nuts and bolts side of the Antonov that was the problem. Old 1930s wooden aircraft such as the Dragon Rapide had no trouble gaining an Air Operator's Certificate – the technical design and original certification records were still filed away somewhere – in Britain. The problem with the Antonov was one of engineering history, and many decades of cold war darkness, and eons of cultural outer space.

Barry Tempest said some unkind things about Russian custom and practice, design and engineering standards, and so on – but how would he know? This was not his personal ball park, and our own experience of the maintenance constraints required for the CAP10 public transport permission was a retrograde step in practical engineering terms. Instead of being looked after by friendly professionals at Farnborough the CAP10 now required to have its checks done by an approved civilian organisation – in our case the people who looked after the Cessnas and Pipers at the West London Aero Club. These complied with the required standard – as they thought fit, and signed the paperwork, of course – but were not entirely suitable for this aircraft. Our 180 hp Lycoming engine was similar to those in a Cherokee model, so it got the same servicing. After one such check I noticed (you couldn't miss it) that the manifold pressure and fuel flow were reading rubbish. A Cherokee air filter had been fitted, but the CAP10 had a fuel-injected engine, requiring something different. The fact that the approved maintenance garage had made two cockpit indications unserviceable was not of interest, so it was six months later that we got the fuel flow and manifold pressure back. More appropriate DIY maintenance is not allowed once public safety is concerned.

However, back to Antonov 2 affairs. In April 1992 James Black and I went back to Strunkovice with a couple of Concorde alternative flying enthusiasts who'd expressed interest; captain Roger Mills (L-1049 Constellation) and first officer Steve Bohill-Smith (Diamond 9 Tiger Moth team). Their Antonov 2 training routine would be the same as before, and we stayed in a local 'privat' again. When the time came for Pavel to send our learners 'solo', he appointed me right-hand seat supervisor, with the one quiet plea: 'look after the cylinder head temperature'. Of the three temperatures that need care from the crew (which include oil and carburettor air intake) this one is probably the most important when it comes to avoiding serious engine damage. Provided the oil cooler is left at 3 o'clock this looks after itself more or less, and the result of incorrect carburettor temperature can merely be surprise misfirings or engine failure due to icing, but probably not engine damage. To the modern airline pilot these are strange and archaic priorities, which I suppose is why he thought of giving me the reminder before he left the aircraft, but in airline terms this appointment was a sort of promotion.

The reader would be wrong in thinking that this is leading up to some facetious frivolity. Not so: this single-engined B17 biplane with the big cockpit was more big aeroplane than Tiger Moth, and this recognition (if that's the word) from an Iron Curtain MiG 15 pilot showed a level of appreciation and respect that I value as a civilian from unknown territory.

On morning three Olin (Oleg) the engineer dug a hole in the ground and it was announced that we would have some fresh lamb that evening. Then a couple of locals turned up in a car, opened the bonnet and out jumped a sheep on the end a rope. It was a rear-engined vehicle, hence the surprise, and the driver duly fetched a rifle from the back seat. The scenario was clear, and there was soon the sound of a single shot. We had to fly, so we gratefully left the locals to what they had to do. This country cooking was more Hawaiian than Bondi Beach Barby, and after a wood fire had burnt itself out in the hole the meat slices plus whatever went on top, covered by the turves from the digging. That evening we ate the result – quite delicious – and next day returned to London, now with four Antonov qualifications in our collective logbooks. We had certainly been in central Europe, and only the gypsy band were missing, perhaps the result of past occupation and its socially improving politics.

On June 12th 1992 the full complement of the Avia Special Antonov 2 fleet (manager, training manager + two others) returned to Strunkovice to collect this almost new biplane OK-VHC for a trial couple of weeks use in England. The main fixture for this enterprise was appearances at the Biggin Hill Air Fair on the 21st and 22nd, so we based the machine at Headcorn, not far away, and James and I cobbled up a display routine which we duly practised on the 18th. Photographs in airfield owner/farmer Chris Freeman's office show rows of escort Thunderbolts and Mustangs parked on this grass airfield in 1944, and on this occasion the flying-friendly farmer-owner was accompanied by a family of young Jack Russells, who would alternate 30 seconds of rest with athletic rushing around – on and off his lap, desk, chairs, table, around the bookshelves, and so on. An entertaining and traditional country scene.

As the boss and most reliably domiciled staff member, James decided that he would initially fly the displays and I would co-pilot. Just flying a transport aircraft up and down is pretty boring – you can go to any airport and see all of this any time – so a routine of non-stop manoeuvring of sorts seemed the best way of displaying the Antonov. The piece de resistance was the hovering part. It wasn't literally hovering of course, but at light weight 50 kph was quite possible, and into whatever wind was available it looked static enough.

As already mentioned, this required a few hundred feet for safety, about half (3 o'clock) flap, and something like climb power to maintain level flight. In fact much of the show was done with plenty of power; not in order to climb or go fast (it didn't look fast anyway), but to manage the drag during the low level steep turns and their reversals. From a 'fast' pass a steep pull up had the speed falling rapidly, during which the appropriate flap was run out and the nose lowered to settle into the slats-out, high alpha, 50 kph, or less, level situation – correct rudder to keep straight and quite a bit of aileron to counteract the roll from the propeller at the power required. But the Antonov was happy to do this, and there was never a sign of tip stalling, even though the ailerons drooped a bit with flap. Of course the propeller slipstream at generous power levels washed plenty of the inboard wings, and provided its own upward force (like a Concorde?) The captain's 'coming out' meant he would lower the nose and multiply the speed by five (+200 kph) in the ensuing dive, for a final 'knife edge' run for pictures (like a Pitts? not really, but you get the idea).

Of course, a short takeoff and landing was also part of the nature of this display, and the only time I saw something conceptually similar in terms of aerial manoeuvring was at Farnborough some years later when the Airbus A380 demonstrator did its thing. The monster trundled for a few yards, lifted off and proceeded to steep turn around the field at about 90kts. That's what it looked like. Of course this is scale effect, the bane of scale model enthusiasts, and here shown in its reverse effect. To its credit, the Antonov stayed more or less in trim during this variety of manoeuvring, but the display routine was quite physical even so – not a one-handed job – which is why a reliable assistant was required to look after flaps, power, cylinder head temperature and anything else. This was, in fact, a good example of CRM, but without any time for the briefings and discussion as required for reputable transport operations. It was CRM without any talking: is this possible? We took the Antonov to Biggin Hill on June 19th for a practice, of which I have no special recollection, so it must have been satisfactory. The next day we returned to this historic airfield for the first airshow day.

An exemplary, jaw-dropping, daren't look away display

Once again I have little recollection of our Antonov runs on the Saturday and Sunday of this international air fair, so they must have proceeded without significant problem. I do remember that one of the days, I think the Saturday, had standard UK display weather – a fresh breeze straight across the runway. One caution I'd picked up from a Czech mentor referred to a long taxi in the Antonov 2 countering a crosswind. Sustained brake on the downwind side can cause the inflatable, inner-tube-like braking thing in the brake drum to overheat and catch fire, leaving you in flames with no brakes. 'For my next trick' might be appropriate, but we managed to avoid this spectacle, and it was another product of the Soviet system that arrested the attention of anyone with a sense of why aeroplanes do what they do – and the possible.

I spotted Anatoly Kvotchur in his light blue overalls (no badges, same as worn by the chocks man) pacing up and down the concrete in front of the red, white and blue Sukhoi 27 demonstrator, mentally rehearsing every possible aspect of his routine and its positioning in this unfamiliar setting. I knew the name from the MiG 29 engine failure, last second ejection and the fiery crash at Paris, three years before. Was this imaginary run-through (fortunately without the hands, or looking into the sky while twirling around) an attempt to get his nerve back, or just showing off? It wasn't like that at all. This was the Sukhoi 27 as a state-of-the-art flying machine. No guns, rockets, rails or external tanks, and probably just enough fuel for the show. For tactical electronics it probably had one talking radio, and the colour scheme was as unmilitary as you could get: was this a marketing charm offensive, or just a fun demo of Russian design capability?

It accelerated down the runway in the usual way, nothing rocket-like, the nose wheel lifted slowly and progressively, and the mainwheels left the ground at quite a high angle of attack; a bit on the slow side, you might think. But as the wheels retracted the nose continued to rise slowly to the vertical, and the speed seemed to remain the same. The nose continued to pitch over until a half loop had been completed – not a large one, and the Sukhoi was still flying, but not particularly fast, or high, then the nose began to coast downwards. Surely not the other half of the loop – too low and slow.

Then something remarkable happened. The nose pulled hard towards the ground and the machine rolled 90 degrees at the same time. Surely disaster would follow, but we got a small quarter clover leaf (a sort of half barrel roll), finishing in level flight, heading away from us at about half the height gained in the loop. The audacity of the man! To pull towards the ground and roll at the same time, from such an unfavourable situation (upside down and nothing on the clock, as they used to say – and none too high), would normally be a death sentence, in anything, but we had just seen a remarkable demonstration of what this large, long and pointy air superiority aircraft could do while flying slowly. I didn't dare look away in case he got it wrong thereafter, but he didn't.

Now on the Y-axis going away from us he then powered up to the vertical and slowed for the tailslide: three lengths I would say, and impressively straight. I happen to know that these jets do suffer from the same engine gyroscopics as a propeller machine during the rapid exchange of nose and tail. Instead of the Sukhoi 26's use of full rudder for its reverse effect, one Sukhoi 27 engine is opened to full power at the right moment, balancing the score-denting yawing moment of the gyration. The show continued in the same style, all well positioned – no long straight bits with associated waiting, a bit of true knife edge, *gratis* the big fins, upside down flying, nice four point rolls, with more heart-in-mouth rolling and pulling at a high angle of attack thrown in here and there, just to show it wasn't luck, and remind us of a unique selling point. 45° attitudes are notoriously difficult to judge, but the slow high drag pass I would put at 35°, a straight and level flightpath, detached flow from the front lifting surfaces of the blended body shape and much thrust-equalling weight and induced drag.

We had a nice Spitfire (Yak 3) approach and landing to finish, but the apparently leisurely takeoff, nonchalant half loop off the ground, little downward clover leaf, then the tailslide said a master at work from the start. Everything done on the limit – but safely. This was the perfect example of an airshow demonstration, by coincidence at the same place where the ill-fated

Douglas Invader had so shockingly been demolished, along with its passengers, a number of years before. What a contrast of skill, judgment, and piloting maturity!

I know Kvotchur takes his job seriously: that's how you get good. Luck doesn't come into it. I mentioned his name to one of the Russian aerobatic people at a later date. 'Ahh, Mr Kvotchur,' he said, looking rather circumspect and serious. But people who perform airshows in grown-up aircraft should take note: if you're not good enough, don't do it. I don't know anything about the degree of electronic assistance in the Sukhoi 27's flying control system. Of course it helps a pilot actually go to limits and be protected to some extent, but the outside world and the laws of physics stay the same, and have no interest in artificial intelligence.

The dangers of electronic assistance

There have since been a number of Sukhoi 27 and derivative public accidents, possibly because the electronic magic makes learning easier, and less comprehensive. The easy throw-around behaviour can shortcut the required learning process, but the 'who is allowed to do what' decisions remain important if fully serviceable modern easy-to-direct aircraft and their unsuspecting contents are not to be wantonly destroyed by human crews. This sentiment applies to airliners, of course. Naturally one has to take into account the differences between the capitalist profit essential and a socialist state defence policy where aircraft development can do as much flying as it likes – not to mention the cash-strapped warbird enthusiast who wants to have a go, and show off a bit at the same time. These environments are as different as chalk, cheese and an occasional vodka.

Hungarian Antonov

Our OK- Antonov 2 went back to Strunkovice after the two-week tryout, and a Hungarian example took its place in August; much older and well-used, but the same basic animal. The July 1992 logbook in between records Concording exclusively, then James and I took British Airways to Budapest to collect HA-ABJ. Esztergom is a town to the north, on the Danube where it forms the border with Slovakia. A look at Wikipedia gives an idea of the timescale of the history in this strategic place, and the claim that the town started as the last ice age retreated makes some sense – 20,000 years ago. The Celts, who preferred something more rugged, continued their migration west as the weather improved – to Brittany, Wales, Cornwall and Ireland via Germany, Switzerland and France. Nothing much has changed in many respects, and when we arrived at the grass field the owner of the operation, a fiery but generous-hearted Hungarian Airlines captain, sent us to drop some parachutists on the airfield as our checkout. The next day we set off with this Antonov for our return to Britain, carrying a few barrels of crude to see us through this dry lease. The traditional Iron Curtain people's engine oil was still in use in much of this region, and could not be mixed or exchanged with Western WD products. It's not crude oil really, but our owner told us to look at the filter at our first oil change – it would be important that we stuck to the rules. He was right. The entire contents were jet black and, like congealed gravy, apparently solid; it certainly was not in a hurry to go anywhere.

The day after we arrived in Britain with the Hungarian BJ the logbook tells me that James and I did a 4hrs 30 trip out and back from Booker in it to appear at the Merseyside Show. There are no more details and the mind is a complete blank about this long-range mission, but it must have been financially important. Airshows are not always about night-stopping and socialising (as must also apply to current long-range US-based peacekeeping bombing missions – you don't even get to see the bang). The two-month session with this machine contained parachute dropping, displays, appearances, and pottering with friends, some of whom were permitted to have a feel of the tiller. Consecutive logbook days in September 1992 show, in order, Antonov 2 (ferry) and Concorde (New York same day, return the next), Hawk (Chivenor), Concorde (New York etc.), Antonov 2 (Duxford show).

Hawk ride

The Hawk opportunity is worth a mention, and proves what can be achieved by old-fashioned diplomacy, a perceived situation of mutual advantage, and managers with an element of personal authority. Concorde captain Stack Butterley, of the Duncan Sandys piloting disappointment, currently flew cadet air experience Chipmunk flights, and contacts enabled him to create the Hawk Concorde exchange scheme with the Chivenor weapons school; a ride for a ride. (He told me he was in trouble at Hullavington for a formation takeoff – not allowed with cadets. The excuse was that both had taxied out and taken off independently; neither, by chance, having seen the other. It's sort of possible, isn't it?) My turn came up and I went to Chivenor to fly with Flt Lt Tony Gent, once a Phantom pilot. By coincidence the student who showed me around was the same person who had given me the ejector seat briefing at Scampton. He had previously been a helicopter pilot, then doing the QFI Effect of Controls parts 1&2 et al: now he was learning the shooting and dog-fighting stuff. They do get around.

I did get a nice introduction to the Hawk because we flew a Valley trainer – unfortunately no gun, therefore no shredding the foliage somewhere around the target – but it did mean that flying per se was the only option. This was an enjoyable and informative 1:05. First, across to Wales and low flying in the mountains, then some aerobatics, my request, in the blue sky over the Bristol Channel above a cloud top of a few thousand feet. This was very pleasant and, as expected, very straightforward; no comment, really. This goes without saying because a pilot with accurate shooting plus his own survival as priorities should not have to waste attention dealing with handling foibles. Within the Red Arrows manoeuvring syllabus there weren't any.

It was time to return to the field. The let down and cloud break were brief and efficient. Tony said 'I've got it, don't worry about the next bit,' half rolled and pulled straight down into the cloud top. The end of the half loop shot out of the cloudbase – 1,500ft? – on the runway centre line and with plenty of speed. We levelled at 500ft, 'You have it,' and he talked me round the break and 1,000ft circuit. A touch and go and another circuit and landing finished the sortie. 117kts was my final threshold speed – I'd expected something faster. It was obvious that instructors of this experience were expected to be able to look after themselves, but during a quick goodbye post-flight coffee before his next Hawk detail, I noticed an American instructor on an exchange posting. Off-the-cuff letdowns tend not to be their style – F15s do a standard instrument approach every time, even in good weather, I've been told. 'What's he like?' I asked. 'If he was a student he'd fail' was the reply. Enough said.

Concorde ear popping

I was reminded of this time-saving and rather elegant cloud break procedure not long afterwards in a Concorde, descending into New York – just the cabin altitude part of it. Tony Gent had warned me of the military pressurisation system before the Hawk flight. The cabin (crew compartment) of the Hawk only began pressurising at 5,000ft, below that it was open to atmosphere, so that in passing this height while coming down during the reverse roll-off (split S, US) in cloud the ears pick up the real ear-popping rate of descent (250kts = 25,000fpm?): not a problem if you're used to aerobatics.

The Concorde equivalent experience was for a different reason, in fact the Concorde design assumption of no possibility of a high cabin altitude means a high degree of pressurisation – from takeoff: the Concorde cabin does not normally even get above 5000ft. On this occasion a management pilot was a passenger. Not familiar with the fabled Concorde novelties and workload, he came up front to witness the deceleration and descent procedure (orbital reentry from a Tiger Moth teenager's perspective) on this sunny day. After the 200 miles of precision action, and at about 8,000ft, skyscrapers in sight, he declared 'That looked easy enough' (*looks easy* an important essential) and returned to his seat. While informing our visitor of the various necessities the flight engineer had done everything required at the same time – except twiddle the cabin down to landing height. At 5,000ft the cabin joined the outside world. We were not diving vertically at the leisurely 250kts required airspeed, but even a sudden 20 downward knots is unmistakeable to the ears; so leisurely descending was required for the remainder of the flight. Nobody complained – just one of those things (unusual, it has to be said, but most of our passengers were very *au fait* with Concording; many of them flew more than us. A way of life – like the Piccadilly Line? – You've got it).

Next month was the return Chivenor compliment and Tony Gent came on a New York trip. As luck would have it we had a reheat fail-to-light at the first London takeoff attempt so the stop, taxi round, give it a blast on the other throttle amplifier and a successful takeoff followed. Did he have a little drive on the way? I'm sure he did, and after we'd checked in at our Manhattan hotel the three Concorders – myself, Les Brodie and Ian Fellowes-Freeman, aka F-squared, plus Tony Gent – set off in the recent enterprise, a crew syndicate road clunker, north to Long Island and West Hampton airfield. There I took the weapons instructor for a flight in Buddy Kohler's Sukhoi 29, the two-seat version of the Su26 aerobatic contest machine. I think he appreciated the manoeuvrability, but was amazed at the small radii and low airspeed (it's all relative, of course).

The difference between the sensations experienced in a highly manoeuvrable light aircraft and the fast jet is the time scale. Lots of speed and lots of g is the manoeuvring jet's safety watchword, but the g goes on for a long time. Unless you are fortunate enough to be chasing a sole target, straight flight can be dangerous. The g suit helps, but only helps. The Sukhoi's 30° recline makes a big difference but there the high g is short term. Gritted teeth and anticipatory muscle are definitely required for the contest scene, but what struck me about a continuous, let's say 6g, in the Hawk was the relentless nature of it, and mainly the difficulty of looking behind at the same time, considering the visual restriction and mass of the helmet. Beginners and airline pilots tend to look straight ahead by nature, but for other sorts of flying this is the least useful direction. Tony Gent explained in the Hawk. While pulling your continuous g you bend your upper body forward, off the back of the seat (inertial reel shoulder straps allow this), bend your head forward and twist your neck as required, and the downward element of now looking back gives you a better view of your pursuer. It works, up to a point, but is very physical, to say the least. He added 'Our students usually develop a larger neck size for their shirts while they're here.' I'm not surprised.

A completely new subject: the Moshe Benshemesh School of Combat

Before this Antonov went back to Hungary during October, Moshe Benshemesh, the experienced Israeli Skyhawk pilot (now a London-based businessman), had already bought his own CAP10, and after a 2xCAP10 practice he came along for a short evening Antonov ride in the right-hand seat. Older AN2 versions do not assume co-pilot takeoffs and landings (rather like some historical airline traditions), so only the captain has brakes. There had been no time for briefing, but with real pilots this is not necessary, and his first chance to take the controls was on the takeoff roll. 'I'll do the power,' I said, 'don't lower the nose (same as a CAP, just keep the ground attitude when we leave the ground' as an adequate takeoff briefing for this aircraft. We trundled, Moshe did his full and free fighter pilot's control check as we rolled (very wise), and once we were climbing away his assessment was 'Vot a bus!' This is correct, but a useful and user-friendly, if slow, bus as well.

As soon as there were two CAP10s (the French Air Force's favourite basic trainer) on the same airfield, Moshe's only reason to fly was the one that applies 'when two or more are gathered together…'; formation aerobatics to start with (loops and barrel rolls), but then, more importantly, one-on-one aerial combat skills: in reality the game of energy advantage. The best pilot will win – for sure. Despite my years of competition aerobatics – pure precision handing – this was a completely new discipline. Even the Tiger Club formation training system as a way of life – station keeping, position changing, even the tied-together line abreast loops in vintage machines was beginner stuff in terms of this tactical science.

I can quite understand why fighter pilots rapidly lose interest in the academic disciplines of competition aerobatics, despite their own potential to excel: it's too clinical and prescribed, and you probably will not win. There are exceptions, but only when the expensive alternative is no longer available. I wonder if Neil Williams would have pursued his competitive quest if he had flown the professional Hunter instead of the Canberra.

I made a promising start. For lesson one the teacher (target) flies a steady circle. The student must visualise this circle as being on the surface of a cone, point down – like an inverted coolie hat. All manoeuvring must stay inside this cone. The object is to get in the correct firing position (pulling lead, of course) with a clear speed advantage. This is achieved by pulling up steeply inside the cone, roll inverted, have a look, pick a point somewhat ahead of the teacher, pull down and dive towards it, picking up speed in the process and dropping behind your target as it proceeds around the circle, but with a clear closing speed. Having got close enough you break off by pulling up again to repeat the process. The idea is to find the rhythm to this up and down, energy exchange routine. Moshe said 'good' and added the refinement that pulling into the shooting position was best done from slightly below. 'The target appearance presents itself with more 'meat',' he said. But after this tick-in-the box for lesson one I seemed to lose the plot. The next attempt did not work so well – had he done something to the circle? Then the circle was not level, but tilted at a considerable angle – much more up and down to it, almost like nonstop looping. The spherical trigonometry was difficult to visualise and it was obvious I was not a real Biggles at all, and at 50 unlikely to become one. Perhaps I should have been a cautious airline pilot after all.

Jonathon Whaley was a military exception for a while, and had tried some contest flying in Tony Bianchi's CAP231. He had flown the Phantom and Hunter in the Royal Navy before becoming a Chiltern Squire, and I asked him about the learning process for this mysterious craft. He concurred about the cone principle, but could not help thereafter, so I gave up on Moshe's course. Jonathon told me of an interesting cautionary experience while low flying over the water in a Navy Hunter. He was flying up the Bristol Channel, with a good sense of the height above the water surface from the consistent channel chop as it whizzed underneath. He was suddenly roused from this peaceful afternoon reverie by the feeling that his groundspeed had increased considerably, for no logical reason. The truth dawned rapidly: the water was getting shallower as Weston super Mare approached, and the waves were getting smaller and closer together: much smaller and closer. Phew! It had been a near thing. In the meantime he bought his own ex-Swiss Hunter.

Moshe made a business trip to Miami by Concorde. I think I wrote an introductory note for the captain; in any case Moshe sat in the cockpit for a takeoff and was suitably impressed by the Concorde's nature for such a big machine. He also told me more about his personal ban on the Skyhawk ejector seat (the two dead-stick landings have already been mentioned). The problem was not the instrument panel (solely), but the effect of the seat acceleration on long femurs. Apart from mentioning the secondary effects of the subsequent parachute landing he did not go into excessive detail, nor will I. Apart from the first Skyhawk glider landing, caused by an Egyptian cannon round from the trenches below going straight into the bottom of the engine, I know nothing more of these exploits, except that on one of them he had enough speed to climb and glide over the conflict border to a friendly airfield (quite close), run off the end of the runway and demolish the NCOs' dining quarters. Otherwise all was well, but perhaps I will stick to flying buses.

I took the Hungarian AN2 back to Esztergom in October 1992, assisted by a helpful Colin Morris. He'd brought his overalls with him (Navy again, I think) and was happy to climb up the footholds on the fuselage side, walk on the roof and out on the top of the top wing (fuel) or over the flight deck to stand on the bonnet (oil). There are other things to do when preparing for the night (control locks, chocks, tie downs), and it is possible to manage this solo, but a co-pilot/engineer makes a huge difference. Our sector lengths from Wycombe, calling at Luxemburg and Straubing, were very reminiscent of the 1960s Comet and 707 days of all points east to Australia – between 3:20 and 4:10. James Black was now working on more permanent plans for Avia Special Antonov 2 operations, and I spent the next five months – until April 1993 – predominantly on the opposite end of the transport speed spectrum. Never more than four hours in the Concorde, and generally a more leisurely, if technically fast, lifestyle.

January 1993. There are now four years to go to that 'It's your birthday! Goodbye!' occasion; like Anne Robinson's *Weakest Link* dismissal. Of course, she didn't mean it. It was part of the job, and no more Concorde would only mean one hobby less and no pocket money (crew allowances). Life had now stabilised into a busy mix of Concorde, its training and operational and social moments, Antonov2 this and that, CAP10 aerobatic joyrides and its management, and continued recreational visits to America and the variety of its flying activities and personalities. To relieve the tedium of the logbook pilgrimage and reader confusion it might be better to describe these topics as separate but concurrent subjects: four parallel hobbies.

CHAPTER 42

FLYING IN AMERICA

Long Island

Ian Groom, who I'd first come across with the Aerobatic and Artistic project in the 1980s, had then moved to a Manhattan skyscraper – 57th floor on E75th street, or was it the other way round? – and now had a pleasant house in the trees in East Hampton as well – more agreeable for flying activities. I can only guess that his major business affairs could spare more time looking after themselves, and did not require frequent appearances in a downtown office. I never knew exactly what he did, but film production seemed to be the long-term connection, and I take this to mean a kind of gambling: investors put up the money to make a film, and divi up the profits when these result. This northern end of Long Island is similar to the fabled Gatsby country and now requires a 1½ hour drive from the city. Scott Fitzgerald actually imagined Gatsby's splendid spread to have been much closer to the Queens Bridge, on the inshore LI coast, and his guests' cars might have made it to Gatsby's in less than an hour in the 1920s, but the escape to greenery and water feeling is similar. The current main road is now made of concrete slabs which have individually tilted under the repeated impacts of commuter front wheels as they jump the inch between one slab and the next, so that the drive is an incessant ka-bump, ka-bump etc.; it's the same thing in both directions. The enquiring mind might ask why, but out and back lanes are separate – there's no automatic levelling here. Whether the Duesenbergs got the same ride I can't say.

I was never a guest at a Gatsby party in the Hamptons, although I did come across Arthur Miller in the pub once, a white-haired eighty-something. I would have liked to ask him about the research for *The Crucible*, written as an allegory of the McCarthy witch hunt for creative communists, because its early source subject matter interested me, but this wasn't the right time or place. In any case McCarthy burned himself out at about 50, so there's a moral in there somewhere – was it worth it? Visitors, like me, came and went at the East Hampton house in the trees, and I did go to a July 4th barbecue at Frank Manelski's beachside home, just south of East Hampton village, and a perfect place to see the settlement's fireworks in the evening.

After a clear and hot day – a traditional family get-together, during which Frank put one of the girls' straw hats on my head at lunch (very considerate as my factor 50 Alligator sun blocker was in Barbados, and I had no hat) – we waited for dark and the appointed time for the Independence fireworks. This was an interesting spectacle because the cold Atlantic at the end of the garden now generated advection fog which may have risen to almost 100ft cloudbase over the land. The whole show was now provided by exploding Chinese rockets, of course, and while we could see the initial climb, the bangs and crackles were somewhat muffled and the explosive detail invisible, but it generated vague coloured impressionistic events somewhere in the 8/8ths overcast, and guessing what was going on up there became quite entertaining. It was, in fact, like Mr Bean's school visiting day chemistry lab. blue explosion behind the frosted glass. Readers who have seen this TV episode will understand; others may be mystified.

Frank Manelski gets a mention because he was a traditional old-style American airline pilot. A local Long Island boy, it turns out, he learnt to fly with the Navy in 1939, joined TWA in 1948, was posted back to Korea in 1953 for a couple of years, then continued with TWA until retirement – 1980s? I don't know, and aviation was not discussed at all, but I have read that he made the first Paris – San Francisco direct. Twenty hours, in an L1649 Constellation, it must have been. That would have been in the late 1950s, but what a long duty day! I did know his son, Lee, however – also TWA. Lee Manelski was in the American team at the 1990 Yverdon aerobatic worlds. He let me fly his aeroplane (one of the several Stephens Acro derivatives) in Texas not long afterwards at the US nationals, but was killed in February 1991 when he collided with a helicopter at Santa Paula, CA, while taking off for an aerobatic instructional flight in his Pitts S2A. Insurance company lawsuits about blame and payouts arose aplenty, particularly because this was a Los Angeles/Hollywood affair. The legal system as a business is simple. Even if they don't win the people with the most money don't lose. Sometimes they pay for the other people's defence to encourage a decision – not to their disadvantage.

Lee Manelski and Santa Paula Ca

Santa Paula airfield is a small, single and short runway airfield next to a seasonal river, and on the other side are buildings, the main road and the town. It's privately owned and available to the public: VFR, traditional values, no control, see and avoid etc. (or wait until it looks safe). It works well, but something fundamental went wrong on this day. We had the same system in our Tiger Moths in 1959, except that we had no radio either – actually this made it easier, even when a Sea Vixen on its maiden flight would sometimes take off. There were no problems that I recall, and Santa Paula usually regards itself as relatively accident free. Radios now being plentiful, their present-day use is for announcing one's actions at uncontrolled airfields – for information to others. Of course, having radio at all creates an additional sense of shared, thus diminished, responsibility, and can reduce the full-time wariness traditional for the totally self-sufficient old time pilot. This does not suggest that radio does not have its uses, and maybe you are reading this heresy here for the first time.

The helicopter pad is abeam the centre of the runway, and maybe 40 yards from it, to the south, towards the river and the rough ground that borders it. If Lee had transmitted the usual 'Pitts 123 taking off Rwy 22', the helicopter must not have noticed, and I cannot believe that Lee did not see the helicopter on its pad, rotor whirling, before he or his student opened up. In any case, the standard helicopter liftoff and transition to forward flight is normally to the south, over the river. While the Pitts rolled along the runway the helicopter lifted off and set off to the north, across the runway. The collision occurred at 40 feet as the Pitts climbed away, still in its nose up attitude, doing, say, 100 mph. Reports say the Pitts attempted an emergency avoiding manoeuvre, but to no avail. It flew through the JetRanger's rotor blades, rolled inverted, dived into the runway and exploded in a fireball, killing Lee and his 18-year-old student. The rotorless helicopter fell to the ground as scrap, and all three occupants were injured. Not one of the three can remember what happened – of course not. Perhaps Bette Davis would have given her evidence in traditional style: 'This... thing' (sweep of the cigarette arm) 'came out of nowhere and hit us.' But she was not on board.

The view from a JetRanger is good, and I do not know which way it was originally pointed on the pad, and helicopters often swivel around in the initial hover (when there is one) to look around before moving off. The official safety board report deals with many possible factors; poor forward Pitts visibility, the risks of uncontrolled VFR (it worked for Lindberg), and so on. It would seem obvious that the presence of the other, in the air, was a complete surprise to both. The Pitts did not expect the helicopter to take off and cross the runway, and the helicopter must have been unaware of the Pitts' presence.

The compensation claims and counter claims went on for some time. Interested or aggrieved parties (or their studio representatives) even sought financial gain from the estate of the dead 18-year-old on the grounds that he might well have been flying from the back seat and was therefore the responsible Pitts pilot. How much dough did the kid have to his name? (Give them my baseball mitt, my chopper bike and my skinny skateboard with the good wheels.) I've no idea, but the makeup of the helicopter team is of major interest to me, and this story is yet another cautionary tale about piloting, the aura of celebrity and the fun of creativity. It's possible to manage all three, but difficult if at the same time.

This was no typical air taxi job; the helicopter was flown by its owner, Noel Blanc, son of the Man of a Thousand Voices, legendary Mel Blanc. Noel continued the tradition of voice actor for Warner Brothers' Looney Toons, and there will be few readers who are not familiar with Bugs Bunny, Sylvester and Tweetie Pie, and many other characters. Was he a good pilot? Absolutely, that's not the point. His passengers were Kirk Douglas and a real Beverly Hills cop, and the professional, social or creative ambience in the JetRanger is completely unknown to me. But the moral is: you must pay the same attention to the job in hand, routine as it may be, regardless of who is on board, and whether you're having fun or not. (This also applied in a Concorde – as David Leney's fleet letter was intended to remind me after my initial route check.)

We do not know what did or didn't happen in the short time between the helicopter pilot pulling collective and nosing over to cross the runway centreline, but it cannot be questioned that he must have been completely unaware of a Pitts in the process of taking off (and hardly in a position for routine avoidance manoeuvring). Following the flurry of lawsuits flying in both directions it was concluded that it was not possible to prove gross negligence on the part of the helicopter pilot, or anyone else's for that matter. The affair seemed to have ended with his offer of $165,000 compensation to the 18-year-old's parents.

Marketing aerobatic training

Ian set up a business teaching aerobatic basics in his S2B Pitts, based at East Hampton. In addition to enthusiastic individuals he also marketed his product to corporate interests, on the grounds that basic aerobatic experience would be useful to professional pilots whose backgrounds did not include it. As someone experienced in the business world, and exuding the confidence of success, he was quite successful in selling this idea, and I would concur that, for the miniscule cost (by corporate aviation standards), the piloting benefit might be indirectly worthwhile, if unquantifiable.

I remember taking the Pitts to White Plains, where a company which operated charter Gulfstreams thought it might be a good idea. There was also an arrangement with a helicopter company, though the helicopter-only pilots found inverted flight systemically alarming. This is logical when one considers that positive loading is essential for the structural integrity of a conventional rotorcraft, and it could also be that some fixed-wing pilots take longer to come to terms with helicopter handling than an *ab initio* candidate. My attempt to fly an airship certainly suggested a supersonic disadvantage, despite my captain's compliments. I can't imagine what other flyers' airship attempts must have been like.

Any association with Concordes has a certain kudos in American flying circles – 'It should have been American,' was a frequent sentiment – and Ian asked me to give a talk about the benefits of aerobatic training when he organised a marketing get-together one Sunday in the East Hampton hangar. There was no other brief, and of course the idea was to encourage more students. I decided not to make much of Concorde skills because any relationship with a Pitts Special is not immediately obvious to many, but spare capacity is always useful (even if invisible). It makes everyday life easier, lowers the stress level and improves working relationships. That was my pitch, anyway. The variety of basic skills taught by some military organisations is intended to produce pilots who will better adapt to different flying challenges in the future: spare capacity. It works, if that's what you want, but the Machine Age has specialised in labour-saving devices which continue to have an exponential effect on human life, its capabilities and thinking. General aviation is but an insignificant example.

Spare capacity – good to have

As a marketing priority first generation general aviation served to reduce aircraft handling skills to a reliance on the car steering-wheel principle, in some areas. There are professional pilots who are greatly puzzled by the vagaries of crosswind and asymmetric power. An inappropriate recourse to the nosewheel when the familiar steering wheel seems to have lost its steering power is not uncommon, even when the jet transport could be travelling at considerable speed, and packing a lot more energy than a bus. This is not a serious problem because aircraft for public use are designed and tested to absorb a fair amount of driver abuse, and a certain level of damage is factored into the commercial equation (as is the acceptable death rate – small as it may appear, except for the unfortunates). But the piloting abilities required – including today's button-pressing as a handling substitute – can also find itself challenged if the pilot frequently has to think at a limiting level during the course of relatively normal flights. An extra level of basic handling skills may not seem relevant to the modern computerised airliner or executive jet, but the extra learning process exercises the brain and extends its capability, a little beyond the bare minimum required, at the least. Learning something new expands the experience boundary. The exact subject matter is not important: the subject here is some spare capacity at all times, something in reserve which will assuredly help when things become more difficult – the extreme case being the surprise. If well enough taught and managed, aerobatics can, and should, be enjoyable and rewarding, although the right equipment, environment and mentor is critical: but this can be done, amply demonstrated by the Avia Special CAP10 AOC aerobatic joyride project (of which more to come).

How my talk in the Long Island hangar went down I don't know, nor did I find out anything about my audience, but rapt attention and no feedback could be a good sign. I did catch the pained and distressed expression on the face of one listener when I gave a recent example of what can happen when a quasi-surprise confronts a crew who have already reached their capacity limit. We all know that transport flying is becoming statistically safer as the numbers progress, but that does not exonerate the serious accidents that we read about on a regular basis, involving fully serviceable modern and user-friendly public transport aircraft going about their daily business. The recent example noted was an instrument approach in a mountainous region that was not successful because of the weather – heavy rain perhaps, or a burst of low cloud. I can only guess that this was a surprise because the correct procedure was not carried out and they flew straight ahead into a mountainside (Ouch!)

What has this got to do with learning aerobatics? Nothing, directly, and I know quite a number of exemplary airline pilots who have never looped the loop in their lives, but this does not imply they did not have the spare capacity to cope with the vagaries of the normal job. And could I have taught them the basics? Easily: that is why they were selected. Had the unfortunate mountain-finders not been at their capacity limit when carrying out the bad weather approach they might have had a clear idea of what to do next if the approach didn't work, and not dropped the ball due to the overwhelming shock of a surprise. Surprise means the unexpected – to be avoided where possible in the air. In all forms of flying the law of averages applies: the more you do it the more likely you are to encounter challenges, surprises indeed – so what's the answer? 'Get some in,' as they used to say. Learn a little more than you think you might need.

On one visit to Prestwick for Concorde base training I visited the fairly new and improved British Aerospace airline pilots' school there. The single-engine flying was planned as usual with the Warrior version of the Cherokee, but there was a bold addition to the elementary fleet; the little Swiss-Italian Bravo. This is smaller and simpler than the Cherokee variants, but there is a different design philosophy – it's not supposed to be a flying car. My guess is that it is easy to fly, gives its pilots a good impression of the outside world from its bubble canopy, but answers its controls in a pleasant, direct and logically responsive way. It does have a revolutionary feature – a joystick coming out of the floor, leaving only the rudder control for the feet – no steering wheel! A metal CAP10 with a nosewheel? Perhaps, but a number of air forces liked it as a basic trainer because of its good handling – with simple aerobatics – and cheapness of operation. The Prestwick school intended to use it as a secondary feature of the single-engine programme, the assumption being that three-dimensional manoeuvring was a specialised and more advanced way to fly. But they told me this had changed; the Bravo was now the entry level machine, because the students took to flying it more readily than to the supposedly safe and easy general aviation product. Safe and easy for whom? This discovery makes sense. The three dimensional manoeuvring of flight is sufficiently different from driving a car on a level surface that this connection should not apply where initial learning progress is desired.

Straight and level and rate one turns (quasi static flying) are, in fact, a specialisation of natural manoeuvring in the air. These subjects are not the easiest things to start with, especially with general aviation aircraft. Birds, as we know them, are a good example. Whatever their hollow-boned dinosaur origins birds are especially good at flying, particularly to avoid predators – and they sometimes travel great distances, it has to be said. But as flying things they learn little from their flightless relatives. Ostriches, and the like, once used to fly, but because of geological changes of residence plus other alterations of lifestyle found themselves to be free of predation and had no need to fly just for safety reasons, so they lost the knack; and walked or ran everywhere instead. This needs less energy and might also be easier. But given the choice would you prefer an ostrich or an eagle to teach you how to fly (and come to terms with all of Newton's Laws of Motion – firsthand)?

My lecture in Long Island was simpler, not as esoteric as this, and stuck to the spare capacity point. I did not find out whether the stirring and disturbing East Hampton address had any effect on school recruitment, but I did get to help out with the odd flying lesson. Jack Ready (Admiral Topgun) came along one weekend, and we went for a zoom in the S2B. This was a year after we had flown Louisa's Extra 300 at White Waltham – the day of the Concorde Dining Society's Dinner. Jack had since retired from the US Navy and was now employed as a consultant for an American consortium to create the future all-purpose do-everything fighter (I think). 'It's like a little fighter,' he said of the toy but 260 HP two-seat Pitts, and Ian hoped that Jack might be interested in a share in the Sukhoi 26 that was soon to arrive.

The Harvard

The father of one of Ian's Pitts students owned an immaculate AT6 (Harvard), and the student used to arrive in it, complete with a small box of simple servicing bits and pieces. A screwdriver, oily rag and a small can of engine oil was adequate (its radial engine was in perfect condition, and the small tin was enough to top it up for the trip home). I had ridden in a Harvard briefly a couple of times. The owner in this case had only authorised his daughter to commute in this example, but Ian suggested I should teach her some suitable aerobatics in it. She didn't say no – and what a flying delight this was! You read all sorts of cautionary warnings about such an aircraft – the same wariness could apply to all interesting machines – but of course it all depends...

This was the perfect device for its training purpose, and I found that 20/30 power, or 2000 rpm and 30 inches – as I remember something less than max-continuous – was quite adequate for the continuous series of looping and rolling combinations which typify some of the training requirements of this era. At three or four thousand feet on a summer's day over the northern end of Long Island, loops, half-Cubans, barrel rolls, quarter clovers, and so on could be flown, one into the other, without losing height or exceeding 180 mph. Could the same thing be done near the ground? Certainly, but with a very strong caution: you'd better be good – not the slightest bit brave or overenthusiastic. Abandon all instinct for something extra for the show. 'Power or pull your way out of trouble?' Not necessarily: even a Harvard's modest 550HP could be a huge embarrassment if improperly applied. 'Lots of speed and g.' No: exactly the right amount at all times, with no unseemly slipping or skidding which will destroy the engine's good work, lose height, and put you closer to the wing-dropping situation. The necessary corrective action in this case is not a problem per se, but, compared with a nimble light aircraft, takes longer, and uses much more height. The steps from Stearman to Harvard to Thunderbolt or Mustang are logical but somewhat exponential in degree, so handling with respect and understanding is best taught early (flying cars were in their infancy in 1938). The P51 Mustang would be slimmer but a similar size to the Harvard, with three times the power and twice the wing loading, and a higher performance wing section. The Thunderbolt had more wing area, nearly five times the power, and could carry a huge load. Both would go to forty something thousand feet so this was what the Harvard pilot could expect to deal with next.

Was the Harvard easier to land than the Pitts? Yes; much, and it is purely by coincidence that I nearly tripped myself up after a Pitts aerobatic lesson with the Harvard daughter. It was a bright sunny day with a strong and gusty crosswind – about 60° off runway heading. The short and stubby Pitts is a fast lander, and the later factory-produced models, with more equipment and bigger engines, are heavier and faster than the early home-built single-seaters. All require good rudder technique on the landing roll, and may (correction: will) run out of rudder power at some stage in a significant crosswind landing. Brake has then to add its effect for directional control. On this occasion I declared that I would land because of the conditions, and so I did. All went well until steering with brake as well as full rudder was required. (Airliner pilots may be disappointed to hear that a grab at the nosewheel steering does not help (nor should it – it's only for taxiing).)

With crosswind takeoffs and landings you can't go wrong with into wind aileron, or so I thought. On this occasion a specially-strong gust blew from the side during the well-on-the-ground part of the runout; maybe 50 mph groundspeed. The Pitts swung immediately, vigorously (and unexpectedly) towards the windward side of the runway and subsequent grass, as if the downwind brake had instantly failed, then, equally suddenly, swung back towards the runway heading. Of course the Pitts has powerful ailerons, two per side. Afterwards I realised what had happened, even though the wings remained level. The gust from the side had been strong enough (40 mph, maybe more) to persuade the little squirrelly thing that it should be flying, and the applied aileron had temporarily taken the weight off the downwind wheel and necessary brake – with no evidence of roll. No sooner had the little beast swung to the left than the mass of the Pitts resisted being swung left and pushed the right wheel down again to the grippy tarmac: saved from more serious embarrassment by Newton.

I would still recommend into wind aileron as a general rule – but not too much, just the right amount. The reader is at liberty to decide how much this is. This cautionary tale is further proof of the true nature of this biography, and I might add that my student of the day, the custodian of the fearsome heavy-metal commuter Harvard warbird, showed no interest in this nano-second manoeuvre. Did she think I'd got it wrong, or that this demonstrated the unobtainable level of skill required to master this demanding toy? Difficult to say.

So what about the Harvard as a stablemate for the three day eventer grazing in the field next to the hangar? I cannot think of a more agreeable companion for the accomplished hobby pilot. But then there's the gleaming silver Mustang I saw make an elegant curved approach to the Toronto Island airport threshold at the perfect delicately-balanced speed for a three-pointer without messing about, taxy to the apron and stop. A lean and elegant grey-suited man got out, extracted his slim document case and walked away to the car that would take him to the financial district. This was a real Mustang – a single-seater. Perhaps one of these could keep the Harvard company. If only…

Florida visits

In April 1993 Ian Groom asked me to join him for a few days in Fernandina Beach FLA. He would be there with the Sukhoi 26 and so would Buddy Kohler with his 29 (the aircraft I'd taken Tony Gent from Chivenor for a ride in). It would be fun. Buddy was a retired entrepreneur from the north east who liked his aircraft for its exotic value. He also flew his loops and Cubans very nicely in it, but had no interest in world championship level competition, or any other sort of aerobatics for that matter. He's the total amateur who enjoys his flying at a level he can afford, and a connection with other flying people perhaps, and leave it at that. Respect. This is the first rule of safe independent flying: understand where you stand, and don't confuse money with ability (your own or anyone else's).

Why we were here, far from home, was not immediately apparent to me, but the stay was pleasant enough. The airfield was the base for T J Brown's Holiday Inn Pitts S2 formation team. I'd seen them in action at a show elsewhere, and the routine was American military in style – tight formation and large figures flown at what looked and sounded like maximum speed and power, interspersed with splits and crossovers. There was the suggestion that I could help them out with a ferry because not all four members were available to do this. TJ explained the finger indication of a radio frequency if you'd got it wrong and found yourself in radio no-mans-land, and also ran through the pre-takeoff checks performed as if in formation, each item called by him over the radio, even though the aircraft were waiting stationary on their wheels at the time. He had flown the F-105 Thunderchief in Vietnam. I can imagine a low level bombing mission could be ruined if the team took off with just one switch overlooked, but my own formation upbringing had not included such detail: a nod when the leader looked at you said you are ready, but those had been the simpler minimum radio days.

There was an L-39 Albatross on the field, and TJ appeared to give lessons in it. This dinky but rather elegant jet trainer was a Czech design, and used all over the Soviet empire. Someone told me the Russians trained pilots ab initio with it. Why not? Difficulty is in the mind of the training staff. TJ gave me a checklist to read. I was later to discover that a well-sponsored display team of these was already looking good at the planning stage, and there was a MiG 15 and a Sabre in a hangar. These were used for a good guy, bad guy airshow routine, and you need not ask who always won, but the fact is that America is an air-minded place, and the business of flying does not have the same British restrictions of geography or notions of social status and the elitism, both positive and negative, that go with the fringe sport of flying. The glamour of historic warbirds in peacetime cannot be ignored, but the flying of them at low level as profitable entertainment does not change their character or piloting requirements. Operating a full-size vintage fighter is expensive, especially if it's a thirsty jet, so someone has to pay. A list of essentials could be piloting ability, experience, maturity and good judgment (at all times), plus money, certainly; and the reader may arrange these in order of priority. This varies.

Ian's interests were moving from Pitts S2 training to flying airshows in the Sukhoi, rather than competing in competition with it. The airshow audience is not as critical as an aerobatic judge, and marketing plus organisation plus a good commentator can put the concept of excellence, glamour, risk, courage, superlative skill... in the mind of the citizen. The impressive and eminently capable TJ was current president of ICAS, the body with responsibility for airshows and those who flew in them. I did not know this at the time, nor anything about ICAS (I for International gives a sense of quality and recognition to an American organisation), but I suspect that Ian making new friends in this area had something to do with Sukhoi displays, and the extra income these might produce. Despite the Concorde association I did not get to ferry a team Pitts or ride in the Albatros. I have no doubt that the impression I gave was disappointingly at variance with the imposing Action Man persona that goes with this part of the world and its aerial activities, which appears to help credibility to go with the words.

But it was a pleasant few days, and I made a couple of Sukhoi practices over the field – to keep the hand in, so to speak. Eventually we returned north in the two Sukhois, led by element lead Groom, whose rather correct radio style gave a sort of TJ military impression: 'Flight of two Sukhois 15 miles south for landing.' No disappointment was expressed when it turned out to be two taildragger light aircraft, but I wondered what exotic warbird expectations had been dashed in the tower.

It was a couple of weeks later, as I prepared to leave my New York hotel room before a Concorde flight, that the TV showed the black Sabre loop into the ground. Subsequent evidence revealed a lack of appropriate experience or judgment on the part of the pilot, who was a successful local businessman and enthusiastic supporter of the warbird display scene. Well, that's show business.

Video replay

Nowadays, air display accidents are invariably filmed by many spectators. The clips submitted to the accident investigation people are extensively analysed and many facts and figures result. Needless to say the findings almost invariably conclude mistake or misjudgment on the part of the hapless pilot. Surely this is unfair? I don't think so. The lovingly maintained work of art, whether warbird or specialised aerobatic machine, seldom gets it wrong. But sometimes the video evidence alone raises questions – the picture does not tell enough of the whole story.

A number of years before this incident, and also seen on the NBC morning news prior to a New York Sunday departure, a home video of an accident the day before at Sydney Harbour was shown. Three Pitts S2s in echelon right formation proceeded from right to left on the screen. The leader made an individual pull up, and was briefly followed by the camera, but this was obviously some sort of break – the majority were now out of shot – so the camera returned to them, still continuing right to left as an echelon right pair. The second one now pulled up, and this time the camera followed it around its 5/8 loop: aha! they're each going to do an individual half-Cuban, one after the other – now we've got it. This machine made its diving half-roll and had just pulled out when another Pitts entered the top of the screen, above it, in a 45 inverted dive and immediately made a snappy quarter roll, the first point of a 2 of 4. In the brief instant of its knife edge attitude it went straight through the front of the #2 man we were following, lost both wings on the relevant side and dived into the water, amongst some moored yachts. The #2 man's engine fell off and this now lighter, aft C of G Pitts floated relatively slowly down to the water in a flat attitude. That is all of the video evidence. My question is: which one was the attacker from above – 1 or 3? Compared with the human's field of view and an ability to mentally zoom in on a subject of interest while maintaining 180 vision the camera is often a limited witness. It only tells some of the story.

A few months after we left Fernandina Beach I read in the paper about the death of TJ Brown. He had been killed flying an L39 in Russia. Very strange: what can he have been doing there to crash? Some ridiculous showing off? I doubt it. It is true that he had referred to this trainer as a 'silly little airplane' in my presence after returning from a Fernandina familiarisation flight with a wannabe PPL jet pilot, but I took this to be light-hearted Thunderchief faux-bravado, and would not have considered this elegant mini-jet any sillier than the Jet Provost. I have since found out that the Russian visit was to arrange purchase of the four-ship Coca Cola display team. 'Give us the money and take them away' should have been adequate, but he was taking a senior officer (this can mean anything) for a ride, came barrelling down the field and rolled inverted. Kids' stuff if you can do it, but the machine immediately pulled into the ground.

Later in this book I will mention the very ancient anthropoid panic instinct. It's to do with survival – usually. In the air the passenger doesn't usually show it. Pilots can be much worse.

Oshkosh 1994

Bob Davis took me to Oshkosh in 1990 when I visited him to ask about chief judging, then in July 1994 I took a Concorde there for the show. This Concorde visit seemed to happen every other year, and although the Concorde was not a display act as such, its presence both in the air and standing in the static park was welcomed. The flights and necessary revenue were provided by a couple of local joyrides (charters) each day, with a Toronto similar fun flight at beginning and end. This arrangement was tacked on to some London-Toronto schedules that were sometimes arranged, thanks to the Canadian government authorising a supersonic route over Labrador and similar snowy Canadian places. Snow would have fallen off the trees, the odd moose startled by large-calibre gunfire sounding closer than you can imagine and maybe a bearded hunter's hut window rattled, but otherwise there was little environmental concern. This three-day Oshkosh visit did not go quite as well as I would have hoped, for two reasons: a technical decision on my part and an industrial one by the caring part of the crew – out-of-control democracy again.

When we collected the Concorde from Toronto there had been some problem with one of the buckets (a secondary nozzle) on the way from London. The electronic box that controlled this gadget would come up with a blue light if something was wrong, the main concern being uncommanded reverse thrust in flight – at any time – but this was not the case as such. I do not remember the details, but the standard fix was to lock the device in one generally useful but not ideal position in that there were minor supersonic fuel performance penalties, but this also meant no reverse on that engine. Engineering opinion on the spot considered that the problem would only occur in supersonic flight, so I opted not to lock the bucket. Oshkosh was OK for us but not over long, and this was high summer in the midst of the razzamatazz of this flamboyant show: Mid-West thunderstorm season, torrential rain, perhaps wind from every direction – this was possible. I'd rather have 4 reversers and a trouble-free subsonic Concorde.

Day One

We arrived at Oshkosh mid-afternoon, a bit late, but our long, thin, very pointy white and quite big flying machine had worked perfectly. The first of the rides around the Great Lakes went well that evening, with our low turn straight off the ground on takeoff, towards the local lake, afterburners blazing; standard procedure for runway 31L at New York. And this second landing of the day was normal: nothing wrong. No problems ahead.

Later that evening our PR man, Roger Mills (otherwise a Concorde captain) was informed that tomorrow the organisers would like the Concorde pilots (flight engineer counts as well – he knows much more than us) to attend the daily evening assembly of EAA (Experimental Aircraft Association) enthusiasts for the traditional Q&A, mini-lecture, tall stories and so on session. Our cabin crew insisted on attending, in uniform, on the stage. Suggestions that this was mechanical interest, afterburners, hair-on-fire-speeds and so on, nothing to do with airline things (supersonic bombers, yes), had no effect. They were part of the crew; an equal, in fact numerically superior part of the Concorde show, and threatened industrial action (going sick for the doctor-free two – or is it three days – that has become a standard BA cabin crew life-arranging ploy) if not allowed to join us on the stage. The EAA said they only wanted the pilots; if that was the case forget it, which was rather a shame for everyone, and I suppose did not endear us to the many fans who would have been disappointed. What did this say of the real captain's authority? Could I call in the police, or rustle up a gang of EAA heavies to physically restrain them? Had I, through my go-between Captain Mills, have insisted that they should sit in the audience there would have been no Concorde flights the next day, or the next. The airline employees present might have understood, but not the thousands of homebuilders, restorers, tinkerers, devoted polishers etc who flock to this mecca of flying enthusiasm. The brave and patriotic military men present might also have had problems with this pathetic demonstration of command behaviour, but this is the freedom they did, and still do, fight for. Anyone want to think about it?

In British Airways the struggle for equality status for cabin crew began with the introduction of the 747. I was there. The isolation of the smaller flight deck crew and the great multitude of plate layers who toiled downstairs in direct contact with our paying customers combined with the on-going, slow-burning English bloodless social revolution, were gaining a momentum that continues to this day. But it was on the next Oshkosh day that the second dent in my sense of identity occurred.

Day Two

Our first flight on Sunday, July 31st taxied out in the midst of preparations for the reenactment of the Great Marianas Turkey Shoot... or was it A Good Day at Schweinfurt? Or could it have been A Gathering of Little Friends, perhaps; even The Complete WW2 Story in Forty Minutes? No, it was bigger than that. Charlie Hillard was Air Boss. He was known to me from world aerobatic championships and just said 'Hi, Mike, it's Charlie' on the radio and left it at that. All was going well, then the dreaded happened. 'Reverse check' is an essential taxi-out item and a blue secondary nozzle light came on. There's no on-the-spot troubleshooting. The situation is simple: you shall not use this engine until whatever's wrong is fixed, or the bucket is locked out. 'Something's wrong with an engine, we have to taxi back and get it fixed.'

Spontaneously, organised chaos ensued. The parallel taxiway in front of and behind us was chock full of single and four-engined taildraggers also taxiing out, but everyone got the message. Assorted fighters bunched up to make space, B17s swerved off the tarmac and lolloped across the grass. Maybe we backtracked the runway between two exits but again we were back on the taxiway, this time headed against the flow, but the same thing happened; old aeroplanes making space.

The basic airmanship all round matched the machinery and the historic tradition: improvise, look after yourself, do what works. The air traffic man might have helped as well as he could, but his ability to police such a scene was limited. Eventually we were parked and our trusty support from New York got on with locking the offending bucket out at 20° as we watched waves of treasured museum pieces sweeping over, enormous petrol-fueled fireballs rising into the sky from the pretend bombs, and so on . . . but the sorting-yourself-out-on-the-grass, no radio, assembling in teams ready for your formation takeoff to the second – five vic biplanes first, box four Turbulents second to make up the diamond nine – reminded me of the Tiger Club non-radio full display opener tradition of thirty years ago, all done on the wristwatch. It can be done, but this is a tradition lost to history, I fear. Tempus fugit, and how!

Day Three

There were more display acts – vintage jets I think, who flew up and down, nothing much in the way of aerobatics – and I remember a boat visit to Kermit Weeks' Sunderland at anchor in the lake. This was a welcome moment of quiet, and the gentle rocking of the flying boat while one relaxed in a large comfortable vintage leather armchair in the downstairs bar cleared the mind and invited immediate sleep. 1930s and the all-points-east days, in every detail.

This Monday, August 1st, was going home day for many of the participants and visitors, but we had a last teatime ride to do. Prior to this we hung about the Concorde showing visitors around, one of whom was Yevgeni Frolov *(Gene, US)*. Since our last 1976 encounter at the Kiev aerobatic worlds he had grown eighteen years older, same as everyone else. I now know he was 24 then, not 17 as I thought, so he was 43 at this Oshkosh meeting, but looked exactly the same as the other quiet, unnoticeable, jacket-and-tie pilot with the thin briefcase who had helped us stay free of cloud in the Ukraine. I would have liked to take Frolov and his briefcase for the Concorde ride on our jump seat, but the charterer had filled us to the gunwales with paying passengers, so no dice. There would have been no surprises for the doyen of exotic jet manoeuvres, but it would have been nice. I think he proves my case about aerobatics and spare capacity.

We set off for this final one-hour jolly and would leave next day, but the busy tower controller thought we were headed for home. 'Bye, thanks for coming' he said as he handed us over to the approach frequency. 'No, we're coming back,' I said. 'Sure you are, see you next year,' was the reply. No time for a long discussion so we continued around our airways route. An hour later, headed south on long finals, I could see plenty of aeroplanes of many kinds crossing our track east to west. A great multitude of flying things was taking off on the easterly runway and many were headed west to the wide-open spaces, nose to tail and side by side as well, all flying between us and the 18 runway touchdown marks. The Oshkosh exodus had begun, albeit more concentrated and orderly than the fabled arrival action. Approach control handed us over to the tower. 'Just keep going and land' I said to Andy Darke, our co-pilot, who was flying. 'I'll watch out for things.'

Despite a coordinated air traffic system (with statutory flight plans), and my after-takeoff remarks, the tower man still thought we had vanished into the distant sky for a year at least, or maybe the usual two. 'Concorde AE on finals for 18' was my opener. After a brief pause his reply was dramatic, 'All you guys on the north side, get the hell out of there, the Concorde's coming!' The sight of a triangle in the sky had a similarly theatrical impact. Like a flock of pigeons that realise you're coming their way, an explosion of metal, wood, some fabric and plenty of state-of-the-art carbon fibre radiated from our projected flightpath. All was well. Andy landed without problem and nobody crashed, I think, at that particular time. Maybe it was something to tell the folks back home about.

CHAPTER 43

BUOCHS 1994: THE BEST PILOTS' AIRSHOW EVER

I had a small part in this airshow, much smaller than would attract attention, but that was no reason to run it down. I had been asked to help judge a Breitling aerobatic competition on August 26th and 27th at Buochs, a 2000m runway field south of Lucerne, and home of the Pilatus factory. Apart from a few Zurich nightstops in the '60s and the Yverdon world championships in 1990 I had little experience of Switzerland, especially its military, or national ability to organise what matters, and let the rest look after itself.

Arrival Day

On Thursday the 25th I made my way to Stans, the nearest town, by British Airways and Swiss Railways. Stans is small as towns go and I knew the airfield was close by – but where was it? Had I come to the wrong place? A walk down what had to be the correct road brought me to a few airfield buildings and a small runway, but what sort of small-scale affair was this going to be? No big fence with barbed wire on top, you could just walk in and wander about, and the valley it was in didn't look big enough for jets; and on the extended centreline, maybe a mile away, was a big pyramid of a hill – definitely a mountain by British standards. Maybe you could get a slow jet in and out of here carefully, but airshow stuff – forget it. I suppose the light aircraft aerobatics will work, but no straying out of the box. But apart from not straying out of the box I couldn't have been more wrong.

The new CIVA (Breitling) contest discipline

I found where the Breitling people were setting up shop, reported to manager Jean-Louis Monnet, got myself signed in, and picked up my Breitling goodies, including a snazzy jacket with a huge work of art on the back signifying this sponsor and my judge status. I first came across J-L Monnet at Yverdon 1990, where he represented Breitling's aerial marketing interests and had their PC7 at his disposal. Jean-Louis had been Patrouille de France leader (and previous member, of course) as well both a Mirage and Jaguar squadron commander, and carried this history with patrician modesty and cultured pragmatism. This new type of FAI-sanctioned contest was based on the traditional four-minute do-what-you-like programme, with a new and artistic twist. Like Olympic ice-skating the performances were accompanied by music, and the aerobatic manoeuvring was supposed to interpret the pilot's choice of musical compilation, the objective being to make aerobatic competition more accessible to the layman, and a new attraction at displays. I had not witnessed this discipline before (apart from the non-musical version). It would not be as easy to judge as it may sound, and, despite my honest judge's sense of rigorous objectivity, I eventually found it more convenient to join the others – and not bother too much about musical interpretation. After all, we were now into show business: the art of illusion.

Across the field, on the factory side, were numerous aircraft, mostly single-engined jets of different types. A long closely-packed line of camouflaged and covered Swiss Hunters looked quiet and parked for the duration. Once Breitling had organised themselves we were taken to our accommodation at what seemed like a large further education college north of Lucerne – find a suitable room for yourself – and next morning were picked up by a Swiss Air Force Puma from the carpark. This was more like it, and it seemed that Saturday would be a practice day available to the public as spectators, and those military flyers who wished to run through their routines, and get used to the substantial natural masonry around most of the small field. Immediately to the south, just beyond a light aircraft circuit width, is the Stanserhorn, 4,600 ft above the field altitude, and beside it the Engelberg valley that runs south to the real Alps – the first one being the 10,000ft snowy Titlis. A few kilometers to the west is Mount Pilatus, a mere 6,500 ft. The groups of parked visiting aircraft suggested aerobatic teams. For visitors, as much practice as you can get makes a lot of sense here. What will they be able to do, at all, was this flatlander's initial question.

Friday

First up for a morning practice was the Spanish instructor's team and their straight-winged friendly-looking Casa C-101 Aviojets. Were there only five? Or maybe six or seven; but these looked like a random selection from the school flight line. Next up were the dark blue Aeromacchis of the famous Frecche Tricolore, without smoke: that's for later. But there was still a cloud layer over the field; not low but below the local mountain tops. They took off in two finger fours and a pair to make ten, all very close. There was no doubt this was a committed close proximity team, and after circling round and getting organised they fired in in their special triangle shape and went straight into a loop. After passing approximately the 40° past the upward vertical stage, they went into cloud. 'Look at that' I said to Jean-Louis. He shrugged, 'Italians' he said. There were sounds of urgent power changing; they emerged on the way down more or less in formation, but not the same one, and quite a bit wider. Something had happened up there in terms of maintaining satisfactory visual contact, I would guess, but the spirited (desperate is a bit too strong) and snappy getting it together on the way down was spectacular theatre – it reminded me of the 1970 Red Arrows' deliberate join up loop in the Gnat – but the spontaneous nature of this example had not been planned, and was all the more exciting for that. Next morning before our pickup I told the leader how entertaining was their closeness and the visible bucking around of the lightly loaded trainers, especially when they make their landing configuration low speed/high power tightly packed pass. 'Yes,' he agreed. 'We like to fly with heart,' placing hand on heart. The others looked on approvingly. He meant it, and by golly they were good at it.

As a first item of the Friday afternoon we had round one of our musical free programme aerobatic competition. The music system required coordination, with a special man to organise the tapes in the correct order of pilots, press the button when the pilot says 'go', and of course make sure the playback is transmitted to the pilot by radio, and fed into the PA system so the spectators can enjoy the 'Artistic Impression', as the ice skaters call it. Generally the skaters and their coaches do very well at this. It's obvious that a lot of work goes into choosing suitable music, and choreographing the figures to fit really quite well with what we are hearing, the idea being to create something balletic. Unfortunately the timing and style of some, not necessarily all, competition aerobatic aircraft does not lend itself easily to this concept. The usual global criteria applied – harmony and rhythm, versatility, execution (how well it was done etc), technical merit (how difficult), positioning – then the new addition; how well did it go with the music? Each of these topics are marked out of 100 (the old ten with more space between numbers, but no easier) and each of equal weight.

The degree to which the flying went with the music was very variable, to say the least (to my ears and eyes). With an unlimited choice of what the word 'music' allows there are great possibilities, but thoughtful and informed advice would probably have helped some competitors. I could see, or thought I could see, some correlation in some cases; little or none at all in others. We would have another go tomorrow.

During the afternoon there were more display practice runs. A Czech Sukhoi 22 (a big fighter) flew around a bit carefully, then three Swiss Mirages took off, a solo followed by a pair. You would expect them to disappear into the sky like rockets, but no. With an informative commentary we had a demonstration of one against two dog-fighting tactics – in the circuit. This was astonishing to see, and I imagined the energy level was scaled down to achieve this, but the barrelling, pulling, scissoring was remarkable to see so close at hand. The tactics (explained in German) were quite beyond me, and how the singleton managed to win I can't imagine, but as a demonstration of communal expertise (with considerable care, I imagine) this looked remarkable to me. Either that or this Mirage version has good handling qualities, Concorde angle of attack range, a variety of useful speeds and plenty of thrust. This makes sense, of course.

Two Red Arrow Hawks appeared in the air, the leader and a #3, and proceeded around a sort of formation programme, but it wasn't exactly attention-getting. Where were the others, and when would they all practise? Why did the two fly away again – weren't they going to land here? These and other questions would be answered tomorrow. That evening, all involved in the display were treated to dinner in the largest steamer on Lake Lucerne. The party took out the whole dining saloon and we had a splendid evening as the vessel made its usual schedule, stopping off here and there, though we could only tell this by the motion of the ship. The Swiss Air Force (called army) must be paying for all of this. With such an observant and politically included population how could they get away with it? There was a reason. (When you order a substantial number of new complex aircraft the manufacturer is naturally grateful.)

Saturday: sticking to the script

The Puma picked us up again, another mixed bunch of passengers, and I sat next to judge John (Colonel) Morrisey and Jean-Louis' two daughters, who were in their twenties. As before, the major in the left hand seat gave us a commentary on the Alpine sights we passed, and as we approached the airfield he told us that the lieutenant (at the controls) would show us a stall turn, imagining that the odd aerobater amongst us would be impressed. There was nothing wrong with the stall turn, but the girls did not like it much and after we landed John asked me what I thought – should he have done that? I was non-committal and he asked: 'What was the mission?'

'To take us safely from the car park to the airfield and not worry anyone,' I said.

'Was it carried out as intended?'

'No'.

'Exactly.'

As a downtown Hanoi Thunderchief survivor, he had a strong sense of sticking to the script, and when it comes to showing off in an unknown environment I agree – however good the Swiss training system.

Yesterday's results

When we assembled prior to the day's contest flights we were addressed by Jiri Kobrle representing the FAI, and there to see fair play. He told us that a pilot had protested about his low marks yesterday. I think they were mine, but Jiri said that all the judges were chosen for their great experience and fairness etc. etc., and that he would not recognise such protesting at a non-national invitational and paid contest (for the pilots). Asking around, I'm sure it was my low score for one pilot's interpretation of the music, of which there was none that I could recognise. Instead of the zero deserved I probably settled for 6 (maybe 59%), but it became clear that most judges had adopted an approximately overall assessment for the impossible judging task anyway, music or no music. I know of one who waited until the end of a routine and scored a whole flight with the same number across the board. This is the ultimate overall impression decision, as in the old days. The pilot who did not like my generous (I thought) music score expected to win, and had flown his usual strong arm and leg series of power manoeuvres regardless of the new criterion, to a totally unsuitable piece of much-loved sun-dappled early romantic rich German teenaged prodigy's charming confection. By contrast I gave a well-deserved 80% for music to a couple of pilots who deserved it, comparatively. I got the impression that the music thing was largely ignored by the judges, and Jean-Louis agreed. He told me he was planning to change the system and have completely independent artistic judges score this topic, but I don't think this happened. Perhaps the (now professional) pilots did not like the idea. To save trouble I did what the others did on this second run; after all, you can't mix entertainment and paid sport if you want realistic judging.

The airshow proper

Before we started, someone high up in the military explained the reason for this year's show. It was to celebrate two things. The rejoicing was for the recent close-run, as usual, result of the public referendum to decide whether to buy the F18 Hornet as the new Swiss fighter. The answer had been yes (cheers and applause). The second reason was to honour and celebrate the legendary and long-serving Hunter, which would be retired (respectful and contemplative applause). Following our judging we repaired to the Breitling hospitality tent to watch the rest of the show, and what a bonanza of entertaining flying it was; good hospitality too.

Of course we had the six Hunters of the Patrouille Suisse, elegant and orderly. This part-time team is flown by full-time instructors currently engaged in teaching the latest equipment. We saw a Venom and some Vampires from olden times, the Spanish team, and the Frecche Tricolore and their sumptuous, over-the-top tricolore smoke-laying (something of a liability in stable autumnal Alpine valleys when fog is waiting for an excuse – but keep it in). There was a rocket assisted Mirage takeoff, more Mirage dogfighting in the circuit plus various solo jet aerobatics, plus assorted historic flying machinery, and the Patrouille de France. This Alphajet team had practised the previous day, but was smaller than usual, and the performance lacked lustre; tentative somehow. I heard rumours; something was not right. I don't know what it was, but I mentioned to J-L that it did not resemble the Fouga Magisters I'd seen at Salon in 1972. He inferred problems, and also said 'Each time they get a new leader the speeds go up by 10kts.'

The Red Arrows appeared, all nine today, running in from the west. Faster and smoother than the Frecche, as befits the higher performance aircraft, but with perfect station-keeping (which makes it look too easy) their display radiated cool professionalism, especially considering the visual backdrop of towering mountains in the distance, but more relevantly, the mere 6,000ft examples very close by. They had based themselves at Emmen, the regular military base not far away, but came over, of course, to the post show get-together party.

I asked the number 9 man what it had looked like from the back, and how they could manage a full show without ever having been to Buochs before. He said the experience was something special and looked fantastic from his seat, but explained the convenient way of rehearsing for a geographically unusual place. They had practised for Buochs quite a lot, he said, at Scampton. Lincolnshire does not look like Switzerland, but his explanation reminded me of the *Dambusters* film and the reservoir models. Now, they superimposed the map of Buochs on that of Scampton, specifically associating the high ground with local landmarks – farmhouses, crossroads etc. The leader redrew the usual routine to accommodate these imaginary hills and mountains, tried it out with a wingman, then practised with the whole team. It had worked well. I've seen a video of the Buochs flight taken from the #9 Hawk. Viewed though the rest of the team bucking around in front (sort of smooth, but like a wobbly big aeroplane), it does look scenically fantastic.

But the day was not finished yet. When the show had as good as ended, and the Breitling stand was buzzing with eager conversation, glasses in hand, Hunters from the other side started taking off – pair after pair after pair. Going home, one would suppose, but this was to be the ceremonial goodbye flypast of these new-looking aeroplanes. Eventually they reappeared from the east, 40 Hunters in perfect formation. The pictures you can google up don't do the real thing justice – they record a practice. On the day there were two at the front leading the four perfect diamond nines making up a giant box 4, discernible as separate diamonds by the merest one aeroplane's width, completely symmetrical spacing. How this was arranged so perfectly I've no idea, but this was flawless Swiss perfection. We will never see its like again, especially from the Hunters. (I happen to know that Claude Nicollier, 4 x shuttle astronaut, was flying #2 in the front diamond.)

As he left for America John Morrisey's conscience got the better of him and he told me that he was sure he had muddled up his score sheets, and given the wrong scores to two or more pilots. 'Please explain to J-L, see if you can sort it out,' he said. I could have done what I thought – what the hell, forget it – but I did mention it to our Breitling boss. He said 'It's too late to do anything, what does it matter, forget it.' Good management potential, I thought.

CHAPTER 44

AEROBATICS FOR SALE

As an amateur pilot by nature I must be thankful for the Concorde hobby as the one that produced a salary (and provided considerable entertainment, one way or another), and supplied a close group of colleagues – a rare privilege in large airline life. It also provided time off to pursue other interests, none of which did I charge for. As an Air Operator's Certificate aviation business Avia Special needed a Training Manager and a Type Rating Examiner – me; and James Black, a real amateur pilot, to represent all the other management functions required for reputable trading. The sole purpose of this AOC work was to conduct enjoyable aerobatic pleasure flights for the general paying public. It worked well, without problem. But for the sake of continuity we start with a happening related to what I believe is a feature of the human condition that killed TJ Brown. It is yet another cautionary tale.

Aerobatic instruction for pilots with a licence did not require the hire and reward qualification, being a consenting adults affair, and an event I experienced while flying with a pilot who I had not met before encourages the telling of this story. Aerobatic instruction was normally a completely different activity from the joyrides, but as an extra project James offered an aerobatic lesson 'clinic' for interested pilots. How different would it be to the aerobatic joyride – not much really? Actually it was – quite a lot.

This pilot owned his own aircraft – a nifty Italian two-seater with constant speed propeller and retractable tricycle wheels, eminently suitable for the elegant military swooping and diving he could easily be doing. The easiest place to start for a complete beginner is the ballistic (aileron) roll, called the 'Champagne Roll' by Peter Phillips when conducting marketing flights in the Victa Airtourer. The instructions are simple, there is no high positive or any negative g, and it gives a comfortable idea of manoeuvring with the scene rotating outside. It finishes where it started – usually.

As usual, I demonstrated an example. Everyone seemed happy. The first attempt started well, no hint of a problem, and the pilot duly raised the nose a bit and applied the necessary aileron. Round we went, sitting comfortably. Then, without warning, my 'student' pulled the stick into the pit of his stomach with astonishing rapidity at the halfway point as the upside-down horizon passed the wings level picture. The CAP10 gave a jolt and stopped flying. In an instant, quasi weightless flight had encountered the positive 6g stall. This event happened to define the manoeuvring speed, and It was fortunate that our basic aerobatic syllabus remained within cruising speed, 120kts, which is close to this parameter. Feeling upside-down is usually more scary than just seeing it, but the picture was enough in this case to trigger this reaction.

Dr Bruno Banzer, the paragliding psychologist, refers to the 'Neanderthal's full stall', indicating a primitive instinct to pull whatever is in your grasp in times of panic (this is almost always wrong in flight). In fact Neanderthal man is alive and kicking (or pulling), and I have seen him traveling placidly on the Swiss bus (the Neander valley is not so far away – just east of Düsseldorf). I believe 2% of human genes are Neanderthal, but the emergency 'pull anyway' instinct comes from our jungly tree-climbing forbears. I have not seen the like before or since in such a full-on and fundamental example, and the nanosecond between apparent normality and the comfort zone circuit breaker tripping can be a surprise. It's lurking in the software somewhere. We were high in the sky: TJ was not so lucky, and without more information one cannot make assumptions about what happened. He didn't pull the stick back, but someone else probably did. It would also be wrong to assume that all Russian pilots are familiar with low-level aerobatics, or not afraid of upside-down flying. Flying with trusting passengers can sometimes be safer than flying with pilots.

The joyride business

This project, by contrast, was a success. The job start-up procedure for staff qualification needed some checkouts and licence signing by suitable Civil

Aviation Authority representatives, the same as the airline six-monthly base check system, and the operation as a whole also had to be vetted with a representative passenger flight. The first time this was arranged a CAA person tipped me off that the particular inspector was a stickler for details. 'Have you got your scales?' my informant asked. Of course our manual covered weights etc, but in aerobatic mode (no fuel in the generous rear ferry tank – it would take you down to the Mediterranean) it was not possible for two occupants to exceed maximum weight. Despite its weight-carrying capacity the little two-seater was designed for two typical Frenchmen. It was not possible to fit two weight-busting bodies inside. But time was now of the essence, and phoning around rustled up some bathroom scales, which I could nonchalantly whip out when the question came up: 'Scales? Of course, I wouldn't be without them.'

Ts crossed and Is dotted, we were in business, so then I had to be checked out as an examiner for this aircraft, to conduct our pilots' base checks. I had imagined that I might get some sort of blanket qualification – all single-engined two-seat aerobatic aircraft up to several hundred HP, let us say – but there was no such latitude. The CAP10B was its own special device. (My Concorde entry said Concorde 136 Variant – where were all the others?) Since my instrument rating examiner course at Stansted in the 1970s the general style of a test debriefing seemed to have mellowed a bit. The original theory was that in order to make your candidate listen eagerly, desperately perhaps, to the pearls of wisdom you wished to scatter you should keep him or her in a position of uncertainty about the pass/fail result until the end of the address (it could mean end of career, in theory). Some professionals seemed to realise that this attitude was a bit spartan and generally unnecessary; after all, we were dealing with civilised professionals, not devious habitual lead-swinging miscreants, as may have been the case in bygone years. 'Go on, tell them they've passed – put them out of their misery'. On the other hand I have to acknowledge that the examining power includes to the public in general, not just reputable chums in the business.

Interestingly enough, the man who conducted my first CAP10 type rating examiner test was old school, and had none of this namby-pamby, be nice, they're nervous anyway approach. Obviously he was an experienced man of the people (he told me he'd spent many hours, years, eons, before the mast in transport command). Also clearly at home with a dinky propeller-driven aerobatic trainer, he had no trouble with the tasks I had set him, and my pretend debriefing was encouraging and positive. But he was not totally happy. 'What about your notepad? You didn't do anything with it. This is how to do it' he said, and plonked his own on the table between us. 'Face down, so they can't see any of what you might or might not have not written on it. Just leave it there. Suspense. It makes them pay more attention'.

True enough, but I have to say that over the several years that I met CAA inspectors and examiners for my own small aircraft base check (every six months), or examiner renewal (was it three years?) – and it was very seldom the same one twice – I was impressed by the practicality and people-handling ease that consistently indicated a wealth of experience in a variety of flying pursuits. You don't have to ask – you can tell. Spare capacity again? Of course: and the closely defined but personally widespread world of airliners did not always run with such professional aplomb. If anyone were to tell me 'You're only an airline pilot', I would understand perfectly.

The product and the customers

As a start up I don't think James and I had a problem with aerobatic competence, but what should we actually sell? The subject conjures up a variety of emotions in the minds of those who hear the aerobatic word. The most pessimistic sentiments probably belong to those with some experience of piloting, especially military learners, maybe of days gone by. Rough and ready manoeuvres-by-numbers instruction will provide exposure to unusual attitudes, speeds and accelerations, and if this is done within a bootcamp environment with much sick bag expectation the result is unlikely to produce the confidence and untroubled acceptance to be desired by more peaceful training organisations. Shock tactics to instil stress inoculation in hapless warriors where time is pressing is another story. I know military pilots who declare that aerobatics is dangerous. Of course it all depends, like many other things in life, on who does it, and under what circumstances.

It's the unusual and unnatural human experiences of flight that promote the sick-making fear associated with aerobatics. My intention was to present this strangeness head on, as the first step in a learning process, and continue from there. It's a marketing job, selling the ideas, and I could not have guessed in advance how well it would work. Side by side seating and good communication are both essential, as is a good strapping in system. The CAP10 had all of these advantages, and could be flown round the basic energy exchange figures with very little control movement. Not like Hollywood flying exploits.

On the climb out the passenger could have a little (unofficial) feel of the controls, and then as a suitable height and place was reached the experience-

and confidence-building began. Feeling continuously heavier was the first totally unusual topic, addressed while a turn was slowly steepened. Arms and legs feel heavier, head feels heavier and so on, making the point that it is not a problem, just different. It is important that they agree with you – they always did, but this acceptance defines the rate of progress. Reducing the bank and allowing a gentle zoom was a chance to introduce the lighter feeling part by slowly easing to a half g nose over – half your normal weight – and the moving picture outside (spare hand useful for pointing out the view) keeping the attention elsewhere but themselves and their currently popular emotions. In a couple of minutes they have accepted a range between 2g and half a g, with the picture changing at the same time. Thereafter a more useful range will be accepted without special comment because attention is focused on other new things. On the strength of this thesis of heavier and lighter, picture moving as well, one can lead seamlessly into a nice barrel roll: sitting straight, feet on floor, the same heavier and lighter – the picture rotating all the way this time, but all smoothly done. It works, and you continue down this road as appropriate and with a logical progression: half-Cubans, the complete loop, the stall turn, even TJ's amazing upside down flying. 'As appropriate' is important, and one could also write a list of pilot requirements for the job. The first is: the pilot must have not the slightest inclination to show how good he thinks he is.

My own first experience of an aerobatic manoeuvre was a good solid 4g+ loop, all the way round, in the Kinloss air experience Chipmunk. Not a problem as such, but no gentle lead up. More alarming was John Stone's first slow roll demo in the Christchurch Tiger Moth, 1959. The roll was good, with the unavoidable 'slow' noticeable, but it was the six inches between seat and trouser that was worrying in the open cockpit and its vintage strap system. A young person stores all these early details for future reference, but a natural human mistake is to consider your own experience a necessary yardstick for others. World championship skills are not necessary, nor is the self-contained obsessive character of the elite competitor. It quickly occurred to me that a successful track record of family fatherhood would be more appropriate, as a first tick in the box for staff recruitment.

Some customers were garnered by advertisement and flown by prior arrangement, but a stall (marketing kind) at an aerial event tended to provide a stream of enthusiasts once the ball had started rolling. 'Do one manoeuvre (easy and recognisable) over the field when you get back', was frequent advice, because the waiting hopefuls, and others, would be impressed by the subsequent happy smiling face of the victim, having observed evidence of the manoeuvre they must have experienced. I remember one customer, expressedly nervous of anything other than cruising around, who I'd got as far as the barrel roll in the short time available. Little by little, and carefully, the logic behind the sensations were revealed, and the final proper figure added almost as an afterthought on the way back to the field – the end in sight. Braced in his seat with the additional help of hands on suitable parts of the structure, he assumed a look of demonic possession; staring glazed eyes, mouth fixed in a devilish grin – expectation and terror in equal parts, no doubt. I hope this is going to work, I thought as we swept up and around, and the victim's eyes followed the rotating scenery in wonderment. But it was the reaction as the airfield and all around it returned to its normal place, just a bit closer, that was dramatic. 'I seen them Red Arrows do that – You bloody idiots! I said,' but the sense of exultation, relief and achievement (his own) was rather touching. A true revelation. Had his day been made? I think so.

Other staff

James had recruited a very nice New Zealand lady, Sue Jeffries, to help with Avia Special admin and I sought suitable volunteer pilots to help out on busy days. Back-to-back trips of 20 minutes without getting unstrapped in between had the potential for a taxing day, and a certain professional stamina was required to maintain standards. Following my shocking 707 lapse and the illegal simulator checks, Avia Special now had a secretary to keep track of base checks as well as statutory maintenance, marketing, crew scheduling and so on.

Jeremy Rendall had started his flying career with Joan Hughes and the Tiger Moth more than thirty years previously, I would guess. He was now a Concorde training captain and had done some CAP10 aerobatics with us fairly recently. Enough boxes ticked. I took the CAP10 to Compton Abbas to fly with Stack Butterley, also Concorde with assorted experience elsewhere. He currently flew the cadets in the Chipmunk and was the link man for the Hawk/Concorde exchange arrangement. We had a jolly zoom around and he would have fitted in well, with a good line in confidence-inspiring and entertaining banter, but nothing came of the audition. Perhaps it would not fit in with domestic arrangements.

Alan Quartly had recently joined the Concorde. Whatever he had done in British Airways was not of interest, but he had been a Hercules pilot, and now flew cadets as well as the rocket. Then there was Chris Mann, also now BA. Also from the Hercules, he had been a Wing Commander, involved in special operations. He was reluctant to comment on the recent scandal of crew members parachuting with the SAS while training in Africa, but the SAS had been so enthusiastic about their jumping, the esprit de corps, and what harmless fun it had been. Totally outrageous, of course: who ever heard of a captain bailing out for fun, leaving his trembling apprentice in charge? But who do we want to do distasteful fighting on our behalf? Politically correct self-serving finger-pointing jobsworths? Apparently yes: but there are some jobs you get on with and do not talk about to the majority voters, ultimately for their own good.

Chris showed the military officer's seamless versatility one morning when we were staying in the Victorian brick-built B&B hotel in Eccles, adjacent to Barton airfield. I seem to remember we had both aerobatic joyrides and Antonov private hires on the go this weekend. On going down to breakfast on the Sunday morning we found Chris already downstairs, taking orders, cooking and dishing up the full English to the handful of guests. 'When I came down I found the landlady in a bit of a state, in tears – domestic/social disaster of some sort, I can't go on, etc. I sent her upstairs with a cup of tea and told her not to worry – I could do the breakfast.' And so it was.

Bartle Frere also flew passenger flights in the CAP10. I see that I signed his 1179 test on Sept. 6th 1994. The Frere family have a distinguished history of explorers, empire administrators, bishops and academics, and Bartle had been a fairly regular learner of ours – possibly starting in Aerobatic and Artistic days: the logbooks would reveal this. More willing boy scout than family father, he was keen and helpful, assisting with Antonov parachute flights, and arranging a successful and interesting private hire session from a farmer's field near Abingdon.

A daredevil foreigner's brush with the CAA

On July 3rd 1994 I went to Humberside with Alan Quartly and the CAP10 to do joyrides. Sue Jeffries drove up there to manage sales and ride scheduling, but we did not do a single one. Near the cold North Sea it was obvious that this could be a hazy place, and although this was high summer, and a cloudless day, the visibility never got near our operating limit of 5 km. And it was an airshow event, observed by the retired Wing Commander, whose name I forget, who was responsible for CAA airshow safety, assisted by Pete Jarvis, now without a licence due to a heart problem, but certainly able to give a second opinion about fouls and touchline infringements.

A Concorde came, driven by one of our new captains. The runway is just over 2,000 metres long, acceptable but not long for a Concorde. I watched with interest; first to spot the aeroplane in the air at all, then how the basic skill of a visual approach, landing and run out would work out in these hot, steamy no wind conditions. Once a primary skill, the satisfactory visual approach and accurate landing, without electronic aids, seems to approach the too difficult level for a number of today's worldwide airline pilots. Our man did well, and no clever comments are called for here, but it was Nicolai Timofeev who stole the show – for all spectators, including the two sage CAA inspectors.

When I had last seen him he was in the process of buying his own special-price-for-locals SU26, and was now doing European airshows to make ends meet. He'd flown to Humberside from Holland, and was going back there after the show. This was the original Russian team model with limited on-board fuel, so he had arrived with the external ferry tank underneath the fuselage. This was an elegant silver streamlined shiny affair which looked just like a bomb, and as I helped him take it off, using the tool kit of assorted spanners that went with it, I wondered what the spectators behind the rope might have thought we were doing. The weather made Quartly and me spectators anyway, and as Timofeev's start time came up I asked him what he thought of the visiblity. 'Are you going to fly?' 'Definitely, I need the money,' he said, 'but I'll only do easy stuff.'

Like Kvotchur at Biggin Hill this was a master at work, but much lower. The only effective visual reference was the ground below, so going high for something clever was pointless in the sunny goldfish bowl. Timofeev wisely restricted himself to basic/intermediate manoeuvres, with guaranteed safety – no negative, no flick rolls – but the easy busking was done with such panache, energy, precision and lowness (all the better to see the ground nearby) that the overall effect was dramatic and inspiring. In fact it had all been playing the ground, courtesy of manoeuvring ability and horsepower. The height over the runway wouldn't have mattered, but after running out of on-axis ideas Timoveef threw in some sort of level circling something - this pads out the time. He disappeared from our view, then reappeared heading back to the display line from behind the crowdline, still at his 50 feet bottoming-out height. He happened to fly over the heads of our veteran ministry men in the process. I walked over. 'We want to see him before he leaves' they said, ominously.

He taxied back to the grass in front of the ropes and I went to help bolt the tank and its various pipes back in their ferry places. Spectators came through the ropes to congratulate, wring hands and declare they were there because they'd seen him before, or that they'd never seen such an exciting display, ever. Sue asked what I thought. 'That was a display of flying with Russian commitment and passion' I said. She thought about it, and understood (I think). As Timofeev and I struggled away with our spanners, dripping petrol, I mentioned the flying over the crowd rule and the required interview. 'I will tell them I am young Russian pilot wishing to learn. Anyway, I don't want to come back to Britain.' He now (25 years later), lives in Florida, and has the same single seater. To some extent I sympathise with him. Rules and regulations are one thing; skill, experience, judgment and maturity are quite another, both in how to apply them, and the piloting itself. It is true that he had flown over the crowd at a low height, although completely under control. It would seem that in the free West, losing control has become acceptable so long as the ensuing crash occurs at a suitable distance from those who have paid to witness the event. Well, you just can't get the quality these days, can you?

CHAPTER 45

ANTONOV 2
1991 – 1997

An airliner of your own

After the rentals of the Czech and Hungarian Antonovs in 1992, James Black decided to buy one. Following the collapse of the Soviet system and general confusion about what 'bizniz' meant, previous state property came up for sale. Having been given the books of a state organisation selling some of it seemed a good way of balancing them, or, even better, buying a luxury property in Switzerland – or even a major football team. James made enquiries of our Czech friends and was offered a machine at a good price, and it was nearly new, so OK-UIN appeared. We started with some refresher practice to get our previous helpers up to speed, and continued with an assortment of rides, outings with friends and parachute dropping.

I see that on May 19th 1993 I made a photo flight with a Cessna for Avia Special marketing. A retired Pete Jarvis came along, keen to fly some formation on the Cessna from the right-hand seat, as the #3 position had been requested by the photographer. And then at the end of that month Steve Bohill-Smith put together a family and friends Sunday picnic outing to Old Warden for one of the Shuttleworth Collection's regular flying days. The weather was not perfect for the delicate exhibits – warm front, rain on and off with west wind – but our journeys to and from were not problematical. We had a full passenger load plus the B-Smith Labrador/Retriever type dog which stood in the aisle to prop itself up. Though getting on a bit there was nothing wrong with it, but it found that lying on the floor was unsettling because of the Wright Cyclone subtle vibro-massage, and preferred to shudder on all fours wedged between the seats next to its mistress, none the worse for the experience.

We parked parallel to the crowd rope facing into wind, to avoid tying down. The huge biplane rocked gently all afternoon but showed no sign of going anywhere, and when we came to leave it was evident that the wheels had gently worked themselves into convenient pits in the soft ground: not too deep – about a tyre's width; only halfway to axle depth. Power would be needed to climb out of these natural chocks, so we waited for other visiting 'light' aircraft parked behind to leave before making our own attempt. The wind had picked up as the cold front approached and backtracking for takeoff distance was not necessary if the full-on short takeoff were to be used. Remaining spectators of all kinds looked aghast as Steve wound the machine up to full power on the brakes, with only about a third of the grass runway remaining. Surely not? It's much too big; but of course after a 40-yard trundle the biplane and its ton of passengers lifted off and made its slow and shallow full flap initial climb. After the carefully-judged clean up in stages normal service is resumed and a circle around the field brought us overhead. The wind at 1,000ft approached 50 kph – perfect for the amazing standing still routine: leave climb power on, run three o clock flap and bring the speed back until the leading edge slats clunk out and put the machine into its landing/parachutal mode, close to 50 kms indicated, and a slight descent – rudder to keep straight and aileron for wings (almost) level. As already mentioned from our training, this configuration is of no normal use except during the landing manoeuvre, but looks like the hover – from the ground.

This day out was reminiscent of the heady days of the thirties, the well-heeled socialising by biplane on grass, the tinkle of tea-cups and laughter, tennis, cucumber sandwiches and champagne, casual elegance with a smattering of erudition thrown in, if you were lucky. Those days have gone, and were not available to all, anyway: but surely many others, even now, would enjoy the sense of minor adventure with aviation history thrown in?

The optimistic hope was somehow to include the Antonov 2 on our Air Operators Certificate, and operate one commercially. This had been resolutely turned down by the CAA because of the complete separation of engineering development and legislation between West and East since the 1917 Rivolutsi. 'Everything in the West is based on what has gone before, and we do not even have a starting place.' As an EU precedent James raised the example of the German Antonov 2 currently carrying fare-paying passengers. It's a special case: it came with the unification of Germany so could continue its work as a qualified East German machine – grandfather rights as a special favour to their newly-liberated DDR brothers and sisters – but EU togetherness does not extend across the Channel. For you this idea is over.

James came up with another idea; a better one. The Antonov maximum permitted weight is exactly the traditional limit for a single-engined private pilot's licence – 12,500lb, 5,700kg in new money. This is two thirds of the weight of a fully-loaded P47 Thunderbolt (single seat taildragger) with a mere 40% of its power, and is theoretically suitable for the required level of that licence. Anyone with a PPL can hire it for their own use, like a Cessna from a club. Take friends and relatives for a ride? Of course, there's no difference, so that's how the private hire system started.

Private hire

The clients didn't actually go solo, and one of us two would occupy a front seat as 'advisor', but as for the money it was the same as the West London Aero Club: the hiring pilot pays. This aeroplane had 12 passenger seats (which could be unbolted from the floor and taken out to make room for parachutists), so up to 12 friends could come along for the novel adventure. Jeremy Rendall was my first conductee on May 16th 1993. This Sunday outing was a birthday celebration lunch at the Rowbarge pub, alongside the Kennet river and canal. We flew to Brimpton, a small grass strip airfield within walking distance; drizzle, wind across – typical conditions – but the appeal of the scale effect, carrying capacity and short field performance of this relatively large and capacious aircraft was immediately apparent. Jeremy's daughter Lucy drove back to White Waltham. Lucy was to join the Royal Air Force and become the third generation of Rendalls to captain the same standard VC10.

Conducting a flight with a pilot of unspecified experience (a licence was the only requirement) was very similar to airliner base training, except that the candidate had no type training whatsoever, and had very likely never flown a taildragger before. But the Antonov was a docile and good-natured beast, with many excellent and quite sophisticated handling qualities. It had, however, much of the ambience of a large transport aircraft and very little, if any, light aircraft feel to it. On September 13th 1992 James and I had been to Duxford to perform our breathtaking routine. David Ross of the Concorde came along and had a fly on the way. Sitting in the sizeable cockpit with its vintage greenhouse windows, instruments and many knobs and switches, growling and trembling across the countryside, he said 'It's just like being in a Shackleton'. Perhaps he was roughly right. He had been a Canberra PR pilot, then Jet Provost instructor, but this comment did give us some idea of what other supersonic colleagues might have done – Hutchinson, Linfield, Butterly, Dixon? Is this correct? Have I missed anyone out? Sorry, but this levity is to give an idea of the Antonov experience as received by *Pilot Magazine*'s target reader as described to me by editor James Gilbert – it's the Cherokee pilot.

A drawing of the Antonov pilot's picture of cowling and air intake box on top against the horizon, a couple of speeds and the fundamentals of steering on the ground by brake was enough for a get-you-going briefing. Other suitable items could mentioned as one went along, consistent with familiarisation progress. Initial attempts at steering on the ground were revealing, but most of the middle rankings made a reasonable beginner's fist of it. Taking off was easier in this respect and, although steering sometimes needed the subtle influence of the advisor's feet, the briefing was otherwise simple and, as the takeoff run was best done in the ground attitude and there were few discernible trim changes, was similar to the Concorde on the runway – leave the stick in the middle. 'Keep the same picture when the machine leaves the ground' is simplicity itself, and much easier than the Concorde's choice of attitudes once the time has come to fly, but with seats occupied with well-fed people the Antonov would leave the ground near a critical aft C of G situation. With every flying kph this control situation improved, in fact the takeoff as described left the ground in a neutral situation (in trim). A misguided Pitts pilot's inclination to raise the nose after liftoff was not a good idea – even if the noise at climb power (normally used for non-critical takeoffs) gave an impression of huge performance: not so.

This super-simple keep-the-picture-the-same advice meant what it said: it did not mean pull, or the 'push like hell' which may be received by some if the additional 'do not let the nose rise above the ground picture' caution was given. Before the reader wonders where this psychological analysis is going, my point is that this kind of simple hands-on supervision is easy if two conditions are met. The mentor, trainer, instructor, supervisor, training captain etc. should understand his aeroplane's behaviour well, not be afraid of it, and also have some intuitive empathy with his customer – whatever their background (which may be a complete mystery). Shakespeare's advice about simple and clear behaviour is very appropriate as a starting place, but you must understand the subject as well.

On the 24th of April 1993 I see that I had a local flying session at White Waltham (the Antonov's current home) with Vince Wyre. Vince was a member of the local flying club and habitué of the Beehive, the pub in the adjacent village. His drinking mates included some bikers, and Vince thought they might like to accompany him to Newbury races in the Antonov of an evening. One attraction of this aeroplane was the engine, which visually resembled a collection (4½ to be precise) of Harley-Davidsons – to some extent. This idea started a number of pleasant outings to the evening race meetings, and the Antonov certainly had presence among the much smaller jockeys' Comanches and Mooneys. The centre of the racetrack oval was mown to make a very respectable runway, and landing to the west, takeoff to the east in the quiet of the evening made for convenient taxiing – virtually none.

A delight of this private hire scheme was a visit to a site where flying was incidental; the unlicensed field where one came and went as if to a car park. No radio, no checking in, no landing fee, no marshaller. The only rule at Newbury was that arrival must be before the first race, and one could not leave until after the last one. This makes obvious sense for a number of reasons, especially as the course had to be walked across to reach the public enclosure or return to the transport home. Sometimes the return would be made at dusk, giving the opportunity to sample the UV cockpit night lighting. This Russian system created a magical effect on the instrument panels, and the pointers and numbers glowed a very clear bluish white, like powerful luminous paint. This was a more effective means of highlighting things that needed to be looked at than flying in daylight, and the other novelty was that the little Anglepoise lamps that shone the UV appeared to be doing nothing. It wasn't until the onset of night that there was proof that they worked. I found this system much more agreeable than the west's red lights at night – those were difficult to see by, gloomy, and made you feel tired straight away. But the cool Soviet glow of the instruments in the dark felt fresh and lively. With no other background lighting inside, outside vision was little affected. Is it true that the West never liked it because the system was highly radioactive?

Small fields

The Antonov tended to look very big in a small field, but its short takeoff and landing potential made it suitable for off-airport fields and strips. The full flap/full power takeoff and its critical initial climb and clean up has been briefly covered, but the proper short landing technique was equally impressive, and apart from the full flap glide approach and landing (forced landing without power), it was not taught on our course. It requires a little more experience.

In many parts of the British Isles modern large field agriculture has not taken hold, and traditional small field grazing and crop rotation is still practised. One such private hire event took place from a farmer's field in Oxfordshire, organised by Bartle Frere. There were a number of pilots to fly, each with their selection of family and friends, and they turned up variously for their allotted time slots. I mention this to point out that our intention was never that one hirer would be used to fly repeated loads of fare-paying passengers: that would be public transport. This topic and the suspicions aroused will be dealt with in due course.

The field in question was surrounded by the traditional trees, and there was a telephone wire crossing one end, inside the trees. This was the approach direction favoured by the light wind. The field size was quite adequate, but would not have looked it to the uninitiated, and the final approach would come over these trees and wire. This required a steepish angle at the right speed. Steepish means full flap and a little power to give a measure of adjustment, and the right speed means not too fast, in fact a small margin above the angle of attack that triggers the Antonov's leading edge slats.

Trigger warning

How to do it

An accurate landing takes place when a flying device touches down on the right spot at the right speed. The aiming is easier to do if the approach is steep, the ultimate example being the dive bomber's vertical attack, except that only the bomb should land in that case. Normal modern transport aircraft have settled for a slope of three degrees, equivalent to driving down a 1 in 20 gradient, and this quite flat approach requires an obstacle-free flight path with runway length to spare. Despite the pilots' best intentions, the place where the wheels touch the ground and the stopping procedure can begin tends to vary. This is life in the fast though usually safe lane, and much general and light aviation takes advantage of this spacious and uncritical luxury. But to do the STOL landing you need a steep approach, a low speed, but enough ability to manoeuvre for turning the descent into a landing; at an even lower speed. The earthwards energy of the approach is washed out by the levelling off manoeuvre, and a soft and slow spot landing should result, thanks to full use of the high lift (and drag) devices provided.

The AN2 represents old technology but careful and thoughtful design. I found that the best way to do this landing was to initially make a normal-looking approach with about half (3pm) flap, towards the field in general, but arranging that, fairly close in, this path would look progressively high, as if heading for the far end. The view downwards over the trees thus opens up, and when a satisfactory line from the eye to the grass is spotted, suitably clear of but not too far in front of the trees and wire, a long press of the button on the throttle runs full flap and the steeper approach begins. Speed will also decrease of its own accord despite the new nose-down attitude, and power and trim should be settled, giving around 100 kph. AN2 aerodynamics will arrange this, more or less. I found it helpful to tweak off some of the right rudder trim (toggle switch) required by the engine, so that keeping straight was just a matter of releasing rudder load when the throttle was closed. This last should be done after the start of the rotate/flare manoeuvre and the engine hand then transferred to the controls for a continuous two-handed steady pull consistent with the approach of the ground. During this procedure the slats will clunk out and the Antonov should sink gracefully the few remaining centimetres to the ground in the three-point attitude and at a low forward speed. The distance between aiming point and touchdown will be less than the 50 metres quoted for our max weight 130 kph glide approaches at Strunkovice, and the landing impressively slow. The very effective parachutal mode slats are automatic, bungeed in their home position and activated by angle of attack.

(In the manual, the engine failure instructions when flying in bad weather with no hope of visibility are interesting: Keep the wings level and reduce speed until the control column is fully back. Keep it there: the Antonov will descend relatively slowly in a flat attitude with virtually no forward speed. Damage can be expected at the pancake landing, but the occupants should survive. Those who have been there will recognise that the vast majority of Russian countryside is flat and unpopulated.)

Attention from the Civil Aviation Authority

The arrangement with the customer was simple: the renter hired the aircraft for his personal use, and passengers could come along at his invitation, but he must pay for the flight. This was explained and he signed to this effect on the booking form. Other, smaller private flights did and still do have a cost share system whereby the occupants, including the pilot, may share the direct costs of the particular flight, but this applied up to a single figure number of occupants. It's now six, but is this scheme also limited by the number of available seats? If so, our twelve in the cabin was way over the limit anyway.

Where the customer pilot got the money from cannot reasonably be researched, and is not normally questioned in polite society. What he could not do was advertise seats for sale on his private flight. You need to have an Air Operator's Certificate to do that, and this was well understood by ourselves – we had one already for the two seat CAP10. But despite explanations and signing of affidavits some of our renters could not understand the difference, and though I never witnessed money changing hands at the door I did hear that a notice had been posted in one of the clubs at Wycombe Air Park offering rides at so much a seat. A day or so after the subsequent flying session an Authority representative phoned me as if he were an old flying mate: 'Look here, Mike,' he started, 'we all know what's going on.' Whatever was going on I was not party to it, and was not inclined to cosy up to an unknown caller in blokey eagerness to sabotage dodgy operators. An attempt at entrapment? Of course, but I had my answer ready. 'Are you aware that I am a director of Avia Special?' No, he wasn't, 'and I will be happy to discuss any topic you have in mind in our solicitor's office in London.' I had been well briefed.

The four-handed meeting – CAA investigator, solicitor, James and myself – went smoothly and amicably, my inferred old telephone mate was perfectly neutral, and we had no further trouble. James' Oxford law degree was not for nothing, though I would agree that logical and unsympathetic application of the rules is not always best outside a courtroom; as I had already found out at the 1990 aerobatic worlds. But when, where and how to change your spots – to achieve the perfect and so often desired compromise – is a rare skill.

Parachuting

In May 1993 I went to Lewknor a couple of times to fly some parachute lifts for a club/school who sometimes operated there. This site was a narrow farmer's strip, aligned N/S (crosswind) on the road between the M40 motorway and Watlington, running along the bottom of the Chiltern Ridge. Apart from the square drop zone at the north end, the strip itself dropped abruptly away into crops either side, so falling off the edge would have been a problem. When I first arrived overhead the man in charge set off a smoke flare to indicate the wind on the ground. Brisk, and mostly across, this clear low-tech method was definitely helpful. Military, I thought, and was not wrong. An ageing white-haired, somewhat bent character told me of his affection for the Antonov; while once doing something parachutal in Turkey he had had 40 of them at his disposal.

It was during a later visit to Lewknor that we discussed my first session of parachute flying from Detmold in 1967 with Ringo, the Rhine Army Parachute Association Rapide. I mentioned the man in charge then, the young, vigorous RASC colour sergeant and excellent parachuting teacher, Mick Turner. Nearly thirty years later in the cold of an English spring evening, I could not believe what this man told me: 'I am Mick Turner.' He sort of remembered me, and I had heard of his accident not long after my German visits; a collision with another jumper in a competition as they both went for the same sandpit target. A back injury can mean a life of increasing pain, but the toll this could take on a life that soldiers on as best it can was a salutary shock. In October 1996 we had a request to do a parachuting drop at Lewknor for a memorial jump and a spreading of the hero's ashes from the sky. Mick Turner, the Bad Lippspringe Chef, had died of cancer. He might have been 60.

Bartle Frere, complete with army boots, spare laces and scout knife came along as Antonov assistant and i/c urn handling. It was on a dull, overcast cold morning that we flew the few miles to Lewknor and landed on the narrow strip, towards the hills, in a stronger than usual equinoctial crosswind. Bartle took charge of the urn and the briefing was for two runs: each for half to jump out, followed by half the Chef's ashes (maybe there's a CAA single drop limit). I told the freefallers that their exit point would be way upwind and started positioning accordingly, but no one seemed to be in charge and they piled out much too early, giving themselves a long walk back to the ceremonial site. I had the feeling that the event had unsettled them a little. Bartle managed the ash runs without problem, I think spreadeagled for safety on the floor adjacent to the large open door so as not to fall out, or worse, drop the urn on the village; and the job was finished once the jumpers had returned from their walk for a ceremonial coffee.

Antonov 2 parachuting economics and its results

It's the aeroplane ride that makes parachuting expensive as a sport. As well as a new sense of adventure this fact (together with advances in wingsuit flying) may explain the growing popularity of base jumping, but parachutists also like the novelty of 'jumping' different forms of transport, and to begin with, the Antonov curiosity and jumper's logbook value produced a number of short-term bookings. In the summer of 1993 we dropped the locals at South Cerney, Weston-on-the-Green and remote West Country places with names like Eaglescott and Sheepwash. Like some of the private hire venues it was the primitive, unlikely-looking unlicensed fields that were the most rewarding to visit with this charismatic people's aircraft, but Weston-on-the-Green – home of the RAF Sport Parachute Association and used for paratroops who static-lined from a passing Hercules during the week – generated its own interest.

Apart from the airborne ride and the parachute, military and sport jumping have very little in common. Despite popular culture, doing something for fun and a similar activity in warfare is not only far more different from the way it is conveniently imagined, but has to be contained within a very different emotional environment. As an outsider I'm guessing, of course, but it seems essential that for warlike success the participants at hit-the-beach level should be more afraid of their supervisors than the enemy, otherwise it's not going to work. Paratroops are taught their parachuting skills by RAF staff, who take on a soldierly demeanour for the job, and there the close connection usually ends. The Weston-based RAFSPA is solely concerned with recreational parachuting, and has a considerable number of civilian members, but do some of the staff have paratroop training connections as well? I don't know, but, like army sport parachuting, the Weston organisation inspired confidence.

After a previous visit or two we went there on August 1st 1993, when a twenty-something linkup boogie was planned. The regular turbo Islander was also present, and demonstrated the enormous performance of the small turboprop engine compared with our petrolhead's Harley Davidson vintage equivalent. After some individual lifting, the formation team assembled for the big experience. The Antonov could reach the standard one-minute freefall 12,000ft, but it would take some time. 'Call me when you reach 10,000ft, I will then take off and join you,' said the Islander pilot, and so we set off with a suitable number of excited jumpers, sitting around the walls on the fold-down seats, or strap-hanging in the centre.

The Antonov version of the Cyclone engine with just the basic gear-driven supercharger can maintain climb power manifold pressure up to 5-6,000ft, as I remember. Then one is at the mercy of open throttle and the atmosphere. By about 8,000ft I realised that it had all gone very quiet; the chatter had ceased entirely. 'What's happening back there?' I asked James, in case they had jumped out without telling us. 'They're quite happy. They've found my *Sunday Times* and have shared out the pages.' Of course they had their own altimeters, so they did not need to visit the cockpit to ask 'Are we there yet?' A very few minutes after we'd reported 10,000ft the Islander popped up alongside us, and we continued side by side, onwards and upwards to the exit point.

It had all gone well, but the time to climb and petrol used indicated that our serious freefall days were numbered. The Antonov 2 is perfectly set up for 800m/2,500ft static line training. It has the red and green lights, buttons and hooter, 12 fold-down seats round the sides, space on the floor, plenty of headroom, ceiling rails for the static line clips, and a big door; but accelerated freefall was already becoming popular. Of course if the government pays, time is not at a premium, and you need to exceed your budget year by year to avoid cuts, so parachuting becomes a different story.

Antonov 28

James arranged a much more suitable bargain rental for the RAFSPA in the shape of an Antonov 28. Now registered in Hungary this example came from Lithuania, had a Lithuanian two-pilot crew and a Hungarian roadie who spoke perfect English. They had arrived from Budapest on August 27th and started the parachute lifting on the 28th, in beautiful weather. I lived not far away and decided to drive over to see how things were going. I got there about midday and things couldn't have been better. Some flights had already taken place and the parachutists were delighted. It looked a friendly enough thing to me, considerably bigger than the Islander, stocky fuselage, two chunky fins on its high-set tail behind the engines, and clamshell doors removed from the back so 17 jumpers could hop aboard and sit on the floor facing rearwards, the first row with their backs against the cockpit bulkhead. To exit they got themselves up and ran straight off the back – perfect. And it had 1000hp a side in comparison with the Islander's less than 400.

The Hungarian majordomo told me the crew were delighted with their Bicester pub B&B, liked the evening food and were happy to keep flying all day, so after I had seen it takeoff and zoom skywards I returned home, my ops inspection finished. Imagine my surprise when later that evening the local news reported a crash near Weston o. G. involving what sounded like the same machine: no one hurt, but machine considerably bent. What could have happened?

I returned next morning to see what I could find out. The airfield was quiet.

What happened? I asked the staff.

Nobody knows.

Where is it?

In a field across the road, looking sorry for itself.

Anyone see it?

Only those inside.

Any video of the takeoff?

Yes, it's next door.

We went into the darkened briefing room and watched the member's video on the wall. I looked for signs of overenthusiastic pull-ups, wing rocking, yaw, roll, nose dropping, hasty pushover etc, but saw a copybook, commendably steady climbout, radiating experience and professionalism. Nothing like an airshow at all.

Outside, there was an immaculately dressed Flight Lieutenant orderly from Brize Norton who was representing military interests. This was August and shirtsleeve order was appropriate, but the accuracy of the freshly-ironed shirt, knife-edge folds in its sleeves, the shorts and exemplary boots below were something to behold amongst flyers. These seemed to be the days of integrated brown and blue as a coordinated fighting force. He reminded me a bit of the beautifully prepared, coiffed and mannered similarly-ranked non-flying officer in blue who commanded Hullavington (balloons) a year or so earlier. Quite charming in a certain way, but I think he overreacted somewhat after finding an empty plastic fuel container in the bushes at the base of the control tower. An IRA bomb? Actually no, but these civvy aerobatic flyers can be so irresponsible, can't they? I had been there to watch the flying, but was not one of them, and cannot disagree; but today's first problem was the Brize Norton fuel. The AN28's paraffin came from this airfield so all VC10, Tristar, Airbus whatever flights were frozen until the fuel could be ruled out as a cause of this surprise accident. Does our fuel smell all right, look all right, no water in it – does it work? These practical judgments are as nought when we're talking politically-correct procedure. Lucky there's not a war on. But before I left, none the wiser and unable to help, I did hear what the Lithuanian pilots had said to the Hungarian in the Russian tongue. 'When we raised the flaps the engines stopped (otherwise we know nothing).'

I had not heard this one before, but it is true. The story can be read in the UK accident report which, apart from mentioning this aircraft's time under Lithuanian registration, is convincing. It's all to do with electrical systems and unreliable earth connections. The flaps and fuel HP cocks actuators shared the same earthing bolt (a manufacturer's, but not designer's, shortcut), but this important metal-to-metal junction had lost its earthing but not mutual connective quality, so, on this occasion, when the flaps were asked to run, the easiest path for the amps was backwards through the fuel HP cocks. As simple as that (and due to inadequate maintenance, incorrect assembly and maybe some Baltic seaside corrosion). What the report does not mention are the massive problems of the wicked Soviet empire (bad) which disintegrated under American (good) influence and attempted to emulate the Puritan capitalist ethic (God wants everyone to own a lot of stuff, starting with me), of whose workings, traditions and disciplines it understood little. This continues to be a major world problem. Could it backfire upon the righteous? Possibly yes.

Faced with this inexplicable surprise at 500 ft in a sprightly climb (the surprise included both engines auto-feathering with each opposite side spoiler popping up) the captain did a good job in finally stuffing the nose down to get what speed he could before landing (as best he could) in a large stubble field (an excellent choice). I do not think there had been time for the required Cockpit Resource Management conference.

A Scottish posting

In September 1995 the parachute club at Arbroath rented the Antonov for a couple of weeks. James took it up there to start things off and I took over from the 18th to the 25th. The experience for us was pleasant but quiet, because it was not worth using the Antonov unless enough jumpers turned up – because of its size and cost – so a routine for the AN2 was repeated each day except the Thursday (weather?) The logbook shows one consistently thirty-five minute flight every afternoon, and the flight time indicates a high climb, but this was not to practise free fall relative work. An eclectic assortment of club members were learning a new community game, 'stacking'; something one associates with military display teams, and obviously an enthusiasm of our dynamic and once Red Devil QJI (qualified jumping instructor?)

I never saw a fully successful stack at Arbroath, but what struck me was the change in parachuting accessibility and things for ordinary people to do, in the thirty years since my first look at 'skydiving' and Mick Turner's school at the horse-hockey pitch, next to the fir trees and the German tank range. Then the four instructors would practise their free fall relative work from 12,000 ft, but if more than two of them got in close proximity during the one minute available, progress was good, and a successful baton pass cause for celebration. Stacking under square canopies was not seen then, because square parachute wings were a rarity (or not yet invented).

This team in Scotland was a collection of very unmilitary-like citizens, from seventeen to seventy: a grandmother with glasses and her knitting, a retired postman or a school leaver from McDonalds. Jump and pull from 10,000ft gives quite a few minutes of gliding time, so there's not the rush of free fall, but the best stackers have to begin the procedure which (I think) is joined from below. If two beginners were to be given the privilege of joining up first, the chances are that no one else would get anything to join up on. My guess is that the Chief Instructor led, and shouted instructions at the others. Rushing down in the aeroplane is not suitable for an air-cooled piston engine so there was time to circle around and watch the attempts as the melee slowly descended. Of the give or take eight amateur stunt-jumpers of a typical attempt, I probably saw three or four wings achieving success by the time landing preparation was required, but the general impression was of moths attacking a candle flame, and cannoning off, of course. They had a nice long glide with plenty of manoeuvring, anyway.

The weather in this eastern part of Scotland is frequently finer and dryer than in the west because the predominantly westerly Atlantic air goes over the Cairngorms first, losing some of its water and strength. On one day we also encountered the standing wave system these mountains can generate. Once above mountain height the west wind is smooth but contains this aerial river swell, downstream of the mountains. Where your climb mysteriously improves, edge over to track north or south across the wind – it's worth an extra couple of metres per second climb.

CHAPTER 46

MORE CONCORDE CAMEOS

Despite its technical complexity and novelty value, the Concorde is not the most significant feature of this logbook story – just one of them. But the fact that it fascinates, intrigues, infuriates, saddens or creates teeth-grinding envy for a very large number of those who have neither flown nor ridden in it is clear from the request 'I want to hear about the Concorde,' so this final chapter (thank God) will consist of more Concorde stories – in no particular chronological order or subject matter. To include essential interest I will break my rule of no name-dropping where no significant distress is likely to be caused, but first we start with an event from the same logbook page as the Scottish parachuting visit with the Antonov 2.

Non-radio arrival at Heathrow

The simple VHF radio talking system is fundamental to airline life, and airliners usually have two sets, or sometimes three. Doing without this communication is something that doesn't happen except when over large oceans or remote deserts. Anywhere within several hundred miles of a major airport it is something you can't do anything without. This event happened on Sept 17th 1995, or the following Oct 7th, which is my best guess. It was a BA 2, the first of the two daily NY-LON Concorde milk runs which arrived in London at about 5pm. A conversion course had not long finished their lengthy training and these were now getting some practice time on normal route flights, and on this occasion co-pilot Keith Strocchi was in the right-hand seat, and doing the flying for the day. We also had a regular first officer aboard to make up the qualified crew. The flight had proceeded normally until the long-range radio man in Ireland, dealing with the eastern half of the Atlantic, told me to talk to London as we entered their airspace. Totally routine, except that we got no reply to our 'Hello London, this is Concorde calling' – nothing. Twiddling the frequency numbers and trying again on both of our 2 VHF radio sets produced no result. Marooned in space – this time by radio?

This is unusual – unheard of. We are speeding towards the west of England at a mile in 2½ seconds at 58,000ft, dragging 100 tons worth of heavy-duty Mach 2 shock wave behind us. It reaches the sea 19 miles behind: the aural effect there is dramatic. Our essential slowing up then coming down point is single digit minutes ahead. Can we stay up here milling around until we've sorted out the problem? Not really: we have to throttle back and come down regardless. Up here in the brilliant stratospheric sunshine we are unlikely to threaten other traffic, but 41,000ft is the highest we can stay, once subsonic; and, even in 1995, other jets could be making their safe, orderly and conforming way about the sky at this height, or even higher. It's just possible.

There was no time to find books and read up about something that usually never happened. What is the basic radio failure procedure? I thought, deep into the past, but quickly. Apart from the radio fail transponder code (already done) I remembered the basics: maintain your last cleared height (the freedom of anywhere between 50,000 and 60,000ft for us), follow the planned route until overhead your destination, circle overhead (London?) for 10 minutes (at 50,000ft+!), then descend and land. There is an alternative in our case – 'Call the last station you could talk to'. Of course: the Shannon man is on a different sort of radio, so I got back to him and told him our problem: also that we would make our normal slow up and descent into the busy airline system anyway. Fortunately he got the message and said 'I'll call you back.'

The weather was perfect down to the ground. If we were observant and quick, we should be able to miss anything we saw as we barged down into the busy London airspace at a reasonably fast bullet speed. We were unlikely to be attacked from behind. There was not time to discuss this – no one felt inclined to suggest alternatives. As we slowed up a 'ding dong' indicated that the man at Shannon was calling. He told me that London cleared us to continue on our normal track and descend to a middling height, say 25,000ft. Perfect.

There was a minor problem with the Concorde flight controls on this descent. One flying control group (outer and middle elevons I think) tended to drop to mechanical signalling. This degrades the sensitivity and accuracy of some of the flying controls, like having a good and bad pilot both try to fly at the same time. It makes the Concorde rock and roll a little (and one is primed with a 'what might happen next' feeling – and the next possibility could be much more problematic). An inconvenient if not a serious problem as it stood, but our new pilot Keith showed his awareness and captain potential by suggesting that I fly and he share the co-piloting functions with the real first officer. I might have suggested this in due course but, if one can cope, why complicate the situation?

The next 'ding dong' signalled some more trans-Irish Sea telephone/crackly radio words clearing us direct to Heathrow runway 9L, 5,000 ft for now. Fantastic. This was going well, and I had every expectation of it getting better. I was reminded of the 1959 simplicity of the Tiger Moth, with a map and no radio. A few minutes later another call from across St George's Channel said that we were cleared for an approach, and that London would flash the approach lights to indicate cleared to land (I took this as meaning clear to land anyway if nothing else was on the runway). Simplicity itself; this was how this aeroplane should be flown – a straight line from here to there at a convenient speed. After landing, a follow-me van led us to our usual place, while our co-pilots attempted to coax some life from the problem radios on the ground control frequency, hearing nothing but managing to block everyone else. Never mind – no harm done, and this had been a faster and less thirsty flight than usual.

This Concorde had given VHF radio trouble for some time, but not as conclusively as this event. It was AG, not the last to be made but the one earmarked for Caledonian, then mothballed. Revived in the 80s, it was slightly different from our others in having an Air France radio power system. Something to do with the radio transmit/receive switchery (so that the two radios didn't step on each other) wasn't working properly. I think it then got fixed. The chief air traffic man phoned me later; not to say get those radios fixed, but to express his amazement that it all went so smoothly. A bit of luck all round I would say.

Back of the cab gossip

London taxi drivers are well known for their garrulous accounts of over-the-shoulder conversations with famous people, many of whom might appreciate the freedom to talk to an anonymous and eager listener from a completely different way of life. The fascinating trivia about the intimate life of a celebrity gives an impression of a lifelong relationship forged between the Savoy Grill and Claridge's.

Margaret Thatcher

It must have been in the late eighties, maybe even early 1990, that the operations man in New York took me aside and said 'You've got Mrs Thatcher, row 1'. This was the second daily flight, getting to London around 9:30pm. Apart from the ongoing Conservative Party discontent and moves to get her to step aside, there had been no special news about her activities, and I did get the impression that this had not been a publicised visit. Security has become an increasing concern over the years, hence the discreet word to me within the confines of the airport, and presumably to the cabin chief. Just another flight.

Something I would never do in a Concorde is put on my captain's jacket and hat and accost the passengers in the cabin. I don't think anyone else did – it's just excruciatingly naff, even if some of our passengers did enjoy visiting the cockpit for a look at the daring flyers who had temporary control of their lives. But that is completely the other way round. The cabin, in my experience, belongs to the passengers, their thoughts and private identities, especially considering the ticket price. Mrs Thatcher did not choose to come to the flight deck doorway, all smiles and coyness, and declare 'Hi boys, my name's Margaret,' or 'Prime Minister', perhaps. But amidst all the quietness and discretion I thought that I should pay my respects, especially as she was chums with our chairman, Lord King. At about 25 west I went to the curtain and slipped, surreptitiously, partly through. This was the winter months and we had been in the dark for some time. All was quiet, the frugal dinner long over, the lights down; Mrs T. was dozing in 1B, eyes closed, half a glass of the amber nectar and soda at her side. Her two suited aides sat side by side in 1C and D. I was in the process of indicating 'OK, leave her alone' as the C man immediately rose, leant over and quietly said, 'The Captain, Prime Minister.'

Bingo! The instant transformation was dramatic, like a light bulb. She sat up, beaming, slipped over to 1A and patted 1B. 'Come and sit here', she said. Sitting down with the passengers is something I would not normally do, but this was not that sort of negotiable situation, and we had a nice chat; about how wonderful the Concorde was, what a great job Lord King had done. Brian Walpole had taken her to Toronto, I think – charming man, wonderful manager etc. I mentioned Norman (Lord) Tebbit who, of course, had spent the end of his flying career on our 707. The look changed slightly, the eyes narrowed, just a fraction: 'Y-e-e-s,' she managed, slowly and quietly. A subtle freezing of the cabin atmosphere? You could say that. Was the look scary? Definitely, though not directed at me; it was the thoughts and recollections I had triggered that were betrayed, the look into the distance. Wistful, really – and the hint of something vulnerable... However, I know nothing about politics: and it was time to say my goodbyes and return to the cockpit to catch up with the machine as they throttled back. Are all the various opinions expressed about the Iron Lady's characteristics true? I think yes, but there's more to it. I perceived genuine concern with the welfare of others, at a domestic level – like a forceful supermum; not to be debated with, but totally relied upon. My overriding impression: she would make a very dependable, stimulating and encouraging grandmother, and your children might well decide that an organised life with granny was better – and prefer to move out.

Leonard Bernstein

I think it was in November 1989 that I saw this name on the BA 4 passenger list, again the New York to London second flight. Best known in public as the composer of *West Side Story*, a look at his televised lectures about music in general will indicate a communicating genius at work (instructors please note). This skill is borne of an instinctive sympathy, understanding and mastery of this vast subject, plus the ability to look back at the position of a ten-year-old who first came across his cousin's old piano, with no family musical background whatsoever. A personal hero, the people's musician of a century? Of course.

'Ask him up,' I sent back before takeoff. The maestro appeared, perfect grey suit to match the wavy hair, and he was wearing the famous hand-tooled cowboy boots: 'Some kind people had them made for me in Texas: I liked them, and wear them everywhere.' Conductor-cool? Definitely, if you can get away with it. 'You must have sat up here many times before?' I asked. 'No, never.' 'Why not?' 'I never liked to ask.' I was surprised, but my idea of celebrity and that of my colleagues must have been different. Once we had powered down 31 left with its 'rotate, positive climb, gear up, turn, 240kts, 3,2,1 noise,' in quick succession – then 'speed at your discretion' from air traffic – we were on our smooth way to London. 'Come back for the landing,' I suggested. 'Certainly,' he said.

He had already told me he was going to London to work with the London Symphony Orchestra, I think for a Candide recording, but this was not discussed, and he duly returned to the flight deck suitably before what passes for top of descent in a Concorde, interested and enthusiastic in whatever was going on. Quite by chance my aerobatic and currently Manhattan-based friend Ian Groom was aboard, in movie mogul mode complete with the successful man's surprisingly light but warm and elegantly cut (and expensive) long length black winter coat. A part of the routine flight which demanded attention was fast coming up on this moonless autumn night, and I sent back the message to ask Mr Groom to step up to the flight deck (to spread the load as informal PR man).

When Groom arrived I pointed at the earphones hanging up behind the jump seat. On the intercom I said 'Look after Bernstein, but don't tell him about my LSO experience.' Out of sheer devilment Ian did just that, immediately. Bernstein was intrigued and wanted to know the details, current orchestra (Oxford Sinfonia pro-am – not bad. 'Town or gown?' he asked) and so on. He also asked permission to quote me with some imagined disciplinary instruction if the LSO needed keeping in order. Of course: and after landing he commented on the speed and drama of this nighttime flying event. Andy Darke (just qualified) had made a good landing, but I think the speed at which the ground approaches at a late stage, and the lack of customary wafting about, feeling for the ground, appealed to the composer's sense of gritty action, together with the idea of the purposeful competence also essential in his line of business. 'That was impressive! We just kind of came straight in and bam! We're down.' Not really, but he liked it. (When you're a Jet/You're a Jet all the way/From your first… and so on. Christopher Walken knows the words.)

Ian later told me that Bernstein had shepherded him through airport formalities arm in arm, and dropped him off at his Mayfair hotel in the Bernstein limo – the best of NY friends.

A few one-liners

Liza Minelli was woozily charming as she would stand in our doorway and say 'Hello, I'm Liza.' Vulnerable femininity itself.

Diana Ross (and her many suitcases) made a point of making us a few minutes late – every time. Empowerment, I suppose.

The flight engineer didn't recognise Richard Gere outside the loo. He took him for a businessman, for that was Gere's demeanour. 'What do you do?' he asked the star. 'I'm in the movie business'. Makes sense.

When someone else (not me) sent the takeoff invitation to Paul McCartney (very frequent traveller) the answer came back 'Is it compulsory?' I'd already agreed with Linda's comments about the boring veg food. Could do better (our own regular choice from NY, Indian Veg, was great).

Michael Winner always told it like it was in his newspaper column. Ditto about the London-Barbados brunch. BA's justification – the ticket's cheap for the distance. Not a good enough answer.

Ginger Rogers was petite and grandmotherly in her fur coat, and took the steward in hold before leaving to lead a twirl in the front galley. 'My God, I've danced with Ginger Rogers!' he said, fanning his face. He had, sort of.

Not all our celebrity passengers were eager for universal recognition. Our VIP lady in the Kennedy terminal once said to me 'You must come and meet the English opera star, Michael Crawford.' 'I've never heard of him,' I said. 'English?' 'Yes'. 'Sorry, means nothing to me.' 'You must have heard of him, he's very famous, he's in *Phantom of the Opera*.' Ah, of course. It's Frank.

We exchanged a few words. 'Do some Frank for us,' I suggested. 'It was very popular in England,' I told her. He sort of laughed and waved his hands in the air. 'No, no,' in mock horror, but he was serious. 'Absolutely not,' he repeated. Not even an acknowledgement of the name Spencer. I could understand. The fragility of a Broadway reputation could be at risk if the Atlantic divide were to be breached. I have to say that the middle-aged man, and the phantom itself, gave no hint of Frank. Betty herself would not have guessed.

No more name-dropping

The name-dropping has now finished, but I cannot leave this subject of the New York mecca of the performing arts without mentioning an unpleasant experience fairly early on in my Concorde career. I never repeated it, and, like the animal world, our brains can learn instant lifelong avoidance behaviour from just one negative experience, if it's painful enough.

It was Christmastime and the crew (minus the first officer) took me to the Radio City Music Hall Christmas show – a traditional rite of passage for mothers, kids, grandmothers and so on. 'You'll love it' they said, 'and there are the famous Rockettes'. I suppose the Rockettes were OK, impressive synchronisation anyway, but sexy? Not really. Great legs, I grant you, and a zillion of them, but what else? And the rest of the show? Let me quote a line from the disaster spoof 'Airplane' (with the problematic fish choice). 'I haven't felt this bad since we saw that Ronald Reagan movie.' Was this line written by

Neil Simon? No, but it could have been. Experiencing the whole show was like drowning in treacle: super-shallow in content, sentimental, mawkish, sugary, sickly-sweet at every turn. I toughed the experience out like a good captain, but the others liked it. 'Wasn't it lovely!' We must have some strange people working for us.

(Incidentally the Reagan quote is clearly a bitchy liberal (their less-right wing), intellectual political dig at the other side. I thought Ronnie the actor was good. I never saw him fall over the furniture, or off his horse. He delivered his lines correctly, and Mrs Thatcher liked him too. Where did he go wrong?)

Different national (and social) concepts of customer service

Concorde customers frequently boarded the aircraft in New York in a better frame of mind than in London. This is not about the passengers themselves. The large majority were multi-directional regulars, even if some of them tended to fly west in a Concorde more than east (a function of time zone direction); but, whoever they were, they were busy and successful people, for whom the Concorde had become a very expensive (by über-democratic standards) part of everyday life – not a once in a lifetime treat, but a well-earned (mostly an unquantifiable) convenience. And it is my belief that our staff in New York – workers from the suburbs with the same immense variety of domestic and financial concerns as the rest of we salaried or pay packet BA staff – retained a conscious and civilised awareness of where their own and their employer's money was coming from, by their very American nature. Other cultures still share the same niceties of judgment. Britain continues to lose out in this area.

(In contrast to French and American revolutionary histories it's the very resilience and apparent stability of British society that serves to conceal the long-term and slow-burning social revolution that has smouldered its way up from ground level since Charles the second returned to the throne. 'Sad but true' as Shnoz Beatty, our history teacher used to say in 1958. The cracks continue to show – not just in the roads of Britain. It's not a good sign for the future.)

It's the delicate balance between respect and resentment that defines different Western cultures and attitudes to their fellow men. A visit to the Concorde lounge at London (accepting that this airport is the British Airways world hub) could indicate the private attitude of the staff to their (very contributory) Concorde customers: 'I'm as good as them, whoever they are. We are all equal. I do my job according to the rules (required standard) and they get what they're entitled (to).' And then the subtle base note – who do they think they are anyway?

In a successful society, capitalist or otherwise, there is an important difference between those paying for a service, how much they are prepared to pay, and those who receive some of that money by providing the service. These three aspects of a trade are not the same, and a satisfactory balance has to be recognised. The fact of the matter is that the London boarders were generally less gruntled than their New York reincarnations. The evidence was subtle but unmistakable, and in their defence, Concorde passengers, as a bunch, tended to be far from troublesome.

These apparently disloyal and critical observations of my colleagues do not only apply to customer service ground representatives. Despite the change in the 1970s of longhaul to shorthaul responsibility for Concorde cabin service – based on flight time, not product – many excellent staff continued to do this job, but the problem for me (as a mere observer) was the variety of style, and the sometimes crass, unconscious and inappropriate sense of propriety and lack of empathy (imagination) that exemplifies, to this day, the social ambience within the fuselage structure. At the time of writing this egalitarianism has become endemic in British Airways (especially the short flights – to give the exceptions their due; sometimes).

Whose cabin is it anyway?

Not so long ago, as a random passenger somewhere near the back of a small Airbus, I was given a questionnaire to fill out about BA customer service in its various forms, based on this flight. After it had been collected a steward came from the back galley, and in the clear earshot of those around, rebuked me for my criticism of the incessant, very audible, pointedly un-self-aware trivial chatter from the back galley. He told me that, as staff, I should not criticise crew behaviour, and, to my astonishment, that the passengers liked it anyway. Not a single member of the surrounding and cowed audience piped up to agree with him, but his reaction clearly indicated a crew's sense of ownership of the device which provides their income. The fact that we passengers have temporarily rented the space for our own use seems to be no longer understood. Out of sight, out of mind is a relevant phrase in this respect, and when it comes to crew members carrying the priorities of their everyday life into the passengers' domain one might consider members a theatre cast engaging themselves in personal and distinctly audible irrelevant conversation once invisible in the wings. It isn't done. The Concorde could be a special case of sonic intrusion.

Concorde crew chatter

Can the female voice drown 160,000lbs of afterburning jet takeoff thrust? If the answer is no, it's only fair to consider the attempt. What did the captive customers think? I don't know, but some explanation is required. The sound insulation in the Concorde passenger cabin was not bad, and once the visor was up aerodynamic noise in the cockpit was surprisingly low, but plenty of engine noise came through the doors, front and back, during takeoff. During one base training session a couple of health and safety men came along to measure the intensity of sound at the rear galley crew seats (in fact sending our trainees aft to sample this experience was normal, just the once). To our amazement the sound men said 'it's not a big deal – similar to a B737?' The cockpit crew communicated via intercom during takeoff and low speed flight for the reasons above – earphones on both ears.

The front doors and galley were quite a long way from the cockpit, and the narrow passageway between was walled by electrical equipment, like a submarine. The two front cabin crew sat in their galley takeoff seats, one on either side by each door, almost opposite each other, but not quite. A small number of feet aft of them sat the first row of passengers – row 1, highest status, for sure, the nearest ears behind the out of sight, out of mind 'we do not currently exist' curtain. One day I pressed my stopwatch and opened the throttles for takeoff as usual. As the eight seconds of engine wind up, reheats lighting and settling, crescendoing roar etc elapsed, raised and strident bursts of high-pitched voice cut intermittently through the din, very evident despite my earphones and the best efforts of the Olympuses. What's going on back there? A fight, a disaster, an out-of-control passenger intent on mayhem?

I mentioned it to the Cabin Service Director later. 'Oh, could you hear us chatting?' she said. More to the point is what did row one, and several others, think of this desperately delivered intelligence about current Tesco bargains, loo (lieu) days, child-minding, next week's inconvenient roster and how to circumvent it? The price of the ticket entitles the passengers, I would have hoped, to their continued reveries: the cloistered meeting to come within the bug-free BA premises on the airport? What to do about the suspected political coup within the extended family? Tonight's rehearsal, tomorrow's performance? Will the auction produce another world record price for a painting? There are many possibilities that enable and encourage them or their government to keep buying Brian and Jock's Concorde tickets.

I considered throttling back next time it happened, taxi round for another try, and explain to the passengers that the very raised voices suggested the sort of trouble best not taken into the air. I never actually did this, even though the same did happen again on occasion; but what's the point? Can one stem the tide of progress? This is just the workplace, anyway.

A terrifying Concorde event (especially if you believe what you read)

Another routine late evening dark arrival at London. Clear weather, everything as usual, and the airfield relatively quiet – only ourselves following a BA 747 on final approach to the runway. The controller explained a late landing clearance for us due to this aircraft in front.

At nighttime the relationship between airliner and air traffic control changes because one cannot see so much in the dark, rather like fog but not so serious. The air traffic system is obliged to provide more help – like sending a policeman to a busy crossroads. Although we could see the jumbo ahead the man in the tower could not clear us to land until it had cleared the runway. We saw it land and trundle, and we continued. Entitled to take its time before turning off, maybe more than usual, our situation started to look more touch and go (almost). Perhaps it would turn off in time, but it might not.

We continued at 190 mph. Experienced co-pilot Tony Heald was flying. 'We can go from the flare, if you like', I suggested, familiar with what is sometimes necessary during training. At about 100 feet the controller, keen to encourage us to land and not power into the sky, said, hastily, 'The-747's-turning-off-you're-cleared-to-land.' He was not completely wrong: it was in the process of turning to the left, but the 200-foot long machine's tail, now swung out to our right across the runway, had not even reached its centreline, and it was moving slowly with beginner caution. Tony decided we had waited long enough and opened the throttles. The addition 18% of rpm required to reach full cold power is available almost instantly. Nothing else is needed to change a Concorde approach into an impressive climb, and we roared into the Hounslow night sky.

Almost immediately the steward from the front galley shot into the cockpit – shaking. 'What's happening?'

'Jumbo on the runway, be down in five minutes.'

He was not reassured. 'But this is not normal, what's gone wrong?'

'Nothing, one of those things.'

After the usual reassuring explanation to the passengers all seemed quiet, we made a quick circuit and landed undisturbed by more jumbos, went home, and I thought no more about it.

Next morning I was phoned by Alan Harkness, our training manager. 'Did you do a go-around at London last night?' This civil transport term one associates with bad weather, and I had to think about what he meant, at first. But how did he know about such a triviality? It is possible that the spy-in-the-sky flight recorder system had flagged up this occurrence – but perhaps not.

'Yes' I said. 'Jumbo was slow to clear.'

'You're supposed to do an incident report – going around below decision height.'

He was politically correct, although this decision height business – 'decide', then a choice of land or go-around statements etc – is usually associated with a low visibility (blind flying) approach. This circumstance was nothing like that in reality terms. Then he asked whether I had seen today's *Daily Mail.* I hadn't.

'Go and get a copy, You're on the front page.'

I did so. I don't think the guilty (or heroic) crew were named, so I was not really on the front page. The only person on board mentioned was Dave Stewart of Eurythmics, currently toing and froing between London and New York, and presumably the source of the story. But it was a typical piece of bigging up the banal on the slimmest of evidence, with little understanding (it's only to sell the paper, isn't it?) The item began something like:

> **Concorde Avoids Collision at London by Inches**
> While landing at London's Heathrow airport last night a Concorde was just inches from the runway when the pilots spotted a jumbo jet and narrowly avoided it by taking off again. *('By Jove, Carruthers, isn't that a jumbo on the runway?' 'Good Lord! Finchley-Hampstead. I think you're right. Better keep your eyes peeled in case there's another one out there somewhere.')* Passengers described the terrifying experience…

I don't have a copy of that arresting report, but you get the idea. If readers wish to research this publication I can do no better than suggest 1988, give or take a year or so.

An author and journalist acquaintance with a pilot's licence was interested. When I explained the flying reality of this reported event, he wrote a substantial *Evening Standard* article, critical of this kind of populist and cynically eye-catching nonsense. It seems to presage the now accepted alternative truth genre – exciting fiction by another name.

Another genuine (but rare) attention-getting possibility

The continuous cycle of engine surging (known as continuous engine surge) at cruising speed was dramatic in that its onset was sudden, and the effect was like having a five-rounds-a-second pom-pom gun joining the flight, someone's hand clamped on the trigger. I believe that much early development work was spent on the complex shape of the Concorde leading edge to minimise aerodynamic causes of engine intake problems, and this partly explains the numbered sections on the Yeovilton Museum prototype. Anything wrong with the delicate positioning of the ramps inside each engine air intake could also easily set off this phenomenon, and one engine surging (trigger warning: compressor flow breakdown) might set off its neighbours as well.

The crew remedy for this occurrence was instant and broad brush; complicated, comprehensive and done from memory, there being no time for trouble-shooting until order had been restored. Apart from a hold-the-attitude piloting demand, the first action was to close all throttles completely. This might silence or quieten the Bofors gun, but the deceleration was more like an emergency stop in the train, suggesting the subsequent vertical fall to the earth imagined by many who have never understood the glider. It certainly would not lessen the sense of battle transforming the previously serene cabin. Diners have been known to write an in-the-moment last Will and Testament on the back of a menu on the way down, to be retrieved from the sea, perhaps, in a Titanic moment – some time later.

The simulator simulated the noise and shaking quite well (I'm inclined to believe), and I only experienced a real but miniature version once when our real engines were throttled back to their first stage Mach 2 slowing up position. The subdued bu-bu-bub and coordinated shaking was unmistakable, but the dials suggested the culprit side, so engineer Bob Woodcock instantly snapped these two throttles shut. The ensuing virtual 'double engine failure in the cruise' was fortunately a non-event at this slowing-up power setting.

A lot of real Mach 2 surging was done during testing. Brian Trubshaw said that at dusk you could see the pom-pom flames coming forward past the cockpit. Despite its drama and the list of immediate memory items required, this surging business was not in the Emergency Checklist, to the surprise and mystification of many crew. Nothing had broken, as such, except the uncompromising supersonic airflow; so the procedure was itemised elsewhere. Could it also be that an unusually long list of emergencies does not encourage the confidence of certification authorities.

Trigger warning *(for the reluctant student)*

Here a short trigger warning feature might help to explain the problem. The jet engine is an internal combustion device, like a piston engine. Unlike the piston version, which compresses its air in a closed cylinder (so it cannot escape prematurely), the jet's series of whirling compressor blades rely on their efficiency and speed to maintain enough air momentum to persuade the compressed air to keep moving along in the desired direction, towards the fiery centre of the engine. The compressor remains open to atmosphere. If this progressive squeezing system does not work properly for some reason the compressed and now very hot air might spot an easier way out – back the way it has come – and escape out of the front of the engine, hence a fiery bang. An external airflow disturbance might do it, or a compressor blade failure, but a faulty position of a variable geometry intake system is guaranteed to cause supersonic trouble. The engine is still whirling round and, now relieved of flow and load, it eagerly packs some more air down the engine – with the same result. The Concorde engine works at a 15:1 compression ratio, and the intake itself contributes 5:1 (or something similar) to the total engine effect, which is where the additional 25% engine efficiency comes from. If this extra intake compression falters, compressed air in the engine will seek the easiest way out – back the way it came in, again and again until something changes.

Lockheed A-12/SR71 Blackbird

Very recently a stewardess on an Airbus 319 told me that the Concorde must have been nice, but rather dated by modern standards. It's not appropriate to compare a Concorde with a B747, an Airbus or a SR71. They are all very different, and designed for quite different purposes, but the Blackbird is worth a mention because of its ingenious supersonic power system. Inside the engine cowling, and around the engine, from front to back, is an open bypass space which becomes a ramjet – an internal combustion engine without moving parts, thanks to supersonic compression and expansion with a fire in the middle. The conical intake moves in, not out, making a bigger supersonic space, and instead of going through the engine, the extra air admitted feeds the ramjet outside it.

Needless to say the usual shockwave, compression and expansion problems have to be met, and the Blackbird's 'unstart' (a germanised English way to say stop) meant, I imagine, that the ramjet airflow rebelled. However, it was a clever idea for 1958, to give Kelly Johnson and P&W their due. And, like the Concorde, making such an aircraft actually work requires a fair measure of genius – not to say much painstaking and tedious toil. (Wasn't the Miles M.52 designed on the same principle?)

Bits falling off

This happened on two or three occasions, though not to me. The evidence could not be concealed, so the events were newsworthy. A typical indication in flight was a thump in an otherwise uneventful cruise. Vibration was reported at speed and there was a slight difference in low-speed handling, but the evidence was obvious when viewed from outside, on the ground – after landing. In two cases a piece of rudder was missing, looking as if it had been bitten off by a giant shark. I believe Air France had a section of elevon disappear in a similar way, but why should these things happen? (The general ban on supersonic Concorde flying over land meant that the pieces fell in the sea, and were not found).

I'm not sure this was ever decided, for public consumption, but the general word was moisture (or temperature cycles, vibration, engine noise) getting inside, causing corrosion and the adhesive (glue) between the honeycomb filling and the metal skin to fail. How long did the makers of the Concorde expect the aircraft to last anyway? And how much research had there been to find out? The reality was that the individual aircraft were lasting longer than had originally been thought of, and was, in effect, an on-going research project as the hours, flights, temperature cycles, years rolled by. In fact the flight crews' pay had a development element built in for this reason, and was supposed to compensate for their 747 long-distance colleagues' long sector bonuses. I don't think it did, but maybe I had more flying fun.

Updating the airliner's equipment

But the interesting knock-on story is about making new parts for old public transport aeroplanes. Technology changes in twenty years. The Concorde's many electrical boxes were hefty things – plenty of coils, capacitors, resistors and especially transistors. In the 1990s I heard that the same functions – engine control, intakes, flying controls, autostability, secondary nozzles, brakes, reheat, plus others (no modern computer stuff) could be replaced by cards, chips, whatever, that would be more reliable and temperature/vibration resistant, and would save five (yes five) tons of weight. That's five tons more load, or 2½ less tons of fuel used every trip. It adds up. The problem was that every single modification had to be proved by 5,000 hrs of route-proving flying, like a new Concorde design. (Can this 5,000 be true? Even 100, gadget by gadget would be tedious) It's easier to make do with the old stuff.

When it came to knocking up some new Concorde rudders, presumably given the original surviving framework to build on, the new copies came unglued quite soon. The knack had been lost, apparently, so some retired Filton craftsmen were reemployed to do a proper cleaning and sticking job – like the old days. The in-flight proving required to certify new, better and lighter technology would have been impractical and prohibitively expensive. Cheaper to get the oldies back to practise their ancient crafts. The English nostalgia disease? Almost.

Lightning strikes

Was I ever struck by lightning in a Concorde? No – sorry; but only today (2019) I read that yesterday afternoon two Swiss airbuses (owned by Lufthansa cheapo division) were struck by lightning, one after takeoff and the other in the cruise, and both returned to Zürich (company policy, the paper said) for a four-hour check, causing their combined 300+ passenger loads a certain amount of inconvenience. The report also said that the airline expects each of its aircraft to get struck by lightning once a year on average. This expectation seems reasonable, but reasonable piloting initiative should also try to avoid this; not the flash and the bang, which seldom did damage, but the potentially destructive turbulence that lurks in such weather, especially at altitude and speed, but immediately after takeoff as well.

My first experience of the stun grenade experience was early on in my Vanguard career, over Watford again, during the descent towards London. Our mild-natured captain, Wacker Payne, stared at the radar picture and steered all over the place to avoid the complex returns, then boom! The light intensity and sound is literally stunning, fingers and toes curl and the body tries to assume its foetal configuration, but normality, vision and hearing resume smoothly and very soon – within a second? Our trusty metal Vanguard continued undaunted, and I've experienced this rare occurrence in 707 and VC10: not always in cloud. On one VC10 approach occasion – in the clear and below cloudbase, but not far from a big black Asian cloud, you could see the brilliant yellow electricity coming our way, zig-zagging, then straight for the nose. Fast, but not at the speed of light. Electric smell of ozone? Sometimes.

In olden metal days one mentioned the strike after landing, no ill-effects? Compasses OK? Maybe burn marks on the radome, and I have seen a dent in the nose, but that's all. Perhaps the modern composite lightweight construction is much more sensitive to the forces of nature. Certainly the computer design is no stronger than it need be.

Wacker Payne's story is tragic. I flew with him only the once. Before I left BEA word got around that he had admitted himself to psychiatric hospital, had walked out one night and stood on the railway line. I know no more. Sad. The nickname was popular in the Royal Navy, I believe, after a cane-happy Eton schoolmaster.

CHAPTER 47

THE CONCORDE'S CHARACTER AS AN AIRLINER

The world has changed a lot since the 1950s. That is the reason for this personal 40-year history of peaceful flying, with its catalogue of relative trivialities from a 15-year-old schoolboy's perspective. In the 1990s I was asked to give a Concorde talk at the annual dinner of the Oxfordshire Army Air Corps Society, Oxfordshire branch. Among the youthful-looking present-day colonels and their sociable ladies were some famous old-stagers, a couple of whom had piloted their gliders to the Pegasus Bridge critical canal crossing, in the early hours of D-day (at night). They landed exactly in the right place; their soldiers only had to run 50 yards and the objective was secured – total surprise. As a lily-livered civvy who'd had it lucky (though only losers think others' good fortune is luck), I thought I would start by acknowledging that it was their skill and bravery etc, and that of countless others (atomic bombs not mentioned), that had enabled me to enjoy a career of agreeable and unthreatening flight – from Tiger Moth to Concorde. I've no idea how my Concorde presentation of supersonic skill, bravery and heroism (with slides from the office) went down (I suppose no complaints is better than the opposite, and it had been my Arnhem neighbour who conveyed the invitation to take the stage), but I cannot deny that I felt a bit of a fraud. Maybe other Concorde lecturers feel the same way – but I'm not sure.

The Concorde was an extension of the technical momentum acquired during World War 2, there having been much British catch-up required once this event appeared inevitable. For interesting views on Concorde inception, the decline of the once substantial British aircraft industry and Edward Heath's gift to General De Gaulle of important design information as a common market sweetener (the answer was still 'non'), I recommend Sir Archibald Russell's *A Span of Wings*. This book also points out that the radical slender delta idea was only supported in limited circles, and many believed that the detached flow principle would not work well enough for an airliner, although the little Handley Page 115 wheeling around at Farnborough with apparent abandon at Antonov 2 speeds was quite convincing. (I believe Neil Armstrong had a go in it in 1970, and survived to tell the tale.)

Anything can be made to fly when it goes fast enough, but it was this design that gave the Concorde much of its low-speed character and handling peculiarities. However, given the problems of making an ordinary pilot's everyday airliner from such an unconventional shape, this was an audacious project in anyone's language, and I must agree with those colleagues who enthusiastically describe the end result as superb, and add that special care, respect and understanding were very desirable in those who made it appear to behave like an airliner.

No one who has not flown this aircraft on a regular basis can fully understand its nature and demands. Of course, the first Concorde training takeoff sells the special experience; even, perhaps, to those who got run away with on early first circuit attempts (4,000ft and 400kts instead of 1,500ft and 250kts). I blame the teachers, not the parents, for this state of affairs!

Before detail 2 of our simulator course in January 1985 Tony Meadows, who had flown the Concorde since the manufacturer's course a decade previously, said that the Concorde rewards accurate flying, and that if the performance got out of hand you only had to throttle back to contain it. 30 years later he said he'd found the Concorde quite straightforward under normal conditions, but very different when things went wrong. I agree with all these opinions, but have to add that, although pilot handling benefited from direct and powerful flying controls and good instrumentation, basic manoeuvring required undivided attention. Marked speed instability and inherent static instability at low speeds meant that a hands-off situation could not be achieved. A good autopilot liked these conditions and flew the Concorde well, provided it was correctly told what to do, but to date (more or less), pilots are still expected to be able to fly their machines themselves, and, one would hope, not regard such a thing as an emergency. The Concorde was very un-airliner-like in many respects, but an excellent supersonic transport, and very agreeable to drive – if you were up to it.

In order to avoid more trigger warning stuff, I will include a letter I wrote to Brian Trubshaw in 2000.

> Dear Mr Trubshaw,
>
> I had just come back from the Interlaken post office having sent my order for your book when I heard the news of the Air France Concorde disaster. The news was a shock but not a surprise.
>
> I retired from BA three years ago having flown the machine for 13 years. We met briefly at the Concorde dinner a few years ago after I had sent you a copy of my instructional handling book – it contained what I would have liked to have been told when I did the course, and I thought I could save myself some time in training briefings.
>
> The aircraft is indeed an engineering and handling miracle; and given a serviceable machine (including hydraulics and undercarriage), a competent crew, a good set of wheels and a clean airfield I would be happy to fly it anytime, anywhere. The salient questions that still have, regrettably, to be asked (maybe you asked them yourself despite the apparent protection of all kinds of civil aviation certification) is whether the world of public transport (flying buses – not flying Ferraris) can, or has a mind to deliver these conditions to an adequate standard for such a masterpiece. I have the feeling that we will not see its like again.
>
> Last week I was in Toulouse at the world aerobatic championships. Most of the French helpers seemed to work at Blagnac and many told me about the effects of the accident on the factory – old retired guys coming in to discuss things: engineers who had done all that work with slide rules? Several said that expert acquaintances privately admitted that they couldn't do the same thing again – just too difficult; even with computers.
>
> The Concorde only tried to kill me once; and it wasn't its own fault. I was the second half of a shared base training detail with John Cook doing circuits at Macrihanish from Prestwick.

After a couple of landings the left gear failed to show locked down and a number of recyclings made no improvement. On the way back to Prestwick I showed John the page that suggested raising the mainwheels and landing on the engines, but he didn't like this. I elected that we land with the wind from the left and our flight engineer left the air pressure from the free fall procedure open (having disconnected the hydraulics, of course – following the checklist etc. I would have thought that green hydraulics was better than 65psi air but there you go). After more faffing around (it was fortunate that this happened at the beginning of a training flight with some fuel to spare) including the flight past the tower and some wing waggling our supporters on the ground said that the gear looked normal to them. Another advantageous thing happened in that we eventually achieved a shortening lock indication where one was absent initially. I think this must provide some resistance to the gear folding, but this was a bit of luck in that this aircraft (AG) was one of several that had the three hydraulic connections at the top of the leg connected wrongly, ie, routed to oppose correct shortening locking/unlocking etc. (I often wondered why the lights did funny things on some of the aircraft – it got sorted eventually). John made a very straight landing and all seemed normal, although a final turn at walking speed had the gear starting to fold. We stopped on the runway and got out. I think we were quite lucky. (I believe that the main gears are toed out a bit. This would have helped us although we weren't as well placed as the Weston-Super-Mare crew and the broken strut incident where I have heard that the leg leant against the engine cowling after landing.)

I was surprised that this unexpected incident had no effect on our passenger services; after all, maybe the same fault was lurking on a service aeroplane (actually one was). Our front office of the two Daves (Leney and McDonald) kept this affair suitably in-house and when I eventually saw the offending components of the failed downlock gismo I was lost in admiration at the precision and delicacy of the undamaged bits and pieces. Clearly weight and quality had been overriding factors in the design concept. The undercarriage cannot fail. But it seemed that a sentence in the reassembly procedure for the side strut had been missed in the translation from the French to the English, so some of our struts had been reassembled by BA with some collet lock gadgets trapped and out of place.

As you suggest in your book, the hydraulic arrangement has always been a subject of concern. The 'one system with three gauges' concept is very artistic and statistically could be argued to be adequate, yet the number of partial losses has been high. It was not so long ago that Chris McMahon suffered green and yellow system total losses from unconnected causes on the same New York service (starting with a serviceable machine). The aircraft therefore arrived with only the blue system and brake accumulator. Chris said this latter pressure disappeared in a flash when he tried the brakes. With no steering or brakes they finally ended up in the sand, undamaged.

Did you hear about the incorrectly set nosewheel speed transmitter that reported 150% of the real speed to the brakes, thus releasing them at speeds above jogging (without a brakes fail warning, of course)? This nearly caught the chaps out on a short runway.

Of course physical damage to any PFCU must be of concern and the reported behaviour of the Air France aircraft suggests that it might have crashed because of a loss of flying controls, whether or not inadequate thrust or fire would have eventually led to disaster. As far as I can gather from the press the authorities are astounded that such destruction could result from a single tyre failure. This is something of a surprise as similar things have happened before, albeit without the same consequences. The condition of the manoeuvring areas of all major commercial airports would give a military man instant apoplexy. My ex-colleague Norman Britton (FOD awareness manager) used to regularly collect a bucketful of metal bits on the stand at New York while the others were doing the departure checks. It seems to me that unless there is an overnight worldwide change of business ethics and practice the same thing could happen to a Concorde again tomorrow, and in a time of sentimentality and accommodation rather than individual responsibility I think such a change highly unlikely.

An ironic feature of the Concorde argument is that despite detractors' claims that it is an old aircraft (and American passengers often would tell me of our spares problems or engine shortage that would cause us to stop operating soon – where did this propaganda come from?) the design concept is as radical and unique as ever; it still looks totally futuristic. The problems for the future do not question the aircraft itself, but the quality of the supporting environment, in all its forms.

Over 25 years we have had a large spectrum of crew members operate the aircraft successfully. Many of us privately felt that a major prang (and it is not in a Concorde's nature to have bumping and scraping accidents) would signify the end, yet even the recent disaster does not seem to have damaged the largely unblemished record of the drivers. One could say that we in BA got away with it for 25 years but it would be truer to acknowledge the astonishing success of your department's development programme, and the concerns and sense of priorities handed over to the initial BA people. On our simulator day one John Eames said 'It took me about a year before I felt happy with the job'. I think he underestimated this a bit. After 13 years I would still have chosen 'Ask me next week'. Laymen, especially the press, ask the silliest questions. In answer to 'What's it really like?' I thought 'It's easily the most user-friendly Mach 2 bomber' summed it up.

Unlike many of my ex-colleagues I think it is reality time. I would be delighted to be proved wrong – but do we wait for the next serious incident (crash)? I don't know. But it was bloody good fun while it lasted – unrepeatable in historical terms.

Yours sincerely,
M A Riley

I retired on Jan 22nd 1997, my 55th birthday. The last Concorde flight had been from New York on January 17th, and this hobby was gone, but the others remained; not for long, however (except the windsurfing).

CHAPTER 48

AFTER RETIREMENT – A LAST TOUR

Apart from a trip to Filton and back with Les Brodie in his Cessna 150 on Jan 21st 1997 (last day of employment!) the remaining logbook pages consist of CAP 10 and Antonov 2 flying, for the assortment of purposes already described, with one nostalgic exception. In April 1997 James Black asked me to go to the Czech Republic to collect Zlin 526 G-AWSH from the Zlin factory where it had been rebuilt.

I had last flown this aircraft (and the type) in the early 1980s, for a few minor airshows. After the Williams 'finding-the-limit' mainspar failure of G-AWAR in 1970 there had first been a main spar warning modification: the centre section tube was pressurised with nitrogen, and a pressure gauge indicated when the tube had actually cracked (No N_2 = time to stop). But a replacement, beefed-up centre section was issued, to be fitted when convenient. I think it must have been round about 1980 when this Zlin was dismantled at Farnborough ready for the sawing, jigging and welding required to replace the factory-prepared part, and that component had waited patiently for several years in its box. But Aerobatics International momentum was dwindling, and the dismantled Zlin slumbered until 1996 when James arranged for the pieces to be trailered to CZ for a complete rebuild – with the yet-to-be-fitted centre section included. I went to Prague via BA on April 20th 1997 and was picked up by Peter Poborsky who drove me far to the east into the rolling and wooded hills of deepest Moravia, to stay in Moravska Trebova where he runs the national aerobatic school.

Then next day it was south west to the Zlin factory, a mile or so west of the town named, not surprisingly, Zlin. On the way he told me of a recent fatal accident at the aerobatic school with a similar ubiquitous Zlin 526. An enthusiast, with some aerobatic experience elsewhere, came to fly, and clearly demonstrated the competence to go solo in this docile ageing trainer. But hardly had he started his aerobatics when he pulled up as if flying a Sukhoi. The wings did indeed fold. This is an example of 'A little learning can be a dangerous thing if not tempered with adequate understanding,' and indicates a culture change in thirty years – in both equipment and individual attitude and expectation.

Before taking the Zlin away I had to sign something about the Czech registration, to the extent that I understood that it would cease to exist once I had landed on the White Waltham airfield (ferry only). I set off for Karlovy Vary, the Zlin vaguely as I remembered it, but still considerably different in character to a number of recent aerobatic machines. There's no doubt that flying specialist high performance, marginally stable, highly powered and highly manoeuvrable (and invariably quirky) aircraft is great fun – and I do not just refer to the Concorde – but what a pleasure it was to taxi out, trundle down the runway and set course over the fields in this gentlemanly trainer that demonstrated the handling expectations that had been developed and accepted as agreeable over the forty years since 1918. Fashion and performance demands change with time, of course, but it occurred to me that, as a basic military trainer this Zlin fitted as a small step-up between the Chipmunk and the Harvard, though considerably cheaper and lighter than the latter. The flight to K.V. near the German border was uneventful, and having tanked up (with tip tanks) for the next day I went into this historic spa town, its river and wooded hillsides, for my nightstop. The food is good here, and guests wander the centre, periodically taking sips of the fountains' magic waters from the spouts of the little china watering cans they carry with them. Pure Belle Epoque. This was touring as it should be – I thought (hoped).

Next morning I returned to the airport, planning to start with the big one – three hours to Maastricht. 'There's a problem with your aircraft,' they said. 'It's leaking fuel.' I went to look at it. It was standing a bit lopsided, and there was a bucket under the lower wingtip. A main wheel had gone flat, and the tip tank on that side was overflowing. So much for the 'as new' expectation. I had only made one uneventful cross-country flight – what next? The Zlin tank system is simple – gravity feed all round, with all the fuel eventually finding its own way to the engine. In this flat tyre case, with one full tip tank lower than the other, fuel finds its way across the span and out of the lower tank overflow. The ground man had arranged a bucket under the lower tip tank to catch some of the fuel, while he went away to find a new 'Ventil' – inner tube valve; which he managed to do. (I had already discovered that there was nothing this man did not know about Antonov 2s, and presumably any Czech and Russian aircraft likely to cross his path.) To give the rebuilders their due it must be said that thereafter everything worked perfectly, including the engine, and after the usual VFR flight plan (times at FIR boundaries, number and colour of dinghies and so on), I was eventually on my way. The met men told me that there was an occluded front coming, and that I should go now, so I did.

After two and a half hours of German fields, villages, hills and woodlands I reached the Rhine, south of Bonn, and the occluded front immediately beyond it. The remaining kilometres to Maastricht head north west over wooded hills, and to continue from here did not look good for VFR flight, at this point in time, so I circled my turning point, Bad Neuenahr. This was another of those single-runway hilltop fields which might have once housed trainers, perhaps Messerschmitts and Focke-Wulfs in olden times. I had been there before for an airshow, probably in the same Zlin, but now there were no signs of life and no answer on the radio, so I landed anyway and waited to see what the future would hold. There was still no sign of life at this airfield, and I walked a little way down the hill towards the town to see if I remembered anything of the geography. It was familiar in only the broadest sense, and I had no idea of where we had stayed, twenty something years ago.

Within an hour the weather improved, the front was passing; it was time to return to the field and continue with the journey. We had already found Maastricht airport to be an obliging customs and fuel place for the Antonov, and this arrival was no different – initially. As I walked across the apron to carry out the formalities I was met by a young man coming to meet me. What for? Perhaps he's a spotter who works there.

'Where were you? You're overdue.'

'I've come all the way from Moravia and Bohemia in a little aeroplane. It's not like an airline schedule.'

'But you're an hour overdue. I've already reported you as missing (in action?) and raised the alarm – notified International Rescue (or its EU equivalent).'

I wonder if he really had. He obviously thought he had, and was quite serious, but there was no evidence of a European-wide mercy mission with no idea of where to start looking. Between the Czech Republic and northern

Holland there is a lot of countryside. I suppose you could only go on reports of unusual fallings from the sky, but I doubt there were any. We got no immense rescue bills from a choice of European states, but what had changed in twenty years? Where was the self-sufficiency that used to be a priority? I suppose I was witnessing the snowflaking of VFR aviation. Like the health service – compulsory protection from cradle to grave, whether you want it or not (or are not even ill).

The remaining two and a half hours across Holland, Belgium, France and the English Channel went without further touring problems. A magazine pictured it at White Waltham, April 22nd 1997, 25 years after I flew this aircraft in the 1972 Worlds at Salon de Provence; now waiting for the gaffer tape letters to be removed.

EPILOGUE

Finished with engines, not with a bang but a whimper

My last powered flight was to conduct James Black's CAP10 base check on Oct 19th 1997, then I lost my licence. I was still 55, and at this final CAA medical the doctor said the same things that had been said since my medical check at Chivenor in 1992 – blood pressure on the limit, and up and down. After each CAA medical thereafter a 24-hour readout from the every-30-minute-machine had seemed to satisfy the next six-month judgment. On this final occasion I made a diplomatic error – I shot myself in the foot, though not on purpose. Concorde flying had only been one of several airborne interests, and when the all-powerful doctor said 'Now you no longer fly the Concorde you won't be needing a licence,' I replied 'Why not? Where do these variable standards come from?' This was the mistake. Instead of gently explaining the CAA policy of compromise and reasonableness, he stated 'If that's your attitude I'll throw the book at you. We'll have a blood test, and you'll get a letter describing future possible medications and licence conditions. In the meantime you're busted as from now.'

Very nice. Very professional I'm sure, and the blood test showed nothing amiss, but I had been less than professional as well. Many flying professionals maintain a long-standing relationship with a CAA-approved doctor, someone you come to regard as a close friend. Judging by their various symptoms and remedies it seems to work, but I had never done this, and discovered that I currently was not on a GP's books either, having recently moved house. You're not allowed to go to the last one – wrong postcode – so, with, the CAA letter, I went to see the new lady I was appointed to. The instant appointment and empty waiting room were convenient, but these were not a good sign. A beautifully-dressed and very composed lady received me coolly. Too precious for words, I thought. Abingdon is an old market town with a Tesco and a Waitrose, but little evidence of the privileged things in life elsewhere. I explained my problem. 'There is no medication without side effects,' she said, in effect refusing to treat me. How professional is that? I could have thought of this statement myself, but perhaps I did not look ill enough. That wasn't exactly the point.

However, after having flown for 40 years, did I want to continue repeating more of the same, and did I want to endure the hassle of a battle with the CAA just to get back to the same place – with cards already marked? No; it was time to give up and see what would happen next.

That is yet another story.

Printed in Great Britain
by Amazon

40141642R00321